THE CORRESPONDENCE OF WOLFGANG CAPITO

VOLUME 2: 1524–1531

THE CORRESPONDENCE OF WOLFGANG CAPITO

VOLUME 2
1524–1531

Edited and translated by Erika Rummel
with the assistance of Milton Kooistra

University of Toronto Press

Toronto / Buffalo / London

© University of Toronto Press Incorporated 2009
Toronto Buffalo London
www.utppublishing.com
Printed in Canada
ISBN 978-0-8020-9955-6

Printed on acid-free, 100% post-consumer recycled paper
with vegetable-based inks.

Library and Archives Canada Cataloguing in Publication

Capito, Wolfgang, 1478–1541
The correspondence of Wolfgang Capito / edited and translated by
Erika Rummel ; with the assistance of Milton Kooistra.

Includes bibliographical references and index.
Contents: v. 1. 1507–1523 – v. 2. 1524–1531.
ISBN 0-8020-9017-6 (v. 1).   ISBN 978-0-8020-9955-6 (v. 2)

1. Capito, Wolfgang, 1478–1541 – Correspondence.   2. Reformation.
3. Scholars – Europe – Correspondence.   4. Humanists – Europe – Correspondence.
I. Rummel, Erika, 1942–   II. Kooistra, Milton   III. Title.

BR350.C29A4 2005   284'.092   C2005-903205-7

This book has been published with the help of a grant from the Canadian Federation
for the Humanities and Social Sciences, through the Aid to Scholarly Publications
Program, using funds provided by the Social Sciences and Humanities Research
Council of Canada.

University of Toronto Press acknowledges the financial assistance to its
publishing program of the Canada Council for the Arts and the
Ontario Arts Council.

 Canada Council **Conseil des Arts**   **ONTARIO ARTS COUNCIL**
for the Arts **du Canada**   **CONSEIL DES ARTS DE L'ONTARIO**

This book has been published with the help of a grant from the
Renaissance Society of America.

University of Toronto Press acknowledges the financial support for its
publishing activities of the Government of Canada through the
Book Publishing Industry Development Program (BPIDP).

Contents

Preface

The present volume covers the years 1524 to 1531, a crucial period for Capito and his fellow preachers, during which the Reformation took root and became firmly established in Strasbourg. It was a turbulent period – 'to preside over tragedies coming in quick succession' as Capito put it.[1] It took a toll on his physical and mental health. He weathered a number of difficulties, some of his own making, others endemic to the process of establishing new confessional boundaries and thus shared by all reformers. Among the latter were strenuous efforts to enlist the support of the secular government, to vanquish Catholic opponents in polemics and public disputations, and to settle internal disputes over the interpretation of the Eucharist.

The first volume of the *Correspondence of Wolfgang Capito* ended with the year 1523, in which Capito relinquished his position at the court of the Archbishop of Mainz and took up the provostship of St Thomas in Strasbourg. His breach with the Catholic Church, long a subject of speculation, became manifest in February 1524 when he accepted the position of parish priest at Young St Peter. He was elected to the post by the congregation of Young St Peter and confirmed in it by the city council (Ep. 189a), thus bypassing the Catholic bishop and ignoring the hierarchy.

One of the principal concerns of the Strasbourg reformers in 1524 was to defend clerical marriage (Epp. 171a, 189). Enjoying popular support, the married preachers held their own against the disciplinary actions of the Bishop of Strasbourg. In April, Capito helped draft an appeal protesting the bishop's writ of excommunication (Ep. 189). Rumours were afloat that Capito himself was about to marry (Ep. 191). He did not take that step, however, until 1 August. His wedding to Agnes Roettel, the daughter of a city councillor, was attended by a large crowd of well-wishers (Ep. 215), but scandalized the

* * * * *

1 Ep. 238: *novis tragoediis sese continuo excipientibus.*

conservative canons at St Thomas and deepened internal divisions between Capito's followers and the Catholic party led by the dean, Nicolaus Wurmser.

A second crisis developed in 1524, when many of the reformers took out citizenship and urged others to follow their example (Ep. 208). In December 1524, Capito published a pamphlet arguing in favour of the clergy giving up their privileges and sharing the financial burdens of the laity (Ep. 230). A decree passed by the council in January 1525, making citizenship mandatory for the clergy, created serious difficulties for Capito at St Thomas.

After negotiating in vain for an alternative solution (Epp. 173a, 216a), a number of Catholic canons at the three collegiate churches of St Thomas, Young and Old St Peter, decided to secede. Wurmser, who was behind this initiative, secretly removed the seal, briefs, and other legal documents and valuables from the vault of St Thomas, with the aim of setting up the chapter elsewhere and branding those left behind as heretics.[2] The splinter group pursued their purpose through legal means, that is, formal protests to the *Reichsregiment*, through public proclamations, and in practical ways through efforts to collect the rents and fees owed to the chapter. A number of the exiles changed their mind when they realized the serious nature of the undertaking and returned to Strasbourg. The alienated property, hidden for some time in Offenburg, was eventually returned to St Thomas, although the Strasbourg canons were forced to strike a new seal to carry on business in the meantime (Appendix 2). Capito described the whole affair in a reply to the *Reichsregiment* (Ep. 237) signed by twenty-one canons and vicars of St Thomas, and in a pamphlet (Ep. 246a), depicting the actions of Wurmser's faction as legally and morally wrong. In this affair, Capito was supported by the city council, which took the position that the collegiate churches had been established for the benefit of the citizens of Strasbourg. The council therefore sent representatives to Offenburg to negotiate the return of the alienated goods and, in March 1528, reached an agreement with the exiles about financial compensation for their lost benefices.[3]

The dissension at St Thomas may have contributed to Capito's decision to resign his provostship, or at any rate the title, in October 1525 (Epp. 248a–d). He himself cites conflict of interest as a reason. He had been accused of putting the material interests of the collegiate church before religious considerations. His mounting debts may also have played a role. At first he attempted to sell both his provostship and his canonry to Gervasius Sopher, the

* * * * *

2 Epp. 233b headnote, 234b, 234c, 235a.
3 The contract is in AST 22, 5–6. For wrangling about the terms of the contract, see Epp. 377c, 431a, 431c.

administrator of St Thomas (Ep. 248a). When this plan did not come to fruition, he handed over the provostship to Lorenz Schenckbecher (Appendix 1c). He retained the right of regress, however, and continued to enjoy most of the usufructs as well as the house associated with the provost's office. According to a contract drawn up by the two men, Schenckbecher was to enjoy the full benefits of the office only after Capito's death. When the new provost demanded financial guarantees in case his title was challenged in court by a former claimant, Jacob Abel,[4] Capito threatened to resume the provostship in 1528 (Epp. 367b, c). A mutually satisfactory settlement was reached, however, and the provostship remained in Schenckbecher's hands until 1540.

To advance the cause of the Reformation, Capito and his colleagues frequently petitioned the council to pass legislation in support of their cause and, in turn, were invited by the council to account for their teaching.[5] Among the most frequently discussed matters were education[6] and the abolition of the mass. The latter involved lengthy negotiations, begun in April 1525 and brought to a successful conclusion in January 1529.[7] In March 1530 Capito wrote a brief history of the developments in Strasbourg (Ep. 406, published under the council's name), showing the crucial role played by the city's proclamations in advancing the Reformation. The council had mandated the preaching of the gospel, abolished the mass, established schools and, finally, taken over the allocation of benefices and the stipends associated with them.[8]

The Peasants' War of 1525 threatened to bring the reformers into conflict with the secular authorities, since the rebels combined social and political demands with Reformation slogans. Erasmus Gerber, a prominent leader in the Alsatian uprisings, contacted the Strasbourg reformers for advice in April 1525.[9] Later on, this contact led to claims that the preachers had abetted the revolts (Epp. 244a, 246). The testimony of convicted peasant rebels seemed to implicate Capito and his colleagues[10] and obliged them to publish an apologia.[11]

* * * * *

4 See CWC 1, Ep. 50 headnote.
5 Epp. 208, 209, 211, 219, 233a, 244a.
6 Epp. 236a, 244b, 246b, 358.
7 Epp. 241, 244b, 244c; 246b, 285a, 358, 359, 364a, 366, 371, 375, 377, 379.
8 Concerning the allocation of stipends see Epp. 366a, 383, 396, 396b, 403a.
9 Epp. 242, 242a, 243, 277.
10 Cf. Dacheux, #4462 : 'The local preachers were called into suspicion by the bishop and his councillors. They are supposed to have advised the peasants and incited them. The preachers complained before the local authorities and asked them to take on their cause ... The city decided to write [on their behalf].'
11 Ep. 280, of March 1526, cf. also Ep. 281.

During the same period, 1524–6, the Strasbourg reformers became the target of Catholic polemicists and were challenged to defend their doctrine at public disputations. In 1524, Capito and his colleagues invited Conrad Treger, the provincial of the Augustinians, who resided in Strasbourg, to meet them in a public disputation. Treger's specious excuses and the abusive pamphlet he published against the preachers enraged the populace and led to a riot. In September 1524, a group of citizens stormed the monastery and brought Treger before the council. He was fined and obliged to swear an oath to keep the peace.[12] The Treger Affair resulted in a series of apologiae and counter-apologiae.[13]

During these years, Capito showed a surprising lack of diplomatic skill and committed a number of gaffes. In 1524 he displayed poor judgment, supporting a notorious confidence man, Hans Jakob Schütz, who alleged that the city council of Sélestat was plotting against the reformers and was eventually executed for his intrigues in 1525.[14] Capito's credulity harmed his reputation, as he admitted to Zwingli: 'My authority and my reputation are diminished because Hans Jakob imposed on me.'[15] In 1526 Capito's indiscreet actions and writings in connection with the Disputation of Baden elicited a protest from the Swiss Confederacy. At the disputation, Oecolampadius, who represented the reformers, had been worsted by his Catholic opponents. In an effort to counter adverse publicity, Capito supplied his relative, the printer Wolfgang Köpfel, with an anonymous account of the proceedings, which was favourable to the reformers. He himself wrote an introduction (Ep. 288a). A candid letter to Zwingli enclosing the pamphlet and requesting further information was intercepted, however. The Catholic apologist Johannes Fabri published a tendentious German translation of the letter, alarming the Swiss Confederacy and resulting in a formal protest to the Strasbourg government.[16] As a result, Köpfel was imprisoned and fined, and Capito was called to account and rebuked by the city council.[17]

* * * * *

12 Epp. 187, 188, 207, 212.
13 Epp. 222, 223, 223a, 223b.
14 Epp. 197, 199, 200, 201, 202, 280.
15 Ep. 234: *diminutae sum autoritatis et existimationis ob imposturam Ioannis Iacobi.*
16 Cf. Capito's response, Epp. 289, 290, 292, 293, and his justification to the Diet then assembled at Speyer, Ep. 300.
17 Dacheux, #4687: 'Decision: Since Dr Capito has gone public without the knowledge of the council of the [Swiss] Confederacy or anyone else, he should be called to account. The [Strasbourg] council will protest before a notary that [the pamphlet was issued] without their knowledge and approval. Wolfgang Köpfel was imprisoned and the books confiscated. Because his wife has recently given birth, he has been set free and fined.'

Capito furthermore caused concern, not to say alarm, among fellow reformers when he manifested Anabaptist sympathies. He advocated tolerance when others called for punishment of nonconformist practices.[18] He entertained a number of men suspected of heterodoxy at his house.[19] People began talking about 'the comings and goings in Capito's house, his many visitors, some suspected of being rebellious minds.'[20] He continued expressing sympathy with Anabaptists who suffered persecution (Epp. 320, 330, 331), although by 1527 he was forced to acknowledge that there were troublemakers among them (Epp. 329, 333, 334).

Capito's public support for men regarded as heterodox, for example, his introductions to Martin Cellarius' *De operibus Dei* in 1527[21] and Schwenckfeld's *Apologia* in 1529 (Ep. 393), may have led to his exclusion from the Marburg Colloquy. He is remarkably reticent about this important meeting called by Philip of Hesse in 1529 to reach agreement on the Sacramentarian controversy,[22] and it was Bucer and Hedio rather than Capito who represented the Strasbourgers at the colloquy. Although Bucer casually mentions in a letter to Ambrosius Blaurer that Capito had recently been indisposed,[23] it is more likely that he remained behind because his views had made him persona non grata.[24]

At the time, Strasbourg was widely seen as a refuge for reform-minded men and women, and a centre from which the gospel message was being disseminated. Accordingly, Capito and his colleagues were asked to recommend suitable preachers to other cities: Mulhouse (Epp. 265, 313a); Memmingen and Solothurn (Epp. 386, 387); and Augsburg (Epp. 429a, 431b, 437, 438). Numerous letters attest to consultations between Strasbourg and the reformers in Zurich (over seventy letters to and from Zwingli) and Basel (over twenty letters to and from Oecolampadius) and, conversely, to the conflict over the Sacramentarian question with the theologians in Wittenberg.

The controversy over the meaning of the Eucharist is a frequent subject

* * * * *

18 Epp. 258, 267. For a full statement of Capito's beliefs, see his so-called Apologia for the Anabaptists, Ep. 431, and his letter to Wolfgang Musculus, Ep. 438.
19 For example, the Anabaptists Wilhelm Exel (Ep. 282) and Ludwig Hätzer (Epp. 321, 322).
20 Dacheux, #4270. Cf. also Oecolampadius' friendly warning, Ep. 450.
21 Ep. 335; cf. his defence in Epp. 338, 342, 343.
22 Yet he acknowledges the importance of the colloquy in Ep. 395.
23 CorrBucer 3, Ep. 257.
24 Cf. Capito's complaints in Ep. 410 that Luther and Melanchthon spoke ill of him at Marburg.

in Capito's correspondence.[25] In October 1525 the Strasbourgers sent a special messenger to consult with Luther concerning the Sacramentarian question (Epp. 247, 252, 252a). They discussed the question also with followers of Luther: Johann Bugenhagen, Johannes Brenz, and Leo Jud (Epp. 248, 259, 270). Capito himself inclined toward the Zwinglian view of the Eucharist being symbolic,[26] but believed that one should not put too fine a point on the interpretation since, as he repeatedly insisted, it was an external matter. He went as far as criticizing Zwingli for trying too hard to find an inclusive formula (Ep. 276).

In 1530 Capito accompanied Bucer to the Diet of Augsburg, but he was clearly ineffective. He was snubbed by his old benefactor, the archbishop of Mainz (Ep. 414). Melanchthon similarly declined to meet with him in person (Epp. 416–18). Both he and Luther agreed to a meeting with Bucer only after Capito had left the city. The tensions with the Lutherans were a consequence of the continued disagreements over the Sacramentarian question. Capito and Bucer had drawn up the Tetrapolitan Confession signed by four cities, Strasbourg, Constance, Memmingen, and Lindau,[27] and presented the document to the emperor as an alternative to the Lutheran confession. Jacob Sturm and Matthis Pfarrer, who represented the city of Strasbourg at the diet, recognized the political implications and persuaded the reformers to modify the clause dealing with the Eucharist. The changes did not have the desired effect. The Strasbourg preachers did not garner sufficient support, and in 1536 signed the Wittenberg Concord to avoid isolation. It is clear from the respective roles played by Capito and Bucer in the late 1520s that the latter's influence in Strasbourg was in the ascendancy.

In spite of the difficulties besetting Capito, he found time for scholarly work. In 1525 he published a revised edition of his Hebrew grammar.[28] Between 1526 and 1528 he produced commentaries on Habakkuk and Hosea[29] as well as a German translation of Hosea. He furthermore wrote a catechism,

* * * * *

25 E.g., Epp. 224, 226, 228, 357.
26 A full statement of his beliefs can be found in Ep. 393; an official statement of the beliefs of the Strasbourg preachers can be found in Ep. 436.
27 Cf. Epp. 414, 415, 420, 420a, 410b, 436.
28 Dedicated to Ulrich Varnbühler (Ep. 238, March 1525).
29 The commentary on Habakkuk was dedicated to Jacob Sturm, Ep. 279, March 1526; the commentary on Hosea was dedicated to Marguerite of Navarre (Ep. 350 to Reader, Ep. 351 dedication, April 1528). For the German translation of Hosea, see Ep. 325.

De pueris instituendis,[30] and answered scholarly questions, for example, from Andreas Cellarius (Ep. 369) and Guillaume Farel (Epp. 388, 389). The latter exchange produced a remarkable disquisition on Jewish funeral practices, which required serious research on Capito's part and provides us with unique insights into his Hebrew library (Appendix 4).

The year 1531 brought tragedy for Capito personally, and for the reformers in southern Germany and Switzerland as a whole. On 17 October, Capito lost his wife to the plague (Ep. 457). On 11 October, Zurich suffered a decisive defeat in the Second Battle of Kappel and lost its leading reformer, Ulrich Zwingli, on the battlefield (Ep. 454). Shortly afterwards, on 22 November, Johannes Oecolampadius, the leading voice of the Reformation in Basel, died (Ep. 456). Capito, who was physically and emotionally drained,[31] embarked on a journey at the end of the year. Travelling officially as an ambassador of the Strasbourg reformers, he visited Constance, Lindau, Memmingen, and Augsburg during the first three months of 1532, but no doubt he also travelled in the hope of finding inner peace. On the advice of his friends, he courted and married Wibrandis Rosenblatt, the widow of Oecolampadius. Capito's travels and his remarriage take us beyond the time frame of the present volume, however.

The second volume, like the first, is based on Olivier Millet's finding list, *La Correspondance de W.F. Capiton* (Strasbourg, 1982). The headnote to each letter provides a brief biography of the writer and/or addressee, notes the location of the manuscript, and supplies publication data if there is a printed text. The footnotes supply biographical data for the persons mentioned in the letter, clarify issues raised, and identify quotations from classical, biblical, patristic, and scholastic sources. As in the first volume, letters easily accessible in modern editions (for example, in the editions of Bucer, Zwingli, Oecolampadius, Luther, and other prominent reformers) are summarized. A full translation is provided for previously unpublished letters and letters that appear in publications with a limited circulation, in particular publications printed before 1900.

As a result of our continued research, some of the letters in Millet's list have been redated.[32] Five new letters (8a, 62a, 156a, 171a, 173a) belonging to the period covered in the first volume came to our attention too late and appear in the section 'Addenda to Volume 1' at the beginning of the pres-

* * * * *

30 August 1527, with a German translation (1527, second edition 1529; cf. Ep. 398c).
31 Cf. his request for medication to Brunfels, Ep. 460.
32 Epp. 235, 262 (already redated by Millet), 340, 345, 370, 376, 397, 397a, 428, 429.

ent volume. In addition, some seventy new letters dating from 1524 to 1531 have been discovered, representing almost a quarter of the letters in the present volume. The numbering of the letters follows that of Millet's finding list. The new letters have been inserted in proper chronological sequence and are marked by an 'a', 'b', 'c', or 'd' after the number. They shed light primarily on the dissension between Catholics and reformers in the collegiate church of St Thomas and on the relationship between the reformers and the city council of Strasbourg. The absence of these letters in Millet's list is, to some extent, the result of a policy decision. Millet focused on Capito's personal correspondence and, as a rule, did not include letters by groups (i.e., letters from and to the preachers or from and to the chapter of St Thomas) unless Capito's personal involvement could be demonstrated. The policy adopted in this edition is more inclusive. It rests on the assumption that Capito was involved in the composition of letters and statements issued by the preachers and, conversely, that he was implicitly addressed in letters from the city or other authorities to the preachers. It also rests on the assumption that Capito was a party, and indeed instrumental, to any letters that appeared over the signature of 'the provost, vice-dean, and chapter of St Thomas' and that he was included in all correspondence addressed to the chapter. Capito was a canon of St Thomas throughout the period covered by this volume and its titular provost until October 1525. Because of the peculiar nature of Capito's arrangements with his successor, Lorenz Schenckbecher,[33] it stands to reason that his involvement in the business of St Thomas remained significant even after his resignation. For these reasons, the correspondence of the chapter and of the preachers as a group are included here.

The volume provides access for the first time to a part of the Archives du Chapitre Saint-Thomas (AST) in the municipal archive of Strasbourg (AMS) that has remained uncatalogued and seemingly escaped the attention of scholars. This is a collection of manuscripts labelled AST 22, which consists of seven folders of letters. AST 22 is identified in Jean Rott's otherwise detailed catalogue[34] only in the most general terms, as 'Sixt Hermann material.' It does, in fact, contain a great deal relevant to our correspondence, including autographs by Capito. Thus, the volume includes a sizable contingent of previously unknown source material. It is hoped that the transcription,[35] translation, and annotation will stimulate new research and generate

* * * * *

33 See above, p. ix.
34 J. Rott, *Extraits et analyses de pièces du XVIe tirées de AST* (1980, revised 1998), research instrument available at AMS.
35 The texts in the original Latin or German will appear on our website, www.wolfgang-capito.com.

new insights into the progress of the German Reformation during a period of crucial developments.

I gratefully acknowledge the financial assistance of the Social Sciences and Humanities Research Council of Canada as well as the material assistance of Emmanuel College (University of Toronto), which provided me with office space and the amenities that go with it. My research would not have been possible without the assistance I received at the libraries and archives whose collections I used, notably the Centre for Reformation and Renaissance Studies at the University of Toronto (Kim Yates; Lena Rummel), the municipal archive of Strasbourg (F. Schwicker; Joseph Fuchs), the Archives départementales du Bas-Rhin, the Zentralbibliothek (Christoph Eggenberger) and Staatsbibliothek in Zurich, the Universitätsbibliothek Basel, the Offenburg archive (Regina Brischle), the Universitäts und Landesbibliothek Sachsen-Anhalt in Halle (Marita von Cieminski), the Staatsarchiv Bern (Nicole Cläy), the Würtembergische Landesbibliothek, Stuttgart (Herrad Spilling), Universitätsarchiv Freiburg, and the Herzog August Bibliothek in Wolfenbüttel (Gillian Bepler, Christian Hogreve). I have received a great deal of assistance from fellow scholars, notably Debra Kaplan and Stephen Burnett, Barbara Henze, Reinhard Bodenmann, James Hirstein, Grantley McDonald, Gerhard Strasser, Reinhold Friedrich and Wolfgang Simon of the Bucer edition, Ranon Katzoff, D.F.S.Thomson, and the members of the advisory committee: Olivier Millet, Jane Abray, Thomas Brady, Herman Selderhuis, and Irena Backus. I would also like to thank Beth McAuley and Shealah Stratton of the University of Toronto Press for their careful copyediting, which greatly improved the manuscript.

My special thanks go to the graduate students who assisted with this project over the course of the past three years: Gavin Hammel (electronic texts, transcription, and translation of individual letters), James Beck (editorial and administrative tasks, index), and Milton Kooistra, whose important contribution to all phases of the edition is recognized in the title of this publication and whose thorough search of the holdings of the archive in Strasbourg has led to the discovery of the majority of the new letters included here.

ERIKA RUMMEL

Abbreviations and Short Titles

Adam	J. Adam, *Evangelische Kirchengeschichte der Stadt Strassburg bis zur französischen Revolution* (Strasbourg, 1887)
AK	*Die Amerbachkorrespondenz*, ed. A. Hartmann and B.R. Jenny (Basel, 1942–)
Allen	P.S. Allen et al., eds., *Opus epistolarum Des. Erasmi Roterodami* (Oxford: Oxford University Press, 1906–58)
ABR	Archives départementales du Bas-Rhin, Strasbourg
AMS	Archives municipales de Strasbourg (now Archives de la ville et de la communauté urbaine de Strasbourg)
ARG	*Archiv für Reformationsgeschichte/Archive for Reformation History*
AST	Archives du Chapitre Saint-Thomas (in AMS)
Baum	A. Baum, *Magistrat und Reformation in Strassburg bis 1529* (Strasbourg, 1887)
BDS	*Martin Bucers Deutsche Schriften* (Gütersloh, 1960–)
BrOek	E. Staehelin, ed., *Briefe und Akten zum Leben Oekolampads zum vierhundertjährigen Jubiläum der Baseler Reformation* Quellen und Forschungen zur Reformationsgeschichte (Leipzig, 1927–1934; repr. New York 1971)
CorrBucer	Reinhold Friedrich et al., eds., *Correspondance de Martin Bucer* (Leiden: Brill, 1979)
CWC	E. Rummel, ed., *The Correspondence of Wolfgang Capito*, (Toronto: University of Toronto Press, 2005–)
CWE	*The Collected Works of Erasmus* (Toronto:1974–)
Dacheux	L. Dacheux, ed., *Fragment des Anciennes Chroniques d'Alsace*, vol. 4 (Strasbourg, 1901)

Eid. Absch.	J. Strickler, ed., *Amtliche Sammlung der älteren Eidgenössischen Abschiede (1521–1528)*, vol. 4–1a (Brugg, 1873), vol. 4–1b (Zurich, 1876)
Ficker-Winckelmann	J. Ficker and O. Winckelmann, eds., *Handschriftenproben des sechzehnten Jahrhunderts nach Strassburger Originalen* (Strasbourg, 1906)
Gény	J. Gény, *Die Reichsstadt Schlettstadt und ihr Antheil an den socialpolitischen und religiösen Bewegungen der Jahren 1490–1536* (Freiburg, 1900)
Gerdesius	D. Gerdesius, *Introductio in historiam evangelii XVI seculo passim per Europam renovati* (Groningen, 1744–6)
Herminjard	A.-L. Herminjard, ed., *Correspondance des réformateurs dans les pays de langue française* (Geneva and Paris, 1866–97; repr., 1965–6)
Ki.Ar.	Kirchenarchiv
Kittelson	J. Kittelson, *Wolfgang Capito: From Humanist to Reformer* (Leiden, 1975)
Knod	G. Knod, *Die Stiftsherren von St. Thomas zu Strassburg, 1518–1548* (Strasbourg, 1892)
Le livre de bourgeoisie	C. Wittmer and J.C. Meyer, eds., *Le livre de bourgeoisie de la ville de Strasbourg: 1440–1530* (Strasbourg, 1948–61)
MBW	H. Scheible, ed., *Melanchthons Briefwechsel: Kritische und kommentierte Gesamtausgabe* (Stuttgart-Bad Cannstatt, 1977–)
Millet	O. Millet, *Correspondance de Wolfgang Capiton (1478–1541)* (Strasbourg, 1982)
Pol. Corr.	H. Virck et al., eds., *Politische Correspondenz der Stadt Strassburg im Zeitalter der Reformation* (Strasbourg and Heidelberg, 1882–1933)
QGT	M. Krebs and H.G. Rott, eds., *Quellen zur Geschichte der Täufer in Elsass* (Gütersloh, 1959–60)
Röhrich	T.W. Röhrich, *Geschichte der Reformation im Elsass und besonders in Strassburg* (Strasbourg, 1830–32)
Schiess	T. Schiess, ed., *Briefwechsel der Brüder Ambrosius und Thomas Blaurer, 1509–1567* (Freiburg, 1908–12)
RTA	Bayerische Akademie der Wissenschaften: Historische Kommission, ed., *Deutsche Reichstagsakten: Jüngere Reihe* (Göttingen, 1962–)

TB	Thesaurus Baumianus (manuscript in the Bibliothèque Nationale et Universitaire, Strasbourg)
VadBr	E. Arbenz and H. Wartmann, eds., *Vadianische Briefsammlung*. Mitteilungen zur vaterländischen Geschichte 24–5, 27–30 (St Gallen, 1890–1913)
WABr	*D. Martin Luthers Werke: Briefwechsel* (Weimar, 1930–78)
Zurich SA	Staatsarchiv des Kantons Zürich
Zurich ZB	Zentralbibliothek Zurich
ZwBr	E. Egli et al., eds., *Huldreich Zwinglis sämtliche Werke*, vols. 7–11 = *Zwinglis Briefwechsel*, volumes 1–5 (Zurich, 1911–35)

Addenda to Volume 1

Letter 8a: 26 October 1517, Ingolstadt, Johann Eck to Capito and Johannes Fabri

Printed in J. Greving, *Briefmappe: Erstes Stück* in *Reformationsgeschichtliche Studien und Texte* 21–2 (Münster, 1912), 224–5. The text of the letter (with a German translation) is also available at http://ivv7srv15.uni-muenster.de/mnkg/pfnuer/Eckbriefe/No48.html. For Eck and his relationship with Capito, see CWC 1, Ep. 1a headnote.

To the most excellent and distinguished lords, the smiths,[1] Wolfgang, doctor of theology, and Johannes, doctor of both canon and civil law, foremost in every discipline and his dearest friends in Basel.

Warmest greetings. Your kindness toward me was so great, most learned men, that I cannot say enough about it to my friends. I would like to return the favour to you, when I have an opportunity. But although I should be the one returning the favour to you, I am compelled again to ask for your help: a month ago I produced a commentary on the *Mystica theologia*,[2] but it does not seem to me in the interest of scholars to publish it in Augsburg, since there is no printer there who has a learned corrector; and how can the printer himself be the judge in such a foreign and most rare matter, which breathes the utmost erudition? I have chosen Froben,[3] the excellent printer,

* * * * *

1 Alluding to the fact that 'Fabri' and 'Fabritius' (Capito's middle name) means 'smith.'
2 *S. Dionysius Areopagita, De mystica Theologia lib. I: Graece. Ioan. Sarraceno, Ambrosio Camaldul. Marsilio Ficino Interpret. Cum Vercellensium extractione. Ioan. Eckius commentarios adjecit pro theologia negativa ...* ([Augsburg]: Miller, 1519).
3 For Johann Froben, the Basel printer, see CWC 1, Ep. 3. He did not publish Eck's edition. See note 2 above.

who stands first among the other printers in Germany. But I have decided on you, Wolfgang, as the corrector, since you have more eyes than Argos.[4] I think that you will readily take on the task because of its general usefulness to scholars. In two weeks I shall send Dionysius via another courier from Augsburg, but you will have to speak to our Froben about the edition. He will do the greatest of all favours to all theologians – the purer and more refined[5] kind. I shall write in full what is necessary and send it with the man from Augsburg. Farewell, my friends, my dearest friends. Farewell. Ingolstadt. 26 October in the year of grace, 1517.

Your Eck, who is most eager to fulfil your wishes.

I held a funeral oration at the official service for the Most Reverend Archbishop of Augsburg;[6] I will send you a copy soon.

Letter 62a: 13 November 1520, Ebernburg, Ulrich von Hutten to Capito

The manuscript of this letter is at the Uppsala University Library, Waller ms. de-02506. There is a digital image of the letter available on the library's website (see http://waller.ub.uu.se/object.xsql?DBID=28502). The manuscript is partially damaged; hence the elision points.

Ulrich von Hutten sends greetings to Wolfgang Capito.

You are very afraid the humanities will be destroyed. Oh, how weak you people are, yielding so easily to your fears! Why don't you rally and, if you cannot do that, at least be sensible? Don't be afraid for the humanities. This will benefit them, add to them, and broadcast them. I am afraid you will soften the strong minds of others with this sort of letter and enervate their strength. I beg you over and over again not to do so. For if I find afterwards that you stubbornly continue in this fashion, I shall say that you have ob-

* * * * *

4 Argos, the hundred-eyed warrior of myth, proverbial for an alert and sharp-eyed person. Capito was living in Basel at the time.
5 *Defecatis,* of chemically purified substances. Cf. the dictionary of the Strasbourg scholar Conradus Dasypodius (1531–1601) s.v. 'Saccarum,' where he uses the expression 'excoctus et defecatus' in the sense of boiled and purified.
6 The bishop of Augsburg, Heinrich IV of Lichtenau, died on 12 April 1517 in Dillingen; on the 14th he was buried in the St Gertrude chapel of the Augsburg cathedral. Eck gave the funeral sermon, and his amanuensis and relative, Michael Eck, edited it. He dedicated it on 23 September 1517 to the abbot Leonhard Widmann of Ottobeuren, *Oratio funebris habita ... in exsequiali pompa Reverendissimi D. Henrici Episcopi Augustensis* (Augsburg: Silvan Otmar, 1517).

structed the humanities much more than the diligent legation of Aleandro,[1] or the bitter letter of Tortosa.[2] Clearly we need courageous men. Cautious men are of no help to us; rather those diligent mentors will harm us. I write this in a friendly spirit for the sake of our common cause.

What you report of Aleandro is news to me, but keep your ears and eyes open to learn what that *Sclavus*[3] says or does against me. Above all, see if you can send me a copy of some papal letter against me. It would help my cause[4] greatly if Aleandro spoke up against me there. I must reply to him in writing.[5] You yourself need only warn me. I very much would like copies of the two briefs of [Leo] X to the archbishop of Mainz.[6] See that they are transcribed for me. They have burned Luther's writings.[7] So what? Rome has

* * * * *

1 On Girolamo Aleandro (1480–1542), the papal legate to the Holy Roman Empire, see CWC 1, Ep. 149 headnote.

2 I.e., the future Pope Adrian VI, who, before he became pope in January 1522, was the bishop of Tortosa, Spain. It is unclear to which 'bitter letter of Tortosa' Hutten is referring. In a letter to Erasmus, also dated 13 November 1520, Hutten mentions a letter from the 'Cardinal of Tortosa' to Leo X, in which Adrian took the pope 'severely to task for suffering you, the master-mind of all this [i.e., introducing humanism into Germany and thus causing the rise of Lutheranism], to remain in Germany' (CWE 8, Ep. 1161:25–7). See ibid., note 3.

3 *Sclavus* may be translated 'slave/servant' or 'Slav.' The editors of CWE 8, Ep. 1161, note 7 speculate that the term refers to his family origins in 'Slavonic' Istria. More likely, however, it is a reference to Aleandro's alleged Jewish descent (in legal terms, Jews were the 'servants' of the emperor). See Hutten's letter of March 1521 to Aleandro (Ep. 229, *Hutteni opera* 2, 12–16) in which he sneered at Aleandro's denial of the rumour.

4 I.e., his plans for an armed struggle against the church.

5 See Ep. 229, *Hutteni opera* 2, 12–16.

6 In letters to Albert of Brandenburg, archbishop of Mainz (*Hutteni Opera* 1, Epp. 176, 179, dated 5 and 12 July 1520), Leo X and one of his officials had requested Hutten's dismissal from the court of Mainz. In a letter to Capito, dated 8 August, Hutten himself wrote of two letters in which the pope had demanded his arrest and extradition to Rome (CWC 1, Ep. 53). In letters to Albert and Sebastian Rotenhan, Hutten continued to plead his case, but Albert had severed all ties with his former protégé (*Hutteni opera* 1, Epp. 180, 191–2; see also CWE 8, Ep. 1135). Thereupon Hutten wrote two works, *Ad Carolum Imperatorem adversus intentatam sibi a Romanistis vim et iniuriam conquestio* ([Strasbourg: Schott], 1520; *Hutteni opera* 1:53–5* and 371–419), which also appeared in German.

7 Shortly after Aleandro's arrival in Louvain at the beginning of November, he ordered Luther's books to be burned in Louvain and Liège, then in Cologne (on 12 November), and later that month in Mainz (on 29 November). In response, Hutten wrote two poems, *Exclamatio in incendium Lutheranum* ([Wittenberg: Rhau-Grunenberg], 1521; *Hutteni opera* 3:453–5) and *Ein klag über den Luterischen Brandt zu Mentz* ([Wittenberg: Rhau-Grunenberg], 1521; *Hutteni opera* 3:455–9).

condemned even Reuchlin.[8] But unless all good fortune deserts me, we shall not all die without being revenged. Sometimes resistance is possible even in causes that are despaired of now.

I am not surprised Sauermann did something stupid.[9] I have never seen him do anything prudent. You have made me afraid for Erasmus.[10] I warned the man in a strongly worded letter to consider his safety.[11] Send me *Hochstratus ovans*,[12] and you will receive in turn *Bulla*, a dialogue which, as far as a fair exchange is possible, will be inscribed to you.[13] I believe it is not without its charm. I have also written a commentary on the bull of [Leo] X.[14] You will shortly have it there [in Mainz]. There is one more thing left to ask for the sake of our friendship: help the monk Bucer get rid of his cowl, which is his dearest wish.[15] He is a very upright man. I travelled with him from [...]

* * * * *

8 On Johann Reuchlin, see CWC 1, Ep. 17. Leo X overturned an earlier acquittal on 23 June 1523.

9 Georg Sauermann (ca. 1492–1527) was provost of the cathedral of Wrocław (Breslau). In 1508, he matriculated at the universities of both Wittenberg and Leipzig. In 1509 he entered the University of Bologna, where he became rector from 1513–14, and on 3 June 1514, he was promoted doctor of civil and canon law. During this time he was also a propagandist for Maximilian I in Italy. In 1519, he went to Rome, and in 1520 to Spain, where he entered the service of Charles V, whom he accompanied to the Low Countries. In the fall of 1520, Charles V sent him back to Rome as imperial proctor at the papal court of Rome. Sauermann died from injuries suffered during the Sack of Rome in 1527.

10 In a letter that is not extant? See the letter Hutten wrote to Erasmus that same day, warning him to guard against the hostilities of the scholastics who opposed both reformers and humanists (CWE 8, Ep. 1161).

11 I.e., CWE 8, Ep. 1161.

12 *Hochstratus ovans. Dialogus festivissimus*, an anonymous pamphlet that was printed probably in Cologne in the fall of 1520. In the dialogue, Johann Eck and Aleandro are reproached for burning Luther's books (see CWC 1, Ep. 63). There is a modern edition in *Hutteni opera*, Supp. 1, 461–88.

13 Ulrich von Hutten, *Bulla vel bullicida* (Strasbourg: [Schott], January 1521), which was published together with *Dialogi Huttenici novi* (*Hutteni opera* 4:309–31). In the end, however, the *Bulla* was not dedicated to Capito, but to Johann II, Count Palatine of Pfalz-Simmern-Sponheim, in a letter dated 15 January 1521.

14 Ulrich von Hutten, *Bulla Decimi Leonis contra errores Martini Lutheri et sequacium* (Strasbourg: [Schott, 1520]; *Hutteni opera* 5:301–33).

15 On 2 December 1520, Hutten informed Bucer that he had written again to Capito regarding Bucer's situation (CorrBucer 1, Ep. 22). For Bucer's requests to Capito for help, see CWC 1, Epp. 61, 65, 74, 85–6. Bucer was finally released from his monastic vows and habit in the spring of 1521 (CorrBucer 1, Ep. 33).

to Speyer, and he delighted me.[16] Help this innocent man, [...] for he is sick
of this hateful garb of superstition, but also because he is in danger from
false brethren on our account, for they have long given him a bad name for
going over to our party. Once I could have helped him myself, when I was
in [Mainz],[17] where I brought you lest that position be opened to some evil
man.[18] Shake up Albert. He will not deny you. If he is willing, it will be done.
Farewell and write back at greater length, especially about people's opinion
of me. Again, farewell. From the Ebernburg,[19] through my secretary, on the
Ides of November, in the year 1520.

Letter 156a: [Shortly after 3 April 1523, Nürnberg?], Caspar [Hedio] to Capito

The manuscript of this letter is an autograph in the Melanchthonhaus Bretten,
Hs. Inv. Nr. 354. Although the inventory at the Melanchthonhaus proposes the
year date 1524, internal evidence suggests 1523, when Capito was still in the
service of the archbishop of Mainz. See below, note 2. For the writer, Caspar
Hedio, see CWC 1, Ep. 47 headnote.

Greetings. On Good Friday I received the enclosed letter, which Lorenz
Nachterhofer[1] sent me to forward to you as quickly as possible. Indeed, it
was good luck that Johann Froben was at hand, to whom I entrusted the

* * * * *

16 The editors of the Bucer correspondence conjecture that Bucer met Hutten for
the first time in Strasbourg in November 1520 (CorrBucer 1, Ep. 19, note 2). The
evidence in this letter suggests that the two men met (earlier?) during a journey.

17 In the summer of 1517, Hutten entered the service of Albert of Brandenburg,
to whom he had dedicated a *Panegyricus* on the occasion of his accession to the
See of Mainz. Hutten left the service of the archbishop of Mainz in the summer
of 1519, but still received a pension from him until his formal dismissal in 1520
(see above, note 6).

18 In 1520 Capito was invited by Albert of Brandenburg to join his court, an invitation that came about through the recommendation of Hutten and Heinrich
Stromer (see CWC 1, Ep. 32).

19 The Ebernburg was Franz von Sickingen's principal castle, south of Kreuznach
in Rheinland-Pfalz.

1 On Nachterhofer, the emissary of Albert of Brandenburg at the imperial court,
see CWC 1, Ep. 134, note 4.

task. Unless there is a mistake in the title, you will have two provostships[2] until *you sell one tunic to someone who does not have one*[3] (but I am joking). Farewell, my dearest patron. My protector, who has recommended me,[4] is gravely ill; I owe him several gulden. After the holidays I shall go up and visit my excellent patron, perhaps not without inconvenience; then, if it seems good, I shall visit old friends in Basel. For I cannot always stay in one spot like a sponge, and it appears advisable to visit Erasmus once.[5] Commend me to him most dutifully. Again, farewell in Christ and make haste to come to Nürnberg.

Yours, Caspar.

Letter 171a: 21 October 1523, [Saverne], Wilhelm von Honstein to the Dean and Chapter of St Thomas

The manuscript of this text is AST 16, #12. For Wilhelm von Honstein, bishop of Strasbourg, see CWC 1, Ep. 174 headnote. It is notable that the letter is formally addressed to the dean (Nicolaus Wurmser) rather than the provost (Capito). This may be due to the fact that Capito's position was in limbo (see CWC 1, Epp. 174, 175), and the bishop no doubt favoured Capito's rival Jacob Abel (see CWC 1, Ep. 50 headnote).

Wilhelm, by the grace of God, Bishop of Strasbourg and Landgrave of Alsace. First, our friendly greeting, worthy, learned, honest, dear, and pious men. We have had a report from a credible source that your parish priest at St Thomas[1] announced to the common people in church last Sunday that he has chosen a wife and that he wishes this to be the first publication of the banns and would celebrate his marriage to her in church the following Sunday.[2] Consequently, in accordance with the decree of the Holy Empire

* * * * *

2 A reference to a benefice in Halberstadt? Cf. Capito's remark in CWC 1, Ep. 157 of 24 April 1523: 'My prince has obtained for me the church of Halberstadt, but I will have no opportunity to take advantage of it. [Albert] knows that I do not want to spend my life there.'

3 Luke 3:11.

4 Sigmund of Hohenlohe, the dean of the cathedral chapter, who effected Hedio's appointment as cathedral preacher later that year. Cf. CWC 1, Ep. 174.

5 Erasmus lived in Basel from 1521 to April 1529, when he moved to Freiburg.

1 Anton Firn. On Firn, see CWC 1, Ep. 171 headnote. Capito, whose duty as provost was to follow up on the episcopal directive, took no action. See below, Ep. 189, note 2.

2 He married on 9 November 1523.

issued at the recent Diet at Nürnberg,[3] I earnestly wish and command you to enforce that decree against the above-mentioned parish priest, as much as you see fit, and to act as you think it is your duty to act. This is our directive to you, and we deign to notify you of it. Given on Wednesday, 21 October in the year 1523.

Letter 173a: [27 October 1523, Strasbourg], The Collegiate Churches of St Thomas, Old and Young St Peter to Wilhelm von Honstein

The manuscript of this letter is AST 22–2 ('p. 62' marked in upper right-hand corner). The date has been added in a different hand. The letter is a request to the bishop to intervene with the city of Strasbourg on behalf of the three collegiate churches. Although Capito is, by virtue of his office, included among the signatories of this letter, he can hardly have approved of the request. On the contrary, he supported the intentions of the city – the subject of the present complaint – to force the collegiate churches to share in the burden of the citizens. For further developments in this matter, see below, Epp. 216a and 228a. For the addressee, see CWC 1, Ep 174 headnote.

Most worthy prince, gracious lord, let us first offer our prayers to God Almighty and our obedient service to you, etc. May Your Princely Grace graciously accept the following humble request of ours:

The honourable council of the city of Strasbourg has some time ago, no doubt with honest and upright intent and empowered by the leave granted them, given an order and passed a law. Among other things, this decree states that one may commute standing taxes, except hereditary fiefs,[1] into a lump-sum payment, as further specified in that decree. Although we are of the opinion that it was not the intention or will of the honourable council for this decree to apply to the three collegiate churches of St Thomas, Old and Young St Peter, or be interpreted as pertaining to the standing tax, it has, in fact, been interpreted in that way. As a consequence of the said decree, the above-mentioned three collegiate churches are bound to pay some of the standing taxes, and the money has been paid into the city's coffers. Yet the above-mentioned collegiate churches have been exempted from the greater part of the standing tax, since their praiseworthy order obliges them to sing and read the service, and they have observed their duty and looked after

* * * * *

3 Of 6 March 1523. See below, Ep. 189, note 19.

1 *ewige zynnss usserthalb erb unnd mannlehen.*

other matters stipulated by their clerical and noble forefathers in the charter of foundation and in the wills, maintaining the practices that have been upheld in the same manner for many years by our predecessors according to tradition and usage. Any cancellation or other change would therefore create considerable irritation and confusion in the above-mentioned order and foundation, which would be rather burdensome, as Your Princely Grace can see for yourself.

Secondly, the honourable council has passed a praiseworthy, necessary, and godly regulation concerning alms to be distributed to poor people, etc. This regulation, which has been published in print,[2] suggests that all collegiate churches agreed to contribute to the alms. In this matter we maintain the opinion that the contributions given by or on behalf of our collegiate churches are subject to the wills and other laws and regulations instituted by pious and honourable nobles and others. Their nature is such that our predecessors defined in writing and contractually their and their descendants' rights versus the rights of the contractual party and their descendants, and the right to approve changes to the circumstances of paying the tax rests with us. May Your Princely Grace consider the potential loss of reputation, the risk, and the disadvantage arising for us and our descendants in the future from those whose forefathers were responsible for the foundation and who still have the documents in their possession.

Furthermore, we of the three collegiate churches have for many years been protected and shielded by the honourable council of the city of Strasbourg, and have always been protected from violence in a friendly and loyal manner. We have been given access to the [city's] law court, which provided us with considerable support and protection against citizens and others. But when the annual term of renewal for the above-mentioned protective service came around, the honourable council cancelled it. Thereupon we respectfully requested several times that they continue to protect us. They refused (we do not know why). This is rather inconvenient for us, for many reasons, which may be surmised by Your Princely Grace and Your Princely Grace's honourable council. Therefore we humbly beg Your Princely Grace, our gracious lord and Ordinary, to support us and deign to intercede with the honourable council of the city of Strasbourg (for, no doubt, they will not lightly refuse you anything that is possible). We hope that you can persuade them to

* * * * *

2 The text of the broadsheet is published in O. Winckelmann, *Das Fürsorgewesen der Stadt Straßburg* (Leipzig, 1922) II: 105–8. The broadsheet is dated 1 October 1523 (the law was approved by the council on 4 August and ratified on 29 September).

deliver us from this difficulty in a spirit of friendship and good will, so that our collegiate churches and their rights and praiseworthy traditions may be observed in the city of Strasbourg, and together with them, as of old, we may live and remain among them in pious concord, enjoying peace and quiet.

We declare our good will and obedience, and wish to be in the service and debt of Your Princely Grace and the honourable council of the city of Strasbourg, as is our obligation to God and as far as lies in our power.

Your Princely Grace's obedient servants, the canons, provost, dean, and chapter of the three collegiate churches of St Thomas, Young and Old St Peter in Strasbourg.

THE CORRESPONDENCE OF WOLFGANG CAPITO

VOLUME 2: 1524–1531

Letter 179: 17 January 1524, [Strasbourg], Capito to Willibald Pirckheimer

Printed in H. Scheible, ed., *Willibald Pirckheimers Briefwechsel* (Munich, 2001), 5:109–11, Ep. 808.

[*Summary*]: Daniel Mieg, who is attending the Diet of Nürnberg, is the bearer of the present letter. He does not speak Latin but is intelligent and a staunch supporter of the Reformation. He will give Pirckheimer the news about Strasbourg and will report back any news Pirckheimer has. Many preachers have married in accordance with Scripture. It is important to be free of the burdensome superstitions the Roman church has imposed on the world, and to uphold only the gospel law. Capito is waiting, either to be exiled (i.e., lose his provostship) or delivered from service to 'Baal.' He is suffering physically from the gout, but his mind is at peace. He asks Pirckheimer to supply him with manuscripts for the printing house of his relative, Wolfgang Köpfel.

Letter 180: 27 January 1524, Strasbourg, The Strasbourg Preachers to the City Council of Obernai

Printed in BDS 1:348–55. See CorrBucer 1:214–15, Ep. 55.

[*Summary*]: After hearing the reformers preach in Strasbourg, the citizens of Obernai introduced reforms at home. This caused conservative preachers to denounce the reformers and their adherents from the pulpit and prompted the council to forbid meetings discussing evangelical doctrine. Two citizens were arrested for violating dietary laws and for speaking up against the superstitious veneration of saints. These men have merely followed the precepts of the gospel, as they should. Anyone who opposes the gospel opposes God. Rather than persecuting such men, the council should support the Word of God. The actions of the council are damaging to the city's reputation. They should instead urge the priests to read and preach the gospel.

Letter 181: 27 January 1524, Strasbourg, The Strasbourg Preachers to [Hans Hesse]

Printed in BDS 1:355–61. See CorrBucer 1:214–15, Ep. 56. Hans Hesse was the parish priest of Obernai.

[*Summary*]: They protest against being traduced in Hesse's sermons as rogue preachers (*Lumpenprediger*) and adherents of false prophets. They are adherents of the gospel truth. The Franciscans of St Ulrich are also preaching against the reformers and spreading lies about them. They should preach the Word of God and draw the people from ceremonies to spiritual piety instead of leading them astray.

Letter 182: [ca. 27 January 1524, Strasbourg], The Strasbourg Preachers to Hans Jacob von Mörsburg

Printed in BDS 1:361. See CorrBucer 1:215–16, Ep. 57.

[*Summary*]: They inform von Mörsburg, the *Landvogt* at Haguenau, that they have written to the council and parish priest of Obernai [see Epp. 180 and 181 above], requesting that they desist from persecuting the Word of God. They ask him to read the letters and support their cause.

Letter 183: [January 1524, Strasbourg], Matthew Zell to Capito

The manuscript of this letter is in the Kongelige Bibliotek, Copenhagen, ms. Thott 497, f. 77. For Matthew Zell, see CWC 1, Ep. 167 headnote.

Today a house fell vacant on account of the death of Peter Oestericher, vicar in our chapter.[1] It is up to the wardens of the hospital to lease the house. One of the wardens is our Nicolaus Kniebs,[2] whom I shall ask – and I would like you to join me in asking – to lease the house to Peter Heldung. This is the same Peter Heldung[3] who is procurator in the Bruderhof[4] and who is now the only one in the chapter who is completely on our side, although he is somewhat discreet about it. He asks especially for a reference. Therefore, write this very night to your friend Kniebs and attest to your and my support for Peter. For the wardens will meet tomorrow. They will be dealing with this and other hospital matters. Farewell, write a few words to the man

* * * * *

1 I.e., the cathedral chapter. I have found no biographical information on Peter Oestericher.
2 For Kniebs, see below, Ep. 184 headnote.
3 Peter Heldung of Obernai in Alsace (1486–1561), was steward at the cathedral chapter, succeeding to the post on the death of his father, Hans Heldung, in 1516. He belonged to the circle of Wimpheling and the literary society of Strasbourg, and set up a foundation to benefit poor girls.
4 I.e., the regular meeting place of the cathedral chapter.

in charge of the lease, that he may see that either one of us is willing to be of service. Farewell.

Master Matthew, sometimes ...[5] when you are here.

Letter 184: [January 1524, Strasbourg], Capito to Nicolaus Kniebs

> The manuscript of this letter is in the Hamburg Universitätsbibliothek, ms. Sup. Ep. Fol.1, f. 364, #117. For the background see above, Ep. 183. The addressee, Nicolaus Kniebs (1479–1552), studied at Freiburg (BA 1495, licentiate in canon and civil law, ca. 1501). He was actively engaged in the affairs of the city, as a councillor from 1512, and after 1519 as a member of the XIII, the committee dealing with political and military matters. He represented the city at the Diet of Nürnberg in 1522, and Regensburg in 1532. He was repeatedly elected Ammeister, the leading position on the city council. Kniebs, who was a public-spirited man and had strong moral convictions, supported the reformers and their agenda. In 1526 he was one of three scholarchs in charge of organizing schools in Strasbourg. In 1528 he was assessor for the *Reichsregiment*, the governing body of the empire sitting in Speyer. After 1532 his increasing deafness prevented him from continuing his active role on the council. When the emperor imposed the Interim on Strasbourg in 1547, Kniebs was among those who preached moderation and tried to calm the people.

Greeting. Matthew Zell, the priest of St Lorenz,[1] believes that I carry as much weight with Your Prudence as he himself does, even though he no doubt deserves that position on account of his own merits. For this reason I have always publicly set the greatest hope on you as a singular patron of pious men. And I ask Your Honour to support this petition and indicate thereby that our efforts are not displeasing to you, and that the small vacant house at the disposal of the wardens should be leased to the priest about whom Matthew gives ample testimony:[2] They say that he suffers unfair treatment from the deputies for the sake of Christ.

I commend myself to you, my most respected and humane sir. May Christ preserve you together with your most chaste wife and child.

W. Fabritius Capito, provost, your sincere admirer.

* * * * *

5 Illegible word.

1 For Zell, see CWC 1, Ep. 167 headnote.
2 I.e., Peter Heldung. See preceding letter, note 3.

Letter 185: 27 February 1524, Strasbourg, The Strasbourg Preachers to the City Council of Strasbourg

Printed in BDS 1:362–5; cf. CorrBucer 1:218–20, Ep. 59.

[*Summary*]: The bishop of Strasbourg has so far refused to give them a hearing, but it is their duty to preach the gospel. They request permission to draw up a summary of their teachings and ask for a date on which they might publicly discuss them. They do not wish to act on their own authority and therefore ask for an official endorsement.

Letter 186: 29 February 1524, Strasbourg, The City Council of Strasbourg to the Preachers

Printed in CorrBucer 1:220–2, Ep. 60.

[*Summary*]: The council is eager to avoid dissension and, in the circumstances, cannot at this time authorize a public discussion of doctrine. They demand that the preachers refrain from further liturgical innovation [such as saying the mass in German], observe in their preaching the mandate [of 1 December 1523], and keep the peace.

Letter 187: [15 March 1524, Strasbourg], The Strasbourg Preachers to Conrad Treger

Printed in CorrBucer 1:222–4, Ep. 61. On Treger see below, Ep. 222 headnote.

[*Summary*]: They have received Treger's *Paradoxa centum ... de ecclesiae conciliorumque autoritate* [see below, Ep. 222 headnote] and ask him to dispute the doctrinal questions raised before a select group, preferably in his monastery. They suggest a meeting on the following day or the day after that.

Letter 188: 16 March [1524, Strasbourg], Capito, Caspar Hedio, Matthew Zell, Martin Bucer, and Symphorian Altbiesser to the City Council of Strasbourg

Printed in CorrBucer 1:224–6, Ep. 62.

[*Summary*]: They inform the council of their request to Treger to arrange for a disputation concerning their teachings [see above, Ep. 187]. Treger is willing to do so, but only if the disputation is authorized by the bishop and the city council of Strasbourg. They herewith request permission to dispute with Treger.

Letter 189: 6 April 1524, Strasbourg, The Strasbourg Preachers to the public

The text of this open letter to the bishop of Strasbourg was published under the title *Appellation der eelichen Priester von der vermaynten Excommunication des Bischoffen zu Strassburg* (Appeal of the married priests against the so-called excommunication of the Bishop of Strasbourg, Strasbourg: Köpfel, 1524) and in Latin as *Appellatio sacerdotum maritorum urbis Argentinae adversus excommunicationem episcopi* (ibid.). The appeal was composed at Matthew Zell's house on 5 April. Capito, who was not yet married and therefore not one of the accused, was present on the occasion and helped draft the appeal. For his involvement in writing it, see his comments to Ambrosius Blaurer in Ep. 192 below.

The translation below is of the German text.

Appeal of the married priests against their supposed excommunication[1] by the Most Reverend prince and lord Wilhelm, Bishop of Strasbourg

The law provides for a person who has been penalized by a judge out of ignorance, or ill will, or some other reason, to have recourse to a higher judge. It is well known and obvious that church councils are superior to bishops and popes, since we know that the community as a whole is superior to any individual. Therefore we, Matthew Zell, Anton Firn,[2] Lucas Bathodius,[3]

* * * * *

1 The bishop had rejected an appeal from the city council and excommunicated the six men named in the next paragraph. On 3 April 1524 he ordered the writ of excommunication posted on the church doors.
2 For Zell (married 3 December 1523) and Firn (married 9 November 1523), see CWC 1, Epp. 176 headnote and 171 headnote.
3 Lucas Bathodius (or Hackfurt, d. 1554) studied at Heidelberg (MA 1513). He was chaplain at Obernai and also had a benefice in Strasbourg. He eventually resigned his posts and opened a private school in Strasbourg. He married in the first half of January 1524. From 1523 on he was in charge of the city's welfare system. He was leaning toward Anabaptism, but renounced his beliefs in 1531. In 1554 he received a benefice at Old St Peter's.

Wolfgang Schultheiss,[4] Conrad Spatzinger,[5] Alexander a former Johannite,[6] and Johannes Niebling,[7] all now priests in the See of Strasbourg, state before you, the notary, and the trustworthy witnesses named below, how some of us through their evangelical pastorate among the people and others through biblical studies have attained an enlightened belief and insight and felt that, in truth, human beings must obey God rather than human beings in matters that concern the salvation of the soul.

And soon after the clear command of God cleansed our eyes, we recognized the repulsive and problematic nature of our pretended chastity. Some of us used prostitutes, and others kept their own concubines at home, causing no small scandal and ill will. We confess what cannot be denied, that some of us offered a semblance of chastity, but in our constant desire sacrificed to the idol Moloch,[8] not without detriment to our belief, for ignorance of God furthers evil strife.

Furthermore, when we were comforted by scripture and grew in hope and strength, we understood what we must do in decency and virtue. We entered holy matrimony, which God not only allowed us but indeed commanded us to do when he sent us out. For the Spirit of God says that every man should avoid being unchaste and therefore have his own wife,[9] and not another man's; and this command applies not only to laymen; everyone is to have his own wife. For a weak and simple man is still flawed in his mind and in his will, even if his body is kept pure (which is, in any case, a rare gift in a healthy man). We took seriously the command that *it is better to marry than to burn*,[10] that is, to suffer desire and restraint or to sacrifice oneself in vain. The only serious obstacle was the wrong attitude of the common people who had long ago become accustomed to our shameful whoring, and rejected the idea of priests entering into an honest marriage.

What was to be done? It was not possible to continue in error, for we had to keep in mind the people, whom Christ held so dear that he died

* * * * *

4 Wolfgang Schultheiss, later vicar of Young St Peter's, was an ex-Augustinian and married on 16 November 1523.
5 Conrad Spatzinger (matriculated at the University of Heidelberg in 1509), vicar at the cathedral, married 5 January 1524.
6 Alexander von Villingen, formerly a Johannite, married on 29 January 1524.
7 Johannes Niebling (ca. 1463–1525) was prior of the Cistercian abbey in Ebrach, then priest of St Erhart's chapel attached to the hospice in Strasbourg. He married in the first half of January 1524.
8 Lev. 18:21.
9 1 Cor. 7:2.
10 1 Cor. 7:9.

for them. We therefore delayed the matter for half a year to accommodate their simplicity and did not make use of our right to turn them from their wrong condemnation of good things. During that time, we revealed the horrid deeds of Satan and with all our might clamoured against the adulterers who broke God's command, in particular, the lovers, whorers, and unchaste people, pointing the people diligently toward marriage which was given to us as a remedy against sin. Thus, they would no longer be able to claim ignorance.

Praise be to God, for he who gave us speech also aided our speech. The people developed a good understanding and began to put less value on the so-called chaste priests among us, even those who had at least the appearance of being pure. This attitude was promoted by the divinely instituted marriage of Martin Bucer, our fellow minister of the gospel and most beloved brother in Christ, and his spouse, the chaste and Christian Elisabeth.[11] At that time the people had acquired a sound understanding and many had accepted the gospel, but our flesh was as weak as before. Should we then have acted counter to the command of Christ?

Should we have accommodated the Pharisees, who seek a scandal in all good things and are a scandal to the whole world through their hypocrisy and malice, feeling no shame at all? What could have kept us from marriage, when it was instituted through the Spirit of Christ and necessary in obedience to his commands, to put an end to the godless customs and do away with the unchaste and flawed clerical chastity? Indeed, there was nothing that could have deterred us from our Christian undertaking. Thus, we each took a wife in defiance of the Antichrist.

At first there was the occasional talk and muttering, in some cases out of surprise at an unheard-of innovation, in others for the sake of malicious, poisonous gossip. For there are always people who slander and criticize what is done in a Christian spirit. Nevertheless it was accepted in the community, as people told each other that our action was legitimate.

The papistical horde, as is their custom, spoke against us in a hateful and insulting manner, calling us scoundrels and heretics. Only the clerics of the collegiate church of St Thomas – not all of them, but only a few who were perhaps led on by other evil people – attempted so many times to drive out their parish priest[12] because he was married, a man whom they previously, when he was a manifest whorer, accepted as a leader of their community.

* * * * *

11 Bucer married Elisabeth Silbereisen in May 1522. She was the daughter of a smith from Mosbach/Neckar and an ex-nun.
12 Firn; see above, note 2.

The truth and sequence of events can be seen from the printed report of the action of the parishioners.[13] All that happened around Christmas.

Thereafter there was peace and quiet about the subject of marriage, and what the married priests said came to be held in higher regard among respectable citizens. Adultery, furthered by clerical celibacy, declined. Christian behaviour was Christian once again, and shameful deeds, which up until then had been preferred to honest deeds on account of the dishonest life of the ministers of the church, were recognized as shameful. Indeed, against the will of our enemies, everything was in accord with true fear of God and righteous Christian life.

Since such progress of the gospel was unbearable to our enemies, they induced several people to incite the bishop against us, and they persuaded him to call us before the law to destroy what we had built up and remove us from the scene. Indeed, he was not unwilling to do this kind of bishop's work. It is reported that he composed a harsh missive on his own and that he was willing to go to extreme ends, making every effort and undergoing every risk, which, however, we cannot bring ourselves to believe at this time. Should he attempt anything untoward, he will attempt it to his own grave detriment and will not be able to obstruct the gospel, for he who is in us is stronger than worldly power. Let him see that one cannot trifle with God.

Let us continue with our account of this business, which is truly worthy of a bishop and his two-cornered hat. Around the end of January, the bishop issued a summons to the effect that we should appear at his court in Saverne within fifteen days to see and hear him explain why we are to be deprived of our priesthood on account of marriage, etc.[14] At first we brought this matter to the attention of the respected council, attaching a request to ascertain that no harm would come to the common weal from it. For our actions were based on the Word of God, whose glory we were willing to sustain throughout the duration of our lives against those whom the glory of the Word has given great honour and possession and their present high authority. We hoped that our Christian zeal would not displease him who was our Christian superior. Yet we worried, though perhaps in vain and without foundation, that our enemies, since they could not succeed with reason and scripture, were

* * * * *

13 I.e., CWC 1, Ep. 177.
14 The summons was issued on 20 January. A copy in German translation is in AST 187, #11. This document also includes an undated reply from Zell, Firn, Spatzinger, Hackfurt, and Schultheiss to the bishop in which they defend their actions.

thinking of using fraud as well as secret and open hostility. They might even bring useless idlers into the city in order to insult the pious citizens, since such agitators against the well-established common weal could easily be found.

We hinted obliquely rather than expressing our opinion openly. We considerately spared the princely dignity of the bishop, in the good hope that any improper actions were the result of weakness rather than malice, and that the prince had perhaps been persuaded by his courtiers, for great fortune is dogged and chased down by flatterers. Next, the honourable council sent several respectable persons to the bishop in order to persuade him to take no action until the conclusion of the present Diet at Nürnberg, when it was hoped that the princes would decide the matter.[15] At that time, the bishop might act with better authority and encounter less ill will [they said]. For at this time, the people believed that any desperate, unchristian action was taken on the initiative of the bishop rather than driven by any necessity. No wise prince would touch such a matter even with the tip of his finger. The bishop could expect honour from staying clear of such an action, and conversely, a lasting bad reputation from pursuing it. Therefore the honourable council would like him to hold off for a time. Once the empire issued its interpretation, things would unfold more properly, and the people would show greater obedience to the powerful lords, especially if their commandments were in accord with Christ. This and other such suggestions were made, we think, by the rulers of the city. But they obtained only one month's delay, which we nevertheless accepted in the good hope that the bishop, who was at that time against us and Christ, perhaps on the instigation of his courtiers (as we would like to think), would acquire a better understanding. For there are people who spur on the running horse, as the future will more clearly reveal, and indeed they are already known to those who recognize the intentions of the devil. Now, however, our simplicity and willingness to be peaceful have been abused, and strife has, as we find indeed, become more intense. For the enterprising bishop thought it best to inaugurate his office by expelling married priests, but first he took care of public opinion, for the people take keen notice of such business and are more willing to speak out and judge than we, the clergy, like them to be. For that reason he issued an indictment against whoring clerics and had it affixed to the church doors, commanding everyone to throw his concubine out of the house within eight days or lose the fruits of

* * * * *

15 See the bishop's negative reply, 13 March 1524 (Gerdesius II, 71). The council made a second attempt to change the bishop's mind (see Ratsprotokoll of 16 March 1524, TB II, 74). The diet adjourned 18 April 1524.

his benefice. In this manner he made sure that the prelates were covered, that is, he put the right lid on the pot, causing the poor priests to borrow houses or exchange them with their neighbours and entrusting their women friends to each other. Even those who had ignored earlier mandates and kept their concubines were now willing to obey, for they were certain that punishment would be dealt out. Indeed, such a command did not at all have the effect the words purported, for the whoring priests were injured by words, whereas the pure, married priests were injured in deed.

Their ruse does not harm us so long as common sense aptly recognizes that the blind are leading the blind, that our great masters and rabbis cannot see – or at any rate, take care that no one else may see or understand – that marriage, which is commanded by God, is far better and more honest than the widespread whoring which has resulted from the greed of the priests. Thus, the bishop thought that by issuing this command, he would make things simpler by eliminating the counter-argument regarding the toleration of whoring, which this very clever judge considered our only and strongest protection. Soon, however, a rumour started that there would be no peace in the future unless he implemented his statute fully, which was perhaps promoted by people who promised more than they could keep. When we heard that rumour, we were desirous of peace and wrote to the bishop in a friendly and deferential spirit,[16] attesting to our belief in scripture. We then requested that he either abstain from unfair legal proceedings or that he order his vicar to give us a hearing, as was lawful, and allow us to show the justice and reason for our position.

It has also been reported that the council reminded him of their former rights and pacts, which had been signed and sealed, which he confirmed and renewed when entering on his office as bishop.[17] These included the provision that the bishop must not pass judgment on a citizen or priest from outside the precincts of the city and must not move the venue from Strasbourg. But those complaints left no impression on him. Why not? The reason has not yet been discovered, except that it is the custom of the clergy not to give a full explanation and habitually to act through ruses, tricks, secret and evil machinations. They try hard to cause dissension among the citizens, for where there is peace and unity, propriety prevails, and foreign authority imposed by force

* * * * *

16 Cf. above, Ep. 171a, for the bishop's first inquiry into this matter, and above, note 14 for the married priests' reply.
17 They referred him to the so-called Speyer Rachtung (Ratsprotokoll 16 March 1524; cf. above, note 15.)

has no power whatsoever. Improper violence increases when public security declines, and tyranny rises everywhere when the rich disagree. It grows out of envy and hatred among the citizens, and is maintained while petty ill will is kept alive. For this condition there is no better cure than salutary friendship among citizens, which serves to strengthen great communities.

Finally, on the third day of this month, the bishop's ban was posted at the cathedral here at Strasbourg, signed and sealed in the customary manner and naming the 14 of March as the date on which the judgment would come into force. This is entirely ungodly and insufferable by the law of God, as our whole community may attest. Indeed, our enemies admit it, for they cite the Fathers but do not refer to scripture even with one word, so as not to slay themselves with their own words. For scripture contradicts their action, and neither popes, nor cardinals, nor bishops, indeed no one in the world, not even the angels in heaven, have been given power over scripture. The judgment of the bishop against us, however, confirms the teaching of the Devil, who forbids marriage and condemns the commandment of the Spirit of Christ. For Christ commands in scripture that each man must have his own wife, to avoid lawless whoring and harmful lust.[18]

For this reason, we, who have been clearly maligned, call out against those who bring suit against us now and any who may do so in future, and we ask that a free Christian council be assembled in the Spirit of God. This council should take its rules from scripture and should not import them from elsewhere. Nor should it suppress the free spirit or prefer its own thinking to the word of Christ, who speaks to us through Moses, through many prophets, through the apostles, and in itself. For the world hopes that such a council will be called soon, as has so often been promised by the princes.[19] Any ruling from such a council we shall willingly accept and obey as the voice of Christ, but we are certain that such a council, if it is ruled by the Spirit, will not decide against us, for we rely on clear scriptural evidence. The Spirit of our Lord, our Lord and God, is unchanging. The bishop in his improper judgment prevents us from keeping God's commandment. For this reason

* * * * *

18 1 Cor. 7:2.
19 Cf. the Nürnberg mandate of 6 March 1523, which contained five points: until a council was called, only the gospel was to be preached; preachers must avoid inciting the population and await a decision of the council; bishops and archbishops must not prevent the preaching of the gospel; until a council was called, magistrates must provide censorship for books and suppress incendiary pamphlets; married priests and those who leave their order are to be deprived of their income from benefices.

we do not acknowledge his trumped-up authority and maintain steadily that neither he nor angels have the authority to touch scripture, which he, in his inexperienced judgment, lessens, overturns, and belittles. Instead of being shepherds, such leaders are cruel wolves, betrayers of the flock in the guise of watchmen, tyrants under the title of fathers.

The Christian reader must understand that, in so far as such men attempt on purpose and with forethought to mar the pure faith with their so-called judgment, the glory of scripture, which was not unharmed even before, is further reduced. For the Church rests on the Word, but that Word is made uncertain by anyone who pierces scripture with the poisonous arrows and blasphemous sentences of his tongue. For scripture is dead and gone as soon as even one syllable is called into doubt. Yet we would rather ascribe such blasphemy to certain ignorant jurists than to the renowned prince, unless he owns it himself.

We appeal not only this judgment but all complaints that may arise from it in the future for us and our community. And we request earnestly notarized statements, firstly, secondly, and thirdly, of all their actions, and in particular we demand that you, the notary, attest to our appeal and all that is written above.

Furthermore, our opponents may cite the laws introduced by popes Pius II and Julius II,[20] which strongly affirm their tyranny by improperly decreeing and prohibiting any appeal to a future council, which is not yet in session. For no one may appeal to a judge who has not yet been born, etc. Anyone who wants to accept such arguments should kindly listen to our reply. Then he will understand to whom one should appeal and why we appeal to the council.

We state, firstly, that those who serve the council and are its members are alive; also: princes and estates appeal to a future diet in the same way as we now appeal to the promised council, for the promise of the princes has given the world hope for a council.

Point 2: We do not know how we can appeal to the archbishops, primates, and the pope himself, for they are enemies of scripture and the cross of Christ, and have earlier condemned the gospel.

Point 3: It follows that one to whom the tyrants of the soul have done violence ought to appeal to a free Christian council alone.

* * * * *

20 The Bull Execrabilis (1459) prohibited appeals to councils; Pope Julius' Bull Suscepti regiminis (1509) proclaimed Pius' bull perpetually valid and declared schismatic any appeal against the papacy to a council.

Point 4: Even without those arguments, we have further reason to appeal, for the bishop bases his judgment on our disobedience, as he states in the pending action, although not a word has been offered in support. The canon laws do not forbid anyone to speak up in matters touching on faith, at the peril of disobedience. For it is indeed a matter of faith, whether one ought to give more credence to scripture or to men's commandments, and this whole business rests on that point. Although the bishop does not wish to refer expressly to this in his judgment, it is its meaning and purport. His judgment condemns scripture and judges on the basis of a papal decree and imperial edict, and places them above a people's conscience.

Point 5: And so he cited us to Saverne,[21] a dangerous and uncertain place, which we may not reach and where we may not walk around without danger to our lives, for we have aroused all children of lies against us by defending the truth. Consider that further, fair reader, etc.

Point 6: He has taken us from here[22] to a place where he has his vicars, official, prelates, judge, lawyer, and advocate, notaries and everything else that pertains to the court. At the same time, however, we cannot have such things in Saverne without considerable cost that surpasses our means, as we have respectfully pointed out to the bishop in writing.

Point 7: It is a violent and improper action for a judge to act fast and without a hearing in the case of a citizen, and to condemn the accused who is willing to justify himself. For we earnestly requested such an opportunity, asking for a term and a meeting here in Strasbourg before a judge appointed for the occasion.

Point 8: He began the action in an invalid manner, for the citation names no accuser. That may have happened for an honest reason, as the fiscal[23] was not at home at the time when some people were cited. He was in Constance to claim a benefice in the cathedral. This may have happened through an oversight of the notaries who (for shame!) did not sufficiently consider all things beforehand.

Point 9: The narrative and account of the matter is untrue, for in pronouncing the so-called ban, it is stated that the bishop took notice of the citation in the presence of the fiscal. This is contrary to the truth. No one is appointed complainant in the citations; rather, the bishop is both complainant and judge, and he himself issued the citation in this matter. Furthermore,

* * * * *

21 The bishop's residence.
22 I.e., moved the court from Strasbourg, where the accused are resident.
23 Not identified.

the entire content of the complaint is a patchwork and construct of lies. How is the divine majesty of the sacred church and of the god-fearing popes violated, when God's will, the commands of the Spirit of the church, and the usage of pious Christian fathers is accepted and maintained?

Point 10: The fiscal, whom he only now appointed as complainant, has been banned by divine, imperial, and papal law, for he is a manifest whorer, with whom no Christian is to share a table.[24] This is the man who has been appointed to accuse us Christian brethren.

Point 11: The judgment goes beyond the contents of the citation and invitation. The judgment bans us, whereas the citation only obliges us to appear and see and hear a declaration[25] that we are already deprived of all clerical privilege, and nothing further.

Point 12: The judgment imposes a greater punishment than is within the mandate of the common and imperial law, even if interpreted in the narrowest sense. They merely deprive a man of his benefice and do not completely ban him. Indeed, the bishop's judgment is quite improper if one looks at the laws which excommunicate the whoring priests and ban them, whereas the married priests are merely deprived of their office but are allowed to remain pious Christians. By contrast, the bishop's judgment condemns and bans us married priests, whereas it threatens the whorers only with a small fine, etc.

We therefore demand to execute this appeal in order to prove by legal means the injuries done to us by the complaint described above and to expose this insidious plot against justice. We are also ready to hear the judgment of the Spirit from every Christian and to yield to it. We are accustomed to yield to simplicity, but we have no intention to yield to the bishop's malice and threats. We are inclined to honour the gospel, but we must go against the enemies of God's honour. They may accept that declaration from us and understand it as truly spoken. Thus, we beseech all Christian princes, dukes, lords, knights and followers, citizens, etc., all peoples and all Christian communities to accept our appeal and subscribe to it. We ask that you protect us and support us with your approval and the confirmation of Christ. And we beg you to resist with heart and hand those tyrants, who blaspheme against

* * * * *

24 Cf. 1 Cor. 5:11.
25 Cf. e.g., the bishop's sentence against Bathodius: *unsern Spruch und erclerung der Rechten, aller geistlichen freyheiten und aller pfrunden beroubt, entsetzt, und von denen abgestossen, beroubt und entsetzt [repeated sic] zu werden, zu sehen und zu hören* ('to see and hear our judgment and declaration in the law that he [Bathodius] is to be deprived and relieved of all ecclesiastical privileges and all benefices'; AST 84, #11).

holy scripture, against the Spirit of Christ, who rush in and assault the salvation of the faithful. You ought to take our side against the blasphemous undertaking of the ungodly popes and bishops, for no doubt all Christians are in our camp. Despise with us the empty bluster and threat of the so-called ban, condemn the condemnation, the thunder and hail. Indeed, we charge you to do so by the salvation of your souls, you who cherish the salvation of your souls, desire it and have committed yourselves to Christ the Lord. Finally, we wish to trust firmly and hope that He himself will destroy the Antichrist with the word of his mouth, as we believe only in the gospel. May he effect that much in our time and effect it soon. Amen.

In the name of the Lord, Amen. Announcement and declaration, etc.

After the above appeal was filed, as no one was present who was willing or had the authority to give this document to the appellants, as requested, I have issued the present document and testimonial brief. This was done at the parish of St Lorenz in Strasbourg.

I, Michael Schwencker of Gernsbach,[26] notary by imperial authority, etc.

Letter 189a: [before 9 April 1524, Strasbourg], Capito to the City Council of Strasbourg

This passage is from a letter read in the city council meeting on 9 April. It is quoted in Wilhelm Horning, *Das Stift vom Jungen Sankt Peter in Straßburg. Urkundliche Beiträge zur Geschichte desselben aus sieben Jahrhunderten (1000–1700)* (Strasbourg, 1891), 20–1. The passage appears in quotation marks, but no archival source is given, and the author has clearly modernized the German. The substance of the letter can, however, be verified from other sources. Compare the official decision handed down on 25 April (AST 69, #52): 'The council and XXI have decreed that the members of the collegiate church of Young St Peter ought to support Doctor Wolfgang Capito as parish priest and preacher.' Compare also Capito's account of his appointment below, Ep. 194.

... On Invocavit Sunday[1] the congregation of Young St Peter came to him and indicated that they had unanimously elected him as their parish priest.

* * * * *

26 Michael Schwencker (d. 1556) studied at Heidelberg (BA 1506). He was a member of the Strasbourg city council (notary from 1518), an employee of the episcopal administration 1518–23, and administrator at St Clara. His wife was a sister of Katharina Zell. He himself was a supporter of the reformers.

1 14 February 1524.

They urged him to take up the position. At first he rejected their request, but they continued to beg him urgently not to withhold from them the gifts God have given him. He accepted, but under the condition that there be no dissension and disruption, and that it be done with the agreement of the council. A few days later, the congregation brought him a positive reply, that is, that he might look after the parish and preach from Easter to the feast day of St John.[2]

Letter 190: [ca. 9 April 1524, Strasbourg], Capito to the City Council of Strasbourg

The manuscript of this letter is in AST 40, fol. 408. For the date see below, note 1.

Strict, honourable, honest, wise, and merciful lords! On Thursday after Quasimodo,[1] the canon Maternus Schmidt[2] and I, the provost of St Thomas, etc., your lords' obedient citizen, went to Count Emich von Leiningen[3] in reference to the matter of Diebold Balthener.[4] Initially, everything was transacted and decided in a friendly manner, since he offered us both a drink. But when we inquired again the next day, Friday, and asked him to refrain from his unjustified request, he insisted that Diebold Balthener should give surety for a man in Rome, who had not instructed him to do so. When he refused to withdraw this request, we offered to settle the issue with him before our lords in Strasbourg or whatever other ecclesiastical or secular court might be appropriate and suitable. But we found him quite indignant. He challenged our friendly request, which had been properly stated, and our offer to settle things in court, which was beyond our obligation. He threatened that he

* * * * *

2 24 June.

1 7 April 1524.
2 Maternus Fabri (Schmidt) of Reichshofen (d. 1527) was a canon of St Thomas and, from 1522, in charge of provisions (*magister granarii*). He took out citizenship and joined the Protestant camp in 1525.
3 Emich VIII von Leiningen (d. 1535), notorious for his temper, was deprived of his estates for his support of the French king against Emperor Maximilian I. He recovered them in 1519, but was later forced to abdicate in favour of his sons.
4 Theobaldus (Diebold) Balthener of Strasbourg (d. 1530) was semi-summissary of St Thomas from 1501 until his resignation in 1517, then summissary. He was one of the canons that remained Catholic and fled the city in 1525 (see below, Ep. 237). In 1528 the city granted him an annual pension of 100 fl for the loss of his canonry. The nature of the present transaction is unknown.

would injure us in body and substance, as soon as he was out of the city, and he threatened especially me, the provost. Then, when I answered in a deferential and polite manner, asking him to excuse me and the collegiate church, he called me a rascal and an evil-doer, and added twice 'you ravisher of Our Lady and the saints,' etc. I then apologized profoundly and asked him not to allow himself to be prejudiced against me and act in this outrageous and unmerciful manner. I suggested that perhaps I had been maligned by people bearing me a grudge. But that did not soften him, and straightaway he said: 'You are a rascal and an evil-doer' and other, worse threats. He said it often, and asked the bystanders to attest to the fact that he had called me a rascal and evil-doer many times, in the presence of others, etc. Finally I answered: 'I too have been in the presence of princes and lords, but nothing like this has ever happened to me before. I ask Your Lordship not to do anything that is unlawful.' Then he was even more upset and uttered other abuses and made abusive gestures and motions. He declared openly that I would never be safe from him, etc., adding words with which I do not wish to bother you, my lords. Finally, Count Georg von Henneberg[5] took him by the arm, and I left the court. Since I am your citizen and Count Emich abused me within your city precincts and himself declared his enmity and feud although I answered him in a decent fashion, mildly and deferentially, and even offered to go to court, it is my respectful request to Your Lordships that you help me obtain justice concerning the count's abuse. I also ask that you provide assurance that I may be safe from violence, for no burgher has ever spoken to me like that. I want to assure you, my lords, of the obedience and service I owe you.

Your servant, Dr Capito, provost at St Thomas

Letter 191: 14 April 1524, Basel, Conradus Pellicanus to Capito

The manuscript of this letter is in the Universitätsbibliothek, Basel, Ki.Ar. 25a, 67. For the writer, Conradus Pellicanus, see CWC 1, Ep. 89 headnote.

Greetings. I welcome, my dearest Capito, all that you have written in reply[1] with your usual candour and openness. You in turn will not condemn my straightforward speech. If I wanted to oblige all my enemies, both enemies

* * * * *

5 Georg II von Henneberg (1492–1526), a graduate of the University of Erfurt, was canon of the cathedral chapter from 1503. He also had canonries at Cologne, Speyer, and Mainz, and was provost of Sts Peter and Alexander in Aschaffenburg from 1512.

1 Pellicanus' letter is not extant.

of the gospel and manifestly evil men (as it appears), I would reject the cowl.[2] Most men, and especially many among my colleagues, desire it, and I would sadden those who are sincerely concerned for me on account of the Truth. However, I would listen to men of perfect judgment, and indeed men like you, but I can satisfy them in another way. Indeed, they will be content if I convince them of the innocence of my soul in this respect. I wish to benefit my neighbours in every way and aid in the progress of the gospel, as far as it is God's will.

I hear that you wanted to write something to me about Johann Bock.[3] I hope it was something positive. Indeed, I wrote to him once or twice in a sincere spirit, and he did not reply. Still, I know his Christian heart, and if your news about him is not positive, I believe that, being a prudent man, he is simply afraid to promote such significant innovation. I hear with great eagerness that things are moving in our direction, so much so, that you have prepared many people to be made perfect in the Word of God. Thus I fear no danger for our cause except from Lutheran radicals, who strive to turn everything upside down, according to their whim. That is a source of great concern for me. I hear different things, but give no credence to them, since I believe ill-natured people are spreading tales about the preachers of the gospel. In our circle, there is no one (no one I know personally, at any rate) whose actions, deeds, and public speech are contrary to the dictates of meekness and humility. Yet they traduce them and say that they are prone to various desires. Even those who profess to be zealous about the preaching of the gospel were reportedly scandalized by some behaviour when they recently returned from Frankfurt. I know how much the papists spread lies everywhere, but I would not wish anything to be said against the excellent servants of God, such as I believe have been given to Strasbourg by God.

I hear that you and some others intend to marry.[4] I do not condemn your intention if it is a necessity and according to God's indulgence, but I would rather that we all devoted ourselves completely and freely to the advancement of the church, especially those who are able to do so, as you are, and men like you, lest they be judged wrongly by the weak, who usually judge carnal men unkindly. I have not yet heard anything specifically about you, but there is general lamenting about preachers disgracing the Word of

* * * * *

2 Pellicanus left the monastery only in 1526, when his position there became untenable and he received a call from Zwingli to come to Zurich and teach Greek and Hebrew there.

3 Johann Bock von Gerstheim (d. 1542), who studied at the University of Freiburg (matriculated 1491), was a member of the city council and the father-in-law of Jacob Sturm.

4 Cf. below, Ep. 205, note 3.

God with scandalous behaviour while teaching purity. Indeed, they publicly claim and boast that their preaching and teaching is inspired by the Holy Spirit. Christ taught us to be modest in our exhortations. I disclose this to you as to a friend and in a sincere spirit, wishing everything to be for the glory of God and to end in spiritual benefit. Farewell. Basel, the 5th day after Misericordia, 1524. I just wanted to write a few words.

Your friend, Conradus Pellicanus

Letter 192: 17 April [1524], Constance, Ambrosius Blaurer to Capito

The manuscript of the letter is in Basel, Universitätsbibliothek Ki.Ar. 25a, #69. The text is partially printed in Schiess 1, 102–3, Ep. 73.

Ambrosius Blaurer (or Blarer, 1492–1564) of Constance, studied at Tübingen (MA 1512) and entered the Benedictine order. Encouraged by his brother Thomas, who studied in Wittenberg, and by Melanchthon, whom he met in Tübingen, Blaurer embraced Lutheran teaching. This led to conflict with his superiors and resulted in Blaurer leaving the monastery of Alpirsbach. Supported by the city council of Constance, he began preaching in 1525 and collaborated in introducing an ordinance mandating social and moral reform in the city in 1531. He was also active in promoting the Reformation in other cities in southern Germany. In 1534 he was invited to reform the duchy of Würtemberg and the University of Tübingen, but after engaging in controversy with Lutheran theologians, he was dismissed by the duke in 1538. Blaurer's refusal to sign the Wittenberg Concord isolated Constance. After imperial troops conquered the city in 1548, Catholicism was imposed on it. Blaurer left for Winterthur, Switzerland, and was put in charge of the parish of Biel (1551–9). In 1559 he returned to Winterthur, where he died.

Greetings. Our friend Zwick[1] gave me your letter, which he himself had

* * * * *

1 Johannes Zwick (ca.1496–1542) of Constance, studied law at Basel and Freiburg. From 1518, when he was ordained, to 1521, he continued his studies in Italy (doctorate in both laws, Siena 1521). In 1522 he returned to Germany, secretly married and, as parish priest of Riedlingen, began preaching reform. He was removed from his post in 1525 and returned to Constance, where he was appointed preacher at St Stephen's. Zwick and Blaurer were instrumental in reforming Constance. After Blaurer's departure, Zwick became the spiritual leader of the city. He was present at the negotiations for the Wittenberg Concord in 1536, but ultimately rejected it for theological and political reasons. The school order of Constance (1538–41) was largely Zwick's work. In 1542 he accepted the position of preacher in Bischofszell (Thurgau). He died of the plague shortly after his move.

obtained from you, my most illustrious Capito. At the same time he told me
about all the affairs of your city. The news was of a kind that greatly pleased
us and also confirmed what we had heard. For these efforts had been anticipated partly by rumours, and partly by your published pamphlets. We
certainly thank our Lord through Jesus Christ that you have come to spread
his gospel and announce your faith to the whole world. And now you are
an example to all the free cities in Germany where the Word is received,
convincing them of the passage in Phil. 1: *He who began a good work in us will
perfect it until the day of Jesus Christ.*[2]

In our community, too, the Word is preached with some success, thank
God, but we would like to see a somewhat more felicitous outcome than
hitherto. Even the little progress we have made must be attributed, not to
me, who neither plants nor waters, but rather, according to God, to our
preachers, to the city council, and to the pious efforts of certain other men.

Since I cannot do anything in that part except what I can do through
prayer and occasionally through counsel, I make no claims for myself and
shall gladly yield that glory, as I ought to, to others who deserve it on account
of their effort and work. My intention is, dear Capito, to make you understand that Zwick recommended me to you more in accord with his friendship
than with the truth, when he said that the business of the gospel appears to
prosper under my guidance among our people. It is now six months since the
council designated me as preacher of St Augustine's. If I appear to undertake
the task rather reluctantly, it is because I recognize that my strength is not
equal to it and will not hold out long. Nor do I know what other disturbances
will come to pass. Moreover, I do not wish to burden my abbot[3] with even
greater unpopularity, when he is burdened enough already on my account.
He has shifted his position somewhat, waiting until things have a different
aspect. Therefore I have been excused from this office of preaching until now.
Thus, there is no reason why your Augustinian provincial[4] should vaunt his
effort or his eloquence so arrogantly, as if the council had distanced itself
from the initiative on his counsel and inducement. On the contrary, the council was all the more incensed the more vehemently he objected, for he is an
impudent and shameless fellow. Indeed, I would have preached even in his
presence, if I had not taken into consideration other factors.

* * * * *

2 Phil. 1:6.
3 Ulrich Hamma, abbot from 1523–35. He retired when Duke Ulrich of Würtemberg reformed the monastery.
4 Conrad Treger. See below, Ep. 222.

We thought we must be circumspect in this matter, more than in any other, lest rashness impede success. Not that we have such respect for those perverse and blinded men, for we despise them heartily, but because we believe that one must show concern for the many people who are as yet weak and foolish. And that is the reason why we have not yet been able to allow superstitions, which are public practice, to fall into disuse or make improvements, lest innovation, which is offensive in many areas but particularly in religious matters, offend the simple people. For if one does not use the greatest prudence and the greatest moderation here, one will break the plant of superstition at ground level rather than pulling it up by the roots, for its roots are deep. But since life is now strengthened by assiduous and truly Christian sermons, at least as far as the people are concerned, we shall soon practise what we cite from the gospel, unless the followers of the Antichrist make a more violent effort. They, of course, are always intent on maintaining their tyranny and doggedly hold us back as much as they can. So far, they still wield bloody power and are strong, as measured by the standards of the world, and we have so far barely succeeded in the face of their ferocity to have the liberty to preach without introducing innovations. For a part – the weaker part – of the council collaborates with them. But to speak frankly, the greater and better part of the council appears in many respects to be more politic than Christian in their respect for the bishop[5] and their consideration for the tranquillity of the world. However, we shall venture something in defiance of the Gates of Hell, especially in those areas in which change matters a great deal, lest you appear to have admonished us in vain.

Farewell, my dearest brother, and if it does not inconvenience you, write to us frequently and strengthen us with your letters. Greetings from my true brother,[6] with whom I believe I live in great happiness. The minis-

* * * * *

5 Hugo of Hohenlandenberg (or Landenberg, 1457/60–1532) held benefices in Erfurt, Constance, Basel, and Chur. He matriculated at the University of Erfurt in 1487. In 1496 he was elected bishop of Constance. He was reform-minded at first, but turned against the reform preachers after 1522. He was unable to stop the movement in Constance and withdrew from the city in 1526. He resigned his see in 1529 and lived at his castle at Meersburg. In 1531, the sudden death of his successor, Balthasar Mercklin, obliged him to resume episcopal duties during the last months of his life.

6 Thomas Blaurer (ca. 1492–1567) studied law at Freiburg and theology under Luther at Wittenberg. He served as mayor of Constance from 1537–47. Forced to flee in 1547, when Catholicism was enforced in Constance, he moved to Switzerland and lived for the rest of his life in Giersberg (Thurgau).

ters of the gospel, who are here with us, salute you, those men who are most prudent and simple and sincere in Christ.

Give our greetings to Hedio, Matthew Zell, Bucer, Lonicerus, Brunfels, and Bathodius,[7] together with the whole evangelical congregation, and pray for us, that the Word of the Lord may spread and be glorified, as it is in us, and that we may be delivered from absurd and perverse men. Constance, 15 Calends of May.

Yours, Ambrosius Blaurer.

Give my kindest regards especially to Hedio. I shall write to him as soon as I am at leisure. For I was very pleased that he spoke so kindly of me in his letter to Zwick. I only wish I were worthy of such a great man – so erudite and good, and at the same time so sincerely devoted to you all.

Letter 193: [End of April/May 1524], Nürnberg, Andreas Osiander to Capito, Martin Bucer, and Matthew Zell

Printed in CorrBucer 1:245–9, Ep. 65.

[*Summary*]: Osiander apologizes for not responding to their letters [not extant]. He did not want to discourage or mislead them since he had only bad news to report. But now, finally, despite fierce opposition, the Reformation has made significant inroads in Nürnberg. He describes what has happened since the arrival of Lorenzo Campeggio, the cardinal-legate at the Third Diet of Nürnberg, on 14 March 1524. The people of Nürnberg responded favourably and eagerly to Osiander's sermon on the Antichrist, and to his two sermons preached on 19 and 20 March concerning confession. Despite opposition from the Augustinians, several thousand people attended a communion service held on 19 March, where both the bread and wine were distributed. Even Queen Isabella of Denmark, the sister of Ferdinand of Austria participated, to the chagrin of Ferdinand. The following day they omitted all idolatrous practices, despite threats of excommunication from Weigand von Redwitz, bishop of Bamberg. The evangelical preachers have divided their sermon duties: Thomas Gechauf preaches at the Neue Spital on Monday and the Benedictine abbey of the Schottenkloster on Tuesday; Osiander preaches at the parish church of St Lorenz on Wednesday, at the Augustinians on

* * * * *

7 For the preachers mentioned here, see CWC 1, Epp. 147 headnote (Hedio), 167 headnote (Zell), 125, note 1 (Lonicerus), 25 headnote (Brunfels), and above Ep. 189, note 3 (Bathodius, i.e., Lucas Hackfurt).

Thursday, and at the parish church of St Sebald's on Friday. The reformers already have the ear of the city council, but he hopes for even more support. Reforms have already been introduced: the old Easter ceremonies of acting out the crucifixion and resurrection have not been observed this year. If the papists accept the reforms, the gospel will have won the day. Conditions in the margravate of Ansbach-Bayreuth are tumultuous. Osiander asks for Capito's, Bucer's, and Zell's prayers.

Letter 194: 4 May 1524, Strasbourg, Capito to Ambrosius Blaurer

Printed in Schiess 1:104–7, Ep. 75. For the addressee, see above Ep. 192 headnote.

The grace and peace of Christ. Today we were meeting at Zell's house.[1] Hedio[2] had just left and I was on the point of leaving, when your letter[3] together with those of other friends arrived. I broke the seal before the company, opened the letter and read it out, for I thought that there was much that many, indeed all people, should know. I cannot tell you, my dear Blaurer, with what pleasure everyone received your letter, not so much because it was elegant (for we are somewhat negligent in the matter of style), but more particularly because it had the aspect of exceptional piety. Indeed, it professed faith purely and simply, and keenly encouraged us to be more diligent, which you certainly made more poignant by that light touch of your free-flowing diction. For what else is it but exhortation, when you say that you thank us for joining in the evangelical faith to the point that we may now serve as an example to other free cities? With such praise you stimulate us, who are dull. You want to persuade us to shine for the benefit of those abroad. It is our duty, then, to pray to Christ: may he have that effect on us, which would make your exhortation not seem in vain. But we shall not be afraid to tell you in a few words about the machinations of the enemy, the clemency God has shown us, and the extent of our weakness. All of this you will clearly see when you come to know what happened after Zwick's departure,[4] especially the more important events, for to go through every detail would be too prolix, as hardly a day passes without new traps being set for us.

* * * * *

1 For Zell, see CWC 1, Ep. 167 headnote.
2 For Hedio, see CWC 1, Ep. 147 headnote.
3 Ep. 192 above.
4 For Zwick, who delivered Capito's last letter to Blaurer, see above, Ep. 192, note 1.

The bishop of Strasbourg[5] has the greatest authority, which he maintains with skilful transactions that are rare and singular in a cleric. He thinks, moreover, highly of himself and is never more indignant than when he is passed over. He believes that as Christ's glory grows, his is damaged. Thus he is terribly worried about a paltry matter, the state of the episcopal stomach, while the people live in folly and error. He makes difficulties for the married priests,[6] whom he denounces openly before the churches with dire curses. And we already thought everything was safe. For he purposely gave us the impression of being placid, that he might overcome us while we were carefree and, as they say,[7] *sleeping on both ears.* His principal aim was to set the people against each other, as one part very much feared the episcopal thunder, the other part totally spurned it. It was at that time that the canons of St Peter fraudulently obtained a mandate from the council commanding me to withdraw from looking after their parish.[8] Furthermore, a strategy was introduced by which they thought they could drive all the married brethren from the city, especially Bucer. They subverted Count von Leiningen the Elder,[9] who tried several times to do violence to my person after first abusing me repeatedly to my face in the most atrocious manner, and doing so within the city precincts, in the court of the papist prelate.[10] But Christ delivered me from all these perils, for when the bishop had published the excommunication, we composed an appeal that same night in the name of the brethren.[11] On the next day we launched the appeal in the presence of the notary.[12] Soon, everything was presented as justified. By this remedy we prevented any dispute among the people about the excommunication. For the bishop had expected that we would pass sentence against him in turn and that we would condemn him and his accomplices, so that the matter would result in open sedition. Such are the talents and the skills of the bishops, to set peaceful people against each other. On the fourth day of that week, the council deprived me of my parish,[13] which I had clearly entered upon

* * * * *

5 Wilhelm von Honstein.
6 See above, Ep. 189.
7 Erasmus, *Adagia* 1.8.19.
8 Cf. above, Ep. 189a.
9 For the affair, see above, Ep. 190.
10 I.e., Count Henneberg's court, cf. above, Ep. 190.
11 I.e., Ep. 189.
12 Michael Schwencker, cf. above, Ep. 189, note 25.
13 Cf. above, Ep. 189a. The council was unhappy with the independence shown by the congregation, but in the end was forced to give in to their wishes.

through the authority of the council. Immediately a rumour started that the preachers of the Word would be cast out. There were meetings, questions, public accusations against the priests, insults were hurled at the council, but only by extremists among the people. Some leaders barely kept themselves from threatening the worst consequences for the priests if they succeeded in exiling us. Although so many things have come to a head at once, I have tried to expedite everything. I gave the task of using calming words and preventing a riot to those whom I knew to be popular. I thus allowed them to say that I would appear before the council and ensure that the gospel suffered no harm, and that matters were not as desperate as they might seem to the inexperienced. These individuals acknowledged to the people that fair decisions were sometimes rescinded for no good reason. Yet, at the same time, they emphasized the fact that the courtiers do not have enough power to induce the councillors to neglect their own citizens in such a pious cause. These things and more were communicated by my messengers in the hope of somehow containing the people's zeal and indignation until we had time to consult about safer plans. And as a result of our consultation I obtained permission from the council to take action. Saturday was agreed on.

In the meantime, lo and behold, another drama took place. My chapter, St Thomas, had been given hope that the council would decide against Bucer being the priest of St Aurelia because he is a married man[14] – that church is under the provision, as they say, of our chapter. I needed to be careful there, lest difficulties should arise from that source. The crudeness of Count von Leiningen upset me even more, although it seems that he was incited by others. For when I was sent to him on Sunday of that week for the sake of composing and settling a lawsuit, he answered me quite peacefully and put the matter off to the next day. Yet when I appeared again at the court of the Lord of Henneberg, he suddenly acted very irate and, with the lord and his nephew and the whole household looking on, attacked me with unspeakable abuse, shouting at me furiously until I was tired of listening. Then he tried to kill me, without anyone doing anything, until God finally delivered me. The danger was acute, believe me, but I was not afraid. I did not change my mien, and I stood my ground bravely, remembering the passage that every hair on my head is numbered.[15] I kept in mind that I would fall or survive according to the Father's will, who did not want anything untoward to happen to his

* * * * *

14 See above, Ep. 189, note 11. Cf. a letter from the dean, Nicolaus Wurmser, and his followers to the council opposing Bucer's appointment in AST 133, #4, 5.
15 Matt. 10:26–31.

son, nor could anything untoward happen against his will. Saturday came. I
dealt bravely with the council, answering all the arguments that my adversaries could possibly raise. There was complete silence, such as is the case
when someone tries to extricate himself from a desperate cause. They then
deliberated for almost five hours, and not without the help of God. For the
same people who had removed me from the parish three days ago appointed
me again for the period up to the day of St John the Baptist,[16] for those had
been the conditions of my initial appointment. Furthermore, they decided to
make appointments for all parishes in a Christian spirit, but we have not yet
obtained the parishes, nor have we obtained the right to profess Christ without enmity. But even so, a marvellous change has taken place: the expressions of the courtiers, who previously sent letters everywhere boasting that
we had been driven out, have become bleak, while the hearts of the pious
have been lifted up from the depth of desperation. Peace has prevailed between the council and the citizens, although truly speaking there had never
been a division. Not a single priestling or woman was moved by the threat of
episcopal excommunication. That is how effective our appeal was. The council negotiated on my behalf with the count. The only result we sought was to
clear myself, at least, of the accusations brought against me. I am quite safe,
but rather disquieted after that ominous week, in which such serious matters
occurred simultaneously. We now expect an interdict, an edict in the name of
the Empire, an imperial ban, the universal force of the devil. I hope, however,
that these turn out to be groundless fears and are stopped in the end.[17] For if
these things occur, we shall have to deal with the bishop, even if he makes a
final stand, and we must do battle as with a cursed enemy.

But I have told you everything at great length. I wish I could tell you all
in even greater detail in person, but I am detained here in the expectation of
the bishop's stratagems and by the uncertain position of the parish priests,
for whom provision will be made before St John's day.

More specifically concerning your letter: Zwick spoke most kindly of
you, and your letter recommends you more than his praise, for it was so
elegant, so pure, so pious that it easily equals, if not surpasses, the German
Advice to the Constance City Council,[18] which I read with great admiration after
your letter. If you committed yourself to preaching the Word, what would

* * * * *

16 24 June.
17 *In nervum erumpere*, Erasmus, *Adagia* 2.6.36.
18 *Ermanung eyn ersamen Rath der Stat Constantz ... ir Gwalt ist veracht* (Nürnberg:
    Jobst Gutknecht, 1524).

you have to offer? Let me plead with you: it is useless for you to swear or argue that you are not equal to the task. No one called to that task will be found lacking when he has God's help. Finally, I am glad to hear that you will reform external matters, which you know have been reformed by the Word in the hearts of the pious. For the Spirit weakens if you do not act on what he has asserted, although you give us proof of your incomparable prudence by biding your time.

Nevertheless, a great deal happened here contrary to expectations and contrary to our plans. Otherwise I would not have thought about delaying, for I attribute perhaps too much to human conjecture in matters of faith.

It was certainly beneficial that Matthew,[19] in particular, disturbed that whole cesspool of the pope without my knowledge. For when I came to know it, I searched the minds of the listeners, and I saw immediately that we had been reduced to a point where it was necessary either to go forward bravely, although we could not foresee the outcome, or to retreat, which could not be done without depressing the spirits of the pious, for they are without counsel and languish when they sense that we leaders are weakening. Therefore we are proceeding with good omens and under the auspices of Christ. For without God's presence we can do nothing.

Yesterday I saw a letter from your brother Thomas,[20] or so I assume. It is entitled 'A young man from Constance to his cousin.' A taste of it evinced the Blaurer eloquence, that is, an easy and subtle eloquence. Please give him and your learned sister[21] my best regards. Her name is famous here. What an excellent family, rich in such great talents! I shall give their regards to all friends who, I know, respect you, and I warmly return your greetings. Greetings to your fellow preachers of the Word from all of us. May you continue successfully in Christ's business. Let us know about your affairs. I have not yet read your letter to Hedio. He is occupied with preparations for his wedding,[22] but I shall make certain that he will read it before tonight. Strasbourg, 4 May 1524.

Yours sincerely, Capito.

* * * * *

19 I.e., Zell.
20 For Thomas Blaurer, see above, Ep. 192, note 6.
21 Margaret Blaurer (1493–1541) received a humanist education, which was unusual for women in her time and evoked general admiration. She assisted her brothers in their work for the reformation of the church. When the plague broke out in Constance in 1541, she worked in a hospital and died as a result of her charitable work.
22 See below, Ep. 196.

Letter 195: 4 May 1524, Basel, Andreas Cratander to Capito

Printed in BrOek 1:277–8, Ep. 193.

[*Summary*]: Oecolampadius returned to Basel from Weinsberg on 31 April. Cratander asks Capito to transmit to him in Basel any manuscripts he might have received from Oecolampadius. He furthermore asks him to send him the Hebrew characters through Wolfgang Köpfel. He needs them to print the Isaiah commentary. [Johannes] Zwick will tell him other news. Boniface Amerbach has just returned from Avignon [to take over the teaching of law from Claude Chansonnette].

Letter 196: 14 May 1524, Basel, Johannes Oecolampadius to Capito

Printed in BrOek 1:279–80, Ep. 195.

[*Summary*]: Oecolampadius urges Capito to welcome Antoine du Blet and Guillaume Farel as they stop in Strasbourg on their way to Wittenberg. Responding to Capito's inquiry, Oecolampadius informs him that his commentary *In Iesaiam* will not be ready for the printer before 1 July. He is now working on a commentary *In epistolam Ioannem primam*, a copy of which Capito will soon receive. Certain pseudo-evangelicals are causing the reformers more trouble than the Catholics do. Some of the reforms enacted in Strasbourg are not being well-received in Basel. He sends his greetings to the brethren in Strasbourg, but especially to Bucer and Hedio, whom he congratulates on his recent marriage. Oecolampadius urges Capito to write a response to Josse Clichtove's *De veneratione sanctorum*, since the latter has accused him of irreverence toward the Virgin Mary.

Letter 197: 23 May 1524, Strasbourg, Capito to Paulus Phrygio

Printed in Gény,124–35, note 2. Paulus Phrygio Constantius (or Konstenzer Seidensticker, ca. 1485–1543) of Sélestat studied at the Universities of Freiburg (BA 1499, MA 1500) and Basel (DTh 1513). He taught school at Sélestat and Colmar and, from 1510, theology at the University of Basel. He became parish priest in Eichstätt and, from 1519, in his native Sélestat. Ousted for his support of the Reformation in 1525, he moved to Strasbourg. In 1529, when Basel accepted the Reformation, Phrygio was appointed pastor of St Peter's there and resumed teaching at the university. In 1535 he moved to the University of Tübingen, where he held the chair of New Testament studies until his death.

This letter contains the first mention of Capito's acquaintance with Hans Jakob Schütz of Traubach, the son of the court scribe Konrad Schütz of Ensisheim, and a notorious swindler. Schütz arrived in Sélestat in the summer of 1523, accompanied by Margrede von Balmus, a former nun, whom he claimed to be his wife. Neither his brother Hans Wolfgang, who was in the service of the bishop, nor his brother-in-law, Stephan von Wangen, wanted to have anything to do with the disreputable pair. In the spring of 1524 they tried to advance their fortunes by ingratiating themselves with the sympathizers of the Reformation. They approached, among others, Paulus Phrygio and Lazarus Schürer in Sélestat, along with Nicolaus Kniebs and Capito in Strasbourg. Schütz then forged a series of letters from the Sélestat Schultheiss Melchior Ergersheim to the government in Ensisheim, indicating the city's willingness to collaborate with the Austrian government and to expel the reformers. Schütz' purpose was to 'expose' the plot and incite the reformers named in the letters to rise up against the city council. He presumably hoped to be rewarded for his role as whistle-blower. Capito believed Schütz' story and informed the council of Strasbourg of the 'plot' on 31 March 1524. Schürer, by contrast, suspected fraud and reported the matter to the city council of Sélestat. On 3 May 1524 Schütz fled to Strasbourg, where Capito attempted to protect him. In June, Schütz was formally charged with fraud and incitement and was obliged to stand trial in Sélestat. He was found guilty as charged and executed on 28 November 1524.

The original Latin text of Capito's letter is no longer extant. The following is translated from the German version made by the city scribe Jacob Wolff for the council. It is likely that the original letter as well as Epp. 199, 200, and 201 were intercepted by the city council in the process of gathering evidence against Schütz. Wolff's translation is rough, and the meaning of several passages remains unclear.

To Paul Seidensticker Constenzer, teacher of Holy Writ in Sélestat, his dearest brother in Christ. Greetings, dearest brother. Jakob Schütz, who is a man of truly noble and Christian spirit, has truly ...[1] a matter, which at first seemed excellent to me, but which would benefit no one if it were to become known. Rather, it would cause damage, and in particular burden you and your friends. Furthermore, as it seems to me (and I am not completely inexperienced in that kind of business), trouble would arise out of the difficulty of uncertain suspicion and harm brotherly love. Consider first and foremost, my dear Paulus, that it is our duty to quiet public indignation, to quell un-

* * * * *

1 The sentence lacks a verb.

rest, and, if we can do so, not to avert the matter but to overcome it through patience. For if things came to a head and to the knowledge of the common people, it would become a concern to take some sort of action against every evil-doer. How ill they would talk of the gospel and how weak they would consider our faith, especially those on the outside. We know for certain that you will do and prompt no good with your scrupulousness and indignation; the more you give yourself and your people over to Christ, and the more you and your community trust in the Lord's protection of the city, the more secure you will be. Now that I have considered the whole matter and have not come up with anything that could in any way be helpful to you, it was on my initiative that he [Schütz] did not write a word about these problems to you. It is proper, after all, for a man of Christian spirit to offer his help, and if he cannot be useful, at least to avoid bringing great shame on the Word. Be content, therefore, in keeping the brethren peaceful and being a preacher of the gospel. Admonish them to avoid evil and be diligent, and you will see, as long as you stop other action, that everything will take its desired course in accordance with God's command, if only you desire what is godly and Christian. I am writing this in accordance with the special affection and good will that bind me to you. My intent is to warn you against such upheavals as the most harmful kind of behaviour, so help me God; and I hope to be of service to you, if you permit me to advise you. May the Lord Christ keep you blameless of such upheavals, for I hope you are without blame if you will otherwise do away with this business.[2] From Strasbourg, 23 May 1524.

Your W. Fabricius Capito.

Letter 198: 25 May 1524, Wittenberg, Martin Luther to Capito

Printed in WABr 3:298–301, Ep. 748.

[Summary]: Luther would not have believed reports that Capito and Bucer disagree with the theologians at Wittenberg had he not heard similar reports three days earlier from colleagues returning from Strasbourg. Luther is vexed that reports of a rift are being broadcast to the detriment of the re-form movement. He is used to such rumours, however, and, if he had time, he would testify in a publication that the rumour is false and that there is concord among the theologians. He is pleased that some monks and priests

* * * * *

2 *wan ir anderst den handel hinweg thun werden.*

in Strasbourg have married. He also approves of the *Appellation der eelichen Priester von der vermaynten Excommunication des Bischoffen zu Strassburg* [cf. above, Ep. 189]. He encourages Capito to continue in the reforms that have been undertaken in Strasbourg. The weak brethren have been indulged, and it is time to act openly. Luther has decided no longer to wear the cowl. He thinks that the false rumour of the disagreement resulted from the publication of a German translation of his earlier letter to Capito [Ep. 131]. Luther states that Capito has changed since that letter: 'Moreover, you were then both another man and a slave of the court, but now you are a freedman of Christ and a slave of the Gospel. You are entirely mine, and I am entirely yours.' He sends his greetings to Martin Bucer, his wife and child, and the other newlyweds, especially Caspar Hedio.

Letter 199: 26 May 1524, Strasbourg, Capito to Paulus Phrygio

Printed in Gény, 125, note 1. For Phrygio see above, Ep. 197 headnote.

Greeting to Paulus Phrygio.

Hans Jakob Schütz has given me news about your and your friends' action, which has distressed me, and I am still greatly distressed today that you are doing things that are contrary to Christian order. Teach patience and consolation in Christ, which is so much greater than the matter which causes you to fear for your fatherland. You will come to regret your dangerous cleverness. I see that the confidential message you sent me has been opened. What is this? By that rash trick things have come to light that should have remained completely confidential and under cover. Indeed, there was a man who told Bucer much about the matter. He must have learned it either from what you wrote or from what Hans Jakob said, and as far as I understand, he says you originated it. We are being warned by friends to be careful not to seek revenge. But it bothers me that you showed more initiative and determination in this public upheaval than was necessary; furthermore, what you have written at various times comes very close to treachery or treason. For the rest, [Hans Jakob] asked me for advice, but on a matter that you had no business to know or consider, a matter which does harm to no one as long as it remains under cover, yet may cause some harm if it becomes public knowledge. That is why I caused him to take back and keep to himself the matter that burdens him and weighs him down. Therefore, dear brother, show a mind and spirit that is in accordance with Christ, and punish those things which are clearly against the Word, and let that be your concern. But you say you will keep the matter to yourself and permit no one to share your knowledge. If you keep it private knowledge, you have acquired it out of curiosity and it is of no use to you. If, however, you reveal it, you will do much evil to your fatherland, although I do not know whether there is anything special in it.[1] Give yourself up completely to Christ and surrender to him your concerns, and matters will be decided in a peaceful manner and to everyone's benefit, even if they appear to be very awkward to our carnal understanding. Farewell and write again. From Strasbourg on Corpus Christi 1524.

Your Capito.

Letter 200: 3 June 1524, Strasbourg, Capito to Paulus Phrygio

Printed in Gény,126. For the addressee, see above, Ep. 197 headnote.

Greeting to Dr Paulus Phrygio.

The matter has been dealt with in a very unwise manner, but perhaps the Lord has decreed it thus for the chastening of our hearts, because we have listened to our desires more than necessary. Hans Jakob would like to come to you and take action. It will be beneficial to you, although it carries a great risk for you also, and if you will not go altogether scot-free, there will be disagreement among yourselves. We shall ask God to appease all things. Hans Jakob is in danger because of his loyalty, but with God's help, he will act more wisely and more safely in the future. Farewell and pray the Lord to preserve the gospel. Strasbourg, 3 June 1524.

Your Capito.

Letter 201: 4 June 1524, [Strasbourg], Capito to Paulus Phrygio

Printed in Gény, 126. For the addressee, see above, Ep. 197 headnote.

Look what unthinking loyalty does for him who has initiated this matter, and how inconstant friendship is among humans. One has warned the other, and now we are under the worst suspicion by God's decree. How ill-natured your council thinks I am, what shameful accusations it has brought against me. I do not know why I am regarded as disloyal – I, who merely advised you out of brotherly love of what seemed to me useful for Christian action and the peace of your community. And in addition, my servant[1] had a letter

* * * * *

1 *ob der furnämlichs in ime habe.*

1 Not identified.

taken from him, which had nothing in it about your business. May God grant this matter a good outcome. But, dear Paulus, pray God that what I have been so careful to avoid will not come to pass, lest we lose the loyal adviser. I feel certain and have no fear, but I do not know what evil will come of the letters that have been taken away. The day will come when all things will be revealed, and ingratitude will be avenged. Many people follow the gospel of the Epicureans, that is, those who find their blessing in eating and drinking. It is their habit and practice to look after their own advantage at great risk. Hans Jakob agreed today to go to you and wait for the justice that is his due, then you will see that he is no frivolous man, but suffers the pain of a loyal heart. Yet the truth will overcome. Farewell, 4 June 1524.

Your Capito.

Letter 202: 4 June 1524, [Strasbourg], Capito to Paulus Phrygio

The manuscript of this letter is in the Bibliothèque humaniste, Sélestat, Corr. B.Rh. 263e. For Phrygio, see above, Ep. 197 headnote.

Greeting. I hoped the matter would proceed differently, but the counsel of the priests and the *Ammann* came to light. They began the business and brought some people back – that is clear. Divine wisdom would break even hard necks. I pray to my God and cast myself down at his feet. Help me with your prayers, that he may give us peace. What I feared would happen, did happen. May this lamentable beginning have a fortunate ending. Let Hans Jakob be strong and of good cheer. I make every effort on his behalf. God will not desert us. Farewell, 4 June, in the year '24.

Letter 203: 15 June 1524, Wittenberg, Martin Luther to Capito

Printed in WABr 3:303, Ep. 750.

[*Summary*]: Melanchthon has asked him to explain to Capito his views on the tithe. He believes that they are justified and should be continued. The remaining taxes should be abolished.

Letter 204: 22 June 1524, Riedlingen, Johannes Zwick to Capito

The manuscript, an autograph, is in Basel, Universitätsbibliothek, Ki.Ar. 25a, #66. For Johannes Zwick, see above, Ep. 192, note 1.

Johannes Zwick to Capito, Riedlingen 1524.

In the midst of the raging and roaring lions,[1] I am awaiting the will of the Lord. One of these days I shall be summoned by the bishop,[2] the ravisher of my parish, either in a friendly manner or violently. Whatever happens to me, I shall write to you. Meanwhile, I ask that you pray to God for me, namely that faith may be confirmed in me and strengthened through his grace. Amen. I can do no more. Greet Hedio and Matthew on my behalf.[3] Farewell, very rapidly.

The bearer of this letter used to be the vicar of Riedlingen,[4] whom I do not know well, yet he seems to be a learned man of sincere heart, having been forced from here because he did not want to swear to certain articles of the Antichrist. If you can do anything to help him in this matter, do it, and love me. Given at Riedlingen, 22 June 1524.

Your Johannes Zwick.

If you are going to write back to me, you can pass the letter on to Blaurer in Constance.[5] But you will perhaps write 'to the parish priest at Riedlingen.'

Letter 205: 5 July 1524, Strasbourg, Capito to Heinrich Stromer

The manuscript of this letter is in the Thüringisches Hauptstaatsarchiv Weimar, Ernestinisches Gesamtarchiv, Reg. O 157b, Bl. 639r–640r. Printed in J.E. Kapp, *Kleine Nachlese einiger zur Erläuterung der Reformationsgeschichte nützlicher Urkunden* (Leizpig, 1727), 2:610.

W. Fabritius Capito to Dr H. Stromer of Auerbach.

Here everything is in commotion. The princes plot against the Lord and his Christ.[1] They work zealously to destroy salvation.

There is a small town six miles from here, from which Ferdinand had a preacher expelled, and one hundred and fifty citizens fled with him.[2] They

* * * * *

1 Cf. Daniel 6.
2 Hugo of Hohenlandenberg. Cf. above, Ep. 192, note 5.
3 For Hedio and Zell see CWC 1, Epp. 147 and 167 headnotes.
4 Not identified.
5 I.e., Ambrosius Blaurer (see above, Ep. 192 headnote).

1 Cf. Ps. 2:2.
2 The incident took place in Kenzingen and involved Jakob Otter. Otter (ca. 1485–1547) studied at Speyer , Heidelberg (BA 1507), and Freiburg (MA 1515; licence in theology 1517). He was parish priest at Wolfenweiler im Breisgau (1520) and after 1522 in Kenzingen. He fled to Strasbourg in June 1524. He later became pastor in Neckarsteinach, Solothurn (from 1529), and Esslingen (from 1532), where he worked until his death.

are now living here. An effort is being made to relieve their misery. For the time being they rely on the charity of others. The town is now held by six hundred armed men. Three men, whom they prevented from fleeing, have been most cruelly tortured in the course of investigating the planned sedition. This is the reason why there are flashes of open war against us. This month pious preachers are harassed everywhere, even in the most densely populated places. Our city has adopted the Word.

Zurich, that most valiant Swiss canton, exemplifies for us the church of old. Nowhere have I seen such power of the Word. Everything has changed: superstition, impiety, luxury, which flourished greatly there, as well as warmongering, in which that people previously engaged like mad. Furthermore, they valiantly reject money. Once we have passed through these tempests, I see that everything will be more splendid, and our enemies will be weakened. Here we adhere to the Word with all our strength and disdain the threats, which are reported to us daily.

Strasbourg is the refuge for exiled brethren. They all come here; they are expelled from everywhere and are sent out again from here as ministers of the Word. But oh! what do I hear? Benno[3] has been victorious and re-emerges into the light of the living through the sacred rites of the papists. He has been canonized by those who are very far away from every canon of religion. Even if all the tyrants unite, we are victorious in Christ. Men have been paid to kill me at their private risk. They have tried twice in vain. I shall not escape, except by a great divine miracle. It is this that has prevented my marriage, to speak candidly.[4] Strasbourg, 5 July 1524.

W. Fabritius Capito.

Letter 206: [End of July/Beginning of August 1524, Strasbourg], Martin Bucer to Capito

Printed in CorrBucer 1:262–3, Ep. 70.

[*Summary*]: Hedio should exhort the people to remain firm in their faith. [Thomas] Murner has set out to prove that the mass is a sacrifice. They will answer him when the tract appears. Murner does not want laymen to be involved in theological disputations. In responding to him, moderation is necessary, but it is not possible to keep silence. Bucer will invite Treger and

* * * * *

3 Benno, Bishop of Meissen (1010–1106), canonized in 1523 by Pope Adrian VI.
4 Capito married Agnes Roettel on 1 August 1524.

Murner to another disputation. He wishes Capito a happy wedding night with his wife, Agnes Roettel.

Letter 207: [Before 28/29 August 1524, Strasbourg, Martin Bucer] to Capito

Printed in CorrBucer 1:264–5, Ep. 72.

[*Summary*]: Capito has undertaken to reply to Treger, but Bucer fears that Capito will be too busy with other things. Bucer offers to write the answer himself, since the matter is urgent. Treger complained that Capito did not reply to his first attack [since the response appeared anonymously]. It is necessary to confess authorship openly. Luther, Zwingli, and others are in the habit of responding quickly and thus overwhelming their adversaries. Bucer has read both Treger's attack and Capito's response and has therefore sufficient information to write an answer. He awaits Capito's instructions.

Letter 208: [End of August 1524, Strasbourg, Martin Bucer] to Capito

Printed in CorrBucer 1:266–7, Ep. 73.

[*Summary*]: Capito should personally attend the discussions with the people and ensure that their proposals are presented in order. Those proposals demand that (1) a public disputation of doctrine should be arranged; (2) only qualified preachers should preach; (3) schools should be set up; (4) the law should be enforced against adulterers, drunkards, slanderers, and gamblers; (5) hoarding of wine and grain by merchants should be forbidden; (6) the clergy should be forced to take out citizenship; (7) mass stipends should be used for poor relief.

Letter 209: [31 August 1524, Strasbourg], The Strasbourg Preachers to the City Council of Strasbourg

Printed in BDS 1:373–6, Ep. 74.

[*Summary*]: The preachers assure the council that they are doing their best to quell the unrest of the people. They thank the council for its support and complain of the stiff resistance of the representatives of the old church, who are *Seelmörder* (murderers of the soul). Their main opponents are [Nikolaus of Bladesheim], the prior of the Dominicans, and the parish priests at St Andreas and St Stephan [Paul Freuder of Ebingen and Vit Kurbach]. They are encouraged by the silence which the preachers keep in obedience to the council's decree [of 1 December 1523, which enjoined them to preach the gospel only and to keep the peace]. They ask the council to renew that decree and add the threat of legal action against those whose preaching is inconsistent with the gospel. Furthermore, it would promote peace among the people if the council demonstrated their commitment to the gospel by stopping abuses. The income from the chapel [of St Erhard], for example, was supposed to be used for educational purposes. Instead, the monks there are still obliged to perform the Catholic rites that are against the gospel teaching. The preachers urge the council to look after the education of youth.

Letter 210: 2 September [1524], Basel, Desiderius Erasmus to Capito

Printed in Allen 5, Ep. 1485; English translation in CWE 10, Ep. 1485.

[*Summary*]: Erasmus suspects that Capito has incited Otto Brunfels against him and is now behind the attacks of [Heinrich] Eppendorf. He covertly threatens revenge. He insists that he is more sincere in promoting the gospel than Capito realizes, but he refuses to support the teachings of the Strasbourg theologians.

**Letter 211: [3 September 1524, Strasbourg], The Strasbourg Preachers to
the City Council of Strasbourg**

Printed in BDS 2:396–8.

[*Summary*]: They urge the council to give them permission to establish schools. They furthermore ask the council to proceed against drunkards and gambling establishments.

**Letter 212: 9 September 1524, Strasbourg, Capito to Willibald
Pirckheimer**

Printed in H. Scheible, ed., *Willibald Pirckheimers Briefwechsel* (Munich, 2001), 5:240–3, Ep. 870.

[*Summary*]: Treger accused the Strasbourg preachers of being Hussites and is personally selling his tract, *Vermanung*. Some 150 citizens petitioned the council to arrest him. The monastery was stormed by irate citizens, who found five prostitutes in the cells, but Treger escaped. Several clerics, Treger among them, were taken into custody the following day. It was decided to hold a public disputation, but Capito does not believe that Treger will participate. The parish priest of Siegolsheim was burned in Ensisheim. Capito encloses a description of the event written by [Felix Ulscenius]. Capito married [Agnes Roettel on 1 August; see below, Ep. 215]. He sends greetings to Osiander, Thomas Venatorius, Bernhard Baumgartner, Albrecht Dürer, and Lazarus Spengler.

Letter 213: [Beginning of September 1524], from [Felix Ulscenius (?) to Capito]

This letter was enclosed with Ep. 212. It is printed in Scheible, ed., *Willibald Pirckheimers Briefwechsel*, 5:244–5.

[*Summary*]: The parish priest of Siegolsheim was condemned to death in the court at Ensisheim and burned at the stake. He had confessed to the accusations under torture, then recanted them. He rejected the consolations of friends, saying he trusted in God. In the writer's opinion he was not given a fair trial.

Letter 214: [September, 1524], Jebsheim, Jakob Kleinlawel to N

The manuscript of this letter is in Basel, Universitätsbibliothek, Ki.Ar. 25a, 120. This is an account by Jakob Kleinlawel, the parish priest of Jebsheim (later documented as pastor of Wangen, 1540–3), of the events reported by Felix Ulscenius in Ep. 213 above. The letter is designated in Millet as 'Jacques Kleinlawell, curé de Jebsheim, à Cap[iton].' The last paragraph shows, however, that it was addressed to an unidentified female relative ('fraw gefatterin') who in turn may have written to Capito (see Kleinlawel's request in the last paragraph of the letter).

Point 1: I asked about Wolff of Siegolsheim,[1] and that citizen of Ensisheim told me that he died as a pious Christian. When they wanted to take away from him the Catholic priesthood, the suffragan[2] was present. Wolff came to him, and when they wanted to put on the alb and the priestly habit, Wolff asked what he was supposed to do. The suffragan replied: 'My dear Mr Wolff, don't be frightened and don't hold it against me that I do what I have to do because of the papal authority, that is, to take away your priesthood.'

* * * * *

1 He has not been further identified. See Epp. 212 and 213.
2 On the suffragan of Strasbourg, Conrad Wickram, see CWC 1, Ep. 72, note 2.

Then Wolff replied: 'If I am evil, then there is no need for it, but if I am a priest before God, then you cannot deprive me of my priesthood, either by the pope's authority or by ours.' Thereafter he was once again led to the dungeon until 1 September. Then he was led forth and brought before the court and condemned to be burned, and when he was being led from the city, he said: 'It is not by justice that I die but by violence, but that will not be the end of it. There is worse to come.' And when the priests gave him counsel, he said that no one need be concerned on his account, for he was going to die as a pious Christian and not as a tempter. At the very end, the priest of Luttenbach came to him and said: 'My dear Mr Wolff, you should commend yourself to God and his mother, Mary.' Then Wolff replied: 'I know very well what I have to do. I have commended myself to God and to my Lord Jesus Christ.' And with these words he surrendered himself into the hands of God Almighty and thus departed from this world.

Point 2: I furthermore asked that citizen whether as many people were killed at Ensisheim as they say, and he told me he saw a priest of Hirsingen[3] being hanged, but he never saw anyone die as peacefully as Wolff. When he was being led to the tree, he spoke so well that there was not one man who did not have tears in his eyes, but when he saw the tree on which he was to be hanged, he fell on his knees and said: 'I greet you, tree, for the corpse of our dear Lord Jesus Christ has blessed you, when he suffered death. Oh tree, shining over the whole world, do not allow me to lose my way like a sheep without a shepherd. I gladly die in order to come to you. Therefore, look kindly on me, and commend your disciple and take me from this world.' And that citizen told me that [the priest] spoke and said a great deal more, but he could not recall it anymore and had forgotten it, but that he died gladly and as a Christian and, as he believed, a saint before God.

Point 3: He told me that several priests were hanged together, among them Hans of Blodelsheim.[4] And when they were led from the city on a cart to the tree where they were to be hanged, Hans of Blodelsheim began: 'You strong knights, whom God has selected to receive a great prize, must not be afraid of temporal death, which is the wage of sin.[5] We must remember that Christ Jesus, our Lord and Saviour, also died for our sins. We must remain steadfast in our faith and in our vocation.' And that same Hans consoled the three until all three were hanged, and he was the last one to be hanged among

* * * * *

3 Not identified.
4 Nothing further is known of him.
5 Rom. 6:23.

them, and when he was led to the rope, he said: 'And who will console me? God alone will console me, my Lord and creator, who has saved this world with his suffering and death. Do not allow me to be separated from you now in my leave-taking and temporal death. Take me into your presence in your kingdom.' And so they died as Christians in God.

May the grace of God be with you always, dear cousin. I send you this as I have heard it from a citizen of Ens[isheim] concerning those men who died in God and love for the sake of holy faith, but as I understood, they died in the worst manner, and I have written nothing of Hans of Wyllental,[6] since you know more about him than I. Dear cousin, I beg you to write on my behalf to a preacher of Strasbourg. I would like to take out citizenship and perhaps in the future move there, for I don't know how I can hold on to my cure, for many reasons: I am not allowed to preach the word of God publicly, and even if I do so, no one wants to receive it. It leads only to trouble, and so I think of Luke 10,[7] and say no more than God be with you, I am overcome.

Jacob Kleinlawel, parish priest of Jebsheim.

Letter 215: 16 September 1524, Augsburg, Urbanus Rhegius to Capito

The manuscript of this letter is in AST 40, #59, fols. 436–7. On Rhegius, see above, Ep. 162 headnote.

Urbanus Rhegius to Wolfgang Fabritius Capito, greetings in Christ.

The letter you wrote to me on 31 August,[1] dearest brother, I received on 16 September. In it I recognize your most honest mind and not only the signs of your old affection, but even an admirable increase. And that is not surprising, for in the old days we were linked by Aristotle, the master of error, and by a love of secular letters and a kinship of thought, but now we are bound by stronger bonds, namely Christian love, which is the bond of perfection.[2] That has changed our minds so that what is yours is as much my concern as what is my own. Recently, when one of the brethren, a good man, reported

* * * * *

6 I.e., the parish priest of Val de Villé.
7 Luke 10:10–11 about unreceptive cities: 'go your way ... shake the dust from your feet.'

1 Not extant.
2 Col. 3:14.

on Capito's wedding,[3] I was delighted beyond belief, for I know that as a result of such examples quite a few will be encouraged to act as is proper

* * * * *

3 The wedding took place on 1 August (see also above, Epp. 206 and 212). The event elicited the following comments from Dean Nicolaus Wurmser: 'Wolfgang Faber Capito married a young woman in the sight of us all. O the great scoundrel! God gave their deserts to everyone who helped make him provost' (AST 192, 21 recto: *Wolfgangus Faber Capito nupsit virgini in despectum omnium nostrum. O des grossen buben! Got gab den lon allen denen, die dar zu geholffen handt, das er probst worden ist.*). In a second notice, he remarked that 'Capito, provost of St Thomas, married on 1 August with great pomp, and nothing happened at church other than that they were joined together and a sermon was held. There was no mass. Bucer gave the sermon. There were some two hundred citizens present to see this abominable deed' (AST 192, 23 recto: *Prima Augusti Capito praepositus S. Thomae duxit uxorem und ist zu kirchen gangen magno apparatu und in dem kirchgang ist nit geschehen dan das man sy bede zusammen gaben hadt und geprediget. Kein meß gehaltet. Hadt die predig gehben Buczerus. Affuerunt ad ii^c civium ad videndum hoc abhominabile facinus*).

On 13 August Wurmser and some of his colleagues tried to deprive Capito of the income from the provostship on account of his marriage, but Capito threatened them with legal action and reminded them that the cathedral chapter had not been able to dislodge Matthew Zell and Caspar Hedio. Cf. the notarized statement to this effect, AST 22 (2): *Quod licet michi hactenus animus fuit, omnia ex re capituli et privatarum personarum agere cum summa concordia, quantus in me fuit, etiam si aliquando potuissem, habuisse actionem, ut michi videtur iuste inimicitie, iam vero quia uxorem duxi contra constitutiones canonicas, Reverentie Vestre, ut audi, presentias et emolumenta michi tam ratione prelature quam prebende competentia reservant. Ceterum, quia in possessione fui et quod feci iure divino, naturali et humano suffultus feci, valde moleste fero me sic de facto sine previa cognitione iuris de possessione per Reverentias Vestras deturbari. Cupio autem tranquille omnia perfici et proscindere causam omnem tum litium tum simultatis, quamobrem Reverentias Vestras exhortor, ut ... expendatis nimirum Reverentias Vestras maximo conatu adversus plebanum Sancti Thome nichil effecisse. Deinde illustres et generosos viros dominos decanum et de capitulo ecclesie maioris Argentinensis magistrum Matheum Zellium dum maritus fieret non suffecisse ut ex plebanatu ... eicerent. Postremoque iidem domini decanus et de capitulo doctorem Casparem Hedionem similiter maritum factum numquam turbarunt ... Quodsi Reverentie Vestre omnino porrexerint me vi eicere de possessione prelature et prebende tunc cogar pro tuendo iure meo constitutiones fortassis aliis adversas similiter proferre.* ('It has been, until now, my heart's desire to do everything regarding the chapter and private persons with the utmost concord, as far as it depended on me, even if I could have taken hostile action sometimes, with justification as it seems to me. Now, however, because I have taken a wife against canon law, Your Reverences, as I understand, are reserving the residency fees and income due to me as prelate and in my capacity as prebendary. Furthermore, because I was in possession [of the provostship and canonry], and because I did what I did based on divine, natural, and human law, I am very annoyed about be-to Christian piety. A good wife is God-given,[4] and I have no doubt that you have obtained a good wife. I too would have married a year ago,[5] if I had not been prevented by the tempests of persecutions, from which I still suffer.

It is a year ago today that I was called back to the pulpit of the church in Hall[6] and fell victim to the plots of the bishop and of Prince Ferdinand. I am popular with the Augsburg city council and with the people. But the bishop of Brixen and the archbishop of Trent[7] leave nothing undone to ruin me. What am I to do in the face of so many hostile plots? I shall escape once more, like the *chosen vessel*.[8] It is now the third time that I have gone to Augsburg, where I have been respectfully received and asked by a large number in the city to expound Paul's Epistle to the Romans. I therefore preach three times a week to a crowd in the church of the Carmelites,[9] not to speak of the work I do besides. Speiser[10] at St Maurice is ill, and I stand in for him frequently on the request of the Fuggers.

* * * * *

---

ing de facto deprived of my possession by your Reverences, without prior judgment. However, I wish everything to be done peacefully and to eliminate every cause of litigation and of enmity. Therefore I exhort Your Reverences to consider … that Your Reverences effected nothing even by the greatest effort against the parish priest of St Thomas; then that the illustrious and generous men, the dean and chapter of the cathedral of Strasbourg, were not in a position to remove Master Matthew Zell from the office of parish priest when he got married, … finally, these same lords, the dean and chapter, have never troubled Dr Caspar Hedio, who likewise got married … But if Your Reverences are determined to deprive me of the prelacy and the prebend, I shall be forced to seek the protection of the law and to cite laws in turn that are perhaps to the detriment of others.')

4 Sir. 26:1.
5 Rhegius married Anna Weissbrucker in Augsburg on 16 June 1525.
6 Rhegius was forced to leave his parish and take refuge in Augsburg after preaching radical sermons during Lent of 1523. Cf. CWC 1, Ep. 162.
7 On Bernard Cles, bishop of Trent, see CWC 1, Ep. 162, note 2; Sebastian Sprenz, bishop of Brixen, studied law and taught at the University of Ingolstadt. He was provost at the cathedral in Brixen 1513–21, then bishop. He fled the town during the Peasants' War and died in exile in 1525.
8 Acts 9:15.
9 St Anna.
10 Johann Speiser (documented 1504–31) studied at Basel (doctorate in canon law, 1511). He was, at that time, procurator at the episcopal court. After moving to Augsburg, he was appointed curate of St Maurice in 1512 on the initiative of the Fuggers, who acquired the right of patronage. When his sympathies for the cause of the reformers became clear, the bishop of Augsburg pressed for his removal. He returned to orthodox preaching and encountered strong opposition among his parishioners. He was eventually replaced by Ottmar Luscinius. Speiser remained in Augsburg, but was reportedly in poor mental health.

I do not quite approve of what has been broadcast in Strasbourg about the unrest in our city. For the city council favours the ministers of the Word. There was a Minorite,[11] a bold and audacious man, who reportedly poured forth certain things quite out of season. When someone wanted to dismiss him, some of the people resisted, I don't know how many, some say a thousand. On 15 September two men who were charged with inciting rebellion were executed;[12] otherwise I am not aware of any disturbance. I hear that there was great unrest in Strasbourg. If they retain the ministers of the Word, this kind of unrest is better than peace. Earlier, I heard some nonsense from the gardener[13] about Satan keeping watch in your city. If Satan cannot hinder the course of the Word, he makes a great effort to make us unpopular on account of the pseudo-brethren. A few weeks ago in public sermons I argued on the basis of Scripture against the gardener's error concerning the Eucharist and baptism, and strenuously discouraged the congregation from reading such stupid pamphlets. Certain impious opinions about the Last Supper have arisen among us through the machinations of the pseudo-apostles, whom I am trying to suppress as well as I can in Augsburg and Ulm. In Ulm, I do what I can through letters; in Augsburg, I speak out personally. There were people who taught that no body or blood was present in the Eucharist

* * * * *

11 Hans Schilling, who was preaching at the Minorite church in Augsburg. In August, the council tried to persuade him to leave, but had to yield to the will of the impetuous mob.
12 Not identified.
13 Clement Ziegler (ca. 1486–after 1551; Strasbourg citizen from 1525). He is first documented in 1522, working as a gardener for the nuns in Krutenau. In 1523 he was one of a group of gardeners who refused to pay taxes, but eventually came to an agreement with the city. In December 1524, the market gardeners of Strasbourg sent him to Weyersheim, but he turned out to be too radical, not only for the members of the local tribunal and Jakob von Salm, but also for the Strasbourg reformers. On 20 December, moreover, there was a confrontation with the episcopal councillors (Strasbourg AMS AA 389, f. 43r.). On 25 February 1525, the Strasbourg city council forbade Ziegler to preach. Ziegler, however, disobeyed their ruling and was arrested by Anton of Lorraine on 2 April 1525 for his involvement in the Peasants' War and unauthorized preaching in the village of Heiligenstein. In 1526 he was working as a gardener in Robertsau. After the death of the local parish priest, the congregation proposed him as pastor in 1528 and again in 1529. The city council refused, however, and sent Conrad Reysser in 1530. Ziegler seems to have respected the decision and kept out of parish matters. He published five pamphlets in Strasbourg in 1524/25 and left a number of manuscripts, the last one dated 1551.

and that it was only an empty sign. I approached their chief[14] and refuted him so completely with scriptural testimony in the presence of many witnesses that he made himself ridiculous. He is called 'Magister' by his people, but when he was obliged to provide proof for his beliefs, he betrayed astonishing ignorance. He had hardly touched chapter 2 of 1 Corinthians. After reading a few books, he was suddenly changed from a layman into a theologian. He is a bold and most vain boaster.

My successor, Matthias Kretz,[15] preaches in the main church of Our Lady. He still turns the mass into a sacrifice and approves of idolatry and super-idolatry. He perpetuates the nonsense of free will, congruous merit, the flames of purgatory, the abuses and tortures of auricular confession, tonsures, vestments, and whatever it is that the Prince of Darkness approves, and maintains it with furious shouting. He has few listeners, a few rich men, some old and crazy Beguines and priestlings, and he has Eck[16] as his patron. Eck recently sent a letter to Augsburg, asking Urbanus to return to the bosom of the church. Johannes Fabri,[17] the courtier, once almost a father figure to me, now hates and tears Urbanus to pieces as violently as possible. With one word he could restore me to the church in Hall, but [he says]: 'That ingrate Urbanus is too devoted to Luther and is unwilling to sharpen his pen against God's men and to write great polemics against the heresiarch in the north, *where every evil is breaking forth.'*[18] That is to say, the madness of the priests is shown to the whole world, and *the man of sin is revealed, the man doomed to destruction.*[19] [According to Fabri], 'That rustic Urbanus does not know how to flatter, he knows only how to rub tender ears with harsh words.' Now you know why the relationship cooled between Fabri and me during the past year. I could have sold my silence for 300 gulden, but my spirit could not

* * * * *

14 Millet identifies him as 'sans doute Karlstadt.'
15 Matthias Kretz (Kress, Gretz, ca. 1480–1543) studied at Vienna, Tübingen (MA 1506, BTh 1512), and Ingolstadt (DTh 1519). He taught Hebrew and Greek at the Augustinian monastery in Polling (Bavaria) from 1513–16, was appointed preacher at the cathedral of Eichstätt, and later Augsburg (1521). He succeeded Rhegius, whose sympathies with the reformers he did not share. Consequently, he faced opposition from his parishioners. He attended the Disputation of Baden in 1526 and the Diet of Augsburg in 1530. After Augsburg turned Protestant, Kretz moved to Munich, where he became dean of the cathedral chapter in 1532.
16 For Eck, see CWC 1, Ep. 1a headnote.
17 On Fabri, see CWC 1, Ep. 110a headnote.
18 Jer. 1:14, a reference to Wittenberg in northern Germany.
19 1 Thess. 2:3.

be broken, being well armed as it is with the armour of Christ. You too have been rescued by Christ from that temptation, for you could have been in the court of the Cardinal Bishop,[20] completely covered with gold and silver, but you regarded those temptations of the world as filth, and would rather serve as priest in the court of Christ.[21]

Now I come to our brethren. Give my regards to Matthew Zell,[22] once my teacher of Aristotle, changed from a pagan into a most Christian man. Give abundant greetings also to Bucer, a man of strong spirit, although a Zaccheus,[23] as far as his weak body is concerned. He is a man of small stature, but he has overcome with his stones and with the slingshot of scripture[24] that Philistine Murnarr[25] and a certain Dreckerius.[26] I hope Hedio is well. Symphorian[27] is known to me from the time, fourteen years ago, when I was in Strasbourg in the service of Zasius[28] and met the man and was most kindly received by him. Let him know that I am the same as I was then, that is, a great friend of Symphorian. Erasmus Schmid of Steinhaus[29] is here with us. He is innocent. The Swiss know it. When the furor has abated, he will return.

* * * * *

20 I.e., Albert of Brandenburg, at whose court in Mainz Capito served 1520–3.
21 Reading *curiefaceret* (*curio*= court priest).
22 For Zell, see CWC 1, Ep. 167 headnote.
23 Luke 19:1–10.
24 I.e., Bucer is compared to David in his fight against the Philistine Goliath (1 Sam. 17).
25 Thomas Murner, spelled Murnarrrrrius, to evoke the German word 'Narr,' meaning crazy man. Murner (1475–1537), a Franciscan, attended the universities of Paris (MA 1499), and Freiburg (DTh 1506), where he also taught. He was appointed warden of the Franciscans in Speyer in ca. 1509, but led an itinerant life, preaching in Frankfurt in 1511, studying for a doctorate in canon law in Basel in 1518, and travelling in Italy. In 1520 he settled in Strasbourg. He published pedagogical and theological works as well as satires against the reformers. When the Franciscan monastery in Strasbourg was disbanded, he moved to Switzerland and received a pension. From 1530 until his death he served as a priest in St John's in Obernai.
26 Conrad Treger, spelled 'Drecker' to evoke the German word 'Dreck,' dirt.
27 Symphorian Altbiesser, see below, Ep. 217 headnote.
28 On Zasius, see CWC 1, Ep. 15b headnote. In 1508, when Rhegius studied in Freiburg, he lived at the home of Zasius.
29 Erasmus Schmid (or Fabricius, ca. 1490–1546) of Stein am Rhein, a graduate of the University of Freiburg (BA 1509, MA 1513/14) had to flee Zurich because of his involvement in the Sack of Ittingen in 1524. He returned to Zurich in 1528 and later became pastor of Zollikon and Reichenweiler (Riquewihr).

Johannes Frosch,[30] my Carmelite host, sends you his greetings. Konrad Adelmann,[31] that patron of the gospel, loves you and yours and sends you his regards. Farewell. Augsburg, 16 September 1524.

Letter 216: 19 September 1524, Nördlingen, Theobald Billicanus to Capito

The manuscript is in Basel, Universitätsbibliothek, Ki.Ar. 25a, #29. Theobald Billicanus (ca. 1490–1554) studied at Heidelberg. His first clerical appointment in Weil der Stadt was terminated on account of his Lutheran sympathies. In 1522 he became city pastor in Nördlingen, where he was instrumental in introducing the Reformation. He initially supported the Lutheran party in the Sacramentarian controversy, but he developed doubts and from 1529 publicly criticized Luther. He was married and continued to serve as a Protestant minister in Nördlingen (see his church order, *Renovatio ecclesiae Nordlingiacensis et ratio omnibus reddita de quorundam institutione per diaconos*, n.p. 1525), while maintaining Catholic doctrinal positions. In 1535 he left the city and studied law in Heidelberg (license in civil and canon law, 1542). In an *Apologia* published in 1539, he claimed that he had never been a Lutheran and had always supported the Catholic doctrine. He was relieved of his duties in 1544 and lived in Marburg without employment until 1548, then was lecturer of rhetoric at the university until 1551. Nothing is known of his final years, but he was buried with a Lutheran ceremony in Marburg.

Theobaldus Billicanus also wishes you grace in our Lord Jesus Christ, most renowned and at the same time dearest Capito, for you were taken some time ago from the court of the bishop and, leaving the world behind, have entered the court of Christ, to promote your brethren there with all your might. Pirckheimer of Nürnberg, whom I visited last year as well as some friends, knows how saddened I was when you were in the court of the effem-

* * * * *

30 Johannes Frosch (ca. 1485–1533) studied in Erfurt and Wittenberg (DTh 1518). He was prior of the Carmelite monastery in Augsburg. He collaborated with Rhegius and Stephan Agricola in establishing the Reformation in the city. He married in 1525. After disagreements with the city council, he was dismissed in 1531 and moved to Nürnberg, where he lived until his death.
31 Konrad Adelmann (1462–1547) studied in Heidelberg, Basel, Ferrara, Tübingen, and Ingolstadt. He held canonries in Ellwangen, Augsburg, and Eichstätt. Initially sympathetic to the Reformation, he turned against Luther. When Augsburg embraced the Reformation in 1537, the cathedral chapter, of which Adelmann was a member, was forced to leave.

inate prince. Yet my sadness was not on your behalf, for I know that you did not lose your strong and sincere spirit, as the letter to Pirckheimer testifies.[1] Rather I was saddened on behalf of the many who could have been helped by you, if it had been possible to tear you away from the wretched court. Indeed, one disadvantage befell you when you were a courtier: you became obscurer and less useful to the literary republic, while others emerged into the light. Yet that was the work of the Holy Spirit, to render you illustrious, not through human glory, but through the cross of heaven. Therefore, thanks be to my Lord Jesus Christ, whom I humbly serve with much toil for the glory and benefit of his church, who led you, my patron and a father to all, back to the office of his church, that you may, together with us, lead the fight to extirpate the heresy of Antichrist, and deliver men's wretched consciences from his snares.

I congratulate your wife,[2] and hope that she will make you the father of a beautiful progeny, since it fell to her lot to marry a servant of the Lord and to live in service to the Word. Our church, of which I am the leader, with God's help, is happily coming to its senses and professes the Lord. Pray for our church, that Christ may render her every day more illustrious through his spirit. Furthermore, since I expound these days the prophet Micah to the people, I have wrangled with some difficulties.[3] Please write to me about certain passages if you have an opportunity. In chapter 4 ('And you are a cloudy tower to the flock')[4] I have translated from the Hebrew: 'And you, the tower Eder, are a stronghold to the daughter of Zion.'[5] This is about the citadel of Zion, according to Gen. 35, where the Septuagint translates in this manner: 'Tower Gader, or Eder';[6] also at the beginning of chapter 5:[7] 'Now, however, you will be laid waste, oh daughter of the robber[8] (this about the daughter of Zion), they have laid siege to us (the Assyrians), they will smite the cheek of the judge of Israel with a rod' (that is, lead the king of Israel into captivity, according to Hosea, chapter 2). This has nothing to do with Christ.

* * * * *

1 Point of reference unclear.
2 Agnes Roettel.
3 Billicanus published a commentary on Micah that year: *Michaes propheta* (Augsburg, 1524; repr. Nürnberg, 1525).
4 Mic. 4:8: *Et tu turris gregis nebulosa.*
5 *Et tu turris Eder propugnaculum filiae Zion.*
6 Gen. 35:21. In its literal sense, the term 'tower of Eder' designates Mount Zion.
7 Mic. 5:1. Billicanus translates: *Nunc autem vastaberis filia latronis* (de filia Zion) *obsidionem posuerunt super nos* (Assyrii) *in virga percutient super maxillam iudicis Israhel.*
8 Now usually translated as 'daughter of troops.'

And in the same chapter:[9] 'When the Assyrian comes into our land, we shall raise against him seven shepherds and eight principal men,' which means according to the Hebrew idiom, I believe, they will raise up sufficient troops to defeat the kingdom of the Assyrians, for that is the meaning of the 'seven' and 'eight.' Therefore, soon afterwards[10] words are added, with a change to the singular: 'And he will free Assyria' (not Christ, for it is not he who delivered them from Assyria, but Cyrus and Darius, cf. Isaiah 45).[11] They are meant by 'seven' and 'eight.' Please write back and let me know what you think about this.

Greet all the brethren in the Lord: Zell, Symphorian, Hedio, Bucer, and especially the most famous man and my brother in duty and spirit, the bishop of Bruchsal.[12] You, my father, farewell in the Lord Jesus Christ and pray for me. Nördlingen, 19 September 1524.

Letter 216a: [ca. 24 September 1524, Strasbourg], The Collegiate Churches of St Thomas, Young and Old St Peter to the City Council of Strasbourg

This letter, requesting protection from the city in return for a payment of *Schirmgeld,* is quoted in full in a report on the tensions that developed between the city and the collegiate churches in the fall and winter of 1524 and led to an exodus of Catholic chapter members (see below, Ep. 233b). The report (in Archive Bas-Rhin, Strasbourg, ms. G 4228) is entitled '*Acta et gesta in negotio expulsionis dominorum trium ecclesiarum collegiatarum S. Thome, Junioris et Petri Senioris Argentinensium*' (Transactions and events concerning the matter of the expulsion of the members of the three collegiate churches, St Thomas, Young and Old St Peter at Strasbourg). The letter is on [11–12]. Another copy of the

* * * * *

9 Mic. 5:5.
10 Mic. 5:6.
11 Isa. 45:1.
12 Anton Engelbrecht (d. 1558) studied at Leipzig and Basel (MA 1518, DTh 1520). He was chaplain at the cathedral of Speyer from 1518 and became suffragan bishop there in 1520. He combined the office of parish priest of Bruchsal with the latter position. He assisted Bucer in obtaining a release from his vows. Because Engelbrecht championed the Reformation, he was dismissed in 1524. He moved to Strasbourg, where he was given the parish of St Stephan. After disputing the role of the magistrate in matters concerning the church, he was dismissed from his post in 1534. In 1536 he was still in Strasbourg, but in 1544 he attended the Diet of Speyer in the company of Bucer's opponent, Johann Gropper. Reconciled with the Catholic church, he lived in Cologne until 1549, but returned to Strasbourg after Bucer was exiled and remained there until his death.

letter in AST 22(2) bears the note 'presented 24 Sept. 1524.' The matter is first raised in Capito's correspondence in Ep. 173a above. In the ensuing negotiations the three collegiate churches offered more money, but the city refused their offer and insisted that the clerical members of the collegiate churches take out citizenship.

Strict, honourable, wise, gracious, dear lords!

Firstly, since the chapter and persons of the three collegiate churches at Strasbourg, St Thomas, Young and Old St Peter, desire and need the protection of the honourable council of the city of Strasbourg, as is evident from their numerous requests and applications, they would be inclined to accept the proposals of the honourable council if it were permitted and tolerable to accept them. However, papal and imperial rights and privileges strictly state that the clergy must remain completely independent of the secular government and should be free from it. If they subject themselves to it, they are guilty of perjury and liable to be deprived of their benefices and thus their sustenance. Thus they have their own, separate government, whose needs, commands, and prohibitions they must respect and obey according to their oath. Since divine, natural, and written law, including the privileges, articles, and regulations of the city of Strasbourg, establish that every resident of the city should be treated according to their rightful privileges, the three collegiate churches of St Thomas, Young and Old St Peter beg, request, and petition [the city] to be allowed to remain within their clerical privileges. They ask that their protection be maintained according to the existing contract, conditions, and regulations, which were established and accepted by spiritual and secular governments, especially considering that some of the persons in the three collegiate churches are not only residents of this city, but also children and close relatives of citizens of the city. It is therefore natural and in accord with human reason and expectation that they will be true and loyal to the city in the interest of their personal security and their property, and that they will further the city's welfare and will be most desirous of preventing any disadvantage to it.

At the same time, they are willing to put their persons and property at the service of the city of Strasbourg and pay, [and offer] for the maintenance of the common welfare a cash payment[1] of 40 gulden per collegiate church

* * * * *

1 *Schatzgeld*, cash levy (cf. Grimm 14, col. 2286) or tax in general, according to E. Haberkern and J. Wallach, *Hilfswörterbuch für Historiker* (Bern, 1964), s.v., but the term may also refer to buying out a serf or commuting a service into a cash payment.

per year. Furthermore, the individuals in the three collegiate churches would pay [according to the following scale]: every provost who wants the protection of the city, 4 gulden; a dean who is under their protection, 3 gulden; a canon who accepts such protection, 2 gulden; and a vicar, 1 gulden per year.[2] They undertake to pay that sum where and when the honourable council deems appropriate for the collegiate churches and is most agreeable to the community. And since it is clearly the council's intention to keep it in their power and authority to cancel the protection of individuals at will, the three collegiate churches ask in fairness that each person in turn have the opportunity to opt out of the city's protection and be thereafter freed of the money to be paid for it. We now ask that you may kindly accept this reply from the above-mentioned three collegiate churches and consider it graciously. We in turn will, etc.

Letter 217: [September 1524, Strasbourg], Symphorian Altbiesser to Capito

The manuscript of this letter is in AST 40, #65. Symphorian (Pollio) Altbiesser of Strasbourg (d. 1533) was parish priest of St Stephan from 1510, then cathedral preacher from 1522–3. He was relieved of his duties because of his Lutheran sympathies. He took out citizenship in 1523 and married in 1524. From 1523–6 he was pastor at St Martin's, from 1526–33 he was at the hospice 'Zu den guten Leuten.' He composed songs paraphrasing biblical texts.

I have made my decision in accordance with your opinion, but I am saddened that the Word has made little or no progress among those who appear to be important in the world. I wish I were dead or did not care for the Word, for we are talking to deaf men and shouting at the dead.[1] I can hardly contain

* * * * *

2 The collegiate churches expanded on this offer on 10 December 1524 (ABR, G 4228, 'Acta et gesta' [21–2]: 'First, the collegiate churches will promise on their priestly dignity to be true and loyal to the city of Strasbourg, to further its benefit and advantage and to ward off and turn away any harm, as far as is in their power, and as far as it is not inappropriate and contrary to their traditional obligations. Secondly, the collegiate churches offer to pay *Ungelt* [tax on goods], *Malgelt* [administrative fee for certifying origin and quality of goods], tariff and impositions, like other citizens. Thirdly, the collegiate churches are willing to contribute to the guilds like other citizens, as long as they are not subject to their commands and prohibitions and will not be forced to be so.'

1 Erasmus, *Adagia* 1.4.87.

myself to let them know how tired I am of this nonsense. They allow their poor to die of hunger, while they waste their money on wax candles and other idolatrous luxuries, but let them do what they want. I shall go to Zell[2] myself and tell him the same thing. For the rest, you say something about being sorry about my losses. It is nothing, I am sorry only on Christ's behalf.

I thank you and your very kind wife,[3] who offered me most agreeable refreshments, and also to our common lord and patron, the bishop of Bruchsal,[4] who is with us in appearance rather than in his heart, as the weak usually are. He very happily colluded. I read the letter he sent me, and I thank the man and wish him peace in Jesus Christ and that he may promote the Word, for I see that he has a powerful spirit. Farewell together with your sweet wife.

Hurriedly, your Symphorian.

Letter 218: [before 1 October] 1524, [Strasbourg], The City Council of Strasbourg to Capito, Caspar Hedio, Martin Bucer, Matthew Zell, Anton Firn, Symphorian Altbiesser, and Diebold Schwartz

Printed in CorrBucer 1: 274–5, Ep. 77.

[*Summary*]: The preachers are asked to produce, within the next five weeks, a statement of their beliefs together with scriptural proofs. The document should be in Latin and German.

Letter 219: [Mid-October 1524, Strasbourg, The Strasbourg Preachers to the City Council of Strasbourg]

Printed in BDS 1:304–44.

[*Summary*]: The preachers are in agreement with Luther on twelve points: the principles of *sola scriptura* and *sola fide*; concerning dietary laws; the priesthood of all believers; the abolition of the mass; the reduction of the number of sacraments; vows; adoration of saints; purgatory; singing; secular authority; power of councils. Of special interest is Article 5, concerning the Eucharist. The question of transubstantiation is not touched upon; the preachers want

* * * * *

2 Matthew Zell. Cf. CWC 1, Ep. 167 headnote.
3 Agnes Roettel.
4 See above, Ep. 216, note 12.

to make only two points: (a) the Eucharist is not a sacrifice, but commemorates the death of Christ, and (b) not only the priest but the congregation as well must partake of the bread and wine.

Letter 220: 9 October [1524, Basel], Johannes Oecolampadius to Capito

Printed in BrOek 1:320–1, Ep. 222.

[*Summary*]: Oecolampadius has read a letter from the Swiss community to the Strasbourg preachers and is now conveying it to Strasbourg. The letter tells of the difficulties of the Swiss. Oecolampadius is glad to hear that Capito is giving free lectures on the Old Testament [at the nascent Strasbourg gymnasium]. He is disturbed that there are so many sects among the Swiss. He sends greetings to Capito, Hedio, and their wives.

Letter 221: 14 October 1524, Strasbourg, Capito to Nicolaus Prugner

The manuscript of this letter is not extant. The translation is of the text copied in TB II: 124.

Nicolaus Prugner (ca. 1488–1557) was an Augustinian monk at Colmar until 1518, then at Mulhouse, where he became prior in 1519. He left the monastery in 1523 and married. He was instrumental in reforming the church in Mulhouse, initiating a public disputation there on 7 August 1524. Unpopular with the city council, which regarded him as a radical, he left Mulhouse in April 1526. In 1527, he became pastor of Benfeld near Sélestat, which was then subject to the city of Strasbourg. When the bishop recovered Benfeld in 1538, Prugner moved to Cologne and entered the service of the Archbishop and Elector Hermann von der Wied. In 1546 he became professor of astronomy at the University of Tübingen and taught there until his death.

Greeting. How I wish that your affairs prospered! I have thought about calling you to us, but so far there has been no opportunity. We are overwhelmed with brethren who have been exiled,[1] so that there are many, some of them indeed needy, whom we can barely support. But I am glad that you continue to preach Christ. This is what must be done in the face of Hell. I beseech you, trust in the Lord, and do not allow yourself to be discouraged by the intimidations of the world. I see that the Swiss will be appeased. Your constancy

* * * * *

1 See above, Ep. 205.

will overcome resistance. We must bear up. Therefore, be of good courage. For that is our lot: to suffer evil, although we deserve good.

I shall think of encouraging words for your people in Mulhouse. We are heavily burdened by the machinations of the provincial.[2] We shall at once reply in an open letter, stating the truth. For you see how we are falsely accused, even in the council of the Swiss. For so far we have never yet departed in defeat, indeed we have trusted in God's Word, through which we remain assuredly safe and will gain a victory. The affairs of Christ are making progress among us, as well as in Esslingen, the margravate of Baden, Ulm, and Innsbruck, and Christ reigns in the remaining lands of Ferdinand against the will of the flatterers, who are all-powerful with the princes of Austria. The margrave Casimir of Brandenburg[3] is holding a synod to discuss controversial articles. His chancellor[4] has great hopes. Everything is carried out by his authority. There is some disturbance at Augsburg. But Urbanus Rhegius,[5] once again an exile, holds sway there. As far as I know, he is a faithful and constant preacher of the Word. Erasmus' *Free Will* very freely promotes the flesh and human powers.[6] Martin Luther will answer him excellently, otherwise men who are less talented, but equal to the task of dispersing such puffs of smoke will do it. This will cause a hard struggle that will go on for some years.[7] We have learned that the Swiss will soon apply themselves to achieve concord, a matter that will benefit both the gospel and you. You, who are close by, are perhaps less able to know such things.[8] I wish you and your family prosperity in Christ. Strasbourg, 14 October 1524. My wife[9] returns your greetings.

Your Capito.

* * * * *

2 I.e., Treger, see below, Ep. 222 headnote.
3 Casimir of Hohenzollern, margrave of Brandenburg-Ansbach-Bayreuth (1485–1527) had issued a 'Resolution' on 25 September containing the provision 'that the holy gospel and divine Word be preached clearly and purely.' He called regional rulers to a meeting at Rotenburg ob der Tauber on 12 October, to discuss the settlement of doctrinal differences.
4 Wolfgang Offner.
5 See above, Ep. 215.
6 *De libero arbitrio diatribe* (Basel: Froben, 1524).
7 Luther answered Erasmus in 1525 with *De servo arbitrio*. As predicted by Capito, the polemic between the two men continued with Erasmus' *Hyperaspistes* (Basel: Froben, 1526).
8 This is what the Latin says, although one would expect the opposite.
9 Agnes Roettel; see above, Ep. 215, note 3.

I hope that Johannes Oswald,[10] the chief scribe, is well, and strongly inclined to Christ. I met him only once, over a quick meal, and remember him to the present day. He is a man who carries much weight. For the public scribes are like the heart of a city. They inspire all members of the city council and give them strength. Please ask him on my behalf to imitate our scribe here, who is a Christian in his heart.

Letter 222: [October 1524, Strasbourg], Capito to the Reader

This is the preface to Capito's *Antwurt auff Bruder Conradts vermanung, so er an gemein Eidgnoschafft jüngst geschriben hat* (Reply to Brother Conrad's admonition, which he recently wrote to the Confederacy, Strasbourg: Köpfel, 1524), f. A1b. This is Capito's first official involvement in the polemic with Conrad Treger over the authority of the church and its traditions.

Conrad Treger (ca. 1480–1542) studied at Freiburg (DTh 1516). He was a member of the Augustinian eremites and prior of their house in Strasbourg from 1517. In 1518 he became provincial of Rhineland-Swabia. He attempted to curtail the influence of Luther in the Augustinian houses under his jurisdiction. In a publication dedicated to Sébastien de Montfalcon, Bishop of Lausanne, *Ad reverendum ... Fabianum de monte Falcone Lausanensem episcopum paradoxa centum de ecclesiae conciliorumque auctoritate* [To the Reverend Sébastien de Montfalcon, Bishop of Lausanne, One Hundred Paradoxes Concerning the Authority of Church and Councils](Strasbourg, 12 March 1524), he accused the reformers of being Hussite heretics. He offered to engage in public disputation with them, but declined an invitation by the Strasbourg preachers (see above, Epp. 187, 188) on the pretext of needing permission from the bishop. The preachers then replied to Treger's pamphlet with the *Verwarnung der diener des worts und der Brüder zu Straßburg von Landen und Stetten, gemayner Eydgnoschafft wieder die gotslesterige disputation bruder Conradts Augustiner Ordens Provinicial* (Warning of the Ministers of the Word and Brethren of Strasbourg to the Regions and Cities of the Confederacy Against the Blasphemous Disputation of Brother Conrad, Provincial of the Augustinian Order, Strasbourg: Köpfel, and Strasbourg: Johann Grieninger, 1524). In May, Treger replied with the aggressively worded *Vermanung* (see below, note 1), published in August 1524 without place of publication or name of publisher. The pamphlet provoked a tumult in Strasbourg. A group of citizens

* * * * *

10 Johannes Oswald Gamsharst (b. ca. 1480 in Kenzingen) moved to Mulhouse in 1486 when his father became city scribe. He studied in Basel (BA 1494) and succeeded his father as city scribe in 1504, serving in the post for twenty-five years. He was a strong supporter of the Reformation.

stormed Treger's convent and brought him before the council, which took him into custody, together with the preacher of the convent, Nikolaus of Bladesheim and three other priests. Another unruly group raided the kitchen and cellars of St Arbogast (see 'Acta und Handtlung so sich zwischen den Burgern zu Straßburg undt Conrado Treger ... in Anno 1524 begeben undt zugetragenn,' AST 173 #3, ff. 18r–20r). On 10 September citizen delegates officially petitioned the council to punish Treger for slandering the preachers. On the intervention of the Swiss Confederacy and the *Reichsregiment* in Esslingen (see CorrBucer 1:278, Ep. 80), the council decreed that Treger should swear an oath to keep the peace and give security for 50,000 gulden. On fulfilling these conditions, Treger was released on 12 October. He returned to his native Fribourg (Switzerland) at the end of 1524. Subsequently, he was present at disputations in Baden (1526), Bern (1528), and Lausanne (1530), but actively participated only in the Bern Disputation, where he used the opportunity to renew the polemic with Capito and the Strasbourg preachers. The controversy produced published responses, not only from Capito, but also from Bucer, Hedio, Katharina Zell, and François Lambert of Avignon.

Dr Capito to the Reader.

The grace of Christ, pious reader. In answer to brother Conrad Treger's last letter,[1] which is completely opposed to Christian truth, and in order to refute his unjustified strong rebuke, I beg you first to take no offence at our simplicity and shortcomings. For such contentious speech and mutual complaints are not fitting for us, to say nothing of such thoughtless scorn. Servants of the Lord (which we all claim to be)[2] should not be combative but rather fatherly toward everyone. 2 Timothy 2.[3] Treger calls us prophets inspired by an evil spirit, prophets who evoke the condemned and poisonous Bohemian heresy.[4]

* * * * *

1 *Vermanung ... an ein löbliche gemeine Eidgenossenschaft von der böhmischen Ketzerei und Antwort auf eine lügenhaft gotteslästrig Buch von etlichen, so sich Diener des Worts heißen an ein gemeine Eidgenossenschaft dies Jahrs im April ausgangen* (Admonition ... to the Praiseworthy Confederacy Against the Bohemian Heresy and Response to a Lying Blasphemous Book by Some Men Who Call Themselves Servants of the Word, Sent in April of This Year to the Confederacy, [Freiburg], 1524).

2 Alluding to the title of Treger's *Vermanung* in which he refers to the Strasbourg preachers as those 'who call themselves servants of the Word.'

3 2 Tim. 2:24: 'But the servant of the Lord must not strive, but be gentle unto all men.'

4 I.e., of adhering to the tenets of the fifteenth-century Bohemian reformer, Jan Hus; the accusation is foreshadowed in the title of Treger's *Vermanung* which refers to the preachers' *böhmische Ketzerei*. See above, note 1.

He calls us falsifiers of the written word, heathens, and open sinners. Then he interprets *publicanus*[5] as rapacious wolves, unprincipled men, and anything else that might make a man hated. Yet his and my office ought to be that of instructors who bear evil-doers with all patience. I wish to be moderate, to refrain from retaliation, and (God willing) remain within the bounds of brotherly love, not to allow myself to become indignant, and to take care *lest I also be tempted*. Galatians 6.[6] And should I transgress, I ask you, Christian reader, to take no offence, but rather to remember that I am a sinful, unsteady man, and thank God that he has given you greater grace, patience, and for-bearance. Also, consider that this matter requires a certain amount of zeal and seriousness. For we should strive for the honour of God. The difficulty lies in holding the middle course when such a heated battle is under way. For vengeance, which is forbidden, can easily present itself in the guise of due resistance. May God grant you an increase in understanding. Amen.

Letter 223: 24 October 1524, [Strasbourg], Capito to the City Council of Mulhouse

This is the second preface of the *Antwurt* (see above, Ep. 222 headnote), which appears on fols. A2r–A4v.

Wolfgang Fabritius Capito wishes the honourable, wise mayor[1] and council of the city of Mulhouse in the Sundgau the grace and peace of the Lord, etc.

Honourable, wise lords and dear brothers in Christ, in reply to Conrad Treger's announcement of a public disputation, which he has however con-sistently rejected so far, we, the ministers of the Word and brothers in Stras-bourg, issued a fair warning last April to the Swiss Confederacy.[2] In it, we point out the ridiculous attacks of that blasphemer and reveal that he abuses certain people's simplicity and sometimes their pride and greed for money to promote dissension in the world. He spreads rumours that we breed unrest

* * * * *

5 Cf. Treger's *De ecclesiae auctoritate*, B ii verso: *qui ecclesyam non audiet, sit tibi tanquam ethnicus et publicanus*.
6 Gal. 6:1.

1 Ulrich Karrer (also called Gerber, i.e., tanner, on account of his profession, b. ca. 1450) was mayor of Mulhouse from 1494 to 1524. He relinquished his post in December 1524 and was succeeded by Acacius Gilgauer.
2 I.e., *Verwarnung der diener des worts ... an die Brüder ... gemayner Eydgnoschafft* (Strasbourg: Köpfel, 1524).

under the guise of preaching the gospel rather than attributing that unrest to his own tricks.[3] This much Brother Conrad's announcement may have achieved: there is dissension everywhere. Since the world aggrandizes its own things, which the Spirit condemns through the pious servants of God, and since the Pharisees speak ill of everything that is going on and give it a sinister meaning, their malice is reinforced every time it is given a semblance of truth. That is the effect of the spirited and quick-witted marvellous speeches of Brother Conrad, which he has offered for discussion. And now Brother Treger has undertaken to give the lie to our warning, using many tricks and slanderous statements, which I shall rebut below in this booklet without returning his abuse. I send you this booklet, Your Honours, in the form of a warning which I intended to write for your benefit in any case and would have done, had I not been hindered every day by the troubles, attacks, and tricks of the enemy. Every one of our days is marked by difficulties and malice. Although the faithful servant of God, Nicolaus Prugner,[4] is capable enough to preach about doctrine, to offer consolation, and improve people through admonition, we nevertheless thought it would do no harm and would in fact be a consolation to find among you other witnesses as well to the resurrection of Jesus Christ, as the apostle says in Act 1.[5] Therefore I do not consider it a burden to write to you on behalf of others, while some of you perhaps still know who I am. For the scribe, Johannes Oswald,[6] and others knew me well when I was preacher in Basel, and perhaps they still remember me. I therefore send you my *Antwurt* responding to the speech of the flesh, which Brother Conrad Treger dares to send against us with many rash words of abuse.[7] The *Antwurt* may be of assistance to laymen, who are deceived by the appearance of the German text in which Treger makes us out to be godless braggards. Many will not yet have seen the clear meaning of Christ in 2 Cor. 4[8] directed against respect for mortals and for the judgment of humans. In their human ignorance, they do not know any better. Indeed, many mislead others and allow themselves to be misled, although we should

* * * * *

3 Alluding to the wording in Treger's *Vemanung* B2r: *geschwind griff*.
4 For Prugner, see above, Ep. 221 headnote.
5 Acts 1:21–2.
6 Gamsharst. See above, Ep. 221, note 10.
7 I.e., Treger's *Vermanung*.
8 2 Cor. 4:3–4: 'But with me it is a very small thing that I should be judged by you or by any human court. I do not even judge myself. I am not aware of anything against myself, but I am not thereby acquitted. It is the Lord who judges me.'

depend on God alone, fear him alone, and love him alone (Matt. 4).[9] But this terrible Pharisee took cover under civil piety, which is only known to the flesh, and turns to external order and honour in morals, customs, and old established traditions. They are indeed valid according to nature and must be maintained by everyone as long as they are not against the justice of Christ Jesus, which is the only thing that counts before God. By all means let us live in order and honour. Christian justice does not wish to injure anyone; it does not want to cause unrest. It does not take away what belongs to others and does not look out for itself, but bears all (2 Cor. 13).[10]

But there is a difference: the reasoning of the flesh does not respect God (Ps. 13) and does not know fear of God's punishment (Isaiah 28).[11] For much that is not right remains unpunished, which bothers even the just (Ps. 36), as can be seen in the prophet Habakkuk (chapter 1).[12] We wretched humans do not want to be treated with contempt, nevertheless we also want to make headway in our quest for salvation. However, we shall not come close to God with such piety, as long as it consists of blood and flesh and is in our nature (Matt. 16).[13] Yet we live in our four walls, for ourselves alone; we rely on ourselves alone forever, and think that God does not care about us. It must be confessed (although it is shameful) that this applies to all natural reason, although it acts reluctantly and wants to gloss over what is ugly. The devout man, by contrast, believes that God is with us, that he punishes injustice *unto the third or fourth generation* (Ex. 20).[14] He fears only God and worships him alone and knows that he will gravely punish the sinner, at the very least through terrible blindness and consequent sin, even if he is not punished here through temporal punishment. Thus Paul writes to the Romans and pagans in Romans 1 that they have no excuse, for they recognized the existence of God but did not praise his divinity nor thank him, and so their ignorant hearts were darkened.[15] Furthermore, the man who fears God feels the power of the law and the help of the gospel, recognizing that all things are done under the influence of sin and unbelief, so that God will have mercy on everyone (Rom. 11).[16] Indeed, we know that his eyes look everywhere

* * * * *

9 Matt. 4:10.
10 Read 1 Cor. for 2 Cor. I.e., 1 Cor. 13:5–7.
11 Ps. 14:1–3 (=13 Vg.); Isa. 28:14–15.
12 Ps. 37:1–7 (=36 Vg.); Hab. 1:2–3.
13 Matt. 16:17.
14 Exod. 20:5.
15 Rom. 1:21.
16 Rom. 11:32.

at good and evil, and that the hair on our head is numbered and that we shall lose none without his knowledge.[17] The Father Almighty has given this knowledge through his Son to all believers who put all their trust in him, and we hope and desire to be participants in it. Thus he has enlightened our foolish reason and forgiven our sins and given us grace and an understanding of his will. For the Holy Spirit of God moves the hearts of [believers], so that they stand in fear of the great wrath of God when they look at their sins. Yet they do not despair, but obtain mercy and forgiveness for their sins through Christ. They fear and doubt for themselves, they feel secure and comforted in the merit of Christ and the promise of God. Thus they have a certain and happy trust in God. The godless man, however, searches in himself for happiness and does not sense God. He puts his hope in himself and none in God, for he believes nothing, or holds an erroneous and wavering belief. Such people think that God will be appeased by our trumped-up works, whereas works fail them and will fail anyone, and when their eyes are opened, they are full of insecurity and despair. Even if there is only a little temptation, they despair, whereas those who fear God give themselves into God's hands with all their heart. In the midst of death they expect all good things from God who has created us for the benefit of all creatures, and who reigns even today. This is the testimony of the Holy Spirit of God in us (John 16).[18] We cannot err, for scripture, which is undeniable, gives testimony despite all reason and cleverness of the flesh. *Ignorant and rash men confuse the divine scripture at their own peril* (2 Peter 3).[19] Indeed, they turn away from it in their dark human folly and remain in their firmly rooted error, which they cover up with an external show of piety. They say: 'We must not disdain tradition. We must not put our understanding before that of the usage and the practice of the church.' It is more appropriate and right, according to them, to come to terms with tradition and thus avoid creating unrest, rebellion, and dissension among the people. One must do what is good for peace, and abstain from anything that can create unrest. They say these things and other such claptrap, as if zealous searching for the gospel truth would bring with it disdain for one's forefathers. We have not been instructed to keep customs, but rather to follow Christ wherever he leads us. For he himself insisted on scripture, and we must not make compromises in any point that goes against Christ Jesus and is clearly written in Holy Writ, which is the touchstone of

* * * * *

17 Matt. 10:30.
18 John 16:13: 'The Spirit of Truth is come, he will guide you into all truth.'
19 2 Pet. 3:16.

our faith. Even if the devil complains violently and incites dissensions, what can we do? We must follow our command, even if there is unrest and no peace. For there is no peace if one is not at peace with God, and there is no divine peace if one acts against his will, as indicated in scripture. That is the aim of our *Antwurt*: to counter the carnal arguments and to show the ugliness of worldly piety, indeed to manifest their godless basis and foundation.

I ask that this be read to other Swiss confederates as well, for no doubt you must suffer many threats everywhere and hear many counter-arguments from godless men. You must suffer much temptation. And yet God preserved the three men from the fire in the Chaldean furnace,[20] and he may and will protect you too from all threats if only you trust and hope in him. God does not allow his people to come to grief. Certainly, if only we can pray, he will see our loyalty and *give his servants the courage to speak* and to act (Acts 4).[21] I have no doubt that we will come to see some gruesome and tyrannical actions, and that your just souls will be frightened and oppressed by their unjust works and persecutions, as was Lot in Sodom and Gomorrah (2 Pet. 2).[22] But this oppression is not without joy and consolation. We know that it is written: *He who endures to the end will be saved* (Matt. 10).[23] Do not lose that glory, pious brethren in Christ, which Paul considers so precious that he would rather die than permit anyone to take away from him such a prize.[24] May God Almighty allow you to grow in his grace and in the understanding of Jesus Christ. Amen.

What actually happened with the Provincial in the aftermath is indicated in the preface to him.[25] Put your trust in it, even if many others state the contrary and say that at the public disputation in Baden[26] the honourable and most learned Provincial overcame us twice, even though he never really wanted to engage with us. Our cause is built strictly on the clear Word of God, which neither the Provincial nor the other scholastic wranglers nor any other creature in Christianity is able to overcome. Our fellow citizens and brethren in Christ send you their hearty greetings. Given at Strasbourg, 24 October 1524.

* * * * *

20 Dan. 3:21–5.
21 Acts 4:29.
22 2 Pet. 2:7–9.
23 Matt. 10:22.
24 Cf. 1 Cor. 9:24–7.
25 I.e., Ep. 223a below.
26 Not the Baden Disputation, which took place in 1526, but perhaps a discussion at the *Städtetag* of August 1524. Cf. also below, Ep. 286, note 1.

Letter 223a: [24 October, 1524, Strasbourg], Capito to Conrad Treger

This letter, one of three prefaces to the *Antwurt* (see above, Ep. 222 headnote), is not listed by Millet. The text is on B1r–B4r.

I wish you, dear Treger, the grace and peace of God the Father and an understanding of our Lord Jesus Christ. *There is no end to the writing of books.*[1] All of us, learned and unlearned, write whatever our bold spirit impels us to write. As a result, many are kept from and turned away from practising the gospel message, which is the only thing that should occupy us day and night. The time is too short to consider every bit of gossip, and curiosity incites a general desire to search for and find out what is going on. When, then, do we have leisure to learn what pleases God? That is the reason, my dear Treger, why we have used our pen less in response to your first wonderful speech[2] and only offered to reply to your challenge orally in the presence of certain knowledgeable men of the honourable council, by the order and permission of the same council. But you have rejected our offer consistently[3] and required the permission of the Reverend Bishop of Strasbourg[4] for a special report and informal discussion, whereas earlier on, when you requested a formal public disputation, you merely asked for security.[5] Therefore people began to suspect the readiness of the gospel Word, which is well prepared to be questioned by anybody. At that point, we could no longer keep silent and permit the Christian truth to be slandered, as if we were reluctant to come before you. We have therefore warned the honest Swiss Confederacy concerning your intent, for your game was aimed at them.[6] And now you incite us again to counter the warning you gave us in the wonderful speech you have published.[7] I, together with Martin Bucer, our dear brother and

* * * * *

1 Eccles. 12:12.
2 I.e., the *Paradoxa* (see above, Ep. 222 headnote), which Bucer referred to as a *Wunderred*, wonderful speech (BDS 2: 42).
3 See *Verwarnung* Biii recto: 'But he answered in the negative, saying that this was forbidden by the imperial estates.'
4 Wilhelm von Honstein.
5 I have rendered the terms 'ernstlich' (serious) and 'frintlich' (friendly) as 'formal' and 'informal.' The reference is to Treger's offer in the *De ecclesiae conciliorumque auctoritate* Aiii verso: 'We are prepared to dispute publicly and even privately in any place, as long as it is safe' (*parati ... publice et privatim etiam ubique locorum modo tutum sit certamen inire*).
6 Treger's second pamphlet, *Vermanung* (see above, Ep. 222, note 1) was addressed to the Swiss Confederacy.
7 I.e., *Vermanung*.

faithful helper in the gospel, will do this. Buoyed by scriptural quotations, I take courage and am hopeful that neither you nor all the gates of Hell can devise lies that will stand up against this. For truth is too powerful and precious. In addition, you accuse us of lying, as if we had slandered you in our *Verwarnung* with untruths,[8] even though we said not a word there that is not borne out by fact. And you carry on with great arrogance and abuse, and agitate against us, so that we must guard against becoming suspect in the eyes of readers who do not know better. It is the habit of clever speakers to make their opponents hated, so that their judges condemn them even before the cause is heard, preventing them from transacting their business in a more propitious atmosphere, as is fair and right. For who would not rather believe you, the pious man of integrity, who never ruffled any feathers? You, of course, are motivated to write a hundred miracle speeches[9] about the power of the holy Christian Church and the holy councils (for which you call on God's testimony) purely out of great concern and indignation about the *dissension that has arisen over the most important articles of our faith, in Christendom and especially in the German Nation*,[10] which has created a schism in the last few years. You are motivated only by concern for the great evil resulting from it: *fire, murder, terror, lament, misery, and deprivation*, all set in motion by the Bohemian heretics, etc.[11] Who would not rather believe the trustworthy honour of such a loyal mind who swears an apostolic oath, rather than our motley assembly, a few rascals, *runaway apostates, frivolous monks* (for to you, we are all 'monks'),[12] who proudly vaunt their great uprightness, their deep understanding, their unheard-of skill in many languages and nevertheless are bleary-eyed, insane, clownish, *shitty prophets, Hussite brethren, raging wolves*,[13] heathens, and manifest sinners? We have introduced the damned, *poisonous, stinking Bohemian heresy*.[14] Our skill is nothing but lies and deceit, to which our spirit impels us. We are shameless and have no regard either for God or scripture and have with our prattling covered up and *painted over the truth*,[15] whether it makes sense or not. In our raging mind we disdain all

* * * * *

8 Treger called it a *Lugenbiechlin*, a book of lies (*Vermanung* Aiv recto).
9 See above, note 2.
10 *Vermanung*, Aii recto.
11 Ibid.
12 Ibid., Fi verso.
13 Ibid., Fi verso, E iv recto, Dii verso.
14 Ibid., Biii verso.
15 Ibid., Bi verso.

Fathers, reject Christian councils, refuse to listen to the holy unblemished church,[16] and give ourselves over only to the Spirit and right understanding of scripture. Our grave heresy causes dissension and unrest because we are inspired by an evil spirit. Under the guise of the gospel we *persuade ignorant people of rubbish.*[17] These and other similar blessed virtues you attribute to us in your truthful book, written neither out of malice nor out of carnal desire. Is that not how you endear yourself to the reader? Your gentle mind knows how to make us presentable and cover our stupidity on account of your sweet love, as Paul teaches in Gal. 6.[18] And you instruct us that we have no need of scripture and need not require it from everyone. And yet you have, in your many pages and among such a great crowd of accusations, cited no more than two or three passages against us, and those only to refer to our madness and pretence of inspiration. Yes, I shall take on even the clear letter of scripture cited in your little book, which required neither skill nor labour to produce. I will do this even though there would be more useful work to do.

I have spent two days hastily writing the *Verwarnung,*[19] addressed to the respected members of the Swiss Confederacy in the name of the public ministers of the Word, so that the merchants travelling to the [Frankfurt] Fair might make it known. I have not even been able to read it over because of incidental business at the parish of Young St Peter and the church community. This may be apparent in the hasty and casual composition of the book. Yet I have written only what is true, as I am bound to do for my lords and betters in the honourable council of the good free city of Strasbourg, and I give proof of it and cite trustworthy witnesses. You, however, accuse us so often of lying and yet, in recounting the affair, although you differ from us, you bring no significant reason to bear, explaining why we should have lied. You simply make assertions and use abuse and waffling as your weapons. You use the colourful and carnal language of a layman to go against the truth and bring accusations against us, which could have been brought at any time against the prophets, apostles and Christ himself. They are of this kind: the synagogue thinks differently and cannot err. Will you be more knowledgeable than your forefathers, the fathers of the church? Are you superior to and greater than our father Abraham?[20] Show us who shares your opin-

* * * * *

16 *De ecclesiae conciliorumque auctoritate,* Aiii verso.
17 Ibid., Aii verso.
18 Gal. 6:1.
19 See above, Ep. 222 headnote.
20 John 8:53.

ion.[21] Does any leader of the Pharisees think like you? Only the people, who know nothing of the law and may be spoken ill of. [You say:]You work no miracles and can show no signs to prove your teaching and make us believe in it;[22] you are a damned Hussite, a frivolous man without honour, etc. Your book belongs on the garbage heap. It is full of that stuff, and has no courtesy in it or humane friendship.

I believe an answer is in order, and I shall take upon me all the risk threatening my brothers and fellow ministers, since I have given you cause to write against me with my 'blasphemy' and my so-called mad, raging, and ill-phrased writings. For I am supposed to have once called you 'Brother Kuntz' and 'Brother Unwilling,'[23] because Your Excellency does not wish to lower himself to common discussion. Even today I would be more inclined to hear from you personally a report on my errors and hope to reply to it, and that is likewise the wish of honest citizens everywhere – those citizens who recently seized you and kept you in custody, so that you might not slip away.[24] They handed you over to their government with the request that you dispute publicly in the German language and show the reason for your expectations of us. They would not have taken you into custody unless there was a rumour that you wanted to flee, which then became manifest. Yet they did not obtain from you any Christian instruction, as they hoped they would if you were kept at hand. Then many realized that you have no fairness or decency, for an honest man should stand by his word and expound the meaning of God's law, and several of us are prepared to show the cause of our belief and hope. No authority can forbid that, for the sword and secular power have no say in matters of the soul, not even one bit. They are in charge only of external things, looking after the public peace and the punishment of rebels. Indeed, the enemies of Christ's cross would have been greatly pleased if you could have made good on your bragging and revealed our blasphemy. And yet you show little respect in your book for the honourable council and honest community of Strasbourg, when you write that they have been misled. You make them followers of a stinking and poisonous teaching, who tolerate malicious rebels in their midst.[25] But the community did

* * * * *

21 *Vermanung* Biv recto: 'You cannot and will not show anyone who in the past thousand years or more believed as you do concerning the principal articles of faith.'
22 Ibid., Biv verso.
23 *Verwarnung*, Di verso; Dii has 'Bruder Aygenwillig' (Brother Wilful) rather than 'Unwillig' (Angry), as quoted by Treger *Vermanung*, Fiii recto.
24 See above, Ep. 222 headnote.
25 *Vermanung*, Aiv verso.

not act on account of this shameful accusation. Rather it demanded in their complaint only that you demonstrate our error publicly and in German, that they might in the future know to avoid us as harmful seducers. You rejected this demand often and strongly, and were hiding behind papal and imperial edicts,[26] although they cannot restrict or prevent anyone from showing the right path to those in error. Rather, they desire that everyone be brought to reason and obedience, and to see this done through the speeches of qualified men (and you want to be regarded as a qualified speaker).

Subsequently the obedient community wanted nevertheless to hear a report of the truth and a clear answer from you, and therefore asked our lords and leaders in the honourable council to instruct you to report in the presence of a few persons and two notaries. That too you rejected, as you rejected everything else, saying that you gave your answer in writing and print, and you expect to carry on the dispute in writing and not orally. The honourable council and honest community accepted that, for they are not inclined to lose a great deal of time on such business, since there are more urgent things on their agenda. They therefore left it at obliging you with an oath to dispute with scriptural evidence and arguments rather than abuse and conceits, which are destructive, etc.[27] The same request was made of us. We were likewise commanded and obligated to be equally sober and moderate, to use no words of abuse and publish nothing until it had been seen by the chancellery and approved. For we clever defenders of the church must learn mildness and Christian patience from the secular authorities. We have accepted those instructions for our part, as is seemly and in accordance with our obligation as citizens. We gave our promise and, in accordance with God's will, will act in a manner that will show that we have strong justification and are respectful and modest in our answer.

Now, since you divided your book into 17 parts, or rather lies, which you yourself have forced on us, we shall number our articles accordingly and simply write a report to keep as much as possible any acrimony from slipping into our words. Firstly, we shall address your preface in which you announce the contents of your book. We expect you to make an effort to reply, according to your undertaking, and answer more fully. However, we expect you to do this without overextending your response and without repeating the reply given in your two abusive speeches,[28] going eternally over the same argu-

* * * * *

26 Ibid., Bii recto: 'it is against papal and imperial prohibition and mandate.'
27 Treger swore an *Urfehde*, i.e., to keep the peace. See above, Ep. 222 headnote.
28 I.e., Treger's two publications, the *Paradoxa* and the *Vermanung* (see above, Ep. 222 headnote).

ment. We hope that you will spare the pious reader who needs to exercise his mind in holy scripture rather than search through such unnecessary matter.

Letter 223b: [24 October 1524, Strasbourg], Capito to the Reader

This is the *Summarium*, attached to the *Antwurt* (see above, Ep. 222 headnote). The text is on f. Niv recto.

Pious reader, to save you some work, you should realize that our disagreement concerns the trustworthiness of scripture, with all sorts of other arguments introduced on both sides. So that you will not be delayed unnecessarily, I wish to indicate to you the order of the most important points. You may want to look at the rest at your leisure.

Concerning Christian and civil piety: A.

Action taken by the citizens of Strasbourg against Treger: Biii.

The gospel does not incite rebellion: Ci, Giii, Li.

The history of the Bohemians: Ciiii.

The Fathers and the councils are not treated with disdain: Eiii.

Concerning mandates: Eiii.

Three abusive statements of Treger and a response to all haters of God: (1) You are divided concerning the main articles; (2) No one ever thought as you do; (3) and you have no miracles or signs to show. All counterarguments: H, J, K.

Concerning scripture and the church, and that the name of the church is suspicious: Mi, Niiii.

Of the clarity of scripture: Oiiii.

Interspersed are many clear expositions of scriptural passages. We await Treger's response, but want him to reply with full scriptural evidence.

Letter 224: October 1524, Strasbourg, Capito to the Reader

This is the preface to *Was man halten unnd antwurten soll von der spaltung zwischen Martin Luther und Andreas Carolstadt* (What One Ought to Think of the Division Between Martin Luther and Andreas Karlstadt, Strasbourg: Köpfel, 1524). For Karlstadt, see CWC 1, Ep. 15a, headnote. The pamphlet was written in the wake of Karlstadt's expulsion from Saxony on Luther's initiative. In October, Karlstadt journeyed through Strasbourg, Basel, and Zurich, where he made contact with Anabaptist preachers. Oecolampadius prevented the printing of a tract by Karlstadt on infant baptism in 1524, but several other tracts in which Karlstadt rejected Luther's teaching on the Real Presence were published. Cf. WA 15: 326–9, 334–41.

Grace, peace, and understanding of the truth, from God the Father, through our Lord Jesus Christ.

There is great joy and jubilation among godless citizens, those 'dear and pious Christians.' They are hoping for a victory against the truth, for there is disagreement between Martin Luther and Andreas Karlstadt. Thus they say among themselves: *Every kingdom which is divided among itself goes to ruin, and one house collapses on the next.* Luke 11.[1] Now Christ is divided into parts. 1 Cor. 1.[2] We will not be able to maintain our honour and pleasure. The ceremony of the mass must be set up again, for where the spirit is extinguished, the flesh takes up all space. But pay no attention to such claims. For you know: if you have believed, he will save you and your kin on the last day. 2 Tim. 1.[3] Just live according to what we preach you daily on the basis of scripture. Follow the example of the holy Word, of faith and love in Christ Jesus, through whom we receive forgiveness for our sins and grace according to the holy call and law of God, and not on the basis of our works. Insist on it with gladness. For our Lord Christ Jesus has been placed by God the Father above all that can be named. Eph 1.[4] In the evening they will return without having been sated, as David says,[5] for they will be deprived of all support and will find that they did to their detriment what they thought they did for their good. Deut. 12.[6] And the end of their way is the way of death. Proverbs 14.[7] Then the joy of their heart will be turned to grief, their joy will end in sorrow and misery. And to speak the truth, I say even now they are full of grief. When Zophar the Naamathite heard the proud hope of the righteous Job and the punishment of the evil men, his thoughts overwhelmed him and his heart was disturbed.[8] When our enemies see our constant hope and peace, they will know that we have received the spirit of God, not the spirit of the world. 1 Cor. 2.[9] He is the spirit of strength, which has all manner of joy in the Lord to lift us up. They will lay their hands on us, as did the Jewish council in Acts 5 [10] with the apostles. They despise us, but we do not care.

* * * * *

1 Luke 11:17.
2 1 Cor. 1:13.
3 2 Tim. 1:12.
4 Eph. 1:20–2.
5 Cf. Ps. 59:14–15.
6 Cf. Deut. 12:30–1.
7 Prov. 14:12.
8 Job 20:1–11. Zophar the Naamathite was one of Job's three friends, cf. Job 2:11.
9 1 Cor. 2:12.
10 Acts 5:18.

We do not mind being scorned by the world as dregs and put on display by the world and the angels, that we may, in this manner, gain the prize that is only God's to give.

Furthermore, they command us no longer to teach this way to our brethren, whereas Christ died for them and we should do good to our enemies. But what are they doing? What strange lies they have made up about us! They accuse one of having been with the servants' concubines, they accuse another of having consorted with his maid and been caught in adultery. They accuse a third one of theft. Now they have started a rumour that we want to overturn all authority, that we teach what is to our own advantage, whereas we only put our finger on their devilish business. They come up with different plans, one after another, as the father of liars and blasphemers inspires them to act.

When nothing succeeds, these brave and precious people say that we are doing our gospel business wrong, that even Luther himself is writing against us.[11] This rumour they disseminated last summer over and over again and recently brought it out once more. A messenger of the Elector, they said, had heard it himself from Luther, who said to him at table that we are doing wrong and he would bring us to our knees with force – this Luther denied in a letter to me.[12] But malicious people are so mulish that often, when caught lying, they know no shame. A thief caught in the act of thieving is terrified in his heart and filled with shame (Jer. 2),[13] but these people, our enemies, the great thieves of our honour, have been caught lying so often and have shown no remorse. But our spirit does not weaken on that account, we are not bowed down. We are standing by the truth. We fear neither lies nor threats, but remain true to the Word with alacrity.

For this reason the devil causes scandal on account of the false brethren, and incites some useless, vain, and dishonest people to turn to quarrelsome discussions, which are in themselves enough to upset the minds of the listeners. They bring up foolish questions, which are not instructive and merely lead to strife (Tit. 3 and 2 Tim. 2).[14] Such a pit of snakes can be found wriggling in Swabia,[15] as is reported; they are enemies of the cross of Christ and leave no clear passage in scripture untouched by criticism. That is the

* * * * *

11 Luther and the preachers of Strasbourg disagreed about the interpretation of the Eucharist. Cf. the negotiations below, Ep. 247.
12 Cf. above, Ep. 198.
13 Jer. 2:26.
14 Titus, 3:9, 2 Tim. 2:23.
15 Cf. below, Ep. 273.

work of the flesh (Gal. 5),[16] which is rude, raw, pugnacious, beastly, unkind, and full of ambition. Even if all his vices are hidden, the vicious man will still be judged for them. They fight on account of greed and pride rather than zeal for the truth and seek only their own advantage instead of the advantage of the community. They are motivated by bitterness against the enemy, whereas zeal for God must be tempered by charity. We must not pay attention to rash teaching, which can be recognized by the fact that it brings about more questions than improvement in faith in God (1 Tim. 1).[17] We must only listen to the commandment of the Lord, the sum of which is: love with a pure heart, a good conscience, and true faith. Anything that does not further that aim leads only to useless blather.

It would be unseemly, however, to leave off preaching salvation under the pretext of being charitable, and resembling an earthly father who allows his child to take up a sharp knife to keep him from crying. This is the principle we have applied so far in deciding what we need to teach. The loyal ministers of the Word have vehemently attacked errors, have urged people to have faith, have made much of the mercy of God, have made little of their own merits, have indicated what is sin and what is righteousness, and have combatted false service to God with clear scripture and with manifold and diligent preaching. They have taken manifest scandal out of people's hearts, first with words, and afterwards, quietly and decently, with external actions. For the Lord wants to slay the son of abomination with the Spirit of his mouth, not with the hand (2 Thess. 2).[18] God has moreover granted us grace and progress with all peace and quiet. The dietary laws concerning specific days are gone, as are popish feast days, abstinence, confession, taking the sacrament[19] – all wilfully introduced service of God has been abolished in our community: burning wax candles, taking holy salt and water, vigils, masses, observing the canonical hours and seasons of the year, penance, pilgrimages, Roman grace and indulgences, all have been eliminated without noticeable upset, a result which no threat of force could have achieved. The honourable council bravely cleared the churches of idols, extinguished many lights and eternal flames and (may God grant it) will, with the same mild measures, soon proceed and abolish all idols.

But why should one rush in and act before the Word is applied? The idols do most harm in the heart, for those who have heard the Word know

* * * * *

16 Gal. 5:19–20.
17 1 Tim. 1:3–4.
18 2 Thess. 2:8.
19 I.e., routinely.

that idols are nothing in this world (1 Cor. 8)[20] and are not scandalized. They leave the images alone as good creations of God. Those who have not yet heard the Word are only embittered and offended if the idols are taken away before they receive the Word. In such a case, they are then even less willing to open their ears to the Truth. For God gives faith through the Word, which is heard by the people, and not through the sudden taking away of idols. Thus great damage would be done without any hope of benefit. For what good is it to tear some idols violently from the walls, when they do no harm to the faithful? For all things harm the faithless, but this action injures them in their hearts, in that they shut out all faith and remain closed to it.

Paul did not take away any idols in Athens[21] and did not lay hands on them anywhere. Instead, he preached of the true honour of God and against the idols, and when they did not accept his teaching, he took his leave and did not touch any idol with his finger. For all our action must start first in our innermost heart and flow out from it, and must not be driven from the outside in. Thus, we do not wish to defend the idols, as some people allege, but are thinking of the simple servants. We wish to act usefully in time rather than with haste, causing damage. Our action, then, is governed by charity and has progressed, for otherwise we will make bitter the sweetness of charity with awkward rebukes, and have no effect.

We shall walk the paths of God, even if an angel from heaven should oppose us, and will be zealous for the honour of God, but with Christian charity, and will not forget our duty to the secular authorities. By contrast, the Antichrist and the haters of God shall enjoy no peace from us, but the good people we shall treat kindly and decently. Let all the devils rue it, for they cannot hinder us by aiding our enemies with their tricks, although they may cause us sorrow and make us yearn for God and call upon him even more earnestly. May God help us. Amen.

It may be that we use the weakness of the community as an excuse, being weak ourselves and not perfectly able to advance forcefully the serious business of the Spirit. In that case, we pray for an increase in grace and wait for the effect of him who effects all things.

Do not be afraid, dear friends, trust in God through Christ. No one can tear you away from his side (John 5).[22] Cease to be children. Do not allow yourself to be driven around and blown about by the breezes of vain men or to fall for the tricks of men and their deceptions, which they would like to use

* * * * *

20 1 Cor. 8:4.
21 Acts 17:16–31.
22 Not John 5; Rom. 8:35: 'Who shall separate us from the love of Christ?'

secretly to lead us astray. (Eph. 4.)[23] The Word of God is stronger than that. Our foundation does not yield as long as we rest on it, and we have no desire willingly to teach anything that is foreign to the Word of God.

I hastened to write this report and consolation for the following reasons: the danger from false brethren is not inconsiderable (2 Cor. 11),[24] and it is coming to a head now. Also, people with vain ambitions may cause an uprising. They talk indignantly among themselves and are full of hate, as was the case in the time of Paul among the Galatians (Gal. 6).[25] Some of them will make sport of scripture and use it to serve the purposes of their immoderate desire. Unfortunately, these people do not care about the scandal they cause, the worry, anxiety, and sorrow they cause to good, conscientious people. Furthermore, there is a disagreement on account of slanderers between Martin Luther, through whom God has advanced and will advance his honour and reveal his Word, and Andreas Karlstadt, whom we also wish to continue to regard as a learned minister of the Word.[26] I believe you are all concerned and anxious about his future, and so I declare ...[27]

* * * * *

23 Eph. 4:14.
24 2 Cor. 11:1–6.
25 Gal. 6 does not seem to be relevant; perhaps Gal. 5:26: 'Let us not be desirous of vainglory, provoking one another, envying one another.'
26 This public pronouncement on Karlstadt differs from Capito's private judgment. See his complaints to Blaurer (below, Ep. 232), to Zwingli (below, Ep. 236), and to Oecolampadius (below, Ep. 249) in which he called Karlstadt a man 'hungry for glory.'
27 A summary of the teaching of the Strasbourg preachers follows:
Point 1: Our belief should not be based on human decrees but on God's Word alone, for we know that human nature is fallible. God subjects us to the present difficulties to separate the good from the bad. We must put our faith in God rather than men. Although Luther 'treats scripture better and with more skill than did anyone in the last hundred years,' we must remember that his gifts come from God. It is wrong to show a partisan spirit; dissent is a sign of imperfect faith. Also, lay preachers claim to be able to interpret the Word of God. It is important not to take sides in human disputes and trust only in God, who knows our hearts.
Point 2: We are saved through faith and God's mercy, not through works. The papists rely on external rites for salvation. We must do away with such superstitions.
– The Mass: We avoid the term 'mass' because of its connotation 'sacrifice,' but we tolerate people who wish to retain the traditional term. We remind people, however, that true service consists in sacrificing one's own person to God and becoming holy and pleasing to him.
– Eucharist: There is some dispute about whether 'this' (in the phrase 'this is

In sum, dear pious citizens, rely on Christ whom our Lord God has shown to us through clear scripture alone, and dismiss everything else that is the product of scholarly envy and ambition, even if the [men who make the statements] are great experts. Our salvation does not consist in words but in the power of God. Troubles are bound to come, for we must be publicly tested, but woe to them who are the cause of the troubles.

Do not allow yourselves to be burdened by the arrogance and pride of godless men. They delight in evil. If only we are patient, we will see the enemies of the Truth shamefaced, for our hope will never come to naught. May God grant you to proceed in his knowledge without giving offence. Amen.

Letter 225: 3 November 1524, Besançon, Etienne Frédelet to Capito

The original manuscript is in AST 40, #61. Etienne Frédelet matriculated at the University of Basel in 1513/14, then studied law at Freiburg (Dr iur. 1519) under Ulrich Zasius. He taught at the University of Basel 1519–21, then entered the service of Cardinal Antoine de Vergy in Besançon.

Most learned man, I hope you too are well. I have most eagerly received your letter,[1] and all the more eagerly, as you provide me most liberally with an opportunity to approach you with my trivial stuff, in that you occasionally remember your Etienne and give an incentive to your brother, who was once your student. I have nothing to say in return other than to note how, in your usual kindness and benevolence, you embrace even those who are less erudite. That is what I write, then, in the short time I have, that you may

* * * * *

my body') refers to the body of Christ or to the bread. We remind the faithful that Christ is invisible and not bound up with external things or signs. 'The purpose of the Lord's Supper is the remembrance of Christ, and to refresh our hope, in which we are one in God with all other believers in Christ. That is why the Lord gave us this supper. To investigate further is superfluous.'
– Baptism: Only water and the words of the Bible are necessary for the ceremony. 'We do not ask at what time or age the child should be baptized, for God grants us his mercy and his gifts in a supernatural way ... where scripture is not clear, we desist from probing the matter. If we need anything further, God will reveal it to us.'
– Consensus: dissent arises from concern for external things and shows that we do not truly have Christ. There is no need to be anxious about theologians discussing 'sacraments, images, and other external things ... it requires much skill and experience, but does not really pertain to salvation.'

1 Not extant.

know that I greet you in turn in the Lord. There is one thing, however, which I find difficult to accept: that you, a priest, are now a married man – you who have so far extolled celibacy as something almost divine. And to hear that you, an old man,[2] are now bound to a woman and involved in domestic cares! It would have been better for you to work in the vineyard of the Lord and restore good literature, as you used to do when you were *removed from care*.[3] If only Strasbourg had not accepted that hitherto unheard-of Lutheran reform, which creates scandal and darkness rather than edification and light. It would have been enough to leave what was doubtful in place until it was decided by the consensus of all. There is nothing more pestilent here among us, nothing more hateful than to even talk about that business. May God, the Best and Greatest,[4] bring clarity to all things and all people for the sake of confirming the truth of our religion and faith. Farewell in happiness, and be indulgent with the writer in your heart. Besançon. 3 November 1524.

Your devoted friend Etienne Frédelet.

Letter 226: [Mid-November 1524, Strasbourg, Capito and Martin Bucer] to the Preachers [of Basel and Zurich]

Printed in CorrBucer 1:281–6, Ep. 81.

[*Summary*]: The Strasbourgers accept only two sacraments: baptism and the Lord's Supper. They would like advice on making ceremonies uniform. There is considerable controversy with Karlstadt concerning the meaning of the words consecrating the bread and wine. They do not wish to decide whether Luther or Karlstadt is right, but they consider the Lord's Supper an 'external matter' (*caena dominica res sit externa*) that should not cause dissension. They are uncertain what to believe or to teach since scripture does not seem to offer a clear explanation. They only know that bread and wine, being external things, 'do not contribute to salvation, whereas the memory of the Lord's death is salutary and necessary, therefore we exhort our people to eat the bread of the Lord and drink the wine for that purpose, disregarding the rest.' They accept infant baptism, but on condition that adults be catechized. They describe the practice they follow in celebrating the Lord's Supper.

* * * * *

2 Capito was in his mid-forties.
3 Lucretius, *De rerum natura*, 2.17.
4 In the humanist vein, Frédelet applies the classical epithets of Jupiter Optimus Maximus to God.

Letter 227: [Mid-November 1524, Strasbourg], The Strasbourg Preachers to the Preachers of Nördlingen and Nürnberg.

Printed in CorrBucer 1:287–8, Ep. 82.

[*Summary*]: Contents substantially the same as Ep. 226.

Letter 228: 23 November 1524, Strasbourg, The Strasbourg Preachers to Martin Luther

Printed in CorrBucer 1:288–97, Ep. 83, and WABr 3:378–81, Ep. 796.

[*Summary*]: They are concerned about the dissension between Luther and Karlstadt concerning the interpretation of the Eucharist. So far they have preached, with Luther, that the bread and wine are the body and blood of the Lord, although they encouraged the congregation to take communion only 'for the memory of the Christ's death; the rest does not benefit them or lead them to salvation, for the flesh does not benefit even if Christ is present in the same form in which he was suspended on the cross.' Some people in Basel and Zurich support Karlstadt's views. They urge Luther to clarify the question.

There is also talk about a disagreement between Luther and Karlstadt concerning infant baptism, a practice they themselves observe. They deplore the fact that there is dissension about external matters. It is shameful, moreover, that they cannot account fully for their practices on the basis of scripture.

They describe the practice they follow in celebrating the Lord's Supper. The diversity of rites gives offence. They hope to achieve some uniformity at least with neighbouring churches.

Treger [see above, Ep. 222 headnote] has publicly accused them of inciting unrest and teaching heresy. There was some commotion, when the people stormed the Dominican convent and removed prostitutes from the cells, but all is quiet again.

There are some protests on account of the clergy being asked to take out citizenship. They say that they may be forced to abandon the city.

Erasmus' work defending free will has stirred up doubts, especially in Cologne, as Hinne Rode told them. They encourage Luther to respond to Erasmus and Karlstadt, but without rancour.

They send their greetings to Melanchthon and Paulus Phrygio. They ask Luther to give their messenger, Nicolaus Merxheimer, a kind reception.

Letter 228a: 1 December 1524, [Strasbourg], The Collegiate Churches of St Thomas, Young and Old St Peter to the City Council of Strasbourg

For the background, see above, Ep. 216a. Like Ep. 216a, the present letter comes from the 'Acta et gesta' in ABR, G 4228, [14–17]. Although the letter is written in the name of the three collegiate churches, not everyone subscribed to the sentiments expressed here, namely that citizenship was not compatible with membership in the clergy. One of the dissenters was Capito, as can be seen from his pamphlet on the clergy's obligation to take out citizenship (Ep. 230 below), which contradicts some of the arguments presented here.

Strict, noble, honest, circumspect, honourable, wise, gracious, dear lords! The honourable council has in the past days written to the three collegiate churches, to the canons and vicars of St Thomas, Young and Old St Peter. They have indicated that they have reason at this time to desire the members of the collegiate churches to become citizens and assume and bear the rights and burdens of citizens, like the others.

Now, the collegiate churches and their prefects have always been eager and willing to be of service and do everything they can for the benefit, honour, and welfare of the honourable council and the pious citizens, and are still willing to do so. But they cannot and will not comply with the honourable council's wish concerning citizenship and the burdens of citizens for a number of notable reasons, especially the following:

First, the collegiate churches do not have the authority to yield or give up privileges and liberties which have been granted to the clergy at large and to the spiritual estate by the spiritual and secular laws, for no individual may yield up privileges which have been given by law for the benefit of the community. If the collegiate churches are to subject themselves to a secular government's commands and prohibitions, the giving and accepting of laws, the giving and accepting of the burdens of citizenship, then they must give up the privileges given by right to the common clergy and the spiritual estate. For example, they would have to give up their recourse to the power of the ecclesiastical law courts, their immunity from the commands of the secular authority, and their exemption from secular prohibitions, among other things.

Secondly, every priest taking on his priestly dignity is obliged to obey his bishop and Ordinary, and so it is not proper that the collegiate churches should withdraw from obedience to the Ordinary and to subject themselves to secular obedience, which they would have to do if they took on the rights and burdens of citizens.

Thirdly, some of the priests in the above-mentioned collegiate churches are under the jurisdiction of His Papal Holiness, and others have taken on their benefices and livings together with certain obligations, which do not agree with secular obligations and the obligations of a citizen, to which they would be subject, and which could not be observed or kept.

Fourthly, if the collegiate churches were to comply with the request of the honourable council, they would immediately cause the complete and irreversible collapse of the spiritual authorities at the most valuable cathedral chapter of Strasbourg. How could they defend such an action before their lords? What disgrace, scoffing, and ill-reputation would they incur with all the authorities, high and low in rank? The honourable council should take that into consideration.

Thus, for these and many other notable reasons, which we omit for the sake of brevity, the collegiate churches with all goodwill, earnestly and humbly beg and appeal to the honourable council to allow the collegiate churches to keep their privileges, old usages, and traditions and to maintain the friendly relations they and their bishop have with the praiseworthy city of Strasbourg, and to leave intact the existing conditions as they have been of old. The collegiate churches and their whole community will be obliged to the honourable council and the pious citizens before God and the world, as far as is in their power. However, the collegiate churches are aware that the community of the praiseworthy city of Strasbourg is somewhat impatient, especially because they have to bear all the inconveniences and burdens of citizens, and the clergy, who lead a more quiet life, live among them free and without burden. Therefore, to put an end to this complaint and to appease and quiet the community, the collegiate churches ask the honourable council to appoint someone from the council as a delegate with whom they may discuss this matter and with whom they may act on this complaint. In that case, they will find the collegiate churches cooperative, modest, and willing to help the community in such a manner that the honourable council and the whole community will not be displeased, and as a result both estates, as in the past, will live with each other in good faith, friendship, and unity and will remain so in future. And although the collegiate churches in all fairness do not expect rejection, they ask nevertheless for a favourable and friendly reply.

Letter 229: 2 December 1524, Nürnberg, Dominik Schleupner to Capito

Printed in Gerdesius II:77–8. On Schleupner see CWC 1, Ep. 154, note 4.

Best of patrons, I received your letter,[1] which is always welcome to me, after my return from Silesia. I apologize for my silence, of which you accuse me. I can justify myself, for you can hardly believe how much is going on every day here, about which I do not think it is necessary to write to you, for I believe it is very well known to you. We, however, are quite ignorant in what state you are and whether the gospel progresses among you still. All we know is this: that it has been given to you as ministers to believe in Christ and to suffer for him. I wish, however, that our brethren could be consoled by the persecutions you suffer, and I ask you from my heart to inform me about the details that concern us.

We sense new troubles, introduced by the so-called prophets, who fight against scripture on the pretext of preaching scripture and miserably tear apart the wretched people by once again introducing the law and free will. I would write more, if there were not a rumour that some of them have migrated to you, and that the leader of their sect, a certain Storch,[2] is there, so that you perhaps understand what they are aiming at. Write about this matter, and tell me what you do in connection with it, whether you disregard it, or whether he keeps his peace.

I am glad to hear that my dear Johannes[3] is faithful and diligent, especially because he deserved such great testimony from you. I have given a loving reception to the young man who suffers from a hernia,[4] the young Silesian, whom you recommended to me. He has obtained a parish through my patronage, indeed through my help, a parish the likes of which not one in thousand has ever heard of, not to mention obtained, so that he is grateful to live free of violence and without grief and is glad to be safe. He himself will tell you about it, so that you will recognize his gratitude toward you. If Osiander[5] writes nothing to you, I must make allowances for him: he hardly

* * * * *

1 Not extant.
2 Nikolaus Storch, a weaver, was one of the so-called Zwickau prophets. He fled to Wittenberg in 1521, but his beliefs were unacceptable to Luther. Storch then migrated to other communities to preach his beliefs. He died after 1536, when he was rumoured to have returned to the Zwickau vicinity.
3 Not identified.
4 Not identified.
5 Andreas Osiander (ca. 1496–1552) studied at Ingolstadt. He learned Hebrew and engaged in textual criticism of the Bible. From 1522, when he was ordained priest, he taught Hebrew at the Augustinian monastery at Nürnberg. He was preacher at St Lorenz and a spokesman for the reformers. He was critical of the Strasbourg and Zurich positions in the Sacramentarian controversy. Although

has time to sleep for all the work. Farewell in Christ, and do not cease to love me. Nürnberg, 2 December 1524.

Dominik Schleupner.

Letter 230: 7 December 1524, [Strasbourg], Capito to the Reader

This open letter comments on the ongoing negotiations over the city's demand that the clergy take out citizenship. For the background see above, Ep. 228a. Capito supported the council's demand and wrote this letter to justify their position. It was printed as *Das die pfafheit schuldig sey Burgerlichen Eyd zuthun, on verletzung jrer Eeren* (That the clergy is obliged to swear the citizens' oath, [and may do so] without loss of honour, Strasbourg: Köpfel, 1524). Capito and seventeen other members of the clergy had taken out citizenship during the year 1523, thus voluntarily assuming the financial burden of citizens, and at the same time putting themselves under the protection of the city. Others followed their example in 1524. On 16 January 1525, the council decided to issue a decree, making citizenship for members of the Strasbourg clergy mandatory.[1] It was agreed that clerics taking out citizenship would not be required to travel on behalf of the city or to render military service. Conversely, they could not sit on the city council.

It is not difficult to maintain before decent people that the clergy may, without loss of honour, become citizens. God's command must take precedence over all human law, and no servant of God is exempted from obeying secular authority, which has been specifically enjoined on him by God in scripture, as is shown below.

* * * * *

not always in agreement with the city council, he represented Nürnberg at the Marburg Colloquy (1529), the Augsburg Diet (1530), the Schmalkald conference (1537), and the religious colloquies in Haguenau and Worms (1540–1). He was the principal author of the Nürnberg school order (1533). On the invitation of Ottheinrich, Count Palatine, he drafted a church order for Palatinate-Neuburg. When Nürnberg introduced a new church order in response to the Interim (1547), Osiander left for Königsberg, where he became pastor and professor at the university under the protection of Duke Albert. His teaching brought him into conflict with colleagues at the university and with the Wittenberg theologians. The controversy outlasted his death in 1552, but his views were ultimately rejected in the Formula of Concord.

1 The decree was promulgated 22 January. For the text, see B. Moeller, 'Kleriker als Bürger,' in *Festschrift für Hermann Heimpel* (Göttingen, 1972), 2:195–224.

In Romans, chapter 13,[2] Paul says that everyone is subject to government and authority, for there is no authority but from God. The authority prevailing everywhere is ordained by God. Also, anyone who resists authority resists the order of God, and those who resist will be judged. Peter writes the same: *Subject yourselves*, he says, *to all human order for the Lord's sake, be it to the king as the supreme power or the governors as his deputies and avengers of evil-doers. For it is God's will that with good actions you stop the ignorance of fools, as free people and not using freedom to cover up malice*, etc. (1 Pet. 2).[3] Or do these passages not concern the clergy? Indeed, they concern all who build their spiritual house on Christ, the cornerstone, the living stone,[4] that is, they concern all Christians, among whom the clergy claim to be the first and foremost.

They argue against that,[5] saying that the clergy must obey the pope, the bishops, and the command of the ecclesiastical court. That may be so, for the Christian must obey all human law, unless it goes against God's precepts. Even if the authorities act sinfully and violently, it is seemly for a Christian to be patient and suffer them. For we must not resist evil. And if we are commanded to go a mile, we must offer to go another one.[6] But if God is mocked, whoever the mocker may be, we must go by Peter's word: *One must be more obedient to God than man.*[7] Since secular authority derives from God, it cannot go against God's will.

God's law requires us to act with brotherly love toward all and have no regard for ourselves. The higher we stand, the more we owe service to everyone (Matt. 20).[8] The princes of this world rule, use force, take or confer freedom according to their will, but the foremost Christian is his neighbour's servant, just as the Son of Man did not come to be served but to give his soul for the salvation of many.[9] Therefore, if anyone commands us, saying that we must not serve our brother by taking on the burdens of citizenship, we do not owe obedience to him but must remain obedient to God.

This commandment of Christ cannot be countermanded by any hu-

* * * * *

2 Rom. 13:1–2.
3 1 Pet. 2:13–16. The phrase 'and to praise those who do right' which follows 'evil-doers' in the epistle is missing from the quotation.
4 Cf. 1 Pet. 2:5–7; Eph. 2:19–21.
5 See above, Ep. 228a.
6 Cf. Matt. 5:41.
7 Acts 5:29.
8 Matt. 20:26.
9 Matt. 20:26–7.

man commandment. Thus we owe no obedience to anyone who says that we must not serve our neighbour by taking on the burden of citizens, but must remain in obedience to God.

It is a bad argument to use as an excuse certain so-called privileges incorporated in the law. For in this matter, no one has the right to command or forbid anything contrary to God's command.

It is clear that no one should grant an exemption that is to the prejudice and detriment of the community – neither king, nor emperor, nor pope, nor imperial estates, nor any secular authority anywhere, for they do not rule the flock of the Lord for their own benefit but for that of the community and should act as faithful servants. Otherwise, good people who complain about such privileges would have to fear those in power, which is against scripture. Tyrants act according to their pleasure, without considering the need of the community. Proper government, which acts in accordance with God, uses the sword to punish the ungodly and honour the godly.

I admit that a community is entitled to exempt anyone, but no Christian provides for an exemption that imposes a burden on someone else, except when such an exemption furthers the glory of God and brotherly love. It is for this reason that bishops were originally exempted, and they accepted the privilege in order to be in a better position to look after and lead their community. There is no need for this in the Empire and in the free imperial cities today. We take care of civic complaints with little expense and through the agency of others, and can still look after our duty without inconvenience, if we are willing. At the time, however, when the servants of the church were exempted [from civic duties], there were no servants of idols.[10] There was no concern or suspicion that there would be one day such a swarm of priests saying mass and offering sacrifice, as we see now.

The privileges granted do not apply to that mob, for according to the written law, such privileges must not be extended to the detriment of other people. Priests of old, being preachers and having the care of souls, were freed from worldly burdens that they might serve the community without hindrance. But how does this apply to that idle mob that merely weighs down the community and is a useless burden on the earth, that is useful only to their own kind and brings disadvantage and detriment to the authorities? A third of the people, and that the wealthiest and most idle part, is exempted without reason and benefit to the community, which is cause for great complaint, but such a foolish exemption is not binding on the descendants [of the

* * * * *

10 I.e., corrupt clergy.

lawgivers]. Both divine and natural law are against such an arrangement, for they require a fair balance among the citizens. Should our forefathers have the authority to exempt the third and best part of the city and put such a heavy burden on the poor citizens, their descendants? Our forefathers were induced to believe erroneously, and to think, quite wrongly, that they might go to heaven merely through the prayer and pompous church service of the said clergy, as if the exemption of priests of the old kind applied to our idolaters and shorn knaves!

Yet there is a royal priesthood of all Christians,[11] and the leaders are merely the servants of the church and not lords in their own right. The defenders of privilege ought to keep this fact in mind, even if they are able to counter with written instruments and legal documents. For if today's honourable council and the respected community of this praiseworthy free city of Strasbourg were to renew the exemption of our clergy for life, the clergy should not accept such an exemption if they wanted to be called Christians. For this exemption is a burden on the community and contrary to the brotherly love and service they owe. Peter says that we should practise brotherly love toward everyone.[12] That brotherly love is not in evidence when rich residents, because they are members of the clergy, further only their own idle, leisurely life and add to the bitter sweat of the poor workman. Christians are obliged to work that they may do good to others.[13] It follows that it is unchristian of them to live a disorderly life, be idle, and live for their pleasure. Paul bids us go about our business quietly, and to mark those who do not do so, and to refrain from intercourse with them so that they may live under a ban (2 Thess. 3).[14] How can it be Christian to protect one's idleness at the cost of the community and to accept exemption from the work of citizens?

Since it is unchristian to accept the privilege when offered, what must we think of those who press for the privilege and pursue it by force and would cause all sorts of upheaval in order not to share the citizens' burden? They give out that one should not eat or drink with those who obey God, calling them frivolous men who have broken their oath. In truth, however, it is unseemly for us faithful Christians to eat or have congress with them [the defenders of privilege], for they have been banned by the Spirit of God for living unchaste and disorderly lives, and are excluded from the Christian community (1 Cor. 5).[15]

* * * * *

11 1 Pet. 2:9.
12 1 Pet. 3:8.
13 Cf. 1 Thess. 4: 11–12.
14 2 Thess. 3:13–14.
15 1 Cor. 5:11.

Let us see whether the privileged lords are good Christians: Christ bids us to put the tunic before the cloak,[16] and these so-called Christians abuse other people's labour and goods to support their leisure. The poor workman is supposed to keep and maintain them at his own cost and, if he is unwilling, they will force him. They, however, the well-to-do clergy, will suffer not a shilling of expense. They hold on to their wealth, and suck the poor sweating man dry. Is that living according to the commandment of Christ? Is that considering one's vows and honour? As if they had sworn to be neither loyal nor kind to the despised layman! Christ delivered up the tax so as not to give offence to anyone and says that his kingdom is not of this world.[17] And the clergy, falsely citing Christ, are unwilling to subject themselves to the government, and want to own and enjoy the wealth of the whole world for nothing.

[They say] that it is for the sake of their conscience that they will not swear an oath of loyalty and good will to the honourable council and observe the commandments or injunctions that have been given for the benefit of the community, for the sake of order and the higher glory of God. What are you saying, dear sirs? Is your conscience so narrow that what the divine Truth demands goes against your conscience? Is it your conscience that obliges you to be neither loyal nor favourably inclined toward the community, and to fight against the law and order established for the benefit of the citizens and the glory of God? Or do you think swearing an oath to the government means they may give orders contrary to natural and divine law? Don't you know better than that? Would the honourable council, some of whom are your friends and relatives, use tyrannical force? What are your thoughts on this? Why are you unduly indignant?

The clergy, I see, refer to the oath they supposedly gave to the suffragan,[18] arguing in this manner:[19] They wish to be obedient to their Ordinary and defend and uphold the rights and privileges of the church. I counter: Then they ought to show more respect for their vow of chastity, and yet they claim that they are not in violation of their oath when they commit adultery, fornication, and other nameless sins. Yet if a man defies the worldly bishop's command and swears to observe the divine command, which accords with communal advantage; if a man does not seek to avoid the common burden

* * * * *

16 Cf. Matt. 5:40; Luke 6:29.
17 Matt. 17:24–7.
18 I.e., the oath of allegiance to the bishop.
19 Above, Ep. 228a.

[of citizenship], then that man is faithless according to these honest and good lords! And, they say, it is not decent to keep company with those who make such demands. That is the substance of their great courage and fear of God. When they swear to keep God's precepts, they give in to their desires without fear, or shame, or consideration for their honour, as for example, by committing fornication, which is forbidden. But when they swear not to do what God has enjoined them to do, then they stick to their oath. They swear that they will uphold the laws and privileges of the Catholic church. If they were investigated according to the law of the church, there would be few among them who would not be under the papal ban and not be judged faithless and in contempt of their oath, for they have no regard for the laws of the church that have honourable aims. They interpret their oath so badly that it binds them only when it serves their interest against the laity and against God's precept, but if the oath urges them to observe Christian probity, they regard it as a matter of church protocol and of little importance.

Indeed, if it was to their advantage, they would find that an oath, according to their written laws, does not bind anyone to do wrong or go against God, and that the legal compulsion to obey the overlord always takes precedence. Why should they not be able to interpret their devilish oath as not obliging them to act against God and brotherly love? They laugh at the dangerous and foolish oaths which are sworn in the schools and which they swear in the papal chancery in Rome and regard them as invalid. But the oath of the suffragan ties them down tightly – o pretended fear of God!

If they really thought that the oath was so important for the sake of God's honour, why are they not equally intent on furthering the honour of God and making certain that the many oaths so lightly imposed by their statutes and books are not sworn in vain?

They cite against us the passage in Jer. 4: *You will swear that the Lord lives in truth, in law, and in justice.*[20] And they believe they may conclude from this that we, who have become citizens, have broken our oath, for we swore off privilege and have voluntarily taken on the obligations of a citizen.

I reply to their argument that neither they nor their ecclesiastical law has ever understood this passage, or else they would admit that none of them can justify swearing an oath, for they do not swear under the conditions specified [in Jer. 4], indeed, are far off the target and the truth. The prophet writes: *If you turn to me, O Israel, (says God) and fear my face, you will not be moved and will swear that God lives*, etc.[21] It follows that a man, who

* * * * *

20 Jer. 4:2.
21 Cf. Jer. 4:1–2.

wishes to swear that God lives in truth, in law, and in justice, acts rightfully and in a godly manner, without deceit and lies. First, however, he must turn to God and discard anything in himself that is displeasing to God: greed, adultery, whoring, self-love, separation from the community, etc. Only then will he be steadfast and able to swear in truth that God lives, etc.

Anyone, however, who seeks other people's harm without regarding God's injunctions, can never swear truthfully that God lives. For that means swearing that one loves the truth best, but such a man loves no one more than himself and lives in the world without God, without Christ, whose yoke he does not want to bear, for he wishes to be exempted from the work of men. There is no law in his eyes by which he is judged or condemned. And there is no justice, for he regards himself worthy and self-sufficient in his own nature and reason, whereas all our efficacy comes from God alone. He sets up his own justice and does not look for the justice given by God.

Since the oath to the suffragan does not regard these conditions and looks only to the oath-taker's advantage contrary to brotherly love, it does not represent a commandment of God. It follows that the oath was not taken truthfully and is not lawful and honest, and therefore not binding when used against the commandment of God.

This is also evident from the commandment in scripture: *You must fear God, your Lord, serve him and follow him, and swear by his name.*[22] This is not simply a command to swear by the name of God, but indicates the conditions that must precede and accompany the oath. The sequence of the text demonstrates that. These elements must precede the oath, as referred to in the text of the law, namely, that you must first fear God your Lord, serve him alone, follow him alone, and that you must not fear men, follow idols or yourself, that is, your greedy and proud mind, or perhaps a shameless whore. In that manner you will swear in the name of God, pay him the greatest honour, and not tie yourself to anything that is against his law. And even if error leads you into an evil situation, the main point is that you still fear and love God and will not allow yourself to be tied to anything against God, whatever words are used.

Since the suffragan's oath seeks only the advantage of the clergy, contrary to brotherly love and God's precept, it follows that the clergy swears and has ever sworn that oath to no good and right purpose, not for the honour of God, but for their own benefit. Furthermore, that oath is not binding on them, for no one is bound by an oath in the name of God that goes against God's honour and his precept. But it is the eternal precept and command-

* * * * *

22 Deut. 6:13.

ment of God not to seek our own advantage and not to seek to rule, but serve everyone for the sake of the Lord, to work and relieve the toil and the needs of others. How could one be obliged by a Christian oath to go against that precept, when an oath is and ought to be for the supreme honour of God?

Long usage and custom does not protect against that. For no usage or custom that is against the law is permitted, not even according to ecclesiastical law. If the passage of time could achieve anything against God, then pagans, Jews, and Turks would have an advantage because they have remained in their error longer than we in our godless oath, contrary to good custom and the law of God, indeed, much longer than the worldly bishops have given their blessing to the sacrifice of the mass.

If it is reported that a man is holding a field without rightful title, his ownership is terminated even if he held it in good faith. It follows that the clergy should not enjoy its privilege any longer, even if it has held it in good conscience until now, since it has now become known and made clear to them that such privilege is against God, against love of one's neighbour, against all right and all nature and all reason, indeed, that it is a burden to the community, whom no one, no matter who he is, should burden.

I write all this on my own behalf and on behalf of my fellow citizens – members of the clergy who became citizens or wish to take out citizenship, but have so far been kept and hindered from doing so by malice, as I have been informed by credible sources yesterday and the day before yesterday. For the adversaries state that they will not eat or drink with those of the clergy who take out citizenship. They want those banned who keep God's commandment, whereas they themselves are truly banned before God on account of greed, fornication, and disorderliness, being useless fools keeping away from work. Let them show their skill and justify why any pious man should, without injury to himself, eat or drink with them, who want to be called Christians. For scripture clearly condemns them. But they prefer to speak in private and do not wish to profess anything before the common people, for lies and untrue slander cannot stand the light.

This I want to be said against those who purposely and wittingly slandered us and first made up stories against us and spread them. My words are not directed against those others who believed them, perhaps without fraud or malice, and repeated what they said. For a common man may go against the truth unwittingly and perhaps be misled by sly people. Those who are responsible for this, however, should respond and refute what I write. I shall not deny that right to anyone.

I write this in good faith and briefly, without being commanded by the written law, which I herewith pledge to answer if anyone undertakes to invoke it against what I am writing. Our opponents may be very learned in the law and in scripture and, in part, experienced in other business, yet I will show them that all scripture and law agrees with us, if they demand it. And I will do so wherever and whenever they wish, in any place, for truth must temper the judge's zeal.

Finally, pious reader, note that we wish to keep firmly and strongly to what we have promised God. If we have sworn anything to the devil or stated any of the aforesaid in error or out of ignorance, we have not done it knowingly, and wish to recant and combat it with body and soul. So help us God. Amen. Given at Strasbourg, 7 December 1524.

Letter 231: 16 December 1524, Zurich, Ulrich Zwingli to François Lambert and the preachers of Strasbourg

Printed in CorrBucer 1:298–314, Ep. 84. For Lambert see CWC 1, Ep. 25, note 33.

[*Summary*]: He apologizes for answering their questions only after such a long delay. In his view, the law must not be preached without correspond-ing emphasis on faith. Preachers who do not preach the gospel or who distort it ought to be dismissed. A nephew might be allowed to marry his uncle's widow, if charity is served and if she is not related to him otherwise. Also, the baptism of children can be justified on the basis of the Bible, since it replaces Old Testament circumcision. Concerning Karlstadt's preaching, Zwingli refers the Strasbourgers to a letter he wrote to Matthäus Alber on the question of the Eucharist. He believes that the word 'is' in the phrase 'This is my body' means 'signifies.' He encloses the letter to Alber, but asks them not to publish it. He approves of singing psalms in the German lan-guage, but cautions them against saying mass and especially against the adoration of the Eucharist. The council of Zurich has gathered the monks remaining in the monasteries and put them into the House of the Francis-cans. The young monks are being apprenticed to learn a trade; the old ones are pensioned off. Leo Jud, Oswald Myconius, Caspar Megander, Heinrich Utinger, and Johannes Aulaeus [Johann Jacob Amman of Zurich?] send their greetings.

Letter 232: 17 December 1524, Strasbourg, Capito to Ambrosius Blaurer

The manuscript is in St Gallen KB, ms. 31/214. The text is partly published in Schiess 1:114–15, Ep. 87. For the addressee, see above, Ep. 192 headnote.

May the grace of Christ be with you, dearest Blaurer. Your most welcome letter, which you wrote in August, was delivered at the beginning of December.[1] That is how negligent the letter carriers are. They certainly neglected and delayed our pleasure, for nothing is more welcome and more pleasant than a letter from you. But by chance I met with this young man,[2] who certainly has a good and liberal mind, and he was willing to deliver this letter to you, even though he was very busy. Yet this is no proper reply to your letter, which is in the hands of friends with whom I shared my pleasure. As far as I remember, you spoke of the state of your church, how atrociously it has been attacked by that Dominican monk.[3] I have no doubt that through your brave resistance the grace of the gospel has been confirmed. Otherwise, we hope that things have improved now. It cannot be long before piety makes the hypocrites cease their lying.

In our church, Karlstadt has caused trouble with his virulent pamphlets.[4] How unrestrained he was in his criticism of Luther! What crime, what misdeed – for he dared to call Luther the messenger and associate of Antichrist, when he will forever be attested as the greatest enemy of the Antichrist. Clement, the gardener,[5] is one of the people earning a little money as a day worker in the gardens. He is quite clever. I am not familiar with the pamphlet he published, for it was printed in Basel, and our magistrate, without our knowledge, prohibited its sale here.

Righteous zeal burns in our city. The people refuse to tolerate fornicators and will no longer suffer the priests to be exempt [from citizenship]. The matter is fiercely disputed on both sides. We hope there will soon be an end to it, for I am certain that they will be forced either to leave or to take on the joint burden of citizens.[6] We shall change the Lord's Supper and the ceremony of baptism in accordance with the pure Word, and we shall do it

* * * * *

1 The letter is lost.
2 Unidentified.
3 Antonius Pirata (d. 1534) was preacher at the Dominican monastery in Constance, and from 1520–3 vicar general of the German Dominicans (non observant). He also preached at the cathedral until the city prohibited the staunch Catholic from doing so in 1527. In 1528, Ferdinand's government in Innsbruck was instrumental in obtaining an income from the Benedictine monastery of St George in Stein am Rhein for Pirata. In 1531 he was preacher at Radolfzell. Blaurer wrote a pamphlet against him, entitled *Warhafft bericht der handlung zwyschent Bruder Anthonyn ... unnd Ambrosi Blaurern* [Augsburg: Melchior Ramminger, 1525?].
4 See Capito's reaction to the difficulties Karlstadt stirred up in Wittenberg, above Ep. 224.
5 Clement Ziegler, see above, Ep. 215, note 12.
6 See below, Ep. 233b headnote.

soon. The remaining papist ceremonies have all fallen into disuse. There are still some statues, which we shall soon cast out. So far we have been quite successful. I shall write more when I am at leisure. At present I have no time.

Farewell to you, together with your most learned brother and most chaste sister,[7] whom I wish a pious husband, although she is capable of celibacy. Let each person bravely battle on his own behalf against the papist kingdom. But the enemy is dogged and does not yield to skirmishes. Strasbourg, 17 December 1524.

Wolfgang Capito.

Letter 233: 21 December 1524, [Strasbourg], Anton Firn, Symphorian Altbiesser, Martin Bucer, Diebold Schwartz, Matthew Zell, and Capito to Every Christian

Printed in BDS 10:23–9 (text on 27–9), #1.

[*Summary*]: The Strasbourg preachers declare legitimate the marriage of Heinrich Kieffer von Aschaffenburg and Elisabeth Frenckin, both parishioners of St Thomas and both separated from their former spouses. Despite the episcopal mandate *Tolleramus* against remarriages, the preachers have formed their opinion on the basis of the inability of Kieffer and Frenckin to live a celibate life. They are following Paul's command to marry so as to avoid immorality (1 Cor. 7:2).

Letter 233a: 26 December 1524, Strasbourg, The Preachers of Strasbourg to Frederick, Count Palatine

Printed in BDS 1:185–280; published as *Grund und ursach auß gotlicher schrifft der neüwerungen ... zu Straßburg fürgenomen* (Strasbourg: Köpfel, 1524?). Frederick II Count Palatine (1482–1556) served in a number of Habsburg campaigns and played an important role in the election of Charles V in 1519. He sat on the *Reichsregiment* of Nürnberg, 1521–5 and was one of the Habsburg commanders in the wars against the Turks, 1529 and 1532. In 1535 he married Dorothea, the daughter of the King of Denmark. The pursuit of her dynastic claims turned out to be financially ruinous for Frederick. In 1540 he presided over the religious colloquy at Regensburg. Succeeding his brother as Elector in 1544, he introduced the Reformation in his territory and joined the Schmalkal-

* * * * *

7 Thomas and Margaret Blaurer. See above, Epp. 192, note 6, and 194, note 21.

dic League. After the emperor's victory at Mühlberg, however, he maintained neutrality.

[*Summary*]: This is a summary of doctrine taught at Strasbourg. It was composed by Martin Bucer and signed by Capito, Caspar Hedio, Matthew Zell, Symphorian Altbiesser, Diebold Schwartz (Nigri), Johannes Latomus, Anton Firn, and Martin Hag.

It begins with accusations against the worldliness of their Catholic opponents and criticism of their unwillingness to engage in disputation with the reformers. Instead, their opponents insist that the teaching of the reformers has been condemned by the imperial estates and the Council of Constance. This is irrelevant. What matters is that the gospel is being preached (*Dann Concilium hin, concilium her, das wort gottes soll man predigen*). The reformers are wrongly accused of inciting rebellion. They support civic authority and public peace.

The following points concerning doctrine and ceremony are clarified: The Eucharist is not a sacrifice but is celebrated in memory of Christ's death. The reformers respect the authority of secular rulers over persons and possessions, but in spiritual matters will obey God alone (*mit leyb, eer und gut wöllen wir aller menschlichen ordnung und gewalt underthenig sein und gehorchen, der geyst aber sol gott ergeben sein, und wie kein mensch den rath und willen gottes wissen mag, also würt uns niemant mögen leren, wie und womit wir im gefallen mögen denn er selb allein*). Mass is to be renamed the 'Lord's Supper,' and communion is to be taken in both kinds and celebrated in memory of Christ's sacrifice on the cross (*das nachtmal nichts dann ein gedechtnuß ist solches opffers*). To avoid idolatry, the host and chalice must not be elevated. Christ's death has liberated Christians from the law and obliges them to serve him in the spirit and through faith rather than external ceremonies. The priest should wear ordinary clothes when celebrating the Lord's Supper, which ought to be celebrated only on Sunday. The liturgy is described in detail.

With respect to the question of the Real Presence of Christ in the bread and wine, the Strasbourgers refer the reader to Capito's pamphlet *Was man halten und antworten sol von der spaltung zwischen Martin Luther und Andreas Carlstadt* [above, Ep. 224]. Summarizing the matter, they emphasize that the flesh does not benefit a Christian; only eating the flesh and blood of Christ spiritually brings salvation. Still, it is important to avoid quarreling over this matter, which concerns externals. The Eucharist is celebrated in memory of Christ, and it is this memory that allows a person to eat his body and drink his blood 'spiritually and truly' (*geistlich und warlich*); the bread and wine are signs and symbols of the new covenant (*zeichen oder figur des newen testaments*).

Concerning baptism: The ceremony is a sign of faith and a rebirth in Christ. Scripture does not specify any time of life when this ceremony should take place. The Strasbourgers support infant baptism. In this point, too, they counsel that quarreling over an external ceremony be avoided.

They have abolished feast days because the Bible commands believers to celebrate God every day; only the Sabbath is mentioned in the Ten Commandments. There must be daily preaching, however. Images must be removed from the churches because they promote idolatry; the vernacular must be used in the liturgy; singing should be confined to the psalms.

Letter 233b: 30 December 1524, Strasbourg, The Chapter of St Thomas to Nicolaus Wurmser and his Followers in Molsheim

This is the first evidence in the correspondence for the secession of conservative Catholic canons and their efforts to set themselves up as the legitimate representatives of the chapter of St Thomas. The move was the result of the city council's refusal to provide security for clergy who were not citizens (see above, Epp. 228a and 230). After negotiations for a settlement with the city failed (see the offer of the collegiate churches above, Ep. 216a), a party under the leadership of Nicolaus Wurmser, the dean of St Thomas, left the city surreptitiously on 6 December, taking with them the seals and papers needed to perform legal transactions as well as some of the valuables belonging to the collegiate church. It soon transpired that the valuables were taken to Offenburg. In Ep. 237 below, Capito claims that the fugitives planned the move as early as March 1524, but the first solid evidence we have dates from 14 September, when Wurmser made this entry in his diary: 'At that time several briefs were given to [Konrad?]Bapst in a box by Jakob Munthart ... and were stored with Jakob' [Kannengiesser? Cf. below Ep. 246a, note 13] (*Sindt zu der selbigen zeidt ouch durch her Jakob Munthart etliche brifen in einer laden die er dem Bapst geben hadt ... hinder her Jakobum gelegen*; AST 192, the so-called Wurmser Protokoll, f. 27; cf. also below, Ep. 235a). Konrad Bapst confirmed receipt of the documents the following day. Cf. the autograph manuscript in AST 22 (3): 'God willing, I shall keep them safe and look after them well' (*Ich will derselben, ob Got will, gutter bewarer und verseher sein*).

The fact that the items were missing was brought to the council's attention at a meeting on 8 December (see 'Acta et Gesta,' [22]). The council immediately took steps to recover the items in question, trying at first to persuade the exiles to return the goods voluntarily. They also wrote to the city council of Offenburg and requested their help in preventing the sale of the goods. Eventually, however, the matter came before a court of law.

For the continuation of the conflict and details, see below, Epp. 237 and 243a.

There are two manuscripts of this letter in 22 (2), a draft with an abbreviated salutation and address, and a good copy. The translation below is of the latter. For the addressee, Nicolaus Wurmser, see CWC 1, Ep. 57 headnote.

To the worthy and learned, respected lords, the dean and other canons of the collegiate church of St Thomas in Strasbourg, who now reside at Molsheim, our dear lords, brothers, fellow members of the chapter, and friends.

Worthy, scholarly and learned, respected, gracious, dear lords and good friends, first of all we eagerly offer you our friendship, goodwill, and service. On Wednesday after Christmas past,[1] the respected council gathered us, the chapter and community of the choir,[2] together and gave us their opinion: they want to take action against us because the common goods of the collegiate church have been removed, which were donated here in Strasbourg, not only for the benefit of individuals, but for the city as a whole. For the donors preferred Strasbourg to other places and their citizens. Therefore, the respected council wished to investigate, but was dissuaded from this action when we, the members of chapter, assured them that we would earnestly and to the best of our ability do everything we could to see the goods returned. Since this has not happened, it is their earnest command and desire that we promise to effect the return of the removed goods within three days, and to show them and give them positive proof that they are here. They have no intention of taking them over or converting them to their benefit, or permitting anyone else to take them over, but will continue to allow them to be applied solely to the support of the persons connected with the collegiate church, etc. We replied to their demand with the opinion that we had tried everything and had written to the absent canons, etc. We had good hopes that the response of the respected council would be brought before the *Schöffen*[3] and accepted, that you would soon appear here in a friendly spirit, bringing along the removed goods, and we asked the council to be patient in the meantime. Thereupon, after some deliberation, the delegates of the respected council said it was their request that we apply ourselves earnestly in order to effect the return of the goods belonging to the community of the chapter within three days, more or less. They also requested that we not remove ourselves or our goods until that came to pass and the common goods of the chapter were returned here. To this, we, the canons,

* * * * *

1 I.e., 28 December.
2 I.e., the canons and vicars.
3 A judicial body, whose members were drawn from the guilds and convened by the council.

agreed after lengthy resistance, and on the following Thursday[4] the vicars likewise, with few exceptions, were forbidden to remove either themselves or their goods henceforth. Our administrator[5] will tell you more orally. Thus, my dear lords and friends, it is our friendly request and loyal advice that you bring the goods of the collegiate church here as soon as possible and join us in our transactions with the city, so that we may both obtain peace. Otherwise, this will lead to disturbances and serious dissent in our collegiate church. Our devoted service to our loyal brothers in our chapter and our dear lords! Given at Strasbourg on Friday after Christmas in the year 1524.

Provost and Chapter of the Collegiate Church of St Thomas in Strasbourg.

Letter 234: 31 December 1524, [Strasbourg], Capito to Ulrich Zwingli

Printed in ZwBr 2:279–83, Ep. 356.

[*Summary*]: Capito read Zwingli's letters only cursorily because he was fully engaged in battling the papists. Some conservative canons have fled the city, taking with them the movable goods of their collegiate churches. Bucer has replied to Zwingli's earlier letters. He now agrees with him, whereas before he was more inclined toward Luther. He has no time to read carefully what Zwingli said about the Eucharist because [Andreas] Cratander, the bearer of this letter, is about to leave. He agrees with Zwingli concerning the legitimate marriage of a nephew to his uncle's widow [cf. above, Ep. 231]. He needs time to think about what Zwingli said about infant baptism. [Andreas] Osiander has given some people the impression that the magistrate has no authority to dismiss priests who do not preach the gospel. They wish to preserve the peace and have written respectfully to Luther [above, Ep. 228]. Capito has also written to [Johann] Bugenhagen. Capito wishes he could serve the interest of the duke [Ulrich of Würtemberg?], but at present his authority is compromised because of the affair of [Hans Jakob] Schütz, in which he was deceived [cf. above, Epp. 197–202]. The city has many financial obligations. It is obliged to cope with a loan to Franz von Sickingen, which cannot be recovered, and another loan, which has been promised to an [unnamed] city. Nor is Capito certain that the city is sympathetic to the cause. Nicolaus Kniebs has succeeded Daniel Mieg as *Amman*. Martin Herlin and Egenolf Roeder are friendly toward the reformers, and he will consult them. They are wealthy,

* * * * *

4 I.e., 29 December.
5 Gervasius Sopher. Cf. below, Ep. 269 headnote.

but cautious. Jakob Strauss of Basel incites the people against paying interest on loans. Feast days have been abolished in Strasbourg, but it makes dating [which used feasts as reference points] awkward.

Letter 234a: [1524/5?, Strasbourg], Capito and the Chapter of St Thomas to the City Council of Strasbourg

This undated letter in AST 16, #19, is identified on the reverse as 'Supplicatio Stifftes Sanct Thoman umb das grebbuch zu St Aurelien' (Request of the collegiate church St Thomas for the parish register of St Aurelia, i.e., the register of parishioners). By October 1525 a settlement in the matter under dispute had apparently been reached, to pay 80 gulden to St Nicolaus; cf. below, Ep. 248d.

Strict, honourable, honest, circumspect, wise, and gracious lords. In obedience to your worthy Lordships' command to provide a suitable income to the two parish priests at St Aurelia and St Nicolaus-jenseits-der-Brusch[1] and to repay the loan previously granted to them, we paid part of the sum and are willing to pay the rest as best we can. For this purpose we have asked the administrators of St Aurelia to deliver to us the parish register and kindly inspect it for the income due to the parish priest and chaplains. They replied that the honourable council ordered the warden to take and keep it until further notice, etc. They freely offered to send the book, including the record of income, anywhere the honourable council instructed them to send it, and thus referred us to Your Graces. Since we have supplied the parish priest of St Aurelia together with his chaplain or assistant with an honest income, our gracious lords, it is our and the above-mentioned administrators' friendly request to Your Graces in this case, as is fair, to effect that the often-mentioned register with its record of income, including interest received and outstanding, be made available to us. Thus we may do what is right in these and other things, for God's honour and the public benefit.

Secondly, concerning the parish priest of St Nicolaus: certain difficulties and misunderstandings have arisen between ourselves and the vicars,[2] which we are unable to settle among ourselves. We therefore beg and request your worthy Lordships to delegate two mediators to settle the matter between us in a friendly manner. We desire to earn this favour from your worthy Lordships with obedience and good will.

* * * * *

1 I.e., Martin Bucer and Johann Steinlein (cf. CWC 1, Ep. 171, note 3).
2 One of the vicars was Florian Betschlin, cf. below, Ep. 237, note 26.

Your worthy Lords' well-intentioned, obedient citizens, the provost, vice-dean, and chapter of the collegiate church of St Thomas.

Letter 234b: [Between 13 and 27 January 1525, Strasbourg], Capito and the Chapter of St Thomas to the City Council of Strasbourg

The manuscript, in Capito's hand, is in AST 22 (2). For the background see above, Ep. 233b. The letter shows that the first efforts to recover the missing goods and the seal from the Catholic party through persuasion were unsuccessful. The canons remaining in Strasbourg under Capito's leadership therefore found it necessary to strike a new seal and officially declare any transactions by the exiles legally invalid. For the terminus post quem see below note 3; for the terminus ante quem see the statement below, Appendix 2, which mentions that the new seal was officially proclaimed on 27 January 1525. A printed copy of the proclamation is in AST 22 (2).

Strict, honest, circumspect, honourable, wise, gracious and favourable lords: on the basis of a recently reported action and the reading of several missives from associates of our collegiate church and the councillors of our gracious lord and governor of Strasbourg,[1] it is abundantly clear, in our opinion, that the dean[2] and the fugitive canons regard and portray themselves as the chapter. They direct the associates of the collegiate church to Molsheim and desire to transfer our collegiate church without regard for our will and move it to another place, namely to Molsheim, contrary to law, authority, and the facts. Furthermore, they have undertaken and dared to start legal proceedings against the praiseworthy city of Strasbourg and to defend themselves. They are also appropriating our rents and moneys and obtaining them, as the councillors and governors of the Lord of Strasbourg have written to the *Schultheiss* of St Peter near Stotzheim.[3] Therefore we humbly beg you, our

* * * * *

1 I.e., Wilhelm of Honstein, the bishop of Strasbourg.
2 I.e., Nicolaus Wurmser. Cf. above, Ep. 233b and Wurmser's claim to this effect in a statement (AST 22–2) dated 6 January 1525.
3 Cf. the letter dated 13 January is AST 22 (2), #17. The Schultheiss of Stotzheim is not identified. St Peter (now Saint-Pierre) is located 2 km away from Stotzheim in Alsace. For complaints about moneys being sent to the exiles in Molsheim, see below, Ep. 235a and a letter from the Strasbourg council to the council of Reichshofen of 22 February 1525 (AST 22–2) requesting that the rents due to the chapter be paid to its administrator in Strasbourg rather than to the Catholic party.

lords and magistrates, to give us, your standing citizens and subjects, letters for all those who are under the authority of the collegiate church. In accordance with the institutions founded in ancient days for the honour of God, the benefit of the community, and the maintenance of the divine service of the collegiate church of St Thomas, we ask that you inform them of the situation in your name. Tell them that some canons together with the dean have recently fled from here, that is, the place normally designated for the chapter. Inform them that these canons claim and pretend to be the chapter and consider themselves the chapter, forcefully exacting rent and moneys, putting them to their own use, contrary to the statutes. May the honourable council issue this warning and state that those in our debt should not make payment to the fugitive canons, but rather to us, who reside here and to whom all documents are made out, according to the opportunity and the readiness of each person's pen.[4]

Secondly, since the canons who are now in Molsheim have appropriated the seal of the collegiate church and taken it away without our knowledge or the permission of the keepers of the keys – for we have two keepers[5] on the basis of the statutes concerning the seal, so that they may jointly apply the seal and draw up legal documents for the collegiate church – we hereby cancel this seal before your strict, honourable, and wise lords, and we affirm that they appropriated it without our knowledge or assent. We furthermore wish to consider null and void any document sealed by them in Molsheim or elsewhere, or to be sealed in future, other than receipts for rents and moneys received by them, or receipts for purchases and sales. We also state that we intend to set up a different seal for our collegiate church in our name and the name of our descendants, which Your Strict Honourable Wisdoms may enclose with the desired writings, as an advisement to the public.

And while they have our seal in hand and claim to represent dean and chapter and carry on all administrative tasks of the collegiate church, it may happen that they touch the capital and sell it, although we do not believe this of them, since they have no right or authority to do so. Thus, for the safety and surety of our collegiate church, we attest and publicly write and wish it attested in view of their past actions, that we have given them no authority and have no intention of giving them authority in the future to buy or sell or take any administrative action. To make this statement more formal, we ask Your Graces, the council, whether we should do this ourselves, or whether Your Graces, being our lords and magistrates, would undertake this action

* * * * *

4 *wie das jeder person gelegenheit und die feder geschickter geben wurt.*
5 One of them was the vice-dean, Martin von Baden. Cf. below, Ep. 237, note 1.

on behalf of your citizens. For that may count more with some people and may strike more fear into our opponents. We therefore beg Your Graces most urgently to look into this matter and come to a fatherly decision concerning us and our collegiate church.

Your strict, honest, and worthy council's willing provost and chapter of the collegiate church of St Thomas in Strasbourg.

Letter 234c: [ca. 27 January 1525], Strasbourg, Capito and the Chapter of St Thomas to the City Council of Strasbourg

The manuscript of this undated letter is in Strasbourg, Archives départementales du Bas-Rhin, G1506, #6. Its contents parallel those of Ep. 234b.

Valiant, honest, circumspect, honourable, wise, gracious lords! Common law, ancient usage, and long-standing approved custom, as well as our well-considered statutes dictate that a dean must not undertake on his own and without the knowledge and authorization of the chapter any transactions concerning matters that involve the whole collegiate church. Yet Dr Nicolaus Wurmser,[1] recently dean, came to an agreement and joint undertaking with several canons and vicars of our collegiate church in a private house here in Strasbourg, which they later confirmed and ratified before a notary in Molsheim and elsewhere in a document written in the notary's hand. Some of them, however, had not thought this over sufficiently at the time, but were moved and persuaded by soft and friendly words. Afterwards they repented, returned to probity and recanted what they had agreed to and promised contrary to what is right.[2]

Dr Nicolaus Wurmser and his followers, then, acted without conferring with the chapter community or the provost, who has the authority and is specifically in charge of administrating temporal goods. They acted without discussion or consultation about the matter, removing our briefs, register, accounts, treasures, and ornaments behind the backs and without the agreement or approval of the stewards of the keys. They also took along the seal of the chapter community and dared to claim they were the dean and chapter. They have the gall to collect our rents and moneys outstanding, using writs from the bishop's councillors. Furthermore, they write, or have written on their behalf, that the dean and chapter have dismissed our administrators,

* * * * *

1 Cf. CWC 1, Ep. 57 headnote.
2 See below, Ep. 237, note 13.

which is not the case. Neither they nor we have ever discussed dismissing the administrators.

We therefore kindly and humbly request Your Honours to inform the various parties of the truth – first of all, princes, lords, and others from whom we or our predecessors have acquired the right to rents and moneys – and indicate to them that we, the provost, vice-dean, and chapter of the collegiate church of St Thomas in Strasbourg, are still resident here in Strasbourg, the place of foundation, and will remain resident here, and that the above-mentioned Dr Nicolaus Wurmser and his followers unlocked our treasury and removed from it, as mentioned above, the briefs, register, treasures, ornaments, and seal, going against common law and our statutes and acting behind the back of the common chapter, and without the knowledge and agreement of the stewards of the keys. They must not use these goods, for they have no rightful title to them. Thus let everyone be warned. Let no one engage in transactions with them in matters concerning our collegiate church, for we, rather than they, are the sole rightful representatives and beneficiaries of our oftmentioned collegiate church of St Thomas, as is apparent and cannot be denied. For this we, your obedient citizens, are in Your Honours' debt forever, for you are our governors.

Your Honours' willing citizens,

The provost, vice-dean, and chapter of the collegiate church of St Thomas in Strasbourg.

Letter 235 is now Letter 233a.

Letter 235a: 6 February 1525, Strasbourg, Capito and the Chapter of St Thomas to Jakob Bapst

The manuscript of the letter is in AST 22–3. For the background see above, Ep. 234b. The addressee, Jakob Bapst von Bolsenheim, is documented as a vassal of the Bishop of Strasbourg for the years 1516–32.

First, our friendly and willing service.

Honourable, kind, dear junker and good friend, we have heard that the councillors and governors of our Lord of Strasbourg[1] wrote to you, asking you to send the annual rent due to our collegiate church and dispersed by you henceforth to Molsheim, etc. to certain persons who have fled from here,

* * * * *

1 I.e., the bishop of Strasbourg, Wilhelm von Honstein.

namely Dr Nicolaus Wurmser[2] and his followers, who claim to be the dean and chapter of the collegiate church of St Thomas, etc. We therefore would like to give you a friendly warning, advising you to give no credence to this message, which has gone to you and others among our rent agents. The authorization was obtained from the bishops' councillors and governors with lies. Rather, pay the rent, now past due, to us and our collegiate church here in Strasbourg, where the collegiate church has been established by order. Do this at the usual meeting place, and hand it over to the usual local administrator, Wolf Graf,[3] who has never been dismissed by us (a trumped-up pretence), and obtain from him the proper receipts, as required. In return we shall represent you against anyone, if need be, and indemnify you, and without doubt act as is proper toward you, our dear and kind fellow citizen. Given at Strasbourg, on Monday after the feast of the Purification of Mary, in the year, etc. 1525.

The Provost, vice-dean, and chapter of the collegiate church of St Thomas at Strasbourg.

Letter 236: 6 February [1525, Strasbourg], Capito to Ulrich Zwingli

Printed in ZwBr 2:299–305, Ep. 362.

[*Summary*]: Jacob Sturm has been appointed assessor [at the *Reichsregiment*]. Luther's letter about Karlstadt has been reprinted in Strasbourg. Capito disapproves of Karlstadt's radical methods. Karlstadt rejects infant baptism while the Strasbourgers support it. Balthasar Hubmaier's reasons for rejecting infant baptism are weak. Capito has read Luther's *Widder die hymelischen propheten, von den bildern und Sacrament* [1525]. He supports retaining images of saints in private homes, 'for the sake of reminding us of them.' The churches in Strasbourg have been purged of images. Capito will write to Luther within two days [not extant] and counsels Zwingli against challenging the Wittenberg reformer.

Karlstadt has caused a commotion in Strasbourg. Capito refers Zwingli

* * * * *

2 Cf. CWC 1, Ep. 57 headnote.
3 Wolf Graf is listed as a notary of official contracts in a statement from the Strasbourg city council of 28 March 1531 (AMS, CH 8587). He is last documented in 1535 as administrator of the *gotshus* in Sesselheim, asking that the persons still living there be pensioned off (document quoted in O. Winckelmann, *Das Fürsorgewesen der Stadt Straßburg* [Leipzig, 1922], II: 78).

to his pamphlet *Was man halten soll* on the controversy between Karlstadt and Luther, and to Bucer's writings on the Eucharist [cf. above, Ep. 224]. Certain preachers in Nördlingen and Nürnberg have stirred up unrest. [Johannes Denck], teacher at St Sebald's in Nürnberg, has been ejected because of his heterodox views on the Trinity. Capito agrees with Zwingli's teaching in principle, even if he disagrees in some details ('I have not read anything of yours of which I disapprove, even if I perhaps think it ought to be phrased a little differently').

The canons who fled Strasbourg [see above, Ep. 233b] have accused the reformers of heresy. [Philip III] of Hanau is calling for a reformation of the churches in his realm. He has invited Capito, but the city council advises against it, thinking the invitation may be a ruse. The preachers have been consulting about the question of the Eucharist. The Strasbourgers originally interpreted the bread as a sign of the body of Christ, but will yield to a consensus of opinions

Capito wrote to Bugenhagen that Zwingli was in agreement with [John] Wycliffe's teaching, but told him not to repeat this in public because of possible misunderstandings. The Strasbourg preachers have written to Luther, informing him of their teaching. Capito emphasizes that the question concerns externals and does not aid in obtaining salvation. He does not have much respect for Karlstadt; Luther, however, has interpreted the articles of faith skilfully. 'We cannot deny that his vehemence has been very useful.' Bucer has translated Luther's postilla on certain gospel passages.

Letter 236a: [ca. 8 February] 1525, Strasbourg, The Strasbourg Preachers to the City Council of Strasbourg

> The manuscript of this report is in AST 324 (Univ.2), #1a, 2ff. It is entitled 'Erleuterong uber ingeleite supplication uff den dritten tag septembris anno 1524' (Explanation concerning the supplication set in motion on 3 September 1524) and bears the note: 'vberantwurt am viii tag febr. Anno 1525' (handed in 8 February 1525). The text is published in BDS 2:399–404. Cf. CorrBucer 2:13–14, Ep. 90.

[*Summary*]: This is a proposal to open up six primary schools for boys and six for girls under the auspices of three or four councillors, aided by two preachers [Caspar Hedio and Jakob Bedrot]. It also includes plans to organize four Latin schools to teach the three biblical languages and finance them, partly through contributions, through the dissolution of monasteries, or through reassigning funds earmarked for ceremonies, such as processions.

Letter 237: 10 February 1525, Strasbourg, Capito, Martin von Baden and the Chapter of St Thomas to the *Reichsregiment*

The manuscript of this submission is in Vienna, Staatsarchiv, Kleinere Reichsstände, Strassburg (Stadt), # 514, ff. 342 recto to 345 recto. It relates in some detail the events leading up to and ensuing after the secession of the Catholic canons of Strasbourg (for the background, see above, Ep. 233b head-note). The submission was printed as *Der Stifft von sanct Thoman zu Straßburg Ußschryben und protestation wider ettliche ungüttliche handlung jüngst vor Keyserlicher Maiestatt Regiment zu Eßlingen fürgenomen* (The announcement and pro-testation of the collegiate church St Thomas in Strasbourg against untoward actions recently undertaken before His Imperial Majesty's government in Es-slingen Strasbourg: W. Köpfel, 1525) . There is also a broadsheet of the *Ußschryben und protestation*, dated 10 February 1525, which was presumably posted in Strasbourg (AST 22–3). The translation below is of the printed text. For signifi-cant variants in the manuscript, see the footnotes.

The majority of the Catholic fugitives had taken up residence in Molsheim and made submissions to the emperor and the *Reichsregiment*, justifying their actions and claiming that the innovations at Strasbourg had driven them into exile (see the summary in Ep. 329a). The *Reichsregiment* (in Esslingen 1524–7, then in Speyer 1527–30) carried on the government in the emperor's absence. It was chaired by the emperor's brother Ferdinand and his representatives (*Statthalter*), Frederick Count Palatine and Duke Philip of Baden. The bishop of Strasbourg, Wilhelm von Honstein, had already lodged a protest with the *Reichsregiment* in September 1524, complaining of the changes introduced by the reformers and of the pressure put on the clergy to assume citizenship (cf. above, Ep. 173a). This prompted the *Reichsregiment* to issue directives to the city to stop the innovations (on 10 January, and again on 3 February; cf . Pol. Corr. I , 94 ff. #177 and #179). The present letter, written in reply to the first directive of the *Reichsregiment*, deals with the legality of removing the property of the collegiate church from Strasbourg. In a separate letter (Ep. 237a below), the reformers justified the religious changes in Strasbourg at length. The *Reichsregiment* issued further orders, but took no decisive steps. By June 1525 several of the fugitives had officially distanced themselves from their leader, Nicolaus Wurmser, and returned to Strasbourg. By September the city was negotiating with the remaining party. The negotiations continued for several years until an agreement in principle was reached in March 1528, signed at Offenburg on pensions to be paid by the city to those who did not wish to return (the manu-script of the contract is in AST 22, 5–6). For legal wrangling about the interpre-tation of the contract see below Ep. 377a.

We, Wolfgang Capito, provost and doctor of Holy Scripture, Martin von Baden,[1] vice-dean, and the community of the collegiate church St Thomas at Strasbourg, offer our willing and obedient service and friendly greetings to each and every person, whatever their standing, office, or duty in the secular or ecclesiastical world. We urgently request you to read our true statement or have it read to you. On the 8 February of this year 1525, a message was received by our gracious lords in Strasbourg from the most gracious governor of His Roman Imperial Majesty and assessor of the imperial government at Esslingen. Enclosed was a supplication[2] signed by Master Sixt Hermann,[3] Diebold Balthener,[4] and Jakob Schultheiss,[5] all three being summissaries of our collegiate church. In it, they claim to be in charge as the commissioners of the three collegiate churches, St Thomas, and Young and Old St Peter, although they never received a mandate from the functionaries of the above-named collegiate church of St Thomas or instruction to act in this capacity. Indeed, their action is not only inappropriate and opposed to right and written law but highly detrimental and adverse to our collegiate church

* * * * *

1 Martin von Baden (d. 1532) studied at the University of Basel, where he graduated in 1495. He became a canon of the chapter of St Thomas in 1500, advancing to the position of vice-dean in 1509. After Nicolaus Wurmser's flight in 1524, he carried on the business of the dean. He purchased citizenship on 11 January 1525 (cf. *Le livre de bourgeoisie*, 2:705, #7539).

2 See the text in Baum, *Magistrat und Reformation*, Appendix, 197–203, which mentions Capito and Bucer by name and describes them as Lutherans (*Luterysche pfaffen*); compare a similar deposition printed in M. Th. De Bussièrre, *Histoire de l'établissement du protestantisme à Strasbourg et en Alsace* (Paris, 1856), 493–6.

3 Sixt Hermann (d. 1527, not as Knod states, 1526; cf. J. Claus, 'Nekrologium und Grabinschriften der Stadt Schlettstatt im Elsaß,' *Freiburger Diözesanarchiv* 26 (1925) 243–96). He matriculated at the University of Heidelberg in 1493 and then at Freiburg in 1512, where he received his MA. He held a number of prebends. In 1517 he is documented as the chaplain of the altar of St Peter in Heiligenstein and in 1519 as the rector of the church in Sessenheim. On 20 August 1517 he became summissary at St Thomas in Strasbourg after the resignation of Balthener and in 1521, canon at Old St Peter. In 1522 he was rector of the church in Alten Molburg.

4 For Diebold (Theobaldus) Balthener or Baldner (d. 1530) see above, Ep. 190, note 4.

5 Jakob Schultheiss (Scultetus, d. 1529) was a canon of St Thomas from 1516. On 21 June 1525 he matriculated at the University of Tübingen. In 1524 the city council attempted to appropriate his income to finance a school. They argued that he had a living in Constance. After prolonged negotiations, the city granted him an annual pension of 100 fl. in 1528.

and would have spelled ruin if God Almighty through his special grace had not protected and kept us safe from them. That you may understand the true nature of their actions and what is correct and what is false in all relevant details, you must first hear the origin of their actions. The matter is as follows:

Last March, in the year 1524, several people in the community of the three collegiate churches, St Thomas, Young and Old St Peter, conceived the futile hope of putting an end to the gospel in Strasbourg and, as they now call it, the Lutheran business, either before Pentecost or at the very latest, on the feast day of John the Baptist.[6] The movement was to be suppressed and extinguished. They may have taken comfort from people in high places who held a grudge and would have liked to (but could not) take action against the Truth; such people are in the habit of giving comfort in writing rather than help in deed! Or perhaps some people who have little faith[7] picked up such news and views from the street, or, as is typical of frivolous people, readily believed things would happen the way they wanted them to happen. Thus it is easy to conceive that they themselves generated the rumour, telling each other tales. Based on such rumours, the goods of the collegiate church were to be transported to a secure place, for it was not plausible that such an upheaval and the suppression of popular opinion, which had embraced the gospel here in Strasbourg, could be brought about without great and mighty resistance. We do not want to assume or claim that their principal purpose was to get at the common property of the collegiate church and make it their own. But one may assume that it was foolish counsel that made them worry about the defence and safety of the collegiate church. They were concerned about avoiding any disadvantage or loss if the good city of Strasbourg were to be struck by misfortune and led astray, and they hoped that, apart from securing the common property of the collegiate church, they would have time and opportunity to save themselves, and by the feast day of St John live in freedom elsewhere without disadvantage. This was what certain persons at the collegiate church attempted and intended to do.

However, it was not concern about a possible upheaval that moved them to take away the common property of the collegiate church, for they did so in March of last year, when there was no unrest of any kind.[8] For

* * * * *

6 I.e., 24 June, the end date of Capito's appointment by the council; see above, Ep. 198a. Pentecost was on 15 May 1524.

7 The manuscript has 'small-minded and of little faith.'

8 However, Gerbel reports in his diary (quoted in A. Baum, 81, note 3) that there were uprisings on 7 and 8 April. Capito himself referred to problems in a letter to Blaurer (4 May, above Ep. 194).

now it is apparent that Dr Nicolaus Wurmser[9] and his followers had this in mind all along and intended to move the three collegiate churches to another gathering place, in case the decision was not in their favour.[10] That is why they acted without reporting to the joint chapter meeting, going against the written law and authorization of our statutes. Without the knowledge and approval of the key-bearers, they unlocked the strongroom and took the documents, letters, writs, accounts, registers, ornaments, and treasures, along with the great and small seal of the chapter, an action that rendered us ineffective and powerless in public. In sum, whatever belongs to and is necessary for the maintenance of the collegiate church they took, partly on the Monday before the Sunday of Letare, 7 March 1524, as we said.[11] They took it to Offenburg, to Konrad Boler, called Babst,[12] *Altstettmeister* and church warden, and others, pretending to do so out of concern and in the name of the whole chapter, as if our bodies and property weren't safe enough in the honest, free city of Strasbourg. And they did this as if the provost, to whose keeping our property and possessions are mainly entrusted by the statutes, and the other canons, who are in constant residence at the collegiate church, were at hand, as if they had been called together at some point by Wurmser and knew of his undertaking.

In the meantime, however, it happened that the above-named three summissaries of our collegiate church, who are followers of the conspirators, presented themselves in Offenburg as the men put in charge by their lords and superiors. They did this, even though the honourable council of the praiseworthy free city of Strasbourg, our gracious lords, and we, the provost, vice-dean, and chapter, had demanded from Jakob Kannengiesser[13] and Konrad Boler, called Bapst, the return of our briefs and the goods deposited with him, by Monday, 23 January.[14] Thus, the three men abetted the fraud

* * * * *

9 For Wurmser, see CWC 1, Ep. 57 headnote.
10 I.e., their representations to the city council in March and the outcome of the negotiations between the collegiate churches and the city in the fall of 1524; see above, Ep. 233b headnote.
11 There is an inventory of the goods of the three churches in AST 22(4).
12 Nothing further is known of Konrad Babst. He is addressed as *Kirchenpfleger* (warden) of Holy Cross in Offenburg in a document of 1519 in the city archive of Offenburg, St A OG 30/1 Pfarrarchiv Heilig-Kreuz (uncatalogued).
13 Jakob Kannengiesser has not been identified.
14 The location of the goods was ascertained when a letter carried by Bonaventura Ersam was intercepted on 4 January (cf. D. Specklin, *Les Collectanées*, Strasbourg, 1890, 506). On 17 January the city's scribe, Wendelin von St Johann (see below, Ep. 246a, note 12), was sent to Offenburg to make an inventory of the

perpetrated against us, for without an order, even of the so-called chapter which was then at Molsheim,[15] they took action on the next Sunday night under the false pretence that they had been ordered to do so. They secretly and behind our backs moved our goods to an undisclosed location and hid them. They acted out of malice, against the will of our collegiate church and chapter, to whom they are strictly bound through an oath of loyalty. Finally, they pledged their persons and goods to the honourable council of Offenburg,[16] with a handshake in lieu of an oath, and promised in addition not to move or sell the goods of our collegiate church, and to attend in a timely manner and cooperate in any lawsuit brought before the councillors of Offenburg by the praiseworthy city of Strasbourg and us or whoever else cited them in this matter. Furthermore, they went to Esslingen, to the most gracious lord, the governor of His Roman Imperial Majesty, and to the governing body (we shall leave it to the pious reader to reflect on the status of their pledge) and there, in the name of the three collegiate churches, lodged a complaint against the praiseworthy free city of Strasbourg and certain individuals, in spite of the fact that we, the provost, vice-dean and other members of the chapter of the collegiate church of St Thomas, not only did not send or instruct them but resisted them. Indeed, among other things, some days ago, we requested them to be in residence, according to the statutes, and to assist here in Strasbourg with the administration of the collegiate church, each according to his assigned task. We asked this in accordance with the contents of the statutes of our collegiate church, to which they had sworn an oath. It is possible that some of our subordinates, persuaded by the glib words and cleverness of the conspirators, joined them and agreed and gave them promises. Some of them were even persuaded to give voice to their agreement, although on receiving better information and remembering their rightful duties, they reneged on their agreement and withdrew from the conspiracy, as can be seen from several notarized documents.[17]

* * * * *

goods and demand their restitution. The move was unsuccessful, and the fugitives managed to sell some of the goods. On 22 January another of the fugitives, Jakob Munthart of St Thomas, was arrested 'together with his cook, during a tryst at night. He revealed where the treasures were kept' (ibid.). Further arrests were made in March: Jacob Schmidthauser of Young St Peter and Wolf Reich of Old St Peter, who were likewise interrogated as to the whereabouts of the treasure (ibid., and AST 111, #13).

15 I.e., the fugitives who claimed to represent the chapter.

16 See below, Ep. 246a.

17 See, for example, the official revocations of Johannes Klotz, dated 7 February 1525, in AST 22 (3) and Jakob Munthart (Pol. Corr. I 96, note 1). Both signed their names to the present letter.

Therefore, we principally state that Dr Nicolaus Wurmser and his followers and the three above-mentioned commissaries did not act on instruction or in accordance with the will of our provost and chapter or the community of the collegiate church of St Thomas in Strasbourg. They appropriated the goods and the administration of our collegiate church in contravention of written and common law, and never called us to discuss any such undertaking. We therefore cancel all their actions and declare them null and void, since they were done and effected behind our back and against our repeated protestations. We do this for all their transactions, past, present, and future, without exception and regardless of how they are phrased or interpreted, whether they concern buying or selling, receipts, legal transactions or other business of the Collegiate Church.[18] Undertakings against the praiseworthy free city of Strasbourg, be they supplications, notices within or outside the law, liens or arrests, are likewise cancelled. This applies especially to the present trumped-up supplication and slander. We also give notice of our intention to go to court against them all, and to obtain compensation on behalf of our collegiate church in retribution for all the collegiate church's costs and damages – the work, effort, danger, and difficulties inflicted upon our goods and reputation – associated with this matter and incurred by persons in the past and in the future. We beg all men, whatever their estate, dignity, or title, to acquit the collegiate church of St Thomas of any guilt in the blamable actions our opponents committed in the name of our collegiate church. We bear no responsibility for their actions, their misdeeds and groundless accusations, and disapprove of them. We do not wish to be associated in any way with their undertaking, nor do we authorize it.

We ask for your support and wish in return to be of service to you, even in greater matters. Given under the small seal of our collegiate church, which we have formally set up to enable us to look after the administration of our collegiate church, and ratified with the signatures of all of us now present (for several were not in residence) in the usual place of the chapter in Strasbourg, on the 10th day of February in the year of our Lord 1525.

The provost, vice-dean of the chapter, and the associates of the collegiate church of St Thomas in Strasbourg, to wit:

Dr Wolfgang Capito, provost and canon

Jakob Munthart, canon[19]

* * * * *

18 *Stifflich* ('of the collegiate church') in the manuscript was erroneously changed to *schrifftlich* ('written') in the printed version.

19 Jakob Munthart (d. 1534), a native of Offenburg, was canon of St Thomas until 1511 (AST 23), vicedean of St Thomas until 1522 and again from 1527. He origi-

Maternus Reichshofen, custodian and canon[20]
Martin von Baden, vice-dean and canon[21]
Beatus Felix Pfeffinger, canon[22]
Lorenz Schenckbecher, canon and cantor[23]
Daniel Messinger, summissary[24]
Adam Held, summissary[25]
Theobald Lehmann, vicar[26]
Joachim Fuchs, vicar[27]
Petrus Rabinolt, vicar[28]
Jakob Reichshofen, vicar[29]
Adam Neger, vicar[30]

* * * * *

---

nally joined the fugitives, but returned and was briefly arrested. He remained in Strasbourg, took out citizenship on 6 February 1525, and became a supporter of the Reformation.

20 For Maternus Fabri of Reichshofen, see above, Ep. 190, note 2.

21 See above, note 1.

22 Beatus Felix Pfeffinger (d. 1554) was a relative of Capito (cf. CWC 1, Ep. 145, note 3). He was a graduate of Heidelberg (BA 1513; Bachelor of Laws, 1518) and a canon at St Thomas in Strasbourg. He turned Protestant and married in 1532.

23 Lorenz Schenckbecher (d. 1547) studied at Freiburg, became canon of St Thomas in 1511 and cantor in 1521. He was a supporter of the Reformation, and on 7 December 1524 took out citizenship. Cf. *Le livre de bourgeoisie*, 2:703 (#7509). In October 1525 he replaced Capito as provost. Cf. below, Ep. 248c.

24 Daniel Messinger of Offenburg (d. 1527) studied in Freiburg (BA 1490) and became summissarius in 1499.

25 Adam Held (d. 1546) became semisummissarius in 1502. He resigned his prebend in 1541.

26 Theobald Lehmann (d. 1560) studied at Erfurt and is first mentioned as a prebendary of St Thomas in 1522. He took out citizenship 4 January 1524. He resigned his prebend in 1544 on account of ill health.

27 Joachim Fuchs (d. 1564) studied in Freiburg. He was vicar from 1515 and also had a prebend at the cathedral; he took out citizenship on 25 January 1525. In 1551 he was deprived of his prebend at the cathedral because he refused to accept the Interim.

28 Petrus Rabinolt is mentioned as vicar of St Thomas in 1522. He took out citizenship on 27 January 1525. He is last mentioned in 1527 and died ca. 1531, when Wolfgang Mossenauer succeeded to the prebend.

29 Jakob Fabri von Reichshofen (d. 1541) studied in Heidelberg (BA 1511, MA 1513). He was vicar from 1507.

30 Adam Neger (Neyger, Meyger; d. ca. 1540), in possession of his prebend from ca. 1522, took out citizenship 1 April 1525. His name does not appear on the manuscript. It is found only in the printed document.

Florian Betschlin, vicar[31]
Walter Kapf, vicar[32]
Balthasar Bock, vicar[33]
Johannes Frentzlin, vicar[34]
Johannes Klotz, vicar[35]
Johannes Summer, vicar[36]
Ludwig Öler, vicar[37]
Wolfgang Dachstein, organist[38]

Letter 237a: 13 February 1525, Strasbourg, The Preachers to the Government in Ensisheim

A summary of this letter is included in CorrBucer 2:14–16, Ep. 91. The full text is printed in BDS 2:432–60.

[*Summary*]: The preachers protest being labelled 'Lutherans' [cf. above, Ep. 237 headnote]. The teaching of Luther is nothing but Christian teaching. They defend their 'innovations' (appointment by magistrate or parish; marriage; leaving the monastery; communion in two kinds; church service in German; abolition of singing, lighting of candles, private masses, and adoration of

* * * * *

31 Florian Betschlin, from 1522 vicar of the St Catherine in St Nicolaus-jenseits-der-Brusch; he resigned the position in 1540.
32 Walter Kapf (or Kaps), not further identified; he took out citizenship on 24 Oct. 1524, where he is, however, identified as 'vicar in the cathedral.'
33 Balthasar Bock (d. ca. 1527) became vicar in 1513 and took out citizenship 18 June 1523. His name does not appear in the manuscript. It is found only in the printed document.
34 Johannes Frentzlin (d. ca. 1532) is mentioned as prebendary in 1522. He took out citizenship 8 December 1524.
35 Johannes Klotz briefly joined the Catholic party, but revoked his allegiance (see above, note 17). He became vicar in 1522 and took out citizenship 31 January 1525.
36 Johannes Summer is mentioned as priest of St Nicolaus-jenseits-der-Brusch in 1520 and as vicar of St Thomas in 1522. He took out citizenship on 31 January 1525.
37 Ludwig Öler of Freiburg had only recently become vicar (January 1525), replacing Christman Usinger who had joined the Catholic party.
38 Wolfgang Dachstein (c. 1487–1553) studied at Erfurt and entered the Dominican monastery in Strasbourg. He became organist at St Thomas in 1521 and left the monastery in 1523. In 1541 he became organist at the cathedral. He accepted the Interim and thus kept his post.

saints; removal of images) as the restoration of practices in conformity with the gospel. They enclose Capito's *Was man halten soll* … [cf. above, Ep. 224] to explain their teaching concerning the Eucharist and his pamphlet *Das die pfaffheit* … [cf. above, Ep. 230] to justify the requirement that clerics take out citizenship. They furthermore enclose Bucer's *Grund und Ursach* [cf. above, Ep. 235] to show that they have always respected the authority of the secular government.

Letter 238: 27 March 1525, Strasbourg, Capito to Ulrich Varnbühler

> This is the dedication of the new edition of Capito's Hebrew grammar, *Institutionum Hebraicarum libri duo* (Strasbourg: W. Köpfel, 1525). The text is on a2 recto–a7 verso. The first edition was published in 1518 and dedicated to Hartmann von Hallwyl (see the prefaces to the first edition, CWC 1, Epp. 11 and 11a). For Varnbühler, see CWC 1, Ep. 49, note 1. Some of the more general educational ideas advanced here reflect the ideals of Christian humanism and resemble the program Capito outlined in an earlier letter, CWC 1, Ep. 8.

Capito wishes Ulrich Varnbühler, protonotary of the imperial government, his friend and dearest brother, grace and happiness.

Greetings, sweetest and most honest friend. I did not begrudge you the effort of writing down a method of learning the Hebrew language, when you requested it for your most talented children. Yet it appears that my effort is not indispensable for this undertaking, especially in our time when books that are quite conscientiously written appear everywhere, from which one may take what is sufficient for the purpose. However, since it is very important that the instructor be a good friend, who is intimately and personally known to your young sons, as I am, I thought it was my duty to spend a little time putting in order this collection of grammatical rules, which I gathered together last year out of the various commentaries of grammarians and authors. If only I had the remainder of the work completed on that same run,[1] when I was fresh from my readings! Then my work would have come forth, if I am not mistaken, with less trouble to me and with much greater benefit to the reader. But it is my fate to preside over tragedies coming in quick succession, from which I cannot absent myself, whatever my intentions and efforts, although I am fully willing and have every reason carefully to avoid them. And so it came to pass that I escaped the preoccupations of a courtier[2] and

* * * * *

1 See below, note 14.
2 Capito served at the court of Albert of Brandenburg in Mainz, 1520–3.

became involved in a more lowly (by the standards of men), but nevertheless dangerous business. I am involved in as many dangers as you who are the principal secretary and indeed chair (*moderator*) of the imperial privy council, and thus are obliged to come in contact with the most diverse characters, and sometimes not the most sincere ones. If only the mountain of my travails were as beneficial to the public as they were bothersome to me privately (or would have been bothersome, had I not made them lighter by bearing them patiently). But now that you have reminded me once more of my promise and asked me again for the grammar, I apply myself to the task. Although it is not a convenient time, I shall oblige you and show my good will toward you by my compliance.

I am greatly encouraged, moreover, to undertake the task because of a most honourable project of our council – in case you are not informed – to establish colleges for the study of the three languages, the humanities, and rhetoric.[3] For experience has taught them, as indeed we tell them every day, that ignorance is the worst bane for a state and the mother of superstition as well as tyranny, an evil which the filthy Antichrist has used to despoil Germany and indeed the whole world. Piety has been extinguished, humanity cast down, ruined and uprooted. These most prudent and Christian men[4] are therefore vigilant, lest the Prince of Lies, who has been toppled and defeated by the Word of the Lord, recover his strength in the face of the stupor of the Germans and attack them even more forcefully than before, ranging among them and destroying the still tender flower of reborn Christianity, that is, the nascent hope of salvation. For they very much hope that the other states will either anticipate or at least follow them in this pious undertaking.

Those impostors,[5] relying on our simplicity and ignorance, have carried on in all matters at will. They display great injustice, living a life of great shame, to which they add arrogance and rashness, so that they are unbearable, not only in the eyes of the august city council, but also in the eyes of rather crass people. No one would deign to associate or converse with such individuals if the old piety still reigned. Indeed, if we believe Paul, one must not even eat at the same table as a fornicator or a greedy man.[6] How, then, must we treat sacrilegious Antichrists, who lie to the Holy Spirit and say, *'Peace, peace', and there is no peace*?[7] How should we treat bragging adulterers

* * * * *

3 See above, Ep. 236a.
4 I.e., the members of the Strasbourg city council.
5 I.e., the opponents of the reformers.
6 1 Cor. 5:9.
7 Jer. 6:14.

and manifest perverts? What shall we do about such crimes and vices, I ask you? And, as everyone knows, there are many people of that sort who fight for an immunity[8] that goes against Christian principles.

Education, especially religious education, then, blocks the path of such contagion. But we recognize that it is also to the detriment of the state if only a few out of so many are knowledgeable. If matters depend on their judgment, popular rule easily changes to oligarchy and from there to monarchy, from which it is only a small step to tyranny. We therefore wish not only a modicum of education for the people, but something even more far-reaching for the common folk and the artisans. This is done to prevent one who has talent, education, and skill from hoping he may stir up a revolution, as do certain criminal minds who for the most part rely on the ignorance of the multitude. In my view, supervising change, reformation, and improvement of things that have deteriorated is the office and duty of the magistrate. Nothing can be done well on the impetuous initiative of the common people; indeed, what was well done has been turned upside down by the licence of common people.

It must be our first concern, however, to see to it that the impious Antichrist does not resume his reign under the pretext of piety, lest the most recent error be made worse than the previous one. May other people take care of maintaining the government, who are better equipped than I with time and experience. It is my proper task to keep the gates safe on all sides and to protect the flock of Christ from raging wolves. And there seems no better method of keeping them off than public preaching. It confirms the timid, and weakens the tales and barbarous lies of the impious papists, with which they have kept the whole world captive for so many centuries. Otherwise we run the risk that those fat-bellies will appear on the scene, who seek profit instead of piety, and simple people will be once again harassed to death by those beastly torturers of conscience. For the sake of making a living, they ineptly feign piety, but they have no qualm to show their true nature once they have conquered public opinion and regard, and have thus obtained the desired end. Their entire struggle is about becoming rich in worldly possessions. They do not believe it is important that a person be pious and good, as long as appearances are kept up, as long as they are allowed to be idle and enjoy the property and influence of pious men. How great will be the gratitude of posterity to our magistracy, which has heeded our timely warning and is staunchly proceeding with the foundation of pious schools of eloquence, which are attached to those of literature. They would have obeyed

* * * * *

8 I.e., exemption from citizenship.

us in the beginning if they had been delivered of resentful antichristians, on whose removal we spent much time. You would not believe, dear Ulrich, the attitude and the violence with which they struggled against the progress of the Word and continue to struggle even now, the adversarial attitude they adopted against alms for the poor because the support money came out of their own pockets and they lost something of their sumptuous luxury. What tricks they tried in order to enable their ruinous errors to supplant both Christian truth and us, its defenders! There was no trumped up crime that they were ashamed to attribute to us. They accused some of the ministers of the Word of adultery, others of patronizing adultery and legitimizing libidinous desires. Some were accused of offering pieces of turnip to the people in the congregation instead of the bread of the Lord, others again, of rejecting baptism and circumcising boys; some were even accused of being thieves, murderers, or traitors of the fatherland. Is there anything that they hesitated heaping on our heads? O impiety, o stupid ignorance!

You followers of Baal[9] intend to destroy the robust truth, which terrifies you, with lies, fraud, tricks, and evil arts since you cannot do it with words or by force. Indeed, the light of the Truth shines too brilliantly in the minds of men to be obscured by your fog and black darkness. To prevent your actions in the future, a proclamation was issued by the council a year and a half ago, when we began our preaching, to the effect that children ought to be taught by suitable teachers.[10] Yet you have made every attempt to delay the course of the Word, using injustice, as I said, obstinacy, and violence, and relying on money, the evil favour of the mighty and your own power. Happy is the day when it will be granted us to see the youth of Strasbourg being instructed in good literature as well as in piety! With the very same sustenance we will nourish both respectable, prudent citizens of this state and free Christians, who are liberated from mental servitude to useless laws and have been assured freedom by the Lord's death. Once we are delivered from ignorance, which was the mainstay of our opponents, they will have no other support, as they well know. They have learned that they can do little with fire and sword, even less with threat and terror, and nothing at all with ideas.

What, then, remains for us to do? Only to safeguard the salvation that comes from pious and honest teaching. A great part of it depends on the knowledge of languages, which we cultivate here with Jesus' help, as far as

* * * * *

9 The image of Baal is also used by Petrus Wickram in CWC 1, Ep. 72, to characterize the conservative canons at St Thomas.
10 Proclamation not traced; cf. the request concerning schools by the preachers above, Ep. 236a.

is necessary, with the intention of putting before tender minds always the best and most approved material. If the more serious minds among the pagans reserved elegy and comedy for an age that was intellectually firmer and stronger, why should we Christians allow youngsters, before their character has been safely established, to meditate day and night on what is lascivious and shameful? Therefore rhetoric must cultivate their minds with virtue as well as an elegant style, and not infect them with temptations, destroy them with unchaste thoughts, or corrupt them with vile desires. Similarly, I believe the knowledge of languages will seem a less dangerous thing if it, too, is based on innocuous authors. It will be aided by grammars, which should be short, lucid, learned, and elegant. Such grammars are available, if I am not mistaken, among the Latins. As for Greek grammars, many people agree with me in giving first place to Johannes Oecolampadius,[11] a man of all-round learning, and at the same time most virtuous. No judgment based on experience has yet been passed on Hebrew grammars. Indeed, not a few men have laboured diligently to bring the holy language to the attention of the world. I do not give preference to my lightweight book over the work of others, although some people, it appears, value it for its order and arrangement, features that promote perspicuity and the ability to be concise, the surest mental aids. For I seem to have somehow gone through all the characteristics of the Hebrew grammar in four books. The first book contains a summary of the others. The second deals with the verbs in more detail. The third teaches the nouns according to type, declension, and significance. The fourth, however, describes at some length the system of vowel signs, accents, and the entire system of prosody. As for the grammar, which I dedicated some years ago to the most elegant young man, Hartmann von Hallwyl, I would now want to consign it to oblivion.[12] It was a premature birth, so to speak, which gave me a great deal of trouble and was of no use to him. He did, at any rate, make closer acquaintance with the Greek Homer and Hebrew Moses. That he neglected sacred writings he owes to me, his obscure teacher, and to my unhappy commentaries, just as he owes a rich store of the humanities to

* * * * *

11 The ideas advanced here on the need to learn the three biblical languages strongly resemble what Capito said in the introduction to the first edition of his Hebrew grammar (CWC 1, Ep. 11). There, too, he praised Oecolampadius' Greek grammar, *Dragmata Graecae Literaturae* (Basel, 1518).

12 See headnote above and the dedicatory prefaces to the first edition, CWC 1, Epp. 11 and 11a. The first edition did indeed receive a bad press (see CWC 1, Ep 11a, note 4, for the negative comments of Wilhelm Nesen and Otto Brunfels).

Petrus Mosellanus,[13] for it was on account of his teacher Mosellanus that he reached the peak of literature and holds fast to it.

I am now publishing the first two books to give the reader a taste of the second two.[14] I shall not keep them under cover once I see that the first two are not displeasing to good and learned men, or certainly once our schools are built on a firmer foundation. What we have begun is still recent and therefore weak.

I dedicate these books to your children, Ulrich, as a monument to my friendship with their father and my special brother. What can cement our relationship more strongly than the existence of a book by which your children are taught virtue and the use of scripture? For the sacred books teach us to speak Hebrew and imbue the heart with piety and right thinking. Unless your love for your children and my hope deceives us both, I believe it is worthwhile to send them forth from your house immediately and entrust them to a good man, who will lead them to a greater harvest of learning and morals, and will further and advance them through appropriate praise, for their talent is incomparable. The paternal hearth, their nesting place, makes young people languid and saps their strength. The soft and caring indulgence of a father nourishes the impudence that comes with security rather than the liberality of a free mind. Farewell in the Lord. Strasbourg, 27 March 1525.

Letter 239: [End of March/Beginning of April 1525?], Strasbourg, Capito to Nicolaus Prugner

> The manuscript of this letter is no longer extant. The basis for this translation is the transcription found in TB IV:153 and printed in Jules Lutz, *Les réformateurs de Mulhouse* (Ribeauvillé, 1904) section V:48, #11. The undated letter is roughly contemporary with the revised edition of Capito's grammar (see preceding letter), which is mentioned here. For Prugner, see above, Ep. 221 headnote.

Greetings, dearest brother in the Lord. I have not replied to your earlier letter because the men who brought it to me did not return before their departure. Yesterday a great rumour arose about Zwingli, eighteen citizens, and two

* * * * *

13 From 1521 Hallwyl studied at the University of Leipzig, where Mosellanus taught until his death in 1524. For Mosellanus, see CWC 1, Ep. 62 headnote.
14 The last two books were never published.

councillors having being killed in Zurich.[1] This was asserted with such assurance that it could easily have taken in a timid person. But we know that man is in the hands of God the Lord, and without his command, *not even a hair on his head perishes*.[2]

I have[3] no dictionary now. I have not seen Caspar's grammar.[4] I hear, however, that it is very comprehensive. I, too, shall waste good time, for I have decided to do some writing and have revised my *Institutiones*.[5] They will soon be printed. I shall leave the completed book to your judgment. Nor do I doubt that learned men will acknowledge the lucidity of its arrangement and the fact that a certain amount of work was involved. Please give my greetings to Oswald.[6] I thank him for his most Christian letter, which quite heartened our church, for I showed it to quite a few people. Farewell. I wanted to write this to you, although I am rather unsettled on account of the most hectic negotiations.

Capito.

Letter 240: [After 8 April 1525, Strasbourg], Capito to [Nicolaus Kniebs]

The manuscript, an original in Capito's hand, is in the Kongelige Bibliotek, Copenhagen, ms. Thott 497, folio 80. For the addressee, see above, Ep. 184 headnote. For the background, see Wencker's chronicle in L. Dacheux, ed., *Anciennes chroniques d'Alsace* (Strasbourg, 1901), 4:126, under the date 19 June 1525 (#4624): 'Closing St Martin's and adding it to the parish of St Stephan. The abbess wants to keep Anton [Engelbrecht], but the councillors want Symphorian.'

Propitious, dear lord, the hospital has now been delivered of the man, who

* * * * *

1 Cf. Ep. 271 below from Zwingli, in which he confirms that he is alive and well and denies a rumour that he has been banished. The source of these rumours is unknown.
2 Luke 12:7.
3 TB has *'habeor,'* which must be an error for *'habeo.'*
4 I.e., Caspar Amman's *Epitome artis grammaticae Hebraeae* (1520, which remained unpublished). Amman (ca. 1450–1524) of Liège, Belgium, resided in Lauingen. He was the provincial of the Augustinians in Swabia and Rhineland, and a reform-minded man, who refused to read the papal bull Exsurge Domine (excommunicating Luther) from the pulpit. He was imprisoned in 1523 and died shortly after his release in 1524. Amman was a noted Hebraist.
5 I.e., his grammar; see the preceding letter for the dedicatory letter to Varnbühler.
6 Johannes Oswald Gamsharst. Cf. above, Ep. 221, note 10. His letter to Capito does not appear to be extant.

until now was in charge of teaching and consoling the poor in the hospice, even though he had no understanding of God.[1] I now ask you, wise and honourable men, to consider how the sick and poor might be offered better consolation. We are thinking of Symphorian,[2] who is ailing, but in his illness is strong and solid in God. In our opinion, he has the greatest skill in consoling people in their troubles and difficulties.

Although parishes are generally not too numerous, the congregation of St Martin might well be divided up between St Thomas and the cathedral. For the said parish is very inconveniently located and too close to the other two. After considering all circumstances, we think it right that you should give consideration to Symphorian, for it would be a suitable and proper position for him. I also ask that you take counsel with Jakob Meyer[3] about this matter. And if you ever need our service, deign to call on us, and we shall make every effort to comply, even if it may be a large undertaking and surpass our abilities. Be commended to Christ.

Your willing W. Capito.

Letter 241: [After 10 April 1525], Strasbourg, Capito to Nicolaus Kniebs

Printed in BDS 2:462–5.

[*Summary*]: Capito asks that the mass and singing [other than psalms] in church be abolished for the honour of God and for the sake of helping the weaker brethren, although some people are stubborn rather than weak and maliciously oppose the gospel. The Lord's Supper is meant for believers. Those who are weak ought to abstain until they have been strengthened by the Word of God. No improvement can be hoped for, however, until 'pagan usages' are abolished. The new order of service should take this form on weekdays when there is no preaching:

1 After a bell is rung, the priest goes through confession and absolution; the congregation answers with 'Amen.' The acknowledgment of their sins is the basis of grace.
2 The congregation sings a psalm, and the minister preaches a sermon for the moral instruction of the congregation.

* * * * *

1 Johannes Niebling, d. 8 April 1525.
2 For Altbiesser, see above, Ep. 217 headnote.
3 Jakob Meyer (Meiger, d. 1562), a member of the city council (member of the XV 1521–4, member of the XIII 1525–62) and appointed one of the three scholarchs in 1526.

3 Silent prayer is followed by the Lord's Prayer.
4 The minister reads a biblical text in German; the congregation responds with 'Amen,' and is dismissed with a blessing.

Letter 242: 17 April 1525, Altdorf, Erasmus Gerber to the Strasbourg Preachers

Printed in Pol. Corr. 1:113, Ep. 199 and CorrBucer 2:16–17, Ep. 92.

[*Summary*]: Gerber of Molsheim writes in the name of the peasants, requesting help from the Strasbourg preachers in spreading the gospel in Altdorf.

Letter 242a: 18 April 1525, Strasbourg, Capito, Martin Bucer, and Matthew Zell to the City Council of Strasbourg

The text of this document (an extract from the minutes of the council, BMS, ms. 745, f. 37 verso–38 recto) is printed in CorrBucer 2:17, Ep. 93.

[*Summary*]: The preachers inform the council of the request received from Gerber [see above, Ep. 242] and ask for permission to address the assembled peasants at Altdorf. They will advise them to disperse and undertake nothing without the permission of Martin Herlin and Bernhard Ottfriedrich, [councillors sympathetic toward the reformers and dispatched by the council to negotiate with the peasants].

Letter 243: [18 April 1525], Entzheim, Capito, Martin Bucer, and Matthew Zell to Erasmus Gerber

Printed in Pol. Corr. 1:114–16, Ep. 201 and CorrBucer 2:17–20, Ep. 94. There is an English translation in T. Scott and B. Scribner, eds., *The German Peasants' War: A History in Documents* (New York: Prometheus Books, 1991), 109–11. The letter is written from Entzheim, then a village near Strasbourg, now the location of its airport. Erasmus Gerber was the leader of the rebellious peasants, who unsuccessfully attacked Strasbourg the following month, and successfully besieged and took Saverne on 13 May. Gerber's army was stopped by Anton of Lorraine, who defeated the peasants at Lützelstein on 16 May. Order was restored by the beginning of June, and the leaders hanged. A new insurrection took place at the end of summer and was at last settled in an agreement signed on 19 September.

[*Summary*]: The preachers counsel the peasants to accept the advice of Martin

Herlin and Bernhard Ottfriedrich to disperse. They point out the problems arising from remaining together: a shortage of food, the danger of strife, as could be seen from the example of the Swabians. The *Landvogt* [Hans Jacob von Mörsburg] and Count Bernhard of Eberstein are willing to promote the gospel and sympathize with the poor. They should listen to the Strasbourg preachers, since the city has shown much goodwill toward them. Herlin and Ottfriedrich are trustworthy and good negotiators and will find a solution. The lords will honour their promise to Strasbourg and allow the peasants to depart without punishment. These are practical reasons; the following is the advice of the Bible: to resist would indicate that they are more concerned with secular than with spiritual matters. They ought not to seek their own advantage by pretending to act for the glory of the gospel. They must trust in God rather than their own numbers. As Christians they ought to seek peace and look to the greater glory of God rather than their own. The preachers assure them of their good will.

Letter 243a: 29 April 1525, Offenburg, Nikolaus Wencker and the City Council of Offenburg to the Chapters of St Thomas and Old St Peter

> The manuscript of this letter is AST 87, #27. For the background see above, Ep. 234a, and below, Ep. 246a headnote. Nikolaus Wencker (d. 1545) was the *Schultheiss* of Offenburg. Cf. Baum, *Magistrat und Reformation*, 145, note 1, and Röhrich, *Geschichte der Reformation im Elsass*, 1:362.

Worthy, most learned and upright dear lords, first we offer you our friendly and willing service at any time.

Dear lords, you are well aware of the mode and manner in which the treasure, briefs, possessions, and goods of the collegiate church of St Thomas and Old St Peter, which were brought to Offenburg at various times, have been placed in our trust. You made a legal claim to the goods, [and they were to stay here] until a settlement is reached in this matter. So far we have kept the above-mentioned goods according to the law. We certainly expected that by now one party would have come forward in the matter of the confiscated goods, to bring the affair to a conclusion, take the goods off our hands and move them to where they belong, and thus deliver us from the attendant troubles and worries. This has not yet come to pass, and matters are rather difficult on account of the peasant unrest going on everywhere in the region, so that no one can be sure what will happen next, and goods belonging to the clergy are particularly at risk. We therefore ask you kindly to come to an agreement with your opponents or settle with them in a manner that will allow you to remove the above-mentioned goods with the knowledge and agreement of both parties and put them elsewhere under proper and good care, so that we may be relieved of the great care and anxiety caused by the matter. Should this message and well-intentioned announcement and request result (contrary to our intention) in any damage to the above-mentioned goods, we formally state herewith that we accept no responsibility and shall answer no claim. We wanted you to be aware of our good and well-intentioned opinion and hope you will take action accordingly. We thus ask you once again to take and interpret our letter in good faith. Our request is motivated by no other reason than what is best for you and us in this pressing necessity. In this matter we trust your good will and will gladly earn it through our friendly services in this difficulty. Given on Saturday after St George's Day, in the year, etc. '25.

The Schultheiss, mayor and council of the city of Offenburg.

Letter 244: 30 April 1525, Strasbourg, Capito to Ambrosius Blaurer

The text of the letter is printed in Schiess 1:119–120, Ep. 93. For Blaurer, see above, Ep. 192 headnote.

May the grace of Christ be with you, most learned sir and most Christian brother in the Lord! Everything here is full of uncertainty. There are so many citizen armies who have been incited to demand, first of all, liberty of the gospel, and secondly freedom from the tyranny under which they suffer wretchedly. The bishop of Speyer has fled to Ludwig.[1] The Elector Palatine is without plan or assistance and relies for his safety on his one stronghold, Heidelberg. Indeed, the people of Speyer have laid down conditions for the bishop that cannot be rejected. The principal condition, after the bishop's expulsion, is that he himself should take up the government. They would then obey freely and with good will, but they would no longer bear the tyranny of the Speyer clergy. Yesterday they negotiated concerning this matter in the presence of the whole army. I shall know tomorrow under what conditions they departed.[2] Anton Engelbrecht[3] is being called back with honour, but he

* * * * *

1 Schiess has 'Bude,' which must be an error for 'Ludwig,' i.e., George, Count Palatine, Bishop of Speyer, fled to his brother, the Elector Ludwig, Count Palatine, in Heidelberg.
2 The agreement, the Compact of Udenheim, made a number of concessions to the rebels.
3 For Anton Engelbrecht see above, Ep. 216, note 12.

labours under the quartan fever, and I fear very much that he will not be of service in these mad affairs. We need strength and the grace of God. No one has been harmed except the clergy. The peasants are looting the monasteries. They demolish them and use the construction material for private purposes. They are occupying many towns now and some citadels. The realms of Stuttgart and Würtemberg[4] have apparently been returned to their prince, if the messengers are not wrong. The anxiety of the papists is amazing, nor is there any less concern among the eager followers of the world. The rich fear miserably for their belongings. Even we in this strong city do not feel entirely secure. Some action of betrayal was set in motion, but in vain, if the men who denounced it are correct, or rather, if the denunciation itself is correct. For the authors [of the denunciation] spoke of some such threats before the magistrate; the magistrate will soon put them to torture to find out the truth. We, however, will nevertheless proceed in the freedom of the gospel, comforted in the Lord.

You will find here only small remnants of the external Antichrist. We are introducing laymen to the apostolic task. Some of them are strong, while others are independent minds whose audacity, we fear, will imperil the church, but we cannot fend them off in this tempest. The man who brings these letters will tell you everything in order. There are an infinite number of things going on, and they are changing by the hour. May Johann Wanner[5] and Bartholomew Metzler[6] and the rest of your preacher colleagues fare well in the Lord, especially your most elegant brother Thomas and your incomparable sister Margaret.[7] Strasbourg, on the last day of April in the year 1525.

Yours, W. Fabritius Capito.

* * * * *

4 The peasants occupied Stuttgart in April, but the Swabian League under Georg Truchsess of Waldburg reconquered the territory by May 1525.
5 Johann Wanner (Vannius, d. 1527/8) studied at Erfurt (MA 1510). He was parish priest in Mindelheim, Swabia, and, from 1521, preacher at the cathedral in Constance. The bishop dismissed him in 1524 on account of his evangelical leanings, but the city council provided him with a salary to preach at St Stephan's. He married an ex-nun in 1525. From 1526 he was preaching in Memmingen.
6 Bartholomew Metzler was at St Stephan in Constance. In 1523 he was threatened with dismissal on account of his Lutheran sympathies, but the city council interceded on his behalf and gave him the prebend of the Leutpriester at the Großspital. In 1527 he obtained the prebend of Johannes Ehinger. The city also asked him to preach at the convent in Zofingen. He married in 1525 and became a citizen of Constance in 1531. He left Constance in 1548 and died 1553 in Burgdorf in the region of Bern.
7 For Thomas and Margaret Blaurer see above, CWC 1, Ep. 89, note 6, and Ep. 194, note 21.

Letter 244a: [ca. 6 May 1525], Strasbourg, The Strasbourg Preachers to the City Council of Strasbourg

The text of this memo is printed in CorrBucer 2:21–2, Ep. 95.

[*Summary*]: The preachers ask the council to put a stop to slanderous tales alleging that they are inciting the people to rebellion against the secular authorities and to claims that the clerics' adoption of citizenship goes against the gospel. They ask that inns be policed because men waste their money on drinking and gambling and neglect their families; the funds of monasteries and convents should be controlled, and those who wish to leave should be allowed to do so. The gospel should be preached in convents, and ceremonies (mass, singing, bell ringing) should be reformed or suppressed. Clergy should be prevented from keeping concubines.

Letter 244b: [Between 6 and 8 May 1525, Strasbourg], The Strasbourg Preachers to the City Council of Strasbourg

The text of this memorandum is printed in CorrBucer 2:23–4, Ep. 96. As a result of the preachers' request, the council decided to collaborate with them on establishing schools; they reduced the number of masses celebrated in the four chapter churches to one a day, and suggested that masses be abolished altogether in the monasteries and convents. The council furthermore promised to act against those who slandered the preachers.

[*Summary*]: Capito, Hedio, Zell, and Altbiesser appeared before the council on 6 May, protesting against clergy who were newly enrolled as citizens and hostile to the reformers, and who contend that gospel preaching would lead to public uproar. They ask the council to support them, to institute schools in which the youth will be instructed in piety and good morals, and to inspect the monasteries to prevent superstitious ceremonies. They furthermore ask that the mass be abolished and the clergy prevented from keeping concubines.

Letter 244c: [Between 6 and 12 May 1525, Strasbourg], The Strasbourg Preachers to the City Council of Strasbourg

The text of this counsel (given in response to a request from the city) is printed in CorrBucer 2:25–9, Ep. 98.

[*Summary*]: Mass in religious houses and collegiate churches should be abolished and replaced by a new rite, including the reading of scripture and a sermon. There is no reason to fear uproar. The city of Nürnberg, where these rites have been instituted, acknowledges that they are in harmony with the gospel. Monasteries should be dissolved; as was done in Zurich, the young men should be taught a trade and the old monks pensioned off. There should be regular preaching in convents; nuns who wish to leave should be allowed to do so. Action should be taken against prostitution, especially involving the clergy. Behaviour in the *Schreiberstuben* (i.e., where the scribes gathered) and public inns should be controlled; early closing hours should be enforced. The institution of schools has been discussed elsewhere [cf. CorrBucer 2: 13–14, Ep. 90].

Letter 245: 28 May 1525, [Strasbourg], Capito to Johannes Oecolampadius

Printed in BrOek 1:368–9, Ep. 258.

[*Summary*]: Capito fears grave danger and recognizes the need to stand on guard for the church. Because of the actions of a few, thousands have been killed [in the massacres of Saverne and Scherwiller on 17 and 20 May]. Some brethren have perished in the upheaval.

Letter 246: [End of May/Beginning of June 1525, Strasbourg], Capito to Nicolaus Kniebs

Printed in J. Rott, *Investigationes historicae: Eglises et société au XVIe siècle* (Strasbourg, 1986), I: 280.

[*Summary*]: Some people hold the preachers of the gospel responsible for the peasant revolts. Capito stresses that they are preaching peace, obedience, and Christian patience. But there is a great deal of resentment because the adversaries ridicule the gospel. They will experience the wrath of God. Many people have been drawn into the rebellion against their will. The magistrate should protect the innocent.

Letter 246a: 8 August 1525, Strasbourg, Capito, Martin von Baden and the Chapter of St Thomas to the Reader

This open letter constitutes round two in the ongoing battle between the warring factions at St Thomas. After the summissaries Sixt Hermann, Diebold Balthener, and Jakob Schultheiss had submitted a complaint to the *Reichsregiment* on behalf of the Catholic party, and Capito in turn had defended the actions of the reformers (above, Ep. 237), the three complainants posted an attack on Capito. It was entitled *Warhafftige verantwurt dreyer Summissarien zu Sant Thoman auf doctor Wolffgang Capito jüngst unwarhafftige, nichtige ußgangene protestation* (True response of three summissaries of St Thomas to Dr Wolfgang Capito's recently published false and groundless protestation). Capito followed up with the present letter, published under the title *Von drey Straßburger Pfaffen, und den geüsserten Kirchen güttern* (Concerning three Strasbourg priests and the removal of the church goods, Strasbourg, 1525).[1]

The Catholic broadsheet, *Warhafftige verantwurt* (manuscript and printed copy in AST 22–3), was posted in Strasbourg at the beginning of August but backdated to 2 March (see below, note 55). In October, Capito was informed that it had been posted in Freiburg as well. Consequently, he asked the city council and university there for permission to post his response, *Von drey Straß-burger Pfaffen*. The authorities not only refused him permission but took steps to have the response burned. On 5 November 1525 Ulrich Zasius wrote to Boni-face Amerbach: 'Capito's insane and pestilent booklet on that matter, sent from the waters of Styx, will be publicly burned here in the next few days on my ad-vice.'[2] On 26 November Capito reported on the burning to Ambrosius Blaurer and Ulrich Zwingli (cf. below, Epp. 260 and 261). For a more detailed account of the affair, see Ep. 280 below.

I, Wolfgang Capito, the provost, and Martin von Baden,[3] vice-dean, the chapter and community of St Thomas, collegiate church in Strasbourg, who appeared to make a statement on 25 February and signed their names,[4] of-fer you, pious Christian reader, whatever your title, position, or estate, our willing and devoted service and friendly greeting. We respectfully request that you listen with an open mind and attentive ears to our reply to a most abusive tract issued in the name and title of Sixt Hermann,[5] Diebold Bal-thener,[6] and Jakob Schultheiss,[7] all summissaries of our collegiate church at

* * * * *

1 An edition of the text by Milton Kooistra can be found in Erika Rummel and Milton Kooistra, eds., *Reformation Sources: The Letters of Wolfgang Capito and His Fellow Reformers in Alsace and Switzerland* (Toronto: Centre for Reformation and Renaissance Studies, 2007), 207–39.
2 AK 3, Ep. 1065: *Capitonis insanus et pestifer libellus eam in rem ex Stygiis undis emis-sus proximis diebus me suasore hic publice comburetur.* Cf. below, Epp. 246d and 246e headnotes for the actions of the university and city council of Freiburg.
3 For Martin von Baden, see above, Ep. 237, note 1.
4 Cf. above, Ep. 237 headnote.
5 For Hermann, see above, Ep. 237, note 3.
6 For Balthener, see above, Ep. 190, note 3.
7 For Schultheiss, see above, Ep. 237, note 5.

the time, in response to our lawful protest.[8] For nothing is so good that it cannot be blackened by a smooth pen and described as bad, and nothing is so bad that it cannot be painted over with fair words and presented as good. This often influences those who are uninformed and inexperienced in these affairs and leads them to unfounded ill will and incorrect judgment. Such was the case with these three former summissaries of our collegiate church at St Thomas and their lying slander regarding our collegiate church, which was recently written by an old hired orator and issued under their name as a justification. In it no method for casting darkness on a clear matter has been spared. They change the true course of events, describing something that happened long afterward as the cause of a matter in the past, whereas things were, in truth, quite different. They mix up the business of our collegiate church with the business of the preachers. They call us a 'conventicle'[9] and 'followers' of our provost, saying that he and his followers must recant. As if anyone of us had ever undertaken to preach, except the provost who must answer for his own actions and words, or as if we had ever said anything to the people that is without support and needs to be recanted! In addition, they attribute to the provost what belongs to the entire community of the collegiate church. These and many other similar tricks are used by them. Such evident untruths, which are inserted throughout their slanderous tract, can be devised without much skill or artifice, as long as a man is without shame and honour. Although the simple truth itself can overcome ornate lies and needs no outside help or outside ornamentation, it is our intention to give a true account of the course and origin of this affair and to allow the prudent reader to recognize for himself what is right or wrong in each party, and to do so briefly, without superfluous words, as far as it is possible and necessity permits. Thus we wish to rebut their groundless accusation and trumped-up slander and can do so easily without seeking revenge.

Their slander rests on three points: that the preachers, through many terrible upheavals, caused the canons to remove the goods of the three collegiate churches, St Thomas, Young and Old St Peter, when in fact there was no uproar in Strasbourg prior to the removal of the goods. Secondly, they claim that they took the goods to Offenburg lest they be removed and taken to a banned government, a claim we cannot understand, since it was the

* * * * *

8 I.e., the summissaries' tract *Warhafftige verantwurt dreyer Summissarien zu Sant thoman auf doctor Wolffgang Capito jüngst unwarhafftige, nichtige ußgangene protestation* (in the following cited as *Verantwurt*), responding to Capito's 'lawful protest,' Ep. 237 above.

9 *Verantwurt*, ll. 3, 52, 97. The line references here and in the notes below are to the printed broadsheet in AST 22–3.

praiseworthy city of Strasbourg that wished to keep the goods on behalf of our collegiate church. By whose authority has Strasbourg been condemned, a city whose practices are all honourable and good and which does not deprive anyone of what is his right and due? Thirdly, they assert that the decision given us orally in Offenburg differed from our written record.[10] We shall reveal the truth: the content of our statement agrees with the oral decision, but not with the decision formulated in subsequent transactions by the pen of others some days later and somehow changed, perhaps not without reason. The fair reader, who is inclined to waste his time on other people's affairs, may see for himself which party speaks the truth and then render judgment. May the truth hold its ground.

On 7 December, or thereabout, of 1524 Dr Nicolaus Wurmser[11] and several canons of our collegiate church fled Strasbourg on the basis of a frivolous and unfounded fear which they raised among themselves or which was instilled in them from another quarter.[12] This prompted us to check the state of our strongroom, brief, seal, ecclesiastical robes, treasures, and all the possessions of the collegiate church. For there was already a rumour that such goods had been taken and sold. And when, in the presence of a member of the community, the strongroom was opened and everything was found missing, the honourable council of Strasbourg, on our request, wrote to the *Schultheiss*, mayor and council of Offenburg. At the time, a rumour was circulating that the goods had been deposited in the strongroom of the church [there] by Konrad Boler, called Bapst, the *Altstettmeister* and church warden.[13] They in turn answered that they had no knowledge of any goods deposited there, etc. When this became known to Dr Nicolaus Wurmser and his followers in Molsheim, they sent a messenger from Molsheim, directing Jakob Kannengiesser,[14] a citizen of Offenburg, to take the goods out of the church again and secretly put them in another place of his choice. But the man was struck by fear that the documents might be damaged by fire or an accident or in some other manner in the place to which he had moved them. Therefore, he quietly handed them again to the above-mentioned Konrad Boler, the warden in his church, and commended them to him at a time when it was believed that

* * * * *

10 I.e., of what passed in Offenburg when the Strasbourg delegates demanded the return of the goods. For a detailed account, see below pp. 129–30.
11 For Wurmser, see CWC 1, Ep. 57 headnote.
12 For the same allegations, see above, Ep. 237.
13 For Bapst, see above, Ep. 237, note 11.
14 See above, Ep. 237 note 14.

the goods had already been secretly transported out of Offenburg. Nothing further was done by us until 22 January 1525, when we sent representatives with full power to Offenburg. The honourable council of Strasbourg sent their secretary, Wendelin von St Johann,[15] and we, the chapter of St Thomas in Strasbourg, sent Gervasius Sopher,[16] our praiseworthy and sworn steward, and Jakob Munthart,[17] who was at the time under arrest by the honourable council of Strasbourg, and the furrier Caspar Nebelin,[18] all citizens of Strasbourg. Their mandate was to demand the goods from Jakob Kannengiesser and, if necessary, from the honourable council [of Offenburg] and have them securely conveyed to Strasbourg. For Jakob Munthart knew only that the goods were being held by Jakob Kannengiesser. Caspar Nebelin, who applied that same Sunday to Jakob Kannengiesser for the goods, anticipated no resistance. But the latter denied that the goods were in his possession and would not say to whom he had delivered them. Whereupon Wendelin von St Johann, together with our administrator[19] and Caspar Nebelin went the next day, Monday morning, before the council of Offenburg. They presented their credentials and the authorizations entitling them to receive such goods, and earnestly appealed to the council of Offenburg, requesting the council and others to prevent any loss to them, according to their directive. If necessary, they would remain until the honourable council of Strasbourg gave them written directions. Then Konrad Babst testified that he still had the goods

* * * * *

15 Wendelin von St Johann (d. 1554) was one of the council's notaries. His transactions are documented from 1517 to 1548. He was at the Diet of Speyer (1526) and kept a diary on the events there (the document is in the Archive Municipale at Strasbourg, ms. AA 407a, #10). After the city's delegates left the Diet of Augsburg because they feared for their safety, St Johann represented Strasbourg there.

16 Gervasius Sopher (or Saufer, d. 1556) of Breisach studied at Freiburg and Basel (BA 1509, MA 1510). From 1508 he worked as a corrector at the press of Johannes Grüninger in Strasbourg and later taught school in Freiburg. In 1523 he became fiscal of the bishop of Strasbourg and, in September, was appointed procurator for the chapter of St Thomas; in 1525 he was the administrator (syndicus sive oeconomicus, Schaffner). He purchased citizenship on 5 January 1524 (cf. Le livre de bourgeoisie, 2:704, #7522). In 1528 he considered taking over the provostship from Capito. See below, Ep. 269.

17 For Munthart, see above, Ep. 237, note 19. He had fled with the Catholic party, but returned and was briefly arrested.

18 Little is known about Caspar Nebel(in), except that he took out citizenship on 12 May 1512. The entry reads: 'Item Caspar Nebel vonn Mittenwalde, der kursener, hatt das burgrecht empfangen vonn Brigida, Paulus Monthart, des kurseners selgen, wittwen, siner husfrawen, wegenn.' Cf. Le livre de bourgeoisie, 2:601 (#6172).

19 Gervasius Sopher.

the day before, but had relinquished them and no longer had them. After much negotiation, the council summoned the *Stettmeister* to appear before our delegates. They went with him to the house of the Brethren and said to the resident there: 'Mr. Bartholomew,[20] tell us whether or not you have the goods of St Thomas in Strasbourg in your possession.' He said he knew nothing of it. The secretary requested that he be tortured. Then the three so-called summissaries said, without having been asked: 'Why are you asking? We received the goods, but they are no longer in the city and therefore not in our possession.' Sixt Hermann and Jakob Schultheiss insisted on that, one on the strength of his oath, the other on his honour as a priest, asserting it contrary to all truth or probability. For the gates of the city were shut when they received the goods on Sunday night, and one might have made inquiries at all the gates on Monday morning and ascertained that the goods did not leave the city, as they now confess themselves in their tract. Indeed, the goods were later located by the honourable council of Offenburg in the Botzheim house where the dean of Young St Peter[21] resided at that time. They were hidden in a corner of the attic. The secretary Wendelin and our delegates then returned to the council in all haste to demand that these honest clerics be required to show that they had a right to the goods. They themselves appeared, asked for a hearing before the council, and were duly granted a hearing, ahead of our representative.

The action against them took most of that day, and those true commissaries insisted shamelessly and doggedly that they had received the goods on the basis of an oral and written instruction, and that they were no longer in the city or in their possession. They stated these things on oath and on their priestly honour. Therefore our representatives, on the basis of their consistent testimony, suspected and opined that the goods had been handed over the walls of the city and perhaps sold among the fishermen, so that things might indeed be as reported. Yet they were unwilling to produce, in response to our representatives' urgent request, any authorization, nor did they have any to show. Nicolaus Wurmser and his followers undertook to send two backdated letters of authorization to those in Offenburg, one after the other, which sedulously thanked and greeted Konrad Boler on account

* * * * *

20 Not identified.
21 The dean of Young St Peter from 1511 was Lorenz Hell of Kirchberg (d. 1529). Hell studied at the universities of Freiburg/Br and Heidelberg (BA 1516). In 1516 Ottmar Nachtigall (Luscinius) dedicated to him a Latin translation of some selections from Lucian, *Ex Luciano quaedam* ... (Strasbourg, 1517), since Hell could not read Greek.

of his action. They were also clever enough to send along some money to be distributed in this matter. As the honourable council of Offenburg presumably knows and understands, anyone who is authorized to act does not need an authorization after the fact based on frivolous, trumped-up reasons, with the date falsified. Rather a citizen swears the truth and nothing but the truth, and his oath should be based on the truth. But those honourable fellows, who swear by their oath and priestly honour, have not given much of a token of their honour or have given it a rather subtle interpretation. Let the patient reader consider how plausible their actions were.

When our representatives appealed to the court and requested that the seized goods be deposited in court, their opponents finally rejected the request and declared themselves unwilling to do so. And now, after the goods have been sent to us by our opponents voluntarily and as a favour, they offer to appear in court with great and glorious words – at a time when the cause for the appeal is no longer relevant and the case is over, for honest people do not wage a useless war. At that time, however, they avoided the law, when our representatives called them before the court on just grounds. They did not ask that the requested goods be brought to a 'condemned' magistrate, as the commissaries pretended, but deposited with the court at Offenburg. What trouble and effort we could have saved ourselves if the commissaries had not denied our rights and fled. We would not have had to consult many seers to dig and search the places they indicated. The sedulous searches of houses would not have happened, although these were not useless, for several of the goods of Old St Peter were found behind a pile of wood and our goods in an attic, as mentioned before. That's how those self-appointed commissaries guarded the goods of the collegiate churches against fire and accident, goods that were supposedly not safe with the council of Strasbourg or Offenburg.

Finally our representatives demanded to have the commissaries arrested and offered to join them in jail to conform with the law,[22] but the honourable council of Offenburg rejected such an action against members of the clergy and gave an oral reply to the representatives' letters of credentials. This was the tenor of their reply: Since, on the urgent request of our representatives, the honourable council spent all day and could not, despite great effort and trouble, make any headway with the three priests, and since they had no right to act against them in that they were members of the clergy, the council finally obtained a concession from the three priests. Instead of

* * * * *

22 The so-called *poena talionis*; cf. also below, Ep. 290, note 42.

swearing an oath, they pledged and agreed and promised not to remove themselves or their goods and possessions from Offenburg until the matter was settled. They also promised to make themselves available to the praiseworthy city of Strasbourg, the provost and representatives of the chapter, to Jakob Munthart or whoever else believed he had a claim on them. They indicated that they would appear before the council or court of Offenburg and would not move or take away the goods of the collegiate church, which were the object of the lawsuit, from the town in which they now were, etc. Wendelin von St Johann replied that it was risky in such an important matter to trust such persons on the strength of a pledge, but he could achieve nothing further and had to take that as a final decision.

This account and none other reached the honourable council of Strasbourg and will be found conforming to the truth. Afterwards the honourable council of Strasbourg supplied credentials to the noble, brave, distinguished, and wise Sir Egenolf Roeder von Diersburg[23] and to Martin Herlin,[24] the *Altstett-* and *Ammanmeister*, together with their secretary, and commanded them to negotiate further with the city of Offenburg concerning the goods. But when the three priests could no longer be found, the deputies said, among other things, that they were surprised, in view of the decision that the priests had been permitted to leave, for they had planned to deal with them in accordance with the decision. The deputies of the praiseworthy city of Strasbourg then negotiated orally on the basis of their credentials, and received an answer in writing from the honourable council of Offenburg, which included a part of the earlier, oral decision. This came into the hands of the commissaries, perhaps as a special favour. The decision noted that the three priests agreed to appear before the court with regard to the goods, if there were any claims, etc., but the principal part was omitted: namely, that in reply to the request of the deputies of the honourable council of Strasbourg and our representatives that they be arrested, the three priests promised – as recounted in person by the *Schultheiss* in a session of the council and as mentioned before – that they would not remove themselves or the goods from Offenburg. The letter, too, is different in the third article of the decision. For the commis-

* * * * *

23 Egenolf Roeder von Diersburg (d. 1550), a member of the council from 1515 and repeatedly *Stettmeister* and member of the committee of XIII, a supporter of the Reformation.

24 Martin Herlin (1471–1547) was a merchant and prominent member of the Strasbourg city council. On 31 December 1524 Capito mentioned in a letter to Ulrich Zwingli that Herlin was friendly toward the reformers (see above, Ep. 234). Herlin favoured resistance to Charles V in 1547.

saries insisted, as said before, that the goods were no longer in their possession nor in the city of Offenburg. For that reason they promised not to move the goods from the town where they were located at that time – not as it says in the written record, that the goods were still in the city of Offenburg. They consistently said the goods were not in the city, but that is not the main point.

That is the truth of the matter, without addition or colouring, and we call for confirmation on the honourable council of the praiseworthy free city of Strasbourg, on the above-mentioned deputies, on the letter, seal, and present information.

For that reason, the so-called commissaries slander us in their tract contrary to what is good and true, and use many types of strong abuse. For they write the following words: 'As matters became more complex and serious, the dean of the chapter and collegiate church of St Thomas, namely Dean Dr Nicolaus Wurmser, Jakob Munthart, Maternus Reichshofen,[25] Hieronymus Betschlin,[26] Lorenz Schenckbecher,[27] Dr Bernhard Wölfflin,[28] Jakob Bopp[29] and Sebastian Wurmser,[30] who were at the time residing at St Thomas and assembled as a chapter, decided unanimously to move the goods of the collegiate church to a place of safety and keep it until peaceful times were restored.'[31] This statement was added to glorious assertions that the honest people of Strasbourg repeatedly rioted and committed undue acts of violence against the clergy and 'liturgical ornaments,' as they call them.[32] The people were reportedly incited by Capito and his followers, and they want

* * * * *

25 For Maternus Fabri of Reichshofen, cf. above, Ep. 190, note 2.
26 Hieronymus Betschlin (d. 1540) was a canon of St Thomas and provost of Old St Peter. He also had a prebend at Young St Peter. He is documented in Rome in 1487 and 1488 (AMS KS 5, f. 117; AMS KS 6, f. 250). He purchased citizenship on 4 April 1525. Cf. *Le livre de bourgeoisie*, 2:720 (#7754).
27 For Schenckbecher, see above, Ep. 237, note 21.
28 Bernhard Wölfflin (d. 1535), matriculated at Basel and Freiburg (JUD 1513), was an episcopal official from 1517–21, was vicar of the choir of the Strasbourg cathedral in 1520, and in 1521 became a canon of St Thomas (nominated by Martin von Baden). He took out citizenship on 3 October 1525, and in 1529 became the rector of Eschau. He died on 1 August 1535 in Waldkirch.
29 Jakob Bopp (d. 1544) matriculated at Heidelberg in 1493. In 1509 he was procurator of the Rota. From 1517–26, he was canon at St Thomas. He was one of the Catholic fugitives but returned and took out citizenship on 31 March 1526. He became a supporter of the Reformation and served as scholasticus.
30 Sebastian Wurmser (d. 1541), studied in Freiburg (BA 1504, MA before 1519) and was canon from 1522. In 1528 the city granted him a pension of 100 fl.
31 *Verantwurt*, ll. 64–7.
32 *Verantwurt*, l. 13.

to suggest that this upheaval became more dangerous the longer it went on, so that it caused innocent clergymen to flee.

The truth is that on Monday after Letare, on 7 March of the past year 1524, the greater part of the goods of our collegiate church were moved from Strasbourg, before there was any fear of an uprising. But what they indicate there[33] happened much later, although much of it happened in truth quite differently. The goods were gone before the provost started to preach in Young St Peter.[34] It happened much later, on a Sunday, when the choir at St Peter began to sing primes[35] during the Lord's Supper, which appeared to go against the people's inclination. Several of the congregation went into the choir and told the priests to be silent, whereupon a part of them left. The others, however, remained in their seats, keeping silent until the service had ended. No one desired to harm them, nor were any of them driven out of the choir by force. They were told to be silent, not to leave the choir. The images, which were the object of ungodly adoration and attention, were removed only after the canons left. This was done in an orderly fashion on the direction of the government of Strasbourg. The images were not, as they write, torn down in a lawless fashion by the common people. The grave at St Aurelia was removed by the whole church, out of Christian feeling.[36] The holy water stoop in the church of St Thomas was overturned by some ruffians,[37] who were severely punished by the honourable council, but all that happened after the canons and the other members of the collegiate church had already left. For the goods were removed more than six months earlier. How, then, could these events have motivated them to act in the aforementioned manner? For they write as if the events just recounted had happened before they fled with the goods to Offenburg and caused them to move those goods

* * * * *

33 I.e., the reference to the uprisings.
34 I.e., April 1524. Cf. above, Ep. 189a.
35 I.e., the early morning service. Here Capito is replying to accusations in the *Verantwurt*, lines 9–12.
36 Here Capito is replying to accusations in the *Verantwurt*, line 13. Cf. Dacheux, 73, referring to the year 1524: *Auch in diesem jar zur selben zeit ward von den gartnern zu Strassburg S. Aurelien grab uffgebrochen, sie fanden aber nichts darinnen dann die gebein.* (Also that year, at the same time, the gardeners of Strasbourg broke open the grave of St Aurelia, but they found nothing in it but bones). Sim. D. Specklin, *Les Collectanées*, Strasbourg 1890, p. 501: pilgrims to St Aurelia believed that the body of the saint was miraculously preserved, but on opening up the grave, a heap of mismatched bones was found, 'so that some people laughed and recognized the fraud.'
37 Cf. the accusation in *Verantwurt*, lines 12–13.

to a secure and safe place. They report everything, moreover, in the most awkward and lengthy manner, as mentioned.

The list they provided of the members of the chapter [present] is not based on reliable memory.[38] For they pass over Johannes Wetzel[39] and Johannes Hoffmeister,[40] who were present at that decision and may have approved of it. Instead they name Lorenz Schenckbecher, whom they called and could not very well pass over, but who consistently rejected their plan and at last spoke against it before the chapter and testified that he did not approve of moving the goods, speaking of the trouble that would result from it for the collegiate church. How can they speak of a unanimous decision, when he consistently counselled against it, and although there were two other canons in residence at the time who were not called, that is Martin von Baden, who acted as becomes a pious nobleman, and Beatus Felix Pfeffinger,[41] who was also found to be ignorant of the matter? Nothing can be said against those two except that the plotters thought they would not agree to such a dangerous enterprise and perhaps, together with others, seriously impede it. [Nor did they call] the provost of our chapter, although he keeps to scripture and is willing to incur danger on its behalf. Indeed, he has always been known as a prudent, honest man in worldly affairs, acting in the affairs of the collegiate church as behooves and becomes him. He would have offered useful leadership to our collegiate church together with his counsellors, if his lawful guidance had been followed. These four men – men who were of some importance – should have been invited in such a difficult matter and their approval sought even if they were absent. But they passed them over and undertook such a dangerous business, which one would more readily ascribe to the bad counsel of strangers, enemies who take pleasure in other people's harm. Indeed, for more than half a year, Martin von Baden never suspected that the goods had been moved elsewhere. How, then, could he, the steward of the keys, have willingly given his keys for this purpose, as those commissaries have written? If they had keys, they would have had no need to break the locks on the chests in the small strongroom. With keys, they could have obtained the goods without doing damage. We write this, obliged to do so by the blasphemous commissaries. We would much rather

* * * * *

38 See above, p. 131.
39 Johannes Wetzel (d. 1538), canon from 1510, also from 1515 dean of Old St Peter; in 1528 the city granted him an annual pension of 30 fl.
40 Johannes Hoffmeister (d. 1528), canon from 1507, was granted a pension of 100 fl. by the city in the year of his death.
41 On Pfeffinger, see above, Ep. 237, note 20.

have omitted it for the sake of maintaining friendly relations. For we have no desire and never had a desire to disgrace the fugitives or damage their reputation, but merely to defend the justice of our own actions.

It was not on account of the sermons of the preachers that the goods were taken from the city. If we, the four named persons, had been called, as required by the law and statutes, and our voice had been heard, we might have found followers among certain people, who were incited by the strange, unheard-of and vain avowals. For the offer of the honourable council to store and guard our goods together with the city's and to return them on our request, would have been sufficient security, and we should have thought that here in Strasbourg, where the preachers exhort the people to charity, patience, and obedience, our persons and possessions are safe and better taken care of than in Freiburg im Breisgau or Offenburg or Molsheim or Saverne. For the unpleasantness to which the three summissaries refer happened much later, as we said, and did not happen in the manner they claim. The honourable council has never permitted anyone to use violence and, with God's help, will not permit it in the future. Anyone who acts within the law need not fear violence in Strasbourg, that praiseworthy free imperial city, which is under such an orderly government. It is therefore far from the truth when they write that certain people, formally and legitimately assembled as a chapter, decided unanimously to move the goods of our collegiate church to a safe place. For four members of the chapter did not give their permission, and perhaps others would have disagreed, who agreed only after they had been incited and persuaded with rebellious talk.

Secondly, it is not true, as they write,[42] that several prelates, canons, and vicars and their servants took whatever they could hastily remove, including the collegiate church's goods, and fled to the countryside within the see. For the goods of St Thomas were moved to Offenburg in March, on the initiative of Dr Nicolaus Wurmser and his followers, through the agency of Jakob Munthart, and deposited with Konrad Boler, called Babst, under the pretense that the whole chapter, with the exception of the provost, requested Konrad Boler to guard it, etc. Jakob Munthart took along Gervasius Sopher, our official and sworn administrator and servant, and revealed to him the undertaking only when they were outside the gates of the city of Strasbourg. We never wanted to blame the theft on them, as the blasphemous commissaries say we do, and do not want to blacken anyone else's reputation. For often a human sentiment leads a pious man astray from the right path. A

* * * * *

42 *Verantwurt*, ll. 22–3.

prudent mind will not count such action dishonourable, but rather ascribe it to lack of skill and experience. That is the spirit in which we reminded the fugitives of the chapter's common law, written law, and statutes to which they are bound by oath. There is no intent to harm in what we write or do. We say that the goods were taken away without our knowledge or the knowledge of our key-bearer and against our will, and that the so-called commissaries were never in administrative charge of the goods, and had no right to touch them, and that we have reluctantly complained in the name of our chapter to the honourable council, our merciful lords of Strasbourg. But for all that we did not want to declare them thieves, disloyal, or dishonest men, as they called us.[43] For the deeds of each man will declare his piety.

Thus the goods, as indicated, were brought to Offenburg last March and on 7 December Dr Nicolaus Wurmser left on foot with a few others, as if he had been driven out. They left for no reason and had no cause for fear except the fear they instilled in themselves or a few petty whisperers suggested, and which they permitted themselves to believe. Thus their claims are not justified when they attempt to claim that goods and persons left at the same time.

In addition, they write that they received the goods from Konrad Boler and Jakob Kannengiesser, which is not the case.[44] Konrad Boler gave the goods to them by himself. One of the priests himself told Jakob Kannengiesser to leave. But how could they have assumed the task of looking after the goods of the collegiate church themselves, which was never their business, over which they never had and still do not have administrative authority? The goods would never have been misappropriated and passed into other hands if they had been entrusted to the honourable council of Strasbourg on their request and with their agreement to have them kept for the collegiate church. [They might have included] the proviso, if anyone of the city of Offenburg applied for them, they would lawfully return those goods and send them to Offenburg. Alternatively, they might have entrusted them to the honourable council of Offenburg, as our representative requested. It was quite obvious in whose hands the goods would be safest. For the citizens of Offenburg and our opponents were themselves glad that the goods safely reached Strasbourg, where they belong and can be guarded. We all could have avoided much cost, effort, work, and trouble, if those so-called commissaries had not willfully meddled, on their own initiative, in the administration of our collegiate church. Through their escapade the collegiate church

* * * * *

43 *Verantwurt*, l. 3.
44 *Verantwurt*, ll. 29–30.

incurred grave danger and concern for its possessions. Yet they claim to have acted in a useful and correct manner.

Furthermore, as commissaries, they also appealed, in the name of the provost, dean, chapter, and community of the collegiate church, to the *Reichsregiment* and demanded a legal mandate, even though they had received no authority from us, the provost, vice-dean of the chapter, and community of the collegiate church of St Thomas, the greater and more significant portion of whom remained in Strasbourg and reside there still, nor did they receive authority or authorization from the others, who were then in Haguenau. Since we, the provost, vice-dean, chapter and community, have continued in residence at the collegiate church of St Thomas in Strasbourg, and since the writ from the representative of His Imperial Majesty's Regiment addressed to the honourable council of Strasbourg[45] may be to the disadvantage of our collegiate church and to us, we have established the truth through our statement. Namely, we have established that the appeal was launched without our knowledge and agreement, and we hereby state that we do not wish to blacken anyone's honour or reputation; rather it is their action that blackens it.

As for the abuse and pressure they suffered at Offenburg, I leave that to the judgment of the experienced reader who knows the skilful mode of operation generally used by the deputies of our praiseworthy free city when they are in a neighbouring imperial city. For the well-being of cities rests on law and order, and none of them wants to tolerate violence. No one would have applied force to the [three priests]. Therefore it would be lawful to leave the praiseworthy city of Strasbourg out of this.

How is it honest when they write in response to the question why they would not need a mandate from us to launch an appeal against the honourable council of Strasbourg in the name of the provost, dean and chapter of St Thomas: 'What law is there that obliges an appellant to seek a mandate and authorization from the party that wishes to accuse them? For Capito and his colleagues are the actual principals who embittered the common citizens against the clergy, and who are the actual reason for our complaint.'[46] Here one can see the honest and true sentiment of the three commissaries, who presume to attack the provost and greatly harm the chapter and the community of the collegiate church. We are the chapter of St Thomas, which the fugitives cannot deny, who finally returned the misappropriated goods of the colle-

* * * * *

45 Cf. above, Ep. 237 headnote.
46 *Verantwurt,* ll. 52–3.

giate church to us after lengthy efforts on our side. We complain furthermore that they have, without justification, drawn the chapter of St Thomas into an action, which does not benefit the collegiate church and its community, and which we never authorized. The provost's followers, indeed, have never embittered anyone against the clergy, as far as the statement is concerned. We are priests ourselves and therefore are unwilling to tolerate the unfounded and bold action of the so-called commissaries, for the very reason that we do not want to embitter the pious citizens against us – unless they think it creates friendly sentiments to bring an untrue accusation before the praiseworthy *Reichsregiment* against the citizens of Strasbourg, as they did. They did not launch this appeal against us at the chapter of St Thomas. Why then, do they make the chapter a party to it? They appealed in our name and title against the praiseworthy free city of Strasbourg. That bothers us, for no one should get involved in a foreign matter unasked, and we have not authorized them. The term 'Capito's colleagues'[47] in their statement should not be applied to the preachers, for the protest has as much to do with the preachers as it has with the king of the Tartars. We, the chapter and the remaining community of the collegiate church, state that anyone who wants to act in the name of the chapter and the community of the collegiate church of St Thomas, must have a lawful mandate from us, the chapter and the community of the collegiate church – what has that to do with the preachers? A man who has a good cause does not mix it up by inserting matters foreign to it. Only a man who harms the truth must resort to such tricks. The pious reader will notice, however, that we of the collegiate church of St Thomas, who complain of the blasphemous undertaking of the commissaries, have nothing to do with the preachers. Yet they raise the suspicion that members of the collegiate church are acting in concert with the preachers. About the provost they write that he has long been under the sanction of a ban and a court judgment, and that if the chapter of St Thomas was cognizant of it, they should proceed against him as is appropriate to God and the law.[48] Until now we have had no such notice that would oblige us to act against him.

Thirdly, to embitter the pious reader against us, they claim that we deviously inserted lies into the written reply of the council of Offenburg, which they call 'recess,'[49] namely, that they promised not to move their persons or the goods out of Offenburg until the matter was settled and that they offered to appear promptly in court, etc. They have concluded that Capito and

* * * * *

47 *Verantwurt*, l. 53: *seine Mitgesellen.*
48 *Verantwurt*, l. 51: *dazu ist er in peen des bans.*
49 *Verantwurt*, l. 84.

his followers who put their name to the protest, that is, the provost and the chapter and the community of the collegiate church of St Thomas, are untrustworthy and without honour, as long as they, the commissaries, will not accept the content of our statement. That is the hot-headed language used by the above-mentioned people. It is a general rule that those who speak too odiously of others make themselves odious in the eyes of the patient reader. But the writer of the *Verantwurt* expresses himself in a manner more pleasing to the ears of his own party, regardless of what may please the judge or the honest reader or may be serviceable to the matter at hand. We never called them untrustworthy or dishonest in our protest or elsewhere. Why, then, was it necessary to make such false claims? The *Schultheiss* of Offenburg[50] said in the final decision that the three commissaries agreed and pledged not to move their persons or the goods until the matter was settled. That is the basis and that was the meaning of the *Schultheiss'* words, and nothing else. They solemnly promised to remain in Offenburg in person with their goods, and to be present in court in the matter of the goods. Even if we did not cite his exact words, we did not stray from the meaning and contents. That is what was heard and was the understanding of Wendelin von St Johann, the secretary of the praiseworthy honourable council, Gervasius Sopher, our syndic, steward, and advocate, and the furrier Caspar Nebelin – all honourable citizens and long-time residents, and that is what the deputy of the praiseworthy city reported to the valiant and honourable council, and that is what we then and now believe. The honourable council of Offenburg will not deny that. The *Stettmeister* himself allowed them to go away, for he gave it as his opinion on Thursday in the council session in Offenburg in the presence of the noble and honourable Egenolf Roeder von Diersburg and Martin Herlin, that there was no obligation, since they were not under arrest and had not been placed under arrest on the request of our advocate, who made an offer of counter-arrest.[51] Anyone who is not physically arrested needs no permission to leave. In this matter we do not wish to blame anyone, for we are all human. We may have erred in our wording or it may have been formulated differently in writing on account of human changeability. We cannot know that, and so we do not wish to impugn anyone's honour. Yet these three priests slander us so grossly. But, God be praised, they do not have such standing that they may deprive us of our honour with empty words alone before staunch people who know us, and their empty words could harm us even less before the law and its strictures.

* * * * *

50 I.e., Nikolaus Wencker, cf. above, Ep. 243a.
51 See above, note 22.

In addition, there was inserted much abuse against certain persons, for example, they write[52] that Jakob Munthart, presently canon of St Thomas, is now married, as if holy matrimony, commanded by God, could deprive him of his canonry. It should be understood that the honest men who make such statements practise dishonest intercourse themselves, engaging prostitutes everywhere, dragging whores around with them and keeping them in their house. They take on whores on the basis of the last will of their friends, abduct women in the service of pious men and prostitute them publicly to the chagrin of pious people. They tempt their daughters in the confessional and are their downfall. They weaken the resolve of young girls, take away the wives of men in their lifetime, and deprive men and orphans of their goods. Then they come to an agreement with the men through the bishop's vicar, who is a party to such transactions, and other such things. Those actions do not harm the dignity of the summissaries, but holy matrimony is so damaging to the canon, that a married man cannot remain a canon! A manifest whorer, by contrast, may remain a respected canon. We do not shy away from the truth, for Christ says: not everyone can accept the precept to live without a wife.[53] Also: *Each man should have his wife, to avoid fornication.*[54] That does not count with our Christian priests, for they teach that a man who needs a wife should bring home a whore and keep his canonry; but if he is no whorer and wants to be married according to the Word of God, he cannot remain a canon, as if our canonry and benefices had been established on the basis of whoring. For no kind of fornication can deprive us of our benefices, but being a married man, according to their statement, deprives us of them once and for all. The pious reader may know that we are not ashamed of holy matrimony. In fact, we wish that our past life, as we hope will be the case with our future life, could have conformed to and agreed with the Word of God and with honour and honesty. For we neither embellish our actions, nor do we blacken anyone's reputation with our statement, and we do not wish to requite their attacks. It is sufficient for us to show our innocence, which is sufficiently clear and demonstrated through an account of our actions, as the fair reader may recognize himself.

Thus they have no right to make public in their name that Capito and his followers are rebellious, do not obey the authorities, are heretical, untrustworthy, that they are thieves without honour, and much more about

* * * * *

52 *Verantwurt*, l. 25.
53 Cf. the Parable of the Great Banquet (Luke 14:15–24), where one of those invited could not attend, saying, 'I just got married, and so I cannot come' (v. 20).
54 1 Cor. 7:2.

our vices, when brotherly love, faith, and the desire to spare pure hearts should have kept them from such descriptions. They felt it necessary to indulge in the old rhetoric, abusing us and using bombastic and tragic insults without shame, for if someone is covered with shit, he likes to fling dirt. We let it speak for itself that they produced their tirade at the beginning of August to post in Strasbourg and elsewhere and signed it in fresh ink 'given at Freiburg 2 March.'[55] In other words, they backdated it by half a year, so that many might think that their statement was issued immediately after our protest, and no one would suspect the truth that they undertook it only after they had once again been defeated, in their vain hope of emerging victorious out of the multiple bloody defeats of the poor. For the ill fate of the world is their comfort. Truth reigns in peace, which they cannot suffer and which harms them. Their power rests on external help, not in their own strength, as the prophet says.[56] The reason why some of us have retracted after courageous consideration what we agreed to in ignorance or as a result of friendly flattery has been duly indicated in the document of revocation.[57] For the sake of brevity, it is not necessary to recount that, for the prudent reader will consider that a decent man must consciously and immediately retract anything that he finds contrary to his legal oath and duty and was done against his will.

We offer to give a satisfactory account of the reason for our action before the law, if anyone wants to hold us to it. It is true – and we admit as much – we did not call the commissaries before the law, for our opponents handed over the brief and the other things willingly and eagerly to us, the provost, vice-dean, chapter and community as the rightful owners, and assured us that they would guard what is still outstanding so that we would find nothing missing. In this matter we, the provost, vice-dean, chapter and community of the oft-mentioned collegiate church of St Thomas, ask everyone of whatever estate, dignity, office, or title not to look upon and judge a person on the basis of hearsay. Rather, before they read the so-called commissaries' abusive accusation, we ask them also to listen to our well-founded and true reply, and thereafter attribute to each party whatever right or wrong they deserve. For we do not wish to appear better or more righteous in our actions than is, in truth, the case. We hope to have acted truthfully. We offer our service in higher matters. And we testify herewith that all our actions which

* * * * *

55 The date had been added by hand to the printed copy of the *Verantwurt* in AST 22–3.
56 Cf. Zech. 4:6.
57 Cf. above, Ep. 237, note 13.

we have taken this year against the three so-called commissaries and others connected with this matter everywhere, first in our former protest and now in this our necessary response, were undertaken for the welfare of our collegiate church. They were done to demonstrate that our actions were lawful and righteous and that they were not intended to bring shame or dishonour on anyone.

As for the accusations brought by the three summissaries of our collegiate church of St Thomas in their statement, I, Wolfgang Capito, shall reply to them in my own name and at my own risk, without detriment to the collegiate church. For I do not care about the empty slanders against my person of which there is a great deal in their reply. My life is known, as is theirs, and our piety is not the world's concern, but God's truth, which concerns all children of the light, is everyone's business.

First, they say that I and my followers at Young St Peter and St Thomas preached Hussite, Wycliffite, and Lutheran heresy under the guise of the gospel.[58] I reply: We preached the holy gospel and the words of the apostles clearly and without human falsification in all the parishes, not only in those two, and we are still preaching as follows: that we are all by nature sinners saved through Christ Jesus, who was condemned on our behalf and truly sacrificed himself for us on the cross, through God's grace alone, without our merit, as God promised in scripture and fulfilled in Christ. We preach that this was done to the glory and honour of God, which is manifest in our sins and in his mercy, so that we deny ourselves and seek not our honour but God's, Jesus Christ's, and our fellow man's. We are saved through faith and trust in the promise of God through Christ, and through nothing else. Secondly, [we preach] the love of God and men, which obliges everyone to do good to all, enemies or best friends, and to suffer evil patiently and with equanimity; thirdly, there is obedience from the heart, both in the eyes of God and toward secular authority, and strict self-control. That is what we teach and profess with great freedom, for we are certain in God and are called to affirm the Truth joyfully. And we state openly: what is contrary to our godly teaching is contrary to God and his anointed, and therefore anti-christian and devilish, and those who impose such teaching on the flock of God are murderers of the soul and blasphemers. We who have the Word of God must not allow it to pass without comment and should not use words of flattery (1 Thess. 2).[59] As commanders of God we are placed above kings, princes,

* * * * *

58 *Verantwurt*, ll. 8–9.
59 1 Thess. 2:5.

lords, and everyone (Jer. 1).[60] We would prefer not to incur hatred and retain the favour and goodwill of the people as long as we may remain servants of Christ at the same time (Gal. 5).[61] We must assert with Paul that anyone who wants to be justified through works based on external commandments, misses out on the grace that is in Christ Jesus.[62] Paul's testimony once and for all condemns all merit, works, intercession of saints, and all human effort. That angers the servants of the book[63] and causes them to slander the Word and to glory in their doomed works, which have been a great source of pride to them so far. This forces us to attest to the Truth more freely than we would otherwise, to reveal their wrong beliefs to all quietly and meekly, without however suppressing certain things. Thus, we showed them on the basis of scripture that their singing and reading was not Christian, for it is not praying or honouring God. The Christian practice is an internal one. Those who pray truly to the Father pray in the spirit and in truth. *God is spirit; those who pray to him must pray in spirit and in truth* (John 4).[64] What can external pomp add to that? In ancient times, the external practices of offering sacrifice and serving in the temple alluded to our future delivery. These things were done by the faithful, not for the sake of works, but for the sake of God's Word. And if they regarded those ceremonies, which God demanded in those times, as works of their own, it was loathsome to God. Indeed, in Jeremiah 7[65] the Lord says that he did not command them to make burnt offerings or other sacrifices, but to listen to the Lord's voice. This is how urgently God desired that in his service one show regard only for his Word. He took no pleasure in the statutory, habitual performance of his long-standing commands if it was done without regard for his Word; these were like the sacrifices offered by the Jews without faith. How, then, can our so-called clergy's singing and piping be a service to God and a work pleasing to him, when they never speak even one letter of the Word of God?

They say: 'We are using the words of scripture.' I reply: 'The sorcerers and fortune-tellers likewise use holy words, but their wickedness is all the greater because they have abused the holy words.' They must admit that their singing and reading is not internal worship of the Father in the spirit and in truth, according to the will of God, and not according to flesh and

* * * * *

60 Jer. 1:18.
61 Gal. 5:22–6.
62 Gal. 2:17–21.
63 *Buchdiener*, i.e., men who observe the letter rather than the spirit.
64 John 4:24.
65 Jer. 7:22–3.

blood (Rom. 8).[66] Their singing may serve human beings, for they accept generous payment for it, like a merchant for his goods and merchandise. This is too crass an abuse of the Word to need further proof, for godliness must not serve profit (1 Tim. 6).[67] Those who introduced circumcision to avoid persecution with the cross of Christ were severely punished by the apostles (Gal. 6),[68] for the grace of Christ was obscured by them, and these new Pharisees have accepted such generous pay so far for their pagan circumcision (for their practices are derived from heathens), that even princes and lords, countries and people enter their service for the sake of their songs, and become bound to them. Oh horror! God in his glory out of sheer mercy delivered us through Christ, who merited all things for us, and this undisciplined rabble has the nerve to oblige other people to serve them. That amounts to casting filth and dirt on God's honour! How can we not bemoan that, when the honour of God must be our concern? How can we not fight against it, crying murder?[69] We, whom God has sent to defend the Word! No, we shall not leave the Word in captivity! We have strength in God, to the salvation of all the faithful. And even if they accept no money – which is not the case, for the larger the crowd present in the choir, the larger the number of prelates – of what use is their Latin singing to the German congregation? For they cannot understand it, just as a Welshman would make no progress and have no effect presenting his case to a German judge. But everything is supposed to be done to edify the Christian congregation (1 Cor. 14).[70] Indeed, Paul does not want anyone to speak in tongues unless as a sign to those without faith and for the sake of interpretation (and even then it is a gift of God). How, then, can it be good to speak in the tongue of scholars, in this awkward manner, and for pay, when there is no interpreter? And when those who speak in tongues are not improved themselves and do not communicate with God, as did those in the time of Paul, is not their heart far removed from God? Nor is it the case that they believe their singing improves them, for in that case it would be improper to take money for it. In their debt calculations and their trading in benefices, they do not understand what they are singing. Some of them may be learned in the law of the world, that is the only thing they understand. The meaning of the Spirit is hidden from them, which is not surprising, since those who are called scholars of scripture never understood

* * * * *

66 Rom. 8:1–21.
67 1 Tim. 6:3–10.
68 Gal. 6:11–16.
69 *Cetermordio.*
70 1 Cor. 14:1–25.

and still do not understand Holy Writ – far from it! What Isaiah said had to be fulfilled: *I shall destroy the wisdom of the wise and strike them with blindness, for they honour me in vain with the decrees of men, says the Lord.*[71] Even if they were gifted with knowledge of God and had experienced his grace, they nevertheless would be unable to wrestle truly with the Word. It would take a month for a person experienced in spiritual exegesis to study in depth the meaning of the psalms and scriptural passages they burble out in a day. Their practice is contrary to the Lord's command: *When you pray*, says the Lord, *do not prattle much* (Matt. 6).[72] And Paul wishes to speak five words in the spirit to instruct the community rather than ten thousand words in tongues. Paul also commands us to speak in tongues for the purposes of being understood by people who use that language, for one's own improvement, and speaking with God.[73] The singers in church likely do not understand what they are braying. Thus, it is a dull and confused noise.

Therefore we must conclude that their undisciplined singing is not inspired by God and quite contrary to the command of the Spirit. We have spoken the truth, especially since he who is not with Christ is against him,[74] and their singing is therefore unchristian and, in so far as they regard it as a good work and to their merit, a grave blasphemy and in contempt of grace. For grace was given us together with all things freely through Christ (Rom. 8).[75] These people are, in fact, enemies of the cross of Christ, which they deny in their deeds. They will not fail to meet ruin, for their belly is their God (Phil. 3).[76] The common proverb shows for whose benefit they sing their songs in church: 'I have my tithe and money for doing nothing, I don't want to be a choir ass.'[77] They would prefer not to sing if they could have their tithe and money without doing so. Their actions tell whether they are singing in the choir for their money or for the honour of God, for they are much more eager to hear sad requiems and songs for the dead than the joyful Gaudeamus.[78]

* * * * *

71 Isaiah 29:14.
72 Matt. 6:5.
73 1 Cor. 14:18–19.
74 Matt. 12:30; Luke 11:23.
75 Rom. 8:1–21.
76 Phil. 3:19.
77 *Eselsarbeit*, donkey labour, is used of unrewarding work (cf. Wander I, 880). The ass-like braying of priests was also the subject of medieval jokes. See, for example, Thomas Crane, ed., *The Exempla or Illustrative Stories from the Sermones vulgares of Jacques de Vitry* (New York, 1971), 22, where a woman reacts to the priest's chant in the choir: 'I am reminded of my donkey which used to sing like that' (*ad memoriam reduco quod asinus meus ita cantare solebat*).
78 Sung at Christmas (cf. Matt. 26:39–41).

For although the organ pipes sound good in both cases, the fee and the holy penny make the sad song for the dead a happy occasion for the servant of the belly, whose devotion evaporates when the holy penny declines. Their regulations declare in themselves that spiritual matters cannot be without temporal things. Their heart and mind are bent on fees, and once they obtain them, they hurry out of the church, toss their choir robe behind the door and join the maid behind the stove. Is that not showing a secular mind? They serve to feed their bellies. Let the Christian reader consider that every song of the clergy is aimed at that.

Anyone who understands Christ must admit that church ceremonies are the more detrimental to the honour of God the holier the matter is. Consider the mass, which they promote as the supreme good work and sacrifice serving the living and the dead. They say it aids in temporal and heavenly things, so that anyone who attends a mass on the Lord's Day is safer and more protected all day – that is how they talk about the mass. How insufferable this foolish talk is to the Truth, and yet it is so common in all the world! In the mass or the Lord's Supper, all trust should be placed in God, whereas in the mass it is drawn from Christ to oneself, which is quite against the command of Christ. Christ has commanded no more than that we eat the bread and drink the wine in remembrance of him, and in them we are given a token signifying the body which was broken and the blood which was shed on the cross. That is, he commanded us to put our trust in the death and blood of Christ, which is the main point and sum of the Christian order, which he wished to convey at the Last Supper through giving out the bread and wine. Trust in Christ alone, pious Christian, and accept the purification from sin through being sprinkled with the blood he shed for us. Likewise, despair of your own works and all creation. That is what it means truly to partake in Christ. In contrast, the mass-priest now turns Christ into a flea market. He turns the mass into something like a pharmacy, a place to obtain diverse serviceable powders and remedies for the salvation of the living and the dead, as well as for any secular concern, such as hail, wind, rain, war, victory, health of cattle and people, and for anything else for which a bold person might pray. To say such things is against our belief, for the living live, each through his faith (Hab. 2).[79] Why, then, do they need the mass-priest's sacrifice? Christ has been sacrificed for them once and for all, and they have found salvation (Heb. 9).[80] The dead have died in the Lord and are in the

* * * * *

79 Hab. 2:4.
80 Heb. 9:28.

hands of God. Why then be concerned with them, about whom we have no commandment, while we allow the living saints, the poor people, to starve and die, in whom Christ suffers hunger and thirst. Through remembering Christ, which is our first concern in the Lord's Supper, man himself dies and looks to Christ alone. Thus, how can it be both a good work and useful in temporal concerns, as their books of the mass claim? And what is worst of all: they have led the people to seek God and his anointed Son most of all in the bread and wine, whereas one ought to seek in it only the remembrance of Christ, who will come to judge the living and the dead, *who has ascended to heaven, that he may fulfil all things* (Eph. 4).[81] That is why he left his disciples: that the Holy Spirit, the comforter, may come to them. We comprehend Christ, not with our mouth, but through our faith (John 6, Matt. 15).[82] One must pray to God alone, and to Christ on his right hand, and that in the Spirit, etc. (John 4).[83] That is why we removed the sacrament from view and cemented up the tabernacle,[84] for wretched people adored it (which is mockery) even after it was left empty. Hezekiah removed the bronze serpent that had been made on God's command.[85] We only cemented up a hole in the wall, which had been set up contrary to God through human blasphemy. Furthermore, Christ sat at the table without pomp, took the bread, blessed it, broke it and gave it to his disciples, saying: *Take this and eat, this is my body.*[86] Now the mass-priests stand there in precious garments and use containers of silver and gold. They say the same words as Christ, 'Take and eat. Take and drink.' But they give nothing to anyone. They alone eat and drink, although one reads nowhere that Christ ate and drank. Rather, he gave food and drink at that time to his disciples. The bread signifies a community of the body of Christ, for we are one bread and one body, as we partake of one bread.[87] They, however, partake in the bread of the mass alone and thus overturn the significance and meaning. Only once a year, but with much incorrect interpretation and usage, do they share the bread with everyone, and sometimes at other times, when someone requests it specifically. But the cup,

* * * * *

81 Eph. 4:10.
82 John 6:22–59; Matt. 15:10–11, 16–20.
83 John 4:23–4.
84 The tabernacle is a receptacle in which the vessels containing the sacrament are kept.
85 2 Kings 18:4: 'And he broke in pieces the bronze serpent that Moses had made, for until those days the people of Israel had burned incense to it.'
86 Matt. 26:26; Mark 14:22; Luke 22:19.
87 1 Cor. 10:16–17.

which is the community of Christ's blood, they allow to no lay person, as if the lowly lay people did not also belong to the community of Christ and did not share in the covenant of his blood. When the delegates of an important ruler come to the pope in Rome, they are so greatly honoured that they are permitted to drink from the cup. These powerful Nimrods[88] honour each other with the legacy of the cross. What? Should we, the servants of the Word and messengers of Christ, refrain from revealing this horror? We are believers and that is why we speak up and say that the mass must be abolished. No honourable oath stands in the way, for the law of God, who is the overlord, is always exempted among Christians. No one can say truthfully 'God lives,' except when he fears and loves God, and would never swear an oath against God. The old founders and sponsors of our collegiate church, who were Christians, wanted to further the honour of God. They did not wish to establish anything that was against God. That is our opinion, and that is how we interpret their undertaking. But if they were ungodly, no Christian has an obligation to fulfil their evil undertaking. A last will that goes against God has no power – their own laws show that – which I want to cite in the case of my own oath. For we preachers instruct no one to go against a vow or oath he has sworn before God; rather, we attest before God that we must not go against God's command for the sake of what is willed by a human. It is true, we advise against living in a monastery and in favour of living a Christian life, that is, in favour of God's rather than man's commandments, in favour of true Christian obedience rather than artificially devised obedience. The former obliges us to serve all human beings, to help everyone, to live according to God's command rather than our own intentions, and to maintain our Christian liberty. The cloistered life, by contrast, requires a temporal type of service, forbidding certain foods on certain days, which are kept on the basis of the devil's teaching (Col. 2, 1 Tim. 4).[89] I will say nothing of the idle manner in which they conduct their superstitious church service, of their greed, or of the burden they place on the poor. One must indeed lead people from the Sodom prevailing in cloisters to the vows made to God, which are of great concern to us.

Furthermore, they write: 'He has forgotten what he said publicly: "and if it rains Lutheran floods, we must nevertheless preserve three things: the sacraments, the hierarchy of the clergy, and the ornaments of the church."'[90]

* * * * *

88 Cf. Gen. 10:8–9: '[Nimrod] was the first on earth to be a mighty man. He was a mighty hunter before the Lord.'
89 Col. 2:8; 1 Tim. 4:1.
90 *Verantwurt*, ll. 89–90.

Did I talk of 'Lutheran floods,' as if we adhered to Luther rather than the Word of God? And they have to make me speak of 'three things,' because rhetoric requires it. If I said that publicly, let anyone who heard it come forward and tell me: 'You said so at such and such a time, in such and such a place.' It is true that I spoke to two canons of baptism and the Lord's Supper as two sacraments, but I spoke to them privately and on their request, saying that those two sacraments should remain, but cleansed and purified, closer to the form in which they appear in scripture. I spoke to them and with those in the higher clergy somewhat more freely about the bread of the Lord. I was prompted by someone who reminded me of the beliefs of Pomponio Leto[91] and other Italian scholars, and I wanted to show him carefully the most certain Truth, such as God will reveal to the whole world in our time, I hope. I did so in private and with the request that they may keep it to themselves, for the common people could not yet understand the shining Truth, just as perhaps my conversation partner was not yet in a position to understand, which I was willing to respect. I did not wish to conceal the Truth, but I wanted to speak to each person at the proper time, for I would rather not shine a light on the sleeper.[92] The blindness of the world has lasted too long. However, I have never spoken in obscure terms before the people of Strasbourg about the adoration of the sacrament and the profitable partaking of it, or about the mass, as I said before. What I said about the authority of the clergy with princes and lords, every citizen in the empire knows, but no citizen has ever heard me say that clerical hierarchy should remain as it is now. Rather, I counselled them to rule their realm well and to establish a fair jurisdiction and government over the Christian community, as is written in Matt. 18, 1 Cor. 5, etc.[93]

As for the ornaments of the church, the reasons and means I used to promote the welfare of the poor is well known, and my definition of true 'church ornaments' was the origin of the papists' ill will against me, for the true church ornaments are in the heart (1 Cor. 6, 1 Pet. 3).[94] Indeed, even canon law forbids silk church ornaments.[95] It may be that, at one point, a

* * * * *

91 The point of reference is unclear. Giulio Pomponio Leto (1425–c.1498), an Italian antiquarian and philologist, taught rhetoric at the University of Rome and presided over intellectual gatherings, the so-called Pomponian Academy.
92 Cf. Eph. 5:13–14: 'Wake up, O sleeper … Christ will shine on you.'
93 Matt. 18:15–19; 1 Cor. 5:9–13.
94 1 Cor. 6:19–20; 1 Peter 3:3–6.
95 Cf. Decretum XXI, 1.4, c.1, deprecating ornate vestments, and specifically those made of silk.

canon often importuned me with accusations that Luther had written a book against monasteries and that I kept my judgment to myself and referred him to scripture and said that no one would give orders to remove possessions by force, for that was what concerned him. I made every effort to win them over to Christ and for that reason suffered them and bore with them but did not wish to speak against the Truth. Why, then, should I have praised church ornaments and clerical authority among those people, when I lamented church ornaments and the ruinous cost associated with them before ecclesiastical rulers when I was a courtier,[96] as many among the low and high nobility can attest?

Next they say in their diatribe: 'It is our firm belief that God will reveal to the people the spirit on which those rebellious preachers pride themselves.'[97] Here they call us rebellious, just as King Ahab called Elijah rebellious,[98] even though it is they alone who disturb the Christian people with their ungodly behaviour and their greed. We consistently preach patience, obedience, and complete equanimity. What authority have we ever destroyed? For no Christian authority could protest against our preference for the supreme authority of God Almighty, our merciful Father, and our desire to put him first and foremost and trust in him to the end. 'Who,' they say, 'did not notice and recognize the final result their sermons produced?'[99] Here you can see their lying statement has been written recently, with the date of 2 March superimposed.[100] For they do not use the future tense, 'the result they will produce,' but the past tense, 'the result they produced.' It is as if they wanted to hold us responsible for the blood that was shed by the poor, as godless men have openly claimed, but against all truth and logic. The praiseworthy city of Strasbourg, and also the poor people themselves who are left here, will attest to the fact that we consistently and earnestly cited (and still cite) passages from the New Testament that confirm secular government, such as Rom. 13, Tit. 3, 1 Tim. 2, 1 Peter 2, Eph. 6, Col. 3, and more of the same.[101] Who caused the disobedience of the people in the Black Forest and elsewhere, where the gospel is not yet being preached, indeed, who for a long time rejected any connection with the Word? And why is there no upheaval here in Strasbourg

* * * * *

96 I.e., when he was in the service of Albert of Brandenburg, Archbishop of Mainz, from 1520–3.
97 *Verantwurt*, l. 97.
98 1 King 18:17.
99 See *Verantwurt* ll. 60–1.
100 Cf. above, note 53.
101 Rom. 13:1–7; Tit. 3:1–2; 1 Tim. 2:1–2; 1 Pet. 2:13–14; Eph. 6:5; Col. 3:22.

and in the Christian city of Zurich, or in other places, where the gospel is being preached? Have there not always been rebellious people? And now these people see an opportunity because many authorities forbid the preaching of the gospel and thus alienate pious minds. That gave evil men an opening to act against the authorities and to incite the people, whereas they would not have had an opportunity to do so if the power of ungodly rulers preventing the preaching of the gospel had not provoked good people with their aggressive action. What Christian can be true to his heart, when he is forcefully turned away from trusting in God? It is true: the poor have used the gospel as a pretense and called themselves Christian brothers, which we criticized with sharp words in their presence and afterwards in their absence in writing. We depicted for them the harm they did to themselves, the wrath of God which they brought upon themselves by inciting rebellion while falsely calling themselves Christians. Unfortunately, it was in vain. The subjects of the city of Strasbourg dispersed on the demand of the honourable council, but the rest, who had also been persuaded to disperse, were kept together by their leader.[102] But neither the trespasses of the poor nor the cruelty of those in power can lessen the Word for those who are good in their hearts. The devil and his followers are in the habit of misusing the Word of God, and yet the seed bears fruit in good hearts.[103]

As for the Spirit on which we pride ourselves, the matter stands thus: Those who are children of God are led by the Spirit of God, for flesh and blood will never possess the kingdom of God. They must be reborn in the Spirit. The member sitting at the right hand of the Father is a new creature in Christ,[104] invisible, the interior person, as created by God, not the external being which will be destroyed. The spirit of God reaffirms and ascertains that we are children of God and allows us to cry from the heart, 'Abba, dear father!'[105] That is what we all pride ourselves on, when we pride ourselves on the grace of God. It creates in us true zeal against all ungodly beings. It was through the spirit that Hezekiah[106] and Josiah[107] did away with the horror of the images, and that Elijah eliminated the priests of Baal,[108] and John the Baptist rebuked Herod.[109] We hope that the same spirit moves the

* * * * *

102 A reference to Erasmus Gerber?
103 Matt. 7:16 and 20; Matt. 12:33; John 15:16.
104 Cf. 2 Cor. 5:17 and Gal. 6:15.
105 Mark 14:35; Rom. 8:15; Gal. 4:6.
106 2 Chron. 29:1–19 and 32:12; Isa. 36:7.
107 2 Kings 23:4–24 and 2 Chron. 34:3–7.
108 1 Kings 18:1–46.
109 Luke 3:19.

Christian government of the city of Strasbourg to remove the images that are being adored and the idols that give offence, and to see to it, as much as they can, that the poor people do not prostitute themselves with stone and wood – a task that is most appropriate for any government. This is the spirit that moved the community of St Aurelia to remove the idolatrous grave,[110] where many sought grace. For our life is saved with Christ in God, and Christ sits at the right hand of God in heaven. We are citizens [of his kingdom] spiritually, we are attached to [the heavenly kingdom] and seek only God's honour, who is our merciful Father and does not suffer sharing with a stinking grave what belongs only to God. God is the living fountain and spring of grace; dust and the foul ashes of bones have no grace in them, except that the bones of the saints will be covered with the cloth of eternity on their day.[111]

This Spirit commands us to profess Christ as the only mediator with the only God (1 Cor. 8),[112] and to save his mother's honour from godless people and to prevent her being made into an idol, for anyone who calls on Mary for grace denies her Son, through whom alone we have grace, according to the testimony of God. But those flattering authors of the response make of her a queen of heaven, which they take from Jeremiah, chapter 44[113] or from heathen books, and they call on her as a patroness of the city of Strasbourg, an idea that has its origin perhaps in the ordinances of a secular court, which allows the accused a patron, or before a soft-hearted judge, a patroness. But Christians know that they are children of God through Christ. If they are accused, they will be justified by God and will never be condemned. For Christ died and rose again and represents us at the right hand of God. Anyone who believes has already passed from death to life and needs no other patron or patroness. Mary, the virgin full of grace, has indeed given birth to the Saviour who represents us before the Father, but she is neither our salvation nor our patroness. That is the role of her Son alone. We have learned that from simple parables and need no acute warning or subtle touches, which are needful at all times to those liars in their response. Our speech must necessarily be foolish to those in the flesh. We speak in simplicity of spiritual matters, which must be folly before worldly wisdom.[114] Thus we teach the gospel, not heretical error under the guise of the gospel, as the commissar-

* * * * *

110 At St Aurelia; see above, note 36.
111 Cf. 2 Cor. 5:4.
112 1 Cor. 8:4–6.
113 Jer. 44:16–25.
114 1 Cor. 1:18–31.

ies claim.[115] Therefore, while they brag that they have preached the gospel
for many years in accordance with the best understanding and for peaceful
ends, rather than in the way we preach, we say that no one must believe
anything but what we have preached, even if an angel from heaven were to
announce a different gospel.[116] For those who set up a divine service on the
basis of human teaching, who insist on the difference between foods, on the
keeping of special days, on splitting up the Christian community, those who
sing in church, using Latin before Germans, who give out that vigils, masses,
and other such things are meritorious works, and direct the poor people to
call upon the intercession of the saints and to adore the images, those people who seek faith always in the blasphemous commands of the papal bulls
rather than believing in the kind precepts of the biblical books, they are the
ones preaching a different gospel.

We, the preachers of Strasbourg, offer to give an account of our hopes
to anyone who asks, and we ask learned and unlearned people alike, for the
sake of God's mercy, not to blaspheme the name of God in us and to correct
their misconceptions about us, especially these commissaries and old Jakob
Wimpheling of Sélestat,[117] who cuts us up badly in his paltry verses, and the
scholars of Freiburg, some of whom were our teachers and preceptors.[118] We
hope that their beliefs do not differ from ours, for they too have read scripture and know that in matters concerning God, we must obey God rather
than human beings. Indeed, we offer to debate our hopes with all people,
learned or unlearned, who believe in the Word of God. For it is proper for
an honest man to conduct his business with anyone openly and refrain from
criticizing in secret what has been done well and lawfully. If we have taught
anything but Christ in Strasbourg, and if we have attached the pious simple
people to us with rebellious heresy and our own stories, let us fare according

* * * * *

115 See above, note 56.
116 Cf. Gal. 1:6–9.
117 Jakob Wimpheling (1450–1528) of Sélestat, studied in Freiburg, Erfurt and Hei-
     delberg (MA 1471; licence in theology 1496), where he taught in the Faculty of
     Art. From 1484–98 Wimpheling lived in Speyer, where he had a benefice and
     was, for a time, cathedral preacher. He then returned to teach in Heidelberg un-
     til 1501, when he relinquished his position and retired to the Williamite monas-
     tery in Strasbourg to devote himself to studies. Wimpheling was at the centre of
     a literary society that included Beatus Rhenanus, Paul Volz, Johannes Sapidus,
     and Lazarus Schürer. He was a staunch Catholic and, in old age, complained of
     isolation.
118 See below, Epp. 246d and 246e, Capito's requests to the University and to the
     city of Freiburg, respectively, to have this apologia posted.

to divine law, Deut. 13.[119] May they punish us bodily as we deserve, let them have no mercy on us.

Thus I, Wolfgang Capito, minister of the Word in the Christian community of Strasbourg, ask all believers who await the resurrection of Christ Jesus not to be upset, for God's sake, by the uncontrolled blasphemy of our accusers and the gossip of other godless people who, through their attacks on us poor men, blaspheme the Word of the Lord. Rather, let them look upon the glory of God, whose representatives we are, and not on our feeble persons, who are well aware of our nothingness. Let them instead think of the Truth made flesh in the Word of God, and what it requires of us rather than what human vanity deserves. For God wants us to look only upon his Word and upon himself, to believe in him alone, to fear him and adore him, as he has commanded. Given at Strasbourg, on the 8th day of August 1525.

Letter 246b: 10 August 1525, Strasbourg, The Strasbourg Preachers to the City Council of Strasbourg

Printed in BDS 2:468–9 (cf. summary in CorrBucer 2:30, Ep. 99).

[*Summary*]: These are the minutes of an oral presentation by the preachers to the city council concerning the institution of a marriage tribunal, schools, rural parishes, the abolition of the mass, and the antagonism between princes and cities.

Letter 246c: 22 September 1525, Strasbourg, Capito to the City Council of Haguenau

The manuscript of this letter is in AST 22–3. This is one of a series of requests (see also below, Epp. 246d and e) to counterbalance the representations of the exiles by publicizing Capito's own account, as given in Ep. 246a above.

Honourable, wise lords: first, I wish you knowledge of God and his Christ, and offer you my willing services.

Honourable, wise lords: Three slanderous priests have brought serious accusations against the praiseworthy council of Strasbourg, the collegiate church of St Thomas, and myself through a false announcement under the

* * * * *

119 Deut. 13:5, 8–9.

deceptive title of an apologia.[1] I understand that it was posted in your city and remained posted on the doors of churches for several days. Thus it is my urgent request, since this calumny was read by the public, to allow this messenger, or anyone else to whom you give the command, to burn it publicly, and to post our rightful and true response. For as the son of a citizen [of Haguenau] I wish to proclaim my and other people's innocence to my fatherland and my fellow citizens, and to defend the divine truth, which was also impugned. This is my obligation as a Christian and should not offend any good person. If you are willing to oblige me, I will, in fairness, oblige you in turn. Given at Strasbourg on the 22nd of September in the year 1525.

Since much counsel is taken on behalf of the gospel, I send Your Honours an announcement recently made by the margraves, my lords Casimir and Georg, in which the matter is discussed in some depth.[2]

Letter 246d: 4 October 1525, Strasbourg, Capito to the University of Freiburg

The manuscript of this letter is in AST 22–3. The university received the letter on 6 October, as recorded in the protocol of the senate (Freiburg, Universitäts-archiv A 10/5). The senate gave an oral reply to Capito's messenger, denying his request to post Capito's justification in answer to the accusations posted by the exiles. They furthermore contacted the Freiburg city council (cf. also Capito's letter to the city council, Ep. 246e below), pointing out certain heretical statements in his justification. On 28 October a proposal was put forward in the senate 'to strike the names Wolfgang Capito, Caspar Hegio [i.e., Hedio], Matthew [Zell] of Kaysersberg and Matthäus [Alber] of Reutlingen from the matriculation records because they did not favour Catholic doctrine' (page 142 of the senate protocol). A decision was deferred, however, because the university wanted to keep a low profile. Enrolment was at an all-time low, and they feared that their actions 'might be misrepresented by certain competitors and used against our university, when there is already a dearth of students' (ibid., 139).

* * * * *

1 Capito uses the word *Entschuldigong*; the title is *Verantwort*. Cf. above, Ep. 246a headnote.
2 On Casimir of Hohenzollern, see above, Ep. 221, note 3. The memorandum on twenty-three articles in which the reformers differed from the Catholics was published in 1524; for the text, see CorrBucer 1:271–4, Ep. 76. George Margrave of Brandenburg (1484–1583) actively encouraged the Reformation in his territory. He was in correspondence with Luther and supported the Lutherans at the Diet of Augsburg in 1530.

Most respected, excellent lords and teachers! In these last days I have been vilified by the most atrocious abuse and lies promulgated in the name of three priests.[1] I have provided a light antidote to remedy this indignity, abstaining from retaliation, as behooves a Christian.[2] I have merely shown the most basic truth of our cause, leaving judgment to the fair readers. Since I acknowledge you as my teachers and friends, I ask you to read the justification of your respectful disciple, for you have recently read the aspersions cast on me, which were published with such arrogance, not only in Freiburg but also in other cities of this realm. May Your Excellencies show favour to this messenger and allow him to affix my justification to the doors of the church and the college. For I will not refuse to defend myself in this matter before a suitable judge, if anyone should challenge me. Farewell in our Christ, who may increase the light of his knowledge in your hearts. Strasbourg, 4 October, in the year, etc. '25.

Yours, Wolfgang Capito.

Letter 246e: [ca. 4 October, 1525, Strasbourg], Capito to the City Council of Freiburg

> The manuscript of this letter is in AST 22–3. For the context see above, Ep. 246d headnote. The city council did not reply to Capito personally, but wrote instead to their colleagues on the council of Strasbourg, warning them 'not to bring such pamphlets into the city of Freiburg, or they would take measures against any messenger carrying such pamphlet' (Protocol of the Senate, Universitätsarchiv Freiburg, A 10/5, 140). In consultation with the university (see above, Ep. 246d headnote), the city council then publicly burned Capito's justification.

Noble, strict, honourable and wise lords, since an abusive publication was recently issued and posted in your city against the collegiate church of St Thomas in Strasbourg and against me, Capito, we have duly answered, without abuse, to spare ourselves and the patient reader. We therefore beg Your Honours to oblige us by posting our reply in turn in your city. It does not impugn anyone's reputation or respectability who is otherwise a man of honour. We offer to defend ourselves also before the law. I will gladly and duly repay the favour to Your Honours, as far as I can. Given.

Wolfgang Capito, provost of St Thomas.

* * * * *

1 Cf. above, Ep. 246a headnote.
2 I.e., *Von drey Straßburger Pfaffen* (Ep. 246a).

Letter 247: [ca. 8 October 1525, Strasbourg], Capito and the Strasbourg Preachers to Martin Luther

Printed in WABr 3:585–7, Ep. 930 and CorrBucer 2:46–7, Ep. 105.

[*Summary*]: The preachers of Strasbourg send Gregor Caselius[1] to present their views on the Sacramentarian controversy. The dissension among the reformers has been detrimental to the church in France, the Low Countries, and Germany. They ask Luther to give Caselius a friendly reception.

Letter 248: 8 October 1525, Strasbourg, Capito to Johann Bugenhagen

The letter was carried to Wittenberg by Caselius (see preceding letter). The text is printed in O. Vogt, ed., *Dr Johann Bugenhagens Briefwechsel* (Stettin, 1888; repr. Hildesheim, 1966), 32–50, Ep. 15. For Bugenhagen, see CWC 1, Ep. 135, note 6.

[*Summary*]: The Strasbourg preachers have sent Gregor Caselius to discuss the Sacramentarian controversy with Luther, but Capito wishes to be more specific about his position, in the hope that Bugenhagen will make a personal effort to achieve concord among the reformers. So far, the reformers have acted in concert. Now, however, the peace has been disturbed, first by those who incited the peasants to rebellion, and then by the tyrannical lords who, encouraged by Luther's book [*Wider die räuberischen und mörderischen Rotten der Bauern*], took cruel revenge on them. Some six thousand people perished as a result. Capito has offered a suitable interpretation of Luther's book and has refrained from criticizing it to avoid giving the impression of dissension among the reformers. The Strasbourgers have been accused of boorishness in spite of the fact that they have urged the city council for two years now to found a college for the study of languages and rhetoric. Erasmus has undermined the gospel by writing against Luther, asserting free will. Capito did not write a reply to Erasmus, because he received no encouragement from Luther when enquiring about the matter. Now Karlstadt is causing uproar in Wittenberg, and attributing views to Luther, which he never advocated: that Christ was not God, that the people had the right to destroy images without

* * * * *

1 Gregor Caselius (d. ca. 1528) studied at Wittenberg and taught Hebrew at Strasbourg. Caselius returned from his mission after 5 November (the date of Luther's reply to the Strasburgers, entrusted to him, cf. below, Ep. 252a) and presented his report in Strasbourg ca. 29 November (cf. CorrBucer 2:71, Ep. 113).

the permission of the magistrate, that infant baptism was wrong. Finally, he has pronounced on the question of the Eucharist, which was discussed previously in Zurich. Capito has sent all the relevant writings and the correspondence that passed between him and Zwingli on the subject to Luther. The Wittenbergers have always emphasized that faith was the decisive factor in taking communion, but until the return of Caselius, the Strasbourg preachers will discourage any more detailed inquiry into the question of the Real Presence. Capito greatly regrets the aggressive tone of Luther's pamphlet against Karlstadt. Balthasar Hubmaier appeared on the scene, preaching Anabaptism. The disagreement over the two issues – baptism and the Eucharist – has disturbed people a great deal. Bugenhagen's letter to the church of Wrocław on the Eucharist contributed to the dissension. In defending Zwingli's opinion against Bugenhagen, Capito does not wish to be adversarial. In Capito's view, the word *est* ('is') [in *hoc est corpus meum*] means 'signifies,' that is, it is a trope. Yet he does not believe in being too inquisitive and investigating the matter too closely. It is enough to remember Christ's suffering, death, and resurrection, and to celebrate the Eucharist in remembrance of him. The cup is a sign; we are delivered from our sins through faith. 'We eat only the bread as a sign of his body' (*tantum panem signum corporis edimus*), the words *benedicere pani* do not mean 'to consecrate the bread,' but 'to thank God for the bread.' Sharing the bread, Christians become one in Christ. They are redeemed by faith, not by eating bread transformed by some miracle into Christ. Capito does not wish to become involved in a dispute about such things, which contributes nothing to salvation. He urges Bugenhagen to work for peace and unity in the church.

Letter 248a: [Before 13 October 1525, Strasbourg], Gervasius Sopher to Capito

> The manuscript of this letter is in AST 19 ('ad 54'). For Sopher see above, Ep. 246a, note 14. At this time Capito began negotiations about relinquishing his provostship and canonry and retaining only his position as preacher of Young St Peter. When he approached Sopher with an offer to cede the benefices to him or his sons under certain conditions, the latter took legal counsel (cf. the lawyer's letter in AST 19: 52). The reservations voiced in the present letter reflect (and in some cases repeat) the legal advice he received. The proposed transaction did not take place, however. Apparently the chapter had reservations about electing Sopher (cf. AST 19, #53). Instead, Capito ceded the provostship to Lorenz Schenckbecher (cf. below, Ep. 248c).

As it is my lord provost's will for me and my children to consider the acquisition of his canonry and the provostship of St Thomas, he has proposed the following conditions to me:

First, that I should give over and pay 800 gulden. Specifically, I should pay 300 gulden in cash and thereafter 60 gulden every year until 500 gulden, in addition to the initial payment of 300 gulden, shall have been submitted to my lord provost or his heirs.

Also, 10 gulden in alms from the provostship.

Also, 10 gulden in alms from the prebend.

Also, that the house associated with the provosthip should, under the conditions discussed, be left to [Capito] for the remainder of his life.

In response, I say firstly, taking into consideration the overall financial situation and the dangerous nature of the times, it is extremely difficult to pay out such a large amount – 300 gulden – in cash all at once and take such a risk. Thus, in these tricky affairs, I, along with my entire household, would like to cover our annual needs for three or four years,[1] come what may, or receive an annuity of approximately 30 gulden as an investment return, etc. Otherwise I might suffer during a time of need or an outbreak of the plague (which is likely to occur soon) or any other misfortune.

Second, I find that the chapter will not heed or respond to anyone regarding the fruits of a prebend unless he has his provision and confirmation, which can only be obtained from the Roman curia. As a result, 100 gulden would be needed for annates, and at least 60 gulden would have to be spent for the purpose of expediting the letter of provision and confirmation.

Further, Abel[2] or the margraves of Brandenburg are still a source of concern. We thus need to be extremely vigilant here, for unexpected and tricky practices and setbacks might still occur in reference to the provostship. Envy is great, and events are changeable.

And even if this does not occur, my son might still have to forgo the use of both the prebend and the provostship for the next three years.[3]

The reason is that he must have, as previously mentioned, at least 100 gulden in order to go to Rome.[4]

* * * * *

1 *ein jar dry oder viere myn lybsnarung haben.*
2 I.e., Jacob Abel, a claimant to the provostship. Cf. CWC 1, Ep. 50 headnote.
3 A reference to the regulation that part of the income in the first three years (the so-called *annus gratiae,* followed by the *biennium*) was to go into the common chest.
4 I.e., it may be necessary to expedite the necessary legal papers in person.

Also, there is the matter of the *biennium*,[5] according to which he must give up 50 gulden over two years, or 25 gulden per year.

Also, 34 gulden for statutes.

Also, 22 gulden for *valete*.[6]

Also, he can only collect half the residence fee.

He must give 10 gulden and 10 florins in alms.

He may only lay claim to the usufruct of the provostship a year after the Feast of Purification.[7]

He must give out at least 10 gulden every year to the almoner.[8]

Every year he must give 12 gulden out of 300 in taxes or, if there is a shortage, 36 gulden every three years.

If corn remains cheap, he must supply a great deal. And if it is dear, it is unpleasant, for where there is nothing, the emperor has lost his privilege.[9] Thus, not an increase, but rather a continued decrease of the chapter's income is expected, just as is obviously already happening to the prebend every day.

First, there is the 200 gulden that must be given to the pastor at St Aurelia.

Also, 200 gulden to the pastor of St Thomas.

Also, 80 gulden to the pastor of St Nicolaus, which must come out of the common purse of the chapter.

Through these things the prebends are reduced in value.

Also, it ought to be taken into account that in any given year, many of the chapter's rental estates either lie fallow or their rents are greatly reduced on account of a lack of people.

Also, there are the penny taxes, which are reduced daily because of the reduction in fields.

Also, there now exists a great deal of uncertainty regarding what sort of existence the chapter will continue to have, or how it will be dealt with in the future, and what changes or ordinances might be enacted regarding it, etc.

* * * * *

5 Cf. note 3. The *biennium* was originally applied to costs associated with the vineyard, then used for other common expenses. Cf. Charles Schmidt, *Histoire de Chapitre de Saint-Thomas de Strasbourg* (Strasbourg, 1860), 118.

6 The papal signature or a final, personal decision by the pope.

7 The Feast of the Purification is on 2 February.

8 *Portator*, originally the man who took alms to the poor people waiting at the gate.

9 German Proverb. Cf. www.sprichwoerter.net: 'Wo nichts ist, hat der Kaiser sein Recht verloren.'

Also, one might earn 6 pounds from the house, once expenses are deducted, but my lord provost retains possession of it.

These and other matters perhaps ought to be taken into consideration, particularly in these dangerous and worrisome times, in which nothing is more certain in the future than great wars, pestilence, and high prices, as well as in view of the current scarcity of cash. Thus, the key, as people say, is not to expose oneself to risk. And since my lord desires to bestow favour and goodwill upon me and my children, for which you will find us thankful, ...[10]

First, that Your Honour should make every effort to place the canonry and the house into the hands of my son with the following conditions, namely that I should pay 200 gulden in cash as soon as the canonry is resigned and my son comes into possession of it.

Also, that an additional 200 gulden would be paid over the next seven years, specifically 30 gulden every year and then in the seventh year 20 gulden.

Also, 10 measures of corn will be paid given as alms during the remainder of the provost's life, as a kind of pension.

Also, for the provostship, 100 gulden in cash.

Also, another 100 gulden to be paid over the next seven years, 15 gulden every year and in the last year 10 gulden.

Also, 10 gulden in alms, for the remainder of the provost's life as a pension, etc.

Also, the house of the provost would belong to him for the remainder of his life or that of my son ...[11]

Letter 248b: [before 13 October 1525, Strasbourg], Capito to Gervasius Sopher

The manuscript of this letter is in AST 19, #50. For the context, see the preceding letter.

I have not yet entirely completed the planned transaction to which I commit-

* * * * *

10 The manuscript is damaged. The gist of the text here is a request for more moderate terms.
11 Damage to the manuscript does not allow a precise translation of the remainder. In addition to charging Capito with the responsibility for the upkeep of the house, it deals with the potential for a situation arising in which Sopher's son might be prevented in some manner from attaining the canonry. It also addresses the possibility of his premature death and the termination of payments in that case.

ted myself with that man.[1] For the man I found to stand bail has introduced some delay. Thus, the need for caution and secrecy. I would like to meet with him tomorrow or the day after tomorrow, for I would like to benefit you more than anyone else.

Capito.

Letter 248c: [ca. 13 October 1525, Strasbourg], Capito to Gervasius Sopher

The manuscript of this letter is in AST 19, #49. This short note, like Epp. 248a and 248b above, concerns Capito's plans to resign the provostship. After negotiations with Gervasius Sopher failed, the provostship went to Lorenz Schenckbecher (for biographical information see above, Ep. 237, note 23). In a statement on his resignation (below, Appendix 1c), Capito emphasized that he had considered giving up the provostship as early as 1524. 'Distracted by various troubles,' he delayed the decision until 13 October 1525. On that date he resigned the provostship in the presence of the chapter, which then unanimously elected Schenckbecher. The conditions set out in Capito's resignation specify that the income of the provostship would be paid to Capito during his lifetime to allow him to continue his charitable activities. These conditions were, however, modified. Cf. the ongoing negotiations documented below, in Epp. 367b and 367c. Capito in turn, agreed to indemnify Schenckbecher for costs arising from any legal proceedings started by Jakob Abel, an old rival claimant to the provostship (see CWC 1, Ep. 50 headnote). Capito reserved the right of regress and, indeed, resumed the provostship (cf. AST 19, #60, of 1538 [?] and AST 19, #78 of 13 December 1540).

Greeting. I shall be there soon, at nine, as agreed with our mutual friend Lorenz.[1] Make sure that a notary is called in, for the dean will neglect to do it, I know. He is amazingly lax, although otherwise a good and upright man. Furthermore, let me have your 300 gulden as soon as possible.[2] For it is now public that I will give up (indeed, have given up) my provostship. Everyone will want to be paid the money owed. My reputation will suffer unless I pay in time what I have promised to pay. For I will give up the provostship today, as quickly as possible; and I shall also cede the canonry. Therefore do not burden me with worries about those 300 gulden, lest I should rue confer-

* * * * *

1 The nature of the transaction is unknown.

1 Schenckbecher.
2 For the canonry? Was its sale to Sopher still contemplated?

ring the benefice on you. For if you show ill will right at the beginning, what can I expect from our future relationship? Most of all, make sure that the notary is on time.

Capito.

Letter 248d: [after 15 October 1525, Strasbourg], The Chapter of St Thomas to [Wilhelm von Honstein]

The manuscript of this letter in AST 19, #61. For the date, see the document concerning Capito's resignation in the Appendix 1c. The letter is a request to the Bishop of Strasbourg to endorse the chapter's election of Lorenz Schenckbecher as their provost. Apparently the bishop did not act on the request (cf. below, Ep. 367b). For the negotiations preceding Schenckbecher's election, see above, Epp. 248a–148c. For Wilhelm von Honstein, see CWC 1, Ep. 174.

Most reverend father in God, gracious lord, first we offer Your Grace, our gracious lord, the humble service we owe you.

In obedience to Your Grace, Doctor Wolfgang Capito has resigned his provostship into our hands – the vice-dean[1] and chapter – in favour of Master Lorenz Schenckbecher.[2] We have accepted his resignation at last without difficulty, in the hope that it will lead to the pacification of our collegiate church, which now suffers grave harm from the ill will and disagreement among its members. Furthermore, Master Lorenz resides at the collegiate church and loyally looks after the business of the collegiate church, whereas Doctor Capito is more burdened with preaching and therefore cannot adequately look after the needs of the collegiate church, as the statutes enjoin him.[3] We therefore unanimously elected Master Lorenz Schenckbecher as our provost and prelate, invested him, and gave him possession through our vice-dean, in the humble certainty that Your Princely Grace will be agreeable. For you are pleased to see our collegiate church prosperous and at peace. We hope that you will, as our gracious lord and bishop, endorse and confirm our transaction, as did your predecessors and as you yourself graciously offered after the old provost had departed. For sending to Rome in these times, as

* * * * *

1 Martin von Baden. See CWC 1, 262.
2 For Schenckbecher, see above, Ep. 237, note 21.
3 A diplomatic formulation. Capito himself gives different reasons for his resignation. See Appendix 1c.

was the practice in former years, would bring upon us much trouble and difficulty with the laity, as Your Princely Grace may graciously see for himself. We therefore beg you humbly and earnestly to confirm our provost, and offer you due obedience and service in turn. Herewith we commend ourselves to Your Princely Grace. May God grant you a long life and felicitous reign. Given at Strasbourg.

Your Princely Grace's humble and obedient vice-dean and chapter of St Thomas at Strasbourg.

Letter 249: 27 October 1525, Strasbourg, Capito to Johannes Oecolampadius

Printed in BrOek 1:405–7, Ep. 291.

[*Summary*]: Oecolampadius will find it easy to argue against transubstantiation (*impanatio Dei*), which has no foundation in scripture. Karlstadt, who acted out of personal ambition, has now recanted and has been reconciled with Luther. Franciscus Irenicus reports that Melanchthon will go to Nürnberg to help with the organization of a school there. Jakob Otter has reported to Bucer a decision by the Count Palatine to permit the preaching of the gospel. Otter agrees with Oecolampadius concerning the Eucharist. Bucer has urged other disciples of Oecolampadius to support their teacher. 'Antonius Peregrinus' [pseudonym for Lefèvre d'Etaples] has read Oecolampadius' writings and approves of them. Capito will report on the success of Caselius' mission on his return (cf. above, Ep. 247). He has written to Claude Chansonnette, whom he believes to be a supporter of Oecolampadius. Luther has written [*Eyn sermon von der zerstörung Jerusalem*], threatening princes who do not support the gospel with a dire fate. Capito's wife sends her greetings. He offers Oecolampadius hospitality, if needed. In a postscript, Capito asks for details about Pellicanus' criticism of 'Bilea' [pseudonym of Erasmus]. He is at a loss what to write to Tilman Limperger, whose words are self-incriminating. He wishes he could speak with Oecolampadius in person and is reluctant to write more plainly.

Letter 250: 28 October 1525, Strasbourg, Capito to Ulrich Zwingli

Printed in ZwBr 2:404–6, Ep. 400.

[*Summary*]: Karlstadt has recanted his views on the Eucharist [see preceding letter], pretending that he had no intention to make definite pronouncements on the matter. Capito sneers at Luther's connivance with this interpretation. He notes that both men took aim at Zwingli. Capito intends to publish Karlstadt's recantation and Luther's preface to it, with an appropriate preface and commentary.[1] He warns Zwingli to be moderate in his writings. 'We seem to have obtained the concession that the clause about faith is not necessary and that Luther himself does not believe in the transubstantiation of the bread (*deum impanatum*).' Capito has written to Bugenhagen [cf. above, Ep. 248]. He assumes that the other Wittenbergers have read his letter as well. Capito will inform Zwingli of their reaction as soon as Caselius returns. Ludwig V, Count Palatine, has opted for the Reformation and allows the preaching of the gospel. The matter will be discussed at the Diet of Augsburg.[2] In a postscript, Capito conveys greetings from Bucer, Hedio, and Farel to Zwingli, Myconius, and Leo Jud.

Letter 251: [ca. 5 November 1525], Wittenberg, Justus Jonas to Capito

Printed in CorrBucer 2:72, Ep. 113. This is a message from Jonas to Capito relayed by Gregor Caselius upon his return from Wittenberg. It runs: 'Jonas to Capito: It is a great thing to be mortified and humiliated. I prefer to be an ignorant disciple of Luther than share in the fame of those men. He will write when there is an opportunity and wonders why Capito has not written to him.'

Letter 252: 5 November 1525, Wittenberg, Martin Luther to Capito

Printed in WABr 3:602–3, Ep. 941. Bucer complained that this letter was first published anonymously in a German translation (Nürnberg, 1527) without giving any context, i.e., without also publishing the letter of the Strasbourgers to Luther, carried by Gregor Caselius.

[*Summary*]: Luther is glad to hear the Strasbourgers' praise of Zwingli and Oecolampadius, whom they call 'holy men.' He makes no such claims for himself, but does take credit for being the first to bring Christ to the people. He does not agree with Zwingli's pronouncements on original sin. It is pos-

* * * * *

1 An edition appeared from the press of Knobloch in Strasbourg, 1525, but without any contribution from Capito.
2 The diet was so poorly attended that it was deferred to Speyer, 1526.

sible that he himself is in error, but they are equally liable to error. Caselius
will report his views in more detail [cf. Ep. 252a].

Letter 252a: 5 November 1525, Wittenberg, Martin Luther to [the Strasbourg Preachers]

The text of this letter, formally addressed to Caselius and containing Luther's
message to the Strasbourg preachers, is printed in WABr 3: 603–7, Ep. 942, and
CorrBucer 2:56–9, Ep. 111.

[*Summary*]: Luther charges Caselius with relating to the Strasbourg preachers 'what he has heard and seen' as well as relaying to them the following
message: He prefers peace, but cannot be silent in view of Zwingli's and
Oecolampadius' publications [concerning the Eucharist], which are disturbing the church of Wittenberg. He agrees that it is desirable to abstain from
abuse, but he must condemn what he regards as wrong. He in turn finds
the terms used by the Strasbourgers offensive [see also below, Ep. 253]. He
rejects the idea of keeping the common people from discussing the nature
of the Eucharist. The Sacramentarian question is crucial: 'It is necessary [to
judge whether] they or we are the ministers of Satan.' There is no middle
position. He will not allow the Strasbourgers to dissimulate about their differences of opinion. They have not convinced him that the word *est* is a trope
and stands for *significat*. The examples they give are not cogent. He asks them
to abstain from teaching their 'errors,' which he likens to the 'madness of the
Arians.' He insists on his moral right to be assertive.

Letter 253: 5 November 1525, Wittenberg, Johann Bugenhagen to Capito

The text is quoted in full in BrOek 1:424, note 2.

[*Summary*]: Bugenhagen supports peace among the reformers, but the Wittenbergers have taught only what can be found in scripture. He is offended
by Capito's terms *esculentus Deus* ('edible God'), *impanatus Deus* ('God in
bread'), and *carnivorae* ('meat-eaters), which he uses in the interpretation of
the Eucharist. He bears Capito and his colleagues much good will, but cannot accept their 'twisted' interpretation.

Letter 254: 8 November 1525, Strasbourg, Capito to Petrus Wickram

The manuscript of this letter is in the Staatsbibliothek, Munich, ms. clm. 10.357,
#24. For Petrus Wickram see CWC 1, Ep. 72 headnote.

Greetings, my father.

Felix Ulscenius[1] has been arrested by the governors of the province.[2] Ulscenius is a pious and virtuous young man, who professes the gospel, and whose life and education have always been above suspicion. I am told that this most innocent man has been miserably tortured, and I fear that this torture for his confession of faith and his Christian virtue will bring much evil to that region. For God lives and reigns as an avenger of innocent blood. It will therefore be your task, my father, to admonish the judges concerning their duty, mercy, and piety, reminding them that they have to give an account to the living God. This may prevent them from making even more atrocious plans against Ulscenius, when his opponents try to incite them against him. They are mostly of the knightly estate and preoccupied with worldly matters and, after the recent danger of the peasant revolts, rather severe and unfair to those who profess Christ, for the rebellious mob have made Christ the pretense for their perfidy, creating a scandal. You, however, are well known. You have a reputation and, indeed, possess knowledge of sacred matters, and you fully understand what advantages and disadvantages the [profession of] the gospel can bring to the community. On account of the respect you command as a doctor and parish priest you will be able, and indeed have a duty, to come to the aid of a brother in trouble. At least use your authority firmly to advise personal friends, lest they bring upon themselves the judgment of the Lord for their inhumane and impious treatment of that blessed man. Farewell and obey the Word of the Lord, my father and brother. Strasbourg, 8 November 1525.

W. Fabritius Capito.

Letter 255: 9 November 1525, [Sélestat], Paulus Phrygio to Capito

The manuscript of this letter is in the Universitätsbibliothek, Basel, Ki.Ar. 25a, 60. For Phrygio see CWC 1, Ep. 44 headnote.

Grace be with you. Your letter,[1] my dear Capito, is very sweet and has brought me great consolation. I feel that you are my only friend, for I have been deserted by almost everyone. I am living in a lion's den.[2] If only the

* * * * *

1 For Ulscenius, see CWC 1, Ep. 70 headnote. Oecolampadius reports his death in a letter dated 15 November 1525 (MBW T2, Ep. 429).
2 The *Landvogt* was Hans Jacob von Mörsburg.

1 Not extant.
2 Cf. Dan. 6.

grace of God would deliver me in the future. There is little hope here, but may the Lord's will be done rather than mine.[3] You remind me, and rightly so, that we must attribute nothing to human wisdom, for the Lord destroys the wisdom of the wise and lays low the prudence of the prudent.[4] God alone works everything in everybody, his word will last forever. Truly, Christ had to die and rise again. I would like you to reflect on the diverse forms of grace in the same spirit.

My dear Capito, I am not my own master. The Lord rules my heart and lips. Far be it from me to attempt or say or do anything without Holy Scripture, so help me God. In everything that befalls me, I entrust myself to God. May he do with me as is his will, as long as he saves me through faith in the Word.[5] May he open my eyes and allow me to recognize his will, justification, and judgment. If it were to please God, I wish I could be elsewhere. Farewell. May God be your comfort. Share with me some time what you have read in Habakkuk.[6] Farewell. Tuesday before St Martin, in the year 1525.

Yours, Phrygio.

Letter 256: 14 November 1525, [Strasbourg], Capito to Ulrich Zwingli

Printed in ZwBr 2:426, Ep. 408.

[*Summary*]: He will see about the apothecary [see below, Ep. 258]. The Wittenbergers answered their request for advice [on the Sacramentarian question] with slanderous accusations. It is rumoured that [Albert of Brandenburg], the archbishop of Mainz, has married. Capito is pleased with Zwingli's response to Bugenhagen, although some pages were missing from the copy he sent. He hopes that the bookseller will send Zwingli's books to the printer Wolfgang Köpfel soon. He sends greetings to Myconius.

Letter 257: 18 November 1525, [Strasbourg], Capito to Andreas Osiander

Printed in *Andreas Osiander: Gesamtausgabe* (Gütersloh, 1975–), 2: 201–4.

[*Summary*]: Capito has heard that the Strasbourg preachers are being criti-

* * * * *

3 Luke 22:42.
4 1 Cor. 1:19.
5 Luke 1:38.
6 For Capito's commentary on Habakkuk, cf. below, Ep. 279.

cized for failing to subscribe to the views of the Wittenberg theologians. He denies that they support the Anabaptists. Concerning the Eucharist, he refuses to take a stand, for fear of creating strife. The Eucharist is a holy mystery. If it were necessary to understand it in detail, God would have revealed those details.

Letter 258: 20 November 1525, [Strasbourg], Capito to Ulrich Zwingli

Printed in ZwBr 2:427–31, Ep. 409.

[*Summary*]: He has not yet received an answer with regards to placing the provost's son with an apothecary [as an apprentice]. If the provost can afford to do so, he should be liberal in paying for his son's board. The peasant rebels have caused much upheaval and are being treated cruelly by the local lords. Capito asks about the disputation with the Anabaptists in Zurich. The Strasbourg preachers are vigilant, and Capito is wrongly accused of favouring the Anabaptist belief. The theologians of Wittenberg bring slanderous accusations against the Strasbourg preachers. A young man fromWittenberg recently wrote to Jakob Bedrot, deploring the fact that the latter lived in Strasbourg among 'the haters of literature.' Another writer from Nürnberg accused them of heretical views on the Eucharist. They have refrained from pronouncements and do not believe that it is essential for salvation to define the nature of the Eucharist. They have asked for a public disputation with their accusers in the Palatinate. Gregor Caselius, whom the Strasbourgers sent to Wittenberg to negotiate peace with Luther, has started on his return journey. Capito asks Zwingli to send his writings to Strasbourg [to be printed by Köpfel; see above, Ep. 256]. He counsels moderation and assures Zwingli of his desire for peace. In a postscript, Capito conveys greetings from Guillaume Farel, Martin Bucer, Antonius Peregrinus [pseudonym for Jacques Lefèvre], Tolnius [pseudonym for Gérard Roussel], Jean Védaste, and Simon Robert of Tournai. Capito sends greetings to Myconius and Leo Jud.

Letter 259: 22 November 1525, Schwäbisch-Hall, Johannes Brenz to Capito and Martin Bucer

Printed in CorrBucer 2:59–70, Ep. 112. Johannes Brenz (1494–1570) studied at Heidelberg (MA 1518) and became preacher in Schwäbisch-Hall in 1522, where he promoted the cause of the Reformation. He drafted church ordinances for Hall, Magdeburg, and Nürnberg and, from 1534, advised Duke Ulrich of Würtemberg on church matters and on reforming the University of Tübingen. After the defeat of the Schmalkaldic League by the imperial troops, he fled to Basel.

In 1553 he became provost and preacher of the collegiate church in Stuttgart.

[*Summary*]: Brenz is surprised that the Strasbourg preachers are offended by the principled reaction of the Wittenberg theologians. They seem unwilling to grant to others the freedom of interpretation they demand for themselves. Brenz favours religious peace, but not at the cost of concealing one's beliefs in order to present a united front to outsiders. He cannot accept their characterization of the discussion about the nature of the Eucharist as frivolous (*curiosae quaestiones*), nor can he subscribe to their interpretation of the phrase 'this is my body' as a trope. He insists on the Real Presence of Christ in the bread. When he preaches sanctification through the Eucharist, he means sanctification through the Word of God. He would like to accept their invitation to visit Strasbourg and meet Lefèvre in person, but is unable due to time constraints. He suggests Gemmingen as an alternative meeting place. He has heard from Theodor Billicanus that Melanchthon will write against Oecolampadius' book on the Eucharist. He hopes that they will not 'pour oil on the flames.' He sends greetings to their fellow preachers and the French refugees, especially Lefèvre, whose contribution to secular and sacred literature he respects.

Letter 260: 26 November 1525, Strasbourg, Capito to Ambrosius Blaurer

> The text of the letter is printed in Schiess 1:124–5, Ep. 98. For the addressee, see above, Ep. 192 headnote.

May grace be with you. I see that your heart is in Christ's business, for you are very solicitous about promoting the churches in other regions. I was delighted with your letter to our Bedrot,[1] which attests to your sentiments. Thanks be to God, who has given such apostles to our most profligate generation. Jakob Bedrot has recently joined our ranks and serves our city in a very modest capacity, but he is soon to be promoted to a better post. It is for that reason that we decided he should stay here: that he may benefit our church, on which a large neighbourhood depends. Indeed, I thank you for being mindful of the man. He is certainly worthy of the most generous provisions and can easily give satisfaction with his bright intelligence, learning,

* * * * *

1 Jakob Bedrot (d. 1541), priest in the diocese of Chur. He taught Greek at the University of Freiburg, moved to Strasbourg at the end of 1524 and taught Greek there from 1526. He was appointed as the first Protestant canon at St Thomas in 1529.

faith, and industry. Johannes Chelius is of the same ilk.[2] He is equally well trained in Greek and has a more than average facility in literature. You may introduce him to your friends in [Bedrot's] place.[3] He will not embarrass you and your friends, for he combines learning with modesty. We used his services when schools were being instituted by the council. In the meantime, Jakob has also been given a church function, a duty to which Chelius could be advanced only with difficulty and after some time had passed. Yet he is very capable of looking after schools, and has for a long time done an excellent job as a schoolmaster. Therefore, my dear Ambrosius, recommend him in Bedrot's place to your friends, to whom you had previously mentioned Bedrot. You will not be sorry for your effort, for he has the full approval of everyone here.

Our church progresses satisfactorily. We are left in peace by the Anabaptists and the other disturbers of the peace. We do not tie salvation to any earthly element. For us, the Eucharist is an instance of remembering the death Christ suffered. We are taking it in that sense and are not worried about what is in the bread, for we know that the words apply to us, not to the bread. Posterity will laugh about the pugnaciousness of our age, when we cause such unrest on behalf of a sign of concord. I have replied to Bugenhagen, certainly a most modest man, in a general way and admonished and encouraged him in Christ's name to take counsel for peace.[4] It is not yet known what the messenger will bring back, whom we have sent to Wittenberg for the sake of making peace.[5] In Freiburg im Breisgau they have burned an 'inept' book of mine,[6] for the sake of disgracing me, although it is unworthy of such an honour. In that manner, certain clerics wanted to satisfy their private resentment rather than prevent any harm to the public. I send you the book, so that you may laugh at the attempt of those silly men. I commend your excellent brother and your most deserving sister to the Lord, as well as your other fellow ministers.[7] Strasbourg, 26 November 1525.

* * * * *

2 Johannes Chelius (d. 1528) is perhaps Johannes Geiger of Seedorf in the diocese of Constance, who studied at Basel (BA 1509). He is presumably identical with the Chelius whose death is lamented by Cratander in his preface to an edition of Cicero (cf. below, Ep. 324 note).

3 I.e., for a position in Memmingen.

4 Cf. above, Ep. 253.

5 Cf. above, Epp. 252 and 252a. Caselius presented his report to the council on 29 November.

6 I.e., *Von drey Strasbruger Pfaffen* ... (Ep. 246a). This is a sarcastic reference to Zasius' description of the book as 'insane' (cf. above, Ep. 246a, note 2).

7 For Thomas and Margaret Blaurer, see above, Epp. 192, note 6, and 194, note 21.

In Tübingen, there is a man who was with you in the Augustinian convent and an Augustinian at that time, but is now a fellow minister here.[8] He sends you his sincere greetings, as does our friend Bucer. Again, farewell.

Your sincere friend, Wolfgang Fabritius Capito.

Letter 261: 26 November 1525, [Strasbourg], Capito to Ulrich Zwingli

The text is in ZwBr 2:438–9, Ep. 413.

[*Summary*]: In the Palatinate some young people are upset about the term *impanatum* ('Christ in the bread'). They use strong words in their response, as Zwingli may have heard from Oecolampadius. [Brenz] has written against Bucer [cf. above, Ep. 259]. Capito has replied, but in more vigorous terms than in his response to Bugenhagen. He has invited them to a colloquy. Capito's pamphlet [*Von drey Strassburger Pfaffen*, above Ep. 246a, cf. Epp. 246 d, e] has been burned in Freiburg. He has explained his position on baptism, in which he completely agrees with Zwingli. He is being attacked for his views on baptism and the Eucharist. He is afraid of war. The Swiss are divided. In a postscript, Capito sends greetings to Oswald Myconius and Leo Jud.

Letter 262

This letter has been redated by Millet. It is now Letter 280.

Letter 263: [ca. 30 November 1525, Strasbourg], Capito to [Johannes Oecolampadius]

The text of the letter is published in BrOek 1:421–6, Ep. 307.

[*Summary*]: Capito sends Oecolampadius the letters he received from the Wittenbergers [cf. above Epp. 252, 253]. He disapproves of their assertive attitude. Karlstadt has come to Strasbourg and started a controversy about the Eucharist, expressing himself in the most authoritarian terms. He reproached the Strasbourgers for their failure to teach the Real Presence 'on account of their custom of making no assertions.' Capito insists that their interpretation of scripture is neither forced nor blasphemous. Luther seized on the term *carnivorum* ('meat-eating'), used by Oecolampadius, to accuse them of being

* * * * *

8 Wolfgang Schultheiss. See above, Ep. 189.

abusive. Brenz has written a long letter to Bucer and Capito [cf. above Ep. 259] in which he makes some concessions to Oecolampadius' interpretation. He asks Oecolampadius to counsel Zwingli to keep the peace. Bugenhagen used a clever formulation when he said: 'I eat nothing but bread and wine, but through the Word I believe in the body and blood (*Edo nihil nisi panem et vinum, sed per verbum corpus et sanguinem credo*).' Capito will send Oecolampadius Brenz's letter and Bucer's response.

Letter 264: 1 December 1525, Strasbourg, The Strasbourg Preachers to the Lords of Gemmingen

Printed in CorrBucer 2:79–86, Ep. 114. The addressees are the brothers Diether, Wolff, and Philipp of Gemmingen, who resided at the castle of Guttenberg/Neckar. They were among the first Franconian nobles to embrace the Reformation.

[*Summary*]: The preachers explain their position on the Sacramentarian controversy: all believers 'receive and eat the true body of Christ,' whether they actually receive bread or not, for 'God has not tied his gifts to anything external.' They discourage parishioners from asking more detailed questions. To prevent superstitious adoration of the bread by those who have no understanding or faith, Zwingli and Oecolampadius have taught that the bread is a 'sign of the body of Christ; the body of Christ is given to believers through the word, such that the mouth eats the bread, and the spirit the body of Christ, through faith.' They are distressed by the discord and dispute over the interpretation of the Eucharist. In their opinion, they are in agreement with the Lutherans on the main issues: 'the dispute was merely about words.' Bugenhagen's views are not incompatible with their own. They trust that the differences with Brenz can eventually be settled. They invite the lords of Gemmingen to discuss their position on the Eucharist.

Letter 265: 2 December 1525, Strasbourg, Capito to the City Council of Mulhouse

The text of this letter is printed in Jules Lutz, *Les réformateurs de Mulhouse* (Ribeauvillé, 1902), Section III:16–17, Ep. 1.

To my dearest governing lords, the protective, honest, and wise mayor and council of the city of Mulhouse:

I wish you an increase in grace and knowledge of God the Father through our Lord Jesus Christ, and offer you my willing service and any honour or favour I may be able to provide, honest, wise, and governing lords. I am grateful to God Almighty that in your respected wisdom you wish to supply your community with a trustworthy preacher who is well versed in scripture and lives an honest and upright life. For such a character is most desirable if the Word of God is to take its course and earn praise. One finds many wicked and unskilled people, who have not experienced the grace of God who preach their own views rather than Christ's teachings. They give the Word a direction in accord with their own carnal desires and their own aims, and abuse it to support their greed, envy, or hatred, or whatever purpose they have at the time. The faithful soon note and recognize this, and stay away from their preaching, regarding them as wolves and seducers. For they have a few clear words in their hearts, which are true and certain, based on their feelings and their experience of faith. And because they know whom to believe, they do not go in for the irrelevant matters, which these false preachers introduce under the pretense of teaching the gospel. They have no desire for more sophisticated teaching, but take care to exercise charity toward their neighbours – and that should be the ultimate purpose of preaching. The false preachers do not harm such people. But they are a stumbling block and a snare for inexperienced and simple people. For secular people tend to judge the teaching of God by the respectability and life of the preacher, until God gives them his grace and Spirit, who leads them to the complete Truth. Then they no longer cling to flesh and blood, but to the revealed Truth itself. It is therefore necessary to supply the weak and the poor common people with a preacher of healthy and true insight, who uses charity as the touchstone of his actions.

Among Christians, government is a gift of God and consists not only of rewarding the good and punishing the evil, but also principally of guiding subjects to the true service of God. Therefore, honest, wise lords, I ask my Lord God to give you grace in this godly undertaking, that people may sense and praise the grace of God in you, which is assured to all who further the honour of God in their hearts; and you wish to establish true service among us, according to the Word of God.

Such is your Christian enterprise and the contents of what you have written to me[1] that I am pleased to assist you and recognize my duty to do so. I have therefore chosen among my colleagues and the many people who are presently here with us, two men whom I wish to bring to your attention, whom we, in God, regard as the most skilled preachers of the Truth:

* * * * *

1 Not extant.

Bonifacius Wolfhart,[2] who hails from Basel and has for some time now lived here. He is an honest man and versed in scripture. We can attest to his skill, faith, charity, and understanding of the Word. The second man with us here is Otto Binder,[3] who never attempted to preach on his own initiative until he was duly called by the cathedral chapter to Börsch, a small town under its authority.[4] There he has remained before, during, and after the revolt, loyally teaching the subjects obedience and fear of God. He himself kept the poor from joining the horde [of peasants] for a while, earnestly warning them that it was improper, indeed, against God, and that God would not let it pass unpunished, etc. Thus the poor and the magistrates in the area, who do not like him, nevertheless gave him a reference. Because he preaches Christ, the peasants in the area come to him, but because he acts only in accordance with scripture, he had to leave without any cause. Thus, the cathedral chapter still considers him a parish priest and has so far supported him. This does not satisfy him, however, for he wishes to preach to the poor, or else not be called a parish priest. He is, moreover, a serious, loyal, obedient man who acts from conviction. That is why we wish to recommend him, and herewith do so.

If you wish to accept our recommendations, I request that you notify me or him, for it is risky for him to travel often. Not everyone is inclined to show kindness to honest men. But if you obtain other preachers, act and proceed according to what is best for the honour of God and yourselves and what you consider your duty. I and my brethren are willing and ready to serve you to the best of our ability. This I wanted you to know, for I am totally yours. Given at Strasbourg, 2 December 1525.

Your Honours' willing servant, Wolfgang Capito.

Letter 266: 20 December 1525, Zurich, Ulrich Zwingli to Capito

Printed in ZwBr 2:464–5, Ep. 423.

[*Summary*]: He sent Capito a letter on 18 December [lost] and is now answering the one he just received [Ep. 261]. Zwingli would like an opportunity to speak to the preachers of Strasbourg in person. Alternatively, he would like

* * * * *

2 For Wolfhart, see CWC 1, Ep 102 headnote.
3 Otto Binder (or Vinarius, d. ca. 1554) matriculated at the University of Basel in 1516 and entered the Franciscan order. He was preacher at Börsch in 1525 (cf. below, Ep. 345), then moved to Mulhouse, where he remained until his death.
4 The parishioners of Börsch elected Wolfgang Schultheiss in January 1525, but the cathedral chapter sent them Binder instead. Cf. CorrBucer 2:12, note 2.

Capito to notify him if a trustworthy person should visit Zurich to whom he may speak openly. Letters are by no means safe, and he is reluctant to offer counsel. Zurich is at peace. According to Oecolampadius, this letter will safely reach Capito.

Letter 267: 27 December 1525, Strasbourg, Capito to Ulrich Zwingli

Printed in ZwBr 2:475–7, Ep. 428.

[*Summary*]: Capito is reassured. He was worried about the fall of Waldshut [occupied by Austrian forces in the wake of the town's involvement in the Peasants' War], for the fate of their neighbours affects them as well. He feared greatly for Balthasar Hubmaier [under whose leadership the people of Waldshut had embraced the Reformation] although he has some reservations about his ambitions. If only Hubmaier would see the error of Anabaptism. He hopes the Lord will restore the Word in Waldshut and end all dissent. So far, the Strasbourgers have avoided open dissent. He thanks Zwingli for his exhortations. The city is rife with rumours, and he knows the mutability of the people. The defection of Waldshut has not discouraged them. The [Austrian government] in Ensisheim continues to persecute the pious. Capito has spoken to a pharmacist [about taking an apprentice, cf. below, Ep. 271]. He charges 16 gulden for board. It seems a fair price. Capito asks Zwingli to contact the young man's father. Capito himself will be his guarantor. The pharmacist will not take him for less than two years. Zwingli will see from the enclosed notice the character of the [Dominican], Johannes Burckhard, who has been accused of fraud and theft. Bucer spent much effort on translating Bugenhagen [the translation of the Psalms appeared under Bugenhagen's name in Basel, January 1526; in the preface Bucer took credit for the translation]. Capito wonders what the reaction will be in Wittenberg. He hopes that Zwingli will write without anger, if he decides to write anything. He hopes that Hubmaier, now in captivity in Zurich, will be judged fairly and charitably.

Letter 268: December 1525, Gemmingen, The people of Gemmingen to the Strasbourg Preachers

Printed in CorrBucer 2:86–95, Ep. 115.

[*Summary*]: They are saddened by the dissension over the nature of the Eucharist. This is a matter that should not be discussed in print or in sermons, but settled among the reformers. This concerns not simply the bread and wine, which are merely external things, but the interpretation of the Word of God. They agree with the Strasbourgers that salvation comes through faith and is not tied to external things. Yet external matters play a mediating role, and people who ask about the nature of the Eucharist deserve an answer. They acknowledge that Paul taught [the message of] Christ, even though he spoke only letters and words. Similarly, we must acknowledge that we eat the body of Christ, even though it is only bread. Some people adore the Word of God in a superstitious manner, that is, they adore the piece of paper on which it is written. Similarly, people may abuse the Eucharist by focusing on externals, such as the piece of bread. But the words of scripture are clear; there is no need to explain the bread as a sign. It is important, however, to teach the congregation in what spirit they must take communion: 'not for the sake of the bread, but for the sake of the Word.' If Zwingli and Oecolampadius agree with that interpretation, there is no need for contention. The Strasbourgers demand a charitable attitude from their fellow reformers, but seem to lack that attitude themselves. The people of Gemmingen cannot accept Zwingli's and Oecolampadius' explanations as cogent proofs. Their preachers continue to believe in the literal meaning of the words, 'This is my body.' Luther's main purpose is to do away with the papistical concept of transubstantiation. If the Strasbourgers teach that the bread is the body of Christ *for the believer*, the question is settled, and there can be no more dissension. It would be better for Oecolampadius to write against Erasmus' book on free will than on the nature of the Eucharist.

Letter 269: [End of 1525, Strasbourg], Capito to Gervasius Sopher

> The manuscript of this letter is in AST # 41, f. 409 (667). For Sopher, see above, Ep. 246a note 14.

Greetings, dearest brother. The creditors are after me. I beg you to make an effort to get the money together. Believe me, the guarantees are very solid, and will bring an ever higher yield with the passing of time. Furthermore, if possible, let me have another 10 gulden to buy wood for the winter. Finally, I intend to call on the provost[1] and his good wife, and on yours, to have a more personal conversation between us. For it is my plan and intention to foster by every means a more special friendship among us. I am not on such good terms with the others, who matter less, in my opinion. Therefore, let me know whether your wife has recovered her health by now, for I certainly

* * * * *

1 Lorenz Schenckbecher. See above, Ep. 248c headnote.

hope so. Please speak to your neighbour about the money so that he may recognize my effort. I fear he believes that I am unwilling and recalcitrant.

Capito.

Letter 270: [End of 1525, Zurich], Leo Jud to Capito

The manuscript of this letter is in the Basel Universitätsbibliothek, Ki. Ar. 25a, #30. Leo Jud (or Keller, ca. 1482–1542), the son of a priest, attended the Latin school in Colmar together with Bucer. He studied at the University of Basel (MA 1512) and became parish priest at St Hippolyte (Alsace), Einsiedeln (succeeding Zwingli in 1519), and St Peter's in Zurich (1523). He was closely associated with Zwingli and remained a leading churchman in the city.

The grace and peace of God the Father through Christ!

You wish to know, most learned man and dearest brother in Christ, my opinion concerning the sacrament of the body and blood of Christ.[1] You seem to me rather unwise, when you seek water from a pumice stone,[2] for what pronouncement can I make, an unformed disciple in the school of Christ who has barely touched Holy Writ with the top of his lips? Nor is it safe to entrust to writing what differs from common usage and tradition. For are there any letters the enemies of faith leave unopened? Indeed, do they not slander even what is taken from the very core of the truth? It is partly for this reason (which you should not consider insignificant) that I waited until now to reply, and partly because I was overwhelmed by a mountain of work, so that I could hardly find the time to write. Do not think, however, that I forgot about it. Our friendship is strong, too solid to need holding together with the aid of letters, although I am fond of reading and rereading your letters. In the matter of your query, I like the opinion of Augustine on chapter 6 of John, where he treats in a learned and Christian manner of the words of Christ, *My body is truly food and my blood truly drink.*[3] And he seems to be inclined toward that party [who interpret] the bread and wine as a sign of the body and blood of the Lord, which the sophists will be forced to concede as well, if they want it to be a sacrament. For either it is a sign, or it is not a sacrament, which they themselves maintain tooth and claw,[4] for they themselves

* * * * *

1 In April 1526, Jud published a book on the Eucharist, juxtaposing and criticizing Luther's and Erasmus' positions: *Des Hochgelerten Erasmi ... maynung.*
2 Erasmus, *Adagia* 1.4.75.
3 I.e., Augustine on John 6:55 in *Contra adversarium legis et prophetarum libri duo*, 1.24.52 (PL 42.636).
4 Cf. Erasmus, *Adagia* 1.4.22.

say that a sacrament is the visible sign of its substance, invisible grace. If it is a sign, it is not a substance – that is the kind of nonsense they say in the collection of Sentences, book four.[5] I, however, think that this bread is eaten and this blood is drunk by faith, not with bodily teeth, for it is food for the soul. What need is there, then, to speak of transubstantiation? It is bread that is eaten, wine that is drunk. It is a sign, just as water is of baptism. Indeed, that food (as Christ says) descends from heaven, but the flesh and blood of Christ does not descend from heaven. Therefore, flesh and blood in themselves are not food, yet they satisfy, refresh, comfort, and enliven the faithful soul when they are eaten with faith, when there is a belief that His body was given for us, His blood shed for us, by whose spirit our sins have forever been washed away. For the flesh does not benefit; it is the spirit which gives life.[6] Therefore, do not fasten your eyes on the flesh, but on that which the flesh covers, namely that which descends from heaven.

But why do I hammer my nonsense into your ears, most learned man? Because it is your wish, brother. Therefore take it with good grace, if in my ignorance I have casually said what is not well thought out. When we have an opportunity to be together, we shall talk about this at leisure and at greater length. In the meantime, we shall pray to our most merciful Father to give us insight into this matter. And if the Spirit of the Lord suggests anything of greater clarity to you, do not deprive me of it. Farewell, dearest brother. Zwingli sends his greetings to you. From Zurich.

Yours, Leo Jud.

I wrote this letter long ago, before you sent me your conclusions.[7] For the man who brought them said he would return to me. I wanted to give the letter to him, but he has not yet returned. I know nothing about a disputation, nor do I know the source of that rumour.

Letter 271: 1 January 1526, Zurich, Ulrich Zwingli to Capito

Printed in ZwBr 2:487–8, Ep. 434.

[*Summary*]: A traveller reports that a rumour is circulating in Strasbourg about Zwingli either having been banished or having gone into hiding. Zwingli confirms that he is alive and well, and ready to take on the Catholic

* * * * *

5 I.e., in the *Sentences* of Peter Lombard, IV, dist. 1, cap.2.
6 John 6:63.
7 Millet suggests that this may be a reference to articles to be discussed at the Disputation of Guttenberg. Cf. below, Ep. 273.

opponents. The Zurich city council imprisoned Balthasar Hubmaier on his arrival in Zurich, [see above, Ep. 267] for fear that he might cause a disturbance. Since, however, he had spoken against the city council when he was in Waldshut, it was decided to meet with him and, on his own request, discuss the beliefs of the Anabaptists. On the day following the meeting he recanted in the presence of two hundred people. Later, however, he took back his recantation and called upon the Swiss Diet, falsely claiming that the recantation was extorted from him. The Zurich council did not turn Hubmaier over to Ferdinand I, although he requested it repeatedly. He was sent back to prison and tortured. His case will be heard on 2 January. Zwingli asks Capito not to forget about the pharmacist [see above, Ep. 267] and [Johannes] Burckhard.

Letter 272: 15 January 1526, [Strasbourg], Capito to Ulrich Zwingli

Printed in ZwBr 2:503–4, Ep. 441.

[*Summary*]: Capito has read Zwingli's letter [Ep. 271] with mixed feelings. He is glad that [Balthasar Hubmaier] has been captured, but detests his inconstancy. Capito is unsure of the outcome of the affair and believes that Hubmaier, once he is set free, will glory in his suffering. He takes comfort in the knowledge that the city council of Zurich is guided by the counsel of the Holy Spirit. He asks Zwingli to report on further developments in the city. The Strasbourg city council is stronger in faith than it has ever been before. They have not yet acted on the preachers' proposals for schools, but Capito hopes that modest initiatives will be taken soon. He reports on the progress of the Reformation: To prevent any return to the old masses, they hold a Christian assembly (*conventus*) every fourth month and a daily assembly in each parish. Attendance is high: first the congregation hears the Word; then time is allotted for silent prayer, 'so that each person may pray to the Lord according to his own spirit.'

Capito has spoken with a highly skilled pharmacist about taking on the young man recommended by Zwingli. He might live with him as an apprentice for two years, at 16 gulden a year. The pharmacist requested a guarantee, and Capito is willing to offer it. [Guillaume] Farel sends his greetings. He strongly opposes the idea of 'God in the bread' (*Dei impanati*), the basis of the Catholic doctrine. The German princes have announced that the Imperial Diet at Speyer shall begin on 1 May.[1] In the meantime, Capito hopes for some peace and quiet. There are rumours of war, but the Strasbourg magistracy

* * * * *

1 It actually ran from 25 June–27 August 1526.

disregards them. Hartmut von Kronberg, living as an exile in Strasbourg, sends his greetings [cf. CWC 1, Ep. 146].

Letter 273: 23 January 1526, Strasbourg, Capito to Johannes Oecolampadius

Printed in BrOek 1:453–9, Ep. 327.

[*Summary*]: Capito is reassured by Oecolampadius' three letters [not extant], which he received all at once. Rumours were circulating that Zurich had restored the mass, conspired against the Word of God, pledged their efforts to the Antichrist, and joined forces with [Catholic] Austria. Oecolampadius' letters show that they are false rumours. As long as Zwingli is alive, the Antichrist is powerless in Zurich.

Capito praises Bucer's faith, learning, and character. The preachers of Zurich, Basel, and Strasbourg are being drawn into a dispute with [Wittenberg] over the [Eucharist]. Capito urges concord and a united front. He is afraid that Zwingli's treatise, [*Eyn klare underrichtung vom Nachtmahl Christi*, Strasbourg, 1526], will exacerbate the dispute. [Johann] Bugenhagen writes with greater determination on this issue than is appropriate. It is said that Philip [Melanchthon] will contribute to the debate as well. Capito believes that the debate focuses too much on external matters, which are not necessary for salvation. Dissent among the reformers aids the cause of their opponents.

Luther has written a vigorous response [*De servo arbitrio*] to Erasmus' [*De libero arbitrio*]. Regrettably, Luther does not seek concord. Capito will not oppose the book if Zwingli agrees with it. Many people appreciate Zwingli's moderate *Ad Ioannis Bugenhagii Pomerani epistolam responsio*.

[Johann] Eck is reported to have made insulting and bragging remarks, but the pamphlet [*libellus*; point of reference unclear] will put an end to them. [Johannes] Fabri may become the next bishop of Basel, and Capito, therefore, advises Oecolampadius to act cautiously. [Theobald] Billicanus' [*De verbis coenae dominicae et opinionum varietate ... ad Urbanum Regium epistola*] and Urbanus [Rhegius' *Responsio ... ad eundem*] are being circulated among the Strasbourg reformers.

Capito is sending to Oecolampadius the [*Syngramma*] of the Swabian preachers. If Oecolampadius writes a response, Capito will see to its publication, either in Strasbourg or in Haguenau.[1] Capito has not heard anything

* * * * *

1 Oecolampadius' *Antisyngramma* was ultimately printed in Zurich by Froschauer in 1526.

about the meeting of the Swabians at Guttenberg [cf. above, Ep. 270]. He comments on [Johannes] Brenz's candour.

[Jacobus] Ceporinus has died. Capito regrets that [Peter Gynoraeus] has been appointed as parish priest of St Alban's. He is glad that [Conradus] Pellicanus has abandoned the cowl. [Johannes Lüthard], the Franciscan preacher, is left behind, but will hardly hold out on his own. Capito expects that the criticism of the Swabians will not upset Oecolampadius too much. Luther has not written against [Andreas] Karlstadt, as far as Capito knows.

The response of the Bern reformers has given Capito hope. He is pleased with the positive news concerning Felix Ulscenius [cf. above, Ep. 254]. As a result of the initiative of the Basel city council, Stephan [Stör; cf. below, Ep. 394] has been captured in Strasbourg. Capito hopes the Strasbourg city council will be merciful to him. Bonifacius [Wolfhart] is like a brother to Stör.

Capito cannot help the young man whom Oecolampadius had recommended to him, since there are many in Strasbourg who need patrons. Hartmut von Kronberg, presently in Strasbourg [cf. Ep. 271], will spend some time with Margrave Ernst I [von Baden] at Breisach. Capito and Bucer commend themselves to Zwingli, and want to reassure him and Oecolampadius that the rumours of war are vain. The Strasbourg magistracy looks out for its city with great vigilance and trust in God.

Zwingli should send the young son of the provost [i.e., the son of Felix Frei] to the pharmacist in Strasbourg. Capito has written twice about the matter since he had promised the pharmacist thirty gulden to give the young man room and board, and instruction for two years [see above, Ep. 272]. [Guillaume] Farel, [Jacques Lefèvre] d'Etaples, Jean Védaste, Simon Robert of Tournai and [Gérard Roussel] are still in Strasbourg and send their greetings. Capito's wife, [Agnes Roettel], pledges her own effort to Oecolampadius.

Letter 274: 28 January 1526, [Strasbourg], Capito to Ulrich Zwingli

Printed in ZwBr 2:510–11, Ep. 444.

[*Summary*]: Luther's *De servo arbitrio* has been published in Strasbourg [by W. Köpfel, 1526]. From what he has read, Capito is impressed by the book's argument and godly character. It is bound to stump Erasmus, who attributes too much power to the human will. Luther has touched on the Eucharist in *De servo arbitrio*. Some church leaders in Swabia oppose his views; some think well of them. Capito fears that the reformers are being drawn into a bitter fight, for which reason they must not dissemble when it comes to their faith. He advises caution and moderation in dealing with the opponents as a means of reaching concord. Capito hopes the disputants may be drawn back to the Christian truth.

[Johann] Bugenhagen's book against Oecolampadius will be for sale at the [Frankfurt] book fair. Capito anticipates that it will either be a herald of peace or a declaration of war, and is prepared for both outcomes. In Strasbourg, the Reformation is proceeding slowly, since the Catholic priests are impeding reform, having gained much hope from the treaty between France and Spain. While writing this letter, Capito received another report that many people are putting their hopes in a general council, which might be initiated at the Diet at Speyer. Capito himself believes that this has little bearing on them, since they rely only on the Word of God.

Capito sends his greetings to Leo Jud, [Oswald] Myconius, and the rest of the brethren, and hopes that Zwingli's wife [Anna] and daughter [Regula] are well. Capito has written twice to Zwingli regarding the pharmacist. He has agreed to take in the boy as an apprentice for sixteen gulden a year, for a minimum of two years. Capito asks Zwingli to pass this information on to the provost [see above, Epp. 272, 273]. Capito has offered to be the boy's guarantor.

There are rumours of war, and Strasbourg is taking appropriate measures. They are negotiating with mercenary leaders. Concord prevails among the citizens. Stephan Stör has been imprisoned [cf. above, Ep. 273, and below, Ep. 394]. He is accused of sowing dissent in the Swiss Confederacy. The Strasbourg theologians hope for legal justice. Guillaume Farel, Antonius Peregrinus, [pseudonym for Jacques Lefèvre d'Etaples] and the rest of the [French] brethren send their greetings. Bucer and Capito hope that Zwingli will respond to the Wittenberg theologians [regarding the Eucharist].

Letter 275: 29 January 1526, [Strasbourg], Capito to Ulrich Zwingli

Printed in ZwBr 2:513–14, #445.

[*Summary*]: Capito is writing on behalf of the widow of Martin Hag, [Barbara von Sargans], an ex-nun, who has been living in Strasbourg for the past two years. The Zurich city council used to support her. Capito urges the council to award her an annual pension, as they have reportedly done for another ex-nun. Marcus the Joannite [of Oltingen] will be looked after, as Zwingli requested.

Capito has found a pharmacist, with whom he has made an arrangement to receive the apprentice for 16 gulden a year, room and board, for a minimum of two years [see above, Ep. 274]. Oecolampadius has written that there will be a Disputation [at Baden]. Capito welcomes the news and hopes that the Truth will prevail. He wishes the Zurich city council could persuade Strasbourg to send a representative, or at any rate, observers. He believes rumours about a treaty between the [Holy Roman] emperor and France are unfounded.

Letter 276: 3 February 1526, [Strasbourg], Capito to Ulrich Zwingli

Printed in ZwBr 2:517–18, Ep. 447.

[*Summary*]: It was useful to read Zwingli's demonstration concerning the terms 'bread-flesh condition' (*artosarkosis*) and 'God in the bread' (*Deus impanatus*), but Capito is afraid that Zwingli is too vehement to create conditions for religious peace. In his opinion, the matter is not an article of faith and does not need definition. He does not want to stand in the way of a reconciliation, however. Capito thinks that the French above all will object to that definition. Johann Eck will no doubt make his position clear at the Disputation [of Baden]. He hopes that the Strasbourgers will be able to attend, or at any rate, observe the disputation [cf. below Ep. 288a headnote].

There has been a [false] rumour that Balthasar [Hubmaier] was handed over to the authorities in Ensisheim, who claim they are not executing anyone for his beliefs [but rather for subversive activities]. Capito hopes that everything will turn out to the benefit of the community.

The Zurich consistory is discussing marriage and divorce. The Strasbourg reformers accept 'divorce authorized by the magistrate as God separating what he has joined.' Capito asks for Zwingli's opinion on marriages involving cousins or permanently ill spouses.

Letter 277: [24 February 1526, Strasbourg], Capito and his colleagues to the City Council of Strasbourg

Printed in CorrBucer 2:98–9, Ep. 117.

[*Summary*]: They deny that they aided or encouraged peasant rebels. They ask the councillors to inform them of the proceedings involving certain insurgents of the Peasants' War who were recently executed at Saverne. They, in turn, will submit a statement of their own actions and of the advice they gave to the peasants [see below Ep. 280]. They are prepared to justify themselves before a court.

Letter 278: 7 March 1526, Strasbourg, Capito to Ulrich Zwingli

Printed in ZwBr 2:537–8, Ep. 457.

[*Summary*]: The letter Zwingli wrote on behalf of Stephan Stör [see below, Ep. 394] is very useful. If his enemies bring the matter to court, Stör will have more lenient judges.

Bucer has reported to Zwingli on the case of [Barbara von Sargans; cf. above, Ep. 275] and on the letters of recommendation from the Strasbourg city council. Capito asks for Zwingli's help. Strasbourg is not as wealthy as reported. The peace [of Madrid of January 1526, between Francis I and Charles V] has given the enemies of the gospel hope, but Capito is confident that fair conditions will be obtained for the religious exiles. Bucer's letter will inform Zwingli about the preachers of Swabia and its environs. Bucer is responding to [Johannes] Brenz's letter. Capito sees no end to their dispute. He repeats the request to Zwingli to help Barbara [von Sargans]. Jodocus Brennwald, a most cultured and obliging young man, is studying Greek. Capito sends greetings to [Conradus] Pellicanus, [Oswald] Myconius, and Leo Jud. He hopes Zwingli's wife [Anna] and newborn son [Wilhelm] are doing well.

Letter 279: 14 March 1526, Strasbourg, Capito to Jacob Sturm

Printed as the dedicatory letter to Capito's commentary *In Habakuk prophetam ... enarrationes* (Strasbourg: Wolfgang Köpfel, 1526), ff. Aiir–Aiiiv. On Sturm, see CWC 1, Ep. 48 headnote.

To the noble and erudite Jacob Sturm, citizen and member of the city council of Strasbourg, counsellor of the *Reichsregiment* at this time,[1] and greatly revered friend, grace and peace from Jesus Christ our Saviour!

During our personal conversations, most distinguished Jacob, you repeatedly exhorted all of us preachers here in the city, and if possible, in the neighbouring cities, to make an effort to treat the scriptures with the same skill and method, for disagreement [among us] would confound the weak judgment of the common people. You argued quite rightly that the people would be divided by the embittered clamouring of certain men with evil intentions; that a handle would be provided to the enemies of the Word to slander our office with their filthy talk. You then concluded your admonition, saying that ministers of the Word are men and subject to passions. You were

* * * * *

1 *Consiliarius* (assessor). See above, Ep. 236.

not offended, and did not demand anything from anyone that was beyond his natural abilities, but you entreated the ministers not to proclaim their human passions from the pulpit, out of season, for in the pulpit only the Spirit should be heard. We, who know that Christ's salutary teaching should be offered, not with insane fury, but with the ardent fire of the Spirit, often and gladly mention this opinion of yours, for you stand first among us in authority.

Mindful of this kind of advice, Bucer and I have initiated a plan to lecture in my home on sacred subjects to our helpers in the Word (the so-called coadjutors), and to do so with a certain informal effort and simplicity, but with faithful care and attention. In short, because we decided not to exclude anyone, the number of people in attendance was higher than we expected, to the point that my dining room could hardly hold them. For that reason, we decided to take our lectures out of the private setting and into the public, and we began to teach publicly at the Dominican monastery,[2] where we did everything to the best of our ability, sometimes lecturing in more detail and more fully than we would have done just among our friends. We have written down some things for those among our listeners who require it, to reinforce their memory. Bucer, in fact, is working on Matthew,[3] because he has decided to make his way right through the entire New Testament, whereas I am working on Habakkuk. I studied this prophet in more detail without yet having established a method of commenting on the Old Testament, for it was much better to see what I could do with God's grace (however little I might achieve in that arena) than to try my hand with a definite method, which, as I said, I did not have, and to set myself a specific task. For the rest, it seemed that certain people were going to publish what they took down from my lectures, although right from the start I was against the idea. But when I had considered how printers today often publish indiscriminately and with very little forethought, motivated more by profit than by a desire to help those who rely on these works, I decided to publish voluntarily what others would have published against my will and over my objections, so that the commentary will appear more correctly printed and be of greater benefit – if any benefit can be expected from a basic commentary of this sort.

* * * * *

2 Cf. below, Ep. 406, reporting that two schools had been established at the Dominican monastery in Strasbourg, one for young boys and the other for clerics. The curriculum included lessons in Greek, Hebrew, mathematics, poetry, rhetoric, and civil law.
3 The first edition of Bucer's commentaries on the gospels were published under the title, *Enarrationum in evangelia Matthaei, Marci et Lucae libri 2 ...* (Strasbourg: [Herwagen], 1527) with his commentary on John appearing the following year.

I am sending this, however insignificant it may be, for you to read and judge when you get some peace and quiet from the *Reichsregiment*. For we most gladly bear with your criticism and greatly welcome it. It has been our custom to admit even the criticism of the general reader, and indeed to invite, demand, and request it on account of the Lord's command. Listen to the decision of the judges, as the apostle says: *Let two or three speak and let the others weigh what is said. If a revelation is made to someone else sitting nearby, let the first person be silent.*[4] We have taken up this law most eagerly and shall strictly prescribe it to others, because we know how much poison has arisen from the practice of everyone without modesty approving and defending his own views, to the harm of the churches. For Paul, in a commandment to the entire church, said: *Test everything; hold fast to what is good; abstain from every form of evil.*[5] And again: *Test the spirits to see whether they are from God.*[6] It is thus necessary to test doctrines; and Christ also made a point of giving this command to his followers. For when he says that we should beware either of wolves showing themselves in sheep's clothing, or of dogs and evildoers and fat-bellies disguising themselves, he means the same thing in each case, telling us to weigh every doctrine.[7] For they entice the simple-hearted and deceive them with pernicious doctrines, they corrupt them with errors, scatter them, tear them apart, and devour them. Thus, it is necessary to use one's judgment when [a court of] justice exposes piety to the ravages of deadly and false claims.[8] It seems to me that I have stated nothing impiously and have touched on the meaning of the prophet. I know at any rate that, in keeping my remarks brief, I impose on readers only once, whereas others, to whom it seems sensible to waste much paper, are a nuisance both by being long-winded and inept in their discussion, to say nothing worse. This is how they evaluate a book: the greater its size, the greater must be its use. Meanwhile, may you, my dear Jacob, fare well. Your most talented mind, which is subtle and acute by nature, steady through education, excellently trained in literature and strengthened by experience, is most suited to looking after public affairs. I ask you to go on and apply your skills most closely to Christian piety, as you usually do. Send my greetings in the Lord to Ulrich Varnbühler,[9]

* * * * *

4 1 Cor. 14:29–30.
5 1 Thess. 5:21–2.
6 1 John 4:1.
7 Matt. 7:15.
8 *ubi iusticia imposturis laetalibus depascendam pietatem maxime exponit* – a reference to the difficulties caused for the preachers by the court hearings in Saverne (see below, Ep. 280).
9 On Varnbühler (1474–1545), see CWC 1, Ep. 49, note 1, and above, Ep. 238.

secretary of the *Reichsregiment* and a man endowed with the most upright faith, graciousness, and authority. All the best to you, too. Strasbourg, 14 March 1526.

Letter 280: [End of March 1526, Strasbourg], Capito and Matthew Zell to the Christian reader

This open letter was printed as a pamphlet entitled *Doctor Capito, Mathis Zellen, unnd ander Predicanten zu Straßburg warhafftige verantwortung uff eins gerichten vergicht, jüngest zu Zabern außgangen. Item von Hans Jacob, der zu Straßburg ge-fierteylt, und dem Büchlin das zu Freyburg im Brissagw [sic] verbrannt worden ist* (A Truthful Response of Doctor Capito, Matthew Zell, and other Strasbourg preachers to the testimony offered in court recently in Saverne; furthermore, concerning Hans Jakob [Schütz], who has been quartered at Strasbourg, and the pamphlet which was burned at Freiburg im Breisgau [Strasbourg: Wolfgang Köpfel, 1526]), ff. Aii recto–[Bvi recto].

The *Warhafftige verantwortung* was written by Capito and Zell in order to clear their names and defend themselves against accusations of being trouble-makers and of having contributed to the peasant rebellions in Alsace. On 8 February 1526, five citizens of Weyersheim – Georg Vetterheim (the 'Bishop of Weyersheim'), Simon of Weyersheim, Georg Volz, Georg Zimmer, and one Behtvogel – were interrogated under torture at the episcopal court in Saverne, and on the same day condemned and executed as instigators and leaders of the rebels. The interrogators obtained from the men the following confession: first, that they did not want to recognize any lord other than God and the emperor; second, that they had received a letter, in which it was written that one should slay all authorities, both spiritual and secular; third, that they wanted a share of the revenues of the nobles and clergy; fourth, that they had consulted with Capito and Zell in Strasbourg; fifth, that the brothers Matthis and Wolf Wurm of Geudertheim had brought preachers to Weyersheim and promised the citizens their help; sixth, that they wanted no more than one parish priest; seventh, that they wanted to destroy all the monasteries; eighth, that the Strasbourg gardeners had sent them a preacher (i.e., Clemens Ziegler, see below, note 16) in December; finally, that they did not wish to pay the tithe unless it went to pay for a Lutheran preacher, with the rest going to the emperor or distributed among themselves.[1] In April 1525, Capito and Zell had indeed advised

* * * * *

1 Johann Adam, *Evangelische Kirchengeschichte der elsässischen Territorien bis zur französischen Revolution* (Strasbourg, 1928), 580. Cf. the testimonies gathered in AMS, AA 389, #46.

Erasmus Gerber, the leader of the revolt in Alsace, who was then in Altdorf, but had urged him and his fellow rebels to disperse and uphold public order (see above, Ep. 243). Despite their efforts to calm the peasants, the Strasbourg preachers continued to be dogged by suspicions that they were inciting the rebels (see above, Epp. 244a, 244b, 246). After the execution of the five rebels in Weyersheim, Capito and his colleagues wrote to the Strasbourg city council on 24 February 1526, again denying any involvement in the peasants' revolt, and asking them to inform them of the proceedings of the interrogation (Ep. 277). They also promised that they would submit their own statement justifying their actions and their advice to the peasants. The following letter, the *Warhafftige verantwortung*, is that promised response. As the title indicates, mention is made also of Capito's pamphlet, *Von drey Straßburger Pfaffen* (Ep. 246a), and of his involvement with Hans Jakob Schütz (cf. above, Epp. 199–202). The *Warhafftige verantwortung*, then, is a passionate appeal to the reader not to believe the claims that the message of the reformers leads to civil unrest.

We, the preachers and ministers of the Word in Strasbourg, wish the pious, Christian reader the grace and peace of God the Father through our Lord Jesus Christ.

Once again we are publicly called villains, especially Wolfgang Capito and Matthew Zell.[2] For in Saverne, several people were recently condemned on account of the uprising of the peasants, one of whom reportedly claimed that they, the rebels, had consulted with us, the preachers of Strasbourg, namely, Wolfgang Capito and Matthew Zell, concerning their actions.[3] Such testimony has often been copied and sent to many cities and principalities, and has supposedly been published at last, as has been reported to us. Now the testimony of the same poor man, who has spoken of us, has been set out and written down in such a way that the simple reader or anyone else, who otherwise prefers to think the worst of us, could not but have understood it in any other way than that we, the preachers, counselled them to give [no] tax or import, to pay no rent or money, to slay all spiritual and temporal lords, to divide up everyone's goods equally among themselves, the same portion for the poor as for the rich, and the like; for articles containing such matters are

* * * * *

2 On Zell (1477–1548), see CWC 1, Ep. 167 headnote.
3 Cf. the testimony of Georg Vetterheim, AMS, AA 389, f. 43 verso: 'that they sought the advice of the preachers Doctor Capito and Master Matthisen [*sic*] in Strasbourg for their actions.'

immediately followed by the testimony that they obtained counsel for their actions from the preachers, Dr Capito and Master Matthew at Strasbourg. Now as the above-mentioned actions are so murderous and unheard of, it may not be unreasonably understood that the peasants principally obtained their counsel from us, and that we, untrue to our own preaching on peace and unity, have now taught them and advised them to overthrow all order and rule, to plunder, steal, murder, and show no respect for authority, especially since it also says elsewhere in their testimony that several people from Weyersheim[4] brought a letter, in which it was written that one should slay all spiritual and temporal authorities. We do not wish to pass judgment on their intention in committing such testimony to paper, but many have the impression and are under the assumption that such a letter was written and issued by us, the preachers, who are presented as advising their actions. Indeed, the general sense and purport of the articles, when compared with others, gives that impression.

So now this poor man, who has given this testimony freely before seven witnesses, has been judged and convicted. What else will people conclude from this other than that we, the preachers, Wolfgang Capito and Matthew Zell, are dangerous folk, who incited the poor rabble, and that the honourable city council of Strasbourg is not displeased with it, since, as our magistracy, they left us alone and did not subject us to painful torture and capital punishment to avoid further unrest on account of us, the troublemakers? Anyone will draw that conclusion from the testimony, especially he who is not particularly well inclined to us or who is otherwise not mentally acute. For that reason, we, who have hitherto suffered slander in silence, are compelled to produce the present declaration.

And I especially, Wolfgang Capito, have not responded to the writings and talk, for how could I possibly have undertaken to incite unrest in the community and council, and to have caused pernicious dissent and unrest in Haguenau, my beloved fatherland, where I have my roots, my relatives, and still have close friends, and whose welfare I am therefore willing to foster to the utmost? I did not respond earlier, although grave suspicion was being cast on me even in print, for the respectable city council, together with the honourable community of Haguenau, knows better. I gladly accept them as judge and jury in this and other matters, and earlier on offered to subject myself to torture in their presence, and am willing to do the same in this case.

* * * * *

4 Weyersheim is situated 18 km northwest of Strasbourg. It was part of the territory of the bishopric of Strasbourg and bailiwick of Kochersberg.

For the same reason I have not responded to the unkind actions in Freiburg, where they burned the Christian pamphlet I wrote, incited by evil people and libellous writings.[5] My pamphlet was publicly burned by the city's messenger on a public market day after several announcements were made from the pulpit with great pomp in the presence of the honourable council itself, the parish priests, their coadjutors, and quite a few of Strasbourg's clergy. I still have not done anything definite about this, although someone brought the ashes here to Strasbourg and carried them around repeatedly, like relics, to much scorn and derision.

I took into consideration that such written responses often incite turmoil, and that such publications can hardly be written in moderate language and without seeking one's own advantage. For the flesh is more concerned about losing respect than preserving the honour of God and his Word, and yet it does so under the guise of serving the Word. Furthermore, I took into consideration that at the end of the aforesaid pamphlet are the following words: 'We offer to give an account of our hopes to all people, learned or unlearned, who believe in the Word of God. For it is proper for an honest man to conduct his business with anyone openly, and refrain from criticizing in secret what has been done well and lawfully. If we have taught anything but Christ in Strasbourg and drawn the pious simple people to us with rebellious heresy and our own stories, let us fare according to divine law, Deut. 13. May they punish us bodily as we deserve, let them have no mercy on us,' etc.[6] That only needs to be said once. But beyond that, although unfair force has been brought to bear against me, I nevertheless offer myself today to Master Sixt Hermann[7] and Jakob Schultheiss,[8] who have reported such things about me earlier on in writing; to the parish priest in Freiburg, his coadjutors, and the university itself;[9] likewise, to Jakob Wimpheling,[10] and to Dr Johannes Fabri of Constance,[11] who is reportedly triumphant, especially against us Strasbourgers, as we hear. I offer myself to all of these individuals, or whoever otherwise sees a flaw in any of my writings or my person and life. If he can find in the said pamphlet half an article that is heretical or rebellious, I will gladly suffer capital punishment at the hands of the magis-

* * * * *

5 I.e., *Von drey strassburger pffaffen*. See Ep. 246a headnote.
6 See above, pp. 152–3.
7 On Hermann, see above, Ep. 237, note 3.
8 On Schultheiss, see above, Ep. 237, note 5.
9 Cf. above, Ep. 246d.
10 On Wimpheling, see above, Ep. 246a, note 114.
11 For Fabri, see CWC 1, Ep. 110a headnote.

tracy and even recant beforehand. Yet I know that in matters pertaining to our faith and hope proper, of which we are speaking and which are at issue, neither angel nor devil, nor any skill, nor the power of the world can in any way refute our reason and rationale. The same declarations have previously been issued in print by us all and have been reiterated. We hereby wish to repeat them again most pointedly and emphatically.

A great deal has been said about me, Wolfgang Capito, in the context of the business of Hans Jakob Schütz,[12] but I have always scorned such reports and passed them over in silence, for my lords, the XIII,[13] know very well of my innocence and of my loyal, friendly, and truthful actions, and I appeal to them. I have never publicly responded to this or other libellous writings and scornful speeches, because I was certain of our innocence and did not wish to cause any hatred or bitterness against anyone.

But the present matter, which concerns legal proceedings, is too important and too dangerous. It is going for the jugular. It creates insufferable ill will among many people, not only for us, but the entire city of Strasbourg along with us. Furthermore, it makes our sermons, which are certainly God's Word, suspect and hateful to many who, in any case, do not bear us good will and have no understanding of our purpose. What is one supposed to think of our preaching, when we are thought to be the instigators of widespread murder, and what are dukes, lords, and local magistrates to think of the city of Strasbourg for allowing us to live here, even though we are regarded in this light? Will they think that the city council was pleased with us, or afraid of the community, and therefore did not punish us although we deserved capital punishment? Neither is the case, and [such a reputation] would burden the whole city in the future. Therefore, we are letting the reader know in brief what advice we gave to everyone, what efforts we made to deal with the peasants' uprising, and also what action we took in this case with respect to the bishop's councillors.

Firstly, because we are obliged to pray for everyone and to ask that each person be saved, it is our custom to advise anyone, who asks us for an account, and we always tell anyone who demands that from us, that our salvation rests in the knowledge of our sins, in being dissatisfied with ourselves and despairing of ourselves in everything that is not of God, so that we might have ultimate confidence and trust alone in the grace of God, which the merciful Father through Christ our Lord communicated to us, through whom we have justification, salvation, and redemption. Therefore, we deter them

* * * * *

12 On Schütz, see above, Ep. 197 headnote.
13 The city's senior privy council.

from human opinions and the teachings of the devil, and earnestly exhort them to rely only on the simple Word of God, in which God is with us and we have life. For that reason, we advised many people to follow Christian preachers, who are not hirelings and wolves,[14] but true shepherds and sensible stewards of the mysteries of God. We also gave the same advice to those of Weyersheim. They gave the impression that they followed our faith in the most Christian manner, for they offered to the Rhinegrave,[15] their canon, to give all dues to the church, more punctually and generously than before, if only His Grace would allow them to be able to obtain a Christian preacher at their own cost, without the parish priest being obliged to depart.

Furthermore, they had taken on a man who claimed to be an evangelical preacher, but of whom we knew otherwise at the time.[16] We admonished and warned them to stay away from him and other people like him, and we forewarned them of what, in part, happened to them afterwards, for the same person has caused no shortage of problems, and is perhaps responsible for many thoughtless undertakings. As a result, afterwards we sent one of us from here[17] to Weyersheim at the request of the poor people, with the command to preach Christ as simply as possible and to urge the people to obedience, peace, and unity. Afterwards, he came back here, and still to this day is willing to give an account of his teachings, his words and deeds, to anyone who asks him for it. Yet, we are sure that his loyal efforts are well known to the episcopal council, seeing that he had earnestly advised the poor people of Weyersheim against siding with the peasants, and that he had done that publicly in their assembly rooms, in the presence of many. But afterwards, the episcopal councillors desired that those poor people should apprehend that same fellow brother of ours, or to help apprehend him as a Lutheran preacher. At their request, we advised them and said that they, as they are obliged, as well on account of their conscience, should humbly offer themselves to the councillors, the representatives of their own gracious lord, that they should be obedient and ready with their persons and goods, and that they should act in all respects in such a manner that the people might sense that the gospel had made them patient and obedient. Apart from that, they

* * * * *

14 I.e., hirelings who abandon their flock at the sight of wolves; cf. John 10:11–13 and 1 Cor. 4:1.
15 The Rhinegrave Jakob von Salm (d. 1557), canon of the cathedral chapter of Strasbourg from 1507. He had the cure of the parish of Weyersheim from 1520, i.e., he was the titular parish priest.
16 I.e., Clemens Ziegler. Cf. above, Ep. 215, note 13.
17 Unidentified.

should beg the councillors, whose authority extends only over their persons and possessions, in the name of God to let the people hear the divine Word, through which God alone rules the conscience. They should furthermore offer not to allow among them any citizen or preacher who proves himself disobedient or rebellious, but faithfully help to punish evil men and see that the people would be obedient to the authorities. That was reportedly transacted verbally and afterwards put in writing, together with a justification for certain articles that were held against them, as the episcopal council well knows – the document might still be in their possession.[18]

How faithfully and how often did we warn and beg them, for God's sake, to cite the gospel only for the salvation of souls, and to seek in it nothing that concerns the world, to live together quietly in peace, and be willing to show themselves more patient than before toward everyone, and not just toward the magistracy! Had the average poor man heeded half of our admonitions and earnest warnings, which we expressed both verbally and in writing, without a doubt this heavy burden would never have fallen on their shoulders. We undertook and did the same not just with one or two people from one or two towns, but with each person who came here. For we always and consistently told them what they owe to God and what to the world, namely their lives and possessions to the magistracy, forbearance toward enemies, willingness to lend a helping hand to anyone; by contrast, matters of the soul pertain only to God, as do things that concern the glory of God proper, and obedience in matters of faith and to his divine Word. People should be more obedient to God in such matters than to human beings, who have no power over souls. Yet we have always indicated that no one should or may seek their own advantage under the guise of the gospel, or raise their hand to defend themselves. We also advised and urged the same before the whole world, and still do, if anyone asked or still asks for our counsel. No honest man can truthfully deny that about us.

Secondly, concerning our attitude during the peasant rebellions, this is the truth: when these grave troubles came to pass, each and every one of us, according to his gifts and abilities, deterred everyone we could. This brought upon us great ill will from certain ignorant people, who did not know better at the time. Several of us were in danger of our lives, and repeatedly so; indeed, we were almost killed. When, however, a group of peasants gathered

* * * * *

18 Cf. the correspondence between the citizens of Weyersheim and the episcopal court of 5 March 1525 (AST 98, #24; Adam, *Kirchengeschichte*, 579–80) and 26 January 1525 (AST 98, #23, printed in Günther Franz, *Der Deutsche Bauernkrieg: Aktenband* [Berlin, 1935; repr. Darmstadt, 1977], 191–2).

together at Altdorf,[19] who proffered the common articles of the peasants, in which they cited the authority of the preachers, some of us would gladly have responded in writing at first and rejected their pernicious error, but we were worried that we would aggravate and spread the matter, as this was in fact what happened. For that reason, we did not write at first. We hoped thereby to deal all the more effectively with the peasants, and that they might refrain from unreasonable actions and keep calm. Yet, at their request and with approval of the honourable city council, as well as that of the magistrates, namely our gracious lord, the *Landvogt*[20] and representative of His Roman Imperial Majesty, several gracious lords of the cathedral chapter and the emissaries of the noble, honourable, and wise city council of Strasbourg,[21] who were in Dorlisheim at that time and were working to turn away the peasants, we stopped dealing with them. On the command of the authorities, we dealt neither with the whole crowd, nor afterwards with their committee. For the authorities exhorted them in as kind a manner as possible to agree to a friendly compromise and to adopt it. We have proof that we acted loyally and with great earnestness, and were perhaps responsible in no small degree for the fact that many withdrew. But, when we realized the true intentions of the leaders and how the crowd was getting stronger and stronger, we left with the knowledge and in accordance with the will of those in power, and went back to Strasbourg. On the way, we considered that our actions on behalf of the Word should be more earnest, for hitherto, we had acted only on the command of the authorities, in the most friendly and polite manner. On the way we stopped off in the village of Entzheim,[22] and on the same day sent back an earnest tract with the following contents: that God has never left unpunished a man who, under the guise of the Word, looks to his own advantage; that a common uprising is always to the disadvantage and harm of the community; also that God, as indicated through scripture, has vehemently punished every uprising against the authorities, even if they were godless and illegitimate.[23]

* * * * *

19 The peasants, under the leadership of Erasmus Gerber, occupied the monastery of Altdorf on 15 April. Gerber was hanged on 17 May. See above, Epp. 242 and 242a.
20 Hans Jacob von Mörsburg, *Landvogt* of Haguenau. Cf. above Ep. 182.
21 Martin Herlin and Bernhard Ottfriedrich were sent in April 1525 by the city council of Strasbourg as emissaries to the peasants. They proposed that the peasants disperse and promised that they would not be punished for their actions. See above, Epp. 242a and 243, as well as PolCorr 1:113–14, Ep. 200.
22 Entzheim, a small village between Altdorf and Strasbourg.
23 The tract is dated 18 April 1525 (Ep. 243).

Next, we cited written historical accounts full of cruel horrors and threats, showing clearly that they had no more grounds to be restless, even if they acted only with an eye to worldly considerations, especially given that the authorities were willing to act according to their petitions, and wanted to reduce their burden in everything, to the extent that it was fair and useful to them and everyone. We forwarded these accounts to Andreas Prünlin,[24] who was parish priest at Dorlisheim at that time, and who, at our command, explained in an excellent manner our brief historical references, and he would have convinced the people to withdraw altogether, had not the leaders skilfully dissuaded them. For they claimed that those under the dominion of Hanau were not yet secure.[25] For that reason, they were supposed to delay for only two days until such people should also arrive at their homes, so that they would not be delivered to the slaughterhouse. In the meantime, the mob was encouraged by outsiders, and there were other reasons why the withdrawal did not take place. We also did not want to deal any further with the matter ourselves, except that we faithfully admonished in writing Andreas Prünlin and others, who looked after the Word and were with the rebels, to turn them away, to vehemently punish the evil undertakings of the poor, as some of them did on their own. Certain noble and renowned men are still saying they were amazed that the preachers were not thrown off the pulpits by the wicked horde when they talked of punishment. Yet, when our tract was read out and after various actions had been taken by the authorities, everyone affiliated with the region of the city of Strasbourg left. It would be tedious to read about all our other troubles and efforts. They are known to a number of decent men, who do not want to hide from the truth, even if we ourselves remain quiet.

Thirdly, as it has come to our attention that testimony was given against us recently at Saverne, we have diligently petitioned and begged the honourable city council, our lords and superiors, to ask the episcopal council for the proceedings along with the witnesses' reports, for the articles against us give only the gist.[26] We are said to have counselled the condemned men in their

* * * * *

24 Andreas Prünlin (Prunulus) was parish priest in Dorlisheim 1524/25. He was condemned to death for his role in the Peasants' War, and hanged in May 1525 by order of Duke Anthony of Lorraine. In his commentary on Habakkuk, p. 20, Capito lamented Prunulus' death, 'whom the tyrant's hand consigned to the noose.' He was succeeded by Johannes Klein, who purchased Strasbourg citizenship on 11 January 1525.
25 The territory of Philip IV, count of Hanau-Lichtenberg (1514–90).
26 See above, Ep. 277.

actions, and yet it is unlikely, and indeed, unusual for an authority to be satisfied with a general statement given under torture. Rather, it has always been the practice to ask about each circumstance, how and when something happened, and no doubt the councillors proceeded in that way. We hoped that they would not find it burdensome to indicate kindly to us what, who, when, and in what circumstances we [supposedly] advised the condemned, and accept in turn our true report with clear and evident reasons, which we wanted to do in such a form that all might be content who harbour suspicion against us in that matter. But perhaps this was not opportune for the council, since the matter concerns a serious and capital offence, and they had in mind a court action. We offered to appear before the honourable council and submit to torture, to keep, maintain, and uphold the law. We offered to submit to the law without protest, in the good hope that the honourable council would not object to accepting our sincere report, or a legal response, for no one has the right to deprive another person of his honour and reputation on account of a vain report. We are obliged to defend our reputation on the basis of the Word of God, for we must have a good reputation before the outside world, etc.

Furthermore, this our supplication was sent to the episcopal council at our costs through a messenger of the honourable city council. It took several weeks for them to meet and consider it, and they have now recently responded to this effect: They had written earlier on concerning the proceedings, but concerning the supplication sent by the preachers, they did not think that they wanted any business or anything to do with the preachers of this age. From this, one might draw the conclusion that they had in mind to act against us at a convenient time, which for some reason they have now decided not to do.

This is the sum of our transactions on both sides, which we truthfully proffer to the general reader, and leave him to judge who are honest men and who are not: we or our opponents. For we are not afraid of the light. For that reason, we then appealed once again and asked the honourable city council to help us obtain an answer and to take note, moreover, whether the same things are said about us by those who are going to be judged in Molsheim. We did not ask for consideration, but on the contrary, that every means be used to make the truth come out, whoever might be affected by it.[27]

To that end, we ask the general reader to recognize that our position is not based on keeping our actions in the dark, but rather in making them

* * * * *

27 See below, Ep. 281.

public, and that we are not wittingly giving out commands for which we need to be ashamed before anyone. As for the rest, we are like other sinners and in need of the grace of God. Therefore, may each one duly reflect that it is our task to direct each person to the Truth, to apply the Truth for Christian purposes, to attempt to help each person, as far as we are able, toward the Word, to improve them, to respond to the Truth, and to remind the authorities to come to know God and to uphold peace, obedience, patience, forbearance, and brotherly love. If we the preachers, be it Capito or Matthew, have done the opposite, let it be immediately indicated to the authorities before any scandal arises, so that we may suffer death through fire or sword, or perhaps be hanged from a tree, as long as the general good is guaranteed. For such people, as many take us to be, based on the testimony issued, are indeed better off dead than alive. The episcopal council, in accordance with their learned understanding, knows that well and no doubt would not refrain from acting, if they had some grounds or plausible charges against us, since they are favourably inclined toward the common good. Their disposition is such, one may assume, that they would not neglect anything of this sort. They do not have such a high opinion of us, nor do they favour us with their friendship. We draw the conscience of the faithful to God and the cross, away from earthly opinions and teachings of the devil, which torment the conscience with human and external commandments. But practices that go against scripture and the Word of God are clear and obvious. Their attitude against us can be sensed from the fact that they write with such suspicion and grave ill will: 'They [i.e., the peasants] took advice from the preachers Dr Capito and Master Matthew concerning their dealings.'[28] For one understands by 'their dealings,'[29] that [we told them] each to take his own, to share everything equally, to do away with all authorities, to slay the nobles and the clergy, especially since they had spoken of these actions earlier on. But if they meant that the little word 'dealings' refers to the actions, which concern the Word, a matter on which we advised them, then it would have been fairer to word their statement as follows: 'The preachers also advised them that they are supposed to be loyal and obedient to the authorities as they are to God himself for the sake of their conscience, and that each man grant, cede, tolerate, and overlook more in earthly matters than before, and to remain steadfast to the divine Truth and to endure what God makes us endure, without any desire for evil revenge.' For we advised them and others in this manner and no other.

* * * * *

28 Cf. above, note 3.
29 *händel.*

There were, however, people who came to us for advice earlier on. Their testimony, too, might be heard to establish whether we, in fact, advised them differently (for these people cannot all have died). Thus, the episcopal council no doubt understands and knows how we advised and helped the poor people of Weyersheim, both orally and in writing. And when some of us said in Altdorf 'Dear friends, your course of action is not evangelical. Do not defend your faith with guns, halberds, and spears,' do you not think that those whom we had advised earlier[30] would have stood up and said: 'Dear men, you have given us different advice earlier. What is the meaning of this? Why are you saying something else now?'

Be that as it may, we ask the patient and Christian reader for the sake of God's will not to harbour any ill will or suspicion against anyone, but consider the gravity of the matters now coming to pass, that even very sensible, clever, and rational laymen of the world and noble members of the council, who are otherwise pious and decent, are running hard against this rock of Christ – people who in secular matters act more honourably and cautiously, indeed, more uprightly and decently. We, who know Christ, are supposed to thank God for the knowledge of Christ that has been given to us, and earnestly pray for our enemies, that God may bestow his grace upon them and let them come to know him, and that there be no hard feelings at all, as I have said, against their blindness. May God the Father through our Lord Jesus Christ bestow upon us all his grace that we may live according to his will. Amen.

Letter 281: [After 26 February, and before 12 March 1526, Strasbourg], Capito and his colleagues to the City Council of Strasbourg

Printed in CorrBucer 2:99–100, Ep. 118.

[*Summary*]: The preachers ask the city council to give priority in their agenda to discussing the upcoming trial at Molsheim of people involved in the peasant revolts, and to defending the preachers against the accusation that they have encouraged the rebels in their actions.

Letter 282: 4 April 1526, [Strasbourg], Capito to Ulrich Zwingli

Printed in ZwBr 2:556–7, Ep. 465.

[*Summary*]: The Anabaptist, Wilhelm [Exel or Echsel], has been at Capito's

* * * * *

30 I.e., supposedly advised earlier to defy the authorities.

house, where they privately discussed baptism three times. Exel talked indiscreetly in public, claiming that the Strasbourg reformers approved of his beliefs. The reformers also had a discussion with Exel's host [Jörg Ziegler?]. The dispute is still ongoing. The Catholics insisted on going to confession during the Easter season, in an attempt to cause commotion. The Strasbourg reformers, by contrast, are striving for peace and quiet. Stephan [Stör] is still in prison [cf. above, Ep. 273]. Zwingli's letter [not extant] was helpful and gave him hope. The courier will inform Zwingli about the reformers in Silesia. The young man Zwingli sent is doing well at the pharmacist's [see above, Epp. 272, 273]. The situation in France will hamper the gospel.

Capito has read Zwingli's [*Ad Theobaldi Billicani et Urbani Rhegii epistolas responsio*, Zurich, 1526] and is pleased with its moderate tone. [Willibald] Pirckheimer has written against Oecolampadius [i.e., *De vera Christi carne et vero eius sanguine ad Ioan. Oecolampadium responsio* (Nürnberg, 1526)]. The reformers in Silesia are on Zwingli's side, even if they disagree slightly about the phrasing. Zwingli's response to Billicanus will help in this respect.

Letter 283: 7 April [1526], Strasbourg, Capito to Nikolaus Prugner

> Printed in Jules Lutz, *Les réformateurs de Mulhouse. VI. Nicolaus Prugner (Troisième Partie)* (Mulhouse, 1912), 16–17, appendix 1. On Prugner, see Ep. 221 headnote.

Grace and peace, my dearest [brother] in the Lord.

I strongly urge you not to set foot outside during these holidays, so that the people may see that your heart is still devoted to the church of God and their city. You can finish the business on which you have set your mind at another time just as conveniently, and with less inconvenience to the church. I do not know yet whether anyone will be sent to you from here.[1] I am bedridden with a slight fever and cough, and so I have been less able to attend to these matters, but I have written to Bucer, and you will know what will happen the day after tomorrow. Make sure to greet our brethren in Mulhouse.

Some rumour – a false one, I suspect – is being spread about you by wicked men and reached me as a vague rumour from an uncertain source; for that reason, I sincerely warn you to find out what sort of suspicion it is and on what occasion it is being spread, to put a stop to the source of this

* * * * *

1 It is unclear where Prugner was at the time of writing. He was too radical for the taste of the city council of Mulhouse and departed some time in April. See also the following note for rumours that he was in Strasbourg.

wicked rumour.[2] For perhaps someone in your household is not above suspicion. I have no doubt but that you are most attached to your wife, and to no other woman than your wife. Make sure you associate with no woman too closely, for the common people can be reassured only with strong evidence. Conversely, I ask you to admonish me in turn, from time to time. Farewell in the Lord. Strasbourg. 7 April 15[26].

Yours, Capito

Send my greetings to your parish priest and write back to us about what hope you have for that man.[3]

Letter 284: 16 April 1526, Strasbourg, Capito to Ulrich Zwingli

Printed in ZwBr 2:565–6, Ep. 469.

[*Summary*]: In reply to a request from Zwingli to review his [response to Theobaldus Billicanus and Urbanus Rhegius, cf. above Ep. 282], Capito approves of Zwingli's approach and argument. He advises Zwingli to continue writing in a moderate tone, with arguments grounded in scripture. Capito is pleased with Zwingli's news about Bern [letter not extant]. The Strasbourg city council has tried in vain to come to an agreement with the fugitive canons [cf. Ep. 246a]. [Philipp von Hanau] is artfully inciting the citizens of Strasbourg. Capito and his evangelical colleagues are discussing with the city council the abolition of the mass (five are still celebrated daily). Bucer and the rest of the brethren send their greetings, especially [Guillaume] Farel, and Tolnius [pseudonym for Gérard Roussel]. In Heidelberg, there are people now who no longer look for the body of Christ in the Eucharist. They ridicule the *Syngramma Suevicum*, calling it the 'Fourteen Patron Saints' (*Fierzehen Nothelfer*).[1] Matthew Zell has been persuaded of the validity of their interpretation [of the Eucharist], but with some difficulty. There are people 'who subscribe to

* * * * *

2 Cf. Dacheux, #4670 (4 April 1526): '[It is rumoured] that the preacher Nicolaus Prugner of Mulhouse is here and has three wives. For this reason the Swiss confederates expelled him. But there was nothing in this; it was only talk.' The rumour is also mentioned in AST 166, #29. Cf. Prugner's apologia, AST 166, #48.

3 Simon Oeler (d. ca. 1528), documented as parish priest from 1524 to 1527, was not committed to the Reformation.

1 I.e., Johannes Brenz' *Syngramma Suevicum* (1525), a treatise in which he defends Luther's position on the real presence of Christ in the Eucharist. It is co-signed by fourteen theologians.

one thing in our presence and affirm another in the absence of their friends.' Capito sends greetings to [Conradus] Pellicanus, [Oswald] Myconius, Leo Jud, and the rest of the brethren.

Letter 285: 16 May 1526, Strasbourg, Capito to Ulrich Zwingli

Printed in ZwBr 2:596–7, Ep. 481

[*Summary*]: Capito reports about the disputation with a layman, the Anabaptist [Hans Wolff], a man who professes Christ and has distanced himself from the Peasants' War. Nevertheless, Wolff kept asserting that the reformers in Strasbourg were 'veritable Pharisees,' and paid too much attention to reforming matters external to faith. He would have them demolish statues, altars, and chapels, eject monks and nuns from the monasteries, and abolish the mass. Wolff's statements aroused a strong reaction, but Capito agrees with him about the necessity of abolishing the mass.

Capito has read Zwingli's response to [Johannes] Fabri [*Uber den ungesandten Sandbrieff Fabers Zwinglis Antwort*, 30 April 1526]. Two copies have been passed around among friends in Strasbourg. Oecolampadius has written to the Basel city council to get permission to attend the Disputation [of Baden] with a letter of safe conduct. Barbara von Sargans [cf. above, Epp. 275, 278] is going to Zurich. She is a woman worthy of Zwingli's patronage and entitled to an income from her former nunnery. Oecolampadius has written about the affairs in France. He is busy reforming the remainder of the masses. Capito announces that the people in Strasbourg now have a true understanding of the Eucharist.

Letter 285a: [18–19 May 1526, Strasbourg], The Strasbourg Preachers to the City Council of Strasbourg

Printed in BDS 2:524–7, no. 11, and summarized in CorrBucer 2:113–14, Ep. 126

[*Summary*]: The preachers outline the reasons why the mass should be abolished.

Points 1–3: It is contrary to scripture and therefore a sin, given that one should trust only in God.

Points 4–9: True service is founded on faith in Christ and on love of one's neighbour. Christ's sacrifice was unique and cannot be repeated in the mass. The mass does not bring salvation, and one cannot make amends for one's sins by paying money. It is therefore an abomination, which the magistrates have to abolish.

Letter 286: 23 May 1526, Strasbourg, The Strasbourg Preachers to Johannes Fabri

Published in *Epistola V. Fabritii Capitonis ad Hulderichum Zuinglium* [Strasbourg: W. Köpfel, 1526], ff. A3v–A5v; printed in CorrBucer 2:114–17, Ep. 127.

[*Summary*]: They reproach Fabri for claiming victory over Zwingli and boasting that he will destroy the preachers of the gospel [at the forthcoming Disputation at Baden].[1] Fabri offered earlier to dispute with the preachers publicly, but nothing came of it. At a meeting in Dachstein, in the presence of the bishop of Strasbourg, [Wilhelm von Honstein], Duke George of Braunschweig and Ludwig von Hohenlohe affirmed that Fabri's offer was genuine and pledged their support for a disputation. The preachers invite Fabri herewith to a disputation in Strasbourg, with the city providing a safe conduct. They are willing to change their ways if Fabri can prove them wrong. They challenge him to bring his rhetorical skills to bear on the matter.

Letter 287: 3 June 1526, Strasbourg, The Strasbourg Preachers to Johannes Fabri

Published in *Epistola V. Fabritii Capitonis ad Hulderichum Zuinglium* ([Strasbourg: W. Köpfel, 1526]), ff. [A6v-A8v] and most recently printed in CorrBucer 2:117–20, Ep. 128.

[*Summary*]: They remind Fabri of their recent invitation [Ep. 286] to come to Strasbourg after the Disputation of Baden and dispute with them as well. He promised to meet with them last year at Dachstein and again at Augsburg, but nothing came of these plans. They question Fabri's sincerity. They hope the meeting in Baden will go forward in spite of Fabri's reservations [i.e., his claim that doctrinal matters can only be discussed at synods, for which he cites papal and imperial decrees]. They offer to defend their teachings, but on the basis of scripture alone. If Fabri needs confirmation that the Strasbourg city council welcomes such a discussion and is willing to guarantee his safety, he may write to them directly. The preachers believe that the city of Strasbourg is, in fact, a more suitable place for a public disputation than the small town of Baden.

* * * * *

1 *Epistola doctoris Iohannis Fabri ad Ulricum Zwinglium ... de futura disputatione Badensi* [n.p., 1526].

Letter 287a: [7 June 1526, Baden], Johannes Fabri to the Strasbourg preachers

Printed in CorrBucer 2:120–1, Ep. 129. This is Fabri's response to Ep. 287 above. When Capito published this response in *Epistola V. Fabritii Capitonis* (see above, Ep. 290 headnote), he related the circumstances in which Ep. 287 was delivered and the reception the courier had from Fabri. Shortly after Fabri's arrival in Baden on 7 June, the courier, accompanied by a servant of Johannes Oecolampadius, tried to deliver the letter. Fabri treated him with contempt and refused to accept the letter, saying that he had already received a number of insulting letters from the reformers. He made mocking references to a grammatical mistake in a previous letter from the preachers and sent the courier away with an oral response.

[*Summary*]: Fabri refused to give them a response in writing for the following reasons: first, they insulted him in their letters; second, they sent him an unsealed letter and did not identify themselves, signing the letter 'The preachers and brethren of Strasbourg'; third, he has learned from [Ulrich] Zwingli to send back letters unread, since Zwingli had recently treated him in like fashion. Fabri had sent him two letters [not extant], one in Greek and the other in Hebrew, through two young men, who were guests of Fabri's at the time. After reading the first letter, Zwingli responded through [Conradus] Pellicanus in German, using Hebrew script. Zwingli did not even bother reading the second letter; fourth, Fabri will be in Speyer within a month and suggests the disputation be held there, when many Christian princes will be present who could act as fair judges. Finally, Ferdinand I's directions were to dispute in Baden and 'not in any chance place.'

Letter 288: 10 June 1526, Strasbourg, Capito to Nicolaus Prugner

Printed in QGT 7:54–5, #50. On Nicolaus Prugner, cf. Ep. 221 headnote. The date is based on Ep. 290 (of 11 June) in which Capito refers to the episode related below (of Wolff interrupting Zell's sermon), explaining that the event took place 'yesterday.'

Today our weaver[1] shouted at Matthew[2] in the cathedral. After Matthew had

* * * * *

1 I.e., Hans Wolff. Cf. above, Ep. 285.
2 I.e., Matthew Zell.

read the text from Deuteronomy, *I give to you the iron heaven*,[3] he added, 'See what disobedience may bring.' Next [Wolff] barked, 'You are disobedient to the Holy Spirit. What you say goes against him and is a lie. In his name I command you to withdraw and permit me to say what the Spirit wishes to say.' I feel sorry for that man, who aspires so madly to make a name for himself. I do not know why he does it. I can think of no other reason than arrogance and vanity. The Spirit of the Lord is not puffed up, nor does it lie, as that man has done today.[4] Indeed, he has often been discovered lying in small matters. Diligently teach the purity of Christian faith and you will do a worthwhile thing. Be a faithful evangelist, I pray. But for the rest, everything here is safe as yet. Farewell. He[5] has again been taken into public custody. Greet the local prefect[6] and the brethren for us.

Capito.

Letter 288a: [ca. 10 June 1526, Strasbourg, Capito to the Reader]

This is the preface to an unauthorized edition of the proceedings of the Disputation of Baden, entitled *Warhafftige handlung der disputation in obern Baden des D. Hans Fabri, Jo. Ecken unnd irs gewaltigen anhangs gegen Joan. Ecolampadio und den dienern des worts*, Strasbourg: Köpfel, summer of 1526 (A true account of the Disputation in Upper Baden between Dr Hans Fabri, Johann Eck and their powerful following against Johannes Oecolampadius and the ministers of the Word).

The Disputation of Baden came about as a result of a challenge issued by Johann Eck in August 1524 to refute Zwingli's teachings in a disputation.[1] In October of that year, the Swiss Confederacy (i.e., the twelve Swiss cantons) designated Baden as the location for the disputation and offered safe conduct to the two men, but Zwingli declined the invitation. In November, the Zurich city council invited Eck to dispute in Zurich instead, an offer which Eck declined in turn. After further written exchanges between the protagonists, there was a lull in the controversy, but Catholic opposition to Zwingli was renewed in the spring of 1525, when Zurich abolished the mass. In October 1525, Eck once again approached the Confederacy with the idea of a disputation, and in March

* * * * *

3 Deut. 28:23.
4 Cf. 1 Cor. 4:6, 18–19.
5 I.e., Hans Wolff.
6 Perhaps Claus Renner, who is mentioned as the prefect in 1537 (cf. Pol.Corr. 1:443–4, Epp. 721–3).

1 Cf. above, Ep. 276.

1526 a meeting in Baden was agreed on. The city council of Zurich, however, did not permit Zwingli to attend, partly because the Catholics were unwilling to accept scripture as the only prooftext, and partly because the letter of safe conduct for Zwingli contained a notwithstanding clause.[2] When the disputation went forward (21 May to 8 June), Fabri and Eck spoke for the Catholics, and Oecolampadius defended the position of the reformers.[3] Oecolampadius was not enthusiastic about attending,[4] and it was generally acknowledged that he made a poor showing at the disputation. To pre-empt adverse publicity, two anonymous pamphlets originating in the reformers' camp appeared in the summer of 1526.[5] They anticipated the official proceedings, which were published with a year's delay, on 21 May 1527: *Die disputacion vor den xij orten einer loblichen eidtgnoschafft ... zu Baden ... stattgehalten unnd vollendet* (Lucerne, 1527). A Latin version appeared the following year under the title *Caussa Helvetica orthodoxae fidei*, edited by Thomas Murner (Lucerne, 1528).

The *Warhafftige handlung*, one of the anonymous pamphlets reporting on the disputation, contains several items: the prefatory remarks given below, protesting the prohibition against private individuals publishing the proceedings (Aii recto–Bii recto), a reprint of the prohibition and other regulations concerning the disputation (Bii verso–Biii verso) with a commentary by the author (Biv recto–Ci recto), Eck's seven theses in German and two theses in German of Thomas Murner, another participant in the disputation (Ci verso–Cii verso), an account of the disputation up to 30 May (Cii verso– Eii verso), and Zwingli's subsequent reply to Eck's theses (Eiii recto–Giv recto). A remark in the 'Annals of Sebastian Brant' (i.e., Jacob Wencker) under the heading '11 July 1526' indicates that 'Capito composed the preface,' but it remains unclear who supplied Capito with the account.[6] A number of historians have attributed it to the Bern scribe Thomas von Hofen, an identification cogently refuted by Staehelin.[7] Capito himself wrote to the city council of Basel (8 July 1526, Ep. 294) that his informant was 'the servant of an imperial lord, as they say' (*eines keyserischen*

* * * * *

2 ZwBr 2, 573–5; Ep. 472, 585–6; Ep. 476, 610–11; Ep. 488' and Eid. Absch. IV 1a, 893.
3 On the arrival of the delegates, see BrOek 1, Ep. 358.
4 ZwBr 2:576-7, Ep. 473; ZwBr 2:596-7, Ep. 481.
5 E. Staehelin, 'Zwei private Publikationen über die Badener Disputation und ihre Autoren,' *Zeitschrift für Kirchengeschichte* 17 (1918): 378–405.
6 Dacheux, #4687. Cf. Staehelin, 390, and CorrBucer 2:137, Ep. 133, note 2.
7 Staehelin, 'Zwei private Publikationen über die Badener Disputation und ihre Autoren,' 388-9.

herren diener, wie man sagenn wil). The formulation would indicate that Capito was not well acquainted with the informant.

The *Warhafftige handlung* was published at the beginning of June. It was known and vigorously refuted in Basel (by Ludwig Baer and others) as early as 10 June,[8] and Oecolampadius mentions it in a letter to Zwingli on 12 June (ZwBr 2, Ep. 495). The Swiss Confederacy protested the illegal publication of the proceedings to Capito (see below, Ep 291), the Strasbourg city council, and the Diet then convening in Speyer. As a result, Köpfel was fined and briefly placed under arrest by the Strasbourg city council.[9] Capito was let off after showing that he had been maligned (see below, Ep. 290 headnote). He did not deny his involvement in the publication, but argued that it was done in the interest of the reformers and was damaging only to the Catholic cause, an argument apparently acceptable to the Strasbourg city council (see below, Ep. 292).

The children of this world are a cleverer sort than the children of the light. That is evident in the worldly papists of our time, whose indolent, superfluous, secure, and riskless life has served only a false god, and still does – a false god whom they wish to uphold forever, if possible, in the face of plain truth. For this purpose, they have never lost any opportunity to fight anyone they can with fear and hope and threats and bribes. The treasures of this world, which are almost completely in the power of the Antichrist, should by now be exhausted, if they were not busy replenishing the veins of the golden ore and increasing their annual income to the point where it cannot be consumed by their vulgar desire. Lies shy away from light, and they seek aid and protection by obfuscating the truth. I can think of nothing they have omitted to suppress the truth. Now they have used bribes and grave physical threats to fight against strong minds, two expedients that, according to scripture, are likely to obscure the understanding of wise men.[10] That is why they have earnestly undertaken to prevent the printing [of the proceedings of the Baden Disputation]. And when neither prohibition nor other means could deter the minds of the common people from the rising light of faith, they threatened future riots, hoping that both parties would get tired and once again willingly take up the Babylonian yoke and yearn for the big fleshpots of Egypt[11] and the worldly life of the Antichrist.

* * * * *

8 Irena Backus, 'The Disputations of Baden, 1526, and Berne, 1528: Neutralizing the Early Church,' *Studies in Reformed Theology and History* 1.1 (1993): 74. This provides a terminus antequem for the *Wahrhafftige handlung.*
9 Cf. Dacheux, *Fragments des Anciennes Chronique d'Alsace,* vol. 4, #4687.
10 Cf. Ps. 26:9–10.
11 Cf. Num. 11:4–6.

They suffered upheavals without complaint, as long as they served to obtain an imperial mandate against the gospel. Some magistrates enforced the mandate and caused honest citizens to turn against the magistrates, for God reduces the power of those who rise up against him. Others tacitly worked around the mandate, and perhaps saw to it that their subjects benefited from the Christian truth. Some, however, in accordance with the Truth, allowed their subjects to be instructed in the faith. These difficulties brought much division in the German nation, for honest citizens turned away from the tyrants of faith. The useless mob, which is not fond of authority in any case, joined them and pretended zeal for the Word of God, whereas their hearts were set on disturbing order and on their own advantage. And so things went awry and magistrates turned against the common people, and finally a rebellion erupted among the common people,[12] so awful and terrible that it would have destroyed both the authorities and the people, had not God protected them. However, these misdeeds of the poor people did not come to pass everywhere, nor did they actually incite murder in many instances. But how many thousand men were slain last summer? All that was clearly the result of the prohibition of preaching and instigated by the tricky papists, not by the Word of God, which brings divine peace and unity and does violence to no one.

At first, the estates came to an agreement at the Diet of Worms[13] and testified in a public edict that they, the magistrates, desired to remain true to scripture and to interpret it in the sense of love and faith, and wanted to ensure that no one taught the common people anything else but fear of God and faith in Christ, love for one's neighbour, self-discipline, obedience to the magistrate even if they gave unseemly commands, and to remain obedient, willing, and patient in the patience of the Word of God. For that and nothing else is commanded by scripture, which punishes and destroys what goes against this command.

If the supporters of the pope had yielded and allowed this to happen and come to fruition through the agency of the magistrates in the German nation, the glory of God would have been furthered, the common estates would have benefited, and the authorities would have been loved by honest men and feared by evil-doers. True, public finances and the trade in ecclesiastical privileges,[14] which has been carried on so brazenly, would have been

* * * * *

12 I.e., the Peasants' War.
13 1521; perhaps a reference to RTA 1:514–17 (19 February 1521).
14 I.e., indulgences.

reduced and necessarily stopped in any case – they cringe at the thought, and confess in their hearts that the peasant has become wise to them. He no longer allows himself to be deceived. Now they are acting like their father, the devil. They will not yield without doing damage. The rebellions are, thank God, over, but where the Word of God had not properly taken root, it dried out in the hearts of many and left room for the noble clerical lords to chase out poor Christ. That was their earnest desire, and they achieved their purpose in many cases. But a true core remains, specifically in Zurich, for God has declared in our day the power of his Word to establish peace and create new creatures. The pensions have stopped.[15] It is no longer allowed to go to war for mercenary purposes, and there are laws against excesses in clothing, eating, and drinking, and all other excesses in the lives of honest citizens. Earlier on, life in Zurich was of a very different kind, and no clever wit can deny that the tree will be known by its fruit.[16] Where there is faith, one follows what concerns faith and the Spirit. Several men have made a great effort to incite dissension in this church: Johannes Fabri of Constance, Johann Eck of Ingolstadt, both doctors, and their followers from neighbouring episcopal sees. Through their machinations, they brought it about that some members of the Swiss Confederacy arranged a disputation on 16 May [1526] in Baden in Aargau. But they acted more boorishly than ever, and used methods that were less than straightforward. For Dr Hans Schmidt[17] refused to dispute with Zwingli before the honourable council of Zurich, and insisted it was unseemly, saying that one must dispute faith only at a synod. He talks as if it was not incumbent on every Christian to give an account of his hope and faith,[18] and was solely the business of the owl-doctors who flee light and knowledge, whereas it is the business of all simple people devoted to God. The learned doctor did not fare well, moreover, and being full of ambition he could not dissimulate for long. He felt obliged to reveal that he was in the service of a great power, that he had effected much and would do more. It was not enough for Dr Fabri to publish a notice in Tübingen on 16 April concerning the disputation, on which some of the Swiss confeder-

* * * * *

15 I.e., payments by foreign powers to influence the decisions of city councillors. Cf. CWC 1, Ep. 109, note 11, and below, Ep. 311. While parish priest in Glarus from 1506 to 1516, Zwingli expressed his opposition to the hiring of the Swiss as mercenaries in his *Das Fabelgedicht vom Ochsen* (fall 1510) and *Der Labyrinth* (spring 1516).
16 Luke 6:44.
17 'Schmidt' (smith) is the German version of Fabri's name.
18 Cf. 1 Pet. 3:15.

ates had decided only two days earlier.[19] That caused suspicion. Furthermore, he wrote in another letter that he requested the disputation. Yet one suspects that he was not serious about disputing, since Zwingli consistently rejected Baden and suggested Zurich, St Gallen, Bern, Basel, Schaffhausen, and Constance as more honest and suitable places, where he had permission to dispute.[20] And, although Fabri wishes to reject Zwingli's letter, he gives no indication why he does not want to dispute in those places. It also raises the question why he wants a disputation now, when he avoided the one in Zurich, especially since he reportedly said that the matter must be settled in a manner other than a free disputation. Perhaps he is referring to the manner he preached in Augsburg, saying that no good would come of it unless one cut down the teachers and preachers.

Now Eck too wants to dispute, although he did not appear at the request of the city of Zurich.[21] That would indicate that he was inclined to pursue another line rather than dispute. Otherwise, there are many pious preachers in the praiseworthy imperial cities, willing to participate in a Christian colloquy, and prepared and eager to defend the Truth. Fabri and Eck neglect to report that they would be safe and be received and treated as honoured guests. They acted cleverly, considering their ultimate goal, for their intention is not to be helpful in this matter, but to further their private interest by disputing before the praiseworthy Confederacy. For their companions and hangers-on are intent on and would like to see a mandate passed by the Confederates against the gospel, or at least to incite dissension among the Confederates so that the business might issue in physical violence. And although they will not succeed, it is nevertheless agreeable and pleasing to this mob to have attempted to trouble the world and create chaos. Those who benefit and obtain glory from the misfortune and difficulties of the poor, think of the world's fortune and welfare as the worst poison, and ponder how to create

* * * * *

19 I.e., Fabri's German pamphlet entitled *Ein Sandbrieff doctor Johann Fabri an Ulrich Zwingli, Maister zu Zürich, von wegen der künftigen Disputation, so durch gmain aidgnossen der XII orten auf den 16. tag may nächstkünftig gen Baden im Aergöw fürgenommen und ausgeschriben ist* (Tübingen, 16 April 1526), which is printed in *Huldrych Zwinglis Werke* 2:2.429–36). The pamphlet appeared in Latin without date or place of publication under the title *Epistola doctoris Iohannis Fabri ad Ulricum Zwinglium ... de futura disputatione Badensi.* For a summary of Fabri's *Sandbrieff*, see Backus, 'The Disputations of Baden ....' 9–10.

20 Zwingli's formal refusal, dated 21 April 1526, was ZwBr 356 n21.

21 On 17 November 1524, Eck declined the offer from the Zurich city council to dispute in Zurich. (Cf. E. Egli et al., eds., *Huldreich Zwinglis Sämtliche Werke* (Zurich, 1905–), 2:2, 414–15).

fear and misery. It is well known that these pseudo-clerics have insinuated themselves with all authorities through their tricks, have incited dissension and pretended to regret the situation. They have interposed themselves as arbiters, since that was partly their right. They have acquired some authority by right and afterwards maintained it with violence and tricks. If tricks did not prevail, their power would not last long. Permission to hold the disputation was given on 16 May, as indicated, even by cities that had, until then, forbidden and rejected it under threat of capital punishment. On 19 May it was inaugurated in the church of Baden, as noted below, and on Pentecost, 20 May, the following article was posted on the door of the church of Baden in the name of the Twelve Confederates.[22]

Letter 289: 11 June 1526, Strasbourg, Capito to Conradus Pellicanus

In June 1526, Capito sent a courier, Johann Büchli, to Basel with copies of the *Warhafftige handlung* (see above, Ep. 288a headnote) and three letters: a letter from Guillaume Farel to Oswald Myconius, dated 4 June 1526 (available in a French translation in Herminjard I, 431–4, Ep. 176); a letter from Capito to Conradus Pellicanus (i.e., the present letter, Ep. 289) and one to Zwingli (below, Ep. 290). When Büchli stopped off in Basel, he also picked up a letter from Oecolampadius to Zwingli (ZwBr 2:627–8, Ep. 496). The final destination of Büchli was Zurich, but he was arrested in Wettingen on account of blasphemous remarks he made about the Virgin Mary. Consequently, the letters he was carrying were confiscated.[1] In Baden, he was interrogated under torture and admitted that the *Warhafftige handlung* was jointly issued in Strasbourg by Capito and his relative, the printer Wolfgang Köpfel. Johannes Fabri, who was in Baden at the time, published a tendentious German translation of the confiscated letters,[2] which was intended to discredit the Strasbourg reformers at the Diet of Speyer. It contained a dedicatory letter to the city council of Freiburg dated 24 June 1526, the

* * * * *

22 Here follow (on ff. Bii verso–Biii verso) six articles governing the proceedings of the Disputation, as posted by the Swiss Confederates.

1 The information comes from a letter from Thomas von Hofen (ZwBr 2:655, #504), and from Fabri's prefatory letter to the reader in his *Neüwe zeitung und heimliche wunderbarliche offenbarung etlicher sachen und handlungen, so sich uff dem tag der zu Baden in Ergöw vor den Sandtbotten der Zwölff örter der loblichen Eydgnosschafft, uff den Sechßundtzweintzigsten tag des Brachmonats. Im jar Tausent Fünffhundert und XXVI. gehalten worden, zugetragen und begeben hat* (without place or publisher, 1526), fols. Aii recto–B[i] recto.

2 *Neüwe zeitung.* For the full title see above, note 1.

German translation, and pointed glosses. Five hundred copies of the book were sold in Strasbourg by Dionysius Entringer, the bishop's procurator. Capito relates (CorrBucer 2:252–3) that he obtained a copy, paying 'not a fair price, not one and half times the fair price, but six times the amount such pamphlets usually fetch.'

Fabri's translation and malicious glosses forced Capito to respond and control the damage to his reputation. He wrote a series of letters to show that Fabri's translation falsified the contents of the letters (see below, Epp. 292–300) and to exonerate himself. He also published an apologetic tract, *Der nüwen zeytung und heymlichen offenbarung ... bericht und erklerung* (Strasbourg, 1526), addressed to the courtiers of Albert of Brandenburg (preface below, Ep. 298), and he reissued the intercepted letter to Zwingli under the title, *Epistola V. Fabritii Capitonis ad Hulderichum Zvinglium ...* (dated 12 August 1526, see below, Epp. 290 and 299), which brought closure to the affair. The scandal taught Capito to be more careful about what he said in letters and whose names he mentioned. On 12 November 1526, he wrote to Zwingli, suggesting the use of coded language when discussing potentially incriminating subjects (see below, Epp. 309 and 314).

The present letter is one of the four letters intercepted and translated by Fabri. Since the original letter is lost, the following translation is based on Fabri's German version in his *Neüwe zeitung*, ff. Ciii recto–[Civ] recto, which also contains his glosses (italicized in the text below). Another German version, with slight orthographic variants, is printed in E. Egli, 'Die zu Baden "niedergeworfenen" Briefe,' *Zwingliana* 2 (1910): 381.

To Conradus Pellicanus, our most beloved brother in the Lord.
Pellicanus used to be a Franciscan monk in Basel.[3]
May the grace and peace of Christ be with you, most beloved brother in the Lord. Your pamphlet on Erasmus and Luther's opinion regarding the matter of the sacrament [of the Lord's Supper] I read with great enthusiasm.[4]
The pious Erasmus never found out who wrote that pamphlet.[5] *Here Capito writes and reveals everything. Without a doubt, they put Christ to shame in the sacrament, but he in turn will put them to shame.*
But more regarding this shrewd response: you should not have any

* * * * *

3 On Pellicanus see CWC 1, Ep. 89, note 1.
4 The anonymous treatise *Dem hochgelerten Erasmi von Roterdam unnd Doctor Martin Luthers maynung vom Nachtmal unnsers herren Jhesu Christ* [Augsburg: Ulhart Sr., 18 April 1526].
5 Cf. CWE 12, Ep. 1674:72–80. The pamphlet was generally attributed to Leo Jud.

regrets about this work. For whether he wants it or not, it must come out into the open. This brother[6] has been dispatched by the printer[7] with my authorization, to find out about your affairs. And if you are able, please effect that this good brother stay on, that he might live without great cost, until Zwingli writes back.

Concerning my Hebrew studies: I now have a Talmud, but no teacher; therefore I earnestly ask you to send me a Talmudic dictionary.

Hopefully you will have better luck now than you had with your grammar.[8]

A dictionary for such a purpose was issued at Rome under the name of Sante Pagnini, but I have not yet seen it.[9] They also say that another one was published in Venice, which I have not gotten a hold of yet.[10] A while ago I saw a Chaldean dictionary at your place, written in your hand;[11] I would like to have that. If you could do without it, could you send it to me, if only for a few months? Please write to us how things are in Bern, for these things are very important for us to know, be they good or bad.

Without a doubt, much was at stake for you at Bern, but now you know the state of things. I will let you worry about whether you and your renegade monks and nuns in Strasbourg are pleased with it. I feel very sorry for those in charge of the city of Strasbourg. Dear Capito, I never did you any harm. Indeed, for sixteen years[12] *I did you much good, but you do not wish to acknowledge me,*[13] *which I am willing to bear. And for the sake of old comradeship, I wanted to forward to you this aforementioned* Neüwe zeitung *from Bern.*[14] *May God let the scales fall from your eyes, that you might believe again in the old faith.*

* * * * *

6 I.e., Johannes Büchli, see the headnote above.

7 I.e., Capito's nephew, Wolfgang Köpfel (active 1522–54). Until 1522 he worked for the printer Thomas Wolf. He published works by Luther, Bucer, and Zell, as well as editions of the classics and the Bible. He leased the city's paper mill. After his death, the print shop was taken over by his sons Paul and Philipp.

8 On the lack of success of Capito's Hebrew Grammar, see CWC 1, Ep. 11a, note 4.

9 Sante Pagnini (1470–1541), *Enchiridion expositionis vocabulorum* (Rome, 1523).

10 Daniel Bomberg (1483–ca.1553), *Talmud* (Venice, 1520–3).

11 A manuscript copy of Sebastian Münster's forthcoming *Dictionarium chaldaicum* (Basel: Froben, 1527?).

12 I.e., ever since they met at the University of Freiburg, where Fabri enrolled in 1509.

13 *Uffsetzen* – the meaning of the word in this context is unclear. Perhaps 'you did not want to trick me, a claim I am willing to accept.'

14 Cf. above, note 2.

Send greetings to all the brethren. Given at Strasbourg on the 11th of June in the year '26. Nigri[15] and the other brethren, especially Bucer, send their warmest greetings.

Yours, Wolfgang Capito.

Letter 290: 11 June 1526, Strasbourg, Capito to Ulrich Zwingli

This is another one of the four letters intercepted, translated and glossed by Fabri (see above, Ep. 289 headnote). Capito alleged that Fabri's German translation was misleading and consequently published the original Latin letter with his own glossary as *Epistola V. Fabritii Capitonis ad Hulderichum Zuinglium, quam ab Helvetiis forte interceptam, D. Ioan. Faber Constantiensis in Germanicum versam depravavit, una cum duabus epistolis, quibus illum concionatores Argentinenses ad collationem scripturarum provocarunt. Quibus cognosces, lector, qua arte, dolo, impostura et perfidia, Capitonem ut opprimeret Faber adorsus sit* (Strasbourg: [Köpfel], 12 August 1526; text printed in CorrBucer 2, appendix:253–66). The translation below gives Capito's letter, Fabri's glosses (in small print), and Capito's reply to the glosses (italicized). Capito was not the only one to complain about Fabri's translation. At the beginning of August, Nikolaus Gerbel related to Martin Luther the fate of Capito's letter to Zwingli. Although he thought that much of it was 'either foolish or unworthy to be written to such a great man,' he also castigated Fabri for translating it 'with such great perfidy, and likewise with such malice, that I do not know whether he understood the Latin, or whether he distorted the translation according to his own whim.' The Latin and German versions were 'diametrically opposed to one another,' he said (WABr 4:103–6, Ep. 1030).

To Ulrich Zwingli, his most revered friend in the Lord.

Grace be with you, dearest brother. The Antichrist is giving us a sample of his final effort; I am not going to say yet whether he is seriously going to do what he says he will do.

Who does not see that he is covertly speaking of war?[1]

* * * * *

15 Diebold Schwartz or Theobaldus Nigri (ca. 1484–1561) of Strasbourg, a Dominican, studied at the University of Vienna (MA 1508). He became a member of the order of the Holy Spirit at Bern, then at Stephansfeld. At the beginning of 1524, he became the aide of Matthew Zell, then preacher from the spring of 1524 to 1550, and finally pastor at Old St Peter's.

1 The point Capito is trying to make is unclear. Fabri's translation is faithful to Capito's text, and there is no gloss in Fabri's text at this point. See *Neüwe zeitung*, f. Biv.

The emperor has given a mandate to the Regensburg alliance[2] and authorized them to defend his interests, along with a magnificent promise that he will soon be in Germany to eradicate that seditious doctrine (as they call the gospel).

Dear Capito, ask the poor, wretched widows and orphans, of which there are many hundred thousand within a small area of the German Nation. Unfortunately, their husbands were slain on account of Luther's counsel and sermons. That is the damned gospel you have preached.

It has long been falsely declared that the gospel truth is seditious. And these days are full of carping critics everywhere, to whose machinations we owe edicts of this sort.

Our bishop[3] is spreading a rumour that he is buying 8,000 sacks of grain in the neighbouring towns in order to maintain a large cavalry; he has reserved living quarters in inns and hostels, and is building stables for the horses in each of his fortresses.

The wise Solomon spoke of a type of human beings which God hates foremost, namely, a man who lies and sows in the wind.[4]

Such rumours have become very widespread in the entire region, not just in our city, to such an extent that certain men thought about guarding against war. Fabri seized on this as a handle here to oppress the Word among the Swiss. For he has a tendency to support superstition,[5] now in decline, with the vainest bit of petty gossip. Who does not know that many rumours are vain? Yet it is no sin for friends to speak lightly among themselves about such things on occasion, although they would be rather embarrassed to speak of them either in public or to a stranger.

What ridiculous plans! Stalwart hearts will not be intimidated by spectres, even if it looks as if skirmishes might be fought on horseback. I do not know how sound that course of action is for them, unless the Lord will make hearts utterly fearful and anxious at the rustling of a leaf.[6] On top of that, they say that Duke Heinrich of Braunschweig has been given the authority and the mandate to fight against the Saxons.[7]

* * * * *

2 The alliance between the Catholic principalities concluded at Regensburg in June/July 1524.
3 Wilhelm von Honstein.
4 Prov. 6:19.
5 I.e., the Catholic party.
6 Cf. Lev. 26:36.
7 Heinrich II (1489–1568), Duke of Braunschweig-Wolfenbüttel, who reigned from 1514 to 1568, but was dispossessed of his principality by the Schmalkaldic League from 1542 to 1547.

If you were a Christian evangelist you should stop, I say, and refrain from writing such grave things, and I see you would be afraid of mummers at a Carnival.

I shy away from bringing shame on even an insignificant man, even if it concerns a well-known matter. Still, what people discuss in their private conversations is no one else's business. And letters written by blameless men are subject to the same rule.

The bishops are most inclined to threaten everything,[8] for they have vast amounts of money. Meanwhile, the truth is ignored. Once the Diet of Speyer is called,[9] it will confirm such plans and bring them into the open, if only they have a chance of winning.

Lo, this prophet knows the future. He knows people's hearts.

I am not saying that the diet was primarily called to confirm these things, but simply that the diet was called.[10] For I do not define why it was called. It will confirm plans of this sort, I said. I made a discreet guess in a letter to a friend, while Fabri made firm assertions before the Swiss, who consequently wrote a letter to the Reichsregiment,[11] stating that they knew they had been called together to eradicate the new error. Fabri first published these letters as testimony against me.

I expect a more serious fight will threaten the city-states, which they have artfully divided.

Once you and your kind have slain practically all the peasants in the countryside, you want to start a war among the cities. I have two pieces of counsel to prevent that: to chase out you and your kind of people, who are enemies of the sacrament, and to reestablish Christian order. If that comes to pass, your prophecy will not be fulfilled.

We often expect what never actually happens. Fabri has translated this as follows: 'A bitter war is in the offing against the city-states.'[12] In this manner he tries unfairly to amplify everything! Finally, he concludes from these words that once the peasants are struck down by us, we will contemplate civil war. The fair reader may judge whether he has drawn the right conclusion.

There is no region in the Rhineland that sincerely supports us: on all

* * * * *

8 Fabri's translation reads: 'The bishops give out much money.' Cf. *Neüwe zeitung*, f. Bii r.
9 The Diet of Speyer ran from 25 June to 27 August 1526.
10 Capito is reacting to Fabri's translation, which is more emphatic than the original: 'But the Diet of Speyer is expected to approve this plan and to act upon it, once they see they are assured of victory' (*Neüwe zeitung*, f. Bii r)
11 I.e., the Diet of Speyer to which the Swiss Confederates wrote on 25/28 June 1526 (*Eid. Absch.* IV 1a, 953).
12 Capito wrote: *Est modo prae minibus acre bellum rebus publicis.* Cf. Fabri's translation in *Neüwe zeitung*, f. Bii r: *Es ist gegen den Stetten ein ernstliche schwertfechtung oder krieg vorhanden.*

sides they are discharging the minor preachers, driven by fear of the upcoming evil.

That is the doing of Bucer, Zell, Hedio, Farel, and other lying brethren in the pulpit, for your tree yields such fruit.

I said: as far as the confession of the Word is concerned, as can be seen from what follows; otherwise the friendship of our city with all the others has been lasting and loyal.

The princes point to blasphemous imperial edicts in their favour, forbidding people even to read scripture, but these too will at last be gone with the wind.

Note well that this evangelist calls the edicts of the Imperial majesty 'blasphemy against God.' We must never forget that.

I simply say 'blasphemous.' Fabri interprets this as 'blaspheming against God' for he adds on his own accord 'against God.' That is, he uses a German word referring to someone blaspheming against God.[13] For the rest, blasphemy is insulting talk, a sense in which it frequently occurs in Demosthenes' Pro Ctesiphonte[14] *and elsewhere, and this word has always been used to mean 'simple insult.' I therefore signified to a prudent friend by this same word that the imperial edicts disparage the Word, for on the one hand they prevent the common people from reading the New Testament, and on the other hand they have made the gospel truth seditious. But I ask you, what does one deserve who calls the prince's edict false or a blasphemy against God, when they are extorted by tricks of this sort, while those in command are telling the story incorrectly, addicted too much to their own cause? The laws allow us to inquire into the rescripts of the princes; indeed, they order us to do so. I am not moved by Fabri's threats.[15] I have written in a private letter what I am compelled to confess openly by faith, even under threat of torture. For so Christ told us: 'He who does not confess me, etc.'[16]*

But the tyrants will never run out of money, *the sinews of war,*[17] and since they have a propensity to harm the neighbouring towns, there will be a reason for war.

Note that he calls the princes 'tyrants' – that is evangelical patience and the Spirit of God! *I call those men tyrants who persecute the Word on their own initiative for*

* * * * *

13 Capito is here complaining about Fabri's use of the term *'gotslesterung'* (blaspheming God), rather than simply *'lesterung'* (insulting) to translate the Latin *blasphema* (*Neüwe zeitung*, f. Bii r).

14 Cf. Demonsthenes, *De corona*, 34.5; *Philippica* 4.35.2 and 36.4; *[Philippi] epistula* 20.1; and *De Rhodiorum libertate* 2.7.

15 I.e., Fabri's remark that 'we must not forget that' (*Neüwe zeitung*, f. Bii r).

16 Cf. Matt. 10:33.

17 Cicero, *Philippics* 5.5.

the sake of their own profit. I would be pleased if the term applied to no one during this tempest! But we know that there are secular princes, and perhaps also ecclesiastics, who wish that the glory of God might progress in public tranquillity, if it were possible.

For it seems that our adversaries are going to say, 'In obedience to the oaths we made to the imperial command, we prohibit new doctrines, while you proceed to assert them freely, on account of which our people are being infected. Either you have to yield and accept our opinion, or we must yield and accept yours.'

If we proceeded according to your ideas, princes and lords would lose all their peasants within three years. One would have to slay them all, according to Luther's teaching and the opinion he gave out concerning the peasants.

I have not been present at their counsels. This is a conjecture. Fabri's gloss confirms my conjecture. He writes: 'If we were to continue,' (he says) 'the princes would be without people, and everyone must be slaughtered according to Luther's teachings and permission.' But, my dear Fabri, explain to me when Luther taught that all peasants should be killed! He anxiously asserts the right of the sword, and he faithfully warns everyone not to rebel against the magistracy in the meantime. If those in charge govern the city for the public good, and the people submit at last to God and even to captious rulers, we will certainly enjoy the most profound peace. That is what the apostolic letters teach us, which Luther has expounded to us.

'Furthermore, [they will say] who can oppose the will of the emperor if such is his command? Indeed, in the interest of public concord, we wish the preachers ejected and the old ceremonies restored, so that both of us may submit to the imperial edicts and be joined together again in religious concord.'

Under the old belief we suffered no evil, but you have done more harm to the whole German Nation than they suffered in two thousand years.

Furthermore, it is ridiculous for Fabri to say that no misfortune has ever befallen us under the old religion. For there have always been wars, and external happiness is not the Lydian stone of religion,[18] but faith in God and a life free from sin is [the proof]. Symmachus the atheist speaks in that manner,[19] as does the pig in Epicurus' flock,[20] but no Christian speaks like that. Out of the abundance of the heart the mouth speaks.[21]

* * * * *

18 The Lydian stone is the proverbial touchstone, cf. Erasmus, *Adagia* 1.5.87.
19 I.e., evaluates happiness by external criteria. Q. Aurelius Symmachus Eusebius, a Roman politician (d. 402), author of discourses and letters, and defender of paganism.
20 Horace, Ep. 1.4.15.
21 Matt. 12:34.

If they did that, how many towns do you think would actually last? Very few: Strasbourg, Ulm, and Nürnberg in this area and perhaps three cities in Saxony and along the North Sea coast.[22] The towns that are situated within the confines of the Swiss Confederacy will follow your lead.

Note how afraid this evangelist is in his heart. He himself believes that their affairs may not last.

The concern of a pious heart for the glory of God among men is not fear but sollicitude. Nor do we complain that the cities mentioned are too far away, a meaning you, Fabri, ascribe to us, so that you may cast suspicion on us of seeking an alliance between the cities.[23] Nor are we without alliances, but rather closely allied and plainly one in Christ Jesus. And yet your faction considers that blameworthy: Behold, [you say] an alliance! And whatever these people call an alliance is most assuredly a conspiracy against the Lord and his Christ.

We see for ourselves here how much hope [our Catholic opponents] are deriving from the divisions among the Swiss. You would think from the way they congratulate each other that they had just won the clearest victory.

Capito, if you had seen the sad and pathetic mob accompanying Oecolampadius and compared it with the magnificent, upstanding Christian host, you would have been sorry for yourself.

The kingdom of the Antichrist has increased through divisions. Therefore they are making an effort to break up the concord among allies, even the most tightly knit allies. Fabri distorts this passage, deprecating the brethren, whom he loathes, and elevating the magnificence of his warriors, as if the Truth depended on the pomp of the world.

We have delayed this course [of action] by this 'foolish' pamphlet,[24] by which the tricks of our adversaries are altogether revealed.

It is true that the pamphlet is small, but the lies in your heart are great and shameful. You ought to be ashamed of such tricks, printing lies against the upright citizens of the Confederacy.

The pamphlet is entitled, A True Report of the Disputation at Baden, *and our adversaries are not bringing any accusations against it other than the fact that that the words of L[udwig] Baer were not cited accurately.[25] For he said something of this sort, and in this case, precisely what he said or did not say has little importance.*

* * * * *

22 Fabri's translation makes no mention of any cities along the North Sea coast. Cf. *Neüwe zeitung*, f. Bii v.

23 This is a response to Fabri's marginal gloss, which comments on Capito's list of cities: 'That is, they would be too far away from you.' Cf. *Neüwe zeitung*, f. Bii v.

24 Cf. above, Ep. 288a.

25 Fabri's gloss does not mention Baer's name. Thomas Murner, in a letter of complaint to the Strasbourg city council, dated 11 November 1526, is more specific.

If we were to act relying on human counsel, we would plainly collapse, seeing how much there is to fear from every direction. But, because we know how deeply the Word has taken root among many people, we trust in the constancy of the people, and we hope that those among them who have fallen will soon rise again. For the [opponents] will not be able to tolerate an expensive and drawn-out war, and they will not achieve anything with a half-hearted effort.

Here, one can clearly see that you would prefer to depend not on the Word of God, but rather on cannons, guns, bulwarks, and great bastions, just as the apostles did, whose descendants you all are.

This passage properly expresses our view. We attest that we depend only on God in such a great affair, regardless of what men threaten to do. Likewise, we place our hope in the constancy of the people, since the Truth has been received from above. But Fabri has drawn the opposite conclusion, namely, venom from the flower and poison from the vine. For he says it is clear from this passage that we strive to have no confidence in the Word of the Lord and rely on war. How blind is an envious mind aroused by hatred!

Last but not least, the pope, whom the defenders of Christ in the bread[26] are propping up ineffectively, has fallen, together with his satellites, and is no longer held in high esteem in the hearts of the people.

You see, blasphemer of God, you want to drive Christ from the sacrament, but you will not succeed. He is too strong. Have you forgotten that you were our preacher in Basel, a light to Christianity, a great rabbi in all languages, that you said mass for five years every day?

Human traditions and ecclesiastical authority are, to a certain extent, bolstered by the novel opinion, which goes against scripture and the ancient canons, of accepting the consecration of the body of Christ by a wicked priest. This is even now being affirmed by some people. The pontiff, I said, leans on this weak crutch, from which he has obtained the utmost authority against the monarchs of the world. Fabri turns this expression around, rendering 'they lightly support him' as 'they will easily be turned away,' as if I despised those who think otherwise, which I am not at all in the habit of doing.[27]

* * * * *

Capito alleges that Baer told Oecolampadius the Catholic protagonists 'dealt with the articles of Christian faith as if they were negotiating about a plot of land' (AST 323, no. 18). Concerning the meeting between Baer and Oecolampadius, see BrOek 1:527, #387, 543–4, #400 and 559–60, #407. Cf. also Capito's letter of justification to Baer below, Ep. 295.

26 *Christi impanati* (Christ in the bread), referring to those who believe in transubstantiation.

27 Fabri writes: 'And to sum it all up, the pope has fallen, along with his supporters, because people have lost faith in him. Thus, those who maintain that Christ goes into the bread will be easily put down.' Cf. *Neüwe zeitung*, f. Biii r.

I wanted to tell you this concerning public disturbances: I see that they are transitory and that their impact will not last long. The weaker brethren have fallen, but the stronger ones will rise again. They are afraid of a new war with France, concerning which many counsels are presented each day. In the meantime, the Lord will advance his Word.

Look, pious Christian, what kind of people they are! They would rejoice if the greatest leaders, the Emperor and the King of France, should go to war against one another just so their trickery might be successful.

My words are spoken with moderation. They are transitory, I say. Discord among the princes does not bring us joy. We pray for them daily, and hope that we may live a peaceful and quiet life under them with all piety and honesty, that their consensus in the Lord may bring peace to the world. We also glorify the Lord, who meanwhile uses pernicious wars for the increase of his Word, and thus suddenly overturns the calculations of the wicked.[28]

Listen to this new strategy of Satan: A few days ago, an altogether illiterate Anabaptist from Benfeld,[29] a town that is subject to our city council, was brought here; he defamed and slandered us[30] openly, and asserted that he was going to force us to recant.[31] Our adversaries in the city council welcomed the fool with great applause, and made sure[32] that we should meet three or four times before the well attended city council.

In the city council there are those who do not yet know that our word is the Word of the Lord, to whom it is pleasing that [Wolff] subscribes to their opinion: they have been united with us in civil concord nonetheless.[33]

The main points of his teachings are: that no magistrate is a Christian; that children should not be baptized; that no godly man may take up arms at the command of[34] the magistracy; and that the devil and all the ungodly must be saved at the end.

While disputing, pernicious men deny the Word of God because it opposes their own conceits, but without it, we cannot be of God. They practically do away with the magistracy, thus destroying civil behaviour and scorning all

* * * * *

28 Cf. Psalm 37:12–15.
29 I.e., Hans Wolff. Cf. above, Ep. 285.
30 Fabri says 'you' (*Neüwe zeitung*, f. Biii v).
31 Fabri says: '… he said that he would convince us that we must be baptized again.' Cf. *Neüwe zeitung*, f. Biii v.
32 Fabri adds: 'with the approval of our followers' (*Neüwe zeitung*, f. Biii v).
33 This is probably a response to Fabri's marginal gloss, which states: 'Note that there are still faithful old Christians in the Strasbourg city council' (*Neüwe zeitung*, f. Biii v).
34 Fabri says: '… in defence of …' (*Neüwe zeitung*, f. Biii v).

the preachers of the Word. They acknowledge as Christians and brethren only those who have been rebaptized; they associate Christian freedom with elements, which Satan has stirred up so that he may convince pious monarchs to enact laws against Christian freedom. But let them weigh up how much damage has been done to the world by spiritual tyranny; let them permit anyone to prophesy, observing due order, so that the rest of the churches may judge.[35] And let them not suppress prophecies with the sword,[36] lest they trespass on what belongs to God, but let them otherwise use it diligently against rebels. Human matters – and these are human matters – cannot last long: soon they will be abolished, with Christ's help.

In the meantime, he launched a thousand assaults against us, charging that the papists are ungodly, but that we exceed them in ungodliness in countless ways, and that there is no one worse than we are now, nor will there ever be in the future.[37] Meanwhile, he announced that seven years from now, at twelve o'clock on Ascension Day, at the first strike of the hour, this world would come to an end.[38] Finally, after bitterly reproving the Word, by which we assailed that insane, vainglorious man, he was sent back to Benfeld under the condition that he refrain from spreading any of his teachings among the people. But in the meantime, he made amazing claims about himself: that he had defeated us and rendered us speechless, and that all erudite men would fall before his spirit; he stirred up many people with such rumours. At last, the city council ordered the prefect of [Benfeld] to throw the man out of town. It was done, and once expelled, [Wolff] came here. Yesterday he was present when Matthew Zell was preaching, and Zell had barely uttered two words, when he began to shout harsh accusations.[39] For Zell was lecturing on some passage in Deuteronomy against those who do not listen to God, and when he was about to start on what was to be his sermon, he said, 'See, how much danger there is in not listening to the Spirit speaking through scripture!' Then that Anabaptist said, 'You are lying about the Holy Spirit, Brother Matthew. By his power, I order you to step down and give me the floor to speak truer things about the meaning of the Spirit.' Then he called the papists just as ungodly [as the preachers].[40] The whole church rose

* * * * *

35 Cf. 1 Cor. 14:29.
36 Cf. 1 Thess. 5:20.
37 Fabri's marginal gloss reads: 'This is as true as if God himself had said it; for you desire to expel Christ.'
38 I.e., Thursday, 22 May 1533.
39 The scene is also described above, Ep. 288.
40 This sentence is missing in Fabri's translation. See Cf. *Neüwe zeitung*, f. Biv r.

in commotion against the lone speaker; a certain citizen laid hands on the
madman and brought him before the magistracy; the congregation followed
suit. Matthew could barely restrain them.

*It was a commotion, not an insurrection or disturbance. When the commotion
had been miraculously calmed,*[41] *the people became suspicious and began to follow
the man who was led away to the magistracy, but the preachers constrained them by
their authority, so that most of them who were there settled down and returned to
their ardent desire for the Word.*

That good-for-nothing fellow offered himself up for *poena talionis*[42] and
most ardently entreated that we should be placed in chains until his case was
ultimately sorted out. He exclaimed from the tower: 'Your preachers will fall,
no, in fact, they have already fallen.'

This letter of yours is proof that this man spoke the truth. Indeed, he is Saul or Caiaphas.[43]

*He added, speaking to the city council: 'and the decrees of the pontiffs and the
external church with all its satellites, that is, its priests, monks, nuns, sacraments,
consecrations, masses, and that sort of thing, are truly opposed to Christ.'*

See how much intemperance roils this simple man, who trusts in himself. On his account, we shall experience some nuisance, but no danger. For
our churches have been forewarned. They know the sum of the Christian
religion and hold fast to it.

That is your talent: to create followers and to make the common people depend upon you
and turn against the authorities.

I wanted to write these things to you.

*From my words 'Our churches know for themselves the sum of Christianity
and hold fast to it,' everyone will understand that we have placed the anchor of our
hope in the knowledge of God and in the well pondered and examined meaning of
Christianity. Hence, the common people, who are by nature fickle, are less vulnerable
to impostors. Fabri distorted these words and drew this conclusion: 'That is your
talent: to set up conspirators and to draw the people to you, turning them against
the magistracy.' O false accuser! I meant that, due to the well understood message of
Christianity, danger from that troublemaker should not be feared. But that most vain
impostor, [Fabri], takes it as the confession of a rebellious spirit.*

* * * * *

41 *Prae miraculo interpellatae commotionis* – the meaning of the phrase is unclear in
   this context.
42 A legal convention to prevent frivolous accusations, whereby both sides in a
   dispute were imprisoned until the case was decided.
43 For an explanation of King Saul and the high priest Caiaphas' roles as unde-
   serving prophets, cf. 1 Sam. 19:24 and John 11:49–52.

Luther has translated the *Syngramma Suevorum* into German[44] and has recommended it with a magnificent preface, in which you and Oecolampadius are reproached.[45] I would like Oeocolampadius to respond with an argument, which you will hear from him personally: namely, that the case should be referred to the Lord, who is trying us in this fashion. In connection with this, we should freely confess how much the Lord has done through [Luther], so that his words are given almost more weight than is due to a mere man. In this way, the Lord would graciously provide the remedy for this evil, having abandoned [Luther] to this error and having allowed him to completely forget charity to such an extent that he gave over to the devil and called 'Satan' those whom he should have acknowledged by the law of charity as brothers.[46]

See how they play false with Luther and praise him as if they would like to make him into an enemy of the sacrament [of the Eucharist] as well.

With these words, Fabri says, we are 'smearing Luther's mouth.'[47] Yet we did not want to counsel anything other than that [Oecolampadius] professes freely and as a friend what the Lord had disclosed through [Luther]. I have said nothing that would make him anything that he is not: indeed, he is a greater man than a wretch like you can bear.

We do not yet have a copy [of Luther's work]. For the Haguenau printer wants to withhold it until the fair.[48] I have devised a scheme and hope that I will soon obtain a copy; then you will have one soon, for we will have to respond.

See, now that is brotherly love, to desire to steal a book published by his brother in Christ, the printer. I consider that Wolfgang's expression of desire are the words of a wolf.

I think it is pious to make an effort to give a brother, on request, the opportunity and the time to speak before the church on behalf of himself and the Truth.

I sent to Oecolampadius what Luther wrote in a letter to one of his

* * * * *

44 *Genotigter und fremdt eingetragener schrifft auch mislichens dewtens der wort des abentmals Christi. Syngramma: (das ist) Vorsammelte schriffte und einhellige vorlegung der achtbarn predigere ynn Schwaben so sich darüber zu Schwebischem-Hall besprochen, zu dem vormertern Oecolampadio prediger zu Basel* (Wittenberg: Jos. Klug, 1526).

45 Luther's preface of 1526 to his translation of the *Syngramma* is published in WA 19, 457–61.

46 Fabri's marginal gloss states: 'Satan's kingdom must be constantly opposed.'

47 I.e., depict him in false colours.

48 Johannes Secer did not want to publish this translation before the September fair at Frankfurt.

followers.[49] O how sure the man is, that he can carry his head so high and disdain anyone he pleases!

Fabri notes that Luther has always been a haughty monk.[50] As far as it pertains to constancy, Fabri's complaint is not entirely unjustified. For nowhere does [Luther] give in to the human tyranny that oppresses free consciences, and otherwise he knows the boundaries of faith. But in explaining the Eucharist he seems to go beyond those bounds, stubbornly asserting, as if he were inspired, a tradition in scripture we do not yet comprehend. I called that, in rather plain language, 'carrying his head so high,' but I said so in private to a discreet friend, lest I detract anything from a brother – and you, [Fabri,] publicly divulged it, going against law. Nor is it a sin, I suppose, to regard a man, however great he may be, as suffering from a certain human flaw. We all easily slip into the vice of obstinacy, growing passionate in the heat of the argument, a label that fits Fabri's teachings, which contribute nothing to edification and which we vehemently detest.

Our printer asks that you send the proceedings of the conference[51] to us if you have them, or at least that you edit this piece.[52] You can steal two short hours from your serious work to do that. For there is a great need for the conclusion of this disputation to be published.[53]

All faithful Christians, and especially the Swiss, will want to keep in mind how these people desire to alter this honourable and excellent business [i.e., the Baden disputation] with their lies. Thus we see and know that they have no interest in the truth. They are only interested in inciting the common people, including those in Swiss territories, to rise up against their lords and masters.

I pray that you will not send our brother away empty-handed.

Fabri concentrates his efforts on the last act [of his play]. It was my plan to ask about the end of the disputation held [at Baden]. But being in a hurry, and for a long time now a stranger to reading literature, I could not think of a convenient phrase to explain myself. I therefore tried to express myself in Greek, saying [gr.] to tēs zētēseōs syngramma – for this is certainly a most commonplace phrase. But I

* * * * *

49 Possibly the letter from Luther to Nikolaus Gerbel dated 26 April 1526, where he deplores the fact that Oecolampadius has let himself be trained by *Schwermgeister* (men claiming to be inspired), cf. WABr 4, 63–4, Ep. 1004.

50 Fabri's marginal gloss states: 'He has always been a proud monk' (*Neüwe zeitung*, f. Biv v).

51 Capito uses the Greek expression *syngramma zētēseōs*. He was interested in the conclusion of the disputation, since the man who provided him with a transcript of the proceedings had left early.

52 I.e., the *Warhafftige handlung* (see above, Ep. 288a headnote).

53 Capito uses the Greek word *katastrophe*, meaning 'ending' or 'conclusion.' Fabri wrongly translated it as 'overturning' (*verkere*, in *Neüwe zeitung*, f. Ci r).

was in such a rush that I either needlessly doubled the first syllable, making it [gr.]
zēzēteseōs, or else I wrote [gr.]tēs syzēteseōs instead of [gr.]zētēseōs (that conjec-
ture is based on my copy and, I think, most likely). My autograph will show whether
that was the case. Certainly there can be no suspicion of fraud. Here, it seems, Fabri
seized a dictionary and, taking what he found next to the word and was suited for a
slanderous translation, though quite remote from the shape of the letters, interpreted
the word, not as [gr.]syzēteseōs or [gr.]zētēseōs, but as [gr.]tēs syssitias or [gr.]
tou syssitiou, which means 'gathering.' And he translated it into German as Geselschafft *[i.e., society, conventicle], a word that smacks of plotting. Next, he left*
syngramma, *that is,* ein Syngramma der geselschafft, *hoping that the difficult*
and foreign word would create a suspicion that something very malicious was being
concealed. Then he deliberately corrupted the remainder, severing it suddenly from
the entity of the sentence – like a member severed from a living body – separating the
two short phrases from the verb. [54]

Furthermore, with Erasmus explaining everything in detail, many learned
gems have become popular, for example, phrases that are taken from their primary
meaning and adapted to another, thus taking on a proverbial cast. Our age, which is
quite imitative, adopted a number of foreign words and made them its own by daily
use, such as catastrophe, *which denotes the last act of a play and which we apply*
proverbially to the end of anything. Older generations used to add fabulae *[of the*
play], whereas our generation generally says only catastrophe.[55] *Since the begin-*
ning and middle of the Disputation of Baden have been published in a pamphlet
that has recently appeared,[56] it seemed worthwhile to have the catastrophe, *that is,*
the end as well, at least to contradict the insulting aspersions Eck cast on the most
pious Oecolampadius, minister of the Word. For Fabri played only a walk-on part
in that play, as it were, except for a few artful asides, as for example, commend-
ing his well-equipped library and praising himself for his victory over the absent
Zwingli, boasting how many of Zwingli's books he had read, and other such things,
which he rehearsed in the conclusion. I therefore thought that making the end of the
Disputation known would serve to refute Eck's and Fabri's vanity, who pour out
self-congratulatory words, claiming victory over the gospel everywhere, corrupting
the simple-minded, who are blinded by such smoke and mirrors. Therefore I asked
Zwingli to entrust to me for publication anything he had put together concerning

* * * * *

54 Fabri says: 'Our printer asks whether you have the proceedings of the gathering and could send it to us, or that you may correct this in two days or a few
short hours. Please do this and apply yourself to the matter, for it is most necessary to alter the disputation' (Neüwe zeitung, f. Ci r).

55 Cf. Erasmus, *Adagia* 1.2.36, *catastrophe fabulae*, the dénouement of the play.

56 Cf. above, Ep. 288a headnote.

that Disputation; and if not, to snatch from his good work a few hours over the next two days and devote it to this lightweight task. Thus the world could see the last act of the play, which Fabri, the director, purposely suppressed.

As for the rest, my translator Fabri gave my words this meaning in German: 'It is very necessary that the disputation be turned upside down.'[57] And he added a shocking exclamation, turning to all Christians and especially to the Swiss, urging them to consider how we intended to pervert the proven Truth with lies, since we acknowledged that we were fugitives from the camp of Truth, for no other reason than to instigate the Swiss people to rebel against the authorities. That slanderer writes as if it were a proven fact that I had instigated the people, although I risked my life in an effort to quell an uprising.[58] I am asking you to consider how impudent the man is, who dared to build up such great slander from words of mine, which he had corrupted, and to arouse the people's anger against my person. Take care, Fabri, lest your perfidy become known and be turned against yourself. For upright men take it ill to be imposed on, as you have imposed on the praiseworthy Swiss people by falsifying my letter.

There is a rumour, albeit unsubstantiated, that the chief city of Hungary has been lately besieged by the Turks.[59] Also: the knights of the Swabian league have been routed by the [peasants] of Salzburg.[60]

I have heard and seen in many places how these eternally damned men rejoice in their hearts when princes and noblemen are harmed. God will not tolerate this situation much longer.

From this, Fabri concludes over and over again that we greatly exult in the troubles of princes and rulers. And yet I am simply telling a friend the rumours generally circulating here, without commenting on my own feelings. And the Lord knows whom I serve, and how much grief we suffer from the disastrous wars, by which the Christian world has been shaken for some time now on account of the temerity of certain people put in charge of government.

* * * * *

57 *das man die Disputation verkere* (*Neüwe zeitung*, f. Ci r). I.e., Fabri misconstrued the word *katastrophe*, ending, and twisted its literal meaning 'turning point at the end of a race course' into 'turning upside down.'
58 Cf. below p. 227.
59 Budapest was captured by the Ottomans under Suleiman I ('the Magnificent') on 10 September 1526, after the defeat of the Hungarians under Ludwig II on 29 August 1526 at the Battle of Mohács.
60 The peasants, who had recently risen up against the archbishop of Salzburg in April 1526 under the leadership of Gaismair, repelled the troops of the Swabian League who had come to liberate the city of Radstadt.

Five thousand foot soldiers have surrounded Milan, waiting for the arrival of [Charles of] Bourbon,[61] who will take over the duchy henceforth,

See how this merchant receives news from the emperor in Spain, from the Turks and the French Swiss, from France, from Hungary, from Switzerland, and from all countries and cities, even from Hell, where they have set Satan free.

on the grounds that otherwise there would definitely be a rebellion among the people.

I think that you would very much like to preach again to the peasants as you did before.

He makes witty remarks on our information gathering, as is his custom. After this he adds: 'I predict that you long for an opportunity to preach to the peasants, as you did before.'[62] But I will not comment on the tricks he uses to distort my words here, for I have said enough about that in German;[63] I put great emphasis on letting the pious reader know that I along with my fellow ministers strongly advised the peasants against sedition. We had been sent and suborned by the rulers of the region [of Altdorf] to defuse the seditious situation. Secondly, while returning home, we were stopped along the way by an army of peasants, until we wrote a missive suitable for the time,[64] which the confessor and martyr of Christ, Andreas Prünlin,[65] read and explained on the same day at around two o'clock to the entire crowd. The ranks of the insurgents would have been altogether broken up, if their leader had not obtained a short delay of two days. For in that interval some of the booty had been divided up, and their fickle hearts grew passionate for obtaining wealth from pillaging.[66] Furthermore, those subject to the rule of our city council yielded when the missive was read to them. Up until that time, the delegates had called them back in vain. There were people who tried to calm them, I quite acknowledge it, but a good part cited the gospel to ingratiate themselves with the rebels, but that was shortly before this evil erupted.

After the peasants had been dispersed, these men paid a small sum to the bishops' commanders, and were soon reconciled and are saying mass again, playing

* * * * *

61 Charles VIII of Bourbon (1490–1527) was count of Montpensier, Forez, Mercoeur, and Clermont, and Dauphin of Alvernia; he was named the constable of Bourbon (1501–27). He was honoured for his courage at the Battle of Marignano in 1515. Later he served the Emperor Charles V in his campaign to drive the French from Italy. In 1526 he was made duke of Milan, and in 1527 he marched on Rome but was killed in the assault. His troops proceeded to sack the city.
62 An allusion to Capito's advice to the peasants of Altdorf. See above, Ep. 280 headnote.
63 Cf. Capito and Zell's *Warhaftige Verantwortung,* f. [A8] v–Bii v.
64 See above, Ep. 243 (summary).
65 On Prünlin (Prunulus), see above, Ep. 280, note 24.
66 The pillage of the abbey of Altdorf, etc.

their old tricks. Nor are they accused of anything, provided that they abjure their wives and cohabit with mistresses in the usual manner of priests. They are absolved of the many shameful actions they have committed, and no one reproaches them for plundering the monasteries. For they set out openly with the marauding horde, like torches of sin, and their companions, already burning brightly on their own, were even more inflamed by their exhortations. On the other hand, pious brethren, those who kept several villages in obedience by virtue of the Word, were discharged or cast out or put in shackles and subjected to torture, the noose, and every kind of death. That is not extinguishing uprisings, but fostering one in the hidden veins of the heart, my dear Fabri. I have said that tumultuous men will reap what they sow. I mean those whom your conspiracy is eager to incite with wicked tricks against the innocent followers of the Word. I call them 'tumultuous men,' not 'seditious men,' as you have translated.[67] For there are dangerous men in these parts, that is to say, unjust wars are profitable for the men to whom I discreetly refer.[68]

If you have any news about Bern or if you see any hope, keep us up-to-date by way of courier.

I will tell you truthfully and not lie. The people of the city of Bern, as well as those in the entire region, who number fully 30,000, have sworn an oath to God and the saints and have given the seven cantons a sealed letter stating that they wish to die under the old faith. Also, they have chased out all of the priests and monks who have taken wives. And on the Monday following the Nativity of John the Baptist, your and Zwingli's brother in the pulpit, the preacher in Bern, professed that he believes that the mass is correct, as we celebrate it. And he swore that the sacrament of the altar contains the true body and true blood of Christ, and promised to hold to and preach the old faith. Have I not given you pause? Your followers know how to judge this. For your Babylonian tower stirs up traps on all sides, and your idiocy will scarcely survive another day.

Farewell in the Lord, most brave soldier of Christ and brother. Strasbourg. 11 June in the year 1526. Bucer and the brethren greet you, especially Farel.[69]

Wolfgang Capito.

Here, Fabri spouted the most manifest lies about the council and people of the city and region of Bern, a fact which I have briefly outlined in my German apologia.[70]

* * * * *

67 *Neüwe zeitung*, f. Ci r.
68 I.e., mercenaries.
69 On Guillaume Farel (1489–1565), see below, Ep. 347 headnote.
70 Capito's *An gemeyne stend des heyligen Römischen reichs* ([Strasbourg], 1526); cf. below, Ep. 300.

The heart of the matter is this: In Bern, Berthold,[71] who is their apostle, preaches the gospel and continues in his office, authorized and salaried by the council. Freedom to preach the Word prevails as the popish faction declines, nor has there ever been in these years a public decree against the gospel, although there, as elsewhere, efforts were made to effect it. Fabri, however, says the opposite of everything, and by implication brings reproach on the sober people of Bern.

On the basis of my letter, which he corrupted, as I said, that sly fellow not only set in motion an evil rumour about me among the people, but has even aroused the Swiss authorities and almost the Reichsregiment *against me in an effort to destroy me, as can be seen from the pamphlet in which I justified myself in German.[72] Do you now, good reader, call Fabri a good man? For how will he escape the accusation of being a falsifier and a most pernicious slanderer? If he knowingly corrupted in his German translation what was well said, he is by far the most wicked man of all, for he takes action with tricks and deceits against the life of a brother who has never deserved ill of him. If he erred through imprudence and ignorance, as many seem to think, he will stand accused on two counts: first, that he was willing to give my words an evil meaning, and second, that he wanted forcefully to twist my most innocent words to give them the opposite sense, even adding short notes. You cannot use ignorance as a defence, most impudent Fabri, for I would respond: Who compelled you to make pronouncements about what I wrote with such certainty, when you do not know the difference between black and white? No one can easily decide whether you have covered me with such great abuse on purpose or through ignorance. For you took care that no one among the Swiss obtained a copy of my writings, which proves that you planned your crime and perpetrated it wilfully. By contrast, you forwarded a copy of them to the Most Serene King of Spain[73] and to Ferdinand, Duke of Austria, etc., they say, which leads to the assumption that you are full of vainglory and were deceived by stupid self-confidence, thinking that you had done right – unless you acted out of contempt for such a great prince, all the great talents of his august family, and the humanities. I leave the whole matter to the judgment of the fair*

* * * * *

71 Berthold Haller (1492–1536) was born in Aldingen bei Rottweil (Neckar) and was a friend and fellow student of Philip Melanchthon in Pforzheim. A moderate reformer of mild disposition, he settled in Bern as a teacher in 1518, was elected chief pastor in 1521 and preached there till his death in 1536, although his life was often in danger. He stood with Oecolampadius against Eck at the Disputation of Baden. Haller drew up the Ten Theses which Zwingli revised for adoption at the Disputation of Bern in 1528.

72 Cf. above, note 70.

73 Charles V, German Emperor and King of Spain, residing in Spain 1521–9; he was represented in Germany by his brother Ferdinand.

reader, but I have added one or two amusing epigrams,[74] *in which a guileless friend*[75] *gives his judgment. For in his opinion you are inept and trying to do the impossible. But he is a poet. He has fashioned with his talented mind verses appropriate to the matter. I shall tarry no longer.*

Letter 291: 28 June 1526, Baden, The delegates of the 12 Cantons to Capito

> Published in Johannes Stickler, ed., *Amtliche Sammlung der ältern eidgenössischen Abschiede*. Vol. 4.1b: *Die Eidgenössischen Abschiede aus dem Zeitraume von 1529 bis 1532* (Zurich, 1876), 956. On the context of this letter, see above Ep. 288a headnote.

Our greetings, etc.

Through one of your couriers, we have obtained letters and printed pamphlets dispatched by you and others to Zwingli in Zurich, which we have found to be critical of the disputation held by us at Baden in Aargau. In these letters and pamphlets there is much that is not true, but rather contrived and mendacious. We would have preferred you to refrain from such pamphlets and writings against us and the Truth, but however this may be, should we find more of these pamphlets and writings, we shall treat the courier as he deserves. We will not show him mercy, as we have in the case of this one. Take such knowledge into account hereafter. Given, etc.

Letter 292: 8 July 1526, Strasbourg, Capito to the delegates of the
12 cantons at Baden

> The original manuscript is lost. What follows is based on a copy in Zurich, ZB, ms. S 17, 24. Another copy is in AST 175. An extract has been published in *Eid. Absch*. IV, 1a, 968. For the context, see above Ep. 288a headnote.

To the noble, strict, pious and firm, cautious, honest, wise, especially honourable and reasonable lords. May my willing service and whatever praise and good of which I am capable be constantly at the ready for you, my noble, strict, honest and wise lords.

The day before yesterday I received a message from you, my strict,

* * * * *

74 Cf. CorrBucer 2, Appendix III, 265. In these epigrams, Fabri is depicted as a 'monster' and 'sacrilegious plotter.'
75 Probably Johannes Witz (Sapidus), cf. Ep. 324 headnote.

honest and wise lords,[1] which you had sent from Baden on the vigil of Peter and Paul.[2] In it, you reported that you discovered my pamphlet and letter on the person of my messenger and found much in them that was contrived and mendacious and directed against the disputation you held [in Baden]. In your opinion, I should not have written such a letter opposed to both the praiseworthy Confederacy and the Truth, And you indicated that if you discovered a similar pamphlet or letter on the person of any other messenger, he would suffer a penalty for it and would not be shown mercy, as this one has been shown, and that I should take that into account. This letter upset me greatly. For it has never been, nor is it now, my intention to oppose the most praiseworthy Confederacy or the Truth. I have frequently lived among Swiss citizens quite happily, and have recently lived for five years in Basel,[3] receiving much honour and goodness from its residents, which I have always remembered. And I have never allowed anyone to belittle the Confederacy, including the people who are in the habit of rarely speaking well of the Confederates. You may know whether Eck and Fabri have always been so loyal and whether they still are today. My goal is simply to express my own sentiment, which, as I have already said, has always been complete good will toward the praiseworthy Confederacy. Why, then, would I want to try to act in a hostile[4] manner without reason, and why at this time, when I would only be hurting myself? For the fact that the clergy likes to play tricks on you and thus undertake to divide the Confederacy ought not to be held against honest citizens, who desire to remain in the faith of their forefathers in all simplicity. For they are deceived by the tricks of the papal party, who claim that their own false belief is the old faith, whereas it is the clear Word of God that is the old faith, whose sole aim is worship of God and belief in Christ. The papists will admit this to be the truth, but the circumstances were awkward. Much happened at the disputation which put the evangelicals at a disadvantage, for example, that the papists preached every day and made the evangelical truth unpopular even before it was discussed. But for all of this Eck and Fabri will be blamed, not the pious Swiss Confederates, although they may have contributed to the situation. Therefore, although, strictly speaking, it is not up to me to defend the pamphlet that was published about the disputation;[5]

* * * * *

1 Ep. 291.
2 I.e., 28 June.
3 1515–20.
4 The manuscript has 'fruntlich,' but the context requires a negative modifier, i.e., 'not friendly.'
5 I.e., the *Warhafftige handlung* (see above, Ep. 288a headnote).

it should not be understood by intelligent individuals as directed against the praiseworthy Confederacy. But it is certainly sufficient for use against the so-called clergy, who want to maintain their falsehoods among you and will never apologize for their libels, unless what happened is allowed to come to light. The Word of God and the Truth do not take refuge in darkness. They find it in their own explication in the bright light of day. People will write and say that the evangelical party was defeated at the contest held by the praiseworthy Confederacy at Baden in Aargau until the proceedings of that day are disseminated for everyone's information. In conclusion, strict, honest, wise, and honoured lords, if there is anything blameworthy in my pamphlet and my private letters, it concerns solely the papists, who instigate violence and the suppression of the Truth through foul means, lies, and murder, since they have no truth or divine message and thus intend to maintain their power against the whole world. Therefore, most favourable lords, I ask that you put away your suspicion of me and believe that I faithfully seek to advance your honour, your interests and your welfare as far as it is in me. If, however, you have any complaint against me, I ask that you kindly inform me of it. For I desire to demonstrate my innocence to your satisfaction. Therefore my lords, may God, his grace and wisdom, be with you as well as fortune and an increase in his honour and glory, which is all we ought to seek in our own affairs. Herewith I eagerly commend myself to your honourable and wise lords. Given at Strasbourg on the 8th of July in the year 1526.

Letter 293: 8 July 1526, Strasbourg, Capito to the Cantons of the Swiss Confederacy

The manuscript of the letter is in AST 175, f. 43. For the context, see Epp. 289 and 290 headnotes.

To the noble, strict, pious, firm, cautious, honest and wise lords my willing service, and what praise and good I am capable of, may it be to the advantage of Your strict, honest, and wise lords.

On 6 July, I received in Strasbourg a letter signed by the representatives of the Twelve Cantons,[1] of which I enclose a notarized copy. In the letter I was upbraided, suggesting that the pamphlet sent to Zwingli and transmitted through my own messenger, was opposed to the whole Swiss Confederacy and to the Truth itself. I have been much pained by this accusation. Since

* * * * *

1 Ep. 291.

I desired to uphold my honour and enjoy the grace and goodwill of all Swiss citizens, I wrote back to the strict, honest, and wise representatives of the twelve cantons, sending my letter to the place where they were assembled at that time.[2] Since I have few means, I sent the letter through a chance messenger in the hope that I might appease them. I enclose with this message a copy of the aforementioned letter, along with my urgent request to read it in the spirit of friendship and as if it had been addressed privately to you, honourable and wise lords. And if any kind of ill will is roused against me, I beg you kindly to overlook it and to recognize that I have made every effort on behalf of the laudable Swiss Confederacy before God and the world. With that, I place my trust in your care and wisdom. Given at Strasbourg on 8 July [15]26.

I remain willingly at your service, strict, honest, and wise lords.

Wolfgang Capito, preacher at Strasbourg.

Letter 294: 8 July 1526, Strasbourg, Capito to Adelberg Meyger and the City Council of Basel

This letter is printed in Emil Dürr and Paul Roth, eds., *Aktensammlung zur Geschichte der Basler Reformation in den Jahren 1519 bis Anfang 1534* (Basel: 1921–50), 2:354–5, #437.

[*Summary*]: On 6 July, Capito received a letter from the Twelve Cantons [above, Ep. 291] in which he was blamed for having written against the Confederacy. He denies that he had any evil intentions or spoke ill of the Confederacy. He recalls with great fondness the city of Basel, where he once lived and where now the gospel is being preached. He encloses a copy of a letter he wrote to the Swiss Confederates [above, Ep. 292] in which he justifies his conduct. The pamphlet that was issued about the Disputation of Baden [i.e., *Warhafftige handlung*] contains nothing that is directed against the Confederacy. Its main concern is to denounce the machinations of the papists. Capito is not responsible for the reference to Ludwig Baer [see below, Ep. 295]. The *Warhafftige handlung* was composed by an imperial servant, who was present at the disputation. The proofreader was told to leave out anything that might be offensive to the Confederacy. Capito himself was too busy with church matters to concern himself with that business. Should any disadvantage arise from his remarks for anyone, he will have them retracted at his own cost.

* * * * *

2 I.e., Ep. 292 above, sent to Baden.

Letter 295: 8 July 1526, [Strasbourg], Capito to Ludwig Baer

Ludwig Baer (Ber, Berus, 1479–1554) of Basel studied philosophy and theology at Paris (ThD 1511). In 1513, he joined the faculty of theology at the University of Basel, where he was dean in 1515 and 1529, and rector in 1514 and 1520. He held a number of benefices: canon of Thann (1507); canon at St Peter's in Basel (1513), provost (1518), and canon at the cathedral (1526–9). He was initially open to the Reformation, but soon became an opponent and presided over the Disputation of Baden (Aargau) in May 1526. When Basel embraced the Reformation in 1529, he, along with Erasmus, Heinrich Glareanus and others from the cathedral chapter settled in Freiburg-im-Breisgau, where he received a lectureship at the university. The original autograph of this letter is in Strasbourg, AST 175, fols. 41 and 45. The letter is also printed in Gerdesius, vol. 2, 107–10.

May the grace of Christ and the knowledge of his might be with you, most famous doctor and friend.

A few days ago, Oecolampadius wrote[1] to me rather sternly and reproachfully concerning the pamphlet that has been published about the Disputation at Baden.[2] Such pamphlets, even if they report the truth, achieve nothing, [he said], and even less so if they offer the sort of empty lies he had seen in this pamphlet. For he had never told anyone the things the author of that pamphlet attributes to you, saying that those remarks were made in the presence of Oecolampadius.[3] I responded to him,[4] saying it was a fact that such pamphlets had only one goal: to make the transactions known to the people without burdening anyone's reputation. Nevertheless, just to be on the safe side, it is in your interest to attest that remarks of this sort were not made by you, lest a handle be provided to an evil man to give trouble to you, etc. – this is my opinion.

Meanwhile, I sent to Zwingli this pamphlet along with a personal letter[5] by my own courier. Unfortunately he was captured, and once they got a hold of the letters and pamphlet, they sent him back with a stern letter

* * * * *

1 This letter is no longer extant.
2 I.e., the *Warhafftige handlung.* Cf. above, Ep. 288a headnote.
3 The author revealed that Baer visited Oecolampadius and suggested that he declare himself defeated on the issue of the Eucharist; as for the rest, some arrangement might be made. The author of the *Wahrhafftige handlung* scoffed at such arrangements: 'Such people feel about faith as if it involved a dispute about a field' (G 3 recto-verso).
4 This letter is no longer extant.
5 Ep. 290.

from the Swiss addressed to me.[6] I do not recall what I wrote [in that letter], but I believe I congratulated Zwingli, that excellent man, on not going to Baden and incurring such great danger. I urged him to profess Christ courageously, and added a warning about Fabri's machinations. For I thought, no, rather, had foreseen that he would flaunt, at the meeting in Baden, the imperial edict, in which the emperor committed himself to eradicate the gospel.[7] This he will never achieve. The Lord will prevent it, and all sorts of obstacles will be introduced on all sides (even by the Gamaliels,[8] which he has among his own bishops and courtiers). Nevertheless, smokescreens of this sort upset and terrify the smaller states, which recently seem to retreat, but which are soon going to return with greater strength. Furthermore, I sent a pamphlet about the disputation so that, being informed about the proceedings, Zwingli might arm himself against the insults Eck used, lashing out at the most innocent Oecolampadius.[9] We were going to see to its publication so that we might thereby bring about the dissemination of the proceedings. I believe the letter contains something to that effect.

But Fabri, bigmouth and empty talker that he is, and already in high spirits from some banquet the night before at the Margrave of Baden,[10] spewed forth horrible threats, saying that our machinations had been discovered and that our pernicious skills had been exposed, that the city council of Basel was thoroughly investigating it, and that I was quite finished and done in. Fabri, in his benevolence, saw to it that this was announced to me, and a knight agreed to be his messenger and report to me the sequence of events. The gist of it was that the city council of Basel was going to persecute me with insatiable hatred. I quietly weighed the matter, asking myself: what if that Thraso[11] reported the truth and Baer was indeed grieved by that innuendo in the pamphlet, in which he was somehow traduced as being a Lutheran?[12] And so I snatched up my pen and am writing these lines to you, as an old friend and close companion, to vouch for my spirit. For I have always been a lover of peace and quiet, as far as it is godly, and inclined to

* * * * *

6 Ep. 291.
7 See above, Ep. 288a, p. 207.
8 Gamaliel, a Pharisee and rabbi (Acts 5:34 ff).
9 In discussing the correct interpretation of the Eucharist at the Baden Disputation.
10 Margrave Philip I of Baden-Sponheim (1479–1533).
11 A character in Terence's play *Eunuchus*, whose name became synonymous with 'braggard.'
12 It is unclear how remarks in the pamphlet could create such an impression.

put up with my troublesome enemies and to overcome them with patience. Far be it from me therefore to turn my friends against me with malice. Your course of action was never as displeasing to me and never as intolerable as certain other people's, for up until now you were content to mind your own business and have brought no bitter accusations in an effort to ruin others. You disagree civilly rather than hatefully, and for this reason I was glad that you presided over the disputation. For I was certain that nothing would be conducted by force under your auspices. If only the rabble of papists had shown equal moderation in acting their parts on stage, there would have been less bloodshed to lament in Germany. Therefore, since you could not be ours entirely and openly profess Christ, it pleased us that you are the sort of man that you are, that you would not support the ravings of those, who have no other purpose than to do away with innocent people who profess Christ. Accordingly, there is no reason why I should wish to see you traduced so hatefully, and if you have really been traduced, it happened without my will and knowledge.

What is to be done, then? Will this inane pamphlet damage Baer's repu- tation? Certainly not. You are above that. You cannot be deprived of your position of honour by such chaff. I, whom the Lord subjects to vicissitudes, have consistently disdained to take notice of much more serious slander and very bitter insults, though the opportunity for revenge presented itself – and I still do not regret my forbearance. For had I avenged the injury, I would have incurred the hatred of many and would have declared to the people that I am hurt by such stings. Once this was known, I would have been the target of thousands of slanderous pamphlets. These people set out to hate me and would attack me wherever I was open to an attack. Think the whole mat- ter through carefully, lest you needlessly come to regret a similar fate, while you strive to prove your innocence in more detail. That pamphlet is quite obscure, and I have not yet read it from beginning to end. It will be given im- portance once you bring serious accusations, for you are pre-eminent in au- thority and erudition. And there are grounds on which I shall justify myself and very firmly dispel the danger. [The author of the pamphlet] is outside the range of fire. Whoever he is, he had much of it copied out by a [secre- tary], whose handwriting we could perhaps identify, if needed. If there is a desire to avert evil suspicion, let the leaders of the Swiss, or rather, those who produced this tragedy with their own players, make an effort to publish the proceedings of the disputation. Things that are conducted openly love the light, and truth, even if kept secret and whispered into the ear of one man, does not shrink from public opinion. Undoubtedly, such rotten pamphlets do no harm unless they impugn anyone's reputation.

The great difficulty is that Fabri spread magnificent lies everywhere, boastfully claiming victory, saying that the Twelve Swiss Cantons had decreed that the gospel should be expelled from their realm and that the people should be prohibited from reading the New Testament. He claims to be carrying sealed letters attesting to a decree of this kind, to be presented to his prince, and perhaps they do not doubt the truth of it. Now, however, the true state of the Swiss, who proclaim the Word purely, will prove his lies even among those who are not aware of Fabri's machinations. The Swiss, who are completely honest, are even now fighting the false statement of Fabri, that most impudent and habitual liar, who claims that they have passed such a decree. For we know very well the public deliberations in this matter of the people of Bern and of your (no, rather our) people of Basel and of some others. But such are the times that the most shameful tricks hold great importance and are regarded as having a great deal of authority and significance even among the most principled people. There will be a time when less will be attributed to such tricks, if only the Word of God will some day have its own dignity. The power of this world in these turbulent times will certainly never obscure the Word; on the contrary, it will shine even brighter when attacked.

I wanted to say these things to you in a simple and candid way. I do not want you to think that I spoke about these matters out of fear or only for the sake of caution. For I do not want anyone for my sake to do or refrain from doing anything that benefits the glory of God or the authority of the illustrious city council of Basel, or anything that helps to establish your integrity. In fact, if someone were to suggest a way of achieving these goals, I would not fail to contribute my share. Wherefore, respected sir, feel free as far as I am concerned, to do what you are doing and what you were going to do, only strive not to do anything that goes against decency and against the glory of God. Finally, if there is anything you want from me in this matter, take care to indicate it, and I shall be even more careful to effect it, as long as it accords with the Christian faith. Conversely, it is clear that you will certainly not ask for anything other than what is fair, since you are a good man. Farewell in the Lord. 8 July 1526.

Letter 296: 8 July 1526, Strasbourg, Capito and the Strasbourg Preachers to Andreas Osiander

Printed in Andreas Osiander, *Gesamtausgabe* 2:105–13, Ep. 5, and CorrBucer 2:128–37, Ep. 132.

[*Summary*]: They thank Osiander for the letter [now lost] in which he proposes a private exchange of views on the Lord's Supper. They were tempted to do this, but the writings and sermons of [Andreas] Karlstadt have thrown everything into disarray, to the great joy of their adversaries. Karlstadt rejects the bodily presence of Christ in the bread and wine. The Strasbourg preachers prefer to recall the death of Christ and his sacrifice rather than to engage in polemics about his bodily presence. They disapprove of those who attacked Oecolampadius' interpretation (i.e., the Wittenberg theologians and [Jacob] Strauss, [preacher in Baden-Baden]). Such polemics raise 'a labyrinth' of pointless questions in the minds of believers. The Strasbourgers still hope that the theologians might come to an agreement: 'Christians will not linger over words, when they are agreed about the substance.' They can never approve of Karlstadt's interpretation, however; Zwingli and Oecolampadius agree in their interpretation of the Eucharist. The Strasbourg preachers have not yet seen the writings of [Valentin] Crautwald. They deplore the prohibition of the sale or reprint of the treatises of Oecolampadius and Zwingli at Nürnberg and call for mutual tolerance. If they cannot agree, 'each man must teach what he believes has been revealed to him, and refute the contrary, but in a generous and kind manner.' They send their greetings to Hector [Poemer], Dominik [Schleupner], Thomas Venatorius, and the rest of the brethren in Nürnberg.

Letter 296a: [ca. 18 July 1526, Strasbourg, The Chapter of St. Thomas to the Strasbourg City Council]

A copy of this letter is in AST 22 (3). According to a note at the bottom of the letter, it was presented to the council on 18 July 1526. The letter concerns the debts of Nikolaus Wurmser, the leader of the Catholic party, to the chapter. For the background, see above, Ep. 233b headnote.

Strict, honest, circumspect, honourable, wise, gracious lords,

In reply to a recent letter from Dr Nikolaus Wurmser to you, our strict and worthy lords, concerning the debt he owes to us and our collegiate church, we have itemized the above-mentioned debt on Dr. Wurmer's above-mentioned written request and application to you, our gracious lords. Herewith we indicate the moneys owed also to you, our gracious lords, with the earnest and urgent request to effect that the above-named Dr Wurmser will indemnify us and our collegiate church, as he forthrightly offers in his letter. The sums are as follows:

Firstly, he must pay 200 gulden to the chaplain of St Egidius at St Thomas, which he apparently received as payment from the heirs of Johannes Man.[1]

* * * * *

1 Cf. below, Ep. 366, note 5.

Also, he owes 100 gulden *ad portam*.[2]

Also, 200 gulden to the office of the dean, which he received in payment of rent attached to the deanship.

Also, 100 gulden borrowed from the chest of the collegiate church, which he received from Lorenz Schenckbecher, our present provost.

Also, 60 pounds to the house of the Beguines, formerly called Zum Wolf, now in Sigytz Street, for a payment received from the abbot of Schwarzach.[3]

Also, 100 gulden into the canonical chest of the legate, received from Jacob Munthart.[4]

Also, 26 pounds, 2 shillings, 4 pfennigs, from the last biennium of Johann Wetzel.[5]

Also, a loan of 40 gulden from the chest of the collegiate church, which he received in connection with the lawsuit against a certain oil producer of Weihersheim.

Also, 11 gulden which Jacob Bopp,[6] a teacher here, paid on his behalf in Rome.

Also, 24 pounds borrowed against the sum realized from the sale of wheat in the previous year, 1524.

Also, 23 pounds of capital to the vicarage of Diebolt Lehmann.[7]

Also, 100 gulden of capital to the chaplaincy in our collegiate church, now in the possession of Master Erhard Stein.[8]

The sum total is 579 pounds, 17 shillings, and 10 pfennings in Strasbourg money.

This calculation does not include the money which Dr Wurmser and his followers took away with them, either from the treasury or from the sale of wheat outside of Strasbourg, which is due to the collegiate church,

* * * * *

2 I.e., in alms.

3 A Benedictine monastery in Rheinmünster, 30 km northwest of Strasbourg in Baden.

4 For Munthart, see above, Ep. 237, note 19.

5 For Johann Wetzel, see above, Ep. 246a, note 39. During the biennium (the first two years of a canon's residence) part of the usufructs of his benefice were reserved for the use of the chapter.

6 For Bopp, see above, Ep. 246a, note 27.

7 For Lehmann, see above, Ep. 237, note 24.

8 Erhard Stein became vicar of the St Adelphus in St Thomas in 1507. He resigned his post in 1520, but seems to have retained (another?) benefice in the collegiate church. He took out citizenship on 30 January 1525, when he was referred to as 'vicar at Young St Peter.'

and which they have received from other sources. Perhaps they will give an accounting and response concerning these moneys at an opportune time. But concerning the sum indicated above, we urgently beg and request Your Graces to see to it that we and our collegiate church are paid and indemnified by Dr Wurmser according to his statement, and that he do so not only in words, but also in deed. For this we shall most humbly be in your debt. We remain your well intentioned citizens, our strict and wise lords, etc.

Letter 297: 24 July 1526, Strasbourg, Capito to Ulrich Zwingli

Printed in ZwBr 2:669–71, Ep. 511.

[*Summary*]: Capito has obtained a copy of Fabri's pamphlet [cf. above, Ep. 289 headnote]. He has exposed Fabri's tricks through a book [see the dedicatory letter below, Ep. 298], which the Strasbourg city council is examining. The council asked him not to write anything to the Swiss Confederates or to the princes without consulting them. The delegates from Lucerne have written a second harsh letter against Capito to the Strasbourg city council, but they sent a copy of the intercepted letter [i.e., Ep. 290]. That is why Capito believes he has a solid case against [Fabri], who twisted and distorted that letter and incited the hatred of the Swiss against him. A response will have to be sent to each of the Twelve Cantons. After all, who will trust a man who opened up a sealed letter [i.e., Capito's letter to Zwingli, Ep. 290], who distorted its meaning in translation, who brought false accusations and statements against him, who caused the Swiss to threaten his messenger, and who wrote behind Capito's back to the Strasbourg city council and to the *Reichsregiment*? The tables have been turned, however. Capito is hopeful that the princes will no longer suffer [Fabri's] lies. He is fearful only that the Diet of Speyer will end before he can clear his name. Zwingli may find out from the courier what else was transacted. [Philip] of Hesse is acting manfully. Saxony has two good preachers: [Johann Agricola and Georgius Spalatinus]. [Franciscus Irenicus], the court preacher of the Margrave of Baden, is of great service; [Adam Kraft], the preacher of Hesse, even surpasses him. If Ferdinand I and the bishops do not desist from pressing for an imperial edict and continue to oppose the Reformation with their machinations, a league between the cities and the princes, in particular, the dukes of Saxony, Hesse and Jülich, will be formed. What is in the making is still secret. Returning to the subject of the intercepted letters, Capito admits that what he wrote may have been foolish, but it was not wicked.

Letter 298: 28 July 1526, Strasbourg, Capito to the Councillors of Albert of Brandenburg

This is the dedicatory letter to Capito's *Der nüwen zeytung und heymlichen wunderbarlichen offenbarung, so D. Hans Fabri, jungst ufftriben, und Wolffgang Capitons brieff gefälschet hat, bericht und erklerung* (Strasbourg, 12 August 1526), f. [Ai verso]. For the context, see above Ep. 289 headnote. For Albert of Brandenburg, cf. CWC 1, Ep. 32 headnote.

Grace and health to you, gracious and favourable lords, junkers and beloved friends. I offer you my willing and devoted service as well as whatever honour and favour I am able to bestow.

After having lived with you at my most gracious lord's court for a number of years as an unskilled advisor and servant[1] and receiving much favour and friendship from all of you, I am obliged and willing to repay your favour and friendship with my own service and goodwill. And I declare myself ready, insofar as I am able, to defend and fight for the advantage of the archbishop. Now, however, Dr Hans Fabri has obtained several of my sealed letters, opened them, translated them into German, and published them. [His translation] contains gross and harmful falsifications, cruelly defaming me before the entire German nation. Indeed, I would have been in danger of life and limb, if I had not received, by God's grace, a verified copy of my letters from the godly Confederates through the honourable city council in Strasbourg. From this copy, the errors in the translation are evident, as Your Graces must see for yourselves, especially in number 28.[2] Therefore, I beg you to remain my gracious lords and benevolent friends, and I pray you do not allow yourselves to be moved by the slanderous writings of the falsifier of the aforesaid letters. I humbly desire hereby to earn this favour from Your Graces. To that end, I commend myself to you obediently and loyally. Given at Strasbourg, 28 July 1526.

Good will and favour, Your Graces, Reverend and Very Reverend Lords, and strict, earnest, honourable, wise sirs,

Yours willingly, Wolfgang Capito.

* * * * *

1 From 1520–3.
2 Capito, *Der nüwen zeytung und heymlichen offenbarung ... bericht und erklerung*, fols. Eii v–Fi v.

Letter 299: 2 August 1526, Strasbourg, Capito to the Reader

Preface to Capito's *Epistola ... Capitonis ad Zuinglium* (Strasbourg: W. Köpfel, 1526), ff. [A1v]–A3r. The letter is printed in CorrBucer 3:249–50, Appendix III. For the context, see above, Ep. 290 headnote.

[*Summary*]: Capito explains that at the request of [Wolfgang] Köpfel, he asked Zwingli to report about the conclusion of the Disputation of Baden (see above, Ep. 290). Capito had been informed that Johannes Fabri was going to spread rumours and slander the reformers at a meeting of the Swiss [*Tagessatzung* 25–28 June 1526], which was to take place at the conclusion of the disputation. In the letter, Capito warned Zwingli about Fabri's plan and related news in confidence, as was customary among friends. The courier was intercepted near Baden and was forced to relinquish all the letters he had in hand, including the letter to Zwingli, as well as letters from [Guillaume] Farel and [Johannes] Oecolampadius. Fabri then produced a tendentious German translation of the letters and had them published along with his own glosses. Since the publication was intended to malign Capito, he decided to publish the Latin original of the letter with his own glosses, so that the reader might recognize his innocence (see above, Ep. 290). He obtained a copy of the letter from the Swiss Confederates, who were convening at Lucerne, and added two letters from the Strasbourg reformers, in which they challenged Fabri to a debate (see above, Epp. 286–7). Fabri rejected their challenge (see above, Ep. 287a).

Letter 300: 13 August 1526, Strasbourg, Capito to the Diet of Speyer

Printed as *An gemeyne stend des heyligen Römischen reichs: yetzund zů Speyr versamlet, wider D. Hanns Fabri Pfarrherren zů Lindaw, etc. Missiven vnd Sendbrief Wolffgang Capitonis* (Missive and letter of Wolfgang Capito to the Estates of the Holy Roman Empire at Present Assembled at Speyer, Against Dr Hans Fabri, Parish Priest at Lindau, etc.; Strasbourg: W. Köpfel, August 1526). For the context, see Epp. 289 and 290 headnotes.

Most illustrious and mighty duke and lord, governor of His Roman Imperial Majesty, most reverend, reverend, most illustrious, illustrious, and noble archdukes, dukes, and lords! Also, praiseworthy, distinguished noblemen, strict, highly learned, best, earnest, wise, etc. most gracious and gracious, especially benevolent lords and good friends! To Your Highnesses and Gracious lords, both grace and friendship, the grace of God and knowledge of

Christ Jesus our Lord and Redeemer, with an offering of my due and willing service.

Dr Johannes Fabri published a private letter written by me, and without authorization translated it into German, with considerable falsifications and insults, thereby harming the reputation of the unfortunate author – that is, my reputation. He told the whole world that the contents was harmful, inflammatory, and containing unheard-of lies, that I undertook to incite the subjects against their authorities, specifically the Swiss Confederacy, and with tricks and strange practices invited a bloodbath, that I preached to, advised, and helped the peasants against their lords and masters, and that I certainly despised the entire ruling class of princes and noblemen, whose ruin I would like to see and was promoting, etc. In each of these points, he twists my words and accuses me wrongly. For it is well known how diligent I and other preachers were in the past uprising, that I condemned the actions and disturbances of the peasants and wanted to appease them. Nevertheless, Dr Hans Fabri, through the falsification of the said letter and other mean practices, brought it about that the honourable city council of Strasbourg intended to punish me and would have executed this punishment, if they had not been sent a copy of my letter, and in my absence recognized, together with other learned men, Fabri's manifold falsifications. Thus, on the advice and through the persuasion of the said Dr Johannes Fabri, the laudable Confederacy brought twisted testimony against me in several letters they sent to Your Princely Lords as well as to the honourable city council of Strasbourg – letters which Dr Hans Fabri then published.

For that reason, it was necessary for me to issue a clarification through the same means, to proclaim my innocence and to deflect such testimony, without wanting to injure anyone. I therefore humbly apologize to Your Princely Lords and Graces, whom I consider in my heart as my most merciful and gracious lords, as rulers established by God, whom I have publicly acknowledged and supported, and whose majesty, praise and well-being I have always wanted and continue to foster, and against which no honest man may speak, whether he be of the upper or lower class. I know I owe obedience for God's sake, and have always obeyed faithfully. Now that I have been repeatedly accused before the entire German nation, I had to respond to all accusations publicly, lest anyone believe that Dr Johannes Fabri has brought any truthful accusations against me. Such a response is necessarily long-winded, although there is no need at all to justify myself before Your Princely Lords and Graces. For that reason, I most humbly pray that You may give heed to the following passages, for God's sake and for the sake of justice:

First of all, to the preface addressed 'To all Christians,' in which the main reason for my letter is laid out;[1] likewise, to the following articles, namely, articles 2 and 37, in which one may see to what extent and by what means I and other Christian preachers, and whoever else, caused unrest;[2] the eighth article, in which I admit that the imperial mandate could be called blasphemous without injury to His Highness;[3] the ninth, which reports that I never called the highly praised princes, my most gracious and gracious lords, 'tyrants;'[4] articles 28 and 55, which give proof and show that I never wanted nor wrote that I wanted to 'overturn' the proceedings of the Disputation of Baden, with an explanation of the harmful lies published by Dr Johannes Fabri, who falsified my letter in word and meaning, and caused it to be misunderstood through his fabricated glosses.[5] And he did this not out of ignorance, although he has no proper skill, but is always trying to make an impression for the sake of glory. Today, praise God, children in the first years of their education understand and recognize [the phrase in question]. For my use of the word *catastrophe*, which he translated as *verkerung* (overturning), is used in all schools, and by all Greek and Latin writers, in the sense in which I used it,[6] and in no other sense, except in some old and outdated word lists, from which Dr Fabri mostly draws his Greek, which contain meanings that schoolteachers have never accepted as plausible. There are still other things, which he also falsified in my letter, to my detriment, but I spare Your Highness from reading them, for you have other business at hand. But if Your Princely Lords and Graces find me guilty and think I spoke and wrote as Fabri says I did – that I indeed encouraged rioting or disobedience against the secular magistracy, or did not vigorously oppose it – then I beg you to

* * * * *

1 Below, Ep. 300a.
2 Capito, *Der nüwen zeytung und heymlichen offenbarung … bericht und erklerung*, fols. [Aiv v]–Bi v; and Gii v–Giii r.
3 Capito, *Der nüwen zeytung und heymlichen offenbarung … bericht und erklerung*, fols. Biii v–[Biv v]. Cf. above, Ep. 290, p. 216.
4 Capito, *Der nüwen zeytung und heymlichen offenbarung … bericht und erklerung*, fol. [Biv v]. Cf. above, Ep. 290, pp. 216–17.
5 Capito, *Der nüwen zeytung und heymlichen offenbarung … bericht und erklerung*, fols. Eii v–Fi v; and Hii v–Hiii r. Cf. above, Ep. 290, pp. 225–6.
6 I.e., 'end' or 'conclusion.' In his defence, Capito cites Mosellanus' use of the term 'catastrophe' to denote the end of the Disputation of Leipzig, as well as Erasmus' use in his letter to Pietro Barbirio in 1521 (Allen Ep. 1225:318–19) in which he used the word *katastrophe*. Capito was right to complain of a mistranslation. The Greek word clearly means 'outcome' in the context in which he used it, i.e., the final phase of the disputation. Cf. Capito, *Der nüwen zeytung*, fol. Hiii r and above, Ep. 290, pp. 225–6.

take my life. And I swear before God, before whom I stand, that I will not flee, and I also say that Your Princely Lords and Graces are obliged to punish me, according to the divine command given in the eighteenth chapter of Deuteronomy.[7]

But if Your Highnesses do not deem me guilty, which I hope to God will be the case, then it is my humble request that you not accept the charges of Dr Johannes Fabri and of other falsifiers of letters, but that I and other pious, honest folk be freed of suspicion, and no credence be given to them without hearing us. For that is the proper way of dealing with people who are not ashamed to write openly and spread untruths to large communities, such as the city of Bern and others. I always want to serve Your Princely Lords, the Electors, to the best of my ability, as well as Your Princely Graces and Graces and earn your favour before God with my prayers and dutiful service and obedience to secular authorities, as commanded by the Word. May God Almighty endow you with his salutary knowledge and give you health and long life for the sake of a godly and Christian government. Given at Strasbourg on the thirteenth day of August in the year 1526.

Good will to Your Princely Lords and Graces, your humble and obedient Wolfgang Capito.

Letter 300a [After 13 August 1526, Strasbourg], Capito to the Reader

> This is Capito's second preface to *Der nüwen zeytung und heymlichen wunderbarlichen offenbarung, so D. Hans Fabri, jungst ufftriben, und Wolffgang Capitons brieff gefälschet hat, bericht und erklerung* (Report and clarification concerning the news and amazing revelation of secrets, which Dr Hans Fabri has recently produced, and his falsification of Wolfgang Capito's letter [Strasbourg, 12 August 1526]), ff. Aii recto–Aiii verso and continued Hiv recto. Although the title page indicates 12 August as the date of publication, the text below mentions an action taken on 13 August (see below, p. 249), which supplies a terminus postquem for the preface. The first preface, addressed to the councillors of the archbishop of Mainz, is Ep. 298. For the context, see above Epp. 288a and 289 headnotes.

I, Wolfgang Capito, wish grace and salvation through Christ to all faithful Christian readers, etc.

Dr Johannes Fabri has recently published a little book with the title *News and an amazing revelation, kept secret, of certain things and actions that came*

* * * * *

7 Actually Deut. 19:15–19.

to pass at the meeting in Baden im Aargau before the delegates of the Twelve Cantons, etc.[1] This title leads the reader to assume that the book reveals amazing secrets and unheard of things, but in fact the book contains nothing that is not already common knowledge and has not already been reported. Indeed, it illustrates that Dr Johannes Fabri is willing, for the sake of his own earthly reputation and glory, to destroy the Christian Truth and to wipe out the followers of the Truth. For the four Latin letters,[2] as you will soon see, contain nothing other than your everyday news and a bit of Christian encouragement and advice. These have been translated inaccurately into German in such a way as to maximize Fabri's ability to denigrate, defame, and discredit. Is it really such a strange situation for a friend to write to another friend regarding general news, such as most people discuss among friends, to privately discuss these matters in a friendly letter, which contains no mischief or malice? Can the whole world really be so greatly astonished at this? The two friends in question have a common matter to discuss, and they also relate news, which a malicious person changes on purpose in order to damage the reputation of both correspondents, changing innocuous expressions into something stronger and more dangerous than they actually were. Is it proper for someone to use heated words in a published tract and in a grave harangue to attack what two innocent men thus discussed between themselves, in private? Is it appropriate to accuse them before the whole world and the leaders of the German nation, as if the whole world cared about their private correspondence, which injured no one? Those particular letters can be taken for nothing other than a private discussion between honest citizens. Indeed, the ancient emperors put people to death for publishing private correspondence which came into their hands, and rightly so.

Have patience, faithful reader, and look over my response. In doing so, you will be able to determine which of us, Fabri or I, produced the scandalous, damaging, and seditious lies and the misleading new teachings that do not come from God, and which of us is not ashamed of using mischievous ploys. You are the judge, you are in charge, for he despised and derided our word, which is truly God's Word, defiling it with his poisonous filth. Indeed, the judgment belongs to the church and to each person individually, according to the saying: *Let two or three prophets speak, and let the others weigh what is said*, 1 Cor. 14.[3] And if anyone can show that I have preached a condemned

* * * * *

1 See above, Ep. 289, note 1.
2 Fabri's book contained German translations of four intercepted letters. See above, Ep. 289 headnote.
3 1 Cor. 14:29.

gospel and have led people astray, ruining them, or that I have destroyed Christian order, opposed the ancient and true faith, or replaced God's Word with something that is not God's Word, then, according to divine law, it is incumbent upon the secular authorities to take me into custody and put me to death. Indeed, if this is the case, I freely offer myself to them.

First of all, hear the cause and content of my writing. On 10 June, Wolf Köpfel, the printer,[4] begged me to help him out by persuading Zwingli or someone else to write material to be added to the first publication of the [proceedings of the] Disputation of Baden. I agreed to write to Zwingli, which I did on the following day, enclosing a copy of the pamphlet on the disputation.[5] We entrusted the packet to a faithful and poor fellow[6] in the pay of the printer, with instructions to take it to Zurich. However, since I was weighed down by much work and poor health – on the morning on which I wrote the letter, I also had to preach, lecture to my listeners for an hour on the prophet Hosea, and, in addition, it was my turn to be in the cathedral by four o'clock in the afternoon in order to preach again – I did not write everything as clearly as I would have liked. As a result, I instructed our aforementioned messenger to ask our beloved brother Zwingli at least to improve the pamphlet. I asked him to add something about the shameful and uncouth language combined with the foul nonsense with which Fabri, Eck, and other enemies of the Truth slandered and defamed both our brother, the pious, inoffensive man of God, Oecolampadius, and the divine Truth itself. [I told him] he need not bother to touch on the points themselves which were argued at the disputation, for they would be brought to light eventually, whether our enemies liked it or not, etc.

I knew, of course, that Fabri would come at the appointed time to Baden in Aargau, and I would have to guard against his usual method and actions. I knew that, by citing the imperial mandate and other news, he would attempt to frighten the simple-minded and that, in doing so, he would further stir up and harden the hearts of his followers against the Gospel. Therefore, I wrote to Zwingli regarding the imperial mandate, and I informed him of other current topics of conversation, with which we do not usually concern ourselves. I did these things so that he could better advise those who are weak in the faith and so that he would be able to anticipate Fabri's tactics, etc.

That is the cause and general content of the letter to Zwingli. Perhaps

* * * * *

4 On Wolfgang Köpfel (fl. 1522–54), the Strasbourg printer, see above, Ep. 289, note 5.
5 I.e., the *Warhafftige handlung*. See above, Ep. 288a.
6 Johannes Büchli. See above, Ep. 389 headnote.

the printer seeks his livelihood and profit. I only wish to shame the papists, so that they will no longer delay the publication of the proceedings of the disputation, about which they have made such great boasts.

And because I sent this letter to Zwingli through a secure channel, or so I thought, and because I knew well that Zwingli was a most blessed servant of Christ, I was less cautious and did not write with the usual care, as one can see from my handwriting, which no doubt looks like a draft. For private letters are in lieu of private discourse, as I said above, which one engages in carefully and cautiously when someone listens in and may be offended as a result. Otherwise, if there is no danger of being overheard, one is less careful and tells what is going on. How I wish that I had kept that letter! Not because I was afraid of danger – there was nothing dangerous in it. Rather, I wish that I had not considered it good enough to be read by Zwingli. Instead, I told the messenger that he should give Zwingli my apologies for my lack of leisure and because I was busy with preaching, reading, and other duties that occupied my time and also because of my poor health. For three days later I fell ill, from which illness I have yet to recover fully. Since I wrote nothing dishonourable or even anything other than what was common rumour at the time, I need not be afraid of a reasonable judge or an intelligent reader. Therefore, I will undertake a word-for-word comparison between the above-mentioned letter to Zwingli and Fabri's version, which was maliciously translated to make it appear blasphemous, and I would like to insert my reasons and the broader context, where necessary. In each place where Fabri has included his nice little glosses, I have countered with an appropriate answer and shown precisely what Fabri has falsified and why. The appearance of the word 'TEXT' indicates that these are the words of my letter to Zwingli, as translated from the verified copy which the confederates of Lucerne sent to the honourable city council at Strasbourg in response to their request and my grave plea. The word 'FABRI' or 'FAB.' denotes Fabri's gloss, and 'CAPITO' or 'CAP.' marks the beginning of my response.

[Here follows the text of Capito's letter to Zwingli, with Fabri's glosses and Capito's explanations:][7]

This report makes manifest what powerful people have put forward in the Baden Disputation against the gospel. It shows the shameless nature of Johannes Fabri, who publishes without authorization private letters written to individuals, falsifying their words and meaning and burdening them with

* * * * *

7 I.e., Ep. 290 above.

mendacious glosses. Indeed, as far as he can, he omits no lies or fabrications that might be useful in ruining a pious and decent man. In addition, Thomas Murner has responded, defending these same learned doctors.[8] They say one can judge the nature of a case by the men who are its patrons. But can it be a honest business if the man defending it harms and insults pious and decent men, that is, all who, in our time, act according to the Word? Therefore, on 13 August, Wolf Köpfel summoned Murner on account of his recently published slanderous pamphlet to state his case here in Strasbourg. He awaited him here. Murner, however, cited his company and refused to give an answer.[9] Perhaps he thought that we might ridicule what he had to say and call him a rascal. Wolfgang Köpfel, however, says that no decent man could honestly say that he had allowed odious pamphlets to be published. He is willing to come before the authorities and maintain his position in an honest manner.

Letter 301: 15 August 1526, Strasbourg, Capito to Georgius Spalatinus

> A copy of this letter is in Bern SA, B III 72, fol. 13–14 Ep. Var. XVII (cf. the transcription in TB II, 277). On Spalatinus see CWC 1, Ep. 29.

May the grace of Christ be with you, dearest Spalatinus. Our church greatly rejoices that you openly profess the Word. For they speak of your amazing constancy and the power of the Lord. Blessed is your piety; thus the profession of faith leads toward salvation. I am especially glad about this because the glory of the Lord is clearly prevailing in that undecided battle. For it plainly prevails where people may profess their faith without fear ...[1]

* * * * *

8 Thomas Murner, *Ein brieff den strengen fursüchtigen ersamen wysen der XII Örter einer löblichen eydtgnosschafft gesandten botten* (April–May 1526) and *Ein worhafftigs verantworten der hochgelerten doctores und herren, die zü Baden uff der disputation gewesen sint vor den xii. ortern einer loblichen eidtgnoschafft: wider das schentlich, erstuncken, und erlogen anklagen Ulrich Zwinblyns [sic], das der fiertzig mal eerloss diebsch bösswicht uff die frummen herren geredt hat und in den druck hat lassen kummen* (1526). Both printed in *Thomas Murner im Schweizer Glaubenskampf*, edited by W. Pfeiffer-Belli (Münster, 1939).
9 I.e., cited the fact that he was in company and could not leave. He added: 'It would not be safe for me to speak and to my disadvantage to keep silent' (*das mir nit wol sicher were zu reden, und zu schwigen auch nachdeilig*; AST 323, #18).

1 The phrase that follows, *qui ex eo malis scilicet[?] hominem formidare possint*, cannot be translated as it stands. The general sense is 'who might otherwise fear human authority.'

Strive, my lord and brother, that there be concord among us humbler people, which will hold fast if we both call on everyone to pursue the principal goal, namely faith in Christ. I acknowledge that many things in scripture are beyond my ken, but we all know what suffices [for salvation]. In fact, *he who believes has eternal life*.[2] What purpose does it serve, then, to be angry and cause a tragic uproar leading to our mutual destruction and the contempt of Truth? Indeed, no one will ever draw me into the arena, unless there is danger concerning faith or charity, the rule by which all of scripture should be interpreted, as Paul teaches.[3] We have held on to this rule tooth and claw,[4] rejecting whatever is not done according to it. As God is our witness: we are acting on the strength of our conscience. It is not for our sake that we deprecate the public discord of the ministers. Our only fear is that the glory of the Lord be diminished on account of our weakness. But the author of all things lives and reigns, and may deal with us as he sees fit.

I am sending you the pamphlet[5] in which I respond to the most impudent Fabri; I am taking our case to the prince.[6] I had the intention of writing,[7] but forgot his title, for monarchs should be addressed with the customary reverence.[8] Join us in fighting the impiety of that most arrogant Fabri; you will do this if you manfully defend the brethren of this region, whom that shameful impostor is slandering most atrociously. What he recently spewed forth against Luther will give you a taste.[9] He used excerpts from scholastic writers impiously to prove his ...[10] For he flatters his own

* * * * *

2 John 6:47.

3 Cf. Phil. 3:15–17.

4 Cf. Erasmus, *Adagia* 1.4.22.

5 I.e., *Der nüwen zeytung ... bericht und erklerung* (cf. above, Ep. 300a).

6 In Ep. 303 below, Capito reports that he has written to the *Reichsregiment,* and that his response was brought to the attention of Ferdinand I. See also above, Ep. 300, addressed to the Diet of Speyer.

7 To the emperor or his representative at the *Reichsregiment.* The text is defective at this point.

8 Cf. Erasmus' comments on proper addresses for monarchs in *De conscribendis epistolis,* CWE 25, 45–50.

9 Perhaps a reference to [Johannes Fabri], *Summarium. Underricht auß was Christenlichen ursachen Doctor Johan Fabri bißher der Lutherischen lere nit anhängig, auch wider das war Evangelion Christi nit gewesen, sunder das selbig gepredigt, gefürdert, und mit der gnad gottes, so vil müglich, gehandthabet hab* ([Mainz: Johann Schöffer], 7 August 1526).

10 The meaning of the phrase, *aliquis scholasticis excerpendo, que testando suam [...]* is unclear.

men, contrary to the duty of a Christian. Please write back to me. Strasbourg. 15 August 1526.

W. Fabritius Capito

Please send my hearty greetings in the Lord to our fellow preacher of
Eisleben, my beloved brother, whom I wish an increase in the grace of the
Lord.[11]

Letter 302: 18 August 1526, Strasbourg, Capito to Ulrich Zwingli

Printed in ZwBr 2:687, Ep. 519.

[*Summary*]: Capito reports that Zwingli's book against Johannes Fabri [i.e.,
*Die dritte geschrifft Huldrych Zuinglins wider Joansen Faber, über das erdicht büch-
lin* (Zurich, 1526)] is an effective response. He has sent two copies to Speyer:
one to Philip of Hesse, the other to Jacob Sturm, both of whom know Fabri's
worthlessness. In his book, Zwingli has been more successful than Capito in
revealing Fabri's tricks. Capito hopes that people will now recognize Fabri's
true nature. Many people have become suspicious of wicked men like Fabri.
His reputation will no doubt suffer.

Letter 303: 25 August [1526], Strasbourg, Capito to Ambrosius Blaurer

Printed in Schiess 1:137–8, Ep. 108. For Blaurer, see above, Ep. 192 headnote.

Greetings, my dear Blaurer!

We are most pleased with your pamphlets.[1] Once the brethren had read

* * * * *

11 Johann Agricola of Eisleben (ca.1494–1566) lived in Wittenberg from 1515 on
and was closely associated with Luther. In 1525 he became rector of the school
in Eisleben, an institution lately established by Count Albrecht of Mecklenburg,
and also served as preacher and pastor of the church of St Nicholas in Eisleben.
In 1536 he was called to lecture at the University of Wittenberg, but became
involved in a bitter dispute with Luther on account of his antinomian views.
He left Wittenberg for Berlin in 1540. Subsequently he was appointed court
preacher by Joachim II, elector of Brandenburg, and was influential in shaping
church policy. He also had a hand in preparing the Augsburg Interim (1547).

1 In 1526, Ambrosius Blaurer published two pamphlets: *Entschuldigung der Dienern des Evangeliums Christi zů Costentz, uff die luge, so jnen nach gehaltner Disputation zů Baden, zugelegt ist ...* ([Zurich: Froschauer], 1526) and *Wider Weltlich
geschmuck und wachait, An die Evangelisch genantenn wyber ain gaistlich lied* ([Zu-
rich: Froschauer], 1526).

them through, we delivered them to the office of our city council, for these writings bring courage to the more timid hearts. The pamphlets came at an opportune time, since Fabri was spreading his insults against me. I, in turn, responded to him without ill temper, but truthfully: I justified myself before the *Reichsregiment*, before several princes, and especially before those who are on the side of the Word.

That young prince of Hesse[2] seems to promote the glory of God with the most ardent zeal. Almost daily, he disputes with Fabri about controversial matters, and wins. He showed Ferdinand our pamphlet.[3] He had it peeking out of his pocket and casually showed it to Ferdinand, who immediately asked to see it. Then our Hesse said, 'I shall willingly present Your Highness with it.' So now Ferdinand is aware of Fabri's crimes. Fabri is notorious in Speyer, and I hope, therefore, that this tiresome man will no longer be a threat to the servants of the Lord. Read [the pamphlet] when you have leisure, so that you may be able to offer a justification on behalf of the Truth and a friend.

* * * * *

2 Philip of Hesse (1504–67) succeeded his father, Wilhelm II, at the age of five. His mother, Anna von Mecklenburg, was regent of Hesse until 1518. At the Diet of Worms, the sixteen-year-old showed himself in full control of his realm; he was, moreover, supported by capable advisors (notably his chancellor, Johann Feige). Two years later, Philip played a decisive role in the defeat of Franz von Sickingen. He was firmly committed to the Reformation, which he introduced in his realm in 1526. He worked toward a rapprochement between the Protestant factions at the Marburg Colloquy (1529) and the Diet of Augsburg (1530). After Zwingli's death (1531) he became an active member in the Lutheran Schmalkaldic League. He was instrumental in ensuring the restoration of Duke Ulrich of Würtemberg to his realm, ousting the Habsburg governor, Philip Count Palatine (Peace of Kadan, 1534). Philip made overtures to Ferdinand I, however, and succeeded in re-establishing friendly relations with the Habsburgs. He was married to Christina, a daughter of the Catholic Duke George of Saxony, and involved in a scandal when his bigamous relationship with his mistress, Margarethe von der Saal, became public. At the Diet of Regensburg (1541) he was obliged to support Habsburg efforts to promote religious peace between Catholics and Protestants, but in 1546 the Schmalkaldic League, of which he was a member, joined battle with the Emperor and suffered defeat at Mühlberg (1547). Philip surrendered and was kept prisoner in the Netherlands until 1552. In the Peace of Augsburg (1555) the German princes finally obtained the right to establish the religion of their choice in their realms.

3 *Der nüwen zeytung ... bericht und erklerung* (see above, Ep. 300a headnote). The events related here took place at the Diet of Speyer, which Fabri attended.

We have accomplished nothing as yet with regards to the brothels.[4] Our city has been a most corrupt place, adultery very widespread, and no street free of whores. How often did we speak out against this abomination! But the Lord diverted our troops elsewhere to deal with new business and disturbances. Hardly any decrees have been passed against adulterers, although a sense of public outrage is beginning to develop. The status of the whores, once untouchable, has been lowered in the public eye, and I am optimistic that someday we shall be seen as a righteous church. We seem to be turning a blind eye to the brothels at the time they are being built or on subsequent occasions; once this filth has been purged from one or the other corner, there is hope it will be completely removed. A pious magistracy cannot establish a brothel on the basis of the Word of the Lord, nor can we let it pass unnoticed forever; indeed, we are bound with all our strength to recall the common people to a blameless way of life. If those who listen to the preachers are faithful, it will be easy to do; if they are unfaithful, as the majority are, certainly we shall be given credit for making an effort to perform our duty fairly. Farewell.

The Word is increasing greatly in Speyer. The committee of the *Reichsregiment*, on whom it is incumbent to deliberate about preaching the Word, partly favours the gospel, partly offers feeble resistance. Yet there are some people who assail it in the most hateful manner, and I know the Lord will destroy them, for they resist the Truth against all judgment. But lately, the Word has been preached with great liberty, especially in Speyer. Strasbourg, 25 August [1526].

Let Zwick[5] send the young man, about whom he recently wrote. Please give my regards to him. Apart from that, we very much hope that your brother and sister[6] may advance in the Lord; for they are worthy of you and distinguished in erudition, uprightness, and faith. Greet your colleagues on behalf of my brethren and me, who hope that you, too, are well in the Lord.

W. Capito.

* * * * *

4 On 16 April 1526, Capito and Hedio proposed to the city council 'to do away with prostitution and divorce.' Cf. ZwBr 2, 799, note 5. A decree against prostitution, gambling, drinking, adultery, and other public vices was passed on 25 August 1529 (printed in Röhrich, *Mitteilungen*, I, 265–81; a copy of the decree is in AST 84, #10).
5 I.e., Johannes Zwick (see above, Ep. 192).
6 Thomas and Margaret (see above, Epp. 192, note 6, and 194, note 21).

Letter 304: 26 September 1526, Strasbourg, Capito to Ulrich Zwingli

Printed in ZwBr 2:724–5, Ep. 531.

[*Summary*]: [Martin] Bucer is in an awkward situation. He translated [Johann] Bugenhagen's Psalter into German before he declared his position on the Eucharist in a published letter to [Johannes Hesse]. Now, Bugenhagen claims that Bucer has twisted his words concerning the Eucharist [i.e., in *Oratio Ioannes Bugenhagii Pomerani, quod ipsius non sit opinio illa de Eucharistia, quae in psalterio sub nomine eius Germanice translato legitur*]. Bucer wants to respond publicly. Capito disapproves. He believes that the protagonists in the dispute should treat each other with civility and concedes that Bugenhagen expressed himself well in Latin, while Bucer did his best to explain the text in German to the general reader. At the time of publication, Capito advised Bucer to keep his explanations separate from Bugenhagen's text, but Bucer did not listen to his warnings. Thus, the need has arisen for a reply to Bugenhagen's oration [published as *Das Martin Butzer sich in verteütschung des Psalters Johann Pommers getrewlich und Christlich gehalten* (Strasbourg, 1527)].

Hinne Rode has married a Frisian woman. The true interpretation of the Eucharist is generally known there. The Turks have reportedly won a battle [i.e., the battle of Mohács, 29 August]. Capito has heard that the proceedings of the Disputation of Baden are about to be published with a misleading preface and peroration by [Konrad Huber], the town scribe of Lucerne, but Capito is confident that the truth will eventually come out [cf. also below, Ep. 313]. The Anabaptists are causing some disturbances, but they will be short-lived, since there is no more foundation [to the claims of the Anabaptists] than to the 'impanated God (*panaceus deus*)' of the Catholics. The Strasbourgers have heard nothing further of Luther. It seems that he is retreating into silence, since he has made no progress with threats and insults. Erasmus has written an irate letter to Capito [no longer extant], but Capito will not respond. He has no intentions of irritating an old man, who calls the Wittenberg theologians his brothers and has removed Zwingli and his fellow ministers from his circle of pious men (*album piorum*). Rumour has it that Philip [Melanchthon] genuinely disapproves of Luther's acrimony against Erasmus, a man who has done so much to advance the humanities. Capito only admires a man who can combine erudition with piety.

Letter 305: 14 October 1526, [Strasbourg], Capito to [Adam Kraft]

Adam Kraft or Crato (1493–1558) was the son of the mayor of Fulda, Hans Kraft, and a reformer of Hesse. Around 1526 he married Agnes Ibach (d. 1544)

and, after her death, Afra Weißmann, née Scheerer (d. 1582). Kraft attended
the cloister school in Fulda, the Latin school in Neuburg (Donau), and matriculated at the University of Erfurt in 1512, where he came under the influence of
humanism (BA 1514; MA 1519). At the Leipzig Disputation of 1519 he came
to know Martin Luther and Philip Melanchthon. From 1523 to 1524 he was
a preacher in Fulda, and from 1524, in Hersfeld. On 15 August 1525, he was
appointed chief preacher of Marburg. In 1526 he accompanied and, after his
departure, represented the landgrave, Philip of Hesse, at the Diet of Speyer; in
1527, he took part in various synods in Homberg concerning the Reformation
in Hesse. In the same year, he introduced the evangelical service in the parish church of Marburg and became professor at the newly founded University
there. In 1529, he participated in the Marburg Colloquy. As superintendent and
general visitor of the Hessian churches, Kraft was involved in the Reformation
of the cloisters, the founding of the church treasury (1531), the composition of
the Church Ordinance of Hesse (1537), and in the composition of the Marburg
Hymnal (1549).

Capito's letter does not appear to be extant. The following excerpt was published by Abraham Scultetus in *Annalium evangelii ... decas secunda* (Heidelberg:
Johannes Geyder, 1620), 51.

We are superior in patience and charity, and not just in our cause. For it is the
cause of Christ and God, not ours. Zwingli and Oecolampadius have a natural modesty, which is of the Spirit, and therefore, perpetual. Luther's ardour
is of the inconstant flesh, which he does not yet understand.

Letter 306: 17 October 1526, [Strasbourg], Capito to Ulrich Zwingli

Printed in ZwBr 2:749–52, Ep. 541.

[*Summary*]: Capito considers it necessary to respond to [Jakob] Strauss'
book [i.e., *Wider den unmilten Irrtum Maister Huldreych Zwinglis*, June 1526;
see above, Ep. 296] and defend the cause. In the book, Strauss reproaches
Zwingli for inconsistency and criticizes him for Latinizing his name, that is,
Zwinglius from Zwingli. Motivated by jealousy, Strauss furthermore took issue with Capito calling Zwingli a minister of Christ, a faithful apostle, and a
chosen instrument of God. Strauss, who used to be a Dominican, has changed
his own name from Friar Jakob to Dr Jakob Strauss. Leo [Jud] should read the
book. He will then see for himself that Strauss is speaking out against scripture and the public peace. Strauss was being held in Eisenach because of his
role in the Peasants' War, but thanks to Luther, [John], Duke of Saxony set
him free. Strauss reportedly encouraged the rebellious peasants to address

the duke as 'Brother Hans.' In his book he tries to ingratiate himself with the Lutherans by agreeing with their interpretation of the Eucharist. He used to criticize them in the past. Capito asks Zwingli to reply in his customary moderate tone, without sacrificing the truth. He asks that the published book be sent along with a letter to [Philip], Margrave of Baden, requesting that Zwingli and Oecolampadius be authorized to sell their books in his territory. Capito will facilitate the matter.

The Strasbourg preachers are reading Luther's *Sermon* [*von dem Sakrament des Leibes und Blutes Christi wider die Schwarmgeister*] to dispel any doubts among the brethren about the error of his teachings. One of them reacted by saying: 'If he has read what Zwingli and Oecolampadius have written so often, then he is extremely insulting; if he did not read it and therefore condemns what he doesn't know, then he is very arrogant.' Nevertheless, Luther deserves their consideration, for his teachings about grace, the law, and the gospel breathe the Spirit of the Lord; his teachings on the Eucharist, by contrast, breathe the spirit of the flesh. Capito beseeches Zwingli to deal with Luther in a patient and moderate way. The Strasbourg preachers are directing all their energy toward the goal of abolishing the mass. Attention is being drawn once more to public vices [see above, Ep. 303]. In that matter, the Lord is giving the magistrates more strength every day. An [unnamed] brother is inspiring the Strasbourg preachers with even greater admiration for Zwingli. Capito asks Zwingli whether he approves of his responses to Fabri [see Epp. 298, 300, and 300a]. Unfortunately, the Diet of Speyer came to a sudden end, which upset Capito's plans to clear his name there. His cause would have been supported by [Jacob Sturm and Philip of Hesse].

Greetings to Leo [Jud] and the other brethren. When Zwingli writes next, he, too, should give his regards to all the Strasbourg preachers. This small courtesy will keep the weak brethren loyal. Zwingli should indicate, however, what is meant for public consumption and what is to be kept private. Capito sends best wishes to Zwingli's wife [Anna Reinhard].

Letter 307: 25 October 1526, Basel, Guillaume Farel to Capito and Martin Bucer

Printed in CorrBucer 2:176–80, #140.

[*Summary*]: Farel relates his adventures on the journey from Strasbourg to Colmar. He lost his way, was hampered by bad weather and separated from his companion. He mentions the conversations he had in Mulhouse with the town secretary [Johannes Oswald Gamsharst], the preacher Jacob [Augsburger], and [Augustin Gemuseus]. Augsburger is in need of an assistant. Oecolampadius suggested that the Strasbourgers send Bonifacius [Wolfhart] to take up that post. Farel himself hopes to obtain Otto [Binder] to assist Berthold [Haller] in Bern. On 25 October, Farel met with Wolfgang [Wissenburger] to discuss the Lord's Supper. Wissenburger taught that the bread is 'a symbol, whether Christ is in it or not.' He was displeased with [Martin] Luther's stubbornness. He wrote twice to Capito [letters not extant] concerning a certain Margarita, but has received no reply. Farel encourages the Strasbourg reformers to write to Marcus [Bertsch] and Wolfgang [Wissenburger]. He believes that their letters would prompt results. In this matter, they should follow the advice of Oecolampadius, however. He sends greetings to Symphorian [Altbiesser], [Johannes Steinlin] Latomus, [Caspar] Hedio, Matthew [Zell], Sebastian [Meyer], Diebold [Schwartz], [Anton] Engelbrecht, Jakob [Bedrot], and [Hartmut von] Cronberg. Farel would have delivered [Michael] Bentinus' letter to his wife, had fear of the city council [i.e., their ban against him] and of the plague not deterred him. Greetings also to Simon [Robert of Tournai].

Letter 308: 8 November 1526, Strasbourg, Capito to Matthäus Alber

The text of the letter is printed in Karl Eduard Förstemann, ed., *Neue Mittheilungen aus dem Gebiet historisch-antiquarischer Forschungen* (Halle, 1845), 7.3: 67–8. The manuscript (autograph in Halle UB, ms. Ponikau, misc. 9, #40) is partially damaged; hence the elision points.

Matthäus Alber (1495–1570) received some of his education at the Latin school in Strasbourg. From 1511–13 he served as an assistant at the elementary school in his native Reutlingen. He studied at Tübingen (MA 1518; DTh 1530) and Freiburg (B Biblicus and Sententiarius, 1521). He served as a priest in Reutlingen from 1521–48 and introduced the Reformation there, instituting German church services, abolishing confession, administering communion in both kinds, and removing images from the churches. He married in 1524. In his interpretation of the Eucharist he followed Luther's teachings. When Reutlingen accepted the Interim in 1548, Alber resigned his position in the church. Under the protection of Ulrich of Würtemberg, he moved to Stuttgart, where he was minister (1549–63) and superintendent of one of the four districts of Würtemberg. He collaborated with Johannes Brenz on the church order of Würtemberg (published 1559) and in 1563 became the first Protestant abbot of Blaubeuren.

To Matthäus Alber, minister in Reutlingen, his respected lord and brother.

... dearest brother in the Lord. The bearer of this letter brings us a great deal of excellent news about the state of your church, above all that the mass has been abolished by the authority of the city council. Although we strive sedulously, the Lord in his clemency has not yet looked upon us, and this is what our sins deserve. Thanks be to God that his Word is advancing [in Reutlingen] at a steady rate, through your agency. How we feared for you on account of the uprisings of the peasants! How vain and unworthy of trust were the rumours reported from all sides, which seemed so true that even good men were inclined to give way to some extent. I see that floods may rise up against you, which you will courageously overcome with the support of the Word, by continuing to do what you have always done – that is, by relying on the Word, which is the safest ground for those caught up in the floods. We fight the mass stealthily, but as always, we are quite free to preach sermons.

There has been a great deal of discussion here concerning the establishment of schools, lest pious literature be disdained, and I hope that something will come of it soon, even if we shall hardly complete the project within a few years.[1] Indeed, there has been hateful opposition from those who should be initiators and leaders of a project that is so advantageous to the city. We shall not allow ourselves to be bothered a great deal by speeches of that sort. Most of us are doing all we can *to make the people ready for the Lord;*[2] we are entirely preoccupied, I say, with the godly, whose ministers we confess to be. In the meantime, we confront people who are defiled through contact with the world, as is proper for us who have professed Christ. What we love most about you, however, is your teaching of a more sincere church, since the Lord has given you the skill to sow the Word. Your fellow citizen, with whom we have spent time repeatedly, is proof of it: he totally breathes Christ, just as his sister stubbornly clings to the Antichrist.[3] Finally, we congratulate you on your fellow-soldier of Tübingen.[4] He will succeed in building concord and consensus in the Lord and give support to the weak. Please greet them when you see them, and tell them of our feelings for you. Bucer, who has left to preach, sends his special greeting, as do the rest of the brethren, who gladly make mention of your name. Strasbourg, 8 November 1526. Please greet your colleagues in the Lord.

W. Fab. Capito.

* * * * *

1 On the establishment of schools in Strasbourg, see also below, Epp. 403, 406, 426.
2 Luke 1:17.
3 The identity of the siblings is unknown.
4 Johannes Schradin, Alber's co-reformer in Reutlingen. On Schradin, see Ep. 364 headnote.

Letter 309: 12 November 1526, [Strasbourg], Capito to [Ulrich Zwingli]

Printed in ZwBr 2:771–3, Ep. 550.

[*Summary*]: Capito has learned about events in Zurich from a letter of [Heinrich Brennwald] to his son [Jodocus].[1] He asks Zwingli to use coded language in his letters, stating confidential information in either Greek or Hebrew to confound casual or curious readers. He provides hypothetical examples of using Greek and Hebrew phrases in this manner. Capito will mention neither his own nor Zwingli's name in correspondence and urges Zwingli to comply with his suggestions. Many people find [Johannes] Fabri's attack on Zwingli [*Christenliche bewysung,* June 1526] ridiculous. They laugh at Fabri's stupidity. The Strasbourg reformers have not yet read it and therefore cannot judge it. They are uncertain of Luther's future actions. The messenger mentioned earlier [unidentified] has not yet returned. He is expected shortly and will report to Zwingli about conditions in Strasbourg. There is pressure on the people to return to the Catholic beliefs and practices. The church at Strasbourg sends greetings to Zwingli.

Letter 310: 14 November 1526, Strasbourg, Capito to Ulrich Zwingli

Printed in ZwBr 2:774–5, Ep. 551.

[*Summary*]: Capito asks Zwingli to exercise caution and be discreet when writing letters to him. He acknowledges that Zwingli must write against Luther [i.e., *Amica exegesis* (Zurich, 1527)], but hopes that he will do so in a moderate tone. The majority of the Wittenberg theologians publicly criticize Zwingli, [Johannes] Oecolampadius, and the Strasbourg [preachers], but there are some who speak up in their defence. Luther relies more on his authority than on scripture. It seems that Philip Melanchthon will take no action against the Strasbourg reformers. He hates bitter disputes and prefers to deal with secular matters rather than with sacred matters in this contentious way. Capito has obtained this information from Martin Cellarius, who is a supporter of Zwingli. Yet Cellarius has his own peculiar doctrines: that the Israelites will possess the land of Canaan; that infant baptism should

* * * * *

1 Heinrich's brother, Felix Brennwald, fled Zurich, returned under a safe conduct to stand trial for making politically dangerous speeches, and was exonerated in October 1527.

preferably be eliminated. Nonetheless, he takes a charitable approach and preaches mutual forbearance. He has discussed the Eucharist with Luther, but was rebuffed. Zwingli's and Oecolampadius' books are for sale in Wittenberg, and some people approve of them. Luther is therefore keeping silent. Many believe that Luther is endowed with God's Spirit. For that reason, Capito urges Zwingli to respond moderately and to avoid publishing what he might later regret. Luther is keeping silent for the same reason. Capito knows that Zwingli can keep his own counsel and needs no reminder to observe moderation. The bearer of the letter is an admirer of Zwingli. Capito asks that he be given a friendly reception. He will write another time of the schemes of bishop [Wilhelm von Honstein], of which they have no clear notion as yet.

Letter 311: 29 November 1526, [Zurich], Ulrich Zwingli to Johannes Oecolampadius, Capito, and the Strasbourg preachers

Printed in ZwBr 2:778–83, #552, and CorrBucer 2:181–4, #141.

[*Summary*]: Zwingli is not familiar with the contents of [Heinrich Brennwald]'s letter to his son Jodocus, but does not think that Oecolampadius and the Strasbourg reformers have reason to be concerned [cf. above, Ep. 309]. [Heinrich] acted out of love for his brother [Felix Brennwald], of whom Zwingli does not approve. At the Disputation of Baden, the city council and people of Zurich were urged to allow at least one mass. When [Caspar von Mülinen] reported this in Bern, a partisan of the Reformation noted that Catholic efforts were in vain. The mass was bound to be abolished. Zwingli reports on the measures taken to break the opposition of those who accept pensions from foreign powers to the detriment of the gospel teaching. These men are traitors and their counsel corrupt. Zwingli has learned of their actions through intercepted letters and through other channels. A committee of eleven has been struck to investigate the matter. Jacob Grebel, the father of the Anabaptist Conrad Grebel, was beheaded for having received more than 1,500 gulden from the pope. Others [i.e., Felix Brennwald and Thomas Wellenberg] fled, but are now trying to return. Zwingli's [*Antwurt über Dr. Strussen Büchlin*] will be published soon [Zurich: Froschauer, January 1527]. Zwingli has not yet begun his Latin response to Luther [i.e., *Amica exegesis ... ad Martinum Lutherum* (Zurich: Froschauer, March 1527)], but will have it ready for the Frankfurt fair. Zwingli considers Plutarch's *Parallel Lives* a useful text. Since the Aldine edition of the text is expensive [*Plutarchi quae vocantur Parallela* (Venice: Aldus, 1519)], he suggests that [Andreas] Cratander reprint them in two volumes, the first of which could be ready for sale at the next Frankfurt fair and the second at the autumn fair. Zwingli predicts that they will sell well in Strasbourg, Basel, and Nürnberg.

Letter 312: 10 December 1526, [Strasbourg], Capito to [Ulrich Zwingli]

Printed in ZwBr 2:798–800, Ep. 557.

[*Summary*]: The Strasbourg reformers are concerned about the church in Zurich, after hearing about the trouble caused by Catholic bribes [cf. above, Ep. 311]. In Capito's view, Zwingli has zealously looked after the affairs of the church and done more than was his duty despite the danger to himself. Capito trusts in Zwingli's spirit and the constant help of the Lord. [Heinrich Brennwald], the father of Jodocus [Brennwald], has described the whole situation in a letter to the Strasbourg reformers, which Capito is passing around to friends [cf. above, Ep. 309]. Capito has not made public the news about the torture [of Thomas Wellenberg] in Winterthur. Capito regrets that Jodocus has become alienated from his betrothed [see below, Ep. 320]. He beseeches Zwingli to take his young age into account. The young woman is good and honest. Capito hopes that their relationship can be mended. The matter requires diplomacy, rather than force. Capito is pleased with the measures the Zurich city council has taken against adulterers and is unperturbed by their use of capital punishment. He will show Zwingli the representations [he and Hedio made before the council on 16 April 1526] concerning adultery. The plague has not subsided. They are expecting a difficult summer. Capito will write to [Andreas] Cratander about printing Plutarch [cf. above, Ep. 311]. The Strasbourg reformers will lecture on it publicly to a large audience. Hans Denck is causing much trouble for the Strasbourg reformers. Capito does not recognize the Spirit of God in him. The question of abolishing the mass remains a difficult issue. The matter may become the subject of a public debate. [Martin] Bucer and the brethren send their greetings. Zwingli has probably received from [Johannes] Oecolampadius the ravings of 'the Saxon Orestes' [Luther].

Letter 313: [18 December] 1526, Zurich [and Basel], Ulrich Zwingli [and Johannes Oecolampadius] to Capito and the Strasbourg reformers

Printed in ZwBr 2:807–8, Ep. 560, and CorrBucer 2:185–7, Ep. 143.

[*Summary*]: Rumour has it that the proceedings of the Disputation of Baden are being printed in Lucerne, with a slanderous preface against Luther and the Swiss reformers.[1] [Thomas] Murner has sent a section of it to [Melchior Fattlin], the suffragan bishop of Constance. Zwingli hopes that the proceedings will expose the machinations of the Catholics. He urges everyone to stand up for their faith. He is keen on doing battle for the Word and believes that victory is at hand. The people of St Gallen have removed the images from their churches and have abolished the mass. The people in Graubünden have followed suit. Zwingli puts his trust in faith, not in human resources. Zwingli dates his letter 'an hour before the lunar eclipse' [i.e., 18 December]. Oecolampadius sends his greetings. [Guillaume] Farel is living and preaching at Aigle. Capito's *Kinderbericht* (Strasbourg, 1527) is well received in Zurich. Adam Petri has published some short sermons [perhaps those of Oecolampadius on Psalm 10 and on the invocation of saints, Basel: Adam Petri, 1526]. Zwingli's apologia to [Jakob] Strauss [i.e., his *Antwurt über Dr Strussen Büchlin* (Zurich, 1527)] is ready for the press, and his [*Amica exegesis ... ad Martinum Lutherum* (Zurich, 1527)] should be available for sale at the Frankfurt book fair.

Letter 313a: 19 December 1526, Strasbourg, Capito to the City Council of Mulhouse

> Printed in Jules Lutz, *Les Réformateurs de Mulhouse* (Ribeauvillé, 1902), 3:24–5, Ep. 7. The original autograph is in the Archives Municipales Mulhouse, tiroir 1, liasse I, #3.

First, may the grace of Christ be with you. I offer you my willing service, honourable, wise, gracious, dear lords.

I read your well-considered and Christian letter[1] concerning Otto Binder,[2] the preacher, to my fellow ministers of the Word, who were at my house when the letter was delivered to me. They were very pleased and, together with me, praised God our Lord that such a man, our fellow min-

* * * * *

1 Cf. above, Ep. 304, where Capito first reports the rumour. The Proceedings were published only in May 1527.

1 *Die Frag, so meine Herren von Milhusen hand gethan an ire Predicanten, von dem usswendigen kirchprängischen aber doch christenlichen Gotzdienst. Die Antwort, die inen geben ist dorauff von iren Predicanten Jacob Augsburger, Otto V. Binder, Bernardus Ronne,* printed in Jakob Heinrich Petri, *Der Stadt Mülhausen Geschichte wie sie im Anfang des 17. Jahrhunderts geschrieben* (Mulhouse, 1838).
2 On Binder, see above, Ep. 265, note 3.

ister of God, should preach the Word in the service of such an honourable and Christian magistrate and community. For this is the reputation you have obtained in many churches because of your loyal adherence to the Word in these dangerous times. I then presented Your Wisdoms' sentiments to Otto Binder, and found him ready and willing. He will follow the messenger in three or four days. He would have gone with him within an hour if the affairs of the reverend cathedral chapter had permitted it. For those benevolent and wise lords wish him to remain in Boersch. The neighbours, however, who want to destroy the Word, have caused trouble for him. Once Your Wisdoms have heard him preach and if you like him, and if it is God's will, please accept him under the same conditions as, I hear, Nicolaus Prugner has been accepted.[3] Those in session shall decide and confirm it. He who serves the altar, shall live by it; he who does not work shall not eat.[4] You know, however, what charity demands if God strikes his servant with illness and he cannot fulfil his command. I suppose you will not be able to come to know the man on the basis of a few sermons, but you will be able to surmise what you may expect of him. I recommend myself to Your Wise Honours. May God maintain you in your belief for his honour. Given at Strasbourg, 19 December 1526.

Your honest, willing Wolfgang Capito.

Letter 314: 26 December 1526, [Strasbourg and Basel], Capito and Johannes Oecolampadius to Ulrich Zwingli

Printed in ZwBr 2:819–21, Ep. 564.

[*Summary*]: The proceedings of the Disputation [of Baden] are about to be published with virulent prefaces. [Martin] Luther and [Ulrich] Zwingli are both heretics in the opinion of the Catholics. It is ironical, considering that the Wittenberg [reformers] recently accused the Zwinglians of heresy because they do not agree with them. Luther is publishing many sermons. His purpose is to show his authority and draw people into his camp. Capito urges moderation toward him.

The Strasbourg reformers held a colloquium with Hans Denck on 22 December. He explained his book [*Vom Gesatz Gottes*] artfully, alternating assertions with denials. It is certain, however, that he does not agree with them

* * * * *

3 On Prugner, see above, Ep. 221 headnote.
4 Cf. 1 Cor. 9:13–14.

on essential matters and is causing difficulties in the church of Strasbourg. Denck has made a great impression on the people with his pretence of virtue and his acute mind. His attacks were mostly directed against Capito, but Bucer defended him skilfully. Denck was ordered to leave Strasbourg, and did so on 25 December. The atmosphere is tense. People do not accept the explanations of the preachers. Capito senses a stubborn resistance. He has heard that two men were imprisoned in Zurich [perhaps the Anabaptists Felix Manz and Georg Blaurock are meant; cf. below, Ep. 329], who continued their agitations in spite of numerous edicts. Capito and his colleagues will give some thought to an [unspecified] colloquium mentioned by Zwingli. He has sent a letter through Jodocus Brennwald and a key to writing in code. He advises Zwingli to use Greek, Latin, and Hebrew, to invert the most important words or state them obliquely, but in such a manner that they can still be recognized and interpreted. Capito is not afraid of the plots of their enemies and would write openly to Zwingli if it could be done without danger to others. The Strasbourg preachers are making public what is happening in Graubünden and St Gallen. The bearer of the letter is a supporter of Zwingli. Martin Cellarius visited Strasbourg. Capito has always considered him a friend of Zwingli.

[Postscript by Oecolampadius]: Hieronymus Artolph delivered Zwingli's letter with that of Capito. They are awaiting the outcome of the meeting in Lucerne [which began on 29 December]. Oecolampadius is preoccupied [with marriage plans]. He sends greetings to [Conradus] Pellicanus.

Letter 315: [December 1526, Strasbourg], Capito to Peter Butz

> The manuscript of this letter is in Strasbourg AST 176, 1061 (formerly f. 511r). The addressee, Peter Butz (d. 1531), was the secretary of the city of Basel from 1521. Cf. CorrBucer 4:90, #292.

Respected sir. Zwingli wrote to me about speaking on behalf of this young woman,[1] so that she may obtain an official reference from the hospice 'Zur Alten Pfalz.' Moreover, it would prejudice her case if anything was done by a spiritual judge, especially in this city, since they believe that he has been instituted by Christ. Furthermore, I would be embarrassed before the holy

* * * * *

1 This letter from Zwingli is no longer extant and the identity of the woman is unknown.

church, for if the matter is not confirmed by your seal, they could easily come to the conclusion that we perhaps have made a beginning on Christianity, but have not gone far enough, since we are leaving untouched the chief part, namely, the arts Satan uses against piety in the household. That is the reason the people of Zurich have taken action against adulterers. I shall send [this letter] after lunch, or perhaps earlier, as well as [news] on the transactions with the pensionaries of Zurich.[2] In the meantime, peruse this small book,[3] in which Oecolampadius has depicted Fabri for us, albeit very modestly, as he is accustomed to do. Farewell.

Yours, Capito.

Letter 316: [End of 1526/Beginning of 1527, Strasbourg], Michael Sattler to Martin Bucer and Capito

Printed in CorrBucer 2:193–5, Ep. 146.

[*Summary*]: Following up on a previous discussion, Sattler indicates twenty reasons why he cannot fully agree with Bucer's and Capito's interpretation of Paul's words in 1 Timothy 1:5, particularly as they relate to the issues of baptism, the Eucharist, excommunication, and the swearing of oaths. He prays for guidance from God in resolving these differences. In addition, Sattler appeals to Capito and Bucer on behalf of certain individuals who have been imprisoned in Strasbourg on account of their heretical beliefs. He argues that Christian correction must take the form of loving persuasion rather than forced recantation.

Letter 317: 1 January 1527, Strasbourg, Capito to Ulrich Zwingli

Printed in ZwBr 3:4–6, Ep. 568.

[*Summary*]: Capito assumes that Zwingli has heard from [Johannès] Oeco-lampadius about the progress of the Reformation in France. [Marguerite of Navarre] supports two Christian preachers: [Michel d'Arande?] and Gérard Roussel. The latter suffers the tedium of living at court to oblige his brethren. Otherwise he would be preaching in Blois. [Louis de] Berquin and [Aimé] Maigret will be set free. [Francis I] favours the Word. [Jean de Lorraine],

* * * * *

2 This enclosure (?) is not extant.
3 *Von Anrůffung der heyligen ... uff ettlicher widersecher, und zůvorab Doctor Fabri, unnutz gegenwurfflich tandt, andtwort* (Basel: Adam Petri, 1526).

the cardinal of Metz, is said to have taken a wife. [Desiderius] Erasmus has written three letters, which were published together [i.e., *D. Erasmi Rotherodami epistolae tres* (Paris 1526)]: the first, to the University of Paris, in which he says that Lutherans are heretics, and indeed, worse than those who deny the Eucharist; the second, to the Parlement of Paris, in which he disapproves of innovators; the third, to [Francis I]. Erasmus prevaricates, writing to each party what he thinks will please them. He does not want the king to concede power to monks and theologians to proceed against good men like Berquin and Maigret. These clerics (he says) will rob the king of his authority under the pretext of fighting heresy and in the name of a council run by scholastics. Capito has not yet found the time to read the letters carefully. He may send a copy to Zwingli. On 3 January, the Strasbourg magistracy will change according to usage. The outgoing council has been tolerable; how much the new council will do for the Reformation depends on the skill of the ministers of the Word. Capito notes that the cities are not yet powerful enough to have a positive effect on the Reformation and restore tranquillity in the Empire. Luther is writing a book against Zwingli and Oecolamapdius [i.e., *Das dise wort Christi ... noch fest stehen widder die Schwermgeister*]. It concerns the Eucharist. Capito urges Zwingli to be more moderate than Luther has been.

Letter 318: 2 January 1527, Strasbourg, Capito to Ambrosius Blaurer

Published in Schiess 1:141–2, #112. On Blaurer, see above, Ep. 192 headnote.

Grace and peace, dearest brother in the Lord. We have seen the *Kalender* of Murner, a work worthy of its author, which sings your praises, since even in his malice he could not invent anything that would be unbecoming in you.[1] As a consequence, he has a stipend of 52 gulden from the Franciscan monastery, on condition that he refrain from traducing any citizen either verbally or in his books. That is why he has kept his fingers off us; for he mentioned my letters, which are not 'citizens,' even though I may have written them as

* * * * *

1 Thomas Murner, *Der lutherischen evangelischen Kirchendieb und Ketzerkalender* (1526). Murner includes Blaurer in the entry for 8 July on 213: 'Blaurer, a monk from Alpirsbach, a promoter of the New Light and preacher of the Word, and nothing but the Word and a servant of a mendacious, distorted and mangled gospel' (*Blaarer ein Münch von Alpersbach, ein verkünder des nüwen lichts und Prediger des Worts, und nüt anders den des Worts und ein diener des verlogenen nüw ausgerißen und zerzerten Evangelions*). Cf. below, Epp. 326 and 327.

a citizen. If anyone brings accusations against him, he will avoid punishment through this ambiguity, even though we laugh at the inanity of this moron. I only wish his impudence were as easy to bear for the Swiss brethren as it is advantageous to us, for the papists are ashamed of his most impudent and, at the same time, most disgraceful audacity.

This young man[2] is suitable for teaching young boys. Many people love him on account of his uprightness; he is capable in Greek and Latin, and has begun to learn Hebrew, but meanwhile he can devote himself to grammar and improve what he has produced. I am sending him on the condition that he return if he does not prove good enough for you, for he may seem rather young, even though he is quite capable of performing tasks. If the citizens had not been so lukewarm about the education of their children, he might have been taken on at our school; but many people now apprentice their sons to artisans, realizing that there is no more hope of obtaining benefices; this is the fruit the gospel bears for the good of the public. Listen to this young man explaining Greek, and also Hebrew, if you like, so that you may afterwards judge him for yourself. Otherwise, we attest to his character, for we have meticulously examined the way he lives. May the Lord protect you. Commend me to Thomas and your most noble Margaret;[3] for I embrace their spirits in the Lord. Give Zwick[4] my regards. I am glad he is your fellow minister of the Word; his heart is exemplary. Strasbourg, 2 January 1527.

W. Capito.

Letter 319: 22 January 1527, Strasbourg, Capito to Johannes Oecolampadius

Printed in BrOek 2: 4–6, Ep. 456.

[*Summary*]: When the scribe of Basel [Caspar Schaller or Heinrich Ryhiner] was here, Capito was in bad health. Yesterday, when it was announced that he was about to leave, Capito sought him out, but the scribe had a previous engagement with the city councillors. Capito could not join him because he had guests himself. Capito still hopes to be able to arrange a meeting with the scribe.

* * * * *

2 Not identified.
3 I.e., Ambrosius Blaurer's brother and sister. On them, cf. above, Epp. 192, note 6, and194, note 21.
4 On Johannes Zwick, see above, Ep. 192, note 1.

Capito believes that marriage is an honourable and sacred matter, especially for a Christian bishop, but the choice of marriage partner is crucial. Capito himself would have preferred to remain celibate, but was obliged to set an example and quell malicious rumours started by his opponents. He wanted to marry a woman of similar age and character as himself, a poor but well-educated woman, but God had other plans. He married [Agnes Roettel], a citizen of Strasbourg and moderately wealthy, because her brothers promoted the match. She is obedient to her husband and to God, an attentive hostess, and inclined to charity. She is pious and listens to moral exhortations, but she is young and Capito is less than perfect, which may offend some people. Capito urges Oecolampadius to marry a godly and Christian woman. He wishes they could discuss the matter in person. 'I would prefer the burden of celibacy over the yoke of an unequal marriage, and it will be unequal, I think, if you marry a woman who is not sincerely and truly a Christian, that is, who is not self-denying.'

The servant has just announced that the scribe will meet Capito at noon. He will be cautious in talking to him, not wishing to give offence to the magistrates. According to the scribe, the reaction from the Basel city council to Oecolampadius' proposed marriage has been mixed. Some people in Strasbourg approve of it, but many disapprove. Their opinion does not matter, however, since the reformers must depend on God. Capito believes that it is right for them to marry a woman in the Lord, if her character and lifestyle are approved by men of integrity. Oecolampadius must not think of his old maidservant. She does not have the right qualities. She is impure, quarrelsome, and intolerable [see below, Ep. 321]. Oecolampadius should use Hans Irmy as his guide and go-between, and entrust himself completely to that prudent man.

Letter 320: 22 January 1527, Strasbourg, Capito to Ulrich Zwingli

Printed in ZwBr 3:25–6, Ep. 578.

[*Summary*]: Capito sends his best wishes to Jodocus [Brennwald] on his marriage, and hopes that the couple will be united in love and piety. He sends his greetings to Jodocus' father, [Heinrich Brennwald]. He asks Zwingli to tell [Conradus] Pellicanus to keep the *Commentaria bibliorum*. Capito has a copy of his own now and cannot afford to buy another. Zwingli's response to [Jakob] Strauss [i.e., *Antwort über Dr. Strussen Büchlein*] is about to appear. A copy will be delivered to [Philip von Baden]. Capito advises Zwingli to respond cautiously to Luther's [*Sermon von dem Sacrament des leybs und bluts Christi*]. He wishes the theological disputes between the reformers could be settled. God has called them to this battle and will settle it again. There has been a rumour that Felix Manz has been executed [he died 5 January 1527], to the detriment of the cause of godliness and truth. Capito asks Zwingli to confirm the rumour. He hopes that the present Strasbourg city council will be inclined to reform the churches. He regards as vain reports that Luther has stopped preaching in order to write against Zwingli and Oecolampadius. Capito sends his greetings to Zwingli's wife [Anna] and their children.

Letter 321: 29 January 1527, Strasbourg, Johannes Oecolampadius to Capito

Printed in BrOek 2:6–8, Ep. 457.

[*Summary*]: Oecolampadius has written to [Ludwig] Hätzer, urging him either to change his immoral ways or stop burdening Capito with his presence [cf. below, Ep. 322 headnote]. He is amazed at Capito's patience with this ingrate. Oecolampadius believes that the church must distance itself from putrid members. They will have to wait and see whether Hätzer will heed his advice and repent. Capito need not be concerned about Oecolampadius' marriage plans, but his advice and prayers are appreciated. Oecolampadius is looking for a Christian wife, 'a phoenix' (that is, a rare bird) or else he will remain celibate. He hopes Christ will not allow him to make a mistake, unless he wants to test him. [Jakob Meyer zum Hirzen] is aware of the matter and agrees with Capito. If only the city councillors of Basel were of the same opinion. Oecolampadius does not think his maidservant is a suitable bride. Neither her morals nor her age recommends her. He has advised her to find another master. However, lest his opponents accuse him of cruelty for dismissing her during the wintertime, he has decided to retain her for a few more months. If only he had known about her character earlier. She spread the rumour that Oecolampadius was about to get married and traduced a widow of good reputation [Wibrandis Rosenblatt?], who loved him in Christ and was willing to serve him. He is approaching the matter carefully and seeking advice from friends.

Oecolampadius thanks Bucer for his letter and greets him and the rest of the preachers. He would like news of Bonifacius [Wolfhart]. He wishes Capito's wife well. The bearer of the letter is an exile, a simple but candid Christian. He has a friend in Strasbourg, to whom he would like to be recommended by the preachers. The wife of Leonhard [Pfister], Capito's fellow-godparent, sends her greetings. Oecolampadius fears that Capito's worries will make him ill.

Letter 322: [Beginning 1527, Worms?], Ludwig Hätzer to Capito

Ludwig Hätzer (ca. 1500–29) studied at Freiburg and became chaplain at Mäd-chenschwyl on Lake Zurich. There he came under the influence of the Zwing-lian Reformation, and in 1523 authored an iconoclastic pamphlet. By 1524 he had embraced Anabaptist views and was expelled from Zurich. In 1525 he was in Augsburg, working as a proofreader for Silvan Otmar. After a dispute with Urbanus Rhegius, he was expelled from Augsburg, and travelled to Constance and Basel. In the late fall of 1526, however, he moved to Strasbourg, staying at the home of Capito (see above, Ep. 321). There he made the acquaintance of Hans Denck and translated Isaiah from Hebrew into German. Expelled from Strasbourg at the end of 1526/beginning of 1527, he followed Denck to Worms and collaborated with him on a translation of the prophets [published in 1527; the work had the distinction of being the first German translation]. His move-ments in 1528 are uncertain, but he was arrested in Constance in November and executed the following year (technically for sexual indiscretion rather than his beliefs).

The text of this letter is published in QGT 7: 71–2, #74.

Look, my excellent Capito, it slipped my mind that you still have three con-tainers, in which our few possessions were transported. I gave them to this Fridolin[1] for the use of his offspring. Furthermore, allow him to take the *pul-pita librorum*,[2] as they are called. Farewell, and I thus urge and admonish you through our Lord Jesus Christ: kindly forgive me, if I have ever sinned against you. I certainly forgive you in my heart anything however grave. Oh Capito, if only we would put off the old man and live in the newness of life.[3]

* * * * *

1 Fridolin Meyer (Meyger, Meiger), a notary in Strasbourg who sympathized with the Anabaptists and who joined them in 1528. He was baptized by Jakob Kautz. His home became an occasional meeting place of the members of the sect, and he was one of their preachers. On 15 December 1528, Meyer was cross-examined by Bucer and Capito on baptism. He was released from prison upon promising not to return to the city, but was seized again at a meeting of the Anabaptists at which Hans Bünderlin and Wilhelm Reublin were also present. In a hearing on 16 March 1529 Meyer denied the intention of the Anabaptists to hold all things in common. He was pardoned and cautioned to desist from his beliefs.

2 *Pulpitum* denotes any wooden platform, here probably a lectern or book stand.

3 Cf. Rom. 6:1–14.

May Balthasar,[4] *the half of my soul*,[5] be commended to you in the Lord, my talented and respected friend! Farewell forever in our Lord Jesus.

Ludwig Hätzer, servant of Christ.

Letter 323: 3 February 1527, Sélestat, Johannes Sapidus to Capito and Martin Bucer

Printed in CorrBucer 3:1–3, Ep. 147. For Sapidus, see below, Ep 324 headnote.

[*Summary*]: Sapidus is indignant about a letter he received from Bucer [no longer extant], in which he reproached him for his relationship with a rich woman, a citizen of Strasbourg. He would like to set the record straight. Some days earlier, Sapidus encountered the woman, dressed in gold and purple, going to a wedding. After the customary exchange of greetings, she wished him good luck in his new teaching position [cf. below, Ep. 324 headnote] and asked the date of his departure for Strasbourg. Sapidus informed her that he was due to leave the next day. She then asked him to meet her for dinner, since she wanted to entrust him with a message. He could not very well deny her request. At the meeting she handed him a letter containing a sum of money, to be sent from Sélestat to Colmar. She furthermore asked Sapidus to make some purchases for her, if convenient. Finally, she asked him to dine with her, which he could not decline without seeming impolite. At dinner nothing indecent was said or done. Afterwards, he returned home.

Sapidus vows that he has committed no wrong. He has no plans to marry the woman, nor would she deign to marry him. He is prepared to marry, but not under duress. His future bride must be a woman of good character and intelligence matching his own.

* * * * *

4 Balthasar Hubmaier (d. 1528) studied at Freiburg and Ingolstadt, where he obtained a doctorate in theology. In 1516 he was appointed chaplain at the cathedral in Regensburg, and later was the parish priest in Waldshut (Breisgau). He introduced German church services and married. He was in contact with Zwingli and Oecolampadius, but disagreed with them on the question of infant baptism. He openly supported the demands of the rebellious peasants of Waldshut in 1525 and fled to Zurich when Austrian troops occupied the town. In Zurich he was arrested and released only after recanting his Anabaptist beliefs. His views remained unchanged, however, and he travelled to Moravia, where he became the leader of an Anabaptist community. The Austrian government succeeded in having him extradited for his involvement in the Peasants' War. He was tried and burned at the stake in 1528.

5 This is a phrase famously used by Horace regarding Virgil, attesting to close friendship, cf. Horace, *Odes*. 1.3.8.

Sapidus was saddened, not only by Bucer's letter, but also on account of his father-in-law's [Hans Knobloch] poor health and his troublesome family. He asks Bucer to share this letter with Capito. He will return from Sélestat in three days.

He continues to defend himself against Bucer's accusations. If everyone were like Sapidus, there would be no adulterers or prostitutes in Strasbourg. [Knobloch] wants him to consider the interests of his niece when making plans to remarry.

Letter 324: After 3 February 1527, [Sélestat?], Johannes Sapidus to Capito

The manuscript of this letter is in Basel UB ms. Ki. Ar. 25a, #41. Johannes Witz (1490–1561), called Sapidus by his fellow-humanists, was a native of Sélestat and studied in Paris (MA 1508). In December 1510 he was made headmaster of the Latin School in Sélestat. He became an enthusiastic follower of Luther, as well as a member of the literary society of Sélestat, and under his energetic direction the school reached a peak of prosperity. In 1525, after a minor quarrel with the magistrates of the city, he resigned his post and moved to Strasbourg. In 1526, the Strasbourg city council appointed Sapidus headmaster of the Latin school at the former Dominican convent. The school merged with the Strasbourg gymnasium founded in 1538. Sapidus wrote a biblical play, *Anabion sive Lazarus redivivus* (published Strasbourg, 1529) to celebrate the opening of the gymnasium. He taught poetry at the institution until his death. His achievements were celebrated in a funeral oration held by Johann Marbach, the superintendent of the Strasbourg church.

To Capito, his dearest brother and lord.

If someone were to trouble himself to follow up adequately on each individual chapter and point that Cratander mentioned in his letter to you,[1] he would need to write a book, not a letter. He wants many men to be made known, and proposes various passages in which the edition should be praised.[2] I know that I lack the strength to offer such things, and that I do not

* * * * *

1 Not extant. Apparently, Cratander wanted Sapidus to write a laudatory preface to his edition of Cicero (see below, note 2), but ended up writing it himself. In it, he thanked a long list of scholars in Strasbourg, Nürnberg, and Basel.
2 The edition in question was produced by Michael Bentinus and Andreas Cratander: *Marci Tullii Ciceronis omnia, quae in hunc usque diem extare putantur opera, in tres secta tomos, & ad variorum, vetustissimorumque codicum fidem diligentissime recognita, ac ultra omnes hactenus visas aeditiones, locis aliquot locupletata*

have the zeal and energy all those things require. In fact, I altogether shrink
from such tasks when I compare my small talent to such an arduous task.
Cicero, the prince of the Latin language, should be commended to the world,
and not obscured by any barbarism or childishness.

You may pretend that it is within my capacity, but I cannot do it now.
I am quite embarrassed and disgusted with the unfortunate plans you and
others have made to find me a wife.[3] In my mind's eye I see what will happen. Although I am not yet certain of your plan, I can guess at it. I am uncom-
fortable, not because I am so ambitious that I cannot suffer to be rejected or
disdained, but because I know that young women have loose tongues. How
easily they sin against their vow of silence, even if they have piously agreed
to keep silent and have given their pledge. They are gripped by a great desire
to spill secrets – in this, they are like women prone to premature birth. They
have their own maidservants, girlfriends, and nurses, with whom they readily gossip and willingly share their plans. Those women then pass them on
to others, so that [the secret] entrusted to one or two women is most often
known to the whole world within a brief space of time. In short, I am now
preoccupied with putting a stop to that bad idea. For I fear that people everywhere will point fingers at me, [saying], 'Here is the man who does not want
to enter into marriage unless it is a splendid and magnificent one,' and other
things of that sort.[4]

If I were a polished writer, I would oblige you more willingly than any
other man. Accordingly, I send you back Cratander's letter. Let him make
use of my talents at a better time and place, and assign me a task more suited
to my shoulders, for even if I made an effort to attempt anything, it would
nevertheless not do Cicero justice. Wherefore, I ask you on account of our
friendship to take it in good and fair part when I retract what I heedlessly
promised yesterday. You will find people who are much more suitable for
this than I, who are not as feeble-minded as I – a vice of which I am unfortunately quite guilty – and who will surpass me by far and in many respects.
Farewell, and I pledge my service to you with a candid heart forever.

Your Sapidus.

* * * * *

(Basel, 1528), 3 vols. The second book of Cicero's letters to Brutus was first
printed by Cratander of Basel in 1528 from a manuscript obtained for him by
Sichard from the abbey of Lorsch.

3 Sapidus wanted to remarry as early as February 1523, cf. CorrBucer 3, Ep. 147,
note 8, and Ep. 323 above.
4 Cf. above, Ep. 323.

Letter 325: 16 February [1527, Strasbourg], Capito to the Christian Reader

Printed as the preface to Capito's German translation of Hosea, *Hosea der Prophet* (Strasbourg: [Köpfel], 1527), verso of the title page. The letter is also printed in J. B. Riederer, *Nachrichten zur Kirchen-, Gelehrten-, und Büchergeschichte aus gedruckten und ungedruckten Schriften gesammelt* (Altdorf, 1765), 2:392, #8.

Wolfgang Capito to the Christian reader.

Grace and peace. Christ our Lord appeared to his disciples on the road to Emmaus and showed how scripture prefigured him, beginning with Moses and continuing through all of the prophets.[1] Since Christ is the end of the Law and the prophets,[2] I have agreed to interpret a prophet, namely Hosea, in a Christian manner – that is, in accordance with the power of the Truth – so that his spirit would enrich us greatly by increasing and strengthening our faith in God. May God grant his grace so that we may be improved by speaking of such things and listening to them, to the honour of the Almighty. Amen. Therefore, I beg you, my listeners, to receive devoutly this interpretation of the Truth and to be diligent. Given on the 16th day of February.

Letter 326: 28 February [1527, Strasbourg], Capito to Johannes Oecolampadius

Printed in BrOek 2:34–5, Ep. 468.

[*Summary*]: Capito has read Thomas Murner's blasphemous and scandalous [*Der Lutherischen Evangelischen Kirchendieb- und Ketzerkalender* (1527)]. He warns Oecolampadius not to respond in the same manner and stoop to Murner's level. His scatological writings embarrass the papists. Greetings to [Jakob Meyer zum Hirzen] and [Kaspar Schaller], the mayor and secretary of the city of Basel, respectively. Greetings from [Martin] Bucer and the rest of the brethren. [Agnes Roettel], Capito's wife, and nurse in his present illness, also sends her greetings.

Letter 327: 28 February [1527], Strasbourg, Capito to Ulrich Zwingli

Printed in ZwBr 3:60–2, Ep. 595.

[*Summary*]: The enemies are spreading rumours about the church in Zur-

* * * * *

1 Luke 24:13–27.
2 Rom. 10:4.

ich. Capito would like to know whether Felix Manz was punished for treason or heresy and whether he suffered death courageously. The preachers
have read [Thomas] Murner's *Kalender* and are treating it with contempt.
They have expected nothing better from Murner, but regret that Zurich is
entangled in this affair. Revenge is not the answer, but the city magistrates
might intercede. Capito predicts that the impudent papists will be brought to
shame. The Anabaptists in Strasbourg have not ceased their teaching, but are
causing no trouble. One must look out for the future, however. The rumours
of an uprising are incorrect: Strasbourg is at peace. Members of the [guild
of the] gardeners were denounced and detained, but the accusations turned
out to be wrong. Apart from that incident, peace and quiet prevails. Some
members of the Strasbourg city council support the reformers. The preachers
are confronted with secret plots rather than open attacks. There is a general
expectation of war. People wrongly believe that the princes are against them.
In Capito's opinion, [Philip of Baden] will eventually come to disagree with
Luther over the Lord's Supper. Capito has written a letter to [Eberhard Ruel],
the secretary of [Philip of Hesse], who has renounced his friendship on account of Capito's views [of the Eucharist]. Luther is doing everything to incite dissent among them. The Strasbourg preachers enjoy support in Baden.
Only [Jakob] Strauss opposes them [see above, Ep. 306] and has recently
banned the sale of Capito's *De pueris instituendis* [see below, Ep. 339]. Capito
plans to discuss the matter with the chancellor, [Jakob Kirser]. [Martin] Bucer
explicitly mentions Luther in his [commentary] on Matthew, a work which
Zwingli is likely to approve.

Letter 328: 18 March [1527], Basel, Johannes Oecolampadius to Capito

Printed in BrOek 2:44, Ep. 474.

[*Summary*]: Hieronymus [Bothanus], assistant [at St Martin in Basel], will
visit Oecolampadius' parents [in Weinsberg]. He knows about the affairs of
Basel and is aware of Oecolampadius' marriage plans. Capito may discuss
private and confidential information openly with Bothanus, as well as anything pertaining to the church. Meetings are being held in Bern to find a
way to establish peace among the Swiss and resist the provocations of the
papists. Oecolampadius is enclosing a copy of his response to [Willibald]
Pirckheimer [i.e., *Ad Billibaldum Pykraimerum* [sic] *de Eucharistia ... responsio
posterior* (Basel: Cratander, 1527)] and some writings of Zwingli that will give
him a taste of the book soon to appear. The first page is missing, he notes.
After Easter, Oecolampadius will respond to [Josse] Clichtove, or rather, to
the Paris theologians. If Capito has a message for Oecolampadius' parents
that Bothanus might convey, he should feel free to do so. Several men were

martyred in Ensisheim in the preceding week. Greetings to Bucer and the rest of the Strasbourg brethren. Best wishes to Capito's wife [Agnes Roettel].

Letter 329: 8 April 1527, [Strasbourg], Capito to Ulrich Zwingli

Printed in ZwBr 3:87–8, Ep. 605.

[*Summary*]: Zwingli's *Amica exegesis* addressed to Luther has been well received in Strasbourg. Capito admires Zwingli's temperate tone. Bucer's worries on that point were unfounded. The preachers will provide relevant comments on the *Amica exegesis*. Zwingli's report on [Felix] Manz [not extant; cf. above, Ep. 327] is persuasive. Capito recognizes that the council acted under duress. The Anabaptists in Strasbourg hold doctrines that are even worse. He would never have anticipated such difficulties. Satan is using the Anabaptists for his own purposes, fostering recalcitrance under the guise of love for religion, but Capito is confident that everything will be resolved to the greater glory of God. He recommends the bearer of the letter [not identified], who has been incarcerated on account of his beliefs and fined 8,000 gulden.

Letter 329a: [Before 14 April 1527, Strasbourg], Capito, Caspar Hedio, Matthew Zell and Martin Bucer to the City Council of Strasbourg

Printed in CorrBucer 3:59–62, Ep. 157. For further developments in Benfeld, see below, Ep. 436a.

[*Summary*]: Meinolf von Andlau has nominated [Friedrich], the curate of Mittelbergheim, for the position of parish priest of Benfeld. Friedrich wishes to continue Catholic rites and lives with a concubine. The city council has to act in such a way that the gospel may continue to be preached in Benfeld. The parish must be allowed to ascertain that the new curate is willing to preach the gospel and marry his concubine. They furthermore have the right to ask Friedrich to come to Strasbourg for an examination. The preachers ask the council to give their attention to this matter.

Letter 329b: [After 2 May 1527, Strasbourg], The Chapter of St Thomas to Wilhelm von Honstein and his Councillors

The text of this letter is in AST 22–3. The letter concerns the continued legal dispute between the chapter of St Thomas and the Catholic party who seceded under Nicolaus Wurmser's leadership in 1525. For the background see above, Epp. 233b and 237 headnotes. For the dating see below, note 3.

Most worthy, illustrious, noble prince! Noble, strict, honourable, learned, respected, most gracious and gracious lords!

We, as provost, vice-dean and chapter of the collegiate church of St Thomas in the city of Strasbourg, where we were founded and established many hundred years ago, have ever and continually, without intermission, looked after the government, administration, and residence, in our capacity as chapter and as was our obligation. Furthermore, we have collected, until now, all of our collegiate church's rents, taxes, and other dues, and used them appropriately and according to traditional usage for our needs and those of the collegiate church, as has been and still is within our rights, authority, and power as a collegiate church. For we have always been in quiet and peaceful possession of the goods and rights, and still are. Nevertheless, several persons in our collegiate church left the city of Strasbourg, and thus caused confusion and difficulties between us and the respected council of the aforementioned city of Strasbourg. We, for our part, are not pleased with this situation and would have liked to avoid it, especially because the [departed canons] are in the minority.[1] They represent no more than nine persons, canons and vicars holding prebends elsewhere. More specifically, Dr Nicolaus Wurmser, dean of our collegiate church, is now also dean of St Margaret in Waltkirch in the See of Constance, where he resides at present.[2] As no member of our collegiate church has a canonry there with him, he has no right or authority, without our request, knowledge, wish and command, to set up a chapter of the collegiate church of St Thomas outside the city of Strasbourg. For he and his followers have no mandate or command from us, the provost, vice-dean, and chapter, the greater part of which (some thirty persons, including canons and vicars) is in the city of Strasbourg. These persons continue to meet and reside in the right old and usual place, the collegiate church of St Thomas. They constitute and represent the true and rightful chapter, through the force and capacity of common law and our statutes. Those [who

* * * * *

1 A statement dated 6 January 1525 (AST 22–2) lists thirteen members resident at St Thomas supporting Wurmser. The list includes Jacob Munthart, who later changed his mind and whose name also appears in Ep. 237, protesting against the claims of the exiles. That letter lists twenty chapter members supporting Capito. His claim to majority support is, however, complicated by the fact that another seven exiles resident at Young and Old St Peter respectively also held canonries at St Thomas.

2 For Wurmser, see CWC 1, Ep. 57 headnote.

have departed], however, go against all that is right, also against all usage and tradition of the Holy Empire. In particular, they contravene everywhere the regulation (containing a notwithstanding clause) of our most gracious lord, the Roman Imperial Majesty, and the estates of the Holy Empire established in Worms. Without our knowledge or consent, they have recently brought out a mandate and inhibition of our respectfully mentioned Majesty in Spain, directed at those owing rents to our collegiate church (no doubt using special tricks, to the great disadvantage of our collegiate church).[3] In this document they made claims [to be the rightful chapter], according to the enclosed copies, that are however unfounded (indeed, the contrary is true). These persons, who have departed from the collegiate church, left us – the city and the provost, vice-dean, and chapter – voluntarily (for, as far as we know, they were not expelled by anyone).[4] They do not constitute even a third of our collegiate church, as said before, and are therefore not lawfully assembled, but rather hold office and prebends in diverse places. Nevertheless, they want to bring the whole chapter over to their side, and are working toward moving it out of the city of Strasbourg, or, should they not succeed, at least to take over our income and revenue (concerning which the briefs, seals, and tokens of legal custody are in our keeping,[5] as we are obliged by law, and of which we have the rightful and peaceful use and enjoyment, and this is the truth, which cannot be gainsaid). They want to transfer this income to themselves, outside the city of Strasbourg, and use it, or in some other form make difficulties for us, to the great detriment of our collegiate church, although they do not and cannot have any right, authority, or power to transfer the collegiate church to themselves and move it wherever they want.

Apart from that, moreover, we are obliged to take on and bear the obligations of the collegiate church, which amount to a sizeable yearly sum: the payment of the contractual dues, rents, taxes, and other such matters. These things are expected from us as the properly constituted chapter in this and in other places, and are paid according to the founders' regulations and according to the wording of our briefs and seals. We shall not mention the

* * * * *

3 Three copies of the mandate, published Valladolid, 2 May 1527, are in Strasbourg, ABR, G 4705. The document directs those owing rents to the collegiate churches to pay them to the Catholic exiles.
4 The imperial mandate reads: 'They indicated ... that they had cause and were forced to move themselves together with their goods, briefs, and seals ... out of the city, on the advice of the Reverend Wilhelm, bishop of Strasbourg' (lines 8–10).
5 But cf. above, Ep. 234b, mentioning the use of a new seal since the original had been taken by the fugitives.

great number of persons connected with our collegiate church, who require and expect support of their persons and residence and their fees from our collegiate church. Furthermore and likewise, we do not wish to deprive the persons who have left the collegiate church of anything that is theirs, but willingly leave them in possession of everything that is their due, as is appropriate according to the statutes to which we both swore – this we are prepared to do at any time. Thus we treat them fairly. If they had any complaint against us, they could have laid it before Your Gracious Lordships and before the highly respected constituted government of the Holy Roman Empire (for we would, no doubt, have attended and had a gracious hearing) rather than take it outside the Holy Empire and act behind our backs. Indeed, the fact that they have a quarrel with the honourable council must not be to our detriment, for if they have any complaint against the honourable council, they should lodge it in the appropriate place and not undertake under that pretext to despoil and deprive us of our traditional possessions without a legal process.

Common sense will tell Your Most Gracious and Generous Lordships that their mandate and inhibition is of such a nature that one can only assume it was obtained from Our Imperial Majesty, our most gracious lord, by applying undue pressure or insinuating themselves with a ruse, for it has not been signed by His Majesty's hand, nor is there a clause justifying the mandate, or an executor who would apply it. In many respects, it has the appearance of a specious and underhanded affair, making a trumped-up claim and suppressing the truth, and containing other irregularities. For such and other reasons indicated above, it is our most devout request to Your Most Gracious and Generous Lordships that you consider aiding and supporting us and our collegiate church in our continued possession of what has been traditionally, rightly, and continuously ours, that is, the government and administration of our collegiate church, as well as the benefit and enjoyment of the said collegiate church's income. We ask that you resist any error that would prevent us and our collegiate church from doing so, or does in fact deprive us of our rights without prior legal action. Also, we beg you to command and request those who are the collegiate church's debtors or obliged to pay them rent to maintain their responsibility to us as before and pay us our due in Strasbourg under our power, authority, brief, and seal. If, however, the above-mentioned Dr Nicolaus Wurmser, the dean, and his followers believe they have any rightful demands on us and our collegiate church, we ask them to appear before Your Most Gracious and Generous Lordships, or before the *Kammergericht* of the Imperial Majesty of the Holy Empire as soon as possible. With our most submissive and devoted obedience,

Your Princely Graces and Gracious Lordships' most submissive and most devout canons, the provost, vice-dean, and chapter of St Thomas, collegiate church at Strasbourg.

Letter 330: 31 May 1527, Strasbourg, Capito to the City Council of Horb am Neckar

Published in QGT 7: 80–7, #83. The text given there is that of a draft in Capito's hand (Universitätsbibliothek Basel, Ki Ar 23a, 157–60) with the corrections entered on the good copy (ibid., 160–1, perhaps written by Matthew Zell).

May God the Father and the Lord Jesus Christ give you, honest, wise lords, the ability to comprehend his grace and mercy and may he preserve you from running against the Word of his kingdom, which is a stumbling block to all the children of destruction. Amen.

News has reached us that certain people have been imprisoned by you and are in the hands of the king of Bohemia[1] because they have interpreted the Word of God in a dangerous sense and have dared to treat the faith in a peculiar manner. Four of these have recently been executed with the sword. The fifth, named Michael,[2] has, as the chief and ringleader, been given three sentences leading to his death: first, that his tongue be cut out in the city; second, that his body be gripped by red-hot tongs in two places and again at the place of execution in three places and that his flesh be thus torn off; and third, that he be burned alive. This has been carried out.

This Michael was known to us here in Strasbourg and, indeed, known to have spoken in error, which we faithfully pointed out to him in writing. And whereas he found fault with us and other preachers of the true doctrine and took offence at some aspects in the lives of the people who desire to be seen as Christians, he did not, in my opinion, take to heart what we thoroughly explained to him in testimony to the truth. Yet he often showed commendable zeal for God's worship and for Christ's followers. He begged

* * * * *

1 Ferdinand I.
2 Michael Sattler (d. 1527) became a Benedictine monk in the cloister of St Peter (near Freiburg) after attending the University of Freiburg. In 1523 he left his order, moved to Zurich, and married a former Beguine named Margaretha. They were expelled in 1525 and travelled to Horb, Rottenburg, and eventually to Strasbourg. In February 1527 he chaired a meeting of the Swiss Brethren at Schleitheim, at which time the Schleitheim Confession was adopted. In May 1527, Sattler was arrested by Catholic authorities in Horb, along with his wife and several other Anabaptists. He was tried and executed. His wife was sentenced to drowning.

the people to be faithful and honest, free from vice, and inoffensive, and he counselled those who fell short of this to become better by walking in God's paths. We never punished such efforts; rather, we praised and encouraged them. We did, however, reject his proposed means and his assertions, and did so in the mild manner owed to a fellow Christian. Even this we did with fear and trembling as if in the presence of God, lest we hastily oppose what truly comes from God. For these are the instructions of the Spirit: to take counsel and act with concern.

Thus, we were not in agreement with Michael. He wanted to make people faithful Christians by means of established articles[3] and external coercion, while we considered this the beginning of a new monasticism. Instead, we desired to progress in the Christian life through the contemplation of God's goodness, just as Moses was encouraged to do good works by remembering God's goodness and his fatherly manner of castigating his people. Deut. 8.[4] This is the rule of salvation: namely, to recognize our sins and know that God has forgiven our trespasses through Christ and wants to give us eternal life through pure grace. As God's children, we are assured of eternal life through the Holy Spirit, who counsels fear and, indeed, instils fear, ensuring that we shall be vigilant in all our actions and do not act in a way that is contrary to God's will. This is the source of wisdom: understanding, counsel, strength, knowledge, and pure, childlike fear, which remains forever.[5] Yet it sometimes happens that God's elect have fear and desire in their hearts to serve God, but have not yet received the spirit of wisdom and do not truly understand that God looks only at the trusting and patient heart,[6] and thus decide instead to please God with works. These people are truly of God and have great zeal but do not yet have the correct knowledge. They ought to be loved as brothers and members of Christ; they ought to be embraced affectionately as feeble creatures, as unlearned folk who are to be informed of the truth in a gentle manner. These are the ones Paul calls us to accept as weak brothers in the faith.[7] For faith and love of God, as well as brotherly love for our neighbour are required of all of us, and the more informed we are, the more it is incumbent upon us to look after the weak vessel and unlearned brother. And we should do so out of true humility and meekness, lest we fall into temptation and are pleased with ourselves, whereas we should only please

* * * * *

3 *zugesagte artikel.*
4 Cf. Deut. 8:5–6.
5 Cf. Psalm 111:10; Prov. 9:10.
6 *Gelossen* (patient). *Gelassenheit* was a key concept for Anabaptists
7 Cf. Rom. 14:1–2, 15:11; Cor. 8:7–12; 1 Thess. 5:14.

other people for the sake of their improvement. Therefore, since knowledge is a gift of God and not the result of our deeds, and since we are wise in Christ's kingdom solely as a result of grace and not at all as a result of our own strength or skilfulness, we owe this diligence even to our enemies, who, like Paul, persecute the people of God out of ignorance.[8] We owe much more to the scrupulous members of Christ, who desire information from us. John writes: *If someone has worldly goods and sees the need of his brother and closes his heart against him, how does the love of God remain in him?* 1 John 3.[9] Likewise, the love of God is lacking in one who neglects to help another, who is in error, to a right understanding.

Now it is reported that after the sentence Michael requested and desired that learned men be sent to him, saying that if they corrected him on the basis of scripture, he would thank them and would still suffer the pronounced sentence willingly. Since some people declared him to be in error, he simply desired someone to correct his error for God's sake. And then, according to reports, someone who was present at the earlier shedding of innocent blood, apparently said to him: 'The executioner will correct you' or 'The executioner must debate with you.'[10] These are fearful reports, if true, and God will pass a cruel sentence on those who brought the law to bear and took the life of a man, to whom they owed brotherly counsel according to God's will. The Almighty God gave Moses the sword of judgment, and yet he only condemned with the sword transgressions that concerned external and civic matters. The Lawgiver punished no internal transgressions, Deut. 27.[11] For public blasphemy concerns the public good, and the Lawgiver punished it with death. However, from our knowledge of their way of life, we know that Michael and his followers could not be suspected of such a crime. They were not blasphemers, unless one considers blasphemy the determination of these wretched people to avoid vain gambling, drinking, gluttony, adultery, fighting, murder, slander, and living according to the desires of the flesh, and to flee what is worldly and carnal.

It is indeed true that they err when they consider external baptism after confession of faith to be necessary for salvation. And they err once again

* * * * *

8 1 Tim.1:13.
9 1 John 3:17.
10 Cf. T.J. van Braght, *Het Bloedig Tooneel of Martelaers* (Amsterdam, 1660), trans. J.F. Sohm, *The Bloody Theater or Martyrs' Mirror of Defenseless Christians*, 2nd ed. (Scottdale, 1999) about Sattler's death: 'The town clerk said: "The hangman shall convince you; he shall dispute with you, arch-heretic"'(417–18).
11 Deut. 27:11–26.

when they say that the government cannot be Christian, that one should not swear an oath, and that the government must not defend itself against an enemy. For our Lord Christ is too great to be bound by water, and our salvation is mightier and more certain, and indeed, God is much too wonderful to be tied to a specific profession or to be restricted from receiving a member of another profession. He wants all people to be saved and will do everything in the name of love; for love is the end of the law.[12] Therefore, no way of life is opposed to Christ that enables us to trust in God through Christ and to serve our neighbour. *The government served the people and bore the burden of their disputes.* Deut. 1.[13] Therefore a government is not unchristian. This is the commandment: that the government should reward good deeds and discourage bad ones. He who opposes this commandment, opposes God Almighty. But when the kingdom of Christ reaches all people (now it is found only among few and far between), then we will all be ruled without intermediary by the righteous David, and we will be pious, righteous, and at peace. Then there will be no need for the sword, since evil-doers, whom the sword was meant to intimidate, will have been rooted out through the Spirit of the divine Word; they will be done away with; they will no longer exist. In these things, our beloved brethren and steadfast confessors of the Truth may have been in error, and the others who are imprisoned in your city are perhaps still in error. In other things, however, they are wonderful witnesses to the Truth and honourable vessels, and they do not block salvation with their errors. For the fact remains: God knows his own, whom he chose before the world was formed.

These people who are imprisoned in your city are certainly among the number of the elect, since they clearly have a fear of God, and they have fallen into error as a result of their seriousness and zeal for promoting the worship of God. The reason for their action is the belief that people should listen to Christ, the Son of God, and believe in him so that they might have eternal life. Therefore, they strive to listen to Christ and believe in him, and thus they gain eternal life. This is a strong foundation in the fight against the gates of hell. But they build upon it with wood, hay, and straw, which fire will destroy; they will be saved, but through fire. 1 Cor. 3.[14] Finally, the matter rests on the first reason, on Christ and on God's grace. Woe to them who persecute Christ in these blameless people and do not strive to expose

* * * * *

12 Rom. 13:10; cf. Rom. 10:4.
13 Cf. Deut. 1:9–18.
14 1 Cor. 3:12–15.

their errors, those who not only harass, but viciously persecute the simple flock of Christ, when they should be fathers and shepherds. Why are they not mindful of the fact that they are the lawgivers of civil society, and have no authority to control faith or to stifle the Spirit of Christ in the heart? Even Moses, the man of God, only ruled the external state, though according to God's command. If we desire to advance the worship of God with the sword, then we should punish adultery, usury, murder, and other crimes, which oppose the salutary teachings of the Gospel. These servants of God flee and avoid these vices, as is manifest and undeniable. It is shocking, therefore, to hear that the witnesses of Christ receive less mercy from Christian governors than was shown under the stubborn Pharisees. In their dispute with Paul, the Pharisees said: *We find nothing evil in this man; but if a spirit or angel has spoken with him, we do not want to struggle with God*, Acts 23.[15] If the prisoners have broken civil law through committing theft or robbery, or inciting rebellion, or some other similar action, they do not concern us. But if their lives are blameless and if they still desire to advance the commandment of love and the worship of God, these innocents should not be punished bodily for their lack of understanding, even if they err in some things. Whoever is able to do so should help them. Indeed, God commands that if anyone should find his enemy's donkey wandering, he should set it on the right path.[16] How much more, therefore, does God desire us to help inform and lead our dear friends, brothers, co-religionists, and co-members of Christ's body in the way of God?

Come now, I beg you: I am labouring on behalf of those who are still alive, whose hearts are tied to God but who nevertheless suffer considerable tribulation. Their faith has been denounced as erroneous, and yet no one has made any effort to reveal to them the nature of their error, offering them scriptural proof. Therefore, it is your responsibility, honest, wise lords, to make every effort to keep your brethren and fellow citizens from being abused and harassed. Use appropriate means to bring to light their innocence and honourable way of life. I am asking humbly on their behalf: let their error not be subjected to capital punishment. Rather, let them receive friendly correction in the matters in which they err, since they err not at all regarding the primary articles of faith and the fundamental points to which all of creation, even the damned, must bear witness at the Last Judgment. And if they have already been corrected once in lesser matters, take additional time, until God

* * * * *

15 Acts 23:9.
16 Cf. Deut. 22:1–4.

finally grants them grace. Indeed, one should not destroy the crushed reed, nor obliterate the smoldering wick.[17] For there are certain sicknesses of the soul that cannot be healed immediately with a single dose of medicine. They are nevertheless confessors of the faith and of the glory of God, and they are thus children of God and must speak in accordance with their beliefs. What, then, would be the use of compelling them through fear to say: 'We have received correction; we recognize our error,' while they continue to hold on to their old views in their hearts? Belief is in the heart; believers strive for a correct understanding, but false piety is a double evil.

I am quite aware, dear friends, that you are no longer the judges. Nevertheless, it is your custom to provide appropriate and fitting assistance to oppressed citizens in secular matters by duly writing a report to the authorities, who are known to harm no one whose innocence is recognized. And surely you would not be blamed if you exercised all due diligence in attempting to set these pious people free. Truly, what you achieve for these poor creatures, you achieve for Christ, who suffers with them. Thus, even if the words of evil people harden the hearts of the authorities, and God wills that these prisoners bear witness to the death of Christ with their blood, you will nevertheless have done your duty, and [they][18] are then bound to bear the punishment without resistance and put up with God's will, in whose power the hearts of powerful princes are. If it is pleasing to him, he will certainly make them receptive to correction and improve their understanding. Otherwise, any attempt to protect them would be fighting against God, just as the opposite party, in persecuting innocent men, fights against God, causing their own destruction. So high and godly a thing is governmental authority that we are even obliged to bear its unrighteous actions for the sake of our conscience, Rom. 13.[19]

In conclusion: may you and your people be commended to the Lord; defend the innocent as your compatriots; and at the very least, make sure they are set straight if they desire it. You are answerable to God for that much. If your brotherly witness does not help, then they must commend themselves to God and suffer imprisonment, until God himself saves [them],[20] who does not remain angry forever and desires everyone to bear his cross patiently, in silent suffering, and to find life in death. Emulate the Jews, who did not rebel against the Babylonian king, who were less troublesome than other na-

* * * * *

17 Isaiah 42:3.
18 The text says 'you.'
19 Rom. 13:1–7.
20 Again, the writer lapses into addressing the prisoners ('you').

tions who desired, in opposition to God's will, to free themselves and defend themselves against tyrants. May God enlighten the hearts of the authorities with his knowledge and the knowledge of his Son, and may he increase our faith. And may he give all those who are in difficulty the ability to persist patiently and serenely in the truth of his worship through all adversity until the end. Amen. Given at Strasbourg on the 31st day of May 1527.

Wolfgang Capito and several Christian brethren at Strasbourg.

Letter 331: [31 May 1527], Strasbourg, [Capito] to the Prisoners at Horb am Neckar

Printed in QGT 7: 87–91, #84.

May the grace, peace, and strength of God the Father be with you, dear brothers and sisters, that you may follow in the footsteps of his Son, our Lord, in all patience and willing acceptance. Amen.

All of us, who serve God with the same Spirit through his Son Jesus Christ, sympathize and suffer with you, and bear your imprisonment and persecution in our own flesh, as people who are one with you in Christ and members of the body of which Christ is the one head. But we rejoice still more for the inner person, who sees and recognizes in the judgment and deliberation of God that this tribulation leads to patience, in which you test your faith, and which, refined by fire, will be proven to be much more precious than perishable gold.[1] Thus, our flesh is in despair and mourns, but our spirit is raised up wondrously and rejoices with you. God is so kind with his chosen people that he promotes in all things that which, according to his fatherly will, is to their benefit, and so he deems you worthy to believe in him, and to suffer willingly for the sake of his name.[2] For you have not been imprisoned for murder, theft, adultery, or other evil deeds, but as Christians, although the poor people who are acting against you perhaps do not yet understand this. Why, then, would you want to mourn or feel shame rather than praise God in these matters? For he begins his judgment with you in the house of God, purifies you through fire, and leads you to a clear understanding and experience of his goodness!

Be vigilant, lest the enemy plunge your heart into impatience and deceive you into thinking that such tribulations originate in men. The hairs on

* * * * *

1 1 Pet. 1:7.
2 Cf. Romans 8:28.

your head are numbered by God, and none may fall to the ground against his will.[3] He loves you as his children and does all things for your benefit.[4] Also take heed, lest the enemy persuade you to adopt a sacrilegious opinion, convincing you that your persecutors, that is, all those who currently abandon or oppose you, are your enemy and followers of the Devil. For Paul himself, who was chosen by God and became a precious member in Christ, helped stone and kill Stephen.[5] He persecuted the Church out of a desire to honour God, for the condemned neither know nor recognize God. It thus may be that these people who currently persecute you through ignorance are, in fact, highly favoured by God and will, in time, become fellow participants in our salvation. Indeed, the children of God will ultimately be united in the revelation of the glorified Christ, a fact which remains hidden from many. Therefore, take care not to fall into the very same blindness. Pray for your persecutors,[6] and do not hate them as enemies, since God is working through them. Most important of all, infuse your hearts with a firm resolve so that they might see that God is with you and that you bear no ill will toward anyone. In this way, you may stop up the mouths of those who speak evil of you. We also hope in the Lord our God that you will bear faithful witness to the precious blood of Christ, through which alone we are cleansed and which alone ought to be prized. Through it alone have we been redeemed into life, into resurrection, and into the kingdom of God, and through it we come to know the marvellous goodness and grace of God, which has no limits and is conferred on anyone who, regardless of how or when, adopts the salvific belief in Jesus Christ, in which resides eternal life without the need for any additional qualification. This understanding will lighten your load and will cause you to grow in the cross.

This alone should be your creed, without any further embellishment, from which you may draw other articles and learn about baptism and the Last Supper and how baptism is a sign of death in Christ and is realized as we die in the Lord. It is an external thing, having as its foundation love, which takes it and prepares it for improvement by God, as order continually commands and promotes.

Also, beloved brethren, as long as evil works continue to exist, earthly authority is established for the purpose of inspiring people to fear evil and cherish good works, and it may be administered in a loving manner. There-

* * * * *

3 Cf. Matt. 10:29–31; Luke 12:6–7.
4 Cf. Rom. 8:28.
5 Acts 7:54–8:1.
6 Cf. Matt. 5:44.

fore, a Christian may be a lord and may serve God in such an occupation. But not everyone is suited to this task. It is thus possible for one person to speak on his own behalf and say that he would not know how to be a Christian and a lord at the same time while refraining from judging other people who may be destined for a higher calling. For God's grace is too full and comprehensive to exclude individual occupations. There are many gifts, all of which are ruled by the same spirit, etc.[7] Therefore, I obey my earthly lords as I would the Lord God himself, and I believe that this secular government is the will of God. And whatever they ask of me, whether it be to take up arms in order to defend the fatherland or some other command, I do it in good conscience, just as the Jews, at the command of Hezekiah, their king, resisted the Babylonian king and were right in doing so.[8] Indeed, it is still the same God, who granted us salvation through Christ and who has a particular method of dealing with the elect which Christ did not alter, but rather fulfilled, for the Son may not contradict the Father. This method is that he, in accordance with his election, places his seed in the chosen heart, causing it to develop patience and the fear of God, which guides the spirit of his children. Then follows trust in God's promise, which is accomplished and fulfilled by Christ, namely that the sins of the world have been laid upon him and that eternal life resides in this knowledge of God and Christ. It is this promise that God shares with all of the elect. This is the method of salvation which God offers to every age through suitable external means, which always urge us to faith and charity. And so there is a transformation of the external things, but the aforesaid internal method remains unchangeable.

Therefore, I myself do not worry about the oath that I take out of obedience and to the benefit of my neighbour without any gain for myself. Rather, I know that I should swear by the Lord's name and accept it; for swearing rightly is to obey God's commands and honour him, a fact which all scripture insists upon, Exodus 20, Deut. 10, Jeremiah 4.[9] Otherwise, in accordance with my understanding of the statement of Christ, I strive to let my words be yes, yes and no, no; anything else has an evil origin and is unrighteous.[10] And for my part, I do not allow myself to swear or take God as a witness for anything, unless, honouring God, I am able to serve my neighbour in doing so. That is the message given me by God's Spirit, regarding which I am certain and sure before God and the whole world. If, however, God has

* * * * *

7 1 Cor. 12:4.
8 2 Chron. 32.
9 Exodus 20:1–17; Deut. 10:12–22; Jer. 4:1–2.
10 Matt. 5:37.

not taught you such things yet, you should continue in the profession of the blood of Christ and pray that these other articles will be revealed to you. In that way, your persecutors shall persecute Christ alone and not anything else in you. Thereby you will please God. For he who has the most august Christ in his heart does not allow external things to confuse him and applies himself for the improvement of his neighbour's faith. He does his work in the fear of God, motivated by a powerful love, willingly and without compulsion.

The point of my admonition is this: that you alone are responsible, as Peter says, for showing the cause of your hope and remaining true to it,[11] which rests on the fact that we have been cleansed of our sins by the stream of Christ's blood. No other article is necessary. Therefore, pray quietly and patiently for divine guidance regarding those things about which you are uncertain, and when asserting your faith, speak in all meekness as if you were before the Lord God. In that way your judges become servants of God and his tools, doing God's will and command, for the advancement of your soul's salvation and the honour and praise of God. Believe this, and remember to hold fast to patience. We will pray eagerly to God with you in order to obtain help and grace, and we ask that you in turn pray for us, for an increase in faith and recognition of him who desires to use all of us for his glory. Amen. Given at Strasbourg.

A true brother and participant in your hope in the Lord, whose name God knows, to my beloved brothers and sisters, who now testify to Christ crucified in their body through imprisonment and suffering at Horb, etc.

Letter 332: 15 June [1527], Paris, Pierre Toussain to Capito

The original autograph of this letter is in the British Library, London, Add. ms. 21 524, f. 176, #73.

Pierre Toussain or Tossanus (1499–1573) was born at Saint-Laurent, near Marville on the northern border of Lorraine, and studied at Basel, Cologne, Paris, and Rome. In 1515 he received a canonry at Metz. There is no precise information about his life over the next years, but in 1524, he was in Basel as a guest of Oecolampadius, with whom he shared a commitment to reforming the church. In spite of his evangelical leanings, Toussain also befriended Erasmus, then residing at Basel. At the end of February 1525, he returned to Metz, but his attempts to introduce evangelical preaching there were met with opposition. As a result, he briefly returned to Basel. In October 1525, he set out for Paris with the official goal of studying Greek. In February 1526, he was captured

* * * * *

11 1 Pet. 3:15.

by the ecclesiastical authorities and imprisoned in Pont-à-Mousson. Upon his release in June, he made his way to the French court at Angoulême and, in spite of the ambivalence he expresses in the letter below, was patronized by the future Marguerite of Navarre for some years. In the summer of 1531, he left France for Switzerland. Between 1532 and 1535, he lived with Simon Grynaeus in Basel. In July 1535, he went to Montbéliard (by then restored to the Dukes of Würtemberg) to reform the church there. Apart from a brief exile at Basel in 1545, he spent the remainder of his life in Montbéliard.

Dearest Capito, a few days ago I received your letter.[1] Nothing could have been more pleasing to me. Roussel[2] is writing to you and to Bucer, so there is no need for me to burden you with many details. You can find out what is happening here from the bearer of this letter. I do not know what Roussel is writing. But I know this much: there is a great deal of talk here, and very little faith and love. Christian courtiers follow their own will and not that of Jesus Christ; in the same vein, Queen Marguerite has married, and is keener to please her husband than Jesus Christ.[3] I am persona non grata to them because I do not share their attitude, but the Truth shall remain forever, and must be served rather than lies. I do not have enough time to write more to you. If there is anything you want to know about my fortune and affairs, you may hear it from this courier. Farewell and give my greetings also to our dearest brothers, Bucer, Simon,[4] and the rest. Paris. 15 June.

Your servant, Pierre Toussain.

* * * * *

1 Not extant.
2 Gérard Roussel (d. 1555) studied at the University of Paris and belonged to the circle of Jacques Lefèvre d'Etaples. He served as a corrector of some of his works and wrote a preface to his edition of Boethius (1511). He himself published a commentary on Boethius' *De arithmetica* (Paris, 1521) and a new translation of Aristotle's *Magna Moralia* (Paris, 1522). Roussel had a living at Busancy, but joined Lefèvre at Meaux in 1521, where he was made a canon of the cathedral chapter. In October 1525, both Lefèvre and Roussel fled to Strasbourg. The following year they returned to France under the protection of Marguerite, soon to become Queen of Navarre. She made Roussel her confessor. Although his preaching caused some opposition, he was championed by Francis I and became Bishop of Oleron in 1536. He remained at Marguerite's court, where he was assassinated by a Catholic fanatic.
3 In 1527 she married the much younger Henry II of Navarre.
4 Most likely Simon Robert de Tournai (d. 1533), a refugee at Strasbourg who stayed with Capito; in May 1528 he and his wife, Marie Dentière, went to join Guillaume Farel in Switzerland, where he became pastor of Bex, then in 1530, pastor in Aigle. Cf. above, Ep. 307.

In your most recent letter you urged me not to be moved by your dispute about the Eucharist. Thank God, I am not so easily moved, my Capito. If I could be moved, there are many things here that could burden me, but the Lord is powerful and will save me. Send my warmest greetings to your wife.

Letter 332a: [ca. 26 June 1527, Strasbourg], Capito and the Chapter of St Thomas to [the City Council of Strasbourg]

There are two copies of this letter with slight variants in Strasbourg AST 16, #20 and #21; the first is marked 'verlesen Mittwoch nach Johannis 1527' (read on Wednesday after the feast of St John, 1527).

Strict, honourable, circumspect, honest, wise, gracious lords,

As a result of an obvious and pressing daily need, we are compelled and driven, strict, honourable, and wise lords, in accordance with our need and desire, to register our humble opinion along with the simple request that you, our strict, honourable, and wise lords, should take that opinion in the best possible way and regard us and the situation of our chapter in a friendly manner. This is our opinion: You, strict, honourable, and wise lords are no doubt aware that since time immemorial, the chapter of St Thomas has always been governed, protected, and managed in both spiritual and worldly matters and concerns by our predecessors and ourselves in a pious, honourable, and honest manner, and has been looked after by honourable people from among the nobility and the common citizenry. As a result, as is evident, the aforementioned chapter has seen continually and throughout that time an increase in religious services, buildings, church ornamentation, and precious objects, as well as temporal goods and properties. There was never any need for an administrator, guardian, or caretaker by any name. Rather, the provost, dean, and chapter (which are the equivalent of the mayor and council in a city or similar office in a guild or university, or judge and court in a public body) have always maintained control and management of all the chapter's goods and possessions, as well as its affairs and transactions without the interference or involvement of spiritual or temporal authorities. This is the usage to which we have adhered thus far without criticism, and we hope to continue in this way, with your goodwill and favour. We hope, just like those who came before us (and without boasting or belittling or despising anyone), to be deemed fit to direct and manage our and the aforementioned chapter's possessions and goods through the help of the Almighty, as well as the protection and assistance of you, our strict, honourable, and wise lords. Indeed, the suggested caretaker role would be more troublesome than advantageous. The reason for this is that there are many issues that require quick resolution. It thus happens that we look out for the needs of the chapter and oversee the vaults and containers [in the treasury] and that we must give daily reports regarding the debts and assets to those who demand such information. Such things could not be done efficiently or effectively by a caretaker whenever the necessity arose.

The stewardship that has been initiated is not in itself harmful to our reputation and respect. You do not regard us as untrustworthy people, requiring a guardian or caretaker. But not everyone understands the matter in this way. The rationale for your displeasure and your desire to foresee and prevent a mistake from happening in the future has been removed and erased. The stewardship is thus no longer necessary. For the changes introduced by some of us, who at that time were not under your authority, were all done for the purpose of preserving and saving the old privileges and freedoms, and from a desire that they may continue. Yet all of us who live here have become citizens and have bound ourselves with promises and oaths to the city of Strasbourg. Both collectively and individually, regardless of status, we, like other citizens, serve the city with our possessions and goods and those of our chapter. We are inclined to serve, and we are also willing and ready to place ourselves and our goods at the disposal of both you, our strict, honourable, and wise lords, and the praiseworthy citizenry of this city of Strasbourg. Therefore, in accordance with the citizenship we adopted, we acknowledge you, our strict, honourable, and wise lords, as our worldly authority, and acknowledge ourselves to be bound, just as other citizens are, to remain faithful and true to this praiseworthy city of Strasbourg, to support its interests and welfare, to defend it from injury, and to obey its laws and proscriptions. Indeed, as honourable men, we and our successors, who will be citizens just as we are, are not permitted to do anything that is antagonistic to the praiseworthy city of Strasbourg or prejudicial to its interests; nor is the chapter allowed to act in this manner. This is proven by the fact that we, as mentioned earlier, are bound to the praiseworthy city of Strasbourg by the same duty as all other citizens of high and low station, of whatever authority they may be. Therefore, in accordance with the reasons laid out here, as well as others which we would like to discuss at length but which we will pass over in the interest of brevity (of which you, our strict, honourable, and wise lords, being most wise and thoughtful, are no doubt already aware), it is our diligent and humble request to you strict, honourable, and wise lords, in consideration of the needs and the situation of our chapter and ourselves, that you graciously release us from what is, in our opinion, an unnecessary and fruitless stewardship. Indeed, we strive for nothing other than honour and goodness for you, strict, honourable, and wise lords, and we hope that our obedient goodwill, which has been shown in all things until now and

·will continue to be shown in the future, will be pleasing in this case as well. To this end, treat us as you do other collectives, such as the guilds or other organizations, or even as other citizens who are free and unencumbered by such things. That would cause us to be forever indebted and humble in your service, strict, honourable, and wise lords.

Your faithful citizens, the provost, vice-dean and chapter of St Thomas in Strasbourg.

Letter 332b: 2 July 1527, Strasbourg, The Strasbourg Preachers to the Elect of God at Worms

Printed in BDS 2, 234–8.

[*Summary*]: The Strasbourg preachers warn the elect in Worms against the seven articles[1] that were recently posted in Worms by Jakob Kautz. These articles reflect the heterodox views of Hans Denck, which he advocated in Strasbourg and which the Strasbourg preachers oppose.

Letter 333: 7 July 1527, Strasbourg, Capito to Ulrich Zwingli

Printed in ZwBr 3:167–8, Ep. 632.

[*Summary*]: Nothing that has been published on the subject of the Eucharist can match Zwingli's book against Luther's slanders [*Das dise wort Jesu* ... (Zurich: Froschauer, 1527)]. People say that [Justus] Jonas will translate Luther's attack into Latin for the sake of the French and the Italians. Capito urges Zwingli to have his own books translated into Latin. He suggests entrusting the task to either [Oswald] Myconius or Leo [Jud]. He asks Zwingli to undo the negative publicity the reformers have received from the publication of the proceedings of the Disputation of Baden [i.e., the official version, which

* * * * *

1. See below, Ep. 336, note 6. The points were:
   1. The inner word is superior to the exterior word.
   2. The word and sacraments, which are external signs, cannot assure one of salvation.
   3. Infant baptism is contrary to the teachings of Christ.
   4. The concept of the Real Presence of the body and blood of Christ in the Lord's Supper must be rejected.
   5. The sin of the first Adam was redeemed by Christ, the new Adam.
   6. Christ's suffering was not sufficient for us if we do not follow his example.
   7. Christ's suffering has no validity for those who do not take it truly to heart.

favoured the Catholic protagonists] published by [Thomas] Murner. There may be people in Zurich who might not be aware of its biased nature.

The Anabaptists are causing much trouble in Strasbourg. Their leader is [Ludwig] Hätzer, who has now moved to Worms. On account of the activities of Hätzer and [Jakob] Kautz [cf. preceding letter], the city council [of Worms] has forbidden all preaching. The Count Palatine, [Ludwig V], has been turned against the reformers. The Anabaptists altogether deny the merit of Christ. [Hans] Denck, the leader of that blasphemy, has easily won over Hätzer. [Martin] Bucer sends greetings to Zwingli.

Letter 334: 9 July 1527, [Strasbourg], Capito to Ulrich Zwingli

Printed in ZwBr 3:171–2, Ep. 634.

[*Summary*]: A few days earlier, Capito informed Zwingli that his book was well received in Strasbourg, even by their adversaries [see above, Ep. 333]. The Strasbourg city council is considering issuing a decree against the teachings of the Anabaptists [passed 27 July 1527; AST 76]. On 8 July, three Anabaptists were taken into custody. One of them, 'a lazy and idle good-for-nothing,' replied as boldly to the magistrate as if he wanted to provoke them into condemning him to death. This was a serious conspiracy against the legitimate magistracy, the ministers of the Word, the authority of scripture, and Christ himself, whose merit the Anabaptists openly deny. There are many innocent followers among the Anabaptists, but also many impostors, who pretend to live a holy life and are like [Aesop's] 'ass in the lion's skin.' There are thieves, adulterers, and conspirators among them, who do not shrink from cursing Christ and the Strasbourg reformers. Capito recently sent Zwingli the articles of Kautz [cf. above, Ep. 332], drawn from [Hans] Denck and [Ludwig] Hätzer. The city of Worms has altogether done away with preaching the Word of God, with the consent of the people [see above, Ep. 333]. Hätzer has caused an uproar, and the Strasbourg Anabaptists praise him for it. Capito is upset that the Strasbourg reformers are being misrepresented by the likes of Hätzer and the Anabaptists, but does not want to burden Zwingli with these matters.

Letter 335: 12 July 1527, Strasbourg, Capito to the Reader

This is the prefatory letter to Martin Cellarius' *De operibus Dei* (Strasbourg: Herwagen, 1527), the first systematic Protestant treatise on predestination, which also includes some novel chiliastic notions in its concluding sections. The letter is found on pp. 2r–[7r].

Martin Cellarius Borrhaus (1499–1564) studied at Tübingen (MA 1515) and Ingolstadt (BTh 1521). In 1521, he went to Wittenberg, but soon developed views at odds with the Wittenberg theologians. In 1526, he established himself in Strasbourg, where he lived for a while in Capito's home. In 1536 he moved to Basel, where he produced several theological works and taught at the university (rhetoric from 1541, Old Testament studies from 1544). He received his doctorate in theology (1549) and was rector of the University of Basel in 1546, 1553, and 1564. Cellarius was close to Sebastian Castellio and Celio Secundo Curio, opponents of John Calvin, and associated with Michael Servetus. He was suspect in the eyes of the Genevan theologians for his unorthodox views.

De operibus Dei was received with caution by fellow reformers, but Capito tried to assure them of Cellarius' orthodoxy. In his personal correspondence, especially with Zwingli, Capito painted a positive picture of Cellarius and justified his own preface (see below, Epp. 338, 341, 342). On 4 September 1527, Berthold Haller in Bern wrote to Zwingli: 'Our Cellarius has sent his book *De operibus Dei*, which up until now has been so highly praised by Capito that it never ceases to amaze me, for the book smacks altogether of Anabaptism; and now Bucer is translating it into our language. Admonish those learned men to discuss this matter among themselves, for once published, they will become seedbeds of unrest' (ZwBr 3, Ep. 652). The German translation by Bucer never materialized, but Capito came to realize that he could not maintain his relations with Cellarius and other heterodox theologians, such as Caspar Schwenckfeld and Michael Servetus, as his latitudinarian approach was causing a rift among the Swiss and Alsatian reformers and becoming an embarrassment for the Strasbourg preachers. On 17 June 1528, Zwingli reported to Capito and Bucer that Sebastian Hoffmeister, a preacher at Zofingen, had informed him in a letter that Cellarius was causing dissent between Capito and Bucer, and exhorted them to remain united in their endeavours. Indeed, on 15 April 1528, Bucer had suggested to Zwingli that Cellarius was having a negative influence on Capito. He urged both Oecolampadius and Zwingli to intervene and draw Capito away from Cellarius (CorrBucer 3, Ep. 186). In September of that same year, he again deplored Cellarius' influence on Capito (CorrBucer 3, Ep. 206). Eventually, as James Kittelson put it, 'a series of personal experiences in late 1531 and early 1532 helped convert Capito to Bucer's firmer policy toward religious dissenters.'[1] In October 1533, Bucer acknowledged Capito's change of heart, writing to Blaurer: 'Capito is wholly ours and well acquainted with the hair-splitting of these people [i.e., the Anabaptists].'[2] A month later he repeated

* * * * *

1 Kittelson, 188–96.
2 Schiess 1: 432–3, Ep. 368.

these sentiments in another letter to Blaurer: 'Capito is wholly ours now; if only it had always been so!'[3]

W. Fabricius Capito to the pious reader, grace and peace through Christ our Lord.

Martin Cellarius, a man of God and especially endowed with the Spirit, has recently journeyed to our city. When he heard of the state of our church and the manner of revelation, in which, through the grace of God, he is powerful in every way, he decided to discuss with us certain dogmas and questions of faith. We readily agreed, met, and conversed among ourselves. Both sides contributed many ideas touching on the glory of God which is to be revealed more clearly in this age. In one or two conversations, he discussed with great clarity, as it seems to me, his belief in predestination, the distinction between vessels of election and reprobation,[4] the children of God and the elect, the perseverance of the saints, the certitude of salvation, the Holy Spirit, the nature and rationale of the sons of God, and other things of that sort, which we, too, explained to our churches as best we could, according to the measure of our faith. He added certain other things, such as, the time when the gospel will be revealed, the method and general nature of prophecy, the perdition of the ungodly, and other things of this sort, some of which we can easily gather by comparing scriptural passages, while others seemed to be, and are, aimed at edification in God, or an analogy of faith, or in agreement with scripture, so that we did not undertake to refute him, even though they were beyond our ken. Therefore, we asked him to write down for us, in order, the sum of his creed and revelation, and lay it out for our independent judgment. In return, we quite openly shared with him what we know about the goodness of God. He was well aware of the proofs for these things, but not on account of his ordination.[5] He accepted what we said placidly and asked for time to ponder them, to consider each point at length, and weigh it in the balance of faith.

He has found, through God's revelation, that the matter is just as we proposed, in fact, he saw the Truth more lucidly than we and was convinced that we must do the same things in order to advance the glory of God. We were altogether filled with joy about our mutual faith and the similarity of our ideas about God, and the mutual recognition of our faith and grace of God. This agreement, once generated, fostered and maintained a very close

* * * * *

3 Schiess 1: 441, Ep. 377.
4 Cf. Acts 9:15.
5 *non ... ex unctione.*

friendship in the Lord. We congratulate ourselves and owe a great deal of thanks to the Lord, who brought to us this light, this Spirit, this concord in the Lord. Soon afterwards, therefore, Cellarius wrote this book, for our use only and for our review. We received the book and read it with a critical eye, evaluated it and approved of it, unless we were taken in by the friendly character of the man, which breathes love for everyone in abundance, or by our endeavour to uphold the glory of God, with which everything he says agrees. For we think that this book is not only useful, but extremely necessary in these times to settle disputes, to do away with sects, and to extinguish the resentment which rages most bitterly among the elect. As far as I know, no one has proclaimed the doctrine of predestination in grander terms. Once this doctrine is understood, the idea of free will, which is the worst bane of true religion, flies away as if it had only been a mere dream. No one has given proof of the Spirit in the hearts of the elect[6] more certainly than Cellarius, whence those who are oppressed by evils derive the most certain consolation. No one has used clearer terms or made matters more perspicuous, even for people of average expertise in spiritual matters (for one may speak the honest truth without feeling jealous), answering the questions: Who was chosen in the womb? Who obtains the Spirit? What charity should be exercised toward a weaker brother, that is, an infinite, steadfast and rock-solid love? Spontaneous acts of charity freely flow from these beginnings. For how many people neglect to love a man, once they are convinced that he is a brother, a partaker in this same glory and a special member of the same body of Christ? Finally, no one has demonstrated a shortcut through the mazes of the prophets by which one might proceed straight to the fortress of understanding, as our man has done here. For the rest [of the exegetical works] all contain very many things that are relevant to the time of the prophets or look at minute details, taking them out of context, the integral and coherent narrative of the Spirit. Moreover, our Cellarius, for I gladly call him ours, is certainly a man of God; he sets straight most wonderfully and unfolds in its sum and entirety the whole sense of Christ lying hidden in the prophecies, laying them out in sections according to the centuries, with great order and clarity. It seems to me that I immediately gained a more cogent and methodical understanding from my first conversation with him than I could ever hope to gain from several months of strenuous effort spent reading books, of which I have the best, especially those in Hebrew.

In sum: Because he has not proffered a vain question in the manner of the Anabaptists, but acts entirely for the glory of God and agrees with those

* * * * *

6 Cf. 2 Cor. 1:22.

who are reborn in the Spirit (and all pious men who read this must admit
that it is so), because he discusses lucidly whatever errors have been touched
upon (I almost said, had to be touched upon), and corroborating our belief
in predestination, he very much strengthens the salutary truth, according to
which, as if by a Lydian stone,[7] one may test minds to see whether they are of
God or not,[8] we decided that it would be conducive to the public good if we
were to make [this book] available to those who were unfortunately unable
to enjoy this great treasure. Therefore, when we urged him not to deprive the
churches of such great gifts by suppressing any longer what he had received
from the Lord for the benefit of others, he readily agreed, so long as it was the
Lord's will. The work was immediately given to a publisher to be printed.
This is, perhaps, not in the best interests of the author, who could have easily polished his style, if there happened to be any unpolished passages on
account of his inexperience. For it is his first attempt, a nascent work, still
rough, which a day, further care, and a revising hand could have smoothed.
But nevertheless, it is in the interest of the pious to come to know this book
as soon as possible, to treat elegant diction as secondary in a book that truly
pertains to the glory of God, as it certainly does. Furthermore, the difficulty
of the subject matter delays the zealous reader, even if it is treated without af-
fecting special eloquence and detailing every significant point. The contents
will penetrate the mind more deeply, if the reader stops to think about each
point than if it had been written in a more fluent style, and he rushed at once
to the conclusion. For such thoughts are written down for the heart, not the
tongue, and they are written not just to be read once, but to be expressed viv-
idly in your life. I give you timely advice, begging and beseeching the elect
to take care not to approve or disapprove rashly anything that is thought to
pertain to religion. Either way is wrong, and it is easy to fall into a trap. For it
is equally abominable to believe nothing as it is to believe everything anyone
says. Avoiding one leads us to the other vice, if the mind lacks the spirit of
moderation.

It is most disgraceful to embrace every doctrine willy-nilly and to be
a beast that has neither cleft hoof nor chews the cud of food digested once.[9]
Moreover, I hardly know whether to place more blame on the iniquity of
those who bitterly criticize what exceeds their abilities or what is not taught
in their name, and yet, as I have said, both faults are committed all the time,

* * * * *

7 I.e., a crucible. Cf. Erasmus, *Adagia* 1.5.87.
8 1 John 4:1.
9 Cf. Lev. 11:1–8.

because human nature is such that credulity is accompanied by levity, and caution by heated condemnation of what you do not understand. Paul warns us, saying: *Let him who does not eat refrain from passing judgment on him who eats.*[10] And again, *Test the spirits to see whether they are of God.*[11] In these verses, he prevents us from both petulant censorship and hasty belief in anything whatsoever. Therefore, let us now follow perfect revelation, the Spirit of counsel, who brings us step by step to a mature judgment, who weighs everything, judges everything, examines everything, and observes everything according to the measure of faith, that is, how much it contributes to the glory of God, to self denial, and how much it moves others to trust in God. One must not struggle in a hateful manner against those who prophesy, except when it is known with certainty, through the sign of the Spirit, that such teachings detract from the glory of God, which the Son, who is in the bosom of the Father, has explained at length. Yet I have no doubt at all that some men, who excel both in learned opinion and in the estimation of the Spirit, will seize on this book and fight against it vigorously, however much it promotes the glory of God, the mortification of the flesh and the comfort of the oppressed. The Lord will direct them against this book, in my opinion, that they may lose the battle and learn at last from the outcome how very far off the target they are. Thus they will be admonished to dwell among the elect meekly and humbly and in fear of the Lord. They wrongly usurp the role of governing the faith of others and want to anticipate the judgment of the Holy Spirit, as if he had conferred all the force of teaching on them. They are led into that iniquity both by self-love and by the false conviction that they have achieved perfection, whereas Paul frankly admits that he has not yet achieved it.[12] These smooth-talking men assert that the glimmer of truth, which is glowing only dimly, is the absolute light of revelation. But they are mistaken, as I have said, misled by self-love and devotion to themselves, which makes them confident and blinds their judgment.

After all, they do not know the Lord, neither in the greatest nor in the least important points. The hearts of the fathers have not yet taken root in the souls of their children.[13] Our sons and daughters do not yet prophesy, since *we know in part and we prophesy in part, but when perfection comes, what is imperfect will come to an end.* Partial prophecies, faulty tongues, imperfect

* * * * *

10 Rom. 14:3.
11 1 John 4:1.
12 1 Cor. 8:1.
13 Cf. Luke 1:17: 'With the spirit and power of Elijah he [i.e., John the Baptist] will go before him, to turn the hearts of the fathers to their children ...'

knowledge, and everything else that is imperfect will altogether give way when perfection comes.[14] That does not depend on excellence of mind; it depends altogether on awareness of one's own worthlessness, on one's calling, and on the grace of God. For *not many are wise in the ways of the world*, etc.[15] Take care that you are sated,[16] *reach for the sign in front and follow it to the prize of the celestial calling of God, through Christ Jesus.*[17] Those who are perfect know this and advance in the knowledge of God, and they strive all the more in their ascent to distance themselves further from the earth and rise to greater heights. Now the nature of God and his power are comprised in scripture, which is infinite and inexhaustible, to the extent that even the man who is perfect in every way lacks something, and will finally be made perfect in his own time, which the Spirit will reveal. Thus I am no less dear to God, because I am not yet admitted to the secret embrace of his knowledge and I miss many things in scripture on account of the slowness of my mind. This I know: that there is nothing in scripture which is contrary to the living sense of my faith. Yet there are some things I understand only dimly, others of which I know nothing, and worse yet, things which I misinterpret and teach in a way different from the dictates of the Spirit. That happens because I want to give the impression that I know everything and use the many passages in my grasp ineptly and feebly, and force everything to serve my purpose, whether it is suitable or not. What then? Will I rage against a youngster who comes forward, better equipped in the knowledge of the Spirit than I, such a great rabbi, and one who is both able and accustomed to discern and synthesize everything more clearly than I?

No, I shall bear him in fairness, unless the Lord snatches away my mind. To avert that, I shall be careful not to do anything harsh or contentious and not to act petulantly against anyone. Indeed, those who are corrupted by such a lack of temperance incite the wrath of the judge against them. For it is not surprising that the elect often give offence, and step up to the very precipice, either because they anticipate their vocation, or because they think better of themselves, and want others to think the same. For both evils insidiously threaten the minds of the pious. The man who pronounces cautiously

* * * * *

14 1 Cor. 13:9–10.

15 1 Cor. 1:26.

16 The text reads *cave satur[atus?] fueris*; perhaps a reference to John 6. 26: *Quaeritis me non quia vidistis signa, sed quia manducastis ex panibus et saturati estis* (you seek me, not because you have seen the signs, but because you have eaten of the bread and are sated).

17 Cf. Philippians 3:13–14, and Augustine, *Confessions* 11.29.39.

and timidly in a civil case and who investigates the matter in depth is rarely deceived. Much less will we be deceived, if we take our time investigating the matter and examine it with a moderate mind, if we do not undertake to define anything which the Spirit in us, which that inner emotional strength, drawing us to the glory of God, does not clearly command us to define. Indeed, nothing disturbs God's elect, even if Judah and Ephraim,[18] that is, the people of God, fight among themselves with the bitterest hatred, for it will be necessary to fight for a long time, until the one comes and is made manifest, who will pacify everything with his blood. Like a sickness, inexperience and ignorance of Christ tear apart the members of one body which are most closely linked, but once Christ is perfectly revealed, that body will once again establish him as the one head joining all members together most closely. In the meantime, just as we distinguish the kings of Israel from those of Judah, so among us, let us, the elect, distinguish as many chiefs and leaders as there are tribes everywhere, who claim for themselves the *ius magisterii* and try to contain the fullness of the Spirit, each according to the small measure of his faith. Thus the Lord will suddenly destroy my own name, such as it is, and the names of others who are respected, that he may bring the glory of his Christ into the open more rapidly, through whom and in whom all things are restored. In order for that to come to pass, I hope, or rather I know, that it will be soon, indeed, I seem to see plainly already that all those, whom the vain voice of the common people elevates with their praises, will be inglorious. God has driven the powerful from their thrones to exalt his humble Christ.[19] This will also be the case with the work of our Cellarius, excellent as it is; with Bucer's Matthew, which soberly teaches many things that are beyond the judgment of the common people;[20] likewise our Hosea, Malachi, and Jonah,[21] in which we pursued to the best of our mediocre ability what belongs to God and the truth, in a style not much different from that of Cellarius. Our work, I say, together with the authors, that is, with us, will sink and perish.

* * * * *

18 Cf. Ezekiel 37:15–23, which speaks about God one day reuniting Ephraim and Judah.
19 Cf. the Magnificat, Luke 1:52.
20 Martin Bucer, *Enarrationum in evangelia Matthaei, Marci et Lucae libri 2* (Strasbourg, 1527).
21 Capito's *In Hoseam prophetam ... commentarius* (Strasbourg, 1528), cf. Epp. 350–1. His commentaries on Jonah and Malachi were not published. Bucer mentions the Malachi commentary in a letter to the Strasbourg city council, 18 March 1527 (cf. CorrBucer 3, Ep. 151, 17), and all three commentaries in a letter to Bugenhagen, 25 March 1527 (cf. CorrBucer 3, Ep. 153, 54, note 36).

We do not object, for that is the human condition. We know this and yet we write for the present use only, until the Lord reveals greater things, just as he will reveal everything at the time, when he will shepherd and guide his own people, when the shadows will yield to the clearest Truth. For the knowledge of the Lord shall fill the earth like water.[22] So far that has happened only in part and to few people. Meanwhile, fare well and uphold the Lord with a tolerant soul in Christ Jesus, who is your comforter. Amen. Strasbourg. 12 July 1527.

Letter 336: 1 August 1527, Worms, Hans Schwintzer to Capito

> Hans Schwintzer (Apronianus, ca. 1500–ca. 1560), was probably born in Schweidnitz in Silesia (modern-day Świdnica, Poland). He was a student of Valentin Crautwald and was with him in Liegnitz (Legnica), where he was cathedral preacher and, like Crautwald, lector. There he also met Caspar Schwenckfeld. When Schwenckfeld settled in Strasbourg, Schwintzer joined him there. He obtained citizenship in 1526 by marrying Apollonia, the widow of the proofreader Hans Niebling, and set up a print shop. He published independently as well as in collaboration with Peter Schöffer, for whom he had worked in Worms. Together with Schöffer, he printed works by Crautwald and Schwenckfeld. Independently, Schwintzer printed Schwenckfeld's *Bekenntniß vom heiligen Sacrament des Leibes und Blutes Christi* (Strasbourg, 1530) and in 1531, a German translation of the *Confessio Tetrapolitana*. Later he held positions on the Strasbourg city council, but in 1556 he was interrogated on suspicion of being an Anabaptist. This is also the last year for which Schwintzer is documented.
>
> The original autograph of the letter is in Strasbourg, AST 40, #64. The text has been printed in QGT 7: 123–5.

To Wolfgang Fabritius Capito, a man of exceptional piety, his lord, and dearest friend in Strasbourg, greetings. To my surprise, I am being called back now to Strasbourg, not without the Lord's counsel, I suspect. For although I dreamed nothing of the sort, that erudite and at the same time pious man, Gerard Geldenhouwer,[1] approached me and declared: 'If only you were of

* * * * *

22 Cf. Isa. 11:9.

1 Gerard Geldenhouwer or Noviomagus (1482–1542), a canon in the order of Croziers, entered the service of Philip of Burgundy, later Bishop of Utrecht. He published a number of historical and geographical writings between 1514 and 1520, and worked for the printer Dirk Martens. He maintained friendly

the same opinion as I – for here I am living a life of leisure, of no benefit to anyone – I wish we could be in a convenient place, where both of us might acquire room and board in exchange for labour. If the Lord were to give us anything in addition, it would have to be shared with the brethren; for you with your skill[2] and I through proofreading (or any other skill in which you might instruct me) could accomplish such things.' I readily agreed, and was filled with much joy that I should live with such a man and that there would be a good reason to return to Strasbourg. And so, we took counsel and, to acquire money to carry out the plan, we went to Lower Germany. There we obtained some money, and everything is still working out well for our plan. I will not be able to make the journey to Strasbourg before the Frankfurt fair, however, for I cannot leave the print shop, where I am a compositor, or else I myself would come and rent a house large enough for the two of us and our wives. But since I can rely on you, who are always doing me favours, I think it will be enough to indicate this plan in my letter and to show what I would like you to do in this matter. Namely, that someone, either a servant of yours or a relative of your wife's, may be on the lookout for such a house, which might be available for us to move into on St Michael's Day,[3] for that is the time, I think, to rent; we shall prepare the details this winter, with the Lord's favour, that at the Lent fair we may harvest the first fruits of our seed. I know that in this matter I have you so ready and willing that I can sleep soundly on both ears.[4] I shall be expecting a response from you. Farewell along with your friends, to all of whom I ask you to send greetings. My wife sends her greetings to you and your wife.

Worms, at the print shop of Peter Schöffer,[5] 1 August 1527.

* * * * *

---

relations with a number of humanists, among them Frans Cranevelt and Erasmus. Geldenhouwer was sympathetic to the Reformation, but only revealed his leaning after the death of his patron, Philip of Burgundy (d. 1524). In 1525 he travelled to Wittenberg and Strasbourg. He married in Worms, where he came under the influence of Hans Denck. He continued to publish historical writings, but found no secure employment until 1532, when he was appointed professor of history at the University of Marburg.

2 I.e., printing.
3 I.e., 29 September.
4 Erasmus, *Adagia* 1.8.19.
5 Peter Schöffer Jr. (d. 1547), a capable die-cutter and Catholic printer, who engaged in his trade at Mainz, 1509–23; at Worms, 1512–29; at Strasbourg, 1530–9; and at Venice, 1541–2. He became a citizen of Strasbourg in 1529 through his marriage to Anna Pfintzer.

Completely yours, Hans Schwintzer.

Our preachers were forbidden to preach, while we were in Antwerp, and at the same time were expelled from the city on account of the disagreement over the Word;[6] one, who had been the parish priest of St Magnus, was captured and detained at Mainz.[7] May the Lord make everything turn out to the best.

Letter 337: 8 August 1527, Zurich, Ulrich Zwingli to Capito

Printed in ZwBr 3:182–3, Ep. 639.

[*Summary*]: Zwingli has been unable to read [Martin] Cellarius' book [*De operibus Dei*], but he asked Leo [Jud] to read it. Zwingli himself was preoccupied with writing his *In catabaptistarum strophas elenchus*. The work will be available at the Frankfurt book fair. The bearer of the letter, [Michael Winckler], has escaped from prison in Vienna. Zwingli has known him for a long time by name and from reports of merchants, who do business in Austria. He comes with a warm recommendation from the cities of Augsburg and St Gallen. Negotiators from those cities are seeing to it that his wife and children, who are still in Vienna, will rejoin him soon. Zwingli asks Capito to offer his support.

Letter 338: 18 August 1527, Strasbourg, Capito to Ulrich Zwingli

Printed in ZwBr 3:191–4, Ep. 643.

[*Summary*]: Franz [Zink] delivered Zwingli's letter [now lost]. Capito offered him hospitality, which [Zink] politely refused. Another man arrived

* * * * *

6 At the advice of Johann Cochlaeus, the city council of Worms decided on 1 July 1527 to banish two Lutheran preachers, Ulrich Preu (called Schlaginhauffen, at St Magnus) and Johann Freiherr. Both Preu and Freiherr opposed Jakob Kautz, who, on 13 June, had challenged his opponents to a public disputation, outlining his views in seven theses, which he attached to the door of the Predigerkirche in Worms. Preu and Freiherr posted their counter-theses on the church doors as well, and put them into print at once. On 2 July the Strasbourg reformers issued a publication titled, *Getrewe Warnung der Prediger des Evangelii zu Strassburg uber die Artickel, so Jakob Kautz, Prediger zu Wormbs, kürtzlich hat lassen außgohn* (Strasbourg, 1527). See above Ep. 332b, note 1.

7 Ulrich Preu, cf. preceding note.

as well, but Capito was too busy to converse with either. Michael [Winckler, cf. preceding letter], the merchant from Vienna, has taken out citizenship. Capito is grateful that such a martyr for Christ was recommended to him by Zwingli and is glad to see that he is free of the errors of the Anabaptists. Martin Cellarius is a far better man than rumour has it. Sebastian's [i.e., Hofmeister's?] accusations are groundless. The Wittenbergers are maligning Cellarius. His views on the Eucharist have upset Luther. Cellarius used to have reservations about infant baptism, but has always been firmly opposed to the Anabaptist movement, which he rejects in his book [*De operibus Dei*]. After a week of living with Cellarius, Capito formed the impression that he was a man of God. The Wittenberg theologians speak ill of him, but he does not retaliate. He speaks ill of no one, not even of the Anabaptists, who harass him in Strasbourg. He openly, but patiently, condemns their errors. He has a godly wife [Odilia von Utenheim]. Capito wrote a preface [to Cellarius' *De operibus Dei*, above, Ep. 335] to counter the negative reports about him. Cellarius debated with [Hans] Denck in the presence of [Ludwig] Hätzer. He expounded Denck's book on free will [*Was geredt sei, daß die Schrift sagt, Gott thue und mache Gutes und Böses*, 1526] in the sense of the apostles. They came to a full agreement. Hätzer, however, continues to criticize Cellarius. Capito writes this to dispel rumours that Cellarius is an Anabaptist. Rather, he is a fellow servant of God, who firmly agrees with the Strasbourg preachers on the justice of [Felix] Manz's punishment [see above, Ep. 327]. Capito does not approve of the fact that Cellarius avoided the [Disputation with the Anabaptists in November 1525], when he was still immature and his judgment impaired. Capito asks Zwingli to read Cellarius' *De operibus Dei* and note down the offensive passages. They will undertake to emend those passages. There is great consensus in Strasbourg with regard to infant baptism. The Strasbourg reformers will give their opinion on [Zwingli's] *Elenchus*, which has recently been published. Any disagreement will be expressed with humility. Capito himself preaches to the best of his ability and hopes for divine enlightenment. Rumour has it that Erasmus is working on a response to [Luther's *De servo arbitrio*; i.e., the *Hyperaspistes*]. They say that Luther is preparing to attack Zwingli's position on the Eucharist [in his forthcoming *Bekenntnis vom Abendmahl Christi*].

Letter 339:

> Under this number, Millet lists Capito's catechism, *De pueris instituendis ecclesiae Argentinensis Isagoge* (Strasbourg, 1527). This publication has no preface, but consult Ep. 398c below, the preface to the 1529 edition of the German catechism.

Letter 340:

Under this number, Millet lists Capito's German catechism, *Kinderbericht*. The 1527 edition had no preface, however. A preface was added to the 1529 edition (see below, Ep. 398c).

Letter 341: September 1527, Strasbourg, Capito to the Preachers of Basel

Printed in BrOek 2:97–9, Ep. 517.

[*Summary*]: Capito is writing this at the request of the bearer of the letter, Wilhelm [not identified]. He congratulates the Basel preachers on maintaining spiritual peace in these turbulent times. The true believer suffers the attacks of the enemy and accepts public disgrace in exchange for eternal glory. They may be exiled from their country, but know their true home is in heaven. They see their brethren die for their faith and are confirmed in their own beliefs. Capito rejoices in the steadfastness of the Basel preachers and in their spiritual gifts. He recommends to them Cellarius' book, *De operibus Dei* [see above, Ep. 335]. Wilhelm will report to them on the state of the church in Strasbourg.

Letter 342: 24 September 1527, Strasbourg, Capito to Ulrich Zwingli

Printed in ZwBr 3:218–22, Ep. 655.

[*Summary*]: Capito has read Zwingli's *Elenchus* with approval. He praises Zwingli's sense of decorum, scholarly skills, and use of scriptural arguments. He will give his judgment in a private letter and awaits Zwingli's private response; there is very little on which they disagree. [Martin] Bucer is faster in giving his opinion and is completely on Zwingli's side. [Martin] Luther's mode of operation is different. He demands compliance with his beliefs and rejects dialogue. Adam [Kraft], who is called 'the archbishop of Hesse,' is unsure about the question of the Real Presence and is withholding his opinion. He first conferred with Capito and then went to the Silesian brethren, but will not be in Silesia for long. [Philip of Hesse?] reportedly said he could not see how Paul's statement in [2 Cor. 5:16] squared with the idea of the Real Presence. All the princes, except for [Friedrich II von] Liegnitz, wish to be seen as supporters of the Word, yet conspire against Luther's articles and decrees. This only helps the cause of the Anabaptists. Word has it that [Jakob] Kautz wrote to [Philip] of Hesse, claiming that none of his preachers so far has preached the gospel. The Lutherans continue to oppose him. Some Anabaptist peasants, followers of [Hans] Denck and [Ludwig] Hätzer, were captured and tortured by [Ludwig V, Count Palatine], but persist in their beliefs regarding Christ and baptism. Capito hopes that Zwingli's and [Johannes] Oecolampadius' views will be endorsed in all of Germany. The Strasbourg preachers have taken action to abolish the last four remaining masses.

Zwingli need not be alarmed about [Martin] Cellarius. He agrees with them in all important points and has recanted his views about [Felix] Manz. Hätzer has traduced him; Cellarius, by contrast, never speaks ill of anyone. Capito is promoting his book [*De operibus Dei*; see above, Ep. 335] not because of its novelty, but because it increases the glory of God. Capito was of the same conviction as Cellarius, even before he met him, as is evident from his commentary on Hosea [see below, Ep. 351], which will appear in the winter [it was published in April 1528]. He has doubts only about one question, which he will submit to Zwingli at a more opportune time. At this time they are beset by the plague and the conflict with the Catholics. Capito mentions Cellarius because there is a rumour that Zwingli will publish something against him [Zwingli is not known to have written against Cellarius]. Capito hopes for concord among the reformers. Franz [Zink] has reported the affairs of Strasbourg to Zwingli. He pledges his loyalty to the Zurich reformers and sends greetings to all the brethren, especially Franz [Zink] and [Conradus] Pellicanus.

Letter 342a: 17 October [1527, Strasbourg], The Strasbourg Preachers to Whom it May Concern

Printed in BDS 10, pp. 47–50, # 3.

[*Summary*]: Felicitas, née Scherenschleger, appeared before them on 10 October [1527]. Her husband, Bastian Stettenberger, was granted the divorce he had applied for after admitting to adultery. He was subsequently banned from the city. In view of his past behaviour, she is not willing to reconcile and requests permission to remarry. The preachers acknowledge that she has been deserted and may therefore consider herself free to remarry according to imperial, natural, and divine right.

Letter 343: 28 October 1527, Strasbourg, Capito to Michael Cellarius

Printed in H. Bornkamm, 'Briefe der Reformationszeit aus dem Besitz Johann Valentin Andreas,' *ARG* 34.3–4 (1937):154–7. For Michael Cellarius see below, Ep. 405, note 1.

[*Summary*]: The Strasbourg reformers were pleased to read [i.e., the unpublished *Vermahnung* of Urbanus Rhegius, Stephan Agricola, Johannes Frosch, and Cellarius] against the Anabaptists. They are a stubborn lot and seduce the hearts of the simple, but the Strasbourg reformers counsel patience and charity. It is important that the reformers maintain concord among themselves. Accordingly, they were alarmed at receiving a letter from an (unnamed) Anabaptist who claimed that the Augsburg reformers did not dare to affirm anything about the Eucharist. The Strasbourg reformers warn them not to give their enemies a handle to slander them. Unity in questions of doctrine is essential. There have been positive reports from England. The people of Bern are making progress [in their preparations for the Disputation of Bern, 1528?] and those of Basel are labouring [over the question of abolishing the Mass?].

Letter 344: 7 November 1527, Strasbourg, Capito to Ulrich Zwingli

Printed in ZwBr 3:299–301, Ep. 666.

[*Summary*]: Zwingli has not written lately, and Capito wonders about the state of affairs in Zurich. He has no doubt that the church in Zurich is stable. The changing climate in Basel only affects the weak; those who rely on God will stand firm [cf. below, Ep. 348]. The Strasbourg reformers preach in favour of abolishing the mass, but have not yet achieved their goal.

Each day more people are joining the Anabaptists and producing new ungodly teachings. Zwingli's *Elenchus* offers effective counter-arguments. Capito regrets that good men become involved and are corrupted by the teachings of the Anabaptists. Some of the Anabaptists are tolerable and uphold their teachings less aggressively than others, but they nevertheless persist in their wrong views. Capito uses scripture as a guide to examine the teachings of the Anabaptists.

Zwingli has greatly advanced the cause of the Eucharist in his most recent treatise [*Daß diese Worte 'das ist mein Leib ...'*]. [Johannes] Brenz, however, persists in his erroneous views. Many people acknowledge that the Strasbourg preachers are friends and supporters of Zwingli. Capito considers that the first step toward unity. Capito's recent report about the drowning of Balthasar [Hubmaier] comes from [Michael Winckler]. On 7 November two evangelical citizens of Vienna were taken to a nearby fortress; nothing is known of their fate. Some Anabaptists have been captured in Vienna as well. Capito is glad that the churches in Strasbourg are moderate and do not condemn anyone rashly. The preachers bear with the weaker brethren.

The plague is raging in Strasbourg. People are leaving the city. A promising student [unidentified] of Capito recently died of the plague. Three of Capito's servants are currently bedridden. Capito sends his greetings to Conradus Pellicanus, Leo [Jud], and the rest of the brethren, with best wishes for the church in Zurich.

Letter 345 is now Ep. 313a.

Letter 345a: 5 January 1528, Bern, Capito, and Martin Bucer to Thomas Murner

Printed in CorrBucer 3:98–100, Ep. 172. At the time of writing, Capito and Bucer were in Bern to attend the Disputation of Bern, in which Oecolampadius and Zwingli were the chief speakers on the side of the reformers.

[*Summary*]: Capito and Bucer declare their solidarity with Zwingli and Oecolampadius, whom Murner has accused of heresy. They indicate that they had been looking forward to confronting him at the Bern Disputation and are disappointed by his failure to attend. They discount the notion that Murner might have feared for his safety, especially in light of the guarantee of safe conduct offered by the Bern city council. They object to his excuse that Bern lacked a qualified judge, pointing out that the people of Bern are Christians imbued with the Holy Spirit and thus able to recognize God's voice. They insist, moreover, that scripture itself is the ultimate criterion of truth. Bucer and Capito furthermore reject as a pretext the claim that Murner's superiors have forbidden him to engage in disputation. They note that this position does not accord with the oath that he swore upon becoming a doctor of Holy Writ. They cite the biblical injunction requiring everyone to correct error and to spread the Word of God to the people. Finally, Capito and Bucer renew their invitation to debate his beliefs with them.

Letter 345b: 6 January 1528, Lucerne, Thomas Murner to Capito and Martin Bucer

Printed in CorrBucer 3:100–3, Ep. 173.

[*Summary*]: Murner declares his willingness to debate with Capito and Bucer, using the Bible as the sole authority. He has asked the *Schultheiss* of Lucerne for permission to go to Bern for the Disputation. Bern has offered him a safe-conduct, but the eight Catholic cantons have not given him permission to go, since they are unwilling to have a matter touching the whole of the Confederation decided by Bern alone. Murner notes that Zwingli did not attend the

Disputation of Baden out of consideration for his safety, nor did Capito or Bucer participate. And now they are proposing Bern in the knowledge that he has been forbidden to go there. But he will not remain inactive. He will ask the entire council of Twelve Cantons [assembled at Lucerne on 14 January] for permission to go to Bern. If he obtains leave, he expects the council of Bern to seek the endorsement of the Twelve Cantons in turn.

Letter 346: 9 January 1528, Frankfurt, Dionysius Melander Sr. to Capito

The original autograph of this letter is in Basel UB Fr. Gr. ms. I 19, f. 47. The letter has been printed in K. Martin Sauer, 'Dionysius Melander d.Ä. (ca. 1486–1561), Leben und Briefe,' *Jahrbuch der Hessischen Kirchengeschichtlichen Vereinigung* 29 (1978): 27–8, Ep. 3.

Dionysius Melander Sr. (ca. 1486–1561) entered the Dominican monastery in Ulm in 1505 and thereafter became a travelling preacher in Swabia, Baden, and Odenwald. He was inclined toward Zwinglian theology and befriended Zwingli, Oecolampadius, Bullinger, Bucer, and Capito. On 13 June 1525 he was installed as evangelical preacher in Frankfurt, and with the support of the citizens and the city council suspended the mass there in 1533. In 1535, he was called by Philip of Hesse to Kassel, where in 1536 he became head preacher and dean of the chapter of St Martin's.

Grace and peace. I have no doubt at all, most learned Capito, that you know clearly the many ways in which Satan attacks the ministers of the Word these days. For when he cannot keep them from the ministry of the Word, he tries to destroy their authority through the lies of his children. This happened to you a while ago, as I have heard with great regret. For there are false brethren who both write and say that the people of Strasbourg and you, in particular, think wrongly about the Trinity and the divinity of Christ.[1] I would certainly have indicated those people to you some time ago, but I did not want to stir up an implacable hatred against you or rouse suspicion of wanting to create discord among brethren. Furthermore, I was unwilling to meddle in other people's business. I defended you and your colleagues, however, to the best of my ability, for I hold you all very dear, esteem you greatly, and respect you as my teachers. I have striven to keep your reputation intact here. I said that you may have a point, that you said perhaps that

* * * * *

1 This may be a reference to Capito's promotion of Cellarius' *De operibus Dei* (cf. above, Ep. 335 headnote). In this context, it is significant that Capito later took an interest in Michael Servetus' antitrinitarian views. Cf. Kittelson, 189.

the word 'Trinity' is not in the scriptures. That did not mean, after all, that you had the wrong concept of God, Christ, and the Holy Spirit. Wherefore, I beg you in the name of Christ, write back or send a message so that I may read what you think about this, and I shall make sure to reply as quickly as possible. For there are those, here no less, who can hardly bear to hear your name mentioned. I would advise you to defend yourself by way of a letter to Hermann Buschius,[2] a man truly pious and upright. Not that he thinks or says anything bad about you, but you would put him in a better position to curb in a politic manner the slander of those at Marburg.[3] If you can bear more and want the names indicated, I'll write to you later. Apart from that matter, the error of the Anabaptists has taken hold here. I opposed it with all my strength, and at last it has been removed; ask my Leonhard[4] about this. There are those in Basel who say that Denck died, stubbornly holding on to the errors of the Anabaptists.[5] Please, write about this too in your reply. We expect a great benefit from the Disputation of Bern, especially in the matter of the sacrament.[6] If you know anything about this, write me a letter to bring me up to date.

Finally, the Lord has rid me of my wife,[7] who, I thought, was born to

* * * * *

2 For Hermann Buschius, since 1527 professor of history at the University of Marburg, see CWC 1, Ep. 46a.

3 Perhaps a reference to the Marburg Colloquy (1529), where the question of the orthodoxy of the Strasbourgers concerning the Trinity and the divinity of Christ was discussed. Capito was not invited; instead, Martin Bucer and Caspar Hedio were sent as representatives.

4 Not identified.

5 Hans Denck (ca. 1495–1527) graduated from the University of Ingolstadt in 1519. In September 1523, he became headmaster of St Sebald's school in Nürnberg. In January 1525 Sebald Beham, one of three artists on trial for making unsound remarks concerning baptism and communion, mentioned that he had conversed with Denck on these matters. After securing a confession of faith from Denck, the Lutheran pastors of the city had him expelled from Nürnberg. In May 1526 he was (re)baptized, and shortly thereafter, he published three brief works defending his beliefs: *Was geredt sey, das die Schrifft sagt, gott thüe und mache güts und böses* (Augsburg: Otmar, 1526); *Vom gsatz Gottes* (Augsburg: Ulhart, 1526); and *Wer die warhait warlich lieb hat ...* (Augsburg: Ulhart, 1526). He went to Worms, where he worked on a translation of the writings of the Old Testament prophets from Hebrew to German (the *Wormser Propheten*) with Ludwig Hätzer. On 20 August 1527 he was present at the Martyr's Synod. He died of the plague on 15 November 1527.

6 The Real Presence and the Sacrament of the Mass were the fourth and fifth theses discussed at the Disputation of Bern, which ran from 6–26 January 1528.

7 I.e., concubine.

do harm and to lie. I am on the lookout for [a wife], and if I find one whose character matches mine, I shall marry her in the Lord.[8] And so, there is no need to write on behalf of that Xanthippe.[9] I do not want to see her, much less to have the beast [back]. For they say I am rid of an evil and that I never had a wife but rather a devil. She took more from me than she ever brought me. Believe me, I expect her to defame you and your wives and your families before ungodly people, if there are any ungodly people among you. I would advise you to exhort the magistrate to banish her from your city. For if she returned here, many (even my enemies) would want to see her drowned. Farewell, excellent father. I have written off the cuff and with my usual candour, as if I were in your presence. Commend me to Christ in your prayers and write back and freely correct me.[10] Again farewell and commend me to the brethren. Frankfurt, 9 January 1528.

Letter 347: [End of February 1528], Strasbourg, Capito to Guillaume Farel

The autograph manuscript of this letter is in the Archives de l'Etat de Neuchâtel, Bibl. past. portefeuille IV, liasse 4, #1. The letter is printed in Herminjard 2: 109–10, Ep. 221.

Guillaume Farel (1489–1565) was the son of an apostolic notary. He studied at Paris (MA 1517) and taught at the Collège du Cardinal Lemoine. In 1521 he entered the service of Bishop Guillaume Briçonnet at Meaux, joining the circle of Jacques Lefèvre d'Etaples. In 1522 he returned to his native Gap to preach the gospel. In 1523 he fled France and travelled to Basel, Strasbourg, and Constance. When his radical ideas created controversy, he was expelled from Basel in 1524, and continued his preaching at Montbéliard and Strasbourg (where he remained from April 1525 to October 1526). In 1526 he migrated to Bern, and was appointed minister of Aigle. He participated in the Disputation of Bern in January 1528, where he must have renewed his acquaintance with Capito. He was instrumental in shaping the Reformation in Neuchâtel and Geneva in the 1530s (it was he who recruited Calvin). He played a leading role in the Disputation of Lausanne (1536). From 1538 to his death he was chief minister at Neuchâtel.

* * * * *

8 In 1537, Melander married Gertrud, the widow of Conrad Meyer.
9 I.e., Melander's alienated wife. Xanthippe, the wife of Socrates, is the proverbial shrew.
10 On the backside of the letter, Capito wrote: 'I responded on 12 February 1528.' That response is not extant.

Grace and peace. I recently received as a guest this friar,[1] a simple man, but a lover of Christ. After eight or ten days of sharing my house with him, I released him from his monastic vow, relying on the authority of the sacrosanct Roman See, an office which I hold in this part, as you know.[2] For we had a man at hand who, for payment, would dye his grey cowl black, and a tailor, who immediately turned him into a French priest; for so he appeared to us in a robe very similar to yours. Furthermore, I have a boarder, who performed the role of a barber, and shaved his head, so that he presented to us a soldier rather than a monk. For I think that a shaved head marks the military man.

And so, to speak seriously, I sent him off to you with a bit of travel money, my Farel, because he is a native French speaker with a godly character, prepared in his mind to undertake any task, unless my guess is wrong, as often happens. Besides, he is suited to preaching the gospel of Christ, for I regard him as a serious Christian. Direct him to find a living in your vicinity in some trade or, if you do not know anyone suitable, tell him to associate with the Savoyans. Even if you have nothing to write, please write more often and tell me what God's plan is for you and for this friar.

There is a rumour that [the king of] France has died, which will be a good reason for the king of Spain to cause a more bitter tragedy.[3] But what does that have to do with us? I am sending as much as has been printed of Hosea; you will get the rest sooner or later. I shall dedicate it to the Queen of Navarre, as I promised Cornelius.[4] Bucer is editing John,[5] but I am afraid that my work will not be ready for the fair, on account of the printer's per-

* * * * *

1 Identity unknown. Bucer mentions him in a letter to Farel, 7 March [1528] (cf. CorrBucer 3, Ep. 181).

2 A facetious comment.

3 The reference is to Francis I and Charles V. The rumour was false.

4 Cornelius was the pseudonym of Michel d'Arande (d. 1539), Augustinian friar at Cambrai, who studied in Paris and, in 1521, entered the service of Marguerite. He was attacked for his evangelical preaching and fled to Strasbourg in 1525. He was made Bishop of Saint-Paul-Trois-Châteaux in the Dauphiné, but his correspondence with Farel shows that he retained his evangelical sympathies. For Capito's dedicatory letter to Marguerite of Navarre, see below, Ep. 351.

5 Bucer, *Enarratio in evangelion Ioannis* (Strasbourg: Herwagen, April 1528). On 15 April 1528, Bucer sent Farel a copy of his commentary on John (see CorrBucer 3: 125, note 1).

fidy.[6] Farewell, dearest brother, and pray to the Lord on my behalf; we will pray for each other. Strasbourg.

Yours, Capito.

Letter 348: 3 March 1528, [Basel], Johannes Oecolampadius to Capito

Printed in BrOek 2:140, Ep. 548.

[*Summary*]: Word has it that [Augustinus] Marius, the suffragan bishop of Basel, has responded to Oecolampadius' apologia [*Widerlegung der falschen gründt* (Basel: Thomas Wolff, 1528)], and that his response [*Wyderauffhebbung der warhafftigenn gründen* (Basel: Johann Faber, 1528)] will be published in Basel any day. Oecolampadius is convinced that Marius' response will easily be rebutted, but at the expense of the people of Basel, who wish for an end to all the infighting. The mass has been abolished in Bern and the idols removed from the churches. The [city of] Lenzburg has not yet followed suit, but will wait and see. Oecolampadius sends his greetings to the brethren in Strasbourg and to Capito's wife, [Agnes Roettel].

Letter 349: 13 March 1528, Strasbourg, Capito to Ulrich Zwingli

Printed in ZwBr 3: 383–4, Ep. 697.

[*Summary*]: [Paul Rasdorfer] came to Strasbourg from Augsburg and stayed for eight days. He has begun to learn the art of weaving and wishes to go to Zurich, where this craft is thriving. Capito recommends him to Zwingli. He holds the correct belief concerning the Eucharist. He is not highly educated, but firm in his faith. Johannes Hylactaèus, who recently came to Bern from Bavaria, attests to [Rasdorfer]'s reputation and renown as a preacher of the Word. The Strasbourg reformers cannot employ him. Perhaps he can be of use in Bern. Greetings to Zwingli's family and the Zurich reformers.

Letter 350: [April 1528, Strasbourg], Capito to the reader

This is the first preface to Capito's *In Hoseam prophetam* (Strasbourg: Johannes

* * * * *

6 According to Herminjard, Capito's fear was well founded. With the Frankfurt fair beginning on 19 March that year, the printing of his commentary on Hosea would have had to be completed by Johann Herwagen before 10 March. It was not published until the month of April.

Herwagen, 1528), which appears on the verso of the title page. For a second preface, see below, Ep. 351.

To the reader.

By reading this, pious reader, you can easily tell how pious my beliefs are about God, about Christ's divinity and humanity, about the mystery of the incarnation, about the kingdom of heaven and the duty of Christ, about the mystical signs of faith, about predestination, and about the slavery of all of Israel and the fullness of the gentiles,[1] and how concord may be maintained among the elect. I sincerely wanted you to be aware of this.

Letter 351: 22 March 1528, Strasbourg, Capito to Marguerite of Navarre

This is the preface to Capito's commentary on Hosea, *In Hoseam prophetam ... commentarius* (Strasbourg: J. Herwagen, April 1528). The addressee, Marguerite of Angoulême, Queen of Navarre (1492–1549), was the sister of the French king, Francis I. Attracted to mysticism, she wrote *Dialogue en forme de vision nocturne* (Alençon, 1533) and *Miroir de l'âme pécheresse* (Alençon, 1531). On account of her writings and because of her patronage of evangelicals, among them Jacques Lefèvre and Gérard Roussel, she was attacked as heterodox by the theologians of Paris. Her brother protected her for some time, but after the Placards Affair in 1534 he was less tolerant of reform thought, and Marguerite retired to her estate at Nérac in Béarn. Lefèvre, who together with d'Arande and Roussel (see notes 5 and 6 below) fled to Strasbourg in 1525, joined the queen at Nérac in 1530 and may have served as a link between Marguerite and Capito.

W. Fabricius Capito wishes happiness to the most famous and pious and chaste Lady Marguerite, Queen of Navarre, Duchess of Alençon, etc. sister of the King of France.

I pray that you, most famous queen, beloved sister, and bride of Christ, may grow in the knowledge of God, who is known by his Son Jesus Christ, in whom lies salvation and eternal happiness. I dedicate my commentaries on Hosea to you, not because of any desire or zeal to teach Your Ladyship the Truth, to which the Spirit of Christ, with which you are endowed, leads you every day. Indeed, you need no human teacher to perfect the teaching of the Spirit, which you already possess and which must grow through divine help. If someone gives further instruction to another concerning the kingdom of

* * * * *

1 Gen. 48:19, cited in Rom. 11:25.

Christ, he will not say, 'Recognize the Lord.' Rather, they will recognize him in everything, from the greatest to the least, for the Spirit, who is superior to the flesh, fills the whole world with the knowledge of God, like water generously poured out.[1] That is what the prophets have clearly foretold. In the meantime, however, the kingdom of Christ, so fully promised, has not yet shone forth, and everything appears to us in bits and pieces. We, the elect, recognize the Father's goodness toward us to the extent that each of us embraces Christ in our mind, and also to the extent that we have put on Christ and have drunk his Spirit.[2] We celebrate the goodness of God every day, according to our individual gifts, and in time we are perfected with his help. Therefore, no human being in the church of Christ, which is taught completely by God, can be given the title 'doctor.' In the absolute sense, that title belongs only to Christ, who is the eternal Wisdom, and, when he dwelt on earth, revealed the name of the Father to the elect, and is powerfully revealed in the elect. Thus it is not my intention to exhort you with authority to proceed bravely on the course you have begun, nor have I taken on the task of assuming that role, for I know what it means to go ahead without being called.

Finally, I have no desire to admonish you or warn you against dangers, although I wish that all the elect everywhere were warned to be on their guard not to slip into error and ungodliness, overcome by the nastiness of malicious men, who defend blasphemous doctrine with the sharp weapons of hypocrisy.[3] For confessing one's beliefs brings salvation. And I know, moreover, that the wall of your faith can never be shaken by the strong arrows of temptation, although you are beset by knaves who feign piety for the sake of sustenance and wealth,[4] whose falseness – obvious from the inconsistency between their words and their lives – gradually weakens the true constancy of the mind professing Christ, softens it, makes it stumble, and thus drives it into error.

What, then, prevents me from admonishing you in a less authoritative fashion? There is, I say, a very good reason. For, consciousness of my weakness, which is perpetually before my eyes, prevents me from wanting to give you advice, indeed, quite deters me from doing so, for I contemplate in my mind the great number of good men you have around you, who are particularly called to this task. If there was a need to advise you, there is Mi-

* * * * *

1 Cf. Isa. 11:9.
2 Cf. Gal. 3:27; 1 Cor. 12:13.
3 Rom. 10:10.
4 Cf. 1 Tim. 6:5.

chel d'Arande,[5] a man of grave eloquence and singular piety and a conscientious but moderate bishop, who does full justice to his office and title. Gérard Roussel,[6] a man of keen judgment and full of ardent zeal for the glory of God, will not omit to say in good time anything that can be of use. Both of these men, as I hear, serve as preachers in the French court, where you live, a singular woman at the side of your most illustrious and heroic mother,[7] equal in prudence, virtue, and greatness of mind to the strongest men. You can listen, moreover, to the dear and piously learned old man, Jacques Lefèvre,[8] in person, whenever you please. And, I hear, it pleases you to hear him very often. Lefèvre, when called upon, holds forth smoothly and gracefully on the mysteries of our faith with a certain pleasant gravity and, if I may say so, an old man's pleasantness. I shall say nothing about the other men in all of France who are given shelter and are kept safe under your patronage from the cruelty and violence of their persecutors – for not all are drones who come flying to your apiary. Each one of them, to return thanks at any rate, is obliged to warn you when you are headed for danger, to direct the actions charity demands of you, to provide knowledge when you are in the process of seeking information, and to spur you on, if by chance you get tired from running the course of the gospel. What could a foreigner like me contribute, therefore, through his efforts? Hardly anything suitable. The reason proper why I dedicate this work to Your Ladyship is the need to make good on a promise. For I promised something like that some years ago to my companions who are in your service, and who command my respect and affection. On this occasion, then, I seem to be doing something worthwhile, although I consecrate to you, my queen, a treasure, not of my making, but of God's wisdom, although you abound in such wealth. For if you read my commentary on the prophet, who is the most difficult of all and yet offers the greatest wealth of sacred wisdom, it will be helpful to you, I believe. And you will read it, for you are most zealous about reading sacred writings. At the very least, you will peruse some of it in passing, if it does not please you to read everything, or if you are detained by more important things, or if your attempt is slowed down by my Latin – iron Latin, as they call it.[9] For I am rather an 'iron' writer who does

* * * * *

5 On d'Arande, see above, Ep. 347, note 4.

6 On Roussel, see above Ep. 332, note 2.

7 Louise of Savoy (1476–1531) was actively involved in the government of France and, after the capture of her son, Francis I at the battle of Pavia, was regent during his captivity in Spain (1525/6). Together with Margaret of Austria she negotiated the Peace of Cambrai in 1529 between Francis I and Charles V.

8 For Jacques Lefèvre d'Etaples (1460–1536), see CWC 1, Ep. 7 headnote.

9 I.e., not of the classic golden age.

not spend much serious effort on polishing his style. Indeed, there are people who will translate into French more felicitously some of the passages that I have turned into Latin. Reading a few passages will at least give you a taste of the whole of this prophet, so that you will not depart from this banquet without a token sample. And to enable you to choose what you please, I have taken care to add an index of topics.

If you deign to inspect anything noted in the index, you will no doubt emerge more certain in your belief. For there you will find described in words what has actually been effected in you when you first entered into the meaning of Christ, and what is being effected whenever you enter into him more deeply. For Hosea shows to the elect, I am tempted to say, in every single phrase, with numerous, and at the same time, most lively arguments, that one reaches the sum of salvation through the greatest suffering. Beyond that, the prophecy of Hosea, which very much applies to all the elect, can hardly be turned into a private message for one individual, for it belongs to all and must not be reduced to a private compendium, and yet I seem to take some pleasure in dedicating this commentary to you as to a shrine of public piety. In the vast kingdom of France your faith is regarded as exemplary, a faith very rare in our time and for many centuries past, indeed, priceless and unheard-of. For you were born and bred to royal pleasure, yet you have always turned your mind to the things of God,[10] have indeed been inspired by fear of God, that seedbed of the children of the kingdom and the beginning of divine wisdom.[11] Roused first by fear of God, you were carried on through various works of superstition, as I have discovered from eyewitnesses.[12] Soon you encountered the discipline of contemplating God,[13] as those times presented them. You pursued it quite felicitously, if there is any felicity in such a system. For I myself have heard and read in Latin the two letters written in French[14] on the essence and power of God, philosophizing quite well in the style of Nicholas of Cusa.[15] Yet experience teaches us not only that the repetitive observance of works and merits is useless and often

* * * * *

10 Cf. Col. 3:2.
11 Cf. Prov. 9:10.
12 Herminjard suggests that Capito is speaking about the French refugees in Strasbourg whom he accommodated at his home during the winter of 1525/26 (cf. Herminjard 2, #227, note 11).
13 I.e., mystical theology.
14 Herminjard suggests that these were probably two letters from Briçonnet (cf. Herminjard 2, #227, note 15).
15 Nicholas of Cusa (1401–64), theologian, mathematician, scientist, and philosopher, matriculated at the University of Heidelberg in 1416, received his doctor-

done without the guidance of the Spirit. Furthermore, everything is transacted in the most scrupulous and calculated manner, for such is the weakness of human nature, whose will the Spirit, being the free gift of God, does
not obey at any time and in any place; and without the Spirit nothing can be
pleasing to God. How they brag that every work is a work of grace! That hypocrisy is most hateful to God, who requires the Truth. But you have already
experienced that a philosophy too refined brings a great deal of trouble and
very little benefit. You may easily gather that much from the uncertainty
and transience of nature. It is not possible that you have failed to notice the
inconsistency of such thoughts. For they bring no tranquillity to believers at
any given point of time, rather, they carry them to and fro on the dark waves
of their vague thoughts, even if they proudly project a stable and consistent
mind to the outside world. They do not rest on that cornerstone, Christ himself, although they religiously name him.[16] The common saying is quite true:
when the cause is weak, the effect is regrettable, and what is born of a mortal
is mortal, whereas the rebirth of us Christians, which happens through the
Spirit, is the only thing leading to eternity, and we must never use any human intercessor as a go-between.

Here it seems to me that your mind has always been affected by the
hand of God. The proud confidence built on your good deeds vanished and
disappeared suddenly as, in your splendid sacred philosophy, you anxiously persuaded yourself to engage in Christian contemplation, looking
toward the eternity to come. But it is necessary that all empty confidence
cease before the internal light that sees hidden sins. Sadness enters into the
place of hope, which besets the repentant mind forever, until that true light
and life of the world, Christ Jesus, begins to illumine the darkness, for on
his advent all darkness vanishes.[17] Indeed, those who are afflicted in the
heart, have always been consoled by the heavenly Father, through the Spirit
of Christ, even before the preaching of the gospel. *For Christ was yesterday
and is today and will be in all eternity.*[18] The soul of the elect flies to him when

* * * * *

ate in canon law from the University of Padua in 1423, and later matriculated at
the University of Cologne in 1425. He attended the Council of Basel (1431–49).
In 1438, he was created papal legate, advocating the cause of Eugene IV before
the Diets of Mainz (1441), Frankfurt (1442), Nürnberg (1444), and Frankfurt
(1446), and at the court of Charles VII of France. In 1449, he was proclaimed
titular cardinal-priest of St Peter ad Vincula. In 1450, he was appointed bishop
of Brixen in Tirol by Nicholas V.

16 Cf. Eph. 2:20; 1 Pet. 2:6.
17 Cf. John 1.
18 Heb. 13:8.

it is overwhelmed either with good deeds or with afflictions. Reading the prophet will make this apparent, and recalling to memory the kind of life you have led, you yourself will easily recognize, as will other people, that you have been placed in the public eye. You cannot do otherwise than often reach the inner recesses of the heart, for you are enjoying God's gifts. You are affluent in everything considered a material good, being the sister of the most fortunate king. Then, leaving behind, as it were, all created things, you ascend to the creator, becoming one with him in an embrace. There you may discern the immense goodness of God, and once you have seen, recognized, and meditated upon it, your heart is inflamed, loving the generous lover in turn. For once good minds recognize their blessings, they are moved to deny themselves and to defer to the maker and giver of all things.

In the meantime, it is quite likely that the mind overwhelmed by calamity (for the fortunes of kings are subject to their own peculiar miseries) takes refuge in the ample heart, in which the salutary rays of grace shine forever through Christ Jesus. For it happens frequently that we overlook our blessings and, burdened by curses, under duress, send our sighs to the Lord our Saviour. If nothing else, you have recognized the beginnings of the Spirit, and moaned under the weight of your stubborn flesh. You must have experienced the Spirit in you, interceding with the Father with ineffable sighs, reproaching you frequently and expostulating with you, pointing to the adoption as God's children and the body's redemption, for the immortal soul is burdened by the mortal element. God who scrutinizes the heart knows our sentiment and, because the Spirit intercedes with him directly, listens immediately.[19] Out of this arises a vivid feeling, which makes us certain that, renewed in the Spirit, we shall have a new body obedient to the Spirit and a stranger to corrupt desires. In this hope we are all safe. The other part, that is, our body, will therefore be increasingly condemned, deadened, and overcome. That is the meaning of obtaining true knowledge of God in this life: through the works of God, through his goodness to us. That other knowledge, however, which human reason laboriously makes up, totally dissolves and perishes, and all the influence that mortal efforts and mortal creatures once had with us is gone, so that on that day, God alone is magnified. Do not be concerned that the flame of your love for the name of the Lord will one day be shut up inside you. It will come forth, it will soon erupt through the fortunate and guiding impetus, through your lips and your hand. Unwilling to hide, it erupts, that is, gives ample testimony in word and deed of

* * * * *

19 Cf. 1 Kings 8:39; Ps.44:21, 139:1–12; Jer. 12:3, 17:9–10.

our inner resolve about God. Of course the sense of his goodness envelops us. Therefore, I believe that Your Ladyship has been led to serve as a safe retreat for our wretched brethren, whom the cruel superstition persecutes everywhere and even condemns to death. Your royal magnificence, with the love of a sister, if I may call it so, aids with your abundant means those needy men, and persistently showers on them your good deeds.

Many seek refuge in your household under the false pretext of being true brethren, abusing your good will. They are strong only when it comes to eating and drinking; they cherish piety only when it requires no more than impious leisure. Otherwise, against the testimony of the soul, they have no scruples to return to the blasphemies they have abjured. The tricky minds of these men angers and almost disturbs us, but we must be strong. To such an extent was it God's will to put everything strong and magnificent to shame through the weakness of the world, through a female vessel. Thus you win the race in the stadium. You put no trust in your own deeds. You disdain human theology, which the great professors admire, and which human intelligence all too gladly displays, showing its madness. You keep yourself for Christ alone, and him crucified. He alone leads you to every good work with his inspiration, and absolves you.[20] In this manner you have come to that height of piety, which is usually called the way of the cross, and of which our prophet has spoken in Israel in many and varied forms. For Ephraim, trusting in his own counsel, publicly blessed the idols of bull-calves to be adored.[21] He declared the city Dan a place suited for this cult.[22] He gave commands to strengthen his position in that realm, which he could have held from the Lord in safety, if he had believed. But all ended badly, and he rued his life. Drawn away from self-love by threats and frequent misfortunes, he at last confessed that God governs everything rightly through his works. This is the end of all piety, as can be seen in the prophet everywhere, and especially in the conclusion.[23] It therefore serves as a great example that Israel, which received so many benefits and was so dear to God, no longer thought then of the favours received, and fell into every kind of vice. Such is our nature as long as we live in this mortal body and are subject to dead works: criminal adultery, oppression of the poor, and ignorance of God. Those were the sins of Ephraim, who was especially dear to God.[24] Therefore I, too, am

* * * * *

20 Cf. 2 Tim. 2:21, 3:17; Heb. 13:21.
21 Hos. 4:17, 8:4.
22 Cf. 1 Kings 12:29–30.
23 Cf. Hos. 14:8–9. The final chapter of Hosea speaks of the blessings that Israel's repentance will bring.
24 Hos. 6:4–10; Hos. 7.

at risk of committing similar sins. For this reason I must be careful not to love my wife and children more than God, to whom alone I owe love and respect, just as Christ loves his church – that it may be improved through me. Conversely, my wife owes me respect, and I try to improve her with respect to her habits of mind. For if I oppress her with unworthy slavery and she is kept away from God, whom alone she must reverence, let her bear that necessity with equanimity, since she is bound to her husband. Let her do her duty willingly in this life, wishing nothing more than to become one with her heavenly spouse. From this correct attitude good habits arise, which will serve, in our daily life together, as a reproach to my own levity, considering that I call myself a man. But woe to the wife who neglects Christ and in her folly is desperately in love with her mortal husband. For she belongs to God and was chosen to be one of the saints. Therefore, let her remain aloof from vulgar love for her husband, from calamity and incidental evils. It would have been better for her to repent on her own accord than to be dragged unwillingly into the street and whipped, although the law allows a newly married spouse a yearly leave, indulging us in our weakness.[25]

As for the rest, my dearest sister, for you acknowledge that name[26] which we consider the greatest token of honour, because we carry around so great a treasure in earthen vessels[27] and in hidden places, we must be very careful. You will hear this counsel from God himself, if you listen closely, for he does not conceal his advice from anyone. The ministers of the Word, however, whom you support for the reason that they dearly regard the glory of God, must not fail to broadcast this message. Their obligation is the greater, the greater your expectation. They will discern this, as we do, for everyone's eyes are turned to you and see that you are recalled daily with hateful arguments from religious thought to vile carnal desires. For it is difficult for a woman to persevere in hard tasks, and even more difficult not to lapse spiritually when she is living in endless luxury, among crafty yes-sayers, and you by necessity are surrounded by such pestilent men. And it is most difficult not to be blinded by the great authority and insistence used with such zeal by the adversaries of the truth.

What shall I say about your most famous forebears (for you are born of kings)? What about the fact that you are the sister of a most generous king, the wife of a most gracious king?[28] What about false brethren, the persecu-

* * * * *

25 Cf. Deut. 24:5.
26 Cf. Acts 4:12; Rom. 10:13; Phil. 2:9–10.
27 Cf. 2 Cor. 4:7.
28 Henry II of Navarre (1503–55).

tors of the Truth, the ignominy of the cross, as it appears to the eyes of the courtiers? Such things might overcome the strongest man, for one cannot teach the end of these things by reasoning. Such is the unhappy error, bound by a triple cord, as they say:[29] the wisdom of the theologians of which the common people are convinced; the specious religion of the monks; and the clear prejudice of the councils and popes. Those are the greatest evils of the French commonwealth. Otherwise, however, France is most fortunate, if it keeps its ambitions confined to its own borders. Our Germany, however, does not fare much better in that respect. If the Word of God is given any freedom, it brings with it a disadvantage: it is blackened by our partiality. We are all zealous for God, for I speak of the evangelicals who have a calling, but we do not all have knowledge, for the Spirit adjusts his gift to the ability of each man, and does not allow anyone's intelligence to exceed his measure, for anything, however piously spoken, is suspect if it is in any way removed from his teachings. Or rather, even what agrees with his teaching is intolerable if it is treated in a manner foreign to the Spirit and with a different stroke. A new ecclesiastical tyranny emerges surreptitiously from such beginnings, worse than the old one.

I confess I am going on in this foolish manner out of zeal for the glory of God, yet it is spoiled by too great a trust in ourselves. Each man thinks he is better than the next and imbued with a more certain spirit. This kind of sin gains strength from the ill will of absurd people, whose noted perfidy readily fills the more cautious among the ministers of the churches with suspicions. Thus caution and zeal for piety becomes a vice for us, and because of the perfidy of evil men, we hold suspect the sedulous effort of good brothers. We must be on the lookout for public peace, but in such a way that we do not stand in the way of the prophets, that we do not extinguish the Spirit, that we do not decry the gifts of God bestowed for the good of the people. Otherwise, our caution is useless and becomes a harmful solicitude for the flesh, when we fall into that all too arrogant talk which we sometimes adopt when we sit in judgment over the ministry of others. They are very learned scholars and do not need our guidance. That arrogant kind of talk begets for the world new constitutions for conventicles, which bring forth new decrees from bishops, new ecclesiastical laws, which attempt to enclose the infinite Truth of God in narrower confines, and to hatch an imperious plot against the words of our teachers. So great is that hidden self-love of us, who preach the Lord's cross and self-denial, that it causes each man to like his own judgment best and dislike that of others. Yet we tell ourselves that we are making every

* * * * *

29 Cf. Eccles. 4:12.

effort on behalf of the unity of the churches and the glory of God, whereas we do everything according to our own pleasure and obey our own will.

The source and root of this evil is this, I think: we do not have, but rather wish to seem to have, an understanding of faith and a concept of God's glory. For we attribute to our intellect and our industry what belongs to God. What, then, is wanted? We support the church and what we have begun we polish and perfect, but not in the Spirit of Christ, through which alone it is born. Where have we left the idea of *carrying everything with the word of his virtue*?[30] And: *Who is Paul? Who is Apollus? If not ministers through whom you believed and as God has assigned to each man*, and more of that kind.[31] I fear that, rushing around and turning in many directions, we will be deprived of the Word of God and end up asserting before the churches what we have not yet received from the Father. For we say not what we have heard, but what we have made up ourselves. Such inopportune diligence, born of the flesh, is harmful, and we are inadvertently a hindrance to you. Bent on imitating the care of the good shepherd, we make an effort to avert any danger through human counsel and cleverness. We block the way to any small offences in the future to avoid all material for dissent, thus confining the spirit of others within the narrow boundaries of what was revealed to us. These are altogether human endeavours, and so they often turn out other than intended, that is, they seriously impugn our unity, and foster the deepest hatred among the elect. We are in great danger of erring, if we depart even a finger's breadth from the ideal of self-denial, that is, as often as we think we are important and arrogate all authority to ourselves, whereas we are only a speck of dust, as they say.[32] We abandon God and cleverly depict ourselves as the preservers and patrons of piety, even though our aim is different, for we still envy the prestige of great rulers and pontiffs, which we should rightly disdain, for faith depends only on God.

If, in the lively knowledge of the Spirit we loved God as the highest good, and walked in his ways everywhere rather than in our ways, if we were convinced that nothing can be done without him, and that he works everything to the best, then we would finally see less upheaval and bring forth more fruit for the churches. We could then look after our flock in peace and quiet and provide solid care, relying on the true shepherd of souls, hanging on his lips, taking the Word from him and giving it to our sheep in turn, for God is made great only by our humility. If we ponder the matter, we see that

* * * * *

30 Heb. 1:3.
31 1 Cor. 3:4.
32 Cf. Gen. 3:19.

there are two causes for the disagreements among us: firstly, there are rulers who either allow preaching or do not forcefully prevent the preaching of the Word, prefer the appearance of the gospel to the true gospel, and govern the state for themselves rather than God. Secondly, and more importantly, we preachers are either inexperienced or lead a life alien from the cross. For the Lord upholds his church splendidly, and advances it felicitously, and unites it most closely through those who, in the past, have died by the cruelty of tyrants, sacrificing their lives to Christ. Among them there is the most complete consensus concerning the glory of God. They seek death for the sake of his grace alone, even if they differ in their zeal about small matters. They profess them together with Christ, but especially and uniquely they profess Christ.

I repeat: unity and concord are ruined by our own fault, partly because we are inexperienced and thus awkward in our dealing with spiritual things, and partly because those of us who are learned are drawn to error by keeping idle at the wrong time. We have been raised by God through the cross, but through malice and self-love have gradually regressed and fallen back into the pit of iniquity. O cross, most fortunate for us, which first cuts through the deceit of our human heart, which puts our insignificance before our eyes! It purifies and cleanses our zeal for the glory of God, which otherwise is infected by turgid, homegrown cleverness, that is, born from our hidden feelings of self-love. It is for this reason, and not without justification, that I have declared earlier: taking up our daily cross is the way to greater glory (a practice wonderfully exemplified by the underground churches in France). That glory will be the more certain in the future the more vehemently it is opposed now. This is the right nourishment for the nascent church, as we know from experience. The greatest hardships are the most tender aid in fomenting Christian shoots, just as harsh weather hardens a crop, which will mature and experience a gentler fortune. Therefore we must carry on bravely, mature in the Spirit and progress to greater strength of mind, that we may be able to *bear all through Christ: plenty, and hunger, abundance and want*, etc.[33] For benedictions recall us to the heart of the law, though only after we have encountered everything that is written in the book of the Law, even curses, which are a kind of preliminary exercise leading to just piety.

Assiduous meditation on the prophets will be conducive to this purpose, for they put before our eyes the fleeting nature of human happiness and in the most certain manner proffer God's counsel, and with it the meaning and evident power of the Spirit. However, because they present his counsel

* * * * *

33 Phil. 4:12–13.

wrapped in corporal metaphors and artfully conceal what is in itself deeply hidden, it sometimes happens that one reads them with a simple mind and is led into shameful errors. These are the most pernicious errors because they are defended with the yardstick of truth, that is, scripture itself. Therefore, I have established what is most important in every action, but especially in reading Holy Writ, and what I see to be of greatest help, and shall clearly explain it. First of all, if it occurs to us to say or do something, we must refer it all to God, I believe, and rely on his counsel. This is what the holy fear of God consistently dictates, who says into my ear whenever I set out to do something, 'Take care! Think of God before you act!' This warning slows down my plans and my actions. It always makes me wary of the harmful cleverness of the flesh. I have often found that human insight is subject to change if it is superficially coloured by sacred reading and a certain spiritual focus. It persuades us to boast of the Spirit with great certainty, though we are inspired only by the cleverness of our own flesh. Secondly, if I have a good idea and am deliberating about an action or pondering a passage in Scripture, I resolve to pursue it to the very end until I reach the depth of knowledge. As I inquire into a matter or into a scriptural passage, I ponder God and hold back for a long time. I occupy my time finding connections between various passages in Scripture, and by comparing them, I become more knowledgeable in Christ, I believe.

Even so, I am no better equipped to reach the kingdom of heaven, for the knowledge I seek is human and does not savour of the chrism. It puffs up the mind and prophanes the Spirit.[34] For a great many things, I find, are acquired in that way. They have the appearance of sanctity and piety, but lack the cornerstone that is Jesus Christ.[35] Such knowledge is diffuse, vague, meandering, and arbitrary, carried in every direction by the breeze of doctrines. If I have a low opinion of myself and lay all my actions and thoughts before the Lord and receive direction from him, I shall soon feel the power of the Spirit, who is with the Father, interceding on my behalf – the Spirit, whom I earlier pretended to have and paid lip service to, instructed by human counsel. Indeed, it is a gift of God acquired through prayer to discover in scripture what is the right sense and what is adulterated and pretence, so that, through the chrism, we have certainty and may make others certain, and that we may recognize our shortcomings and pray with greater devotion that he who embodies the fullness of the divine nature may supply what is lacking in us.[36]

* * * * *

34 Cf. 1 Cor. 8:1.
35 See above, note 16.
36 Cf. Col. 1:19, 2:9–10.

In this manner you must commend yourself to the Spirit, our teacher, that you may ask wisdom from him, who bestows it, that is, bestows the wisdom of God. He bestows it simply on all and does not offer proof. For man cannot teach what is of God, but the Son leads us to the whole Truth through the Spirit. When he is silent, however, it happens that the flesh insinuates itself and interferes. For this reason, I believe we must exercise the greatest caution and ensure that the ideas we embrace are derived from self-denial and will lead us, with Christ as our mediator, to celebrate the glory of the Father.

Nevertheless, I believe that I must teach these things to others – cautiously and carefully, lest my ignorance burden them. I wish I never failed and never offended those best of hearts. I offend them inadvertently, in my stupidity, and I wish I did not supply evil minds with so many occasions for slander, for they traduce our church everywhere with their lies. I realize what happened: I inveighed against the contemptible flesh in my brethren in the name of the Spirit. I am now more modest, bearing the dissenter's opinion in matters which I know to be otherwise, either because it was revealed to me, or from the analogy of God's glory, or on account of faith. I think to myself: my brother suffers now from the imbecility I suffered earlier, and perhaps to a more dangerous degree. This way of thinking keeps me from quarreling if the desire arises in my mind.

I wanted to speak to you in my preface of the power of the prophet and the need to emulate him. And now I beg and beseech the Lord to increase the fire in your heart, which is already burning with zeal for his glory, to increase his grace, and to keep you safe for the glory of his goodness. Strasbourg, 22 March 1528.

Letter 352: 29 March 1528, Strasbourg, Capito to Ulrich Zwingli

Printed in ZwBr 3:406–8, Ep. 705.

[*Summary*]: Capito sends Zwingli a copy of *In Hoseam prophetam ... commentarius* [see above, Epp. 350, 351]. If the commentary does not agree in all points with Zwingli, it should not affect their Christian concord. He has not mentioned Zwingli in the commentary because Bucer counselled against it. If Luther or the papists attack Zwingli in the wake of the Disputation of Bern [in January 1528], Capito will defend him. He regrets that Bucer has not mentioned Zwingli in his commentary on John [published April, 1528]. Instead, he celebrated his victory over Treger in the preface. The published proceedings of the Disputation of Bern will reveal the prowess of Zwingli and Oecolampadius. Some people hope for discord among the reformers, but they will be disappointed. Capito appreciates Zwingli's integrity, faith, and 'truly bishop-like qualities.' The Strasbourg preachers intend to show patience in the face of Luther's furious criticism. The news Capito gave Zwingli [in a lost letter] concerning the Swabian League turned out to be false. Zwingli will soon see Luther's [*Vom Abendmahl Christi Bekenntnis*]. There will be an opportunity to respond. He asks Zwingli to write frequently. His letters are read by many to great benefit. Bucer sends his greetings.

Letter 353: 9 April [1528], Basel, Capito to Johannes Oecolampadius

Printed in BrOek 2:171–2, Ep. 566.

[*Summary*]: [Vincentius] Opsopaeus has sharply criticized Oecolampadius. Luther's *Vom Abendmal Christi Bekenntis* has appeared, in which he treats Zwingli with contempt. The two men agree on many things, but Luther emphasizes the differences. Capito deplores Luther's attitude and hopes that Oecolampadius will be discreet in his reply, indeed pass some things over in silence, and thus preserve the peace. It is important to let the general reader know on what points they agree and what points have been quietly conceded. Many readers are offended by the controversy between the reformers. Capito includes a letter to Oecolampadius' wife.

Letter 354: 14 April 1528, Strasbourg, Capito, Martin Bucer, and Jakob Bedrot to Joachim Vadianus

Printed in CorrBucer 3:118–22, Ep. 185.

[*Summary*]: They congratulate Vadianus on the departure of the parish priest [Benedikt Burgauer] from St Gallen to Schaffhausen, and are sorry for the congregation there. They urge him to complete his *Chorographia sacra* [Zurich: Froschauer, September 1534]. They are pleased to hear there is no danger of the Swiss confederation breaking up. There is hope that the city council of Strasbourg will take steps against superstitious practices [i.e., the mass]. Mercenaries have been hired in the vicinity for the war [between Charles V and Francis I] in Italy. In the Netherlands, there is war between Gelderland, aided by France and England, and Brabant. The Hague has been sacked. This is how God avenges the death of his martyr [Wendelmoet Claes, burned at The Hague on 27 November 1527]. There are rumours of war in Germany and plotting among the secular and ecclesiastical princes. Word has it that [John III], the Duke of Cleves, [Philip of] Hesse, the dukes of Lüneburg and many other noblemen and bishops are plotting against the marriage of [John Frederick], Duke of Saxony, and [Sibylla], the daughter of [John III]. They say that [Franz I von Braunschweig], the bishop of Minden, and [Erich von

Braunschweig-Grubenhagen], the bishop of Paderborn, have taken wives. There is danger of an upheaval in Germany, although George of Würtemberg, who has recently returned from Hesse, does not think this will come to pass. Capito and his colleagues fear that Philip of Hesse will suffer the same fate as Franz von Sickingen if he goes to war. They believe that the gospel will be victorious through patience rather than armed combat. Martin Luther, meanwhile, has published *Vom Abendmahl Christi Bekenntnis*, a book that is aimed against the beliefs of the Strasbourg preachers. Luther speaks of a 'sacramental union' (*unitas sacramentalis*), which is no different from saying that it is a 'union of the sign and the signified' (*unitas signi et signati*), and that is what the Strasbourg preachers are teaching. [Johannes] Brenz teaches the eternity and omnipresence of Christ's humanity, a doctrine of which they disapprove. Bucer is sending along his commentary on John, although it has been hastily edited. He finished the book in a rush on his return from Bern. He would have liked to say more about the Disputation of Bern [January 1528] in his preface, but the printer demanded the manuscript. They send greetings to [Christoph] Schappeler and Dominik [Zili].

Letter 355: 15 April 1528, Strasbourg, Capito to Ulrich Zwingli

Printed in ZwBr 3:424–5, Ep. 712.

[*Summary*]: Luther's criticism has offended people and confirmed the preachers of Strasbourg in their own beliefs. Philip of Hesse wants Luther, Oecolampadius, and Bucer to discuss the Sacramentarian question in his presence, but he has to deal with territorial disputes [i.e., the Packsche Händel] first. He plans to restore Ulrich von Würtemberg to his rule. People think that Zwingli will not venture on the journey because he has too many enemies and would endanger himself. Everyone hopes that Zwingli will respond to Luther with moderation and not in a spirit of revenge. The reply must be written in such a way that the laity can understand Zwingli's arguments. Bucer will defend Zwingli in [*Vergleichung D. Luthers und seins Gegenteils vom Abendmahl Christi*, June 1528]. Capito will do what is required of him. He sends greetings to [Wolfgang] Mangold and [Diethelm] Roist and asks Zwingli to comfort Oecolampadius, whose marriage is opposed [by his wife's family].

Letter 356: 22 April 1528, Strasbourg, Capito to Ulrich Zwingli

Printed in ZwBr 3:442–3, Ep. 717.

[*Summary*]: Capito has shown Zwingli's letter [lost] to his friends. In Strasbourg, they are negotiating about the abolition of the mass. He has expressed

his views in the commentary on Hosea [see above, Ep. 351]. He wants
Zwingli to attribute any errors to ignorance rather than evil intent. He hopes
that Zwingli's reply to Luther will be moderate. There is no call for feelings
of revenge. It is best to stay away from arguments ad hominem and concen-
trate on the doctrinal question instead. Zwingli's views have broad support.
There are rumours that the peasants of Saxony are preparing a rebellion. The
princes are putting money and power ahead of the gospel. Capito hints that
important matters will come to a head on 1 May [concerning the mass? Cf.
below, Ep. 358]. Capito sends greetings to [Diethelm] Roist, [Wolfgang Man-
gold], and [Johannes Schmid, parish priest of Dällikon?].

Letter 357: 17 May 1528, Strasbourg, Capito to Michael Cellarius

> Printed in H. Bornkamm, 'Briefe der Reformationszeit aus dem Besitz Johann
> Valentin Andreäs,' *ARG* 34.3–4 (1937):157–9. For Michael Cellarius, see below,
> Ep. 405, note 1.

[*Summary*]: On Capito's initiative, Bucer has replied to [Michael] Cellarius
at length [cf. CorrBucer 3:135–41]. He advises him to reply without passion.
The Lutherans pay too much attention to the letter [in the Sacramentarian
controversy], insisting that sinners, too, partake of the body of Christ. When
Christ spoke of eating the bread, he meant spiritual eating, through faith. The
ultimate purpose of the Supper is the commemoration of Christ's death. The
teachings of the Anabaptists are intolerable, but persecution merely makes
them more stubborn. They must be taught patiently and treated with lenity.
It is the only way of achieving peace. Once they understand that they are of-
fending the command of God and doing harm to the churches, the better sort
of men will make concessions. The Sacramentarian controversy, driven by
both Lutherans and papists, has caused much disturbance. Peace comes with
freedom of conscience (*in summa enim libertate summa pax vere persisteret*). He
sends greetings to Cellarius' nephew, Johann Hylart.

Letter 358: [ca. 29 May 1528, Strasbourg], The Chapter of St Thomas to the
City Council of Strasbourg

> The manuscript of this letter is in the Universitätsbibliothek, Basel, Ki.Ar. 25a,
> 158. Millet dated this letter 1 June 1528, but a draft in Capito's hand (AST 16,
> #23) notes that it was presented on Friday, 29 May 1528. That draft differs from
> the final version (given here) in the conclusion. See below, notes 6 and 7.

Strict, honourable, circumspect, honest, wise, gracious lords!

On Monday Your Graces sent us, through a message from the honourable council, an ordinance concerning the divine service,[1] and we agreed to put in an appearance next Wednesday to indicate to the honourable council our intentions. Nothing has been done about this until today, on account of the illness of our vice-dean, Martin von Baden,[2] who has not summoned us. We ask that you take this in good stead, and believe that we at St Thomas are most willing to obey Your Graces in all appropriate matters, and especially when we are asked to increase the glory of God. We have now diligently perused the ordinance in question and find, as the preamble says, that it proposes a divine service that greatly serves the improvement of the community. But there was no indication of what should be done about the mass, although we assumed that it was your intention to abolish it, for you wish to abolish false services and any attempt to serve God in a way he has not commanded, as is the duty of every godly magistrate. Nevertheless, it would not be seemly for individuals like us to undertake anything on our own initiative and to compel the people among us when we are few and have no jurisdiction and authority. What concerns the community should be commanded by the magistrate, who have to answer to God for their actions and omissions, and pay the penalty when they are found wanting. We also take into consideration, if your ordinance is accepted and observed alongside the mass, that it might be rather burdensome and rightly considered too much for any Christian citizen, for they might infer from it that we wish to reinstate our previous practice. Furthermore, it would go straight against Your Graces' intentions, for you appeal in your preamble to God's glory, the common public peace, and law and order, which should be upheld and defended by any magistrate or authority. It would not do that an untoward thing like the mass be celebrated anywhere under Your Graces' auspices; rather a true divine service, according to Scripture, must be instituted and maintained. We therefore beg you humbly to indicate to us your pleasure, for if it is your intention (which we do not hope) to maintain the mass side by side [with the reformed service], we are determined to beg Your Graces most diligently to release us from such an ordinance, since it would not accrue to the glory of God, nor appease and soften all the ill will now felt between secular and ecclesiastical estates. It is a long time now that we have abandoned the mass, each after his own interpretation, and we would furthermore have to endorse singing as well,[3] which would be quite awkward and ungodly.

* * * * *

1 Cf. CorrBucer 3, Ep. 194 and notice on 157–8.
2 On Martin von Baden, see CWC 1, 262, note 12.
3 I.e., in Latin by the clergy, without participation of the people.

Secondly, if it is your command to accept this ordinance instead of the mass, we state that we are willing to obey and have nothing further to say than that the ordinance is Christian and according to Scripture and the old traditions, but we remind Your Graces to think of the opportunity given to the public church of Strasbourg, and what could be maintained and retained to great benefit. For the ordinance includes the instruction that we should come together twice a day and each time sing something specific and, with it, have a brief exposition teaching the people from the pulpit for half or a quarter of an hour. That is indeed good and right and well conceived by you on the basis of the first epistle of Paul to the Corinthians, chapter nine,[4] but since numerous German sermons[5] are being held in all the churches every day, as, for example, in many churches the morning prayer, and in close succession, the mid-morning sermon at St Martin and the daily sermon at the cathedral, as well as the Latin reading at the Dominicans, attended by some of us, it would not be regarded as an improvement to institute anything new, which would impede traditional good practices, for the other sermons would then have to be omitted, and the associates of our collegiate church would be kept from a better practice. This would make no sense. Furthermore, we give consideration to the fact that our people have more need of exegesis and less of singing, for we are not much practised in the Scripture. That is why, in consideration of Your Graces' intent, we gather in the morning for about a quarter of an hour and sing a psalm in Latin, as is done in German by the congregation everywhere in conjunction with the German sermon, and to use the remainder of the time for a Latin sermon and exegesis. Thus the Word of God is not shortchanged, nor does one sermon get in the way of the other. St Thomas and the cathedral are in close proximity, and the glory of God and the common welfare is truly furthered by this practice, since many skilled people may be trained here to remedy any future lack of qualified people, and we could find successors to well-known and trained people – how can that be achieved by singing to them in Latin and doing a little German exegesis? That would surely be unpopular and suspect, and rightly so. We have in mind, gracious lords, to support with money from our collegiate church the great glory of God, and next the welfare of the public, and to restore our collegiate church to its first beginnings, for the collegiate churches were schools, where people were sent to be trained for both ecclesiastical and secular office, and we hope that this will be a beginning of such a Christian and useful enterprise. That was the reason why we wished to give instruc-

* * * * *

4 Cf. also 1 Cor 14:12–14.
5 *Prophezei*, that is, sermons and instruction in biblical exegesis.

tion that readings be added to the sermon, for it has yielded considerable benefit: a sound and clear and fair understanding in all ministers of the Word and, in part, in the whole community. Singing a great deal in Latin would only embitter the common people, and German sermons would displace the other necessary sermons, as we said. But Latin exegesis would yield much benefit without hindering anyone.

Thirdly, one might read in Hebrew and Greek after dinner and, further-more, institute a public lesson in rhetoric. There is, however, a public sermon in the cathedral at four o'clock, which is attended with benefit by some of our people, who could not be kept from it without creating a disturbance. Therefore we thought we should not have lectures after dinner at this time and wait for an improved situation and further orders from you, our lords and superiors, so that all things might come to pass for the better, according to you own desire and inclination.

Fourthly, although there is only one Christian church and it is assem-bled on Sunday, we are of the opinion that we should not have a separate rite on Sunday, to avoid the semblance of division, which would bring no bene-fit and much trouble and ill will. We are called Latins, but we understand German, and we know that we are all, each according to his gift, members of the same body, a belief that should link each man with the community, without establishing a separate church. We hope that all this accords with Your Graces' intent, with the glory of God and the public welfare. We have changed nothing, for we don't attribute anything to ourselves. We obey the command of God and act and live to benefit the city, so that all collegiate churches may be respected, even though they have fallen into abuse. We ask for your friendly and helpful response to discover whether the above-men-tioned form of the divine service meets Your Graces' approval. If that is the case, we are willing to accept and practise it.[6] We do not want to be regarded as men who are unwilling to yield to what is fair, as we are bound to do as obedient citizens. We are most willing to use our persons and possessions to the greater glory of God and the public welfare, and offer ourselves and our collegiate church humbly and obediently to Your Graces.

Your Graces' well-intentioned citizens,

The provost, vice-dean, and chapter of the collegiate church of St Thomas.[7]

* * * * *

6 The words 'and helpful ... practise it' appear only in the final version (added in the margin of the Basel manuscript). They are absent from Capito's draft.

7 Capito's draft is signed: 'In my, W. Capito's, name.' This is followed by a post-script, which is listed as a separate letter by Millet (Ep. 359) and may have been presented as a separate note to the city council.

Letter 359: [1 June 1528, Strasbourg], Capito [to the City Council of Strasbourg]

The manuscript of this letter is in the Universitätsbibliothek, Basel, Ki:Ar. 25a, 159. Cf. above, Ep. 358, note 7.

Dear lords, I am speaking as a preacher and commander of God. I ask you, for God's sake, to press on and abolish masses and idols, which are a public scandal and a grave accusation of blasphemy. Thus we shall better provide for improvement and will avoid God's wrath, for God wishes to be respected alone, and hates all who serve two lords[1] and do not want to put their trust entirely in him. The logic of the world must yield and subject itself to faith, etc.[2]

Your willing servant, Wolfgang Capito.

Letter 360: 17 June 1528, Zurich, Ulrich Zwingli to Capito and Martin Bucer

Printed in CorrBucer 3:162–4, Ep. 195.

[*Summary*]: Zwingli reports that he received a letter from Sebastian Hofmeister, preacher at Zofingen, informing him that Michael Cellarius [see above, Ep. 357, and below, Ep. 361] is causing dissent between Capito and Bucer. He exhorts them to remain united in their endeavours. He asks them to assist the bearer of the letter in his legal wrangles with Johannes Burckhard.

Letter 361: 28 June 1528, [Zurich], Conradus Pellicanus to Capito

Printed by R.G. Hobbs, 'Monitio Amica: Pellican à Capiton sur le danger des lectures rabbiniques,' in *Horizons européens de la réforme en Alsace* (Strasbourg, 1980), 81–93. The text of the letter is on 91–2.

[*Summary*]: Pellicanus warns Capito not to put too much trust in Hebrew exegesis. He criticizes a passage in Capito's commentary on Hosea [see above, Ep. 351; the passage is on f. 72r], in which he speaks of a return of the Jews to Palestine. He believes that this reflects Michael Cellarius' views. The passage should be interpreted metaphorically, that is, that the Jews will recognize

* * * * *

1 Literally 'carry on both shoulders.'
2 1 Cor 1:18.

Jesus, and this is indeed a desiderandum. He asks Capito to take this criticism in good part. He wishes Cellarius and his wife well, but hopes he will not attribute to the Spirit what is merely human wisdom. Zwingli is too busy with lectures on Isaiah and Ezechiel and too occupied with responding to Luther's attack to read Capito's writings, but when Pellicanus brought the point about the return of the Jews to his attention, he too wondered that any Christian could interpret this literally.

Letter 362: 29 June 1528, Liegnitz (Legnica), Valentin Crautwald to Capito

> Printed in QGT 7:164–73, Ep. 141. Valentin Crautwald (ca. 1465–1545) was canon and lector at the cathedral in Liegnitz, Silesia from 1524–37. Together with Caspar Schwenckfeld, he promoted an inner spiritual renewal and opposed Lutheran sacramentalism. His teachings are summed up in *De cognitione Christi* and *Novus homo* (both 1529).

I wish you knowledge of our Lord Jesus Christ according to the Holy Spirit, amen! We praise the Lord and Father of our Lord, who is one with him and who has effected through his grace that everything Schwenckfeld[1] and I sent to you and wrote to your fellowship was welcomed by you and found a place among you, not the place it deserved, but that which your charity accorded to our writings and missives.

It pleases you to have us write either by way of Augsburg or Nürnberg, and we ourselves decided on this beforehand, although it is more difficult for us to write through the men in Augsburg and more convenient to do so through those in Nürnberg. Yet we suspect that the ministers there hold opinions different from ours[2] and would criticize our effort, not to speak of what could happen as a result of their desire to know of the affairs transacted between us in charity.

Dominik Schleupner,[3] my compatriot and a long-standing acquaintance, is a close friend. I had no hesitation to speak freely and sometimes seriously with him about many controversial matters, but so far I am in doubt what Dominik will do in this respect, even though he is my compatriot and such an old friend.

* * * * *

1 Cf. CorrBucer 3, Ep. 189. On Caspar Schwenckfeld, see below, Ep. 393 headnote.
2 The majority of the Nürnberg preachers, and especially Andreas Osiander, were Lutheran partisans.
3 On Schleupner, see CWC 1, Ep. 154, note 4.

I also know that Haner[4] is in Nürnberg, a man wonderfully devoted to letters and piety, and as far as this matter is concerned, completely favourable to Oecolampadius and his views. Being the man he is, I do not know whether he should be exposed or burdened through our letters. Therefore I ask that you take some steps in Nürnberg to allow us to obtain our wish and take the trouble to write to us through them. Spengler[5] is a close friend of Dominik in Nürnberg, as Dominik himself confirmed some time ago when he visited his hometown.

The [proceedings of the] Disputation of Bern have reached us.[6] The publication struck the followers of Luther hard. Indeed they say that Luther himself was gravely concerned that the disputation had been initiated and ended in this manner. I have read the discussion about the Eucharist up to a point, lest I stay away too long from the holy books. Even the pontiffs realize that the disorder of the pontiffs has provided the reason for these disturbances; yet some people somehow defend the matter itself in apologiae and justify it under various pretexts.

In my opinion, Schwenckfeld's letter and book should be suppressed for the time being,[7] since not everything can come to fruition so quickly. Press ahead and reason forcefully: I prefer to be slow rather than precipitate. Indeed I would rather err on the side of being too slow in this matter than too hasty. I have experience in both approaches, and I know that it is safer to take one's time.

Furthermore, those Fathers and old bishops wrote their interpretation of Scripture for their own time and for the people who lived then. But when some things (and there are not a few) are not ripe and would be regarded as

* * * * *

4 Johannes Haner (ca. 1480–1549) was at the time close to Oecolampadius and Zwingli. He studied in Ingolstadt and in 1525 became cathedral preacher in Würzburg. In 1526 he joined the reformers and moved to Nürnberg, where he was preacher from 1526 to 1534. In the thirties he corresponded with Georg Witzel and, on account of his rapprochement to the Catholic church, was ousted from Nürnberg. He settled in Bamberg, where he obtained a Catholic benefice and became cathedral preacher.

5 Lazarus Spengler (1479–1534) of Nürnberg studied at the University of Leipzig, returned to his native city in 1507 and became town clerk there. From 1516 he was also a member of the city council. He was a leading advocate of the Reformation and a strict follower of Luther.

6 Held in January 1528; the proceedings appeared in Zurich at the end of April.

7 The letter is not extant. The book is Schwenckfeld's *Ein Anwysunge das die opinion der leyplichen gegenwertigkeyt unsers Herrens Jesu Christi im Brote wider den ynnhalt der gantzen schrifft gericht ist*, published in Zurich by Froschauer in August 1528 without authorization (see CS 3, no. 1).

oracles by posterity, you are not unaware of the damage they could do. As far as I am concerned, I do not want to publish anything until the Lord commands me, and it will bear fruit. For I beseech him and pray that he direct all our and your affairs to his glory.

Luther, moreover, leaves nothing undone that would further his control and has written earlier to our prince[8] in a manner not much different from that which he adopted in writing to your council.[9] He also wrote to certain other people who had begun to share our views and had earlier on been his sworn followers. I hope he will increase in us the sanctification of the divine name. But there is no reason why anyone should think that his actions against Karlstadt,[10] the peasants and others, which were unfriendly not to say unchristian, will remain unpunished, for God's glory has not been obscured at all. It usually increases through insults cast on our name and our devotion, and vice versa.

It is because of the disagreement among the elect that everyone looks more often to the heavenly teacher and conducts the rites in fear of the Lord, and is vigilant in his prayers, hoping that self-confidence and trust in the flesh may gradually decrease and cease completely. *There must be heresies,*[11] and we must urge everyone to be solicitous about unearthing the truth, which they have started to cover with the ashes of the smoky human fire. And who can tell what advantages will arise from their disagreements? For I would contend that they are great, especially in our time, so that I do not hesitate to prefer disagreements to the peace we all desire and demand to be granted quickly, or at least I do not hesitate to compare and contrast them with peace. But may the Lord command the sea and the wind, that there may be great tranquillity, amen.[12]

I have always been unconcerned about the Anabaptists, or at least about those who have persuaded themselves that piety and sanctity can be promoted by this ceremony of initiation. Indeed I feel that my sentiments are somewhat like those the Lord has imparted to you. I have never approved of the tyranny against them, neither the tyranny used by those who are addicted to rites and have incited them with ministries or letters, nor the tyranny used by the powers of this world against their lives and possessions.

* * * * *

8 Friedrich II of Brieg-Liegnitz. Luther's letter to him is not extant.
9 *Brief an die Christen zu Straßburg wider den Schwärmergeist* (Wittenberg, December 1524).
10 For Andreas Karlstadt, see CWC 1, Ep. 15a headnote.
11 1 Cor. 11:19.
12 Cf. Matt. 8:26.

Nor can I be persuaded to be baptized again or ask to have the external ministry of baptism repeated.

For I know, if there was an error or variant in matters that pertain to salvation and truth, it cannot be restored or mended by an external symbol or through a rite; the Spirit is needed; an internal new beginning through Christ is needed, not an external repetition through a rite. For Christ says, *the man who is washed need only wash his feet*.[13] Indeed, from this and through the immense goodness of the heavenly Father, I have begun to recognize that cleansing power of him, who washes us with his blood and imbues us with his Spirit, and does so not only to our feet, but also to our hands and head.

If anyone wishes to adduce reasons for his re-baptism, although I know there is only one washing,[14] or for immersion or its representation through water or through the sign of the cross, I do not fight him, even less if anyone, crossing a papistical church, carelessly sprinkles himself with the water kept in various places and in stoops, or even if he does so on purpose in memory of that baptismal washing, which happens through water and the spoken word.

For I do not see that sprinkling with water should cause death to those miserable people – the sprinkling I mean which was free among papists, yes free indeed, which the priests used to pour out for holiness on certain days and in certain rites, sometimes profusely, sometimes sparsely. I furthermore wonder about the reason why those, who were baptized in the vernacular language, were during those years rebaptized by the papists without trouble, as were those who abandoned Lutheranism in neighbouring Poland; and in Austria where they uttered dire threats against the Anabaptists, they were baptized again and much water was poured over them, without anyone arguing against it or complaining about it. Among the papists, being bathed repeatedly promotes piety. Among others those who have been baptized twice are dipped a third time. The water serves only as a reminder to the crowd, as long as it is not done through our stupidity and in ignorance of the divine mysteries. But that is enough about the water of baptism of those who are re-baptized.

Baptizing children is certainly intolerable, nor can it be proven in any way on the basis of scriptural passages or examples, however hard many people try to assert it and make a great effort, including our Bucer. The children of the heavenly kingdom must be born from God. Not through generation but through regeneration do they become Christians. No one is reborn

* * * * *

13 John 13:10.
14 Cf. Eph. 4:5.

before he is born. Nor can children be brought into the kingdom of heaven through us inscribing or taking them in. Another kind of sign is needed.[15] We have received no ministry and no command to sign children into the kingdom of heaven. If anyone doubts it, let him diligently ponder his vocation and his mission, then he will remember that it is the task of the prudent and faithful steward to distribute in the service of his Lord, not what he himself has signed or drawn up, but whatever food or grain, measured in time, the Lord entrusted to his care.

Nor does circumcision protect the Hebrew people. Circumcision and baptism are different sacraments, nor is anyone baptized in a mystical manner, unless the foreskin of his heart has been removed earlier.[16] In Colossians Paul says concerning the sacrament, that those who confuse circumcision and baptism with what happens internally, are greatly mistaken.[17] For among other things they attest to the fact that they have not yet understood Paul in this passage. For they do not see that Christ said in the last chapter of Matthew: *go forth and teach all nations.*[18] Why do they not pay attention to the word 'teach' and take care to make those disciples first who are to be baptized? Why do they not see that there is a difference between what Christ calls *matheteuein*, teaching, and *didaskein*, ordinary instruction? Why don't they see that discipleship has always preceded apostolic rite?

Truly, this pertains to my friend Bucer proper, who has taken it upon himself to maintain these views together with others. Let them recognize how solid their ground is, when the Lord has opened their minds and understanding more widely. I have written to you, however, who has already received the gift from the Lord, so that you are in a position to pronounce more freely about these things. Consider well and see whether your admonition can excuse you before the Lord, or whether you may act other than in accordance with the master's teaching, or whether charity ought to be exercised in these grave matters, or whether one ought to give in to the requests of the people, and whether we should be excused when necessary, or whether we must do what is useless in sacraments, in the church, in the people of Christ, namely things that do not edify, do not benefit,[19] to say nothing more. I write this, indeed, not to lure you into a trap, but to enable

* * * * *

15 Cf. John 6:27.
16 Cf. Jer. 4:4.
17 Cf. Col. 2:11–12.
18 Matt. 28:19.
19 Cf. Rom. 15:2.

you to pronounce in matters of which you approve, blessed with the words of Paul, Rom. 14.[20]

Luther's opinion about the power of the sacraments will be defeated if the Lord completes what he has begun in you, when you forcefully argue and prove that the grace of God comes only through Jesus Christ in his human nature, is given only through him, that he is the source of grace and plenitude, from which we all draw; grace is not transmitted through creatures, is not in them, nor joined to them; all creatures, even the unborn, are incapable of grace; the privilege of man and flesh is in the flesh of a man only through God, so that he drinks a sip of divine grace through the flesh of Christ; grace cannot be conferred through the elements; indeed no spiritual or salvific power can be inherent in external things.

I have seen that Bucer in his commentaries on the gospel of John[21] has undertaken to vindicate this injustice to the divine grace, and I am very glad of it, for I have learned from his commentary that you have truly entered the school of Christ's Spirit. The Spirit will glorify me, Christ says,[22] and I see that the Lord will supply you with battle rams and catapults, and you will bravely fight endowed with grace, which belongs uniquely to the man Jesus Christ. I have learned from the same guide that the dogma linking grace to the elements and devolving it from the old creature to ourselves is completely impious, and I have recognized how completely adverse it is to true piety.

Therefore I have gathered passages from the New Testament, which say that the grace of God is revealed in Christ, and have considered whether, through the command and aid of the Lord, grace has perhaps been asserted in Christ; all the oracles of human wisdom will depart in confusion, not only in this point, but even more so in the whole matter of [Christ's presence] in the bread or rather that fictitious and Geryonic union.[23] May the Lord grant that this be resolved opportunely according to his will, amen. I praise your concord and pray that it be according to the Lord, not according to men.

You have experienced Fabri's great machinations,[24] his handiwork.[25] Now we are experiencing it. He has explained in some booklet why Balthasar

* * * * *

20 Rom. 14:22.
21 *Ennaratio in evangelion Johannis* (Strasbourg: Herwagen, April 1528).
22 Cf. John 8:54.
23 Geryon, a mythological creature with three heads.
24 On Capito's troubles with Johannes Fabri, see above, Ep. 289 headnote.
25 *tractet fabriliter* – a pun on the name of Fabri, which meant 'smith.'

Hubmaier died, burned publicly in Vienna, Austria.[26] In that passage he seriously impugns Zwingli, as if Balthasar had been bound and tortured when he was in Zurich, on the initiative of Zwingli. If that pamphlet has not yet come to your hands, you can write to Nürnberg for it.

I would like to make notes on Cellarius' book,[27] when I have leisure to reread it, although I have no doubt that anything that is imperfect there can be erased in a more perfect second edition, or rather can be supplemented, as long as we do not fall away from the magisterium of the Spirit and grow and walk in the fear of the Lord.

I need not explain why I would like to see the gospel of Matthew in Hebrew, if that is possible, or translated into that language from the Greek.[28] I too have noted that the rabbis have written purposely against our teaching and have demeaned what is Christ's. I know this from observing the customary replies I receive from Jews in familiar conversation whenever I initiate a debate with their teachers among them about the Messiah. But I do not have much time for the rabbis.

I do not know whether to be sorry that our age is so dependent on them. I only know that God is disdained thereby, and it does not escape me that their table has been turned into a snare, and the same is going to happen to us, or something even worse, unless we learn and seek to be filled with the magisterium of the Spirit, which is in Scripture and which they blaspheme.

One must exercise a great deal of judgment in reading the rabbis. This caution is especially necessary for those who wish to hunt in their commentaries for something more than grammatical points and something of equal value; and most of all if anyone wants to transfer or adapt anything to Scripture in these commentaries that is based on human wisdom, not to say error or illusion. I have no doubt that you already possess what I desire. The whole world will come to know this at some time, especially those who want to maintain everything and adore everything rabbinical in Scripture.

Christ's Spirit is more present to us than the rabbinical spirit; he teaches us with greater certainty about the truth than they do in their disagreement. Scholastic and sophistic folly have been driven out. If God does not look out for us, rabbinical and Judaic perfidy will succeed them. I wish there were no

* * * * *

26 *Adversus D. Balthasarum Pacimontanum* (Strasbourg, 1528), f. XCV r-v; Balthasar Hubmair (see Ep. 322 above) was burned at the stake in Vienna on 10 March.
27 On Martin Cellarius and his book *De operibus Dei* (prefaced by Capito), see above, Ep. 335 headnote.
28 The idea that Matthew wrote his gospel in Hebrew (rejected by the majority of modern scholars) goes back to the Church Fathers, e.g., Jerome PL 23, 643B.

example of this anywhere, but to my grief, there is an example even in our Bucer. Inspired by the observations of the rabbis and by Ruffinus' statement that the churches disagreed about the matter of Christ's descent to hell, Bucer dared to call into doubt Christ's descent to hell.[29]

I know what the rabbis prate about Sheol, but they did it to obscure Christ's descent and to elevate the kingdom of the lower regions above Christ. I shall proceed to show him sometimes in a friendly manner and with the good will becoming to brothers, how he wronged Scripture, Psalm 15 and Acts 2,[30] hiding behind the protective arms of the rabbi.

Whatever scriptural passages affirm the resurrection of Christ from the dead, will also prove that he descended to hell, to the lowest regions of the earth, the abyss. For the dead are thought of not only as decaying bodies in their sepulchres, but also in terms of the souls of the dead, which migrate to another place. Christ, therefore, of whom it is written that he was among the dead and rose from the dead, was not only in the sepulchres of the dead, but necessarily also visited that other place of the dead, which is alive and remains in existence. I shall point out to Bucer that he has spoken boldly, if I remember to do so when writing to him.

Perhaps you will urge me to publish my writings, but your example is a warning to me. We must shortly be the disciples of the Spirit and become more and more afraid of our own work, even hate it. Just as you wish that I take in good part whatever you write, I in turn ask you for the same thing, although I want to be more concerned about being absolutely certain of my interpretation and of my way of life, lest there be anything in my writings or in my action worthy of reproach. But let that not create any difficulties between us, I ask you. Let charity prevail and truth rule supreme, amen.

It seems that my fatherland[31] will take the side of Luther in the near future, which Jesus Christ, our common Saviour and Lord, may prevent, I pray. There will hardly be a place left for me in my country.[32] If it is the Lord's will that I go into exile and migrate from here, I shall hurry to you and hide away in some corner until this iniquity passes. Give my greetings to all

* * * * *

29. See Martin Bucer, *Enarratio in evangelion Iohannis* (Strasbourg,1528) in *Martini Buceri Opera Latina*, edited by Irena Backus (Leiden, 1988) 2: 525–7; see also Douglas H. Shantz, 'The Crautwald-Bucer Correspondence, 1528: A Family Feud within the Zwingli Circle,' in *Martin Bucer and Sixteenth-Century Europe: Actes du colloque de Strasbourg (28–31 août 1991)* (Leiden, 1993) 2:635–44.

30 Ps. 16:10 ('For you will not leave my soul in hell') cited in Acts 2:27.

31 Silesia.

32 Schwenckfeld was obliged to leave Liegnitz in February 1529.

your dearest brothers and ask them to pray jointly to Christ on my behalf. Do not forget Cellarius. I would be pleased if he saw fit to write to me himself. At any rate, dear Capito, urge him to write.

Furthermore, I thank God for the edition of certain good authors and am grateful to you as well for the titles. I have learned to use them under the brilliant sun of righteousness. As for the scriptural exegetes, I know what value to ascribe to them: in Tertullian[33] I have seen much truth and traces of pristine piety; a great deal of sacred erudition in Hilary;[34] I would prefer to read Chrysostom[35] in Greek rather than Latin; I wish those passages that are missing in Cyril's commentary on John could be restored.[36] For his commentary makes clear how vastly superior Cyril is (and many others of the ancient exegetes) to us in the knowledge of Christ. Yet he has lost much of his lustre through the fault of translators, who lacked training in biblical studies, and introduced a lot of awkwardness. I hope our friend Oecolampadius will be more fortunate in the labours he impends on Cyril than he was with Vulgarius,[37] although there are things even there that merit the approval of the spiritual reader. Moreover we must seek out the consensus of our forefathers in the matters, in which we think rightly and in accordance with God. We must not disdain that aspect.

You see, I go on rather long conversing with you. Christ says in John 5: *You search the scriptures.*[38] Many think the Greek verb *ereunate* is in the imperative mood, whereas it is in the indicative, as my friend Schwenckfeld also observed.[39] The context shows this: it shows that Christ calls all to himself, but he wishes to be sought in Scripture. He does not, however, direct us to Scripture there. And if you interpret this only as referring to the glory of Christ, you take away a great deal of authority, which is arrogated to scripture in our time on the basis of this passage. Indeed, you will be a bad and novel exegete, or something like it. If you use Cyril's testimony to shore up your interpretation, you will have a strong case against your adversaries. For

* * * * *

33 Quintus Septimius Tertulllian (ca. 16–ca. 225), African Church Father.
34 Hilary of Poitiers (ca. 315–67).
35 John Chrysostom (ca. 347–407), Bishop of Constantinople.
36 Only fragments were available of Book 5–8 of Cyril's (d. 444) commentary on the gospel of John.
37 Oecolampadius published an edition of *Opera Cyrilli* (Basel: Cratander, August 1528); he published an edition of Vulgarius' (i.e., Theophylactus, bishop of Bulgaria in the eleventh century) *In quatuor evangelia enarrationes* (Basel: Cratander, 1524).
38 John 5:39, traditionally interpreted as an imperative: 'Search the scriptures!'
39 See CS 2:490 and 3:15.

Cyril in book three, chapter 4 of his commentary does not want this passage to be read as an imperative, and I trust his work. Here is judgment and the freedom of the Spirit.

I do not approve of all the teachings of the Anabaptists, but I warn you to consult among yourselves about the liberty of the Spirit, which is in the faithful through the spirit of Christ. For concerning our so-called freedom of the will I believe neither Erasmus nor Luther have written correctly.[40] Anyone will understand with certainty the nature of that freedom, whether there is such a thing, if he has a good and precise understanding of the fall and restitution of man, of the double aspect, the old and the new man, and if he feels in himself the force of the Spirit, by which the sons of God are impelled.

May he, who made a dwelling place for the Spirit in our flesh, make this come abundantly true in us, amen. Farewell now and live well. Given at Liegnitz, on the day before the last of June 1528.

Letter 363: [May/June 1528, Strasbourg], Capito to [Nicolaus Kniebs]

> The manuscript of this letter is in Copenhagen, Det Kongelige Bibliotek; ms. Thott 497, f. 78; Kniebs was at that time assessor at the *Reichsregiment*. For Kniebs, see above, Ep. 184 headnote.

May the Lord bring you back safe and sound, most upright sir and patron. Please give these 25 gulden to Varnbühler.[1] And if there is any news, especially concerning the gospel, please communicate it to me, too. I shall write frequently to you, if only you will not get tired of reading [my letters]. In the meantime, we bravely continue to say mass.

Capito

Letter 363a: [June/July 1528, Strasbourg], The Strasbourg Preachers to [Balthasar Mercklin]

> This open letter to the imperial vice-chancellor and bishop of Hildesheim, Balthasar Mercklin, was published under the title *Kurtze summ aller lere und predig, so zu Strasburg gelert und gepredigt würt*. It is printed in the appendix of

* * * * *

40 Erasmus in *De libero arbitrio diatribe* (Basel: Froben, 1524) and Luther's reply, *De servo arbitrio* (Wittenberg: Lufft, 1525).

1 On Ulrich Varnbühler, a protonotary in the *Reichsregiment*, see CWC 1, Ep. 49, note 1.

CorrBucer 3:378–85 and is connected with the visit of Mercklin to Strasbourg from 28 June to 2 July 1528. The letter, listed in Millet as Ep. 376, has been renumbered to reflect those dates. For Mercklin, see CWC 1, Ep. 55, note 3.

[*Summary*]: They assure Mercklin of their respect for the authority of the emperor, but it is their task to uphold the honour of God and the truth of the gospel. The sum of their teaching is this: They encourage people to put their faith in Christ and to submit patiently to the authorities. They recognize the sacrament of baptism and of the Eucharist, which the believer 'eats as bread and body in the Lord' and 'in remembrance of [Christ's] death.' They encourage the people to pray and fast in the true sense and to honour the saints, although only Christ can intercede for them. They say nothing about purgatory because it is not mentioned in Scripture. They counsel people to confess to God and men, but to men only for the sake of Christian advice. External matters, such as food, drink, and type of clothing are unimportant. They exhort the people to keep the vows they have made if possible, but they free them of those that have been undertaken against the will of God. They teach the people to obey human laws, but in divine matters they cannot wait for the decision of councils or other human beings. They are obliged to preach against those who believe that they can earn God's grace through the mass and other ceremonies. They must act against those who would obscure the Word of God; at the same time, they are intent on 'observing order and Christian charity.' They offer to defend their teaching on the basis of Scripture and, if convinced of error, to suffer capital punishment. It is their desire to please God and the authorities, but God first and foremost.

Letter 364: 6 July 1528, [Strasbourg], Capito to Johann Schradin

The manuscript of this autograph letter is in the Universitätsbibliothek Halle, ms. Pon Misc. 2° 9, #41, and printed in Karl Eduard Förstemann, ed., *Neue Mittheilungen aus dem Gebiet historisch-antiquarischer Forschungen* (Halle, 1845), 7.3:68–70.

Schradin (d. 1560/61) was teacher at the Latin school in his native Reutlingen. Nothing is known of his early life or studies. He was a follower of Luther and correspondent of Johannes Brenz and Philip Melanchthon. He attended the Marburg Colloquy in 1529, signed the Augsburg Confession in 1530 and the Wittenberg Concord in 1536. After the Augsburg Interim he was forced to leave Reutlingen and, in 1553, became preacher at the court of Georg of Würtemberg-Mömpelgard. In 1557 he returned to Reutlingen, where he died.

To his respected brother in the Lord in Reutlingen.

...[1] The man who brought your letter to me was steadfast in the discussion with the Anabaptists here, who involved him against his will. In this we see the care and diligence of our beloved brother Matthäus[2] and of your sodality, in which we regard you as one of the leading men. For the rest, do not misunderstand me, for I admonish you from the heart. I am candid and frank. I was disturbed by your rhetoric and the juvenile style of your letter, in which you insult me with such arrogance. Your attitude is quite different from your style of writing. I know from others about your faith and your zeal for piety, but you are inspired by the wrong spirit, and that has affected your modesty. I ask you to make an effort not to slander the gift of God in any man. The Lord is zealous and powerfully protects his glory from those who seek to seize it. Luther is God's pre-eminent tool. Through him he has brought light to the world and advanced it to a higher level, from which many have benefited. But believe me, it is true that Zwingli preached the gospel truth before he had ever heard of Luther. At the same time, he promoted the affairs of the church, as becomes a good pastor. I do not wish anyone to be maligned, except by evil men. Some criticize Zwingli for not reading Luther's works. Before the Sacramentarian controversy, in which Luther dealt with everything in his own manner, people thought everything would go more smoothly once Zwingli came to know Luther's spirit more intimately. Luther did not disdain anyone. He was everything to everyone. He combined invincible constancy with a rare mildness,[3] even if he was by nature and disposition rather ardent and impulsive. Nor does anyone among us disdain Luther, my dear brother. We do not know how to dissemble. What we do not believe and what cannot be accepted by analogy of faith or does not promote anyone's faith, we consider outside the faith. Yet we do agree with some things in Luther's last publication, if we understand him correctly.[4] We are particularly saddened by his harsh manner of speaking and wish he would reserve such aggression for the enemies of Christ and not for his elect members. His erudition and eloquence, in a manner of speaking ... you are wrong ...[5] we attribute less to eloquence. Our only desire is to be changed in the image of God and to be free of idols, that the [divine] image may shine forth more clearly in us. We congratulate you on your faith and spirit, which we recognize in part, and pray that they may advance day by day. We have

* * * * *

1 The manuscript is damaged at this point.
2 On Matthäus Alber, see above, Ep. 308 headnote.
3 *morum placiditas.*
4 *Vom Abendmahl Christi Bekenntnis* (cf. above, Epp. 352, 353).
5 See note 1.

not yet achieved them. But if you permit us to do so, we admonish you to live a just life in the faith and spirit, that is, to be modest concerning yourself and full of peace and charity toward your neighbour, which covers a multitude of sins. Far be it from us to slander your good deeds; [we are speaking] out of obedience and deference to God. The main point is not to make leaders of sects out of excellent ministers or to reproach what is without doubt a gift of God, the giver of all good things.

Finally, if you write anything conducive to edification, I shall diligently respond as far as I can and faithfully suggest what I think may benefit your church. I have no mind to do battle, especially in matters of religion. We are called by the God of peace. Give our greetings to our dear brother Matthäus and your other fellow ministers. As for the rest (I almost forgot), proceed with care against the Anabaptists. You will effect nothing with commands. They are more likely to yield at the first skirmish if you take diligent action and show respect for liberty. 6 July 1528.

Dearest brother, accept what I have candidly written in God's presence and knowledge and in God's sight.

Yours, Capito.

Letter 364a: [Summer of 1528, Strasbourg], The Strasbourg Preachers to the City Council of Strasbourg

Printed in CorrBucer 3:185–7, Ep. 203.

[*Summary*]: Their teaching is founded on the Bible, which obliges the citizens to be obedient to the authorities. Piety is given by God to the elect through his grace and not through works. Furthermore, the Bible commends marriage for everyone, including the clergy. There are only two sacraments recognized in the Bible: baptism and the Lord's Supper, which is celebrated in remembrance of Christ's sacrifice. The mass is a human invention. Singing in church ought to serve the purpose of edifying and instructing the faithful.

Letter 365: 31 July 1528, [Strasbourg], Capito to Ulrich Zwingli

Printed in ZwBr 3:515, Ep. 742.

[*Summary*]: He informs Zwingli that the container and the money belong to Paul Rasdorfer, [parish priest of Betschwanden]. Oecolampadius will tell him the details. He has received Zwingli's letter [lost] and read it to Bucer. He is optimistic about his affairs and will write a longer letter [Ep. 366] the following day.

Letter 366: 31 July 1528, Strasbourg, Capito to Ulrich Zwingli

Printed in ZwBr 3:516–18, Ep. 743.

[*Summary*]: The Strasbourg preachers hope that the mass will be abolished soon. There is some disagreement, but it does not disturb the peace. One must distinguish between two kinds of Anabaptists: the leaders, who avoid Capito and whom he dislikes because they are schemers; and the simple people who are willing to be guided and should be led gently to a true understanding of the Bible. He does not support the likes of Balthasar [Hubmaier] or [Hans] Denck. The truth will win out. He himself is devoted to the study of the three biblical languages, but at present he is 'exhausted by the thorny problems' of Hebrew. Whatever errors he commits are simple errors and free of malice and obstinacy on his part. He will carefully study Zwingli's commentary on Isaiah [published in May 1529] and admires Zwingli's skill. He will also read [*Gemeinsame Schrift Zwinglis und Oecolampads*] against Luther, but will not judge it since he has not yet heard the other party. He asks Zwingli to have Paul Rasdorfer's goods [see above, Ep. 365] brought to him.

Letter 366a: [between 11 and 26 September 1528, Strasbourg], Caspar Hedio, Capito, and Martin Bucer to the City Council of Strasbourg

The manuscript of this letter is AST 69 (# 19). Cf. CorrBucer 3, Ep. 204a, where this letter is referred to as lost.

Strict, honourable, cautious, honest, wise, gracious lords!

When it became public knowledge that the position of preacher at St Helen[1] had recently become available due to the death and demise of Balthasar,[2] who was the most recent person to occupy that position, we considered how we might, by your leave and through the simplest means, ensure that your poor subjects be provided with a Christian pastor. We therefore had a friendly conversation with several of the councillors. But

* * * * *

1 In Schiltigheim, which was under the jurisdiction of Strasbourg.
2 Balthasar Loß (d. September 1528). In an undated complaint (AST 43, #95) Loß refers to himself as chaplain of the altar of the virgin in St Martin (collated by Bernhard of Eberstein) and complains that he was refused his residency fee on the pretext that he was not living in the city.

Jakob Riecker[3] claims a legal right to this position, a right he holds according to a papal decree. We, however, have chosen a faithful servant of the Word of God, one who will certainly be pleasing to Your Graces and to your subjects. You should thus allow Wolfgang Schultheiss,[4] the assistant at Young St Peter's and the person whom you previously preferred, to enter into his full rights so that no uncertainty will be caused by the papists and so that you, our lords, will not have to tolerate further unrest. Indeed, this matter should not be delayed, which is why we sent a message to Your Graces first. We therefore beg Your Graces to select Wolfgang Schultheiss or some other man who seems fitting to you, so long as he is known to live a Christian life and adhere to its teachings and beliefs and is known as a zealous adherent of the evangelical movement. In terms of your involvement, you are accountable to both God Almighty and your poor subjects. And indeed, the assistant entering on this office would not be to Your Graces' disadvantage or to that of your subjects; rather, this appointment would advance and benefit your affairs. Therefore, do not allow yourselves to be disturbed if people say that Johannes Mann,[5] the rightful possessor of the benefice, is still alive. For if he were still alive (which no one knows), he would no longer be the possessor, since Balthasar took over legitimate possession of the office, and Johannes Mann has been promised an annual pension [as compensation]. Jakob Riecker has indeed triumphed in Rome, but not according to the prevailing rights, for he has received possession through the abbess of Eschau.[6] But why go on? Your Graces now have the opportunity to establish this preaching position on the most Christian terms. And if you do not, you will be held accountable. Therefore, it is our most humble request that you should expedite this matter faithfully. For if you desire to avoid angering the Lord God, you ought not to have any consideration other than the honour of God and the welfare of your subjects. Thus, we have revealed our humble opinion

* * * * *

3 Jakob Riecker of Heiligenstein, studied at Freiburg, was canon of Young St Peter's since 1507, chaplain of the altar of St Lorenz in St Thomas, and titular rector of St Helen's Church. On 1 May 1525, he took out citizenship through his father, a boilermaker. Cf. his letters to the council asserting his rights in AMS II 12 (43).
4 On Wolfgang Schultheiss, see above, Ep. 189, note 4. Riecker eventually ceded his rights to him.
5 Johannes Mann of Sélestat matriculated at the University of Basel in 1507. He held multiple benefices and served for some years at the papal court.
6 I.e., the abbey of St Trophimus in Eschau.

in order to report to our gracious lords the state of affairs, and we proclaim ourselves ready and willing to prove our servile humility.

Your Graces' obedient subjects,

Caspar Hedio

Wolfgang Capito

Martin Bucer, etc.

Letter 367: 13 September 1528, Strasbourg, Capito to Ambrosius Blaurer

The text of the letter is printed in Schiess 1: 167, Ep. 125. For Blaurer see above, Ep. 192 headnote.

Grace and peace. This good man[1] has lived a blameless life among us for a long time, causing no problem for our church. Bucer can fully attest to this, and more specifically Bedrot,[2] a man of excellent judgment. Therefore, give him a friendly welcome and assist him with verbal as well as substantive support. I find among the Anabaptists men of very good heart and prepared for true piety, whom you may join to your little flock by using lenience. They have left it rashly, through ignorance of Christ, an ill from which practically all the world suffers nowadays. Furthermore, the greater part is involved not only in error but also in malice. They are intent on restoring the Mosaic law and thereby creating commotion. It is necessary to guard carefully against those people and fervently pray for them. For some deny that there can be a Christian magistrate, others attempt to set up leaders for the purpose of inducing the people to slay Lutherans, Zwinglians, papists, in a word, all who do not subscribe to their seditious views. They spout words that have the appearance of being pious; they speak of 'the spirit of Elijah,'[3] 'a return to first beginnings,' and other things of this sort, to make us embrace their idolatry and take up the sword of Gideon.[4] How hard is our lot, if we are not strengthened by the grace of God! I stand up like a wall against such preying spirits. As for the rest, I am of an opinion very similar to yours, indeed of the same opinion completely, and will not involve innocent people in the same odium. I write this in passing. Give my regards to your respected family and

* * * * *

1 Unidentified. The remainder of the letter would indicate that he had, at some time, been involved with the Anabaptist movement.
2 On Jakob Bedrot, see above, Ep. 260, note 1.
3 Cf. Matt. 11:13–14, 17:12–13; Mark 9:11–13; and Luke 1:17.
4 Cf. Judg. 7:14.

your brother[5] in Constance. Many greetings to Zwick[6] and all the best for the future to yourself. Strasbourg, 13 September 1528.

Yours, W. Capito.

Letter 367a: [14 September 1528, Strasbourg], Capito to Ambrosius Blaurer

This is a postscript to the preceding letter, Ep. 367. Cf. Schiess 2: 779, appendix I, #27.

The day after I wrote this,[1] a monk from the monastery at Alpirsbach[2] called on me. He announced that another of his ilk,[3] a prior, would come two days later. I wanted you to know this, for your exhortations were not in vain. I will offer my service to the exiles if I have an opportunity. It is likely that they will be laid low by a deep mental depression because of the new and unusual circumstances in which they will have to live. They therefore stand in greater need of consolation.

Yours, Capito.

Letter 367b: 1 October 152[8], [Strasbourg], Lorenz Schenckbecher to Capito

The manuscript of this deposition is in Basel, Universitätsbibliothek, Ki.Ar. 25a, 152. The document appears in Millet as Ep. 397a and is assigned to the year 1529. Since Capito in his response (see below, Ep. 367c) states that Schenckbecher has held the provostship for three years, and Schenckbecher notes in the present document that he entered the office on 16 October 1525, the deposition must be redated to 1528.

I, Lorenz Schenkbecher, canon and elected provost of the collegiate church St Thomas in Strasbourg, profess herewith in my own hand: On 16 October of

* * * * *

5 I.e., Thomas Blaurer, see above Ep. 192, note 6.
6 On Johannes Zwick, see Ep. 192, note 1.

1 I.e., Ep. 367.
2 Blaurer had been a member of the Benedictine community at Alpirsbach (dissolved in 1535 by Duke Ulrich von Württemberg). The abbot at the time was Ulrich Hamma (1523–35).
3 I.e., a Benedictine?

the year 1525 past,[1] it happened that the worthy and most learned Dr Wolfgang Capito, my dear friend and brother, laid down and totally divested
himself of the provostship of St Thomas for an excellent reason, to avoid,
for the sake of the word of God, much unpleasant talk among the common
people.[2] For that purpose he asked Master Gervasius Sopher, our mutual
good friend in confidence, to take the said provostship as a favour to him, for
he was at that time burdened with much debt.[3] Finally, after many requests,
I agreed and took the provostship without qualifications, and took possession on the basis of a free election of the honourable chapter (done for the
sake of my own person). However, until now Dr Wolfgang Capito has had
the use of 10 gulden a year from my income of the provostship, as a token
of my goodwill and agreement. He used it for his benefit according to his
pleasure. Since, however, the provostship is still under litigation and Jacob
Abel believes he has a claim to it,[4] I am at risk at any time of being asked for
the received income from the provostship since I am the possessor and have
signed for it. We therefore agreed that Dr Wolfgang Capito and his wife, Agnes Roettel, would give me a promissory note for 300 gulden, guaranteed by
Ulrich Roettel, administrator of the Dominicans here, and his brother Hans
Roettel, both [Capito's] brothers-in-law, and that they be co-debtors obliged
to pay at the end of the term, as signed in the brief deposited with the notary
Jakob Schmidt[5] today. Thus I promise with this, my own signature, that I
or my heirs will not demand the said debt, unless we were to lose a lawsuit
against Jacob Abel or anyone else who believes he has a claim on the provostship and were forced to pay. Such a lawsuit should be pursued and defended
at the cost of Dr Wolfgang Capito and his heirs and without any cost or damage to me and my heirs. Then, and not earlier, may I or my heirs demand the
said 300 gulden and enforce the promissory note. And in order that I may be
certain of the rest of the income in the future, it was agreed, with Dr Wolfgang Capito's consent, that any money coming to Dr Wolfgang Capito from
the provostship should remain with me and be kept for a future lawsuit, as
said above, until Jacob Abel's death or else until a settlement between him
and Dr Wolfgang Capito is reached. That is, once there is no more claim

* * * * *

1 Cf. Appendix 1c, where Capito gives the date as '15 October.'
2 On Capito's motives, see Appendix 1c.
3 Cf. above, Ep. 248a.
4 A document in which Abel tenders his resignation on 2 June 1529 is in AST 19,
  #63 but the claim was still (or again?) before the courts in 1534. The city, however, refused to honour the papal decree on which Abel's claim was based. No
  final judgment is extant. On Abel, cf. CWC 1, Ep. 50 headnote.
5 Jakob Schmidt, documented as 'notarius contractuum' in 1528 only.

from Jacob Abel's side or any other person on the provostship, then and not earlier will the said promissory note over 300 gulden be null and void. I have delivered this document to the above-named Gervasius Sopher.[6] It is in my own handwriting, sealed with my seal at the end, and meant to maintain this agreement and to avoid future misunderstanding. Given on Tuesday after St Michael the Archangel, on the first day of the month of October after the birth of Christ, our dear Lord and Saviour, 152[8].

Letter 367c: [Shortly after 1 October 152[8], Strasbourg], Capito to Gervasius Sopher

This letter, numbered Ep. 397 by Millet, has been redated on the basis of internal evidence. Cf. also above, Ep. 367b headnote. The manuscript of the letter is in the Universitätsbibliothek Basel, Ki.Ar. 25a, 152. It indicates Capito's desire to resume the provostship unless a satisfactory settlement with the present holder, Lorenz Schenckbecher, can be reached. For the background, see above, Ep. 248c headnote.

My dear Sopher, you will hear in the following articles why it is that I suddenly request the provostship, and furthermore, how and under what title I mean to possess it in the future, and also the conditions that would satisfy me if my lord and friend, the provost Lorenz Schenckbecher, wishes to retain it.[1]

1. The thought of taking up the provostship again in person originated with the undertaking concerning the promissory note for 300 gulden.[2] This made me consider the sequence of transactions between us from the beginning to this point and the fact that I feel more burdened every day so that it might at last become unbearable for me.

2. For when I promised you the provostship and canonry and Lorenz Schenckbecher accepted the provostship,[3] and after he was elected by the chapter, he agreed to provide irrevocable procurators for the

* * * * *

6 Cf. below, Ep. 367c.

1 For Schenckbecher, see above, Ep. 237, note 21.
2 I.e., a promissory note given as surety in case Schenckbecher's provostship became the subject of litigation. See below, note 9, and Appendix 1c.
3 Capito initially offered the provostship to Sopher. See above, Ep. 248a.

purpose of resignation. For his effort and labour concerning the collations, the seal, and other incidentals he was to have 10 gulden a year.[4] (I had specified these 10 [gulden] previously in the presence of Bucer and Obrecht[5] of [St] Thomas. The procurator offered nothing.)[6] You know that I asked in your presence and in the presence of several good friends, who will still remember it, that he should keep the provostship under the same title and condition ... at his pleasure, since he had already been elected [by the chapter] and [is] in possession and I, at the same time ...[7] still preferred to divest myself of the title.

3. He accepted that, and promised religiously with humble gestures that he would make no collations without my consent: 'You will be the provost, not I.' But I omitted to demand procurators, as discussed. Our business was based on trust and friendship, and in the first year I accepted without objection the use of the 10 gulden, which the provost agreed to give as a gift.

4. In the second year, on Candlemas day,[8] however, when I requested my money, the provost complained, saying he was concerned because he signed for the full amount. Jacob Abel[9] might sue and obtain the complete amount of the benefice from him or his heirs. After much discussion, we agreed that in the future the sum should be registered and an undertaking put in writing about it, indicating the place and person with whom and in whose name the document should be deposited.[10] For Schenckbecher insisted on keeping the matter secret and refused to trust me, but I did not want it to be deposited with him, as he kept asking, since I have come to experience some of his cleverness this year. It was then deposited with the financial officers. All summer I did not do anything about the undertaking or about fulfilling the above-mentioned condition.

* * * * *

4 The exact nature of the financial arrangement remains unclear. Cf. Appendix 1c, which mentions 20 gulden to be paid to Schenckbecher (i.e., over two years?). From the statement in item 3 below, however, it would appear that Capito retained the money. Cf. also above, Ep. 269.

5 Wolfgang Obrecht studied in Leipzig (matriculated 1501) and became vicar of St George in 1522.

6 The passage in parentheses appears in the margin.

7 The manuscript is damaged at this point, creating lacunae in the text.

8 2 February 1527.

9 Abel was a claimant to the provostship. Cf. CWC 1, Ep. 50 headnote.

10 Cf. the draft document dated March 1527 (date of day left blank), AST 19, ad 55.

5. Since it was a business between friends and brothers, I looked after my larger affairs and quite forgot about our agreement. For I am much burdened with the business of the church and the poor brethren, and therefore agreed to put the incoming money toward the payment of some debts.

6. Then you approached me in a conversation that would be too long and tedious to relate, telling me of Lorenz Schenckbecher's many complaints, which rather surprised me.

7. After some negotiations in your house for the purpose of reaching agreement on the matter, and on your suggestion, we added up all the money I had received and would receive until Candlemas Day 1529, which amounts to 300 gulden, and put them into a promissory note, as if I promised to pay back money lent to me, making me [Schenckbecher's] debtor and having my two brothers-in-law, Ulrich and Hans Roettel, together with my wife sign as well, while Lorenz was to give me an undertaking in turn.

8. An undertaking ... an account of the truth ... trusting in your honesty and upright nature ...[11] for one must have some check and balance for such a tremendous undertaking and guarantee.

9. But the provost's account[12] is different and goes against mine. It supports the promissory note, saying that he has been elected provost, that I wanted to divest myself completely of the provostship, that I asked him through you, Sopher, to take on the provostship and that he was elected out of regard for his person, without any qualification. That is his account supporting the promissory note. He threatens me with dishonour should I or my heirs refute it in the future, and that is also the intent of the words that follow.

10. The undertaking states that I had, thus far, enjoyed the usufruct of the 10 gulden by his assent and agreement and was entitled to use them for my advantage and benefit, according to my will and pleasure. These words give outsiders the impression that the money is the provost's rather than mine, for I divested myself completely of the provostship without qualification, and he was the possessor on the basis of a free election, and authorized my use of the money. Such passages could also be cited, etc.

11. The risks the provost fears are briefly noted, but they are specifically connected to the promissory note and the debt.

* * * * *

11 See above, note 7.
12 I.e., in Ep. 367b above.

12. [He states] that, in case of an eviction, he could demand the total sum of 300 gulden, actually meaning, 'as much as is granted to the adversary by law or settlement.'

13. [He states] that he should keep the remaining money and does not mention that the remainder belongs to me according to the contract, and that the promissory note would become null and void at that point,[13] but not earlier.

14. Thus, the whole undertaking is phrased to protect Mr Lorenz in his authority and right as provost unconditionally, that on special request and knowledge the 300 gulden ... for my use and benefit ... and nothing further about the remaining deposit ...[14] other than in case of a future dispute. The aforementioned narrative may give the impression that it was the right of the elected provost after the agreement, etc. Anyone who wanted to be particular, as the jurists are, for whom such an undertaking is meant to be kept, may further find, etc.

15. In the final article[15] it is stated that I went to the council office and demanded a change to this effect in the records, but the provost referred me to a future date, when the income from the provostship came due again. In any case, we would have to give each other a mutual undertaking. I had to be content with that, for the severe promissory note was already signed. And no one knew of the undertaking except you alone.

16. Had I retained the last article, the account would be necessarily different. And all the other points would have been taken care of as well, I hope. Just think what it means to sleep with such fleas. I am written down for a debt of 300 gulden with guarantors, although I owe not a penny of it. And just as I was eager so far on behalf of the church to rid myself of the title of provost, the honour of God compels me to do away with the promissory note and to take on the provostship myself and look after its administration myself. The soup I give to the poor makes me happier than this useless talk and the gossip of useless people, and these anxieties about the provostship.

17. These are in general the reasons, which are further explained in these articles, why I have decided to take over the provostship

* * * * *

13 I.e., when a settlement is reached with Abel.
14 See above, note 7.
15 Point of reference unclear.

and come to terms with Lorenz, unless he were agreeable to the articles and method described below.

18. This is the form in which Mr Lorenz might divest himself of the provostship in a dignified manner and without loss, and the manner in which I may take it on with due care:

19. He ... should complain to certain people about the provostship ... and say that he hoped to divest himself of it again ...[16] and return it to me, in the form and manner in which he gave me to understand last summer. Next, I will speak in a friendly manner to our founders, explaining the circumstances and asking them to elect me again, should I not succeed in having you take on the office.

20. I believe they will not refuse to do that, for the other election merely established a precedent to elect a provost, but one act does not make a law. It was therefore of no use to insist that the provostship has a different aspect and nature; that is outdated and has long been abolished.

21. And even if they did not want to elect me, I would nevertheless be and remain provost and, with God's help, would know how to maintain my right before honest judges, in the face of Abel[17] and all the courtesans,[18] during my lifetime. The election was not followed by a confirmation, etc.[19] Here I shall repeat what I said in the first articles.

22. This does no harm to the provost. He took on the provostship by proxy and gratis as a steward, and he gives it to me, the principal, as he is obliged to do. He has had the provostship for three years now without loss to him, on account of the collation and seals, etc. If he had any deficit, I will satisfy him to the last penny he has expended.

23. As provost of St Thomas, he enjoys respect among clerics and laymen and has been preferred and had no disadvantage in his marriage.

24. A vice-dean has to expend much work and effort, and does not have the rank of prelate ... the dean's house is not owned, but requires an annual rent ...[20] but Mr Lorenz Schenckbecher is now ...

* * * * *

16 See above, note 7.
17 See above, note 9.
18 A derogatory reference to the members of the papal court.
19 Cf. the chapter's request for the bishop's confirmation of Schenckbecher's election, above Ep. 248d.
20 See above, note 7.

and has the prelacy, has no problems ...[21] and all work which he
would otherwise have to do, the work we all do as canons, etc.
And he has the collation and the investitures and the right of the
seals in addition, and is the certain heir, after my death, of the
complete benefice without anyone being able to raise an objection.
God may bring me death whenever it is his will. I live in great
danger. On Monday night I inhaled such a miasma from a man
sick with the plague, and even today I feel rather heated and
feeble in body. But I have no intention to die sooner on account of
the provostship. I will wait for God's call and not depart without
God's grace.

25. On Monday in the chapter I was heartened by the honest admonition of my lord Lorenz in his capacity as provost, and I know it is
my duty to serve everyone. Therefore, I myself put it to him that
there would be no danger if he held the provostship as agreed.
We would know how to defend ourselves against the courtesans
during our lifetime. Our heirs, being citizens, would surely be
defended as well without great effort, so that I have no concerns
whatsoever, etc.

26. However, to allow him to feel secure and at peace, I would be
willing to have the provost issue a public statement, in which an
account of the affair is given in the proper order, as can be seen
from the first articles, and you yourself were pleased to accept,
etc. And that the use of 10 gulden be specified as my stipend in
the future, on convenient terms, so that the matter would be made
my business and that of my heirs. If anyone wanted the income
returned, he would have to look far and wide, in all countries and
kingdoms, in short, the challenger will find no other law [to support him] and will have to yield to the regulations of the city.

27. Furthermore, [Schenckbecher] would have to constitute irrevocable procurators, as has been agreed, to resign [the provostship]
to me or when I agree to accept such matters, etc. Therefore we all
... not that I would want anything counter to usage, rather ... nor
the nature ... to do everything humanly possible ... yet one ought
to exercise caution in these things ...[22] procurators are necessary.

28. Thus, the promissory note and undertaking would come to an
end, and both parties would have it in writing and deposited in

* * * * *

21 See above, note 7.
22 See above, note 7.

the record office and need no longer cause each other concern. That is, roughly, the answer to your request, and we hope that Lorenz, the provost, will soon make up his mind. It is not convenient for me to wait until Monday. I cannot devote my attention to God's spiritual business, while God keeps my mind uneasy and involved in such secular concerns.

29. I understand, however, that the provost has not fully considered how risky and burdensome the undertaking is for me. I am compelled to act in the said matter and am motivated by godly considerations and can and will no longer suffer the tension.

30. There is no need to indicate my further plan ...[23] for I hope for a decisive answer in the future and to have it deposited with a discreet notary, such as Schwencker[24] is said to be, who would, in any case, have some knowledge of the matter. Thereafter I would not want [Schenckbecher] to be at risk, however, and will always show myself a god-fearing man. Return this account to me on Friday, so that I do not have additional work. For I will keep it until the matter is settled.

Letter 368: 15 October 1528, Basel, Johannes Oecolampadius to Capito

Printed in BrOek 2:237–8, Ep. 607.

[*Summary*]: Although the principal task of the preachers is spiritual, they may be excused for taking an interest in secular affairs as well. He therefore raised the question (on Zwingli's initiative) why the Strasbourgers were not seeking an alliance with Zurich. Constance, St Gallen, and Mulhouse have already joined them, and Bern has moved away from accepting pensions [from the French]. He wonders how much influence the incoming bishop of Constance, Balthasar Mercklin, will have [for his negotiations with Strasbourg, see above, Ep. 363a]. Rumour has it that he entered into negotiations with Jacob Sturm. He hopes Capito will intercede. He may want to consult by letter with Zwingli, who is staying in Basel at the time. He sends his greetings to Bucer and Bonifacius Wolfhart. Damianus Hoeman [Damianus Irmi?] has left for [Austria?] and will not return to Venice before Easter. He has no other contacts and therefore cannot oblige Capito's request to obtain a bibli-

* * * * *

23 *der merkt/mecht wirt us leren komen/konen*: reading and meaning of phrase uncertain.

24 For the notary Michael Schwencker, see above, Ep. 189, note 26.

cal commentary. The bearer of the letter, a displaced person, wishes to work for his living. He asks Capito to assist him in finding work. He sends Wolfhart a cap and thanks him for helping another exile whom Oecolampadius recently recommended.

Letter 369: [October 1528, Wasselonne], Andreas Cellarius to Capito

The manuscript of this letter is in AST 40, #66, f. 444. Andreas Cellarius (or Keller, 1504–62) was born in Rottenburg/Neckar. When he began to preach the gospel in 1524, he was expelled and took refuge in Strasbourg, where he became deacon (*diaconus*) at Old St Peter. From 1525 to 1536 he was pastor in Wasselonne. From 1536 until his death he was pastor of Wildberg in Würtemberg.

May the Father's favour and goodwill be with you through Christ, Capito, best of men! The brother,[1] whom you sent to me some time ago with a letter of reference, is still with us. With God's favour, the knight who is in charge here[2] will appoint him minister of the Word in the village of Bischwiller, since Gervasius[3] has been obliged to leave it. To speed the matter up, either you or others (I would prefer it would be done by you rather than by others) should write to the knight, asking him not to tarry or change his mind on account of the complaints and threats of our adversaries. For the papists in the chapters are very much opposed to it. The vacancy concerns Old St Peter in Strasbourg, for they have the right of collation for the parish of Bischwiller. On the other side, a certain citizen of Strasbourg, by the name of Beger,[4] also opposes the appointment. He holds a part of the jurisdiction there. The people, however, are very desirous of the Word and have asked repeatedly for someone to come and preach the Word to them. Therefore, see to the matter and consider how it should be approached. If you write anything about the matter, do not say that you have been prompted by me; say that you know about it from common report. The knight's proposal is no secret, for he wrote

* * * * *

1 Erasmus Beyer, who remained pastor of Bischwiller until his death in 1544.
2 Fabian von Eschenau (d. after 1541), administrator at the castle of Reichshoffen and later of Wasselonne, Seigneur of Bischweiler-Hanhoffen.
3 I.e., Gervasius Schuler, cf. CWC 1, Ep. 44 headnote.
4 Matthias Beger of Blayberg (d. 1532), who had a say in the collation. He was the last of the Beger family, who held numerous fiefs. The family's castle was the Schwarzenburg.

ΒΑΣΙΛΕΙΩΝ ΔΕΥΤΕΡΑΣ.

Κεφάλαιον ά. ι.

Καὶ ἐγένετο μετὰ τὸ ἀποθανεῖν σαοὺλ,
καὶ δαβὶδ ἀνέστρεψε τύπτων τὸν ἀμα-
λήκ. καὶ ἐκάθισε δαβὶδ ἐν σεκελάγ
ἡμέρας δύο. καὶ ἐγενήθη τῇ ἡμέρᾳ τῇ
τρίτῃ καὶ ἰδοὺ ἀνὴρ ἦλθεν ἐκ τῆς παρεμ
βολῆς τοῦ λαοῦ σαοὺλ. καὶ τὰ ἱμάτια αὐτοῦ
διερρωγότα. καὶ γῆ ἐπὶ τῆς κεφαλῆς αὐ
τοῦ. καὶ ἐγένετο ἐν τῷ ἐλθεῖν αὐτὸν πρὸς δαβὶδ, καὶ ἔπεσεν ἐπὶ
τὴν γῆν, καὶ προσεκύνησεν αὐτῷ. καὶ εἶπεν αὐτῷ δαβίδ. πό-
θεν σὺ παραγίνη. καὶ εἶπε πρὸς αὐτόν. ἐκ τῆς παρεμβολῆς ἰσραὴλ
ἐγὼ διασέσωσμαι. καὶ εἶπεν αὐτῷ δαβίδ. τίς ὁ λόγος οὗτος
ἀπάγγειλόν μοι. καὶ εἶπεν ὅτι πέφευγεν ὁ λαὸς ἐκ τοῦ πολέμου
καὶ πεπτώκασιν πολλοὶ ἐκ τοῦ λαοῦ, καὶ ἀπέθανον. καὶ σαοὺλ καὶ
ἰωνάθαν, ὁ υἱὸς αὐτοῦ ἀπέθανε. καὶ εἶπε δαβὶδ τῷ παιδαρίῳ
τῷ ἀπαγγέλλοντι αὐτῷ. πῶς οἶδας, ὅτι τέθνηκε σαοὺλ, καὶ ἰω-
ναθαν, ὁ υἱὸς αὐτοῦ. καὶ εἶπε τὸ παιδάριον τὸ ἀπαγγέλλον αὐτῷ.
περιπτώματι περιέπεσον ἐν τῷ ὄρει τῷ γελβουέ. καὶ ἰδοὺ σαοὺλ ἐπεστήρικτο ἐπὶ τὸ δόρυ αὐτοῦ. καὶ ἰδοὺ τὰ ἅρματα καὶ οἱ ἱπ
πάρχαι συνῆψαν αὐτῷ. καὶ ἐπέβλεψεν ἐπὶ τὰ ὀπίσω αὐτοῦ καὶ
εἶδέ με. καὶ ἐκάλεσέ με. καὶ εἶπα ἰδοὺ ἐγώ. καὶ εἶπέ μοι τίς εἶ
σύ. καὶ εἶπα. ἀμαληκίτης ἐγώ εἰμι. καὶ εἶπε πρός με. ἐπίστηθι δὴ
ἐπάνω μου καὶ θανάτωσόν με ὅτι κατέσχε με σκότος δεινὸν καὶ
ἔτι ἡ ψυχή μου ἐν ἐμοί. καὶ ἐπέστην ἐπ' αὐτὸν καὶ ἐθανάτωσα αὐ
τόν, ὅτι ᾔδειν ὅτι οὐ ζήσεται μετὰ τὸ πεσεῖν αὐτόν. καὶ ἔλαβον τὸ βα
σίλειον τὸ ἐπὶ τῆς κεφαλῆς αὐτοῦ, καὶ τὸν χλιδῶνα τὸν ἐπὶ τοῦ βρα

Biblia. Tēs theias graphēs ... (Strasbourg: Köpfel, 1524–6), fol. 38v.
Photograph courtesy of the Universitätsbibliothek Basel.

about the business to the provost and dean of the collegiate church of [Old] St Peter, although they have not yet responded.

Furthermore, as I go through Hebrew concordances, I constantly come across those three letters [waw, gimel, waw][5] – I cannot conceive their meaning. Similarly, in the Greek Bible published by Wolfgang Köpfel,[6] I find abbreviations which I have never seen before, which puzzle me. I do not know how they ought to be read. Among them I have noted ['S'], which I take to stand for [the Greek prefix] *epi*, and ['G'], which I read as [Greek] *et, eph, es,* etc.[7]

What is happening concerning the mass in your Strasbourg? Let me know in a letter, if you have time. Farewell, and give my regards to your family and brothers.

Yours, Andreas Cellarius.

Letter 370 is now 396a.

Letter 370a: [Before 1 November 1528, Strasbourg], Capito to Johannes Oecolampadius

> This letter (now lost) is quoted in a letter of 8 November 1528 from Oecolampadius to Zwingli (ZwBr 3, Ep. 774, lines 2–15), which begins: 'I have faithfully done what you advise, my dear Ulrich. I have hinted to Capito that [Strasbourg should] approach our city,' i.e., to conclude an alliance. Capito reportedly answered:

I do not know what to say in reply to your letter. We are not sluggish cowards, but one must act in season. People have various complaints. The rule of the people is a many-headed monster. Many abhor the uncertain actions of our friends. There are those who hope that Constance will be an ally in the future on account of their profession of Christ.[1] But all innovations are suspect to those in the know. Now listen to another thing: certain people from Metz came here and declared that there was a prominent rumour in

* * * * *

5 A contraction meaning 'etc.'
6 *Biblia. Tēs theias graphēs* ... (Strasbourg: Köpfel, 1524–6).
7 Cellarius is correct in his surmises about the Greek ligatures. See illustration p. 361.

1 Constance had concluded an alliance with Zurich in December 1527 and with Bern in January 1528. Cf. above, Ep. 368.

their city about an alliance being discussed between the cities.[2] They say that the articles have been written down and have practically been ratified. But in our city there is complete silence about this. Yet we do not doubt that this has been decided among the leaders of the cities in our Germany. You may guess the rest and arrive at your own conclusion about the nature and circumstances.

Letter 371: 1 November 1528, [Strasbourg], Capito to Ulrich Zwingli

Printed in ZwBr 3:593–4, Ep. 773.

[*Summary*]: Capito recently wrote to Oecolampadius concerning the proposed alliance of cities [Ep. 370a]. The abolition of the mass is still pending. People fear losing the subsidy of the princes. Capito and his colleagues are prevented from preaching openly in favour of the abolition of the mass. The nobles are looking out for their own advantage. The bearer of the letter is the husband of a Swiss woman, whose own marital status is unclear.[1] He asks Zwingli to intercede on her behalf. Capito would like Pellicanus to give him an account of the beliefs and practices in Zurich regarding the Lord's Supper. The preachers of Strasbourg would like to adopt them.

Letter 372: 19 November [1528], Basel, Johannes Oecolampadius to Capito and Martin Bucer

Printed in CorrBucer 3:256, Ep. 617.

[*Summary*]: Oecolampadius was glad to welcome Jacob Sturm and his companions in Basel. Together they travelled on to Bern where they were well received. [They were to help in the negotiations between Bern and the rebels in the Oberland]. Capito's letter was brought by the Constance physician [Conrad Nyder?]. He fears the 'feigned piety' of the Anabaptists.

Letter 373: [December 1528?, Strasbourg], Capito to Nicolaus Kniebs

The manuscript of this letter is in Copenhagen, Det Kongelige Bibliotek Thott, f.

* * * * *

2 The rumour was correct. Negotiations were on the way between Augsburg, Nürnberg, Ulm, and Strasbourg, but the representatives of Strasbourg did not support the terms (cf. Pol. Corr. 1, 310).

1 Perhaps this is Felicitas Scherenschleger mentioned above, Ep. 342a.

76. It concerns the efforts of the preachers to have the mass abolished. See also below, Epp. 375, 376. For Kniebs, see above, Ep. 184 headnote.

May God strengthen you, dear sir, in your endeavour, which we share and heartily support, but we must patiently suffer God's will, which makes us better men. Consider it God's means of urging you on to walk in his ways more courageously. Aid the glory of God! And if there are more objections, to which there appear to be no answer, send them to me that I may reply at leisure and examine them attentively.

W. Capito.

Letter 374: 12 December 1528, [Strasbourg], Capito to Ulrich Zwingli

Printed in ZwBr 3:618–19, Ep. 785.

[*Summary*]: Capito thanks Zwingli for his letter [lost]. He hints at possible alliances between the cities that have embraced the Reformation. This will not be possible, however, unless the mass is abolished. The matter was discussed by the Strasbourg council on 7 December. The burden of maintaining the position of the preachers rested on his shoulders alone because Bucer is engaged in studies, 'perhaps more than is to our advantage.' He approves of Strasbourg sending a delegation [to assist with the negotiations with the Vier-Städtebund]. He hopes that Bucer [at St Aurelia at the time] will soon be called to a post 'within the city walls.' He is making every effort to obtain such a post for him.[1] Bucer sends his greetings.

Letter 375: [27 December 1528, Strasbourg], Capito to the City Council of Strasbourg

The manuscript of this letter is in AST 80 (#15). It is entitled 'Capito's justification addressed to the council of Strasbourg concerning his statement that the mass must be abolished even if the magistrates did not abolish it.'

Strict, noble, firm, honest, wise and favourable lords! The noble and hon-

* * * * *

1 Cf. the submission made by the preachers on his behalf ca. 3 March 1529 (CorrBucer 3:249, Ep. 218). Cf. also below, Ep. 383.

ourable Jakob Zorn[1] and the honest, wise Hans Hug[2] have reproached me for reportedly saying, 'the mass must be abolished, even if you, our wise lords, will not abolish it.' They demanded that I indicate under oath whether I knew about any people who intended to act in this manner in the face of the honourable council and to name them, for this might give rise to much work, trouble, and danger for my lords.

Thereupon, after some back and forth, I replied, telling them about the circumstances in which I made the statement, which I am now indicating to you in writing, gracious lords, that you may have a better understanding of my inclination and good will, for the statement was not made in this way, although the content is correct. I request that this be graciously read out and that the council proceed as God directs them. I hope they will not blame me and my brethren for being rather zealous in our preaching in these times. We seek only the glory of God and the welfare of the city, for otherwise we would appear before the world in a different and more peaceful manner. The business of God will suffer a setback and will be more deeply hated, if action is not taken at this time.

We have often pleaded humbly with Your Gracious Lordships to abolish the four masses,[3] which are against God, divide the city, and partly offend foreigners, partly incite them against Your Graces, but it has not yet been Your Gracious Lordships' pleasure to consider the disadvantages. In the meantime, the resentment among the people increases, for those who do not obey the gospel, if they attend the sermon at all, come to church with an impious and disdainful attitude, and gravely abuse the honour of God. This is an injury to our church, and some people become impatient as a result, for temperaments vary.

We never cease to counsel patience and often express hope for improvement. It is true, our opponents are dogged and our hearers are given more strength by us every day, and that is why I said yesterday that our sermons incite them against the mass. For one cannot praise the grace of God, the merit of Christ, and brotherly love without condemning the mass, either publicly or covertly, since it is counter to the true service of God. Everyone

* * * * *

1 Jakob Zorn zum Riet (d. 1531), member of the council, Stettmeister 1525/26.
2 Hans Hug is documented as a witness to a deposition on 26 October 1514 (AST 12, #43: 73). I have found no other information on him. The Hug family was prominent on the city council. Philip Hug (d. 1532), for example, was *Ammeister* in 1520 and 1526, and a member of the XIII from 1521–31.
3 Still celebrated daily in Strasbourg; cf. above, Ep. 284 of April 1526, which mentions five masses being celebrated. Cf. also above, Ep. 358 for the preachers protesting the half-measure of celebrating mass alongside evangelical service.

understands that and cannot very well tolerate that in the same place where God's grace is praised, the opposite is maintained in deed. The mass hampers the conscience of the weak brethren and prevents them from improving their lives, and they become careless and remiss.

It is on account of the celebration of masses that we are unable to establish general Christian law and order; nor are we able to punish manifest vices. Diverse sects arise, and we have to worry about the general public welfare, unless the matter is considered in the required and proper manner, which in turn moves us to be zealous in our enforcement.

Now, my gracious lords, I said, the mass must be abolished even if you, our lords, wish to delay. I also said: 'If Ahab will not abolish Baal, Elijah will have to do it.'[4] Indeed, I fear the rumours coming from the ignorant mob. I have no fear of honest, reasonable, and God-fearing citizens, who accept the Word of God. They will not permit anything dishonest, for the sake of God.

I am, however, very much afraid of the wrath of God, who likes to put down human cleverness in transactions and usually afflicts the affairs of the world. Thus, if you, our gracious lords, as magistrates, omit to improve things, private zeal must take action. For God's work will certainly not be left undone, even if we are left behind and must give our life for it, especially since the mass prevents all improvement, and the whole city is weakened and its welfare obstructed. And rather than having the disorderly mob act incorrectly, I prefer taking the risk myself, together with a few pious Christians, but all that would be done more properly through the agency of you, our gracious lords.

We beg you, for God's sake, not to think that we wish to govern the city in secular matters, for that is hardly fitting for us and would be dangerous, although we might have remained in the enjoyment of honour, greater security, and earthly benefits if we had chosen it, and if God's honour had not been more important to us. We work only as messengers of God's rule and to spread his law. In that task, we take precedence over princes and lords, kings and emperors, for we are the commanders of the almighty God. Anyone who listens to us in this respect, listens to God, for we speak for him, and we offer to prove and explain this on the basis of scripture and on the testimony of the conscience of the elect. If our opponents are found right, we rightly deserve death, and you are bound to punish us. If you listened to God speaking through us and obeyed de facto, you would not find yourself dimished in your government and dignity. In sum, dear lords, we would re-

* * * * *

4 Cf. 2 Kings 10:18.

frain from preaching if we were not certain that all who belong to God must do as we say. If the imperial mandate[5] was brought here and looked into, one would come to the conclusion that our action does not go against the imperial edict, and might say: 'It has to be that way.' But the majority among you is convinced that the mass is blasphemy. As for the other part, our appeal has deprived them of any excuse for pleading ignorance. If we voiced our opinion and told the people to obey God and do what they owed to God and the common city, it was in your honour and not to inveigh against you. We, too, have sworn to maintain the welfare of the city. Why should we not be zealous when we know that you lead the city into ruin if you do not abolish the mass? Every other imperial city, in which sermons have been preached as long and as earnestly as here, has abolished mass among princes, lords, and cities.

We do not want to disdain the world, which is made of flesh and blood and is a child of folly; rather, we do not want God to be disdained, for no one can withstand his power. Let everyone look out for himself and take care not to disdain God. He wishes to be more feared than the emperor. Your faith, or lack thereof, is imputed to the whole city. If you do not turn to God, the city will be brought to ruin, for he is above all creatures and wishes to be feared above all.

We have discovered from the threats and abusive talk of the opponents to the Truth and, partly through messages from the imperial government, that there are negotiations taking place concerning the mass. The imperial government knew of it and therefore sent an official delegation here to reinstate the mass.[6] Now that we know of the tricks and plotting of our opponents, we cannot and will not desert the cause of our Lord Jesus. Rather, we must earnestly defend his cause with the sword of his Word. For error must yield to truth, and Christ and the mass cannot, at length, stand side by side. You cannot call this haste. Three years ago, it was decreed to abolish the mass, as you yourself acknowledge.[7] One might have kept the four masses for three or four weeks, while a Christian ordinance was established in the city. It is only out of human consideration that the mass has been maintained to the present day. In the meantime, there were many procrastinations and promises of diets, councils, and other meetings, and nothing ever came of them. Meanwhile, the devil seeks such excuses to find occasion to re-establish the whole false practice, to put down the Word of God and to drive us away and allow the wrath of God to fall on you. We cannot obey those who

* * * * *

5 I.e., the mandate of 20 January 1522 against religious innovation?
6 Cf. above, Ep. 363a.
7 Cf. above, Ep. 233a.

do not regard God alone in divine matters. However, I am satisfied and comforted, for I understand from my lords, that this business will be brought
before the *Schöffen*[8] and citizens. I have asked humbly for this, and am still
pleading that the honourable council may announce this officially and set a
date for the confrontation between the devil and God's glory, earthly fear
and earthly comfort, before the *Schöffen* or assembled guilds as soon as possible and that Your Graces act upon it. Loyally admonish your subjects and
point them to God, as is the duty of rulers and men in office, to whom I
herewith commend myself obediently, and ask them in a friendly manner
to consider what God's honour, the continued welfare of the city and the
urgent need of the poor people demand, for we do not know how we can
support them without violating God's honour and causing dissent among
the common citizens, which God may forfend. Amen.

Your Graces' obedient servant,
Wolfgang Capito.

Letter 376:

This letter has been renumbered. It is now 363a.

Letter 377: [3 January 1529, Strasbourg], Capito to Nicolaus Kniebs

Printed in Rott, *Investigationes* I, 282.

[*Summary*]: All God-fearing men seek Kniebs' support in their quest to have
the mass abolished. He hopes that he will present the matter in a persuasive
manner to the *Schöffen* [on 4 January, cf. above, Ep. 375, note 8]. A decision
needs to be made. The city must either endorse the papists or shut them out.

Letter 377a: [Between 7 and 15 January 1529, Strasbourg], The Strasbourg Preachers to the City Council of Strasbourg

Printed in CorrBucer 3:222–4, Ep. 215.

[*Summary*]: The imprisoned Anabaptists Jacob Kautz and Wilhelm Reublin
have met with Johann Sturm and Franz Bertsch. Since they are respected
men, the preachers ask that they be allowed to address a select group of

* * * * *

8 Cf. Ep. 377 below. The *Schöffen* voted for the abolition of the mass on 20 February 1529.

learned or interested people or to submit their beliefs in writing. They furthermore ask permission for a public disputation. [The request was rejected.]

Letter 377b: 23 January [1529, Strasbourg], The Strasbourg Preachers to the City Council of Strasbourg

Printed in CorrBucer 3:224–40, Ep. 216.

[*Summary*]: In response to a submission [by Kautz and Reublin on 15 January; see above, Ep. 377a], the preachers declare that the division between the visible and invisible church is not based on Scripture. The church of the elect is visible and recognizable by the fruit it bears. It is based on the Word of God and on the two sacraments of baptism (of children) and the Lord's Supper (interpreted in the spiritual sense). Kautz does not want ministers of the Word bound by loyalities to any city, but this recommendation applies only to the apostles; their [own] mission is to improve the people of Strasbourg. Kautz accuses the preachers of being unwilling to take up the cross, but only God can judge their intentions. The true fruit of faith is peace; suffering for one's beliefs is not a 'fruit of faith' – even Jews and Turks are willing to die for their beliefs. The preachers object at length to the Anabaptists' arguments in favour of adult baptism. Nevertheless, they ask the council to move Kautz and Reublin from prison to a private house to allow them to regain strength. Once they are restored to health, the preachers would like to interrogate them and discuss their beliefs further.

Letter 377c: 4 February 1529, Strasbourg, The Chapter of St Thomas to Balthasar Mercklin

The original autograph of this letter is in AST 22 (5–6). The letter concerns payments negotiated between the chapter and the Catholic party, which had seceded in 1525. It is addressed to Mercklin in his capacity as vice-chancellor of the Empire. His authority is also invoked by Nicolaus Wurmser, cf. below, Ep. 386a. For Mercklin, see CWC I, Ep. 55, note 3.

Most reverend prince, gracious lord, first we most studiously offer our obedient and willing service to your princely Grace.

Gracious lord, we have received with due reverence and taken cognizance of Your Princely Grace's letter dated the last day of January,[1] con-

* * * * *

1 Not extant.

cerning Petrus Wickram,[2] summissary of our collegiate church. In reply, we ask Your Princely Grace to hear our well-meaning and subservient opinion: the above-mentioned Dr Petrus has no difficulties or quarrels or discussions about debts with us, as far as we know. We came to agreeable terms with him in Offenburg, as we did with our other fellow-canons of the collegiate church who left [Strasbourg]. The terms of our agreement were as follows: in settlement of all his demands for the years past he would be paid 80 gulden, from which anything he had received previously should be deducted.[3] We shall leave it at that, gracious lord, since the last article of our Offenburg contract has been confirmed and ratified by Your Grace in a document drawn up later.[4] (Article Number Twelve says that the contract discussed and agreed upon by the appointed parties, Johann Bock,[5] Jacob Sturm,[6] Claus Meyger,[7] and Nikolaus Wencker, *Schultheiss* at Offenburg,[8] is and shall remain in force). Should the repeatedly mentioned Dr Petrus wish to make new and different demands on us, and should he inform us of them, we hope to reach an agreement with him, that Your Princely Grace may be spared the effort and be relieved of the work and negotiations. We are most grateful to Your Grace for your recent efforts and labour, and wish to show our obedience and goodwill. We and our collegiate church remain at the command of Your Princely Grace. Strasbourg, 4 February 1529.

Your Princely Grace's obedient and willing servants,

The provost, vice-dean, and chapter of St Thomas at Strasbourg.

Letter 378: 13 February 1529, Basel, Johannes Oecolampadius to Capito

Printed in BrOek 2:280–84, Ep. 636.

[*Summary*]: There has been an uprising. The people occupied the main plaza and guild offices after the city council refused to give in to the requests of the preachers. Two councillors fled. Johannes Irmi spoke on behalf of the people. While the council deliberated about the reinstatement of [the cathe-

* * * * *

2 On Petrus Wickram, see CWC 1, Ep. 72 headnote.
3 Cf. the contract signed in Offenburg on 27 March 1528, AST 22(5–6), which mentions that sum and provision.
4 Perhaps a reference to the official statement in AST 22(5–6), 18 March 1528. Cf. also Wurmser's mention of the confirmation below, Ep. 386.
5 For Johann Bock, see above, Ep. 191, note 3.
6 For Jacob Sturm, see CWC 1, Ep. 48 headnote.
7 Not identified.
8 Cf. Ep. 243a headnote.

dral preacher] Tilman Limperger, armed members of the public entered the cathedral and began destroying the images. Ignoring the warnings of the councillors, they moved on to other churches. At last the council gave in to the demands of the people and removed twelve councillors: [the mayor, Heinrich] Meltinger, [Lux] Ziegler, Bernhard Meyer, [Hans] Egloff Offenburg, [Hans] Oberriedt, [Hans] Lucas Iselin, Hans zum Brunn, Franz Baer, Andreas Bischoff, [Hans Murer] Silberberger, Johannes Stoltz, and [Kaspar] Thurneysen. Afterwards, it was decreed to remove the images from the churches and to abolish the mass. Peace was restored. The people did not steal money; they vented their fury only on the images. They heaped them on nine pyres and burned them. Representatives from Zurich, Bern, and Solothurn are present in the city. Oecolampadius fears more tumults. His enemies call him the source of the evil. [Heinrich] Glareanus is preparing to leave and take his students to Freiburg [he left on 20 February and obtained a position as teacher of poetry at the university]. Ludwig Baer has already left [for Freiburg]. Oecolampadius sends greetings to Bucer and Hedio. He fears for the life of his son Eusebius [d. 1541], who is in poor health.

Letter 379: 21 February 1529, Strasbourg, Capito to Ambrosius Blaurer

Printed in Schiess 1: 183, Ep. 137. For Blaurer see above, Ep. 192 headnote.

Grace and peace, dearest brother. Yesterday the mass was abolished here on the majority vote of the Three Hundred.[1] Thanks to the Lord, who has finally enabled us to disdain the empty threats of the tyrants. We shall write soon of the tricks the adversary will use to impede us. For when I realized that there was someone who could conveniently bring this message to you, the messenger was already at the point of departure. We hope the remainder will go well. All the best. Farewell with your brethren and the whole church. Strasbourg, 21 February, in the year 1529.
     Capito.

Letter 380: 6 March 1529, Basel, Johannes Oecolampadius to Capito

Printed in BrOek 2:285–7, Ep. 639.

[*Summary*]: He is jubilant that the mass has been abolished in Strasbourg

* * * * *

1 I.e., the *Schöffen*. Cf. above, Epp. 375, 377.

[see above, Ep. 379]. He asks Capito whether he knows of a dedicated man to send to Solothurn to fight for the cause of the gospel. There are citizens and some members of the nobility who will protect him. [Kaspar Schaller], the city scribe of Basel, will soon travel to Strasbourg [cf. Ep. 382 below] to discuss this matter with them. He hopes that, by that time, they will have a candidate prepared to go to Solothurn. He is glad that Bucer has written to Philip of Hesse [concerning plans to organize a colloquy]. His father is well; he praises his wife's character; his son [Eusebius] is sickly. Konrad [Hubert] will travel to Strasbourg in the following week. He sends his greetings to Bucer.

Letter 381: 15 March 1529, [Strasbourg], Capito to Ulrich Zwingli

Printed in ZwBr 4:71–2, Ep. 821.

[*Summary*]: Capito has heard of Christopher's[1] complaint against the Swiss confederacy. He alludes to the difficulties of the preachers in Strasbourg and the delegates at the Diet of Speyer. They will send [Johann] Mantel and [Melchior Ambach] when the former returns from Würtemberg at Easter. The bearer of the letter will tell Zwingli whom they have in mind for Solothurn. He has dipped into Zwingli's commentary on Isaiah [*Complanatio Isaiae*, Zurich: Froschauer, 1529] and approves of it, but asks him not to neglect the Hebrew commentaries.

Letter 381a: [Middle to end of March 1529, Strasbourg], The Strasbourg Preachers to the City Council of Strasbourg

The text of this letter is in BDS 2, 411–12 (= CorrBucer 3:252–4, Ep. 220). Capito first raised the matter of the location of Bucer's residence in December 1528 (see above, Ep. 374). A request to obtain another house for Bucer was presented to the council around 3 March (cf. CorrBucer 3:249, Ep. 218).

[*Summary*]: Bucer and Capito have been lecturing daily on theology [at the Dominican monastery]. Bucer, however, lives a fair distance from the monastery [i.e., at St Aurelia]. His other duties leave him short of time, and he cannot afford to lose time on commuting. The preachers therefore request

* * * * *

1 The printer Christopher Froschauer (cf. Eid. Absch. IV 1 b, 88 ff.) or Christophe Ballista, who had been sent to Aigle by Zwingli (see below, Ep. 389).

that he be given accommodation closer to the monastery. His presence is also needed in discussions concerning the Anabaptists.

Letter 382: 29 March 1529, [Strasbourg], Capito to Ulrich Zwingli

Printed in ZwBr 4:84–6, Ep. 827a.

[*Summary*]: [Johann] Mantel and [Melchior] Ambach [see above, Ep. 380] will tell Zwingli of the conditions in Strasbourg. They will soon find a suitable candidate for Solothurn. Capito assures Zwingli of the loyalty of the Strasbourgers and alludes to the alliance planned by Philip of Hesse. Oecolampadius can tell Zwingli more. The Basel city scribe, [Kaspar Schaller], was recently in Strasbourg [cf. above, Ep. 380]. At the [second Diet of] Speyer there was a fierce debate about banning the Zwinglians and the Anabaptists. The two 'heresies' were being treated as one. Mantel will tell Zwingli the rest. Thirty-nine Anabaptists have recently been imprisoned; rumour has it that another eighteen have been seized today. [Hedio, Bucer, and Zell laid a formal complaint against the Anabaptists before the council on 20 March]. Capito asks Zwingli's pardon for his recent remarks about the latter's commentary on Isaiah – they were based on the judgment of others.[1]

Letter 383: [Between 15 March and 9 April 1529, Strasbourg], Capito to Nicolaus Kniebs

The manuscript of this letter is in AST 40, #42, f. 410. For the dating see below, note 1. On Kniebs see above, Ep. 184 headnote.

Worthy, wise sir. It is up to you to consider my friendly request and to effect, first, that the worthy council send a message to the congregation of St Aurelia about the change in the parishes, and address them in a calm and friendly manner in their name to make them comply peacefully and willingly. Otherwise, there is the risk that the congregation of St Aurelia will appeal to you, my lords, asking to retain Bucer, etc.[1]

Secondly, please support our request that the worthy council assign the

* * * * *

1 Cf. above, Ep. 381, but the phrasing would indicate that Capito made specific suggestions, perhaps in a letter now lost.

1 Cf. above, Epp. 374 and 381a, a request to have Bucer moved. Bucer became pastor at St Thomas on 9 April 1529.

stipend of Georg[2] to the collegiate church of St Thomas for the time being, that is, until they may obtain a benefice to further finance the position. In this manner, Bucer's work, industry, and grave expense can be taken care of, as required by his need and his routine. He, in turn, will loyally promote God and the community, as he has properly done so far.

Thirdly, there is no accommodation for Bucer other than the small house of Dr Sebastian,[3] which has only one room in which he is supposed to live with his children and to study, which is quite impossible. And it is not convenient to move Master Anton,[4] for he should remain in residence near the parish. But if the collegiate church is accommodated in the matter of Georg's pension, I would attempt to find a solution in the matter of accommodation myself.

Fourthly, I ask that you consider Dr Sebastian, who has always served zealously and shown good will and loyalty concerning the honour of God and the well-being of the community. For it behooves you, as Christian men and magistrates, my dear sirs, to provide for his upkeep, or at least to see that he can live in the Gutenleutenhaus[5] at a gulden a week. If the worthy council makes other provisions on its own account, they will act honestly and in a praiseworthy manner, and will give evidence that they consider without prompting the effort of a good man of merit, which will make others more willing to serve, although everyone should give first consideration to God.

Fifthly, I ask that, for propriety's sake, a positive reply be given to the collegiate church of St Thomas, that they may set this in motion on Monday and the honour of God and the advantage of the community may thereby be furthered – as I reported to my lords in person in so many words. May you act to please God and honest citizens.

Your Wolfgang Capito, willing to oblige you.

* * * * *

2 The request was granted, cf. below Ep. 384a. Georg Hoffmann, provincial of the conventual Franciscans of Upper Germany, residing in Strasbourg, died at the beginning of 1529. After the dissolution of the monastery in September 1525, Hoffmann was given a pension of 50 florins. That pension was granted to Bucer on 19 May 1529.

3 Sebastian Meyer (or Major, 1465–1545) was a former Franciscan with a doctorate in theology from the University of Freiburg. He taught in the Franciscan monastery at Strasbourg, became preacher in Bern in 1521, was expelled for his reformist leanings in 1524, and returned to Strasbourg. From 1529–31 he was chaplain of the hospice Gutenleutenhaus. From 1531–5 he was in Augsburg, from 1536–41 in Bern, and finally resettled in Strasbourg.

4 Anton Firn (cf. CWC 1, Ep. 171 headnote). Firn, who had been pastor of St Thomas, stayed on as Bucer's assistant.

5 Cf. above, note 3.

Letter 383a: [End of March/beginning of April 1529, Strasbourg], The Strasbourg Preachers to a Commission of the Council

Printed CorrBucer 3:259–61, Ep. 222a. The commission addressed here had been charged with replacing the mass with other services.

[*Summary*]: The cathedral chapter, as well as the chapters of Young and Old St Peter, object to the new service, whereas the chapter of St Thomas is cooperative. Therefore, St Thomas should be allowed to arrange for daily obligatory Latin instruction in biblical studies prior to the sermon in the cathedral. This programme will serve as training for future preachers. Thus, St Thomas will set an example to the other chapters and follow the example of Wittenberg, Marburg, Zurich, and Basel. The preachers furthermore suggest afternoon instruction in Greek and Hebrew.

Letter 384: 13 April 1529, Liegnitz (Legnica), Valentin Crautwald to Capito and his colleagues.

Printed in QGT 7: 237, #182a and CorrBucer 3:264, Ep. 224.

[*Summary*]: Although Crautwald had decided some time ago to recommend Schwenckfeld [cf. above, Ep. 362], he has only now found the time to do so. When Schwenckfeld arrives in Strasbourg, he will be 'a living letter.'

Letter 384a: 14 April 1529, [Strasbourg], The Chapter of St Thomas to the City Council of Strasbourg

Printed in CorrBucer 3:265–8, Ep. 224b.

[*Summary*]: The chapter has received the church order from the council [sent on 10 April; cf. AST 80, #27] and will obey it. That is, they will (1) have a lecture in the morning and will eventually institute afternoon instruction in Greek and Hebrew [cf. above, Ep. 383a]. At this point, Bucer and Capito cannot undertake this additional work because the latter is in poor health and the former does not have the energy. Hedio and Sebastian Meyer [cf. above, Ep. 383 note 3] should be delegated to help them. (2) The council suggested reading a text from scripture, followed by a Latin exposition; the preachers suggest a prayer or psalm of the reader's choice instead. (3) They would like Bucer's salary to be raised, and ask that they may be allowed to use the pension of the late Georg Hoffmann for this purpose. [Cf. above, Ep. 383, note 2; this request was granted 19 May 1529.]

Letter 385: 19 April 1529, Strasbourg, Capito to Johannes Oecolampadius

Printed in BrOek 2:318–19, Ep. 655.

[*Summary*]: Capito is concerned about the church in Basel. They are sending Bonifacius [Wolfhart] to assist Oecolampadius. His own preference would have been to send Wolfhart to Solothurn, but the Strasbourgers were against it. Hedio will replace Wolfhart as Hebrew teacher. Writing in code [see also above, Epp. 309, 314], he refers to Ferdinand's pact with the Catholic Swiss cities. He has heard that there is much disagreement at the Diet of Speyer. There is talk of a colloquy on the Sacramentarian question and of restoring the old rites. He prays for a good outcome.

Letter 386: 19 April 1529, [Strasbourg], Capito to Ulrich Zwingli

Printed in ZwBr 4:104–7, Ep. 835.

[*Summary*]: It is difficult to find good preachers. Zurich has only the one Zwingli. Capito regards it as a compliment that Zwingli has proposed him as preacher for Memmingen, but he feels that he owes it to his congregation to remain with them. They will soon send Jakob Otter, who may serve in Solothurn or in Memmingen. [Johann] Mantel, who is of advanced age, will make a good assistant. There are many capable men in Strasbourg, but he hesitates to recommend them for such a challenging position. For Memmingen, he would like someone who can assist, but is not inferior to, Simprecht Schenck. He is glad to hear that Johann Heinrich Winkeli, [formerly] prefect of Dornach, has embraced the Reformation. He has no serious criticism of Zwingli's commentary on Isaiah [cf. above, Ep. 382], although he differs with him in a few points. 'But words do not matter so much, as long as each man attempts to observe the rule of the Spirit.' He has dined with Johann Caspar von Bubenhofen, a worthy man, who will report to Zwingli what cannot safely be entrusted to a letter. Capito hopes for a good outcome [of Bubenhofen's lengthy lawsuit now before the courts]. Zwingli will hear the rest of the news from Basel. He refers in coded language to the difficulties of the Basel church.

Letter 386a: 25 April 1529, Offenburg, Nicolaus Wurmser to the Chapter of St Thomas

The manuscript of this letter is in AST 22 (5–6).

Reverend and most learned lords, in an agreement drawn up and established between the honourable council of Strasbourg on the one hand and the provost, dean, and the persons attached to the three collegiate churches residing outside of Strasbourg on the other hand, it is stated that the contract drawn up at Offenburg[1] between the persons of the collegiate church of St Thomas, residing in or outside the city, will remain in force. This contract expressly states that the exiles are guaranteed payment of their past personal stipends and residency fees, as noted in the appended invoice, to be paid to them and to their heirs. The contract also provides for future payments, as required, for personal stipends and residency, and to pay to the best of your ability in case of prohibitions, arrests, wars, and other such difficulties. And although we sent delegates to Speyer, who were properly furnished with a directive from us concerning the recent agreement, the honourable council would not allow them to bring the matter to a conclusion and put their seal to it before you have signed and sealed it. Still, Jacob Sturm,[2] my lord and father, and also some priests and the *Altammeister*[3] promised and pledged before the most reverend prince and lord, Balthasar,[4] Bishop of Malta, and His Majesty the Roman Emperor's commissary and ambassador, that he would do so on our request, and I have no doubt that he will. I therefore humbly and earnestly beg Your Reverend Lordships, that you will act on this in writing without delay and name a suitable place for a meeting, to hear the matter and seal it, that we may draw up an account as soon as possible and that the collegiate church be aided thus, which we all ought to be inclined to do. And although I do not anticipate a rejection of my request, I nevertheless ask that you give me an answer in writing[5] and send it to me at Offenburg, that I may know how to act. Given at Offenburg, Cantate Sunday, 25 April, in the year 1529.

Letter 387: 28 April 1529, [Strasbourg], Capito to Ulrich Zwingli

Printed in ZwBr 4:112–13, Ep. 837.

[*Summary*]: The Strasbourgers have sent Jakob Otter to Solothurn on the request of [Caspar Schaller] the city scribe of Basel. Alternatively he could join Simprecht Schenck in Memmingen [see above Ep. 386]. Capito refers cryptically to a fortunate occasion allowing them 'to undo the chains and alliance

* * * * *

1 For the contract signed in Offenburg, see above, Ep. 237 headnote.
2 On Jacob Sturm, see CWC 1, Ep. 48 headnote.
3 I.e., Nicolaus Kniebs, see above, Ep. 184 headnote.
4 On Mercklin, cf. CWC 1, Ep. 55, note 3.
5 The answer was given in Ep. 398b below.

concluded with impious men in bad faith.' A letter from Christian Fridbold, [representative of St Gallen at the Diet of Speyer], will tell more about their hopes. Martin [Germanus] has accepted Zwingli's teaching and will travel to Zurich to speak with him personally. Bucer sends his greetings.

Letter 388: [Before 10 May 1529, Strasbourg, Capito to Guillaume Farel]

> The text of this letter, an autograph, is in Zurich SA E II 446, f. 73r–74v. For Farel, see above, Ep. 347 headnote. Some of the references in the footnotes have been supplied by Stephen Burnett and Debra Kaplan.

Greetings in the Lord. I now know what you wish to know about the Jewish custom of burying. Twenty years ago, I saw a copy of that ominous shroud[1] at the Carthusians in Freiburg-im-Breisgau. It is a ridiculous fraud and has recently begun to make the rounds, so that I now am reminded that I heard of it then. Therefore, I shall describe the burial practice observed by German Jews; then, how it squares with the age of Christ and the subsequent centuries; finally, what affinity that nonsense of a superstition has with the evangelists, although you do not need me to do that. Yesterday, I listened to the account of a Jew,[2] reporting as you will see in the following:

1. The body is moved from the bed and placed on a sheet spread on straw or on the paved floor.
2. After the body has become cold enough, it is carefully cleansed with tepid water, but only the part that is being washed is uncovered – that is to say, they handle the body with modesty.
3. The white of one or two eggs, thickened with water, is smeared across the entire head, because this tends to give it brightness and sheen.

* * * * *

1 After the Fall of Constantinople in 1453, numerous unauthenticated relics were brought to the west, among them, purported burial shrouds of Christ. The most famous example is the Shroud of Turin, which in the sixteenth century belonged to the House of Savoy. It was kept at their castle in Chambéry until 1578, when it was moved to Turin.
2 Perhaps Josel of Rosheim (1478–1554), a leader of the Alsatian Jewish community. His representations to the emperor led to a certificate of rights for German Jews in 1544. He attended some of Capito's lectures in Strasbourg. See S. Stern, *Josel of Rosheim: Commander of Jewry in the Holy Roman Empire of the German Nation*, trans. G. Hirschler, (Philadelphia, 1965), 178.

4. Presently, they put [on the corpse] a long under-tunic, extending all the way down to the feet; linen socks are pulled over the feet; the head above is wound with a linen headband, as used by sleepers.

5. A linen shawl is placed on the body and another garment is put on top of that, in accordance with the Law. The Jews call this linen shawl a *tallith*,[3] a four-sided linen cloth with phylacteries at its four corners, in Hebrew *tzitzith*.[4]

6. A linen sheet is placed on the bier or casket, which is buried with the body. It is wrapped around the whole body, after it has been prepared in the aforesaid manner. The hands are fully stretched out and laid close to the sides of the body, which lies flat on its back, with the face turned upwards.

7. After the body is washed, the eyes and mouth are closed; on both eyes is placed either a small piece of pottery or a small rock or a small chunk of earth, and a stone is placed under the chin to keep the mouth shut.

8. They then close the whole bier or coffin, in which lies the body so that no earth can befoul what they regard as sacrosanct relics. So much about burials of this day and age.

9. Furthermore, if the person was killed by force, they must bury him as he was found, omitting the rest of the ceremonies; similarly a woman who has died in childbirth or a priest[5] are buried unwashed, etc.[6]

I shall now enumerate the points in which this custom agrees with that of the ancients and the source of the changes, as I see them:

1. They now remove the body from the bed and place it on the straw; formerly, the funerary bier was to be overturned. The prescription runs: *avel hayav be-kefiat ha-mitah*, that is, 'the mourner is required to turn the bier over' (that motion represents not simply a turning over, but dejection and distress). For they seem to indicate by such a ceremony that the dead person may go to another place.[7]

* * * * *

3 The term is given in Hebrew script and in transliteration.
4 Num. 15:38–9. The term is given in Hebrew script and in transliteration.
5 Capito writes the Hebrew term, *kohen*, in Hebrew script.
6 The information in the nine points enumerated here closely parallels *Shulhan Arukh, Yoreh Deah* 364 (Kitsur Shulhan Arukh 197–9). For Capito's use of this work, see below, note 8.
7 Cf. Talmud, *Moed katan*, 26b–27a.

2. They wait for the body parts to cool down. For it has been especially prescribed that they should not disturb a living soul in any way or minister to it through funeral rites, that is, they should not wash the body, or anoint it or close its eyes, etc. Otherwise it will be regarded as homicide, according to the author of the book, *Yoreh Deah*.[8] Washing is done in place of purification.

3. In this day and age, the head and face are washed in wine and crushed egg white, which seems to be done in place of anointing. For in the land of Israel, they were enjoined to anoint the dead body with perfumed and aromatic balms.[9]

4. The ancients did not clothe the body in the clothing of those living, *ela malbushim tachrichin bishtan*,[10] but clothed them in wrappings made of bandages. So says Maimonides in book 14.[11] This can also be seen in the burial of Lazarus and Christ in the gospel of John.[12] It is relevant to know that a *tachrichin*[13] is a wrapping-up of the whole body, except for the head, just as the *atiphath*[14] is for the head (this is found in *Maseches Moed Katan*).[15] After the time of

* * * * *

8 *Tur, Yoreh Deah* 339 (Kitsur Shulhan Arukh 194, 4). The author, Ya'akov ben Asher (1270–1340), was the son of the great Jewish legalist, Asher ben Yechiel, with whom he studied. He grew up in Germany, living within the Ashkenazi tradition, which challenged many of the positions of Maimonides. In 1303, he and his father moved to Toledo, Spain. Ya'akov ben Asher wrote a comprehensive commentary on the Torah, to which he added numerous *gematriot*, numerical insights into the text. *Yoreh Deah* was a part of his major work, a legal code called the *Arba'ah Turim*, the Four Rows. It divided Jewish law into four sections: *Orach Chayim, Yoreh Deah, Even Ha-Ezer,* and *Choshen Mishpat. Yoreh Deah* covered dietary laws, usury, idolatry, and mourning.

9 Rema, *Yoreh Deah* 352 (Kitsur Shulhan Arukh 197, 4) mentions the egg and wine mixture.

10 The phrase is given in Hebrew and transliteration. It means 'these are the garments of shrouds made from linen.'

11 Moses Maimonides (1135–1204) or Rabbi Moshe ben Maimon (Rambam), renowned physician and scholar, was born in Cordoba, Spain. To avoid persecution under the Muslims, his family fled first to Morocco, later to Israel, and finally to Egypt. Maimonides is the author of the *Guide to the Perplexed* and the *Review of the Torah (Mishneh Torah)*, a law code, which became the standard guide to Jewish practices and may be regarded as the most important work in the post-Talmudic period. Book 14 of Maimonides' code (trans. A.M. Herschman New Haven, 1949, 1740) mentions only a simple shroud.

12 For Lazarus, John 11:44, and for Jesus, John 19:38–40 and 20:6–7.

13 The term is given in Hebrew and transliteration.

14 The term is given in Hebrew and transliteration.

15 The title appears in transliteration.

Christ, the custom was to leave free and bare the head of the rich who had died from a natural cause, but they ruled that the head of a person who has been killed be covered to hide the shame and ugliness, especially if they had died a horrible death; for in the case of suicides and those who have died a violent death, vestiges of grief appear on their faces. Their faces appeared wrapped up in a separate piece of suitable linen and sewn together at the top, as can be seen anywhere if one reads anything about the history of the Hebrew people. Therefore, the body of our Lord was not veiled in the way that your superstitious shroud claims. The author of that lie did not notice (whoever was the first one to make it up) that Peter meant that a small cloth was placed apart from the linen sheet, for the gospel writer calls it a *sudarium* [sweat cloth] in Latin, because it covered the face.[16] For you generally wipe the sweat (*sudor*) off your face with a piece of cloth, which is why that type of cloth is called a *sudarium* in Latin. It is the equivalent of the one used to veil the head and cover the face.

5. But they tie a linen shawl around the undershirt; they used to sew it together with a linen thread. The shroud itself is carefully wrapped around the body, a tradition Rabbi Moses the Spaniard[17] handed down in the book *Shofetim*,[18] under the title *Avel*.[19] A *tallith* is a linen cloth which has four corners to which are attached notes of the Law. They used to place that type of vestment upon the top of the body. Rabbi Nathan seems to explain this.[20] For the dead will rise in the future in the same clothes in which they were buried. The Jews, therefore, want to be buried in an honourable and holy vestment. That is the superstition of the Jews, which I do not begrudge telling you, especially a judicious brother like you, keen to learn about their history. For this reason, John writes that Peter saw the linen cloths lying there. They sewed up the body in a linen bandage, but they wrapped the sewn-up body in another linen

* * * * *

16 John 20:7.

17 Maimonides, *Mishneh Torah*, the Book of Judges (*Shofetim*), [Laws of] Mourning (*Avel*). See above, note 11.

18 The title is given in Hebrew script and transliteration.

19 The term appears only in Hebrew script.

20 R. Nathan as cited in the Jerusalem Talmud (Tractate Kilaim, ch. 9, halakha 3, p. 32, col. b; Tractate Ketuboth, ch. 23, halakha 3, p. 35, col. a; this is cited in the Tur, *Yoreh Deah* 352, where Capito may have seen it). On burial with talit, see also *Yoreh Deah* (Kitsur Shulhan Arukh) 197, 1.

bandage, which is a *tallith*.[21] Otherwise, the evangelist would have written *linteamen* [sing.] and not *linteamina* [plural].

6. The hands are placed flat against the sides, like someone lying down quietly. This was commanded in the Talmud in *Moed Katan*.[22]

I shall now sum up briefly fraudulent claims. It is not a *sudarium*, as the mystagogues call it, for a *sudarium* does not apply to the body; nor is the shroud said to refer to the face but to coverings of the body. It is not a *tachrichin*[23] or a covering of the body, for that was bound very tightly to the body. It is written in the passage of the Talmud cited in the *Perek ve'Eilu Megalchin*[24] that two people bestowed their efforts on looking after the corpse, one to wrap up the body in linen, and the other to tie the knots, that is, *umikascher haisch*.[25] And indeed, with all their strength they fastened that linen bandage around the body. This is apparent from the fact that they sanctioned that the body of a dead woman be wrapped up by a woman, but that it be bound by a man, so that the knots be sturdier. Therefore, because only an effigy of shoulders and chest and a bit of the shins is visible on that false shroud (*sudarium*), why do they not see the whole body they claim was pressed against it, and the position of the hands, as they are stretched out toward the feet?

When he was still alive, Gregor Reisch,[26] a Carthusian from Freiburg and visitor of the Order throughout Germany, said that it was not a *sudarium*; that [Christ's] sacrosanct body was not wrapped up in it, but was placed upon it after being taken down from the cross, before the funeral rites even

* * * * *

21 The term appears only in transliteration.
22 Cf. Kitsur Shulhan Arukh 197, 5. The title is given in Hebrew script and transliteration.
23 The term is given in Hebrew script and transliteration.
24 The title is given in Hebrew script and transliteration.
25 The term is given in Hebrew script and transliteration. This is also recorded in Tur, *Yoreh Deah* 352.
26 Gregor Reisch (c. 1467–1525) first studied at the University of Freiburg (MA, 1489) before entering the Carthusian Order. During the years 1500–2 he was prior at Klein-Basel; from 1503 to shortly before his death he was prior at Freiburg. He was also visitor for the Rhenish province of his order and confessor to Maximilian I. His chief work is the *Margarita philosophica* (Freiburg, 1503), an encyclopedia of knowledge intended as a textbook for young students. It contains in twelve books a Latin grammar, dialectics, rhetoric, arithmetic, music, geometry, astronomy, physics, natural history, physiology, psychology, and ethics. The form is catechetical: the student asks questions, and the teacher answers. The book was popular on account of its comparative brevity and accessible format.

took place. This makes little sense. For if the body had been washed in such a cloth, many bloodstains would have remained. Yet he reports, I believe, only three drops. See the second article [above]; furthermore, Mark writes: *When evening had come and since it was the Preparation*, etc.[27] He calls 'evening' the time when the sun has almost set. It was not permitted either to shave off a beard in the evening or even to continue an activity until nightfall, since it was the beginning of the Lord's Day or Sabbath. For the Passover happened on the Sabbath Day, as Mark shows. Jews do not disagree, and the order of the church observes it thus. Likewise, anything that has the appearance of work is prohibited. Moreover, it is a form of work, in fact, work proper, for Jews to wring water out of a damp cloth. Therefore, if a dead person needed care that required work from Jews on the first day of the feast, the care customarily given to persons of higher standing, it was established to see to it that the body be placed on a beam or plank without covering it with a linen cloth, as in article [1] above. Instead, they covered the body to be washed with straw, and rubbed it and cleansed it [in that manner] to avoid wringing out the moistened linen. This is called *le-sehita*.[28] So writes Rabbi Israel in his book entitled *Pesaschim U-Khetavim*,[29] and before him, Rabbi Mordecai.[30] Thus, what is not permitted on the feast day is prohibited on the eve as well, a custom honest men would not readily have disregarded without reason. The Feast was approaching; therefore all actions were done in headlong haste, and they took care not even to embark on any work. Furthermore, this was all done out of consideration for Christ's dignity, for Joseph and Nicodemus were disciples of Christ, who regarded him very highly and looked up to him as one [who was] more than man.[31] Therefore, it is not likely that they would have abandoned his true praise and busied themselves in vain triflings, such as the shroud. If it were true, they would have been occupied with the preservation [of his reputation]. The Gemara says,[32] for the sake

* * * * *

27 Mark 15:42.
28 The term is given in Hebrew script and transliteration. The correct term is *sehita* (no *le* prefix). It refers to the prohibition of wringing out wet cloths on the Sabbath.
29 I.e., *Pesakim U'Ketavim* 5 (title given in Hebrew and transliteration) of Rabbi Israel ben Petahia Isserlin (1390–1460), a Talmud scholar, born in Regensburg. Isserlin was forced to flee persecution and settled near Vienna.
30 Mordecai ben Hillel (c. 1250–98), German legal authority and author of a commentary on the Talmud.
31 Joseph of Aramethea and Nicodemus oversaw the preparation and assumed the costs for Jesus' burial, cf. Mark 15:42–7 and John 19:38–42.
32 The Aramaic gemara (meaning complement) is a commentary on the Mishna and part of the Talmud.

of honour, a message should be placed at the head, where mention of the deceased and mention of his good deeds is made, but lasting fame will, in any case, outlive an illustrious man. What have those [who are] taught about spiritual matters to do with the worthless remains and relics of a dead person, when they will later only recognize [Jesus] sitting at the right hand of the Father? Are we to believe that such great men were occupied with such frivolous triflings? It certainly does not seem that Christ taught this to his followers. From these things you may construct the strongest proofs with your skilful mind, comparing, if you have leisure, Jewish practices with those of the evangelists. I shall give an account of the rest to make the entire burial procedure comprehensible.

The eyes and mouth are closed; among the ancients the nostrils were, moreover, blocked up with a small amount of earth. So the ancient tradition says, which is derived from this [text] of Genesis, and thus they conform with it: *Dust you are*, etc.[33] Furthermore, it is written in the Jerusalem Talmud that the often-mentioned Rabbi wanted the bier used in the funeral pierced and perforated underneath, because that would be in accordance with the precept *keburath karka*,[34] that is, a burial of earth or a basis of the earth. For *karka*, soil, is not *afar* [dust],[35] as Ya'akov ben Asher writes in chapter 374 of book 2. For this reason they place earth on the eyes and mouth, and then upon the entire prepared body, but only a little. After this, they cover the body to be buried with a flat piece of wood,[36] so that no soil may defile the body, for it is regarded a disgrace to the deceased if it is immediately defiled by earth. These are the great absurdities in which the unfortunate superstition persists.

Letter 389: 10 May 1529, Aigle, Guillaume Farel to Capito

Printed in Herminjard 2: 177–80, #257. For Farel, see above, Ep. 347 headnote.

Greeting, grace and peace in God. May he shine his light more fully on the world, lest the heart, which is one, be divided into fingers, hands, feet, eyes, noses, ears, and arms, and lest the variety make the beginning manifold.[1]

* * * * *

33 Gen. 3:19.
34 The terms are given in Hebrew script and transliteration. The reference to the Jerusalem Talmud is from Tractate Kilaim, chapter 9, halakha 3, p. 32, column a.
35 The two terms are given in Hebrew script.
36 Cf. *Yoreh Deah* (Kitsur Shulhan Arukh) 197, 5.

1 A vague reference to 1 Cor. 12:4–27.

I have read what you have gathered with such effort concerning the burial of the Jews.[2] And this superstition, diverging far from the truth and vain itself, assumes the right to condemn the vanity and impiety of the idolaters! I am grateful for your labour, for I know it was very tedious. I read the passage in the book you suggested to me,[3] but I guessed more than understood what you are about. I wonder that those acute dissecters[4] have not progressed further. Our friend Cellarius has cut the knot for us and explained it very clearly.[5] How bright the light would shine if all devoted themselves to the glory of God and to charity toward their brethren! Instead, they attack their brethren with evil intent, trampling on the lamb and muddling the waters. May God settle the strife.

I don't know what to write about Christophe.[6] A great, soft belly cannot be satisfied with a few hard crusts. But he came to live here two months ago, crying for the cowl and saying that he would gladly return to it, perhaps in the hope that we would pay more attention to him and try to tie him to us, or perhaps because he really wants to return to the monastery. I see no signs of truthfulness in him. He has been sent to the neighbouring region.[7] I can only communicate with him by letter; I see him rarely. May the Father who is omnipotent move his heart and mind that he may devote himself wholly to serving the gospel! If we cannot report anything positive, we can at least say that, in this manner, the wolf has been cast out.[8] Guillaume, Marguerite's husband,[9] has come here, solicitous about Christ, and zealously preaches the Word. Other brethren are joining in the work as well, and I hear the neighbours are seeking a minister of the Word,[10] but I am afflicted by a number of ills and dare not invite anyone. I only pray to the Father and Lord of the harvest that he will provide us with labourers,[11] which he will easily do,

* * * * *

2 Cf. above, Ep. 388.
3 Capito cited a number of authorities in Ep. 388. It is unclear which book Farel had in mind.
4 A reference to Jewish commentators?
5 For Martin Cellarius' *De operibus Dei*, see Capito's introduction above, Ep. 335.
6 Christophe Arbaleste (Ballista), a physician of Paris, fled to Strasbourg where he made the acquaintance of Bucer and Capito. He practised medicine in Zurich for a while, then accepted a position as pastor in Chessel in 1528.
7 I.e., Chessel.
8 I.e., the Catholic priest; cf. Farel's letter to Bucer (CorrBucer 3, 277, Ep. 228): 'At least we achieve our goal: the wolves are kept away by the merchants.'
9 Little is known about Guillaume Du Moulin, an ex-monk from Flanders and a colleague of Farel in 1528/29. He became pastor of Noville in 1529.
10 I.e., the Pays de Vaud.
11 Cf. Matt. 9:38; Luke 10:2. Farel uses the word *extrudere* for 'provide,' following Erasmus' usage in his *Paraphrase* on Luke 10:2.

whereas human beings can achieve nothing, even by working themselves to death.

I have heard that Pierre Toussain[12] has been called by the people of Metz. I would rejoice if he brought forth any fruit there, preaching Christ. For I cannot see what he can achieve in France, under such an insane king,[13] who permits the people being prevented from reading the New Testament, thus being deprived of any means of learning the Truth. No books, no teachers show them the way. The almighty Father knows the time, and no one can prevent him from perfecting his will. He allows his people to recognize his will more fully and to follow it in perpetuity.

Farewell, my Capito, and promote peace and concord, as you always do, so that everything comes forth into the light in its own time, in the friendly spirit of Christ. You see how many people who believe in Christ are zealous, not for the law, but for external matters and traditions – you know well what to think of them. When God opens up heaven, there will not be such contention over water and bread, nor over wheat. Once the siege is over, food will be cheap. May the Lord bring it about that his knowledge speedily fills the world. Give my regards to Cellarius and his co-workers; greetings also to your wife and your family. Aigle, 10 May 1529. Our brethren and, not least, our friend Claude[14] greet you.

Your Farel.

Letter 390: 13 May 1529, Strasbourg, Capito to Ulrich Zwingli

Printed in ZwBr 4:119–21, Ep. 840.

[Summary]: Capito uses coded language to express his fear of the machinations of the papists at the Diet of Speyer, and his disappointment about the difficult negotiations for an alliance between Zurich and Strasbourg. He hopes that there will be no public unrest. The papists are trying to foster dissent.

* * * * *

12 For Pierre Toussain, see above, Ep. 332 headnote.
13 Francis I.
14 Claude Dieudonné (Deodatus), an ex-monk from Metz and correspondent of Heinrich Agrippa. He was sent by his order to Paris, where he was associated with the circle of Jacques Lefèvre. He left his order and is perhaps identical with the pastor of Ollons (attested there 1528–32).

Letter 391: 18 May 1529, Strasbourg, Capito to Ulrich Zwingli

Printed in ZwBr 4:124–6, Ep. 842.

[*Summary*]: Caspar Schwenckfeld, who breathes the spirit of Christ, has arrived in Strasbourg. He complains about Zwingli having published his tractate on the Eucharist [*Ein anwysunge, das die opinion der leyplichen gegenwertighheyt ... ist ... widder den ynnhalt der gantzen schrifft*, written 1527, published Zurich: Froschauer 1528]. Capito uses coded language to allude to Fabri's machinations at the Diet of Speyer and his attempts to foster dissent among the reformers. Zwingli's letter [ZwBr 4, Ep. 839; the letter was sent via Strasbourg] will soon reach Philip of Hesse. Luther will be obliged to meet with Zwingli. Capito asks Zwingli to write to Schwenckfeld.

Letter 392: 12 June 1529, Worms, Peter Schöffer to Capito

Printed in QGT 7: 238–9, #185. Peter Schöffer (ca. 1480–1547), a member of the well-known family of printers in Mainz, moved to Worms in 1518, then to Strasbourg in 1529, where he collaborated with Johann Schwintzer and Matthias Apiarius. He specialized in publishing music scores.

To the most learned Wolfgang Capito, minister of the Word in Strasbourg at Young St Peter, his commanding lord, greetings in Jesus Christ.

First, my most willing service, gracious dear sir. I read your recent letter addressed jointly to me and to Johann Schwintzer,[1] and gather that he has told you about our planned collaboration in printing books. He will fully explain to you why this has been deferred until now, for we have now come to another agreement, which we shall execute next winter, if God wills it. We trust that you will help us by providing us with copy[2] and anything else that is not to your disadvantage. We, in turn, will do our best to be of service to you and your friends. May God's spirit grow in you. Given on 12 June 1529.

Your willing Peter Schöffer at Worms.

Letter 393: June 1529, [Strasbourg], Capito to the Reader

This is the preface to Caspar Schwenckfeld's *Apologia und erclerung der Schlesier* (Strasbourg: Beck, 1529), f. AIIverso–AIVverso. The text is printed in CS 3,

* * * * *

1 For Schwintzer, see above, Ep. 336 headnote.
2 *Exemplare*, i.e., manuscripts.

394–7. Caspar Schwenckfeld (1489–1561) was a descendent of a noble Silesian family. After studies in Cologne and Frankfurt/Oder, he entered the service of Duke Friedrich of Liegnitz. In 1518 after a conversion experience ('awakening of God'), he began to preach the gospel and persuaded the duke to introduce the Reformation in his territory. In 1523 he organized the pastors of regional churches, including Valentin Crautwald, in a Brotherhood for study and prayer. Schwenckfeld disagreed with Luther over the Sacramentarian question. A visit to Wittenberg in 1526 resulted in an open breach between the two men. In the following years, Schwenckfeld befriended Anabaptist groups. In 1528, Zwingli published his book on the Eucharist without authorization (see above, Ep. 391). The work aroused the ire of King Ferdinand, prompting Schwenckfeld to write the *Apologia und erclerung*, addressed to Duke Friedrich. To save the duke any embarrassment, however, he went into voluntary exile. In 1530 he wrote a criticism of the Augsburg Confession, and objected to Bucer's formula for concord between the Zwinglian and Lutheran factions. He travelled throughout southern Germany, debating doctrinal questions with preachers, and in 1533 settled in Augsburg, taking up residence with Bonifacius Wolfhart (see CWC 1, Ep. 102 headnote) and studying Hebrew. He resumed his travels in 1534. Because of his continued resistance to Bucer's plans for concord, he was ousted from Strasbourg and settled in Ulm. Predictably, he refused to accept the Wittenberg Concord of 1536. In 1539 he was forced to leave Ulm. His teachings were condemned and he remained in hiding. Taking refuge with the Laubenberg family near Kempten, he wrote his *Great Confession On the Glory of Christ*, disseminating the manuscript among the reformers. From 1542 he lived with Georg Ludwig von Freyberg at Justingen under the protection of Philip of Hesse, but continued to be attacked by Lutherans (Sebastian Coccius, Johannes Brenz). After the defeat of the League of Schmalkald and the imposition of the Interim (1547), he fled to Esslingen and was once again forced to remain in hiding. The Peace of Augsburg (1555) outlawed non-conformists like Schwenckfeld. At the Colloquy of Worms (1557) he was condemned by all parties and died in exile.

Wolfgang Capito to the Reader:

Pious, good-hearted reader, I ask that you diligently read the apologia and confession of the noble and honourable Caspar Schwenckfeld, my dear brother. Consider it and rate it according to your own God-fearing judgment. As far as I understand at this time, he addresses in it the matter of the Lord's Supper, as he stands before God with a faithful conscience. He describes, depicts, and places many things before our eyes, not only out of scripture and the sayings of the Fathers, which clearly show the error of our flesh, but also many other things based on his own thorough experience of our Christian belief, through his skill and vocation[1] and a spiritual understanding of our salvation and the meaning of our Lord Jesus Christ elevated on the cross – which, after proper judgment, no one may attack without harming himself.

Glory be to God our Father, from whom Schwenckfeld no doubt has received both an understanding of divine things and a measure of skill to bring it out for our improvement. In this piece, he provides a much-needed apologia and, in doing so, he touches in passing and with a few words on the trumped-up and slanderous accusations against him. But principally and with the greatest diligence, he aims the contents of his writing at an understanding of scripture and the knowledge of a spiritual Christ, our Lord, who is our head, our salvation, and our eternal life. I am hopeful that his modest reply will exonerate him in the eyes of the Christian prince, Duke Friedrich von Liegnitz,[2] to whom it is addressed, and principally in the eyes of His Majesty, the King of Bohemia and Hungary,[3] before whom he has been groundlessly and treacherously accused, as is explained in part here in this booklet. For quiet and peaceful innocence cannot long remain suspect before an experienced and prudent ruler. Furthermore, this will serve to contradict the malicious rumour that is being spread about us among both papists and Lutherans, as well as among general readers, namely, that we object to the eating of the blood and body of Christ in the Lord's Supper, and that we are divided among ourselves, for there is nothing in this rumour. By God's grace, we know how near or far Christ is with and in us, perhaps better than our opponents know or think they know. But let each man who reads Schwenckfeld's apologia pass judgment, weigh and judge it. Let each man speak according to his conscience and decide whether we or our opponents are dealing with these mysteries of faith more righteously, more truthfully, and more honestly. For the content of this book points to Christ and his Holy Spirit; it moves the heart, and agrees with the certainty of faith of every right-minded believer, while its opponents take refuge in the physical bread, the material word and dead letter, in the priest and the binding or loosening of other things, for which no reasonable evidence can be shown.

We are not divided into sects. We are fundamentally one in the recognition of the Truth and in agreement about it, and for this we praise and celebrate God Almighty through Jesus Christ, who has given us one heart, one mind, and one Spirit, and has given us uniform knowledge in the Holy

* * * * *

1 *Salbung*, i.e., unction, ordination.
2 I.e., Friedrich II of Liegnitz (1495–1547); the dedication letter to the duke follows Capito's preface on Aiv verso to Fiv recto.
3 I.e., Ferdinand I, in whose territory Duke Friederich's realm lay.

Spirit. Otherwise, such unity could not have come about, for we live within a circle of a hundred miles, and could not have agreed if we had depended on human counsel rather than on God and the Truth.

For what our listeners hear about these matters from us in our daily sermons, the Holy Spirit depicts in the written word through this dear brother as if through the use of a dearly-beloved tool. And this is accomplished in such a lucid and clear fashion that turbulent consciences disturbed by all manner of carnal zeal may be freed and live in peace now, for nothing is lacking in the truth and honour of Christ. Rather, a great deal of light and understanding grows and arises from the discovery of holy mysteries and from the spiritual discernment of divine things. He gives proof of this through divine power, and not only in the words of this book, as far as I have heard.

Our salvation-bearing brethren have never ceased to show us such salutary and living use of the body of Christ, and have therefore compared the sixth chapter of John with the Lord's Supper.[4] They have pointed out that the words there indicate that only Christ himself is recognized as spiritual food, which draws us closer and strengthens us for our own good. True believers are reminded of his death and its consequences as they break the bread. All of us have consistently held to the word of Christ, therefore, and have never denied it, but we have resisted with all our strength the gross error and abomination derived from his words. We have always accepted the mystery and certainty of faith, according to each man's gift and grace, for the improvement of the common good. They, on the other hand, want to give the body of Christ, who is spiritually at the right hand of God, to human beings in the form of earthly bread, to give it into their hands and to be handled by godless and condemned members of Satan. Then Zwingli and Oecolampadius got to the bottom of the matter and undertook to show the abomination and error of the belief in the corporal presence of the body of Christ in the bread at the Lord's Supper. Interpreting the words of the Lord's Supper, Zwingli says: 'est' means 'significat,' that is, 'is' stands for 'signifies,' and Oecolampadius says: 'corpus' stands for 'figura corporis,' that is, 'body' must be taken figuratively. Both men are desirous of the divine Truth and have not detracted from a clearer understanding. They have added value and context to it, insofar as it is held in this matter that the earthly bread is not the substance and body of Christ, but is rather taken as a symbol. The true bread of the Lord is recognized as that through which the hearts of believers will be led and directed beyond themselves to Christ, who himself

* * * * *

4 John 6:25–59.

is the spiritual and heavenly bread that endures for eternal life.[5] This is sufficiently indicated and explained in their own books. Schwenckfeld and the other Silesians, however, understand the demonstrative pronoun 'hoc,' the little word 'this' in the spiritual sense, saying that the mind of the believer is thereby drawn from the external to the true heavenly bread that is Christ the Lord himself. They are all in agreement concerning this interpretation, that the body of Christ is not to be understood as corporal in the actual earthly bread, nor is the body contained under the species of the bread, as the papacy teaches, but rather that he is truly in the Supper of the believers, through the word of the Holy Spirit. Just as in the natural order bread nourishes our body, so the body of Christ (broken for us in the living word, with which he is one) is heavenly bread alone (John 6)[6] and according to the spiritual order, is nourishment for the believer's soul and for true Christians. True Christians are those in whose hearts Christ the Lord lives through the true faith. They are truly fed by him spiritually in his Supper and are nourished with his body and blood to eternal life. Through the visible sacrament, or the bread of the Lord, they are admonished to remember the Lord and reminded eternally to praise and thank him for his spiritual meal and his favour. This concerns only the believers, for the body and blood of the Lord is enjoyed only through the right and true faith.

Anyone who does not look for strife will find in the writings of all these men, and especially in those of the preachers in this land, an improving message and will not listen to our adversaries but accept this true interpretation and learn the truth. Tumultuous people, however, will not be satisfied, but will look only for strife and misunderstanding everywhere and will effect nothing according to the well-founded divine truth or the precepts of charity. For charity leaves spiritual things in their order, and willingly accepts from each man the words of interpretation, as God has given them to him, whatever they may be, as long as they do not diverge from Christ Jesus and the true faith. One should, however, come close to the rule, etc. And every Christian should make use of such fair thinking, etc.

Finally, although many people quite readily remember the article of faith, that Christ has risen and is sitting in heaven at the right hand of God, they wrongly introduce beyond, and indeed, against our faith and against Scripture the corporal and carnal presence of the body of Christ in the bread. Thus, Schwenckfeld has taught his dear brethren about the right hand of God and the two natures of Christ, and for the honour of God fought against

* * * * *

5 Cf. John 6:27.
6 Ibid.

the error of those who say that the body and blood of Christ is everywhere and in all creatures, here and there, etc.

I had this printed for the honour of Christ and for your improvement. Thus I beg you again, Christian reader, to allow me to commend this book to you. Read it with a fair and impartial mind. Consider the contents diligently in the fear of God, and ask God to give you and all others the truth and increase it further. May God Almighty, to his eternal praise and honour, reveal to all who may still lack it the knowledge of Christ for the sake of charity and for their edification, and rouse in us all an honest zeal for the Christian life, which flows alone from true understanding. May he effect that we take each other's hand and stand in God's fear for the building up of the body of Christ,[7] without strife and carnal desire. Amen. Given at Strasbourg, in June of the year 1529.

Letter 394: 2 August 1529, Baden, Stephan Stör to Capito

The manuscript of this letter is in AST 40, #68, folio 446. The letter concerns Stör's efforts to obtain a temporary release from the *Urfehde*, that is, a sworn promise not to enter the territories of Strasbourg or Basel. The writer (d. 1529) was at one time parish priest of Liestal near Basel. A document recording the *Urfehde* (AMS, AA 389, Nr. 31; copy AST 176, Nr 139, f. 343 recto, dated 19 July 1526) states that Stör wrote a letter to the Basel city council, which was likely to incite unrest. He was accordingly arrested and set free only after the Duke of Würtemberg and other persons in high places spoke up on his behalf. The condition of his release was a ban on entering Strasbourg and Basel.

May the grace of God be with you. Worthy sir and beloved brother, I have at last understood your reply. I had great hopes that it would be better, considering the kind recommendation of my gracious prince and lord[1] and my enduring poverty and misery, but if God commands it thus, I shall accept it with much thanks, and continue commending my cause to his divine will, etc. Should my position in Liestal be restored to me, however, through my gracious lord of Basel,[2] I will have to go to Basel in person, for I cannot deal

* * * * *

7 Cf. Eph. 4:12.

1 The document in AST (see headnote) has a note added at the end: *Porro Philippus Landgr. Hassiae pro eo scripsit* (furthermore, Philip, duke of Hesse, wrote on his behalf).

2 I.e., the bishop of Basel, Philip of Gundelsheim (1527–53), who never entered Basel, however, and lived in exile in Freiburg/Breisgau.

with this matter through a messenger. I was deprived of my house and possessions on short notice, and I still have to settle accounts with many people and divide the property with my stepdaughter[3] – but how can I do that when a ban and *Urfehde* of the magistrate of Strasbourg blocks my way, and there is no possibility to get at my property, unless your people in Strasbourg will earnestly help me? Thus I beg you, dearest brother, help me as much as you can to convince my gracious lords of Strasbourg, for God's sake, to suspend the ban for a month and allow me without hindrance to travel in both sees, addressing to me a safe conduct to this effect. Once you have obtained the document, please have it sent to me quickly in Baden at the house of Michael Nesel.[4] I will go to Basel that very hour and obtain a declaration that I have been released from my *Urfehde*. And once the strict and wise lords have done me this favour, could you request them to add another, namely that I may look after my affairs for one month and settle my accounts with pious people there; when the month has passed, my ban and *Urfehde* will come in force again, and I will act in obedience to it, as I have zealously done so far. Hurry in this matter, so that I can complete the whole affair before the Frankfurt Fair starts. Please look after my affair as best you can. I have written in great haste. Given in the margravate of Baden, before dawn, on Monday, 2 August in the year of our Lord 1529, etc.

Your Stephan Stör, fellow worker in preaching the gospel Christ.

Letter 395: 4 August 1529, Strasbourg, Capito to Ulrich Zwingli

Printed in ZwBr 4:240–2, Ep. 888.

[*Summary*]: So far, Capito was against Zwingli attending the [Marburg Colloquy].because of danger to his life, but he has now been convinced that Zwingli can make his way safely. He also sees the importance of a personal meeting between Zwingli and Luther. Philip of Hesse has written to [Jacob] Sturm to use his influence to persuade Zwingli of the need to attend. Sturm will explain the plans for his safety: he will be protected by [Ludwig], Duke of Zweibrücken-Pfalz, and from there pass into the territory of Philip. On the return, Wilhelm von Fürstenberg will see to his safe journey to Constance. The Marburg Colloquy will offer a unique chance to achieve concord.

* * * * *

3 Unidentified.
4 Unidentified.

Letter 396: 6 August 1529, Strasbourg, Capito to Ulrich Zwingli

Printed in ZwBr 4:247–8, Ep. 891.

[*Summary*]: On 4 August the city council took over the right to appoint candidates to vacant benefices and will no longer accept papal appointments. Jakob Bedrot, [see above, Ep. 260, note 1] professor of Greek, was given a canonry at St Thomas on 6 August. He hopes Zurich and Strasbourg will soon enter an alliance. He recommends the [unidentified] bearer of the letter.

Letter 396a: [After 27 September 1529, Wasselonne], Andreas Cellarius to Capito

The manuscript of this letter is in Strasbourg AST 40, #75, f. 458. On Cellarius, see above Ep. 369 headnote. Millet dated this letter 1528. It has been redated, based on the death of the Bishop of Speyer, mentioned below (see note 5).

Greetings. I have read your letter, in which you express the belief that the abbot[1] has perhaps granted this privilege to that nobleman[2] as a favour to the prince,[3] but it is nothing of the sort. When the abbot was here recently, he was quite ignorant of the fact that I was still paying that pension. He was convinced that I had that parish[4] free and without any pension since the death of prince George,[5] for when [the abbot] returned the second time to us from Strasbourg, he invited me to a meal. By chance the topic of the annual pension came up, which I pay his steward without fail. When the abbot heard of it, he said for all to hear: 'Are you still burdened with that pension?' I responded that I was. He was surprised and indignantly poured forth these words: 'So that's what it means to be an officer of the court! May God destroy those rascals, for I thought that you were in possession and free of obligations.' The chief scribe of the prince heard this, and was himself of the same impression. After the meal, the abbot and I talked about the matter among ourselves. He asked whether the nobleman had given me collateral letters. I said yes. He asked me to bring them. I brought the letters, and he read them.

* * * * *

1 I.e., of Hornbach: Johann Kindhäuser (d. 1540).
2 Ludwig von Eschenau, councillor of Ludwig von Zweibrücken-Pfalz. See next note.
3 Ludwig von Zweibrücken-Pfalz, reigned 1514–32.
4 I.e., Wasselonne.
5 George Count Palatine, bishop of Speyer, died 27 September 1529. He was the titular rector of the parish.

After he read the letters, he asked for the chancellor to be called. When he came he showed him the letters. The chancellor said he did not recognize the handwriting of the writer of those letters. He told the abbot that they were a forgery. Finally, the abbot said to me: 'Take courage, I shall see to it that the parish is freed of the pension,' etc. Farewell, but I shall write to the nobleman, as you told me.

Yours, Andreas Cellarius.

Letter 396b: [November 1529, Strasbourg], The Chapter of St Thomas to the [City Council of Strasbourg]

The text of this letter is in AST 19, #66.

Strict, honest, providential, honourable, wise, gracious lords!

The most respected, honourable and wise lords, Nicolaus Kniebs, *Altammeister*,[1] and Paul Balthener,[2] delegates of the honourable council, requested us at St Thomas to elect Master Jakob,[3] lecturer in Greek, to the prebend vacated by the death of Ulrich Bertsch,[4] which has already been bestowed on him in an oral communication. We would have been most willing to do so, had we not been handed a papal brief by Stephan Usinger,[5] vicar in the cathedral. In the beginning, such papal briefs were merely presented as a friendly request to the collegiate churches, prelates, princes and lords, but later they were imposed on us as a legal obligation. However, the Council of Constance did not recognize papal appointments, and afterwards they were curtailed.[6] After an agreement was drawn up between the pope and the German Nation, they were no longer accepted by many rulers and princes, for example in Austria, Mark-Brandenburg, Würtemberg, and other regions, which abolished them afterwards. Moreover, recently at Nürnberg, the estates appealed against the pope's demands.[7] As a result, the Margrave of

* * * * *

1 On Kniebs, see above, Ep. 184 headnote.
2 Paul Balthener (d. 1535) was active on the city council from 1521; he was a member of the XV at this time.
3 I.e., Bedrot (see above, Ep. 260, note 1).
4 Ulrich Bertsch (ca. 1460–31 July 1529) studied in Erfurt and Freiburg, where he obtained an MA. He lived in Rome for twenty years from 1483. He held a canonry at St Thomas from 1487, as well as other benefices in Vendenheim, Rust, and at Young St Peter.
5 I have found no information on Stephan Usinger except his matriculation record at the University of Freiburg in 1503.
6 This may be a mistake for 'Council of Basel.' See below, Ep. 403.
7 Cf. the estate's reply to the papal legate, RTA 3, 435–43 (5 February 1523).

Baden[8] and several cities in His Grace's realm invalidated all transactions by papal courtiers and other such briefs, for it is now apparent to all the world that such iniquitous papal briefs strongly militate against the interest of the whole German Nation and of all decent men. Thus, we have taken these steps without Your Graces' further approval and assistance, lest we be left without resources, and the city of Strasbourg together with us suffer damage, ill repute, and mockery.

But since, in our opinion, the papal complaint goes completely against the Word of God and is contrary to what pleases God and what you, the honourable council, and the whole city have undertaken to uphold, and since it is also to our detriment and causes much effort and labour for you, our lords, we thought we would, with special goodwill, put before Your Graces and Reverences the following articles, with the request to consider them further:

First, such *gratiae*[9] or papal briefs may have a legitimate basis but are clearly maintained to the detriment of our fatherland, even if they are legitimate and admissible. They support our opponents in their blasphemy, so that they conceive even greater hopes of imposing their will on the honourable council and the citizens at large, for once a foothold is gained, progress can easily be made, and everything which has been abolished for the honour of God may be restored.

Secondly, such tricks of the courtiers are counter to public welfare, for undeniably the collegiate church has been instituted as of old here at Strasbourg for the benefit of the city, that the children of the pious, whether of high or low estate, may be guided to fear God, be taught well, and develop good morals. We at St Thomas, who have so far gladly obliged the honourable council in everything, have shown respect and have been at their service as far as we could, to bring about such practice in our collegiate church, but the bulls and briefs from Rome hinder our actions. The pope promotes and obtrudes on us every ostler and donkey-driver and hampers every pious scholar. He does so in an effort to acquire more servants and keep the truth hidden from common understanding, for the whole lot of courtiers never serves without getting in the way of the established government, and they live in luxury, as Rome teaches them.

Thirdly, if the financial machinations of Rome continue to be tolerated, the honourable council will have much work, for although you, our gracious lords, will not allow us to be harassed by such tricks, but rather treat us as

* * * * *

8 Philip I (1479–1533), ruling as margrave 1515–33.
9 I.e., appointments made by the pope, *ex gratia papae*.

citizens, since we (or some of us, at any rate) showed ourselves obedient and, following Your Graces' mandate,[10] took out citizenship, have desisted from our errors and vices and have entered into matrimony. On that account, as Stephan Usinger argues, all our benefices are now justly demanded back by Rome. The [Catholic party] is only waiting to see whether such *gratiae* will once again be accepted here in the city of Strasbourg. If that were the case, they would use the precedent against us, although it is contrary to divine, natural, and secular right. It would indeed be a hardship to admit some papal bulls and reject others, although they are in all aspects the same, that is, useless and contrary to reason.

This is the object of our humble request: see to it that Stephan Usinger, a citizen of your city, desist from maintaining his so-called right, which is void and contradicts Your Graces and our common city, and that he freely relinquish the right to you. He cannot object to it, for he can see for himself that Your Graces have so far disregarded the pope in matters and laws concerning God, and would not in this case, on the pope's instance, accept matters that go against God's honour and the welfare of the city. Nor does Usinger suffer injustice since his claim is based, not on law, but on wantonness and a travesty of the law. Furthermore, it is understood that he has no complaint on the basis of his qualifications. Let him show how he can use and maintain the fief he has from God in a godly manner.

Now is the time, gracious lords, to supply the city of Strasbourg with useful people who serve the common interest – now that we are working toward and fighting for improvement. Otherwise, we would have to take on once again unbearable burdens. Either you, the honourable council, will become the rulers of our city, or you will be subject to the growing and excessive power of ecclesiastical rulers. To find relief afterwards will cost great toil and effort and distress many people. Yet you have nothing to fear these days from the courtiers, neither action nor complaint before His Majesty the Roman Emperor, the electors, princes, and lords – people are not inclined toward them, and they do not even have the favour of the ecclesiastical princes. If, however, you sit still and say nothing, it will shortly happen that the collegiate church of St Thomas will feel toward you as the others are currently inclined. For we, who wish you well, will be overwhelmed and outnumbered, unless Your Graces protect us from that which would lead to unrest. For people currently flee from a mere shadow of unrest. We beg,

* * * * *

10 Promulgated 22 January 1525. Cf. above, Ep. 230 headnote.

therefore, that you may give us a favourable reply in this matter, for we are inclined to offer our complete good will and service to Your Graces.

Your willing and obedient citizens,

Lorenz Schenckbecher, provost,[11]

Jakob Munthart, vice-dean,[12]

Jakob Bopp[13] and Wolfgang Capito, canons of the collegiate church of St Thomas.

Letters 397 and 397a have been redated and are now 367b and c.

Letter 398: 14 December [1529], Strasbourg, Capito to Ulrich Zwingli

Printed in ZwBr 4:352–4, Ep. 942.

[*Summary*]: He is appalled that there are so many difficulties still about the alliance between Zurich and Strasbourg [concluded 5 January 1530]. He alludes to negotiations with Basel [concerning supplies of corn and gunpowder]. They ought to realize that they will be at war with Germans, not with the French or the Italians. Friends warn that all of Europe is conspiring against them, but so far nothing has come to pass that they cannot handle. He begs Zwingli to do what is in his power to bring about this mutually beneficial alliance. The count [Sigmund von Hohenlohe or Wilhelm von Fürstenberg] has not yet returned from Philip of Hesse.

Letter 398a: 16 December 1529, Strasbourg, The Chapter of St Thomas to Hans Schachtel

The manuscript is in AST 22(5–6). Hans Schachtel (d. 1542) was vicar of St Thomas from 1522. He joined the Catholic party and fled Strasbourg in 1525, then settled for a payment of 30 gulden per year. The terms of that payment are the subject of this letter.

First, our friendly greeting. Dear Mr Schachtel, we acknowledge the contents of the letter you have recently written to us.[1] As far as the request for the

* * * * *

11 See above, Ep. 237, note 23.

12 See above, Epp. 233b; 237, note 19.

13 See above, Ep. 246a, note 29.

1 Not extant.

stipend is concerned, which you think should belong to you, we make no concessions. There is no evidence. Therefore you should desist and refrain from such a groundless demand, for we owe you nothing of the sort now and have no intentions to acknowledge a debt in the future. If we came to an agreement with Theobald Lehmann,[2] who is in charge of the second *annimissaria*, we did so voluntarily rather than out of any legal obligation. As for the second point, concerning what is owed to you on account of your residency last year, we will pay you, as we do the other persons of the collegiate church, at set times and terms, and to the extent established in the Offenburg agreement.[3] As for the redemption of your stipend, it is your task as the possessor to make every effort to obtain another lawful *censiten*.[4] The capital, after a suitable deposit has been made, may be used as security. If you have a *censit* and indicate this to us, we will take the proper action. We did not wish to withhold our opinion on the subject of your letter.[5] You will know what to do. Given at Strasbourg, 16 December 1529.

Letter 398b: 16 December 1529, Strasbourg, The Chapter of St Thomas to Nicolaus Wurmser

The manuscript of this letter is in AST 22 (5–6). For Nicolaus Wurmser, see CWC 1, Ep. 57 headnote. The business to which this letter refers is likely connected with Wurmser's letter to the chapter, above, Ep. 386a.

First, our friendly service and goodwill, reverend, most learned, gracious, dear lord and friend. As far as the account is concerned, which you have presented to us in the matter of ...[1] and which we have examined and perused, we appoint a day for the negotiations between us: the next feast day of Bishop St Hilary.[2] However, should this day not be convenient for you, please name another suitable day either before or after the above-mentioned

* * * * *

2 For Lehmann, see above, Ep. 237, note 26.
3 Cf. above, Ep. 237 headnote.
4 I.e., an auditor?
5 *haben wir euch uff ewer schryben nit verhalten wollen.*

1 The word for 'in the matter of' (*belangend*) appears in the margin of this draft. Obviously, the matter in question (cf. above, Ep. 386a) was stated in the copy sent to Wurmser.
2 13 January. Cf. below, Ep. 400a, which mentions that Wurmser attended a meeting in Strasbourg.

St Hilary's Day. We await your reply and wish to indicate that we hope the matter will come to a good and useful conclusion. We ask that you reply in writing. Given at Strasbourg, 16 December 1529.

Letter 398c: 1529, Strasbourg, Capito to the Reader

> This is the preface to Capito's German catechism, first published as *Kinderbericht und fragstuck von gemeynen puncten Christlichs glaubens* (Strasbourg: Köpfel, 1527). The first edition did not have a preface. The present letter appears on the verso of the title page of the second edition (Strasbourg: Köpfel, 1529). It is printed in F. Cohrs, ed., *Die Evangelischen Katechismusversuche vor Luthers Enchiridion* (Berlin, 1900), 100. For the Latin version of the catechism, see above, Ep. 339.

To the Reader: Our *Kinderbericht* may be summed up in this way: The world should desist from its actions and turn to God our Lord. It should seek from him forgiveness of sins, justification, and blessing through Christ, and should put its hopes in him alone, that the name of God may be blessed and that our lives may serve as examples of piety and honesty. Others may know differently, or believe they have such knowledge, for our talents vary, and strange talk may arise, but I ask, for God's sake, that there be no dissension on that account. Whatever gifts anyone has received from God, let him peacefully apply them to the improvement of the church. The church, guided by the Spirit of God, will then pass judgment and adopt what is best, so that there be only one master and teacher in heaven and remain the spirit of Truth for all of us. If anyone has any other complaints against me, let him indicate them orally or in writing, and seek punishment. With God's help, he will find me willing and ready to establish the Truth. I will not defend my flesh with sharp words, for I am a worthless man. Let God who is one lead us with his only Spirit, through his only son, Jesus Christ, to the true eternity of faith. Amen.

Letter 399: 13 January 1530, Strasbourg, Capito to Joachim Vadianus

> Printed in VadBr 4:201–2, Ep. 592.

[*Summary*]: Simprecht [Schenck] vouches for Nikolaus [Guldi's] character. He has left the Anabaptist sect. They have sent Guldi to Zwingli [see below, Ep. 400] to ensure his safe journey to St Gallen. Bucer, who does not generally favour such men, will write more. Capito asks Vadianus to aid Guldi in his search for a living. His conversion may serve as an example to others.

Letter 400: 13 January [1530], Strasbourg, Capito to Ulrich Zwingli

Printed in ZwBr 4:397–8, Ep. 957.

[*Summary*]: Capito is pleased that an alliance with Zurich has finally been concluded [on 5 January 1530]. There has been trouble with the Anabaptists. The bearer of this letter [Nikolaus Guldi, cf. above, Ep. 399] or Bucer's letter will tell him more. Caspar Schwenckfeld has returned to Strasbourg and is engaged in fierce debates. The images will be removed from the churches, once the Strasbourg representatives have returned from [Zurich]. [Ulrich] Funk will tell Zwingli more. Capito is amazed that the people peacefully accepted such great changes.

Letter 400a: 21 January 1530, Strasbourg, The Chapter of St Thomas to Wilhelm von Honstein

The manuscript of this letter is in AST 22(5–6). For Wilhelm von Honstein, Bishop of Strasbourg, see CWC 1, Ep. 174 headnote.

Most Reverend Prince, gracious lord, first we humbly offer our goodwill and service at any time.

Gracious lord, upon receiving Your Princely Grace's written document containing an understanding with respect to a contribution requested by His Imperial Majesty, our most gracious lord, we recently sent to Your Princely Grace the reverend and most learned Dr Bernhard Wölfflin[1] and Master Beat Pfeffinger,[2] our fellow canons, with earnest instructions to explain to Your Princely Grace the scarcity of our means and that of our collegiate church.[3] On that occasion we humbly offered the necessary apology for refusing to pay the contribution upon receiving the instruction. We understand from the above-mentioned Master Beat Pfeffinger that the supplication was presented (in the absence of his colleague, the above-mentioned Dr Bernhard, who had to remain here on account of a sudden illness). Your Princely Grace informed us, however, that our dean has spoken differently[4] and proffered a diverging opinion before Your Princely Grace, namely: he and other fellow

* * * * *

1 On Wölfflin, see above, Ep. 246a, note 28.
2 On Pfeffinger, see CWC 1, Ep. 145, note 3.
3 For other complaints about their difficult financial position, see below, Ep. 404c.
4 I.e., Nicolaus Wurmser, the leader of the Catholic party who left Strasbourg and accepted pensions from the city in lieu of their stipends.

members of the chapter would be willing and ready in these and other cases
to oblige His Imperial Majesty, our most gracious lord, and Your Princely
Grace, as long as this was supported by the persons of the collegiate churches
residing in the city of Strasbourg. We therefore give Your Princely Grace our
humble opinion, namely that we wonder what caused our dean to say that,
for he was with us when both the canons in residence and those coming from
abroad were formally assembled as a chapter,[5] and he participated in the deliberations and counsel, as well as in the ensuing decision and finally offered
to take the reply of the assembled chapter to Your Princely Grace, agreeing
that it was right and appropriate in view of the collegiate church's needs.
He had instructions from us in writing to indicate this duly to Your Princely
Grace, in the good hope that Your Grace would not take it amiss, after receiving a full account. And it was our understanding that he would properly explain our common decision and the poverty of the collegiate church.
However this may be, we humbly beg Your Princely Grace to regard us all
no less willing and ready than the dean to show due obedience to the Roman Imperial Majesty, our most gracious lord, and to Your Princely Grace,
in every possible matter, even if some of us might give a different impression in the present crisis (although they have said nothing to justify such an
impression). Rather, we have significant and honest reasons [to act as we do],
as our delegates have reported in the supplication presented in our name, as
Your Princely Grace will remember, and we are clearly prevented from com-
plying [with the imperial request]. Since it is completely impossible for our
collegiate church to comply, we most humbly beg Your Princely Grace once
again graciously to accept our necessary apology, and to defend us and represent our position before the respectfully mentioned Imperial Majesty and
our gracious lord of Malta,[6] etc. or where and before whom you are inclined
to do us this favour. We wish to remain for all time in Your Princely Grace's
debt and service. Given at Strasbourg, 21 January, in the year 1530.

Your Princely Grace's obedient and obliging,

Provost, vice-dean, and chapter of the St Thomas in Strasbourg.

Letter 401: 27 January 1530, [Strasbourg], Capito to Johannes Oecolampadius

Printed in BrOek 2:414–15, Ep. 722.

[*Summary*]: He asks Oecolampadius to find a tutor for a seventeen-year-old

* * * * *

5 Cf. above, Ep. 398b, which suggests 15 January as a date for that meeting.
6 I.e., Balthasar Mercklin, bishop of Constance, Hildesheim and Malta, see CWC
   1, Ep. 55, note 3.

[unidentified]. He will pay about 8 gulden per annum, which is all he can afford. If the young man does well, he will try to obtain a more generous subsidy from the council. Their aim is to find stipends for students as well as professors [see below, Ep. 404]. Erasmus has attacked Gerard [Gelden-houwer in the *Epistola contra quosdam qui se falso iactant evangelicos* (Freiburg: Faber Emmeus, 1530)]. Some people counsel Geldenhouwer to write a reply, but it is perhaps better to let it go because the papists do not trust Erasmus anyway. He asks for Oecolampadius' opinion in this matter. He has also written about the young man to Paulus Phrygio and [Andreas] Cratander.

Letter 402: 3 February 1530, Basel, Johannes Oecolampadius to Capito

Printed in BrOek 2:415–17, Ep. 723.

[*Summary*]: People are not lacking who will reply to Erasmus' slanderous invective [against Geldenhouwer, cf. above, Ep. 401]. Oecolampadius hopes they will do so in moderation. He does not think that he can be of assistance to the young man [mentioned in the preceding letter, Ep. 401]. He may in fact dismiss the 'half-French' amanuensis he has now. If, however, the young man is a relative of Capito, he will do what he can. Hieronymus [Bothanus] will write to Capito and ask for access to the writings left behind by the Anabaptist Nikolaus [Guldi]. Oecolampadius' wife, [Wibrandis Rosenblatt], thanks Capito for the prayer book he sent her. She is expecting.[1] Berthold [Haller] will preach in Solothurn. The Anabaptists are more trouble to the reformers than the papists. Phrygio wrote to him concerning the young man; Cratander did not. He is perhaps upset because Oecolampadius gave his commentary on Daniel to another printer.[2] He advises caution about reply-ing to Karlstadt.

Letter 403: [Before 23 February 1530, Strasbourg], Capito to the Reader

This is the conclusion of Capito's *Des Conciliums zu Basel satzung und Constitu-tion, wider pfrundenhändel und Curtisanen practick* (The Decrees and Decisions of the Council of Basel against Commerce in Benefices and the Tricks of the Courtiers [N.p.: 1530]). The publication contains an introduction (Ai verso–Bii recto), which explains the historical context of the decrees concerning church benefices passed at the Council of Basel (1431–45) and defends the idea that

* * * * *

1 The child, a daughter named Irene, was born on 21 March.
2 It appeared from the press of Johann Bebel and Thomas Wolff in March 1530.

conciliar authority is superior to papal authority. This is followed by an annotated German translation of the decree 'Placuit' (Bii recto–Di verso), dealing with the granting of benefices. Next comes a 'Beschluss,' that is, a conclusion (Dii recto–Fi verso), which overlaps to some extent with Ep. 404 below. It is a proposal to extend the provisions of the Basel decree, which was concerned with funding positions in universities, to funding education in general. The author criticizes traditional universities for turning out useless graduates and for corrupting rather than edifying youth. He notes that reforms have now been implemented, for example, at Heidelberg and Basel, which promise better results (Diii verso–Div verso). Since the church has failed in its mandate to support learning through benefices, it is incumbent upon secular authorities to take matters into their own hands and bestow the benefices falling vacant in the so-called papal month on worthy recipients (Eii recto). Benefices should be used to support parish priests and their assistants, teachers, and administrators, as well as students and apprentices (Eiii verso–Fi verso). The volume further contains *Concordata principum: Vertrag Teutscher nation mit dem stul zu Rom uber verleihung der pfrunden* (Concordat of the princes: a contract of the German nation with the See of Rome concerning the appointment to benefices) and *Des heiligen bapsts Leo bescheyd wie und wem man Pfrunden verleihen soll* (The holy Pope Leo's decree how and whom one ought to appoint to a benefice). In the conclusion, which is given here (Liii recto–verso), Capito identifies himself as the author and addresses the reader directly.

Finally, pious reader, it is my request and friendly counsel not to take the contents of this booklet in ill part. Rather, you ought to learn from it how the world serves God, to show more earnest respect for God yourself and to ask him for mercy, for he alone can help us. Everything else is in vain and bears no fruit. In addition, make an effort to follow these instructions for improvement without causing unrest or tumult. I have shown you the image of a corrupt church with all its councils and decrees, popes, bishops, priests, etc. and all their undertakings. These are intended for no other purpose than to promote God's kingdom, but God's name is used as a pretext to obtain worldly riches and to control them. This will become obvious to you from this booklet, which merely indicates the facts and does not attack or endanger anyone. I, Wolfgang Capito, will respond to anyone who has doubts about individual points and needs further information, and will give him proof on the basis of undeniable historical facts, the writings of the Fathers, and written canon law (insofar as it is good). I only know that I have indicated everything with consistency and truth, more or less as it flowed from my pen. Farewell, and fear the Lord.

Letter 403a: [Before 6 March 1530, Strasbourg, The City Council of Strasbourg to Capito and Caspar Hedio]

The manuscript of this letter is in AST 324, #2b. A copy of the letter (lacking the final paragraph), written in a later hand, is in AST 324, #2c. Capito and Hedio replied to the letter in Ep. 404 below. For Hedio see CWC 1, Ep. 47.

Dear friends, as you know, we decided some years ago together with you and the whole community, through a majority, to permit the preaching of the Word of God as a nourishment of the soul, based on divine scripture and unmixed with misleading human decrees, for this is appropriate and should be executed according to God's will.[1]

We recognize our weakness and how far we have erred from the path of the Lord, and in addition must ponder that our error was greatly promoted by our leaders in the Word and especially in the collegiate churches and parishes, through masses, through their teaching, and through their character, which was not as their high calling would have required. This is how the pope and his courtiers act: The courtiers serve some years in Rome, gadding about, driving donkeys, and other such things in their usual manner – things that do nothing for the honour of God or the maintenance of peace and concord, but further only their own advantage and pomp – and after they have served to the scandal and detriment of all honest citizens, they bring along a dubious brief obtained for their service, which is of no use to us or our people. On the strength of such briefs they expect to be given salaries, prelacies, canonries, parishes, and other benefices. And although this was done at first on the basis of special pleas, those briefs became so prevalent as the power of the clergy increased that these people seized benefices established for learned, pious, and peaceful people beloved of God, fought for them, kept them, and enjoyed their usufructs, although others who deserve far greater respect for their learning and character and should have been preferred for such benefices had to yield to the Roman servants, the so-called courtesans, even though the majority of them were neither suitable nor capable to look after the available benefices, especially the prelacies and parishes. Indeed, rather boorish and ignorant people were appointed, and seized the usufructs of the best benefices and moved the others aside into lesser positions. Consequently the common men, pious and honest citizens,

* * * * *

1 The decree was passed on 1 December 1523. Cf. below, Ep. 406.

were angered when they saw that the patrimony of Christ had been turned into trading goods and were fought and quarrelled over. Thus, many heterodox sects and opinions arose and came about, which damaged the glory of the Almighty and hindered true service to God. For who would want to become learned in true Holy Writ when such trumpery is valued more highly than the truth? This was also noted at several imperial diets by our electors, princes, and secular estates, including the delegates of the city of Strasbourg. They bitterly lamented and complained in a hundred articles of complaint,[2] adding warnings and cautions: if these conditions were not improved, they would not tolerate or permit them to go on. The final decree specifically concerning benefices runs as follows: [...][3]

For these and other necessary reasons, which are passed over here for the sake of brevity, we have been moved, first of all, to see to it that our children are instructed and taught by learned teachers and men skilled in the Greek, Hebrew, and Latin tongues, that they may thoroughly learn the fear of God, Christian discipline, honest behaviour, skill, reason, and virtues, as well as service to the common weal. We did this in the hope that afterwards, when they reached maturity, they might be employed in the parishes, collegiate churches, and in the public business of our city. For we found that several of the children of our citizens were endowed by God our Lord with a suitable natural talent for learning, but were kept from obtaining it through poverty or their parents' lack of means, and thus were unable to attend school. This caused them to become apprentices and enter into diverse manual labours, and yet we know and are aware that such a gift is a special grace of God the Lord, which may be given to the child of a poor man as much as to that of a rich man.

Thus we decided on the following policy to increase God's honour, maintain and promote the citizen's concord, a praiseworthy and excellent thing, and to put an end to the cunning practices of the courtesans which are against divine, natural, and imperial law, and have no honest basis. Hereafter, when a benefice becomes available in this city or the benefice of a cathedral canon falls vacant in the papal month,[4] the usufruct of that benefice will be used to apprentice the children of citizens or to further pious, learned men, who can be put to good use. We shall not permit these benefices to go

* * * * *

2 The Grievances of the German Nation, presented at the Diet of Worms, 1521.
3 The decree itself is not cited in the manuscript, i.e., was presumably inserted in the copy sent to the preachers.
4 I.e., the month in which the pope had the right of assigning any benefice falling vacant.

to Roman servants and courtesans, or be obtained with papal briefs acquired
through tricks and simony, nor shall we permit the chapters of the collegiate
churches, monasteries, or colleges to obey and follow such briefs. Furthermore, we shall see to it that no notary or other person, who is asked to serve
them in this matter, will aid them. In this matter one must consider the consequence of allowing the courtesans to go on as before exerting their power.
All sorts of quarrels would arise if the usufructs of the benefices in the chapters (which are for the benefit of the community and have been established
long ago by our forefathers for the sake of God, to be given to learned people) were to be alienated by such courtesans, who act quite contrary to our
Christian intent and are very much against it. In this fashion, these benefices
would be lost to the city and wasted on their pleasure, while our children
and other pious, capable persons who might be able to learn a great deal of
discipline and good character, would come to naught and be thwarted. This
is our will and opinion in this matter, but we do not wish to deprive anyone,
whatever his status, of his proper gift or right of bestowing this honour, the
so-called *ius patronatus*.[5] When benefices fall vacant outside the papal months
or the right of nomination applies to both months, we do not want to hinder
anyone. Rather, we are inclined to protect them, who are our fellow citizens.
We also wish to state that our initiative will only last until a Christian council
is assembled in future, as has been decided at recent diets.[6]

In the meantime, dear friends, our Christian and well-grounded, pious and circumspect decree may be helpful against the courtesans or others
like them, or anyone who wishes to aid them against us or our people with
papal and other processes and briefs, as with the papal ban, and thereafter
with attempts to execute it and act on it. Should this happen, some people
…[7] through which troubles and error arise, we have initiated this and wish
to hear from you what is your pleasure and will take our lead from you.

Letter 404: 23 February 1530, [Strasbourg], Capito and Caspar Hedio to the City Council of Strasbourg

The manuscript of this letter is in AST 324, #2a. For Hedio see CWC 1, Ep. 47.

* * * * *

5 I.e., the right of presentation.
6 I.e., the diet and the emperor desired a general council, but successive popes
  prevaricated. The Council of Trent was finally called in 1545. Cf. below, Epp.
  407, 409.
7 The meaning of the phrase *mancher das ihn so in itz liegt in zit der anfechtung laid
  wurdt lossen sin* is unclear.

This letter appears to be a reply to Ep. 403a. The proposals presented here are based on the decrees of the Council of Basel, discussed in *Des Conciliums ... satzung* (cf. above, Ep. 403 headnote). For literal parallels between that publication and the present letter, see the footnotes.

Strict, noble, earnest, honest, wise, ruling lords,

It is our humble request to bring the following proposal to your attention for your consideration, namely how and in what mode and manner you ought and could further the glory of God and the common weal by means of ecclesiastical possessions and collegiate churches, without detriment and loss to prudent and honest citizens.

First, reasons have been given in print[1] and elsewhere why it is seemly for you to become involved in granting benefices along with the regular patrons and to abolish and do away with the papal month.[2] No law gives this right to the pope; the councils have abolished it,[3] and experience shows that the pope does not look to God's honour and the benefit of the church in granting these benefices, and has no intention of doing so.

Also, it is the task of Christian governments to see to it that all of God's gifts are used to further common welfare and the law. This happens when benefices are granted to, and the collegiate churches' money is used by, those who are beneficial and of service to the public or may become useful. For the basic mission of the very first collegiate churches was to supply the public with leaders in office and with teachers, to look after the training of youth, the maintenance of the poor, and to supply administrators and servants in other positions. It is the obligation of every government to see that this happens. It would therefore be most useful, while you decide about granting benefices during the papal month, which has already been done in two collegiate churches, also to deliberate about ways and means to be consistent and to make every effort to ensure consistency.

The prelates, even those in the cathedral chapter, would have no reason to complain if the honourable council asked them and requested that they deign, for the sake of God and the community, to give up every other month, which until now they had to concede to the pope.[4] For their own welfare

* * * * *

1 I.e., *Des Conciliums zu Basel satzung*, described above, Ep. 403 headnote.
2 Cf. above, Ep. 403a, note 4.
3 *Und keyn Curtisan hette rechtmessigen titel zu seiner pfrunden nutzung so sie von bästlicher [sic] heiligkeyt durch ire hoffdienst erlangt oder sunst erkaufft haben (Des Conciliums satzung* a i verso).
4 I.e., transfer the right of presentation from the pope to the council.

and honour depends on the church being well supplied [with educated men] and on the number of learned and knowledgeable people. After all, the more knowledgeable the community, the greater the respect paid to them. They cannot prevent this from happening even if they doggedly resist, and it is thereafter your task to take care that benefices are well allocated.

For this reason, one must consider whether it is desirable for the honourable council, as is done in other important matters, to assign to efficient men on the council the task of investigating and discovering the circumstances and the potential of people who might, at any given time, be granted a benefice as teachers, lecturers, and in other capacities. They ought to reflect on this and then indicate their thoughts to the honourable council to avoid that the matter be brought before the plenary council unprepared and unexamined, and ensure that better care may be taken of Christian interests.

Thus, when a benefice falls vacant, they might, at your request, at any time indicate to Your Graces reliable, honest, and useful men, who can be employed in the service of the church and the community and in official positions. And when all positions are duly looked after, they may also consider children of citizens who are to be apprenticed and show that they are honest and well-behaved, and give their names to you, our wise and honourable lords. These children may then be supported with money from benefices under the conditions and to the extent explained below. In this matter, one must not take into consideration the wealth or poverty of their parents. This is to avoid too much innovation in our practices, which would be the case if only the rich or only the poor were to be apprenticed, etc.

Furthermore, Your Graces must consider whether it would be expedient to admonish the guilds and the citizens in general not to importune the patrons of the said benefices with requests, but to allow those in charge to indicate to the honourable council people to be taken on as apprentices, as long as they have been found suitable after diligent inquiry. People should be accepted from all guilds, for there are able children to be found among all of them. Also, the common alms are to be supplemented with money from the benefices, as ecclesiastical law commands.[5] We must ensure that a servant or student does not obtain a whole benefice,[6] but that the holders of the benefice are given a portion by the delegates of the honourable council, that on their command and in their name, as much of the benefice money be given

* * * * *

5 *das ... nutzung den armen zugeeygnet werde, dann der kirchen güter seint der armen* (*Des conciliums satzung* Fi recto).

6 *Das beschicht wann man nitt iedem eyn gantze pfrund gibt* (ibid., E iv recto).

as they may deserve and need, for example, 20 or 30 gulden[7] for a teacher of children, depending on his industry and skill, for awarding the same amount when industry and skills vary would be harmful. Furthermore, 10 or 20 gulden would be appropriate for a boy who lives with his parents, unless he is older and needs books or other things. Furthermore, 25 gulden or 30 or 40 would be adequate for those who are sent elsewhere. Those amounts are approximate and depend on the circumstances, and if they continue industriously, they deserve to be loyally supported. One should, however, consider in time how the collegiate churches might be encouraged in this sentiment and have no disadvantage from it. For they have an obligation to benefit the community, which is the basis of their collegiate church and the original endowment.

Those in charge of assigning the benefices should retain a portion of the annual stipend, so that if during the ordinary beneficiary's month a benefice was terminated, from which five or six persons are supported,[8] the benefice might nevertheless be maintained from the reserves until a new benefice became available.

We are pleased that you do not intend to interfere with the ordinary patrons of a benefice, as you are entitled and have the right (for they ought to be ousted, since they hold their benefices improperly, according to the Council of Basel),[9] but we hope the honourable Christian council will make them understand that they must act appropriately, or else be obliged to apply the benefice to a good and right purpose.

Anyone granted a benefice by the councillors should immediately on his appointment set up legal representatives who will, upon your request and command and in your name, whether the holder likes it or not, make him relinquish his benefice. This should be done with or without grounds, as it benefits the community and the honourable council or pleases the lawful patrons of the benefice in the name of the council, lest once again we support an idle and useless mob, such as has been supported thus far from the ecclesiastical possessions. Nevertheless, one ought not to apply this rule at the risk of the ordinary patrons of the benefice, which Your Graces will not ask for, and which we would not like to advise.

Your Graces will take this proposal in good part, for we speak our mind

* * * * *

7 *also dass eynem knaben zehen, zwentzig oder dreissig gulden seiner gelegenheyt nach jars geben würden* (ibid.).
8 *domit werden sechs oder acht jungen von eyner pfrund der gmeynd gottes auffgezogen* (ibid.).
9 Council of Basel, Session 21, 9 June 1435, 'De pacificis possessoribus.'

truthfully and simply. If you wish to bestow benefices, as the other patrons and the pope himself habitually do, it would serve no purpose. For if you give the use of the whole benefice to idle people or to young, inexperienced fellows, thus giving them an opportunity to live freely and according to their whim, what would we have achieved with all our effort? The people would say that we have traded the papacy for a worse kind, that we abolished the pope in Rome, and appointed the masters and the council of Strasbourg to be our new popes. And if Your Lordships wanted to endow useless and inexperienced youths with canonries in the cathedral and with benefices, and allow them, as before, to live like lords and knights in idleness, you would rightly be called the new popes and corruptors of the church. You may reflect on that point yourselves. We speak freely, but you, our wise and honourable lords, will understand that our intentions are good.

It makes no difference whether those useless people, who are supported by God's gift, are foreigners or citizens. One may think that they benefit the community because they are obliged to spend their money here, and thus spend the church's possessions here, but both do equal harm through their bad and irritating example. What is even worse, it would cause plotting and divisions in your city. The pious youth would be neglected, and the common people embittered against you. They would think that you worry about yourselves and not about the commonweal if you only appointed your own children and those whom you favour, and that you forgot about benefitting God.

This will be the outcome eventually, but even now it would not be to Your Graces' credit to endow the children of citizens with benefices in order to benefit yourselves and your beloved children, whether they are suitable or not, while a suitable child of another pious common man is left without support, although he deserves to be trained for a higher office even if his father cannot manage it. Furthermore, even if a child is suitable, if he is given a whole benefice and established in it, he would be corrupted on account of the surfeit of possessions. It is necessary to keep a tight rein on youth.

Your Gracious Lordships are in the habit, and rightly so, of appointing persons to offices on account of their suitability rather than their family. That is even more important in granting benefices, which have been established to further the honour of God and for the benefit of the community, and should be used only for that purpose.

One can support many teachers out of the income from one canonry at St Thomas, at Young or Old St Peter. As a result, they may more devotedly teach the children of poor citizens. There are teachers now who suffer hard labour, great want, and hunger. This should arouse pity in us and make us glow with shame. How would it further the common good to give a benefice to an inexperienced young jackass for life, who could live in his new popish pomp, thumbing his nose at the community and fail to benefit anyone?

Conversely, it will benefit the public and the citizens if the benefices are granted as we propose and as we also indicated in print.[10] It will motivate common citizens to bring up their children in a virtuous and disciplined manner, and they themselves will be more industrious and obedient and listen obediently to our teaching, hoping that they will receive support in the future and will be rewarded, just as men in office are more attentive to their duties if they are amply supported. Reward encourages the worker and keeps him willing.

But if Your Graces would make, even once, an inexperienced youth without merit a man of importance, in order to do a favour to his parents or for reasons other than the young man's merit and suitability, and if you give a benefice to a young person whether he is learned or not, you would cause the officials much bother, work, and danger, day and night, and perhaps disgruntle the common people in your service. Your Graces would certainly discourage the youth from learning and cause many to try new tricks, for everyone would think, as stands to reason, that he might have pleasure without work and would stop working if his work provides no reward and generates only ill will and disgust. Even if the pious servants of the Spirit, who looked to God Almighty as their Lord, left no work undone (for the Christian heart does not value secular belongings), they would nevertheless become weak and dull and lose heart on account of the injustice, especially when our government wants to be regarded as Christian, and most people regard you as such. Thus, you should hand out God's external gifts, that is, earthly possessions, in a Christian manner. That is your duty, or you may expect punishment from God [if you do not fulfil it].

Finally, my lords, we are certain that such an arrangement for the granting of benefices will please God Almighty and cannot ever be criticized by any prudent government. You must not even respond to our opponents, for how can one maintain God's honour and the welfare of the city, if one plays favourites and thus increases the idle mob? Who would believe that you intended all changes for God's benefit if you kept the possessions of priests and monasteries for yourselves and your families and friends, rather than applying them to the general betterment? What could you say in response to the imperial estates of His Imperial Majesty or anyone else in defence of your action? We ask you to reflect on that.

* * * * *

10 See above, Ep. 403 headnote.

We speak in this manner, not because we doubt your understanding and intentions, strict, honest, wise lords, or because we suspect you of such undue and selfish action. We simply wish to warn you that such things do not come to pass without effort and planning. You have many affairs to look after, and the enemy does not bring about improvement but always seeks to hinder it. We, however, are called shepherds. Therefore, we think it is our task to be watchful. We speak out of a desire for peace; and a warning, even if given unnecessarily, has never harmed anyone. Especially in a matter that concerns God, one must carefully watch the flesh and omit no opportunity to utter a warning. May God give us the grace to act out of fear of God. Amen.

Letter 404a: 6 March 1530, Strasbourg, The Strasbourg Preachers to the Community

This open letter, published in pamphlet form as *Das einigerlei Bild bei den Gotgläubigen an orten da sie verehrt, nit mögen geduldet warden* ... (That the Veneration of Certain Images Cannot Be Tolerated By Believers in These Places, Strasbourg: [J. Knobloch Jr.], 1530), justifies the removal of images from the churches in Strasbourg on the basis of scripture and patristic exegesis. The text of the pamphlet is printed in BDS 4:161–81 and summarized in CorrBucer 4:25–6, Ep. 276.

[*Summary*]: The decree of the city council concerning the removal of images from churches [passed on 14 February 1530] was prudent and in accordance with God's command. So were the decrees abolishing private masses passed four years ago and public masses one year ago [21 February 1529]. Some people, who lack the necessary understanding, are opposed to these measures. The preachers have therefore undertaken to justify and explain the actions of the council in their pamphlet, first published in German and now also in Latin [cf. below, Ep. 404b]. They encourage the citizens to read these publications and pray that Christ may enlighten them.

Letter 404b: [After 6 March 1530], Strasbourg, The Strasbourg Preachers to the Community

This is the introduction to a Latin translation of Ep. 404a above: *Non esse ferendas in templis christianorum imagines* ... ([Strasbourg: J. Prüss], 1530), trans. by Jakob Bedrot. The letter is printed in CorrBucer 4:26–9, Ep. 277.

[*Summary*]: The preachers urge those who do not approve the removal of images to read Bucer's justification [Ep. 404a], which has now been translated into Latin.

Letter 404c: [9 March 1530, Strasbourg], The Chapter of St Thomas to the City Council of Strasbourg

The manuscript of this letter is in AST 16, #31.

Strict, honest, circumspect, honourable, wise, gracious lords,

We have recently looked into the accounts of our collegiate church and studied its affairs to consider ways and means how the collegiate church might continue to serve the interests of the whole community. We find that in the last five or six years we have reached a low point as far as rents and income are concerned, and have suffered a reduction of some 6,000 gulden, the greater part of which the collegiate church still owes, as we have indicated in a supporting document (and this does not include the reduction of income of the parishes). We furthermore contribute 450 gulden to the maintenance of the parishes, from which we had an income of 100 gulden in the past. Our collegiate church incurred such expenses because we, the majority of the chapter, obeyed the honourable council and did not make common cause with the exiles, who established a second chapter outside the city and in all affairs of the chapter bitterly fought and intrigued against us, while we remained on your side and honoured God, for the benefit of the honourable council and respectable citizens. Perhaps they thought they were right and had the authority to do so, and the said financial damage was the result of a misunderstanding – Your Graces are not ignorant of the facts. Since we have ended up and, for the most part, are in such difficulties and carry such burdens on account of our obedience and goodwill toward the honourable council, we have no doubt that you are willing and inclined to help us recover our footing, for you have treated us with paternal care before. Trusting in this, we confidently beg you to do us this favour and act in the interest of the collegiate church and allow us to sell the treasures of the church, its so-called ornaments and treasure, which are useless now, and put them to better use, that is, to pay our debts and preserve our capital. Otherwise, we would have to touch our capital or else suffer more damage and destroy the praiseworthy collegiate church – a collegiate church that is supposedly 'permanent.' Indeed, gracious lords, the collegiate church is in dire straits and in danger of ruin. It is our constant endeavour to turn it into an institution that honours God and benefits the common good, as we have partly shown now and will continue to show, God willing. Thus, an increasing number among us supported the idea of making such a request. Indeed, we would rather have asked to use the pompous ornaments of the church, which are a scandal, for the benefit of the poor folk, which is their proper use. As long as our entire collegiate church is looking to the honour of God (and as time passes, ever more so) and serving the interests of the poor people, and as long as God gives us his blessing and Your Graces support us, we thought we should use the said treasure – with your permission – to maintain our collegiate church. We will not, and indeed must not make use of it in any other way than to honour God and further the interest of the poor people. We can think of no other way to maintain this glorious collegiate church for the honourable council. Rather, it would deteriorate day by day in our hands. This would surely discourage all people of good will, whereas all our opponents would be pleased, for their sole desire is to see us, who were always obedient to the council, perish first. This is what Your Graces must consider, and we commend ourselves and our collegiate church to you.

Your Graces' well-intentioned citizens,

The provost, vice-dean, and chapter of the collegiate church of St Thomas.

Letter 405: 19 March 1530, Augsburg, Wolfgang Thalhauser to Capito

The manuscript of this letter is in Zurich SA E II 358, 71. Wolfgang Thalhauser, who had studied together with Paracelsus in Ferrara, was municipal physician in Augsburg, and from 1540 professor of medicine at the University of Tübingen (dean of the faculty of medicine in 1541). He was a follower of Schwenckfeld.

Salvation and grace through Christ. I have never been at leisure so far, dearest Capito, to write you even one word to let you know that I will always remember your kindness to me. For when I came to Strasbourg and greeted you briefly in the name of our friend Michael Cellarius,[1] you received me with great kindness in accordance with your liberality. However, the hard and unavoidable need to look after my business will excuse my being remiss. Ah, my brother, I have an amazing desire to write to you, but I do not

* * * * *

1 Michael Cellarius (ca. 1490–1548) studied in Leipzig and became parish priest in Straubing and Wasserburg/Inn. He was obliged to leave on account of his evangelical preaching and moved to Wittenberg in 1524 and to Augsburg in 1525. He had a caustic style of preaching and writing, which involved him in a number of polemics. In 1525 he published *Frag und Antwort etlicher Artikel zwischen M. Michaelen Keller und D. Mathia Krezen ... newlich begeben*. In 1527, Duke Wilhelm of Bavaria attempted to have him arrested; he faced difficulties from the Catholics also during the Diet in Augsburg and left the city for Constance. In 1531, he returned, however, and resumed his preaching.

know how to begin, although I cannot leave you ignorant of these things, nor would it be appropriate because of the admirable judgment of God. Hear, therefore, in a very few words what has occurred, and praise God together with us: These days, that is, on 13 March,[2] our Cellarius sat down after the sermon to fill his empty stomach, as he usually does around noon. He had hardly eaten a bite or two, when a great fear overcame him and he trembled in his whole body. After a while, a burning fever ensued and he lay until the middle of the night, not unlike a man bereft of his senses. I, however, was occupied with other business and absent from the city. When by chance I heard about his condition from a messenger, whom Rehlinger sent to me,[3] I travelled all night on horseback. Rushing back to him, I found him lying like a dead man. But when I looked at him and saw the veins pulsing with life, I saw that he was not in danger of death. Rather, the force of the disease had gone to his head and put his mind into a fog, so that he was labouring under noxious fumes, about which I shall say nothing at present.

I can only say that people had different opinions about the case. A rumour spread through the whole town that Michael had been taken from us through a sudden death. Some said he was agitated and furious earlier on. Even if I wanted to, I could not tell you a fraction of the great jeers all pious men suffered at the hands of the opponents. But God, who does not disappoint the hope of his people, transformed the joy of the impious into a reproach, for they said he had been carried off to hell, but now they had to hear that all his weakness had disappeared, that Michael had returned from the nether regions. Forgive me, brother, necessity prevents me from writing any more, but this messenger will tell you everything. But as soon as I can, I shall write to you fully about everything through another writer, and especially about the fact that you must reproach Cellarius for his overzealous studies and work, which exceeds his strength. Farewell, together with Martin Bucer. Please give many greetings to him in my name, as well as to your wife. Augsburg, 19 March 1530.

Wolfgang Thalhauser, physician.

Letter 406: 31 March 1530, Strasbourg, The City Council of Strasbourg to the Public

Millet included this document, although it is a statement rather than a letter and was issued in the name of the city council. The manuscript, entitled *Copey*

* * * * *

2 13 March 1530 fell on a Sunday, the second week of Lent.
3 For Ulrich Rehlinger, see below, Ep. 456 headnote.

eins ußschribens aller newerong halb so durch gotts wort zu Straßburg inbracht und im namen eins ersamen rhatts beschehen mocht (Copy of an announcement on account of the innovations that were introduced in Strasbourg through God's Word and made in the name of the honourable council), is in the Universitätsbibliothek Basel, Ki.Ar. 25a, 139 (ff. 217–37). It is a hastily written draft, with many cancellations and marginal additions, mostly in Capito's hand (with insertions in a second, neat hand on ff. 219 verso, 232 verso–234 recto). The contents closely resembles Bucer's advisory Ratschlag D (BDS 3:346–57), written in preparation for the Diet of Augsburg. See below, Ep. 409.

[*Summary*]: The reforms instituted in Strasbourg have resulted in slanderous accusations, which make a defence necessary. When [Matthew Zell] first began preaching the gospel in 1522, he was accused of heresy by the bishop's official, [Jacob von Gottesheim]. This caused dissension in Strasbourg. An edict passed on 6 March 1523 at the Diet of Nürnberg gave authority to the council to censor books and maintain peace until a general council decided the issues under dispute. The relevant section of the Nürnberg edict is cited. The city council therefore called on the preachers and their Catholic (*päpstler*) opponents to explain their respective positions. The latter declined, however, insisting that the matter was not to be discussed before lay persons. The council protested in vain that it was their duty to look into this matter. On 1 December 1523 the council passed a decree forbidding the preachers to teach anything but the gospel and ordering them to refrain from personal attacks. The preachers taught the people that true justification comes through faith and warned them that works were not sufficient for salvation, arguing on the basis of scripture, patristic writings, canon law, and conciliar decisions.

The council instituted a public system of alms. 'For the first time public almsgiving was instituted, for the following reason ... If each individual wanted to help everyone without correct assessment, for which they do not have time, the pious would have to suffer, and the good poor people would still not be helped. Therefore a public system of almsgiving for the poor in the community is needed, for we are all called Christians and are deemed to be Christians' [f. 221]. For this purpose, that is, to do away with begging and to help the sick and poor according to predetermined criteria, a commission of three men was appointed: 'one of the nobility, one of the permanent councillors,[1] and one ordinary councillor, to assist the administrator of alms (*Schaffner*). They are to be called wardens (*Pfleger*)' [f. 222v].

* * * * *

1 *Ewige Räte*, i.e., members of the XV or XIII, who were members for life.

Obligatory auricular confession has been abolished ('No man or angel can forgive sins. That is up to God alone,' f. 223) as have fasting, the use of holy water, blessed salt, and the lighting of lamps before images.

On 6 January 1525, the council required all clergy to become citizens. They argued that the commandment to love one's neighbour meant sharing the burdens of the residents of the city. In the secular realm, obedience was owed to the secular authorities; in the spiritual realm, obedience was owed to God alone. The refusal of certain members of the three collegiate churches to take out citizenship and their subsequent flight from Strasbourg led to legal action in the *Reichskammergericht*.

On 15 March 1525, a decree was passed against clerical concubinage. At first there was considerable opposition against married priests, but the preachers showed that marriage was commended in Scripture. 'No person had the right to forbid marriage to a particular estate or person ... and no vow was binding that went against God's Word' [f. 225v]. Monasteries were dissolved because 'idleness benefits only the individual, and segregation was against brotherly love' [f. 226v]. The inmates were either pensioned off or allowed to reside in specifically designated convents, according to an edict of 2 September 1525. The portion of the income from monasteries that was not needed for pensions was used for the public good. On 7 May 1525 singing in church was forbidden, except during the four daily masses in the collegiate churches. The preachers taught that the mass was an abomination and harmful because of the claim that Christ's sacrifice on the cross was repeated at mass, whereas he died for sinners once and for all. The mass misrepresented the Lord's Supper. The preachers taught that 'we come together in his name, eat his bread and drink his wine to commemorate his death ... and that we are truly nourished by the Lord's body and blood for eternal life' [f. 228v]. Schools were established for the education of children and the training of future pastors. There boys are taught virtue and self-discipline as well as Latin and Greek. Those who were in training to become ministers were taught Greek and Hebrew, as well as mathematics, poetics, rhetoric, secular law, and biblical exegesis. A church order was established, providing for morning prayers and sermons in five parishes and two sermons in the cathedral, one in the morning, the other in the afternoon on days when there are no lectures. On Sunday, there are two morning sermons in the seven parishes, a noon sermon at the cathedral and at St Aurelia, and evening prayers in four parishes, as well as catechism after the sermon in the cathedral. The Lord's Supper is celebrated every Sunday in the parishes. The preachers teach that there 'is present in the Lord's Supper the living, true body of Christ, a true nourishment, and also his true, heavenly, living blood, which is a certain and invigorating drink for believers' [f. 230v]. The preachers have abandoned

Latin and the use of salt and chrism in the ceremony of baptism and have taken care to admonish the parents and godparents to ensure a Christian upbringing for the child baptized. On 9 February 1527 three cemeteries were created outside the city walls.

On 9 January 1529 the question of the remaining four masses was raised by the city council and relegated to the *Schöffen*, who decided on 20 February 1529 to abolish the mass. On 25 August 1529, a decree was passed regulating morals and instituting a marriage tribunal. On 14 February 1530, a decree was passed to abolish idolatry, to remove images and altars from the churches ('our hearts are the altar and sacrificial stones,' f. 235v). A defensive alliance has been formed with Zurich, Bern, and Basel. The purpose of all these measures was to safeguard the honour of God and assure the welfare and salvation of the community.

Letter 406a: 3 April 1530, Bern, The Council of Bern to Martin Bucer and Capito

Printed in CorrBucer 4:69–70, Ep. 281.

[*Summary*]: They send 10 gulden to support the Latin and Greek studies of Simon Sulzer [1508–85; later teacher at Bern] and ask for a character reference and progress report.

Letter 407: 22 April 1530, [Strasbourg], Capito to Ulrich Zwingli

Printed in ZwBw 4:546–51, Ep. 1012.

[*Summary*]: From a letter sent from Italy to Philip of Baden at Speyer, Capito has discovered that Zurich and Bern sent delegates to Venice, warning them against the power of the emperor. Capito thinks that such a matter should not have been discussed in public. Those in power will believe that Erasmus was right, when he predicted that the evangelical teaching would open up the way to mob rule (*democratia*). He urges Zwingli to use code when writing about sensitive issues. 'For counsel is no counsel if it is spread among many.' Philip of Hesse will not attend the diet.[1] He has appointed three delegates: [Philip] von Waldeck, chancellor [Johannes Feige], and Erhard Schnepf. Their mandate is to settle or defer the discussion about the Eucharist among

* * * * *

1 He changed his mind, arriving in Augsburg on 12 May.

the reformers. References to a future council appear to be only a delaying tactic. [Johannes] Fabri is up to his usual tricks. The delegates are to give their opinions in their own name, but refrain from restricting the freedom of the gospel or acknowledging the pope as head of the church. They are not to agree to anything contrary to their beliefs. Capito believes that a general council will never come about. Some people believe that all depends on the emperor, but Capito has his doubts. He points out that Charles speaks neither Latin nor German. He wonders who will represent the cause of the French, for 'monarchs listen only to other monarchs.' Philip of Hesse is the only one who looks after the cause of the gospel. It is important that the reformers present a united front. The [Marburg preacher Hartmann] Ibach laments the military plans of Philip of Hesse. Schnepf will be pitted against Fabri. The Strasbourg delegates will be [Jacob] Sturm and [Matthis] Pfarrer

Letter 408: [End of April 1530, Zurich], Ulrich Zwingli to Capito and Martin Bucer

Printed in ZwBw 4:556–7, Ep. 1014a, and CorrBucer 4:89–91, Ep. 292.

[*Summary*]: [Felix Brennwald, a former mayor] would like to apprentice his son, [Hans Jakob Brennwald] to the Strasbourg city scribe, [Peter Butz]. Zwingli recommends the skill and character of the young man. He regrets imposing on Capito and Bucer with his request, but the Brennwalds are relatives to whom he cannot deny this favour. If Butz cannot take the young man, he hopes they can find another suitable place for him. The parents are willing to pay up to 20 florins. Matters in Zurich are well, except for a poor. harvest.

Letter 409: [End of April 1530, Strasbourg], Capito, Martin Bucer, and Jacob Sturm in the name of the City Council of Strasbourg to Charles V

Millet included this document, which is a statement of beliefs rather than a letter, and formally addressed by the city council to the Emperor. Printed in BDS 3:342–64, Ratschlag D, Fassung A. Cf. also CorrBucer 4:91–2, Ep. 293.

[*Summary*]: The city explains its religious beliefs and practices and hopes for the convocation of a general council to settle the remaining questions. They ask the emperor to receive their statement graciously. It is not meant as an act of disobedience, but rather as an expression of their Christian belief. [For a more detailed account of the contents, see above Ep. 406.]

Letter 409a: [End of April/beginning of May 1530, Strasbourg, Capito, Martin Bucer, and Jacob Sturm in the name of the City Council of Strasbourg to Charles V]

This is an alternative version of Ep. 409 above (Fassung B, Printed in BDS 3:364–92 = CorrBucer 4:92, Ep. 294).

Letter 410: 15 May 1530, Strasbourg, Capito to Ulrich Zwingli

Printed ZwBw 4:580–2, Ep. 1025.

[*Summary*]: Karlstadt has recently come to Strasbourg. Capito approves of his views on the Eucharist, but he has no prospect of obtaining a position in Strasbourg. Zwingli will find him lacking in only one respect: his dialect. He will be content with modest means. Capito feels sorry for Karlstadt on account of the persecution he suffers from Luther. Luther has also spoken harshly about Zwingli and, in a recent letter [not extant], against the Strasbourg theologians and Oecolampadius. He criticized Capito personally at the Marburg Colloquy (*Scio ... quae idem palam asseruit de me Marpurgi*). Philip [Melanchthon] is hypocritical (*fucata dictione praeditus est*). He has spoken abusively about the Strasbourgers, alleging that they deny the divinity of Christ. He said, moreover, 'that he would rather come to terms with the papists than with us heretics.' Philip of Hesse instructed his delegates to urge concord among the reformers and to refer questions to a future council. He does not expect the Diet of Augsburg to establish a definite date for such a council. The emperor will seek a financial subsidy. Capito asks Zwingli to find a position for Karlstadt. He sends his greetings to [the mayor, Diethelm] Resch [or, Roist]. The departure of [Jacob] Sturm and Matthis Pfarrer for Augsburg is imminent.

Letter 411: 23 May 1530, Oldersum, Ulrich von Dornheim to Capito, Martin Bucer, Caspar Hedio, and Martin Cellarius

Printed in CorrBucer 4:103–5, Ep. 300. The writer, Ulrich von Dornheim (ca. 1470–1536), lord of Dornum, Esens, Wittmund, and Oldersum in East Friesland, promoted the Reformation in his territory.

[*Summary*]: Their letter adds to his pleasure of receiving a letter from Karlstadt. He has suffered persecution from Count [Enno I of East Friesland], but hopes to be aided by letters from [Philip] of Hesse and to benefit from the support of Strasbourg. He sends greetings to the community in Zurich and Basel, and to Ulrich Zwingli and [Johannes] Oecolampadius personally.

Letter 411a: 23 May 1530, Augsburg, Gereon Sailer to Matthew Zell, [Capito, Martin Cellarius, and Martin Bucer]

Printed in CorrBucer 4:106–11, Ep. 301. Gereon Sailer (ca. 1500–63) studied medicine in Ingolstadt (doctorate in 1527) and shortly afterwards became town physician in Augsburg. He represented the Augsburg city council in their search for a suitable preacher, unsuccessfully negotiating with Ambrosius Blaurer in 1530 and Urbanus Rhegius in 1535, and finally, successfully, with Johann Forster of Wittenberg. He continued his scholarly work, publishing a treatise on the plague in 1535 and collaborating on a handbook of medicine, *Conclusiones et propositiones universam medicinam per genera comprehendentes* (Vienna, 1538).

[*Summary*]: Sailer has not written earlier because no messenger was available. Philip [Melanchthon], [Justus] Jonas, [Georgius] Spalatinus, and [Johann Agricola] of Eisleben are diligently working for the cause of the Reformation. Agricola is preaching every day. [Philip] of Hesse has brought [Erhard] Schnepf; George of Saxony has brought [Johannes] Cochlaeus; and Joachim, the Elector of Brandenburg, [Konrad Wimpina]. [Johann] Eck, who has sent the emperor his *404 Articles* [Ingolstadt, April 1530], is expected to arrive soon. Philip of Hesse has invited Michael [Cellarius] and Urbanus [Rhegius]. He hopes to create a semblance of peace among the feuding Protestants. So far, the Saxons have refrained from preaching about the Eucharist. It is to be hoped that they will not raise this thorny issue in their sermons during the diet. Bucer's pamphlet [*Non esse ferendas*] is circulating together with Bucer's letter [cf. above, Epp. 404b]. Sailer wishes the letter was available in German as well. He urges Strasbourg to send representatives to Augsburg, since the emperor will want to discuss the question of the Eucharist. François Lambert has died of the plague in Marburg. He asks that [Caspar] Schwenckfeld be treated well. He hopes for a letter from Bucer.

Letter 412: 24 May 1530, Strasbourg, Capito to Ulrich Zwingli

Printed in ZwBw 4:590, Ep. 1029.

[*Summary*]: Capito recommends the bearer, [either Jacob Hilari or the Philip mentioned below, Ep. 413], who served as a priest in Brandenburg and was ousted because of his beliefs. He is an upright and godly man, but Capito cannot recommend his industry. He hopes that Zwingli will help Karlstadt.

Letter 412a: [May 1530, Strasbourg], Capito to [Daniel Mieg]

The manuscript is in AST 40, #43, f. 411. Daniel Mieg (1476 or 1484–1541) was a member of the city council from 1520, representing the guild of bakers. In 1523/4 he was a delegate at the Diet of Nürnberg (see above, Ep. 179). From 1527 he was repeatedly *Stettmeister*. In 1529 he was the city's representative at the *Reichsregiment*. At the time of writing, he was presiding *Ammeister* in the city council.

Honourable, wise, circumspect, and ruling lord. After Christmas 1525, my gracious lords of the honourable council asked me to move from the house I had to Young St Peter and gave me the house of Lorenz Hell,[1] at the time dean, that I may better preside over the parish, keep the community in order, and serve Your Graces more properly in the Word of God. I willingly complied and have lived there for about four years and five months. Now a citizen of Freiburg,[2] who is reportedly the warden of the above-named dean's children, demands from me 20 gulden yearly rent for the house, which would amount to more than 80 gulden. I consistently and throughout referred him to the *Ammeister*, but he did not comply and yet keeps up his demands. In this manner, I and my heirs are kept in suspense and under obligation to pay what he demands. For that is what he claims in his demand. It is my earnest request to Your Wise Honours to negotiate with the chapter of Young St Peter and to request that they immediately satisfy the above-named warden of the children or other heirs of the dean, that no one may have a claim on me or my heirs. I ask this especially because the parish has an obligation to look after this, and it was Your Lordships who put me into the house. Otherwise, I would perhaps have preferred to remain in my own house, which was more convenient and appropriate for my needs, if it had not been for the honour of God and your favour, my lords, and for the advantage of the community, which made me move to the above-named house. If this is not done, my opponent will continue to have a claim on me and my heirs. I therefore ask Your Wise Honours to help me in this matter. I am willing to earn your favour.

    Your Wise Honours' willing servant,

      Wolfgang Capito.

* * * * *

1 For Lorenz Hell, cf. above, Ep. 246a, note 21. W. Horning, *Urkundliches über die Jung-St.-Peter-Kirche und Gemeinde* (Strasbourg, 1888), 6, cites a manuscript in the 'Stadtarchiv, Lade 47, Nr. 11' which refers to this transaction on 3 February 1525. On that date, the city council 'authorized Daniel Mieg to put Dr Capito into the house of the Dean ... which is located at the entrance to Young St Peter.'

2 Unidentified.

Letter 413: [ca. 20 June 1530, Strasbourg, Capito] to Ulrich Zwingli

Printed in ZwBw 4:622–4, Ep. 1044.

[*Summary*]: Philip [unidentified], whom Bucer and Capito jointly recommended, has returned and relies on their help. He relinquished his Catholic benefice and married on their recommendation and must now look for a means of making a living. He is destitute and, on the advice of Melchior [Macrinus?], wants to travel to Zurich. He has asked Bucer for a letter of recommendation, but is now worried because Bucer hinted that he was an Anabaptist sympathizer. Capito would not want to recommend any man who is seditious. He admits that he has sometimes been wrong in his judgment of people. He and Bucer are preparing to depart for [the Diet in] Augsburg. He believes he will be of use there because of his former connections with courtiers. He is preparing for the journey by reading Luther's writings, an unpleasant task. He is at present reading Luther's [*Grosses Bekenntnis vom Abendmahl* of 1528]. Luther has also written against the bishops [*Vermanung an die geistlichen, versamlet auff dem Reichstag zu Augsburg*, Wittenberg, 1530], but the sale of this book has been prohibited by the Augsburg city council. Luther is indignant because the Strasbourgers dared to reply to his arrogant writings. No doubt, Luther's writings will be translated into Latin and French. Capito is pleased that Zwingli approves of Karlstadt. Valentin [Ickelsamer] is staying at Capito's house. He has been ousted on the initiative of the Lutherans [Friedrich Myconius and Justus Menius, on suspicion of being a supporter of Karlstadt] and was unable to obtain an audience with Luther, even though Justus Jonas and [Georgius] Spalatinus spoke on his behalf. Luther's tyranny has increased in the wake of the Marburg Colloquy [of 1529]. Philip of Hesse attended the sermons of Michael Cellarius ('one of ours') in Augsburg and ignored Johann Agricola von Eisleben. Bucer will reply to Leo [Jud].

**Letter 414: 7 July [1530, Augsburg], Capito and Martin Bucer to the
        Strasbourg preachers**

Printed in CorrBucer 4:124–32, Ep. 308. For security reasons, Capito and Bucer travelled to the Diet of Augsburg separately. They arrived there on the 23 and 26 June respectively (see CorrBucer 4:118–22, Ep. 306, note 3) and remained incognito for the time being (see below, Epp. 415, 420).

[*Summary*]: The emperor has not yet pronounced on the [Confessio Augustana]. [Philip of Hesse, referred to in code as 'Candidus'] was reproved by the emperor for not enforcing the Edict of Worms. The emperor was in the company of [the vice-chancellor Balthasar Mercklin], and [the imperial secretary] Alexander Schweiss. Philip noted that other principalities shared his views and demanded scriptural proof that they were wrong. The [Edict of Worms], he noted, had never been applied rigorously. Discussing his views on the Eucharist, Philip of Hesse assured the emperor that he believed in the Real Presence. The emperor in turn admonished him to obey his final decision in this matter. Afterwards, Mercklin hinted that a favourable decision concerning 'the Nassau affair' [i.e., the contested region of Katzenelnbogen] might be forthcoming if Philip severed his relations with the Lutherans. He stood firm. Philip also spoke with [Matthäus Lang], bishop of Salzburg, the papal legate Cardinal Lorenzo Campeggio, and others. Capito and Bucer fear that the conciliatory attitude of Philip Melanchthon will merely strengthen the hand of the Catholics. The Confessio Tetrapolitana has been signed (with the article on the Eucharist revised) by Constance, Memmingen, and Lindau. They will shortly present the Confession [i.e., on 9 July 1530] to the emperor, who is being advised by the theologians [Johannes] Fabri, [Johannes] Cochlaeus, [Konrad] Wimpina, [Konrad] Köllin, and [Balthasar Mercklin] who has just been installed as bishop of [Constance]. [Christoph von Stadion] tried to persuade them to make further changes. They feel embattled. The Lutherans are inimical toward them. They admonish their brethren to remain strong. Urbanus Rhegius will go to Lüneburg. Johann Agricola has reportedly left for Nürnberg. Michael [Cellarius] has been prohibited from appearing in public. Capito wrote to [Albert of Brandenburg], the archbishop of Mainz, and was granted an audience, but when the appointed hour arrived, the archbishop excused himself. Capito will attempt to set up another meeting. They asked Philip of Hesse to arrange for a meeting with the Lutherans, but he could achieve nothing because 'they clearly regard him as a Zwinglian.' Matthis [Pfarrer] and [Jacob] Sturm are acting with all diligence. Michael [Cellarius] is in danger.

Letter 415: 12 July 1530, Augsburg, Capito and Martin Bucer to the Strasbourg Preachers

Printed in CorrBucer 4:138–42, Ep. 312.

[Summary]: They have not yet made a public appearance. Zwingli sent his [Fidei ratio] to the emperor [on 3 July]. On 9 July, Georg von Truchsess invited the Lutherans, on the emperor's behalf, to add a section on the power of the pope. This they did in the blandest terms, fearing that a stronger statement would endanger acceptance of the whole document. On the same day, the emperor invited those who protested their faith at the Diet of Speyer to discuss their reservations and follow up on the document they had sent to the emperor [on 7 September 1529]. Also on 9 July, the Confessio Tetrapolitana [see above, Ep. 414] was presented to [Balthasar Mercklin], now bishop of Constance. The emperor is said to have vowed to sacrifice his life rather than accept the proposals of the schismatics. It is rumoured that he has sent envoys to the Turks to negotiate a three-year peace in the hope that he might suppress the gospel in the meantime. They are pleased to hear that the altar of Young St Peter in Strasbourg has been removed.[1] They send greetings to Symphorian [Altbiesser].

Letter 416: [15] July 1530, [Augsburg], Philip Melanchthon to Capito and Martin Bucer

Printed in CorrBucer 4:142–3, Ep. 313 and MBW T4/1: 378–9, Ep. 972.

[Summary]: [Johannes] Brenz has reported to him about his conversation with Capito and Bucer. He cannot meet with them personally because he does not want to burden the Lutherans with the odium adhering to the Strasbourg teaching. Zwingli's [Fidei ratio] was inappropriate in tone and unfortunate in its timing. He wishes to settle their disagreement about the Eucharist, but invites them to submit their opinions to him in writing.

Letter 417: [15 July 1530, Strasbourg, Capito and Martin Bucer to Philip Melanchthon]

This letter fragment, which was apparently not sent off, is printed in CorrBucer 4:144–7, Ep. 314 and MBW T4/1:383–6, Ep. 974.

[Summary]: They would prefer a personal interview rather than providing a written explanation of their views on the Eucharist. They agree with the Lutherans on the Real Presence. If Zwingli denies it in his statement to the emperor, he merely means to deny its presence in a specific place and dimension (dimensionibus suis et loco praesens); when he says Christ is present 'in the contemplation of the faith,' he means that Christ's body is eaten 'through the benefit of faith,' which the Lutherans will not deny. From the enclosed pamphlet [i.e., Oecolampadius' Quid de Eucharistia veteres ...], he will see that Oecolampadius denies only the natural consubstantiation of body and bread.

* * * * *

1 I.e., in the course of removing images from the churches.

Letter 418: 18 July 1530, Augsburg, Capito and Martin Bucer to Philip Melanchthon

This letter, which was sent instead of the unfinished Ep. 417, is printed in CorrBucer 4:152–7, Ep. 317 and MBW T4/1:394–9, Ep. 980.

[*Summary*]: They prefer to speak to Melanchthon in person. As for Zwingli's [*Fidei ratio*], it contains nothing that he has not also written elsewhere. He has in common with all reformers the determination to put Christ above the pope, which is what makes them unpopular with the emperor. If Zwingli has shown passion, so has Luther in the past. That does not mean that he is not inspired by God. It is true that Zwingli's disagreement [regarding the Eucharist] goes beyond words, but only if it is interpreted in the rather primitive (*crassius*) manner, that is, 'uniting Christ's body with the bread or placing him in the bread.' Surely this cannot be the Lutheran interpretation. They insist that Christ's presence is real, but not localized. They themselves do not deny the Real Presence and cannot see what difference there is in their respective opinions except 'that we cannot as yet agree on the words through which the mystery is to be explained; for how could it be that those who are taught and inspired by the Spirit did not agree on such an important matter?' If the participants at the Marburg Colloquy [of 1529] had been allowed to explain their views at greater length, they might have reached an agreement. They have heard that Melanchthon accuses Zwingli of departing from what was agreed on at Marburg. This is incorrect. They would like a personal meeting in the presence of Brenz and Sturm.

Letter 419: 22 July [1530], Augsburg, Capito and Martin Bucer to Ambrosius Blaurer

Printed in CorrBucer 4:157–9, Ep. 318.

[*Summary*]: There can be no doubt about the loyalty of [Konrad] Zwick, [a delegate to Augsburg]. They enclose a copy of their letter to Zwingli to save themselves repeating the report. Both Catholics and Lutherans are hostile toward the Strasbourgers. The bishops fear war. They send greetings to [Johannes] Zwick and the other brethren in Constance.

Letter 420: 22 July [1530], Augsburg, Capito and Martin Bucer to Ulrich Zwingli

Printed in CorrBucer 4:160–4, Ep. 319 and ZwBw 5:37–41, Ep. 1068. This is the last letter written jointly by Bucer and Capito from Augsburg. Capito presumably departed shortly thereafter. He arrived in Strasbourg on 5 August 1530 (cf. Ep. 420a below).

[*Summary*]: The emperor is pressuring the electors George of Brandenburg and John of Saxony to revert to the Catholic faith. They have not yielded. He has not called in [Philip of Hesse], perhaps because the earlier interview [cf. above, Ep. 414] made him despair of success. The *Confutatio confessionis Augustanae* has been presented. The Catholic princes are afraid of war and are looking for common ground. They may do nothing about married priests, allow communion in two kinds, and declare a moratorium on the mass until a general council can be called, but the emperor will object. He is prepared to go to war against the 'heretics' with the financial help of Henry VIII. Capito and Bucer have gone public and presented the Confessio Tetrapolitana. They have talked with Brenz. They have not been able to arrange a personal meeting with Melanchthon. They fear they will be unsuccessful in their efforts to present their views to the rulers [of Saxony, Brandenburg, and Lüneburg] who support Luther. Philip of Hesse is on their side. They also talked with two courtiers of Albert of Brandenburg, archbishop of Mainz: [Caspar von Westhausen and Michael Vehe], but found them intransigent. Zwingli's [*Fidei ratio*] has offended some people.

Letter 420a: 8 [August 1530], Augsburg, [Martin Bucer to the Strasbourg Preachers]

Printed in CorrBucer 4:181–5, Ep. 322. This letter is included here because Bucer assumes Capito's presence in Strasbourg (p. 185, lines 1–2: *habetis, ut spero, iam Capitonem*) and therefore includes him in his address.

[*Summary*]: The emperor called the representatives of the evangelicals and offered to present them with a response on condition that they accept this response as final. This was not acceptable to the evangelicals. Joachim of Brandenburg, [Heinrich] of Braunschweig, and others offered to negotiate with the emperor on their behalf, but the evangelicals said they needed no negotiators since they were not enemies. On 6 August Philip of Hesse left on the pretext that his wife was fatally ill, which caused the emperor to tighten security. The Confessio Tetrapolitana has been given a harsh reception. Bucer asks for prayers that they may remain firm in their response. The emperor is powerful, but he cannot go against God. They cannot expect help from any of the princes, with the possible exception of Philip of Hesse. He hopes that Capito has arrived and informed them of what he saw in Augsburg. There is a rumour that the emperor will make concessions to the princes and cities until he can obtain a truce from the Turks.

Letter 420b: [25 August 1530, Augsburg, Martin Bucer to the Strasbourg Preachers]

> Printed in CorrBucer 4:228–32, Ep. 330. The letter, a German translation by Caspar Hedio, has no address or signature.

[*Summary*]: Philip Melanchthon met with Gregor Brück and Sebastian Heller. Bucer finally obtained a personal interview with Melanchthon through the intervention of Argula von Grumbach. He asserted that they believed in the Real Presence and gave Melanchthon a written statement to be transmitted to Luther. He has written to Zwingli and Oecolampadius. Eck said that he preferred the devil and the Turks to the evangelicals. No response to the Confessio Tetrapolitana has been received. He asks them to pray for Johannes Schneidt, parish priest of Holy Cross, who has been incarcerated as a disturber of the peace. The churches of Detwyler and Dossenheim [two villages under the jurisdiction of Strasbourg] have not yet been looked after. The preachers should admonish the council to communicate with their delegates more often. Bucer is afraid that he might be obliged to flee Augsburg.

Letter 421: 30 August 1530, Basel, Capito to [Nicolaus Kniebs]

> Printed in Pollet II, 161–2 (with some errors and omissions); cf. the facsimile of the manuscript (AST 40, #13) in Ficker-Winckelmann I, 57.
>
> After his return from the Diet of Augsburg, the council sent Capito to Basel and Zurich (cf. below, Epp. 424, 426) to consult with the reformers on a joint course of action. This is his report to Nicolaus Kniebs. The letter was sent through Caspar Hedio, whose name appears as the nominal addressee on the verso. On Kniebs see above, Ep. 184 headnote.

Circumspect, honest, wise sir, we arrived in Basel yesterday around nine, and before sitting down to dinner, I came to a full agreement with Oecolampadius concerning the articles.[1] Jakob Meyer, the mayor,[2] Balthasar Hilt-

* * * * *

1 I.e., concerning the Sacramentarian question. Cf. E. Dürr ed., *Aktensammlung zur Geschichte der Basler Reformation* (Basel, 1921–50), 4: 570–1, # 617, #618.
2 Jakob Meyer zum Hirzen (d. 1541).

brand, the *Zunftmeister*,[3] and Bernhard Meyer[4] joined me for a meal at the inn; in the evening we were at Oecolampadius' house and were fêted with wine, no doubt, to honour Your Grace. I thanked him and accepted, also to honour Your Grace. After breakfast, the mayor asked me whether I was in agreement with Oecolampadius, for the honourable council had in mind to send him along [to Zurich]. It would be very good [he said] to be in agreement and to act unanimously in Zurich. And when I indicated to him that Oecolampadius was well pleased with me on the whole, and we wished to continue our discussion, he asked whether I was agreeable to the council writing for a preacher from Bern as well,[5] for that was the considered opinion of the honest council. I said it was my pleasure, for I was worried that Zwingli would make no decision without consulting the people of Bern, and the matter would suffer delay while he wrote from Zurich to Bern. Thus a messenger was sent to Bern with instructions to ride all night long and to present the letter today to the XII or to as many of them as possible. Therefore I fear, gracious lord, that we shall have to remain in Zurich for three or four days,[6] but I have no doubt that God will bestow his grace on us, so that peace will not be obstructed, as far as lies in us. Thus I commend you to God and offer my ready service. I ask you to thank my lords of Basel for their effort and the honour they did us. Given at Basel, 30 August 1530.

Your Grace's obliging Wolfgang Capito.

Letter 422: 31 August 1530, Zurich, Ulrich Zwingli to Capito

Printed in ZwBw 5:98–9, Ep. 1085. Apparently, Zwingli was unaware of the fact that Capito and Oecolampadius were on their way to Zurich, where they arrived on 31 August (cf. above, Ep. 421, and below, Ep. 426).

[*Summary*]: He is glad that Capito has arrived safely in Strasbourg [i.e., from Augsburg]. He assumes he has already heard from Bucer about the inter-

* * * * *

3 Balthasar Hiltbrand was master of the guilds from 1530.
4 Bernhard Meyer (1488–1558) was a delegate to Zurich in April 1531 (cf. Corr-Bucer Ep. 414, note 7) and mayor from 1545 to his death in 1558.
5 I.e. Caspar Megander (1495–1545), who studied in Basel (MTh 1518), was chaplain at the Zurich hospital from 1519, and married in 1524. He was a supporter of Zwingli and participated in the disputations of Zurich (1525) and Bern (1528). In 1528 be became preacher in Bern and taught at the university there. Cf. also below, Ep. 424.
6 I.e., while waiting for the arrival of the preacher from Bern.

view with Melanchthon [see above, Ep. 420b]. If they had met earlier, they might have achieved consensus. Zwingli will write at length to Bucer. He will accept the Real Presence if it is stated that Christ's presence is not corporeal, but spiritual and sacramental through faith, for Melanchthon more or less conceded that. He has responded to Eck's violent denunciations [in the *Ad illustrissimos Germaniae principes Augustae congregatos de convitiis Eccii epistola* of 27 August]. It has been printed. Perhaps Christoph [Froschauer] has a copy with him. He asks for news from Strasbourg. The Anabaptists are causing problems in [Bremgarten]. He sends greetings to [Caspar] Hedio.

Letter 423: 3 September 1530, [Zurich], Capito to Friederich Myconius

> Printed in Otto Clemen, 'Die Brücknersche Sammlung von Briefen aus der Reformationszeit,' *ARG* 27 (1930): 264, Ep. 6. Friedrich Myconius (ca.1490–1546) was a Franciscan turned Lutheran theologian, active in Weimar, Gotha, and Leipzig. He was instrumental in the reformation of the Thuringian church. In 1538 he travelled to England to persuade Henry VIII to support Luther. He was the author of a history of the Reformation (*Historia reformationis*, published posthumously in 1715).

[*Summary*]: Myconius had asked him to discuss the abolition of secret confession, but there were more important matters on the table. People must explore their conscience in private. This is what the Strasbourgers teach young people. The next step will be to teach the older generation. They hope to settle the Sacramentarian controversy. Capito asks Myconius to pray for concord. Bucer sends his greetings.

Letter 424: 4 September 1530, Zurich, Capito to Martin Bucer

> Printed in CorrBucer 4:264–7, Ep. 337.

[*Summary*]: Capito reports on his meeting with Zwingli, the Zurich ministers, Oecolampadius as representative of Basel, and Caspar Megander as representative of Bern. They hope to come to an agreement with the Lutherans concerning the Eucharist by adopting the formula of a 'sacramental union.' They will overlook the fact that various interpretations and practices were adopted in spite of what was agreed at the Marburg Colloquy [1529]. They believe that Luther misunderstood their point of view. They hope that this has now been clarified in the written statement sent to him [by Bucer, see above, Ep. 422]. Their position can also be seen from the enclosed statements [by Zwingli, Oecolampadius, Jud, and Megander; cf. below, Ep. 428].

Letter 425: 5 September 1530, Zurich, Capito [on behalf of Zwingli]? to the Five Catholic Cantons

Printed in M. Schuler and J. Schulthess, eds., *Zvinglii Opera* (Zurich, 1828–42), 2.3:77–80. The letter was written (see below, Ep. 425a) and carried by Capito to the meeting of the cities in Baden, where it was presented on 13 October (cf. Oecolampadius to Bucer, CorrBucer 4, Ep. 353) in Zwingli's name. The 'Fünf Orte' addressed here are the five Catholic cantons of Lucerne, Uri, Schwyz, Zug, and Unterwalden. They had formed a league in November 1528, and in April 1529 entered a secret alliance with Ferdinand I.

[*Summary*]: The reformers urge the Catholic cantons to maintain peace. They impose no demands on their preachers except that they preach the gospel rather than popish errors about purgatory, indulgences, and idolatry. Secular governments recognize that they must protect the spiritual welfare of their subjects and promote the gospel, so as not to arouse the wrath of God. It is their task, moreover, to protect the worldly goods of their subjects. This being so, the Five Cantons ought to permit gospel preaching. The lack of God's Word is the only thing that divides them. They invite them to embrace peace and concord. They ask that this statement be read in their assembly.

Letter 425a: [Between 6 and 11 September 1530], Strasbourg, Capito to the XIII of Strasbourg[1]

Printed in BrOek 2:484–7 (first half) and E. Staehelin, 'Oecolampadia,' in *Basler Zeitschrift für Geschichte und Altertumskunde* 65 (1965): 179–81 (conclusion).

[*Summary*]: Capito arrived in Basel on 29 August [cf. above, Epp. 421, 424] and met with Oecolampadius. It was decided that Oecolampadius and a representative from Bern [Caspar Megander] should accompany him to Zurich. They arrived in Zurich on 31 August and stayed until 6 September. The city of Schaffhausen did not send a representative [cf. below, Ep. 426]. On 4 September Zwingli received a package with letters from [John], the Elector of Saxony, and Philip of Hesse, with replies from Philip Melanchthon and Johannes Brenz concerning an agreement among the reformers. In the afternoon the preachers were joined by four city councillors. Capito presented Bucer's articles ['Ratschlag A,' cf. CorrBucer 4:92, Ep. 294], urging concord. Zwingli presented the papers he had just received, which showed the hos-

* * * * *

1 See above, Ep. 280, note 12.

tile attitude of the Lutherans. Although Capito pointed out that the attitude of the Lutherans had changed in the meantime, no agreement was reached. The meeting concluded with a request that each representative should put his views in writing. On 5 September, Oecolampadius, Megander, Jud, and Zwingli each presented their views on the Sacramentarian question. In Capito's view, these position papers were too explicit (*zu ganz usgetruckt und zu vil heiter*) to be accepted by the Lutherans. Capito did not present a separate position paper and kept to Bucer's articles, since they had been presented to and approved by Melanchthon. In the end, it was decided that Capito should write to Bucer [Ep. 426], enclosing a summary of what had been discussed, phrased in a manner acceptable to the Lutherans but not diverging from their own interpretation (*das si Luther mochten angenehm und der worheit unabbrüchlich sin*). They did not instruct Bucer to write new articles for presentation to the Lutherans, as Capito had requested. The letter and summary was sent to Bucer on 4 September. A copy is enclosed. Capito also encloses a letter composed by himself but sent in the name of Zwingli and the preachers of the four reformed towns to the five Catholic towns [Ep. 425]. A disputation is planned in Solothurn,[2] to which Conrad Treger has been invited. The preachers offered to send a representative and sent a message to this effect through [Urs Stark; cf. above, Ep. 426]. He pleaded [Johann Büchlin's] case, asking that he be allowed to travel in Switzerland [cf. Ep. 289n]. They discussed at length the question of imposing church discipline on the towns. Johann Eck has slandered them, saying that they dissolved monasteries and divided the goods among themselves. They will defend themselves, arguing that the original purpose of the collegiate churches was to support education [cf. Capito's proposals above, Ep. 404]. Zurich, Bern, and Basel were urged to look after their clergy. He hopes that Strasbourg will do the same for the local clergy.

Letter 426: 13 September 1530, Strasbourg, Capito to Martin Bucer

Printed in CorrBucer 4:275–86, Ep. 340. Bucer was still in Augsburg at the time of writing.

[*Summary*]: Capito gives a fuller report of his journey to Basel [see above, Epp. 421 and 425a] and Zurich [see above, Ep. 424]. In Basel, the mayor [Jakob Meyer zum Hirzen] and the master of the guilds, [Balthasar Hiltbrand], de-

* * * * *

2 The meeting did not come to pass.

cided that Oecolampadius should join Capito at the meeting with Zwingli in Zurich. They also sent a messenger to ask for a representative from Bern, either Berthold Haller or Caspar Megander [Megander joined them; see above, Ep. 424]. The Zurich reformers asked for a representative from Schaffhausen, but the council, which is hostile to the reformers, made excuses. They assured them, however, that they would accept any decisions made at Zurich. Capito arrived in Zurich on 31 August and remained until 6 September. He and his companions were received hospitably and accommodated at public expense. Capito praises the discipline kept in Zurich. Oecolampadius' efforts to introduce a system of church discipline in Basel have so far been unsuccessful. The Franciscan [Johannes Lüthard] and Marcus [Bertsch, parish priest of St Leonard's at Basel] are preaching against him. Capito would like to discuss with Bucer the possibility of introducing church discipline in Strasbourg.

The question of coming to an agreement with the Lutherans was on the agenda. Oecolampadius accepted Bucer's formula, with some reservations. Zwingli, who wrote a sharply worded letter [not extant] to Bucer, is somewhat more amenable to his position now that he has heard Capito's interpretation. While they were waiting for the arrival of Megander, a packet of letters came from Philip of Hesse with a proposal concerning [the Schmalkald League] and its rejection by the Elector of Saxony; also Bucer's proposal [Ratschlag A, cf. CorrBucer 4:94–5, Ep. 296] with Melanchthon's and Brenz's response. On 2 September, Capito reported to the Zurich preachers, in the presence of four councillors, about their negotiations in Augsburg with Melanchthon, Brück, and Brenz [see above, Epp. 416, 417, and 420b] and Melanchthon's readiness to seek a formula on which they could all agree. Zwingli insisted on reading certain materials written by the Lutherans against Zurich and the Zwinglians, which greatly offended the councillors present. He furthermore reminded them of the hostile reception he had in Marburg. Capito emphasized that the attitude of the Lutherans had changed. They were more inclined to make peace after the discussions they had with them in Augsburg. Zwingli resented Capito's efforts to promote peace at first, but finally agreed to have Bucer draw up articles for discussion. At that point, Capito wrote the official report to Bucer [i.e., Ep. 424], which he hopes will give Bucer an opportunity to continue negotiations with Zurich, in person, if necessary. If he does, he must first speak to Ulrich Funk (cf. above, Ep. 400) and Leo Jud and get their cooperation.

Capito is glad to hear that Bucer will have an opportunity to speak with Luther personally [on 26 September at Coburg]. He has made a presentation to the Committee of the XIII in Strasbourg concerning the matter of organizing schools, and has received a positive reply from them through Egenolf

[Roeder von Diersburg]. While in Zurich, the preachers wrote a joint letter to the [Five Catholic cantons; see above, Ep. 425] to urge peace. There will be a disputation between the reformers and Catholics at Solothurn [cancelled because of the Kappel War]. Oecolampadius and Capito talked to a magistrate from Solothurn [Urs Stark?], who happened to be in Basel when they returned. They must carefully monitor the situation in Solothurn, where the Catholic party is strong. He hopes that war can be avoided.

Fridolin Meyer [public notary of the bishop and a sympathizer of the Anabaptists] has died of the plague; Martin Herlin's wife has died of phthisis. Bucer's family is well. Jacob Rieher reports that Johann Schneid has been set free [see above, Ep. 420b]. Ideally, the apostolic creed should be a sufficient basis for Christians. Capito regrets the need for further articles. He wishes for a more charitable approach. He has received a letter from Erasmus [not extant] and has read his [*Responsio ad epistolam apologeticam*, 1530] a reply to Bucer's [*Epistola apologetica*, 1530]. He has not had time to read it carefully, but he can see that Erasmus is a 'virulent creature' (*virulenta bestiola*). He regrets the slow progress in Strasbourg to institute elementary schools; he finds the council more cooperative in other matters. He misses Sturm and Pfarrer [who are still in Augsburg] and other supporters who are busy at the Frankfurt Fair. He has read Luther's two letters [not identified] to Melanchthon, which are cryptic. The Elector [Johann Friedrich I of Saxony] is staunch in his support of the reformers; the emperor relies on Fabri and Eck. He wishes Bucer would return with news of peace with the Lutherans. He sets his hopes on the personal meeting between Bucer and Luther. If Luther sees Bucer's sincerity he will, no doubt, be moved. It is regrettable that Luther is surrounded by flatterers and does not recognize his own shortcomings. Capito will see to it that Bucer's letters are transcribed and shared with Oecolampadius and Zwingli.

Schwenckfeld, who is on his way to Silesia, asks to have the enclosed letters transmitted to Christian [Fridbolt, master of guilds in St Gallen]. [The jurist Franz?] Frosch is impoverished. He asks for Bucer's support. Gerard Geldenhouwer [cf. above, Ep. 336] is in a similar position.

Letter 427: 27 September 1530, Strasbourg, Capito to Ulrich Zwingli

Printed in ZwBw 5:161–3, Ep. 1107.

[*Summary*]: The enclosed letter [below, Ep. 427a] will inform Zwingli of the affairs in Augsburg. The imperial party is planning to make war on Strasbourg. Capito is glad that the Lutherans are now showing more fairness toward them. Bucer left Augsburg on 19 September to meet with Luther [in

Coburg] – he hopes, with good results. In an earlier letter, Bucer vowed to fight for the truth and convince Luther of the legitimacy of their position. Capito is keeping up his spirits, although conditions in Strasbourg are difficult: the harvest was poor and the granaries are empty. They are being put under pressure by speculators. The *episcopales* [the Catholic canons?] refuse to come before the city's courts. He writes this in confidence. Erasmus has aggravated matters for them with his [*Responsio ad epistolam apologeticam*, Freiburg, 1530] in reply to Bucer's [*Epistola apologetica*, Strasbourg 1530; cf. above, Ep. 426]. He expects the return of the delegates from Augsburg.[1] On their return, he hopes the alliance with [Philip of Hesse] will be concluded. He exhorts Zwingli to do everything possible to persuade the Swiss towns to maintain concord. Their enemies rejoice at the dissension among the reformers. He asks Zwingli to send him 'songs, even those composed for the lute.'

Letter 427a: [After 23 September 1530, Augsburg?], N to Capito

> This letter was enclosed with Ep. 427. The writer is not identified. The text is printed in ZwBw 5:164–6 (Beilage zu #1107). The letter was conveyed by Capito to Zwingli on 27 September.

[*Summary*]: John and George of Saxony planned on leaving Augsburg on 19 September, but were persuaded by the emperor to remain until 23 September. On 22 September they had an interview with the emperor in which he demanded that they support the punishment of Karlstadt and Zwingli, but they declined. Martin Bucer left on 19 September for Nürnberg and Coburg to meet Luther. If they had come to an agreement about the Sacramentarian question at Marburg or in Schmalkald [1529], matters would be easier now. The writer has not written to Capito for some time, but is with him in spirit. He wishes he were in Strasbourg or Nürnberg. Papists and reformers are far from agreement. The situation is tense. In a Latin postscript, Capito adds in his own hand that the messenger will leave for Basel. Philip of Hesse wishes to deposit money with the Strasbourg merchants for future use against his enemies.

Letter 428 is now Ep. 425a.

Letter 429 is now Ep. 412a.

* * * * *

1 Matthis Pfarrer left at the beginning of November; Jacob Sturm travelled on to Schmalkald and Nürnberg and returned only at the end of the year.

Letter 429a: 27 December 1530, Augsburg, The City Council of Augsburg to Martin Bucer and Capito.

Printed in CorrBucer 5:116–18, Ep. 365.

[*Summary*]: The council thanks Capito and Bucer for the letter dated 13 December [not extant], in which they recommend Wolfgang Musculus and Bonifacius Wolfhart as preachers. Shortly afterwards, the council sent Balthasar Langnauer, syndic of the city, to invite Musculus and to come to an agreement with him about the terms [cf. below, Ep. 431b]. They stand in need of preachers in Augsburg after they had to dismiss the evangelicals to satisfy the demands of Charles V during the Diet of Augsburg.

Letter 430: [1530], Strasbourg, Capito to the City Council of Strasbourg

This manuscript is in AMS II, 13a (44–45) 6, folios 11–12. It concerns a complaint by Daniel von Zweibrücken, a graduate of the University of Heidelberg (BA 1520), who held a benefice at Old St Peter. He is documented in 1528/9 as a student attending Bucer's and Capito's Bible studies and signed his name to a petition asking that Bucer be given a house in the city (AST 69 #21; cf. above, Ep. 381a). He remained a canon of Old St Peter's and is mentioned in that capacity in a document of 1540 (AST 109, Nr. 83), where he is styled 'Magister.'

Strict, honoured, honest, wise, gracious and governing lords, I beg Your Graces to consider favourably Daniel von Zweibrücken's suit against the chapter of Old St Peter and aid him in bringing about a positive conclusion.

First of all, he has sunk into great poverty and debt through the illegal seizure of his possessions, and as a result of this painful affair he was at last driven from the city some two years and four months ago. He has been deprived of his benefice and yet is obliged to pay 25 gulden in pension money.

Secondly, the representatives of the chapter are going after the seizure of goods in a matter protected by law,[1] and some people use this as an example that anyone who fights a decision of the honourable council is at a greater advantage than he who submits and obeys.

Thirdly, as the governing authority you have an obligation to protect a man against such use of force, and to defend the oppressed against force and calumny, for one cannot paint over the fact that Daniel has been subjected to pressure.

* * * * *

1 *Ufzug suchen in eim spolio, das ist in einer solchen sach, die von Rechten gefreiet ist.*

Fourthly, the community should apply the public law equally to all. The canons of the chapter have sworn to their statutes and taken a vow to them, and not a penny is taken from them although they do not keep the statutes. But Daniel has been deprived of half of his benefice under the pretence that he had gone against the statutes, which none of them observes.

Fifthly, if one wants to make an issue of the fact that he is married, it should be noted that other priests are allowed to have their wives and are being kept on. Thus others enjoy the income from their benefices at St Thomas and Young St Peter, who are not ordained according to the statutes and have no intention of doing so, and what is right for us should not be illegal and criticized in others.

Point Six: Daniel has incurred this difficulty as a result of a command from the honourable council which inhibited ordination by the bishop. First of all, then, you forbade improper cohabitation and commanded marriage. Secondly, you commanded all inhabitants of your city to take out citizenship. Thirdly, you commanded that the gospel be preached and lived by. Therefore, Daniel married in this city in the presence of creditable citizens, and publicly took his wife to church and took out citizenship, and preached and lectured on the gospel. These three factors prevent him from being ordained, even if he wanted it, for anyone who desires ordination, must swear, according to the new decree of the bishop, something to the effect that he will not diverge from the decrees of the pope and the bishop and the constitution of the papist church, and that he will not recognize other secular authorities. But Daniel is a citizen now and, in accordance with several decrees passed by you, does not accept papal law.[2] Let my gracious lords take that into consideration.

Point Seven: The honourable council agreed to maintain us clerics in the chapters in our habitual rights and protect us from harm, also in the changes in ceremonies and other forms of obedience, at a time when Daniel was in full possession of his benefice.

Point Eight: It is apparent from the agreement between those of the clergy and the chapters who left [the city], that as long as they did not object to the changes in the ceremonies or the form of divine service and did not go against the decree of the honourable council, their administration should remain intact. But is that not going against the wishes of Your Graces when they deprive a man of his livelihood only because he wishes to be obedient to you?

* * * * *

2 Daniel von Zweibrücken took out citizenship on 26 July 1525, where the entry records him as a canon of Old St Peter.

Point Nine: When a pious government forbids an evil, they desire complete obedience. Thus, the mass is forbidden until the clergy or someone else proves its validity on the basis of holy scripture. In the same way, ordination has, through your power, been suspended, as being preliminary to saying the forbidden mass. Indeed, a man who gathers straw and powder, in order to set a fire when he has a better opportunity, will be punished in the same way as a man who set the fire right away. The intention is there and there is proof for it, and that is what secular and natural law punishes, not the deed in itself.

Point Ten: Daniel and I cannot but regard it as going against our obligation as citizens to accept ordination and to demand it from others, for we have sworn to be obedient to the commands and prohibitions of the honourable council. We both recognize that the mass has rightly been abolished by you according to the Word of God, and your command to take out citizenship and your prohibition of scandalous concubinage is in accordance with divine and ecclesiastical law. However, if you, my lords, were to make a decision in the presence of the *Schöffen* and the *Amman* and command something that is against God and our conscience, we can only conclude that we would have to renounce our citizenship on the basis that we have sworn not to act against God and to act only in so far as God calls us and gives us strength to aid his Truth. Indeed, God would give us spiritual power and scriptural proof for that purpose. The clergy[3] can do nothing against it, for they have agreed to the changes in their contract and by living in the community, and yet they renege on it and fight against it. But Daniel, a good man, obeys your lords with good conscience, as every pious Christian citizen is obliged to obey. And no one should suffer harm on account of his obedience, for the government may prevent such harm, and why look on any longer while this poor man comes to grief?

Point Eleven: It is my belief that tolerating the tricks of the opponents will in time lead to disruption of the whole government and the ruin of the praiseworthy city of Strasbourg, which God may forfend. For if the decisions of the *Schöffen* and the *Amman* are opposed with word and deed by sworn citizens, and no one is punished for it, then a tumultuous mob may proceed to oppose other things, which I do not wish to describe further, but only ask you to consider.

Point Twelve: Therefore, may it please Your Graces to help us to obtain a positive reply, for we wish to complain once more before the honourable

* * * * *

3 *Pfaffheit*, i.e., the Catholic clergy.

council about our difficulty and oppression, and if we are not helped, we will commend the matter to God and patiently suffer the injustice, for we do not know how we can fend it off by legitimate means.

Please consider this written with friendly goodwill, for I am willing to serve the welfare of the community and Your Graces and know what I owe you. If this matter needs to be brought once more before the honourable council, it is my and Daniel's submissive request to allow this written request to be read, to remind my lords of the business, for our opponents' game is to keep up the delay and at last trick us with an illegal confiscation, and the poor fellow has no place to live. I commend myself to Your Graces.

Your gracious, honest, honourable, and wise Lordships' willing servant, Wolfgang Capito.

Letter 431: [Strasbourg, 1530/31], Capito to N

> Millet included this document (autograph in the Universitätsbibliothek Basel, Ki.Ar. 25a, 138) in his list, although it is not a letter but an undated draft of a memorandum concerning the punishment of Anabaptists. A copy in Zurich (ZB, Hs. S 18, N. 122) labels it 'Capito's apologia for the Anabaptists' (*Capitonis apologia pro anabaptistis*) and dates it 31 May 1527, connecting it with the (German) letter Capito wrote to the mayor of Horb (above, Ep. 330). There is, however, no evidence for this conjecture. Since the present document is written in Latin, it was presumably meant for fellow reformers. The allusions it contains to the persecution of Anabaptists in Würtemberg may refer to events in the spring of 1530 (see below, note 1). However, the sentiments expressed here also agree with those voiced by Capito in the spring of 1531 in Ep. 438 below. The text is printed in QGT 7: 284–8, #233, where it is dated 'ca. 1530.'

On the question of whether the Anabaptists endure punishment on account of madness or as a result of fervent piety.

Those Anabaptists recently apprehended in the duchy of Württemberg, who are of all ages and of both sexes, have chosen to undergo various punishments rather than simply acknowledge their error in words, even though a clause was added permitting them nevertheless to believe what they wished.[1] For they would not knowingly tell even the smallest lie and

* * * * *

1 Capito may be referring to the execution of Augustin Bader in Stuttgart (30 March 1530) and other executions that took place in Tübingen that same year. For his involvement in the affairs of Bader's widow, see below, Ep. 451.

believed that a death earned for confessing what they believed ought to be preferred to a life bound up with such a lie.

Then, the duke of Bavaria[2] prohibits speaking about their beliefs but does not prevent people from holding them, and yet they continue to rush toward their destruction with unfettered speech.

Finally, the man who suffered punishment in Heidelberg would not allow himself to be persuaded by Frecht's friendly plea[3] to save his life by freely affirming Christ but recanting his baptism, which is an external manifestation of the world. Indeed, having been instructed and supplied with these arguments by Frecht, he offered himself up to the executioner to be persuaded.

Through such things, it is made clear how they hate the rhetoric of the gowned[4] and how little they care for their life, both of which are reasonably clear evidence for their incomparable madness, if one believes what is affirmed.

My Opinion:

I believe that the Anabaptists err gravely, as they are more concerned with the letter than the spirit, and that they are most offensive in the boldness of their speech against anyone who disapproves of their form of baptism. Yet, at the same time, I admit that in many of these people there is evidence of the fear of the Lord and of true submission and genuine zeal. For what sort of benefit can they hope to gain from exile, torment, and the infliction of unspeakable punishments on the flesh? I testify before God that I cannot say that it is insanity rather than the divine spirit that leads them to disregard this present life. It is not complete madness, for there is nothing rash or hot-tempered about it. Rather, as confessors of the name 'Christian,' they encounter death consciously and with amazing patience. This same type of vice was attributed to the early martyrs because their blamable stubbornness provoked the executioners. Look, for example, at Cyprian concerning the

* * * * *

2 Wilhelm IV (1493–1550), duke of Bavaria (1508–50).
3 Martin Frecht (1494–1556), studied in Heidelberg (BA 1515, MA 1517, DTh 1531), and taught theology there from 1529. He moved to Ulm in 1531 and became the city's chief reformer. He participated in the Wittenberg Concord (1536), mediating between Luther and the Strasbourgers in the Sacramentarian question. He also participated in negotiations between Protestants and Catholics in the colloquies of Worms and Regensburg (1540, 1546). Since he objected to the Augsburg Interim, he was arrested in 1548 and, in 1549, banned from Ulm. In 1552 he was appointed professor of theology at the Unversity of Tübingen.
4 *Prolixum vestitum.*

libellatici,[5] at Tertullian concerning the knight who refused the crown,[6] thus endangering his life, and at those who refused to throw even a little bit of incense with three fingers into the live coals placed before an idol.[7] What place will remain for professing Christ when such a window for denying Christ is left open? Yet the meaning of the following must be considered: *But brothers, if I still preach circumcision, then why am I still suffering persecution? For in that case, the little offence of the cross has been abolished.*[8] And again: *Those who desire to appear pleasing in the flesh are the ones urging you to be circumcised, lest they suffer persecution on account of the cross.*[9] Indeed, Paul did not give in when his flock was being infiltrated by false brethren and spies on liberty, who were scheming to bring Christians back into servitude.[10] Thus he ensured that the truth of the gospel remained among his followers. In a similar way, the brethren, who are dear to my heart even though they err in other things, cannot yield, lest Christ be withdrawn from them. For according to the apostle, in circumcision Christ is meaningless. But according to these men, their beliefs are negated if baptism is negated.

Thus, after hearing the preachers and receiving the testimony of Christ through his messengers, they gave themselves to Christ, in whose faith they were afterwards baptized. In this case, baptism is not an empty ceremony for these people. It is an act of faith tying them to Christ and a sign of obedience to be witnessed by Christ's followers. They promise to obey those who admonish them to expect a time when they will have to attest to their beliefs with their lives and blood. For either their faith is shaken and they deny in their current crisis what they believe in their hearts, or they persevere inflexibly when their soul is threatened with death. There is no third option once

* * * * *

5 The *libellatici* were one of three classes of *lapsi*, a term applied in the third century to Christians who relapsed into paganism by sacrificing to heathen gods or by other external acts of apostasy: the *sacrificati*, those who had actually offered a sacrifice to idols; the *thurificati*, those who had burnt incense on the altar of the gods; and the *libellatici*, those who had drawn up or had caused to be drawn up certificates (*libelli*) stating that they had offered sacrifice without, however, having actually done so. Pope Cornelius and St Cyprian of Carthage, who wrote a treatise entitled *De lapsis* (PL 4.0463D–0494B), favoured the readmission to the church of repentant *lapsi*, and it was agreed in the synods held in 251 that they should be readmitted after performing certain acts of public penance.
6 I.e.,Tertullian's *De corona militis*.
7 In contrast to the so-called *thurificati*, see above, note 5.
8 Gal. 5:11.
9 Gal. 6:12.
10 Gal. 2:4.

they have become accustomed to having the mortification of the flesh connected with baptism. For every time they deny the truth, which they were
never made free to deny, the soul of each one cries out to them: 'Self-love is
the reason you abandon your way of life.' What they take to be the testimony
of scripture reassures them, as does the tradition of the apostolic church, the
harmony and truth of the sign and sacrament, the innocence of their companions, and their determination to live Christ. We, by contrast, are in many
ways divided and inconstant, negligent in amending our lives, whether privately or publicly. We are involved in flattery and in collusion with men of
the world, with whom we are more readily drawn to scandal than to zealous
emulation of the type of life that is worthy of Christ. For no one is a non-
Christian in our eyes so long as he subscribes to our ministry, and no one is
chastised for their behaviour more seriously than the person who does not
praise all things. As a result, those who yield to the difficulties of the times
often repent and expiate their shameful deed and are penalized by their community as if they had denied Christ himself, so that they become much more
constant thereafter.

In sum: their focus is the cross, the sign of the mortification of the flesh,
and they have tasted something of life in the resurrected and reigning Christ.
Hence, they have surrendered themselves to Christ, and baptism has become
for them a symbol of surrender, indeed a symbol of the mind fixed upon the
death of Christ. I think we ought to look into their hearts and acknowledge
the generous gift of God, because they are strengthened against the flesh and
Satan insofar as it involves love of life. I say again that they err: *Let each man
be fully convinced in his own mind.*[11] For the apostle considered it sufficient that
weak people should please themselves in deciding whether to distinguish
between days or not: for either is regarded as clear evidence of error.[12] I ask
whether those, who refused to do battle under the Maccabees on the Sabbath
and were slain for their error,[13] ought to be thought of as stirring up sinful
behaviour or whether this action should instead be given praise as proof
of a gift of strong faith? Indeed, one may deplore the weakness and lack of
judgment in such great men, just as I deplore it in our Anabaptist martyrs.
Yet I do not criticize the fact that they go to their punishment as if bound by
the fear of the Lord, lest we thereby excuse our own faint-heartedness. For I
fear that in making such a judgment, we completely obliterate the judgment
of the Spirit. For we ourselves have often experienced that secular studies

* * * * *

11 Rom. 14:5.
12 Cf. Rom. 14: 14, 20, 23.
13 1 Macc. 2:34–8.

obstruct the course of divine grace and the Word of God. There is good reason for saying: *Not many are wise according to the flesh.*[14] Indeed, reading often transforms the naturally malleable mind, inclining it to soft sentiments, to humane thoughts, and leniency. This is the disadvantage we, too, have experienced on account of our zeal for secular learning: through the help of the Holy Writ we are imbued with a tinge of piety, but we lack the essence and marrow of piety. For what ardour shall we feel for mortifying the flesh if we support and assent to the counsels of the flesh? We rarely take seriously the need for prayer, unless we are moved by such adversaries as these and by the tumults of our people. We are too complacent.

The Son of Man is the Lord of the Sabbath,[15] but the sabbath is a ceremony. Yet to these people, baptism is not a ceremony. It is a sign, a seal, a testament, a covenant made in good faith,[16] through which the Spirit certainly sees our submissive faith and our desire to be obedient to God's authority. They do not grant this status simply to the act of sprinkling water. Rather, they are mindful of the sacrament. They never consider these things outside the context of the sacrament, just as we do not allow the letters of the Word of God to be considered without the eternal Word of God. In short, they embrace the beginning of faith and grace through the sign of baptism, and they reject any other use of this sign as an affront to God.

Indeed, on account of their simplicity they do not know how to differentiate between things that are distinct in nature, since they are everywhere joined together in Scripture, and they perceive baptism, not as a ceremony, but as a sacrament of the New Testament. It embodies the death of the flesh and is the life of the spirit, a present image of rebirth by means of celestial waters, when faith makes all things present in nature.

Add to this the fact that certain very simple people, who led a commendable life, are being executed. For they are instigated by people, who provide for themselves in this world. No one finds life sad and difficult, except through vices, even if being joined to the spirit bothers the flesh. Can I say, therefore, that their desire to die in testimony of Christ is madness, when I see that they put such a price on faith in God? For they are inclined toward the truth, not toward pretence. They take seriously what the common people only boast about, and give themselves over to Christ. Whereas others pay lip service, they focus on the genuine thing. How speciously people speak of repentance! The word is twisted in their mouth; one can see that they have something else in mind, something that serves their worldly goals.

* * * * *

14 1 Cor. 1:26.
15 Matt. 12:8.
16 1 Pet. 3:21.

Letter 431a: 2 January 1531, Waldkirch, Balthasar Mercklin to the Chapter of St Thomas

The manuscript is in AST 22(7). For Mercklin, see CWC 1, Ep. 55, note 3. Mercklin succeeded Hugo of Hohenlandenberg as bishop of Constance in 1529 (see above, Epp. 414, 415). For the chapter's reply, see below, Ep. 431c.

Balthasar, by the grace of God, bishop of Constance and Hildesheim, etc.

First, our friendly greeting, reverend, most learned, dear and pious lords. On our arrival in Waldkirch, Dr Nicolaus Wurmser complained to us that you rejected his claim, contrary to the Offenburg contract, which was confirmed by the commissaries of the Roman Imperial Majesty and ratified in writing as he indicates to us.[1] We have read the contract and do not find it reads as you indicate. It says only that the persons mentioned, whether canon, summissary, or vicar, should not collect residency fees in two places, which is reasonable. These words need or require no further interpretation or exposition. It is therefore inappropriate and wilful of you to withhold from him what is his. We also informed him of the statement we provided, explaining that he does not receive residency money from us here at our chapter in Waldkirch, and never has.

Thus, it is our gracious request kindly to allow him his money and to look after the matter in good faith, which we trust you will do, for should we be contacted again, we would see cause to write to the honourable council about it and seek other means to see that his claim is taken care of. For he is under our authority, and has been implicated in this matter to his great disadvantage and inappropriately, and should be compensated. We shall graciously acknowledge your action and expect no refusal. We have asked [Wurmser] to inform us in writing, should you persist in your action. Given at Waldkirch on the 2nd day of January in the year, etc. '31.

Letter 431b: 11 January 1531, Strasbourg, Capito and Martin Bucer to Mayor Ulrich Rehlinger and the City Council of Augsburg

Printed in CorrBucer 5:177–9, Ep. 374.

[*Summary*]: Capito and Bucer have received the council's letter [Ep. 429b] through the syndic Balthasar Langnauer and obtained permission from the

* * * * *

1 I.e., the contract of 27 March 1528, which settled matters of compensation for the Catholic canons of the three foundations. The document is in AST 22 (5–6).

city council of Strasbourg for Musculus to depart for Augsburg. They praise his character and learning and expect that he will soon adapt his speech to the Augsburg dialect. They pray for the progress of the church in Augsburg.

Letter 431c: 12 January 1531, Strasbourg, The Chapter of St Thomas to Balthasar Mercklin

The manuscript is in AST 22–7. This letter answers Ep. 431a above.

Most Reverend Prince, gracious lord, first we offer Your Princely Grace our good will and service at any time and with the greatest readiness.

Gracious lord, we have received and perused Your Princely Grace's letter concerning the reverend, most learned Dr Nicolaus Wurmser, our dean. In reply we give Your Princely Grace our humble opinion and account. We have been obliged to discuss the article regarding residency contained in the Offenburg contract,[1] not only with respect to the above-mentioned dean, but also on account of Dr Petrus Wickram.[2] We can see from Your Princely Grace's letter that Your Princely Grace regards that article as lucid and clear and thus needing no further interpretation among educated people, or so it would appear to anyone who was not present himself at the negotiation. Since, however, *the reason of the law is the soul of the law*,[3] we have no doubt that in this article the intention of the parties to the contract and our sentiment and intention was different from the sense our previously mentioned friends, Dr Nicolaus Wurmser and Dr Petrus Wickram, want to read into it now. And so we consider it best that the signatories to the above contract, who can be reached without special work and effort, should advise both sides of what is right and proper, and by their declaration decide and put an end to the ambiguity. We shall gladly accept and stand by their decision as shown to us, in the hope that both our dear gentlemen and friends will be content with this honest offer, and together with us accept the decision of the oft-mentioned signatories to the contract, and not reject what we most earnestly offer to do. We wish to assure Your Princely Grace of our dutiful service in response to his letter. Given at Strasbourg on 12 January in the year, etc. '31.

Your obedient and willing provost, vice-dean, and chapter of St Thomas in Strasbourg.

* * * * *

1 See above, Ep. 431a, note 1.
2 For Wickram, see above, Ep. 377c.
3 'Ratio legis anima est,' a common legal phrase.

Letter 432: [January 1531, Strasbourg], Capito to Nicolaus Kniebs

Printed in QGT VII: 299–300, #238. For Kniebs see above, Ep.184 headnote.

Honourable, wise lord, the bearers of this letter failed to raise their hands on the day of oath-taking,[1] and have therefore been reprehended. They have explained to me the motive of their action. I answered them that they were in error and were dividing Jesus Christ the Son of God from the Father, although he is one with the Father and cannot be at odds with him. I also told them that the passage in Matthew 5, *You must not swear by anything*,[2] is said by Christ, not by God the Father, who says earlier in the prophets that one ought to swear an oath in the kingdom of Christ, and that the passage is meant to reprove the Pharisees, who committed perjury, swearing by heaven, earth, the city of Jerusalem, etc. and did not keep it like an oath. Against them Christ says: *You must not swear by anything*, that is, not practise justice like the Pharisees who pretend to swear an oath. Swearing an oath in fear of God, however, is the greatest glorification of God (see Deut. 6, etc.).[3] That answer satisfied them. They thanked me kindly and asked that I request Your Honour to allow them to take the civic oath free of charge. Therefore I ask you to have mercy on them. I do not have time to talk to you in person, or I would come to you, as is seemly. I feel sincerely sorry for the poor people, for they are zealous for God's honour.

Your obliging Wolfgang Capito.

Letter 432a: 19 January 1531, Speyer, Nikolaus Geylfuß to the Chapter of St Thomas

This autograph is in AST 16, #33. The address reads, rather oddly, 'To the Dean and chapter of St Thomas in Strasbourg.' One would expect this to be addressed to the provost, vice-dean, and chapter, since the dean, Nicolaus Wurmser, was not resident in Strasbourg and not among those named below as being present at the discussions Geylfuß had with the chapter. Nikolaus Geylfuß was, from 1518, vicar of St Thomas. He joined the Catholic party and fled the city in 1525. In 1528 he agreed with the city on compensation for the vicariate. The terms of payment are the subject of the complaint in this letter. At the time of writing he was vicar at the cathedral of Speyer.

* * * * *

1 The *Amman* was elected on the first Thursday of the year; the oath of loyalty was taken the following Tuesday.

2 Matt. 5:34.

3 Deut. 6:13.

Reverend, most learned, gracious, dear lords!

I appeared before your reverend lords personally in Strasbourg on Monday after Quasimodo Sunday of last year[1] and there asked you, my reverend lords, in a respectful and friendly manner for payment of my personal stipend and residency fee for the period preceding my departure from the above-mentioned city of Strasbourg. At that time, the majority of the reverend lords of the chapter of St Thomas in Strasbourg, namely the provost, Master Lorenz Schenckbecher, Jakob Munthart, Master Hieronymus Betschlin, Jakob Bopp, Dr Bernhard Wölfflin and Master Peter Wickram,[2] canons of the said collegiate church, were called together on my request at a formal chapter meeting and appeared in the usual place of assembly at the chapter. There they responded in a gracious and friendly manner to my request. We came to an agreement that you, my reverend lords, should and wish to pay me the due amount for my personal stipend and residency fee, according to my peaceful and friendly request, as said before, the sum of 86 lb, 7ß, 1d, as was accepted by Your Reverences and ratified in good faith.[3] It was agreed that Your Reverences should pay that sum in two payments or two terms, the first payment, of 46 lb, 7ß, 1d on the said Monday after Quasimodo, which I received immediately in cash from your administrator,[4] for which I gave the said administrator a receipt. The second payment was due last Christmas, and that date passed without it. I therefore send another humble, subservient, and earnest request to you, reverend gentlemen, to be so kind as to pay the outstanding 40 gulden to Cristman Usinger[5] or Hans Frentzlin[6] on my behalf, on either man's or both men's request or application. I myself will do whatever seems best to Your Reverences. According to your need and pleasure, they may give a receipt before a notary or in some other form for the whole sum, and I have given them plenary power to do so. I will be

* * * * *

1 I.e., 25 April 1530.
2 On Schenckbecher, Munthart, and Betschlin, see above, Ep. 237, notes 23, 19, 31; on Bopp and Wölfflin see above, Ep. 246a, notes 29, 28. On Petrus Wickram see CWC 1, Ep. 72 headnote.
3 I.e., in the Offenburg contract. See above, Ep. 431 a, note 1.
4 Gervasius Sopher.
5 Cristman Usinger, from 1514 vicar (altar of St Leonard) at St Thomas. He was given leave to study in Heidelberg in 1524. He joined the Catholic party, but had a change of heart and took out citizenship in 1525. In 1530 he became vicar of Sts Michael and Peter in Strasbourg.
6 Hans Frentzlin, vicar of St Thomas (altar of St George) from 1522. He took out citizenship on 8 December 1524.

forever in Your Reverences' debt and offer you my poor service most obediently and earnestly and commend Your Reverences to God Almighty, who
may grant you peace and health. Given hastily at Speyer on Thursday after
Priscae Virginis, in the year, etc. 1531.

Your most willing and obedient Nikolaus Geylfuß, vicar at the cathedral in Speyer.

Letter 433: 22 January 1531, Strasbourg, Capito to Ulrich Zwingli

Printed in ZwBw 5:312–16, Ep. 1159.

[*Summary*]: He is pleased that Zwingli's plans for a 'Christian union' have
not been laid in vain. The Saxons object to the election of Ferdinand as Roman king. They ignore [Luther's?] warnings against a political pact. They
have made contact with Strasbourg. First, however, it is necessary to come
to an agreement about the Sacramentarian question. The Strasbourg position
on the Real Presence is acceptable to them: Christ's body and blood is 'eaten
through faith, as far as it concerns eternal bliss, and nourishes believers.'
Capito refuses to use the terms *substantialiter, essentialiter, realiter* since doing so would foster dissension. The political pact does not contain articles
of faith. 'Much is being resolved by maintaining silence.' He knows that Luther will not sign any more articles. He hopes Zwingli will give a suitable
interpretation to the way they are phrased now. All the important elements
on which they agree are there, 'the body of the Lord, the spiritual eating
for the purpose of eternal life.' Zwingli should not reject them because of
Luther's 'made-up [concept of Real] Presence' (*commentitiam Lutheri praesen-
tiam*). Capito commends Karlstadt to Zwingli [cf. above, Epp. 410, 412]. He
asks again for the hymns composed by Zwingli [see above, Ep. 427], which
he wishes to bring to Bernhard [Ott]friedrich.

Letter 434: 10 February 1531, Darmstadt, Johannes Lindenfels to Capito

The manuscript of this letter is in AST 40, #22, fol. 499. The letter is printed
in Fritz Herrmann, 'Drei Briefe eines Darmstätter Zwinglianers aus der Zeit
Philipps des Grossmütigen,' *Archiv für hessische Geschichte und Altertumskunde*,
n.s. 9 (1913): 142–4. Hans Lindenfels was a teacher in Darmstadt from 1531–6.
He is last documented in 1556 as administrator (*Keller*) in Lichtenberg.

Peace and perpetual happiness through the Lord, most venerable sir and
dearest brother in Christ.

I am sending my greetings through your messenger,[1] who was conveniently at hand. I would like to tell you about the insanities of a most fierce blatherer (I should have said, preacher) at our court,[2] not because I want to slander someone behind his back, but because I thought it would be a good thing (if he deserves it) to stop the mouth of this impudent man with a friendly complaint and tell him not to condemn what he is incapable of judging and cannot understand at all. Now that he has obtained a post at court, he thought he would please his prince[3] if he lashed out as much as possible against Zwingli, and now he acts with the persistence that is the way of this type of soldier. He goes on raging even if the prince gainsays him every day. He has no standing with the prince and would long have been sent elsewhere, if he did not fear that this would be interpreted by the papists as inconsistency in the matter of the gospel. Among the people and his own accomplices he is, as you can see, an egregious censor. Here, our parish priest is pious and sincere. He is a close friend of Hedio.[4] If you regard us worthy of a reply, please let us know what Martin Luther replied.[5] Farewell in eternity with all your brethren. 10 February, in the year '31. In haste.

Yours, Johannes Lindenfels, teacher in Darmstadt.

Letter 435: 12 February 1531, Zurich, Ulrich Zwingli to Capito and Martin Bucer

Printed in CorrBucer 5:261–6, Ep. 389.

[*Summary*]: Zwingli disapproves of concord based on dissembling (concordia *hypoulos*), which will not hold. He, too, believes in the Real Presence. He explains his own position: Christ is present in the supper, but not naturally or corporeally, but sacramentally and symbolically, and only 'in the contemplation of faith.' They may agree on words, but if they interpret them symbolically and the Lutherans literally, the agreement is not sound. What-

* * * * *

1 Not identified.
2 Millet suggests that this is Nicolaus Maurer (1483–1539), who was canon at St Andreas in Worms from 1523 and assistant in Weissenburg in 1524/5. From 1526 he was in Darmstadt, between 1527 and 1529 he was superintendent, between 1529 and 1536, he was pastor at Zwingenberg, and from 1536 until his death, pastor at Frankfurt.
3 Philip of Hesse.
4 Perhaps Bernhard Weigersheim, who became pastor in Darmstadt in 1529.
5 I.e., to Ernst of Lüneburg, rejecting Bucer's proposal for concord: WABr 6:28–29 (1 February 1531).

ever phrasing is used, it needs a clear interpretation. At the next meeting in Nürnberg [which was cancelled], they ought to state that Christ's body is eaten spiritually and sacramentally. If they make concessions now, all the old erroneous opinions will be revived. He notes that they do not mention Andreas Osiander's letter [not extant?] and wonders whether they received it. Zwingli does not understand the involvement of the city council in this question. Is it relevant to their plans for a political alliance? He has no objection to Bucer's letter [to Ernst of Braunschweig-Lüneburg, written in German; CorrBucer 5, Ep. 368] being published, but he sees no need for it and is afraid of misinterpretations. He asks them to take his letter in good stead.

Letter 435a: 18 February 1531, Saverne, Wilhelm [von Honstein] to the Chapter of St Thomas

> The manuscript of this letter is in AST 16, #34. For Wilhelm von Honstein, bishop of Strasbourg, see CWC 1, Ep. 174 headnote. The letter is addressed to the vice-dean, Jakob Munthart (see Ep. 237, note 19), and the chapter rather than the provost, perhaps because the bishop regarded the matter of the provostship as unsettled.

Wilhelm, etc.

First our friendly greeting. Reverend, honourable, dear and pious lords, we have a credible report that several persons in your chapter are in the process and have decided to sell the treasures and ornaments of St Thomas, etc.[1] As you no doubt know yourselves, you have no authority whatsoever to do so without our authorization and endorsement. It is therefore our gracious request and earnest command that you desist from such a plan and leave the above-mentioned treasures of the collegiate church untouched. We wish to inform you of this duly and with good grace, and we ask for your written response. Given at Saverne, on the Saturday after Valentine's Day, in the year 1531.

Letter 436: 20 February [1531], Strasbourg, The Strasbourg Preachers to Ambrosius Blaurer and the Preachers Assembled at Memmingen

Printed in CorrBucer 5:277–89, Ep. 393.

[*Summary*]: They would have liked to attend the meeting [in Memmingen]

* * * * *

1 See the chapter's request to the city above, Ep. 404c.

but were not authorized by the city council. They hope to meet in Ulm and later in Nürnberg [neither meeting took place]. To compensate for their absence they are sending the present statement of their beliefs. In turn, they ask for a detailed report about the meeting in Memmingen. It is of the utmost importance to reach agreement on the Sacramentarian question. They delineate their own position: 'The true body of Christ is truly exhibited in the supper, but as food for the soul.' In support they cite biblical passages and refer to Oecolampadius' collection of patristic passages, [*Quid de Eucharistia veteres* ... July 1530]. They follow traditional beliefs when they deny that the body of Christ is united with the bread in a natural manner and note that the body of Christ is in heaven. Christ offered up his body for our redemption and offers it to us in the Supper as nourishment for the soul. They remind the brethren that 'whatever occurs in the mind can only be expressed through metaphor. When Christ decided therefore to call his flesh true food and to call the offering he made to the disciples during the Supper, an offering of his body and blood, why should we be reluctant to use these metaphors, as did Paul and the whole church of old, and why should we be reluctant to state that he is truly present and we are truly eating?' To avoid strife and giving offence, it is important to adapt one's language to the understanding of one's audience. The apostles showed a spirit of compromise, and they must do likewise. As long as they are permitted to interpret the presence of Christ in the bread as a Sacramentarian union, there is no reason for further dispute, 'for we confess the Real Presence of Christ's true body and our eating thereof.' As for Luther's demand to include the formula *manducatio impiorum*, that is, that the impious, too, eat the body of Christ, they may come to an understanding, if one distinguishes between sinners who believe in the sacrament and therefore receive the body of Christ, but not for their salvation, and nonbelievers who merely eat the bread. This needs to be discussed among them before they meet at Ulm, and with Luther before they meet at Nürnberg. Zwingli will not stand in the way of religious peace so long as it is stated that the body of Christ 'is not localized in the bread' and Oecolampadius has already approved what they state here. Rites should be standardized as much as possible to show that they are all inspired by the same Spirit. Church discipline coupled with the authority to excommunicate, such as instituted in Basel, may be useful. They should also discuss a public creed to be taught in the catechism. They hope that Ambrosius [Blaurer], Simprecht [Schenck], and Konrad [Sam] will come to the planned meeting in Ulm.

Letter 436a: [ca. 21 March 1531, Strasbourg], Capito and Martin Bucer to [the Bailiff of Benfeld]

The manuscript of this letter is in AST 98, #38. It is not included in CorrBucer.

Honest, wise, noble, strict lord and Junker, we have examined the parish priest of Benfeld[1] and found him neither unwilling nor disinclined to preach the gospel clearly and purely, but rather timid and without sufficient understanding of scripture. This office should not be entrusted to such a man. We told him that the honourable council requires clear preaching according to God's honour and said we would be satisfied with him (and he understood this from you), if he agreed to preach the gospel well and in due form. It became apparent, however, from our personal conversation and his own admission, that he did not yet have sufficient understanding of the gospel and scripture. Furthermore, the Holy Spirit forbids appointing a novice as bishop or parish priest, and it would be embarrassing for him suddenly to condemn the mass in Benfeld, when he had said mass elsewhere just a few days ago. There would be considerable doubt about the reason he had changed his mind, whether it was on account of the advantage of holding the benefice or through the agency of the Spirit of God. It would therefore be good, in our view, for him to accept the parish and move to Benfeld with his household and his servants (with Your Lordship's permission), but not serve as parish priest there himself. Rather, we would like him to stay with us here in Strasbourg for a year, listen to sermons and lectures, and acquire other skills that a parish priest needs. Thus we said he should, after due consideration, indicate to us that he has accepted from our lords a delay of eight days; that he is eager, in view of the characteristics we attribute to him, to learn the truth; and that he wishes to comply with our request because the reasons we gave are of concern to him. He has replied now and expressed his agreement, asking that we indicate this to Your Lordship, but with the proviso that Junker Meinold von Andlau,[2] his lord, may present him to the benefice, that he may be in residence there and personally look after the parish. He promises to come here next Thursday, to await the further decision of Your Lordships. For (he says) it would not be proper for him to act other than in agreement with his lords. Now, we are of the opinion that it is not necessary to importune Junker Meinold especially since, as a resident of Benfeld, he is subject to the same collegiate church, and would serve the desire of our lords on the honourable council and the good will of the community of Benfeld in his own person and through others. For his lord does not want anyone to take leave, nor do we ask leave for anyone in the case. Rather, the period he would spend here would be to the benefit of the parish and its associates, whereas some people might want to spend time living elsewhere for their pleasure and entertain-

* * * * *

1 Ulrich Würtemberger (d. 27 October 1541).
2 From 1434 the nobles of Andlau, in this case Meinolf von Andlau (d. 1548), held the right of presentation in Benfeld.

ment. But Your Wise Honour may report to Junker Meinolf, if you think it seemly, that the honourable council is inclined toward this parish priest and pleased with him, and we hope that he, too, will be satisfied. And to reassure the parish priest, for he is worried that this might go against his lord's will, you might tell him that in your opinion he needs to reside here at least for a year, yet he may keep his household in Benfeld. There will be another priest[3] who, with the knowledge and agreement of the parishioners of Benfeld, will look after the parish, and [Würtemberger] may go back and forth as opportunity affords. He would also preach from time to time and be heard personally from the pulpit. This would not be counter to his endowment and agreement, and you may, at a suitable time, convey this opinion to Junker Meinolf yourself.[4] Thus he would no less be in residence, etc. In this manner he will be satisfied. We hope he will not turn out an unsuitable parish priest. May God bestow his grace on him and us all. Amen.[5]

Martin Bucer and Wolfgang Capito.

Letter 437: 4 April 1531, Strasbourg, Capito to Ulrich Zwingli

Printed ZwBw 5:398–401, Ep. 1191.

[Summary]: The Turks are reported to be preparing an attack on Austria. The emperor is gathering military resources, but they are aimed at the reformers, according to the reports of Dutch merchants. Merchants from Venice report that a truce is being negotiated with the Turks. Some people say that Zurich is in great danger of being attacked. It is necessary to come to an agreement with the Lutherans. Philip [Melanchthon] has adopted a hostile tone toward Bucer in his letters to Nürnberg. There is fierce opposition against them in Augsburg as well. Duke [Ernst] of [Braunschweig]-Lüneburg is urging concord. A rumour was spread and reached Luther and Johannes Bugenhagen, that Bucer had reneged on the agreement reached in Marburg [1529]. He implores Zwingli to keep silent in the future on the question of the Eucha-

* * * * *

3 The records given by M.-J. Bopp, *Die evangelischen Gemeinden und Hohen Schulen im Elsass und Lothringen von der Reformation bis zur Gegenwart* (Neustadt/Aisch, 1963), indicate that Nicolaus Prugner was pastor of Benfeld 1527–38, and Würtemberger his 'Helfer' (i.e., his assistant).

4 Meinolf of Andlau gave his permission in a letter to the city council of 15 April 1531 (AST 98, #39).

5 The phrase 'Given at Strasbourg, 21 March 1531' is cancelled. It is possible that there was delay in sending the letter, so that the date had to be changed.

rist. They do not wish to compromise on the Truth, however, while seeking concord. In Augsburg, at any rate, a change has taken place. The council has rejected the Lutherans and embraces the Strasbourg beliefs. They have been invited to send two preachers to Augsburg [see above, Ep. 431b] and will send two more men shortly. Jacob Sturm, [a delegate at the Schmalkald meeting], has not yet returned. Sebastian [Meyer] will depart for Augsburg.

Letter 438: 17 April [1531], Strasbourg, Capito to Wolfgang Musculus

This extract appeared in the seventeenth century collection of Fecht, VIII, 843–4, #34 and has been printed more recently in QGT VII 331–3: #248. The manuscript does not appear to be extant. For the year date of the letter see the arguments there, p. 333.

Wolfgang Musculus (1497–63) left the Benedictine monastery at Lixheim in 1527 and came to Strasbourg, where he began an apprenticeship as a weaver. He came to the attention of the reformers and was appointed Matthew Zell's helper at the cathedral in 1528. In January 1531 he was called to Augsburg on the recommendation of Bucer and Capito and preached there until 1548. He did not accept the Interim and therefore had to leave the city. In 1549 he became professor of theology in Bern.

... I very much approve of the fact that you pity these wretched people.[1] For what they do is not without reason. I always shy away from the free action my brethren take against them, when I know how reverently Paul proceeded, and what exceptional awe he felt. I do not in any way want Christ to be harassed with abuse, for he suffers in his members. It is characteristic of a worldly man to put pressure on his opponent through action. It is the part of a demagogue to magnify the fault of the guilty; it is less than human to attribute to malice what people do under duress and to abuse them vehemently. There is no complete agreement concerning the oath, which is exacted here from the Anabaptists. Daniel Mieg[2] takes this from the sermons of our brother Bucer. I would almost say he fully contends that everything must be taken from them. I, conversely, object, saying that we must leave it to God's inspection, who wishes the Truth to be sacrosanct, and does not yet wish them to swear off their errors summarily. I always say: to judge about faith is too exalted a task for me.[3] My aim is not to go against the polity. As

* * * * *

1 I.e., the Anabaptists.

2 For Mieg, cf. above, Ep. 412a headnote.

3 The letter is in Latin, but this sentence is in German: *Vom glauben zu urtheilen ist mir zu hoch.*

for the rest, they are inclined to exact the following [from the Anabaptists]: (1) They must not traduce the Word publicly; (2) they must not assemble in secret; (3) they must not talk against the public oath, but obey the commands of the magistrate as good citizens.

What good is it to exact the rest and muzzle the spirit? I do not care if they go against us, as long as the public peace is not disturbed. We shall achieve the rest through the power of the Word and our offices. Nor do I doubt that everything would have calmed down sooner had we explored more accurately the consciences of those people. For matters are often carried on as if this were a secular case, and carried on by people who rely on the prejudices of others and carelessly condemn what they do not know. So far I have tried in vain to keep them from their radical course. Bucer agrees with this, but he wants a decree about infant baptism, which I do not wish to be decided at this time. For we have not made sufficient efforts to reach them with private admonition, yet I will not refuse to sign a decree as long as I do not discover afterwards that the proofs for infant baptism are weak. I am looking for arguments in every case that are based on an understanding of Christ, and not on scripture twisted by imagination to suit whatever is proposed. Whether we want it or not, we must allow the pious to separate themselves from the world, or we are found to do violence to Christ. Yet I wrangle with those who think of separation, for they do not yet have the Spirit, which could prove their piety to their colleagues through clear spiritual gifts. I aver that we must contribute our small measure in public, so that as many people as possible may come to know and embrace Christ. Indeed, it is necessary to explore the character of their piety and to use brotherly admonition to improve those with whom we are on a familiar footing. Let us leave censure of the remainder to the Lord, until he himself reveals the recesses of their hearts. I have not yet been able to consult with Bucer at length, but we shall take up the topic one of these days. If we agree on anything more firmly, I shall let you know in detail. In the meantime farewell, and go on leading the life you do, that is, a blameless life. Strasbourg, 17 April, at dawn. All our brothers return your greetings. The wife of Matthew[4] is gravely ill. I shall have a little more hope if she survives until noon today. Give my regards to Mayor Rehlinger.[5]

* * * * *

4 Katharina Schütz (ca. 1497–1562), wife of Matthew Zell, active in the Reformation, editor of hymn books and Reformation pamphlets.
5 For Rehlinger, see below, Ep. 456 headnote.

Letter 439: 18 April 1531, Baden-Baden, Gereon Sailer to Capito, Caspar Hedio, and Martin Bucer

Printed in CorrBucer 5:353–5, Ep. 416. For Gereon Sailer, see above, Ep. 411a headnote.

[*Summary*]: Sailer and Sebastian [Meyer, cf. above, Ep. 437] are at the house of Kaspar [Glaser], tutor at the court of [Bernhard III] of Baden-Baden. They are impressed with Glaser's qualities and ask for the Strasbourgers' help in bringing him to Augsburg. They hope to meet Johannes Schwebel, the man who attended the Marburg Colloquy [1529] together with Bucer and Hedio. Schwebel has been driven out by [Ludwig II], Count Palatine. Glaser would like to work together with Schwebel. Sailer asks the Strasbourg preachers for their opinion of Schwebel. Glaser is willing to go to Augsburg on the conditions offered, but is uncertain whether his employer will give him leave to depart. They must thank Jakob Kirscher [chancellor of Baden-Baden and librarian at Pforzheim] and Nikolaus Gerbel for promoting their cause.

Letter 440: [After 18 April 1531, Strasbourg, Capito to Martin Bucer]

Printed in CorrBucer 5:355–7, Ep. 417. This note, written in Capito's hand, appears as an addendum to Ep. 439 (AST 157, #157).

[*Summary*]: He asks for Bucer's advice on what to write about Johannes Schwebel, whose views on the Eucharist are reportedly not sound. Johannes [Wahl] von Odenbach complained about him in a letter. He will meet with Bucer the following day. Bonifacius [Wolfhart's] wife will depart soon. His own health is improving.

Letter 440a: [Between 6 May and 26 June 1531, Strasbourg], The Chapter of St Thomas to the City Council of Strasbourg

The manuscript of this letter is in AST 16, #32. It bears no date, but cites an agreement with the city signed on 6 May 1531 (see below, note 1) and contains a request for funds, which was approved by the council on 26 June 1531 (see below, note 4).

Strict, honourable, respected, wise, gracious lords,

We recently came to an agreement with the honourable council and made a contract concerning the parishes, which we both ratified and confirmed. Your Graces have the sealed letter in your keeping now. This document states, among other things, that we in the collegiate church of St Thomas should pay into the treasury 150 gulden a year for the support of a parish priest and his assistant.[1] We gladly and willingly offer, to the best of our ability, our counsel and support to the commonweal of this city and the honour of God, and at the same time are maintaining the collegiate church, which we hope will be in the future more useful in furthering the honour of God and the commonweal. This we have indicated repeatedly in a previous supplication, begging the city to take measures to relieve the collegiate church, for otherwise we would suffer irreversible damage and loss. For this reason, there was discussion whether the income from the *fronmesserei*,[2] which has fallen vacant after Diebold Balthener's death[3] and concerning which our chapter has the right of collation, should be used for the benefit of the parish and the collegiate church, that we might supply the parishioners with a more capable and honest parish priest.[4] Thus we plan – with your advice, favour, and agreement, gracious lords – to add and incorporate the said benefice, together with its annual usages and income, which is equal to the income of one of our canonries, in the income of the parish priest. In this manner, each parish priest will look after his parish and preside as long as (and no longer than) he is suited and able. The benefice will be applied to this purpose, together with all its income. He will have the use and enjoyment of it, together with the use of a house, as was assigned to the priests earlier on. Each parish priest should keep his house in order, that is, look after the stoves, windows, chimneys, wells, roof, and other such details, in accordance with the daily needs. As for the rest, which concerns the main owner, the collegiate church will look after it, and will annually pay any taxes levied on the house. In the same manner, each canon is obliged to take care of his property and to keep the building sound and to bear the costs. As for the assistant and co-minister of the Word, however, we request for him the two yearly residency fees that were previously paid annually to the parish priests and assistant by the chapter, that is, approximately 20 pounds each per year, that is, 40 pounds altogether, a fair compensation, so that the assistant will have nothing to complain of. In addition we ask that he be assigned the accommoda-

* * * * *

1 The document is AST 16, #35, dated 6 May 1531.
2 I.e., the stipend for saying the *Fruehmesse*, the service celebrated at 5 a.m. in the summer and 6 a.m. in the winter.
3 8 November 1530. For Balthener see above, Ep. 190, note 4.
4 The council approved of making Balthener's stipend available for the purpose requested. The document is AMS, CH 8590 (copy AST 16, # 39), dated 26 June 1531.

tion (including payment of taxes) that was in the hands of the late Diebold Balthener, but to require him to look after the upkeep duly and properly, as the daily need arises, as outlined above with respect to the parish priest. We hope that this will be agreeable to you, our worthy lords, and that the stipend of 150 gulden of the parish priest and his assistant at St Thomas, previously assessed and taxed by the honourable city council, will now be exempt in response to our above-mentioned writing. We will then assign the said benefice, with its complete annual income to the parish priests and their assistants in the terms stated, free and unburdened of all payments for statutes, *annus gratiae*, *biennia*,[5] and other such burdens, so that a benefice would be available for every parish priest and would permanently be used for their benefit. In the same way, the above-mentioned two annual residency fees would be given to an assistant and co-minister of the Word, for his support – in our opinion, a fair compensation. Thus the parishes will be supplied with respectable and authoritative persons until the honourable council will come to our further aid and relieve the collegiate church of its pressing and ruinous obligations. In this matter, we wish to hear your worthy lords' intention, good opinion, and gracious reply.

Your worthy lords' well-intentioned and obedient citizens,

The provost, vice-dean, and chapter of St Thomas, collegiate church at Strasbourg.

Letter 441: 8 June 1531, [Strasbourg], Capito to Ulrich Zwingli

Printed in ZwBw 5:469–71, Ep. 1220.

[*Summary*]: Capito is glad that Zwingli supports Ludwig Carinus. He has departed for Bern, according to Zwingli's instructions. The bearer of the letter is Francesco Negri of Bassano, whom Bucer recently recommended to Zwingli through Oecolampadius. He is a solid and learned man. He is working as a tailor, but is being taught biblical exegesis by Bucer and Capito. He has applied himself sedulously and is sound in his beliefs. They hope that Zwingli will commend Negri to [Johannes] Comander and Antonio Transverso in Graubünden. Negri is well suited to preaching but can also be employed as a teacher. He may even carry the evangelical message into Italy. Bucer is in Ulm. He is making progress, but is opposed by the parish priest of Geislingen, [Georg Osswald], who will be ousted.

* * * * *

5 See above, Ep. 248a, notes 3, 5.

Letter 442: 27 June 1531, Zurich, Ulrich Zwingli to Capito

Printed in ZwBw 5:497–8, Ep. 1232.

[*Summary*]: The bearer of the letter [not identified] will report on conditions in Zurich. They are still blockading food supplies to the Fünf Orte [cf. above, Ep. 425]. Zwingli has heard nothing from Ulm. Rumours about the emperor vary. Some say that he will soon return to Spain; others say that he is preparing an attack on Hesse or Nassau. Zwingli asks them to inform him as soon as they hear anything certain. They put their trust in Strasbourg to such an extent that recent rumours about the hiring of mercenaries in Lorraine were discounted because nothing had been mentioned about it in reports from Strasbourg. He sends his regards to Bucer, should he have returned from Ulm.

Letter 443: 7 July 1531, [Strasbourg], Capito to Ulrich Zwingli

Printed in ZwBw 5:505–22, Ep. 1235.

[*Summary*]: He is worried about the affairs of Zurich, but the emperor's court is ineffective and corrupt. In the opinion of Philip of Hesse they are safe. The strife between Solothurn and Basel [the 'gallows war' over jurisdiction in capital cases] will delight their enemies. He assumes that Zwingli knows about the feud in Friesland between [Balthasar van Esens] and Ulrich [von Dornum], a patron of Karlstadt. There is a false rumour about 12,000 Spanish infantry having been raised. He has heard another rumour through Matthis Pfarrer that the emperor will depart for Spain in September. The emperor sent a reply to the Schmalkald League [on 30 June 1531] and is amenable to a truce. [Ludwig], Count Palatine, and [Albert of Brandenburg], archbishop of Mainz, are negotiating on his behalf. Strasbourg supports the peace efforts. A meeting has been deferred to 24 August. He hopes that it is not a ruse on the part of the emperor. There is no military initiative in Lorraine [cf. above, Ep. 442]. Metz is being harassed by a robber baron, [Nikolaus of Heu]. The Strasbourg area is full of unemployed mercenaries, which would indicate that the situation is peaceful everywhere. Philip of Hesse is no longer regarded as unstable (*nullae nunc agitant intemperiae*).

In Augsburg, the Anabaptists have recanted. The council is divided over two preachers, Michael [Cellarius] who is on their side, and Stephan [Agricola], who is a Lutheran. The men they sent from Strasbourg [Musculus, Wolfhart, Meyer, cf. above Epp. 429a, 437] have no authority as yet.

The affairs at Ulm are prospering. Martin Frecht [cf. above, Ep. 431], 'the glory of the university of Heidelberg,' preaches there. A Greek teacher [Wolfgang Bindthäuser] has been called to Ulm from Ingolstadt. The churches have been purged [i.e., the images removed] and the mass will be abolished or may already have been abolished – Capito last heard from Bucer eight days ago. [Georg Osswald; cf. above, Ep. 441] proffered Eck's *Confutatio* at the request of the council. The reformers answered him in their sermons. Dithmarschen [in the duchy of Holstein] has embraced the Reformation.

Capito expects Bucer to return [from Ulm] within five days. [Jacob Sturm], Bernhard Ottfriedrich, and Matthis Pfarrer send their regards. The reports about the Reformation instituted by the Swedish king [Gustav Vasa] are correct. He has forced the bishops into subjection. Ludwig, Count Palatine, received the *Landvogtei* of Haguenau as a reward for his support of Ferdinand's election.

Letter 444: 18 July 1531, Strasbourg, Capito to Joachim Vadianus

Printed in VadBr 5:13–14, Ep. 639.

[*Summary*]: The bearer of this letter [Alexander Berner, cf. below, Ep. 445] has been sent to seek information on the administration of alms in other churches so that they may improve their own system. Bucer recently returned from Ulm, where the Reformation has now been established. He sends his greetings.

Letter 445: 18 July 1531, Strasbourg, Capito to Ulrich Zwingli

Printed in ZwBw 5:436–8, Ep. 1247.

[*Summary*]: Bucer has returned from Ulm. The Reformation has been established there. Soon negotiations will begin about an alliance between Strasbourg and Ulm. The Swabian alliance is not solid [it was dissolved in 1534]. Ottheinrich of Palatine-Neuburg is engaged in a feud with the [Cistercians at Kaisersheim]. A date is to be fixed for the next Diet in Speyer or Worms in September [it was held in Regensburg, January 1532]. The emperor has in mind to corroborate Ferdinand's election before returning to Spain. The bearer of this letter is [Alexander Berner; cf. above, Ep. 444], who is in charge of distributing alms, and has been asked by the council to investigate the system of alms in other churches. Bucer sends his greetings.

Letter 446: 16 August 1531, [Strasbourg], Capito to Ulrich Zwingli

Printed in ZwBw 5:573–5, Ep. 1261.

[*Summary*]: He describes negotiations to gain support for Ferdinand's election preceding the diet [then set for September at Speyer, but moved to Regensburg]. The emperor has commissioned Joachim I of Brandenburg to appease Albert of Prussia and has sent Wilhelm [Capito calls him 'Philip'] of Nassau to talk to the Elector John of Saxony and persuade him to rescind his alliance with Philip of Hesse. Wilhelm III von Neuenahr, the brother of [Hermann von Neuenahr] has been sent to the court of Hesse by the emperor. The official agenda of the diet is religious peace, but the real agenda is the confirmation of Ferdinand and the increase of papal power. The situation is difficult for Strasbourg. He advises Zwingli either to come to an agreement with the Five Catholic cantons or to declare war openly. He will show Zwingli's letter [not extant] to [Jacob] Sturm. Bucer sends his greetings. Strasbourg has not yet been invited formally to attend the diet.

Letter 447: [20–21 August 1531, Strasbourg], Capito to Simon Grynaeus

The manuscript of this letter is in the Zurich SA, E II, 349, 206. It is printed in CorrBucer 6: 60, note 30. The writer, Simon Grynaeus (1493–1541), was a fellow student of Philip Melanchthon's at the Latin school in Pforzheim. He studied in Vienna, then worked as teacher and librarian in Buda. In 1523 he was in Wittenberg. From 1524–9 he lived in Heidelberg, where he taught Greek at the university. In 1529 he was called to the University of Basel. In July 1531 he visited Strasbourg on his return from England, where he had gone in search of Greek manuscripts. In England he was instructed by Henry VIII to obtain opinions from the reformers on 'the King's great matter,' the legality of his marriage to Catherine of Aragon, the widow of his brother Arthur (d. 1502).

The marriage, which was against canonical law, had gone forward after Pope Julius II issued a dispensation. The couple had one surviving daughter, Mary. The need for a male heir and the king's attachment to Anne Boleyn led him to seek an annulment of his marriage to Catherine. The situation was fraught with difficulties, not only because the papal dispensation had to be set aside, but also because Catherine was the aunt of Emperor Charles V. When the first round of negotiations with the papal court broke down, Henry VIII requested numerous universities to pronounce on the matter. Most of those consulted in 1530 pronounced in favour of the king; the prestigious universities of Paris, Salamanca, Leuven, and others in Charles' realm, however, pronounced against it. During the subsequent disengagement of the English from the Roman church, the king decided to seek the opinion of Protestant theologians. Thus, his instructions to Grynaeus to collect the opinions of reformers in Germany and Switzerland. The correspondence between Grynaeus and the reformers shows that they were far from united in their opinion (cf. below, Epp. 448, 449, and 459). The theologians of Strasbourg and Wittenberg variously stated that Old Testament law (i.e., Lev. 18:16, on which Henry VIII based his arguments) did not apply to Christians, or that a discreet bigamy was preferable to an annulment or a divorce, whereas Zwingli and Oecolampadius advocated a separation. The Sacramentarian controversy made it imperative for the Strasbourgers not to aggravate the differences between the Swiss and the Wittenberg theologians, but after the deaths of Zwingli and Oecolampadius at the end of 1531, they were free to offer their independent opinion (cf. Ep. 459 below).

[*Summary*:] The Strasbourg preachers have read Grynaeus' letter to Bucer [CorrBucer 6:56–61, Ep. 447] and will give their answer within three days. They believe that the marriage between Henry VIII and Catherine was just and consensual and according to divine law. A divorce *in speciem* might be possible, or else one might have to think about repudiation or some other form of separation, even polygamy. Luther might approve of it, but it is a solution fraught with difficulties. It might be condoned in monarchs, however. It would be less embarrassing for the queen, if she retained her rank and honours. She might afterwards remarry. There was much unhappiness and disagreement among them. Grynaeus should perhaps hold off until he has heard their definitive opinion [cf. below, Ep. 459]. They expect they will agree with Zwingli.

Letter 448: [Between 2 and 7 September 1531], Basel, Symon Grynaeus to the preachers of Strasbourg

Printed in CorrBucer 6:95–7, Ep. 457. For the context see above, Ep. 447.

[*Summary*]: The reply to [Henry VIII] has been prepared. It is up to the Strasbourgers to send it in this form or give it more consideration. Nothing will be done until the king sends his personal messenger. He doubts that Philip [Melanchthon] will supply an answer. He has already written to him twice. Grynaeus himself cannot advise them of the best response. He will follow their advice.

Letter 449: [10? September 1531, Basel], Simon Grynaeus to the Strasbourg Preachers

Printed in CorrBucer 6:107–10, Ep. 461.

[*Summary*]: Grynaeus' advice is to send off the responses to [Henry VIII; cf. above, Epp. 447–8], even if they are not complete. The king will send a special messenger, [Thomas Cranmer], to listen to their views. The responses will be kept confidential. Grynaeus does not expect the theologians of Wittenberg to provide a response. The response of the Strasbourgers cannot be faulted. It focuses on the question of the king's conscience. The universities of Italy and France have given their opinion; so has Zwingli, who draws on arguments from natural and divine law. The messenger will go to Frankfurt. The Strasbourgers have Grynaeus' permission to revise his letter to the king. He asks Bucer to finalize and copy his last two letters and have them ready by the morning of the following day.

Letter 450: 17 September [1531], Basel, Johannes Oecolampadius to Capito

Printed in BrOek 2:681–3, Ep. 932.

[*Summary*]: Oecolampadius can see that Capito is offended. He meant well and merely wrote to warn Capito that his reputation was at risk. There was no need to compare him with Luther, Erasmus, or Melanchthon, who have not reciprocated Capito's friendly feelings. Oecolampadius, by contrast, is a constant friend. Capito has satisfied him concerning his beliefs and his character. Oecolampadius is worried only about the people [i.e., the Anabaptists and their sympathizers] Capito receives into his home. Capito needs to decide: if he approves of the teachings of the reformers, he must not consort with their opponents. Capito's tolerance may turn out to be the cause of dissension rather than peace, which he desires. He hopes that Capito will relieve his anxiety without reproaching him for taking the liberty of admonishing him.

Letter 451: 18 September 1531, [Strasbourg], Capito to Joachim Vadianus

Printed in VadBr 5:17–18, Ep. 644.

[*Summary*]: The weaver Augustin Bader was condemned to death as an

Anabaptist in Stuttgart [on 30 March] 1530. He left a widow and children.[1] He deposited 16 gulden with the tailor Hans Witzigman, who recently entered the service of Conrad Glantzen. Capito asks for Vadianus' help in recovering the money, since the widow is in dire need. Nikolaus Guldi has been living in Strasbourg for a month and remains a true believer. Capito commends him to Vadianus. Bucer sends his greetings. Capito has written to Dominik [Schleupner] and asks Vadianus to convey the letter to him.

Letter 452: 7 October 1531, Strasbourg, Capito and Martin Bucer to the City Council of Augsburg

Printed in CorrBucer 6:182–4, Ep. 483.

[*Summary*]: Sabine Bader, the widow of Augustin Bader, who has been executed in Stuttgart [cf. above, Ep. 451], has lived in Strasbourg quietly and piously, but cannot make a living there and is therefore returning to Augsburg. They ask that the city accept her recantation [accepted 24 October 1531] and permit her to take up residence in Augsburg.

Letter 453: 10 October 1531, Strasbourg, Capito to Joachim Vadianus

Printed in VadBr 5:21, Ep. 648.

[*Summary*]: He is pleased with the man [unidentified] recommended to him by Vadianus. He is free of the Anabaptist superstition. [Sabine Bader, cf. above, Ep. 451] will shortly move to Augsburg. He has been tutoring her and has written to the Augsburg council on her behalf [cf. above, Ep. 452]. He recommends a young man [unidentified], who wishes to take up residence in St Gallen and perhaps take over the shop of his master. Bucer, Bedrot, and the other co-ministers send greetings. Bucer has not yet completed his Latin apologia [of the Confessio Tetrapolitana, BDS 3:187–318].

Letter 454: 22 October [1531], Basel, Johannes Oecolampadius to Capito

Printed in BrOek 2:699–700, Ep. 945.

[*Summary*]: He agrees with Capito about reforming the universities. There is

* * * * *

1 I.e., Sabine Bader, who so impressed Capito that he considered marrying her after he was widowed himself. Cf. CorrBucer 7:217, Ep. 544.

a need to distinguish between good and mediocre students, but there must be no excess. Times are difficult: there are many good lecturers, but few students. The Five Catholic cantons are at war with Zurich. Zwingli, together with the abbot of Kappel [Wolfgang Ioner] and [Konrad Schmid] of Küssnacht, have been captured and put to death. The enemy committed worse cruelties than the Turks. Ioner's eyes were pricked out. Someone reported that Zwingli was torn to pieces. He asks for the prayers of the Strasbourgers and sends greetings to Bucer, Hedio, and the other preachers.

Letter 455: 28 November 1531, Strasbourg, Capito to Anna Reinhard

> The manuscript of this letter is in Zurich SA E II 356a, fol. 86(87); it is printed in J.H. Hottinger, *Historiae ecclesiasticae saeculi XVI pars secunda* (Zurich, 1665), 2:666–7. This is Capito's letter of condolence to Zwingli's widow, Anna Reinhard (d. 1538). Zwingli secretly married the widow and mother of three children in 1522 (marriage made public in 1524). They had four children.

To the widow of the late Ulrich Zwingli, his dear sister in Christ. My dearest lady, I feel for your grief and suffering, as you can imagine. For you were aware of our affection and good will toward each other. It is, moreover, a great loss to all churches. Our whole gospel has suffered a decisive loss through the death of your dear husband. You have suffered all this grief and trouble once, but we are more heavily burdened and affected by this grief, which becomes more sorrowful to us every day. You have lost your husband, that precious man, as well as your son, son-in-law, brother-in-law, and brother. Who would not commiserate with you? But God be praised who gave you such a husband, who maintains his honour even in death, and has won lasting fame which should benefit your children. For people will not forget him. Everyone will cherish his family always. Given at Strasbourg, 28 November 1531.

Letter 456: 10 December 1531, Augsburg, Ulrich Rehlinger to Capito

> The manuscript of this letter is in AST 160, #234. Ulrich Rehlinger (1471–1547), an Augsburg patrician, and from 1523–35 (in alternate years) mayor or Baumeister of Augsburg. He favoured the Zwinglian branch of the Reformation. He tried to protect Michael Cellarius (see above, Ep. 405, note 1) who was arrested in Augsburg in 1527. On Rehlinger's request, Strasbourg sent two preachers to Augsburg in 1530/31 (see notes 2 and 3 below). Rehlinger was instrumental in encouraging Augsburg to join the League of Schmalkald.

First, grace and peace from God the Father through Jesus Christ, our deliverance and salvation. Honourable, well-meaning, dear sir and brother, first I would like you to know that I have heard, with sincere regret, of the death of your honest, dear wife.[1] May God Almighty see to her resurrection, as no doubt he will, and may he grant you relief. Furthermore, dear sir and brother, you have no doubt heard through letters from my dear sirs and brothers, Bonifacius[2] and the other preachers, how things stand here with our church. May God Almighty improve things daily, that we may look only to him and not to human beings. Bonifacius and Musculus,[3] I hear, consider it good, for many reasons, to have you here with us for a while and have written to you at length to this effect, which I, for my own person, would like very well. I, too, regard it as very good and beneficial and would like to see you here. It would be beneficial for those who are not well grounded in the article concerning the Lord's Supper. For this reason, it is my earnest request to Your Honour to come, if there was an opportunity and you were able and willing to do so. I would also want to obtain permission from your lords at Strasbourg to have you stay at my house, which would be a favour and a service also to my wife[4] and would please her a great deal. You need not worry about the nature of my offer. I know that I will greatly benefit from you, which I will take into account, my dear sir and brother. You must consider that you should look for comfort in your grief now and become cheerful again, and at the same time do good, render a favour to my wife, and give pleasure and service to myself. She will be at Your Honour's service and wishes you well and likewise laments the death of your honoured and dear wife. My dear sir and brother, I beg you most kindly not to be offended by my faithful counsel and my imperfect understanding. It is because God Almighty has called our dear and faithful servants of God and his eternal Word from this sinful world, namely Johannes Oecolampadius and Master Ulrich Zwingli, whom God Almighty may grant resurrection, as he no doubt will.[5] Dr Martin Luther opposed them on account of the sacrament and in other matters. That same matter now rests with my dear sirs and brothers, you and Martin Bucer, as the pre-eminent men. God Almighty has no doubt effected earlier on that you and Martin Bucer came to the point where Dr Martin Luther listened to you two through Bucer and

* * * * *

1 Agnes Roettel died on 17 October 1531.
2 Bonifacius Wolfhart, cf. CWC 1, Ep. 102 headnote.
3 Wolfgang Musculus, cf. above, Ep. 438 headnote.
4 Rehlinger married Ursula Gossenbrot in 1497.
5 Oecolampadius died on 22 November 1531; Zwingli on 11 October 1531.

had a friendly talk.[6] With God's help the matter was brought to the point where the two parties approached each other and came together, and Dr Martin curtailed his heated writing about this article. I heard that the princes and cities of the Christian league will shortly meet[7] to see whether through God's grace and help the matter may be brought to a compromise and consensus, without the Word of God and the Truth being curtailed. All who are of a Christian mind must pray that this will come to pass, and surely my two sirs and brothers will be the means of effecting it, for which God will grant you both his grace. Certainly the gospel will benefit at the future diet,[8] for you two, the most learned men, know what harm and disadvantage the schism has caused and will cause in the future. May God Almighty prevent it henceforth. Thus I commend myself forever to your service. I beg you also to offer my best regards, service, and expression of good will to my dear sirs, Jacob Sturm and Matthis Pfarrer,[9]and wish all the best to my dear sir and brother Martin Bucer, as well as Caspar Schwenckfeld,[10] if he is still staying with you in Strasbourg. Thus may the Lord God be with you and all of us. Given at Augsburg in haste on 10 December, in the year of the Lord, 1531.

    Ulrich Rehlinger Sr.

Letter 456a: [After 16 December 1531, Strasbourg], Capito and the Strasbourg Preachers to the City Council of Strasbourg

The manuscript of the letter is in AST 84, #6. Printed in CorrBucer 7: 118–26, Ep. 525.

[*Summary*]: On the invitation of the council, the preachers offer the following suggestions concerning church discipline: they ask the council to prevent public criticism of their preaching and lifestyle, which might create dissension among the people. They would like the council to assure the emperor that they respect and obey their superiors, but owe obedience to God first. They must speak out against the enemies of the Word of God. They repudi-

* * * * *

6 Bucer met with Luther in Coburg in September 1530.
7 I.e., the Schmalkaldic League, which met in the spring of 1532 at Schweinfurt.
8 In Regensburg, 1532.
9 For Jacob Sturm, see CWC 1, Ep. 48 headnote. Matthis Pfarrer (1489–1568), member of the city council, from 1525 on the committee of XIII, repeatedly *Amman*. He drew up the Strasbourg legislation concerning alms and represented Strasbourg at the Diet of Augsburg (1530) and on other diplomatic missions.
10 For Schwenckfeld, see above Ep. 393 headnote. Schwenckfeld was in Strasbourg, with interruptions, from 1529 to 1534.

ate the accusation that they are 'murderers of the gospel and of the soul' (*schrifft und seelmörder*) and administer sacraments 'that are not the sacraments of Christ.' The council should invite those who criticize the preachers in guilds and chapters, to lodge an official complaint before the council so that the preachers in turn may defend themselves against such accusations. They are willing to undergo any punishment if the council finds them guilty of any trespass.

Letter 457: [Before 25] December [1531, Strasbourg], Capito [to Leonhard von Liechtenstein]

Printed in QGT 7:363–86, #290a. This letter is the result of a request by Leonhard von Liechtenstein, the lord of Nikolsburg, for an evaluation of Oswald Glait's *Vom Sabbath*. I have not been able to trace a copy of the work, which may have remained in manuscript (cf. below, note 1).

Nothing of substance is known about Glait before 1525, when he arrived in Nikolsburg (Moravia). Apparently he had been expelled from Austria because of his heterodox preaching. An evangelical congregation had formed at Nikolsburg in 1523 with the encouragement of Leonhard von Liechtenstein and under the leadership of the preacher Hans Spittelmaier. Glait became Spittelmaier's associate. He attended a synod at Austerlitz in March of 1526 and wrote a report on the discussions between evangelicals and utraquists in *Handlung, yetz den XIV. Tag Marciy dis XXVI jars, so zu osterlytz ... beschehen* (Zurich, 1526?). Glait, who leaned toward Anabaptism, accompanied Hans Hut to Vienna in 1527 and attended the meeting of the Anabaptists in Augsburg ('Martyrs' Synod') in the same year. Few details are known of Glait's later career. *Vom Sabbath*, the work discussed below, led to a polemic with Valentin Crautwald. Neither Crautwald's attack nor Glait's response is extant. The controversy is known, however, from the intervention of Glait's disciple Andreas Fischer (*Bericht und anzeigen ... vom Sabbath*, manuscript in the Schwenckfelder Library, Pennsburg, PA). Glait preached in Silesia until he was ousted in 1542. In 1545 he was imprisoned in Vienna and executed (by drowning) the following year.

Andreas Fischer's promotion of his mentor's teachings prompted Leonhard von Liechtenstein to seek an opinion on Glait's book from Capito and Caspar Schwenckfeld. Schwenckfeld's sharply critical review (CS 4:444–518) is dated 1 January 1532. Capito supplies an approximate terminus postquem for the present letter, stating that he wrote it one month after Leonhard's request reached him at the end of October. He left Strasbourg ca. 25 December (see below, Ep. 458), which supplies the terminus antequem. However, this time frame is at odds with Schwenckfeld's claim that his critique antedates Capito's: 'Since he [Capito] was burdened with significant affairs and could not oblige [Leonhard von Liechtenstein] as fast as he wanted and supply an answer, he thought it was better that I should give him my verdict.' Schwenckfeld's statement would indicate that Capito began the present letter at the end of November but left it unfinished (see below, note 71).

Dear friend and brother, I wish you and all who fear God true enlightenment of the gospel through the light of Jesus Christ. For fear of God protects us against error and keeps us close to the one who is the only path to eternal life. And may we thus continue on the path without deviating and without wilful presumption. Amen.

It so happens that the booklet *Concerning the Sabbath* which you sent here,[1] reached me at a time when the Lord was visiting his grave paternal punishment on me, for my dear sister and wife Agnes, my loyal helper in all services to God, was sick and died during those same days.[2] She died peacefully, quietly and in full devotion to God, but her death did not fail to elicit great disquiet and grief from me. For I recognized it as God's punishment, and I repented of my sins. God thus used this situation in order to encourage me to take stock of myself. Let eternal praise be to him who chastises me in a fatherly manner, who has eternally proven his constant compassion on the cross, and who shows me my sin. Nonetheless, for several days, I and others were able to contemplate nothing else but that God would want to put an end to my existence and take me from this earth as well. Thus, I laid aside your letter and the booklet for almost a whole month and did not concern myself with it.

Now as I take it in my hands again, reading it over and pondering it, I can see in it no other use than to make me more vigilant and make me pray to God with great earnestness to protect simple men from such bad, presumptuous, and ambitious minds through the distribution and increase of his gifts. Otherwise, these people will incite a great deal of trouble and will give rise not only to Jewish superstition but even to pagan frivolity, since these people hit both extremes. Indeed, as soon as the letter of the law is abolished, they forget about God, since they do not rest in Christ's teaching and are thus unable to have a true God.

It would be a good thing, my lord, to take notice of this warning from the holy apostle John: *If anyone comes to you and does not bring this teaching* (referring to the teaching of Christ), *do not bring him into your house, and do*

* * * * *

1 Schwenckfeld (CS 4: 453–4) relates that he and Capito were sent a manuscript of the book (*ein geschriben Exemplar*).
2 Agnes Roettel died on 17 October 1531.

not greet him, for whoever greets him makes himself a participant in his evil deed.[3] If the teaching of Christ concerns us, we shall not take pleasure in anything that is against it. No one likes to hear his friend slandered. Therefore, just as under the law those who have been banished on account of their teaching remain outcasts and no one pays attention to them in order to show that the understanding of the whole church is opposed to their error, so, likewise, the apostle desires Christians to be gracious to all those who acknowledge Christ's majesty and to flee all who live and teach things opposed to the Son of God. If we fail to do so, our friendly interaction shows that we, too, take pleasure in their blasphemy.

As for this booklet *Concerning the Sabbath*, it is clear to any orthodox believer that it is not in accordance with the teaching of Christ. For Christ's teaching always brings to light our dark hearts, our hidden sin, our old, natural curse that comes from Adam, together with his evil plans and inability to do good, as well as a compulsion and desire to do mischief, all of which the apostles clearly explain through the death of Christ. Yet through the spirit of his resurrection, Christ's teaching also shows how, by the grace granted to us children of God, our depraved nature along with the cause (that is, with the old creature) will be completely uprooted, and in its place will be planted a blessed bounty of gifts. It shows us how to break free from our past sins, revealing what it is to be justified before God and what it is to be received as heirs of heavenly blessings. His teaching discloses what it is to be made a new creature before God in terms of good works and an enlightened heart. It relates how we arrive at faith and how a renewed heart and the inner man will be shaped in accordance with God's will. It declares what beliefs may or may not be abandoned. Christ's teaching distinguishes between those who have put on or have manufactured their faith and those who are true disciples of Christ, who stand in the recognition of the Truth. It reveals the nature of Christian freedom and shows the difference between the law and the gospel, between the written and natural Word of God, and between appearance and truth. It demonstrates how the human Christ, who is currently in the immortal and divine nature of the Father, ought to govern our hearts, and it makes clear whether he does so himself or through the mediation of his creatures, through external words and sacramental signs. His instruction makes known the proof of true faith and shows how and if faith creates new and heavenly people. It reveals the nature of constancy in faith, where the faithful progress and reach perfection, and how the Father draws, the Son

* * * * *

3 2 John 1:10–11.

enlightens and the Holy Spirit sanctifies the elect. It explains Christ's purport and the glorious actions continuously pursued by the apostles. Yet all these are a horror to this booklet, which disdains all spiritual matters. Is it possible that anything of the understanding of Christ exists in men with such an attitude, who call the seventh day and the dead letter a firm rock on which to build, a sign and seal of the hope between God and man through which we will be made righteous? Beware, lest we receive a false Sabbath in exchange for the true one! What role will Christ play, if the seventh day is our hope and our intermediary between God and man, the firm rock and foundation of our spiritual building? O, the misery! Shall we blaspheme the divine majesty of Christ's name and invest empty elements of this world with such great dignity – dignity that is owed to the divine power of Jesus Christ alone? What presumption and lack of understanding! How low we have fallen, merciful Father, that such assertions should find not only readers and listeners, but even followers! May God have mercy on these poor souls, who are sadly still imprisoned by their error and sin. Indeed, they are even more horribly entangled in the devil's chains through such presumption, which masquerades as the fear of God. May God help them and us to find the truth in Jesus Christ. Amen.

Thus, dear sir and brother, when someone engages in prophecy, we should not extinguish the spirit, but rather, we should test all things and hold fast to the good.[4] More importantly, we should hold fast to the Truth and the power of God, not looking to the shadows and the dead letters of Moses. We should freely accept those things that God teaches us and that the Holy Spirit instils in us – namely, those things that serve to improve us and build us up toward God, that are in accord with our belief in Christ – and we should not pay attention to the empty gestures and pompous, arrogant words that strive to give a great deal of importance to things other than the internalized, living and reigning Christ. For while a Christian should always accept only those things that lead to his improvement, he must still let go of many things that may be good in themselves and might also lead toward the worship of God. For it is a special gift to discern who has the Spirit in the whole community, 1 Cor. 12,[5] and not everything suits every person at the same time. There are many examples of this in the treatment of vices: whereas one person must be firmly and earnestly compelled, another must be gently encouraged to proceed and to pay attention to the Lord God.

However, the author [Glait] and others like him are not to be hated,

* * * * *

4 1 Thess. 5:19–21.
5 1 Cor. 12:10.

since there is much that remains covered in darkness. We all declare with the mouth that Jesus Christ is our salvation. Yet he will progressively reveal to us the nature and form of his power in today's world through his Spirit, and he will suggest it in our hearts through the working of our conscience. He will do this, not so that a new, peculiar idea will come into being from these or any other meaningless things, but rather so that God's Truth should also become and remain the eternal, constant Truth in our hearts. This is not the case with those who are completely engrossed in the flesh.

Such disputations, which do not lead to Christ the Lord, are of little concern to Christians. I myself would have liked it if festivals such as Easter and Pentecost as well as Sundays and other holy days had been considered differently in the past. For now they have turned people against one another and have almost instigated a conflict, through which the external image of the rightful master, the Holy Spirit, as it is drawn up in Scripture, would be completely devastated, and his office abolished. It does no harm for me to wish for a different conception of these holy days, but that is not the point, and it is not my place to incite rumour and create unrest. The Law of Moses still exists, from which I gain a witness of my life and salvation. Why would the customs of the external world – that is, external practice – disturb me, regardless of whether or not they are taken from Scripture? He who believes in Christ has eternal life;[6] what else does one need? All other things are of little concern, since faith grasps God's grace, which is the promise and the inheritance.[7] It creates new hearts, true worshippers and servants of God, well-suited to good works, whose good works flow from an active love and not from the letter of the law or fleshly concerns.

However, in order that I might set my own understanding against this booklet and thus clearly negate its argument with truth, I have decided to write (in accordance with the order in which you asked these questions in your letter) regarding the following: first, the difference between the Law of Moses and our gospel; second, the extent to which the entirety of Moses continues to apply after our Lord Jesus Christ has risen and the manner in which it applies; and third, I will write to make clear the main point of the booklet and to reveal its error. Yet, by the grace of God, I hope to direct my comments not at this booklet alone but also at the many confused minds and at the Jews, who have instigated the same argument in a similar fashion. In this way a satisfactory response may be provided to this challenge once and

* * * * *

6 John 3:16.
7 Cf. Gal. 3:17–19.

for all, either to give satisfaction or to reveal the limits of my skill. Indeed, this business is not new to me; others have spoken up against this booklet for other reasons.[8] For it satisfies neither Jew nor Christian, neither letter nor spirit. Rather it is an evil, arrogant argument, which reflects more than a little badly on the writer. Therefore, since I wish to write for the benefit of everyone, I will henceforth not address my words to you but rather to the general reader, who is trapped by many misconceptions. I will dare to speak from my soul and heart.

Concerning the law in itself, which the gospel encompasses.

Regarding the first point. The Law is the eternal will of God to punish evildoers and bless the elect with his grace. He made this Law known to the patriarchs internally and then to all people publicly in the writing of the Ten Commandments on Mount Horeb. These same things were shown clearly at the tabernacle and were further revealed through the many statutes in the five books of Moses, which in themselves are a description of the Law of God. And the end of that Law is Christ. He who believes in him is righteous and has fulfilled the righteousness of the Law, which may be proffered through Moses and the prophets, and perhaps I also bear witness to it.

Concerning the law observed without regard to Christ, which is opposed to the gospel.

However, Israel strove for such a law of righteousness and was unable to fulfil it. For they sought the law not in faith but rather in the works of the law, etc. Rom. 9.[9] Thus, the works of the law, which by their very nature include Christ, became their – that is, the Pharisees' – own form of righteousness, and, as a result, they were unable to subject themselves to the righteousness which God recognizes, namely, God's grace. The result was that the apostles distinguished between law and grace, between Moses and Christ, the means and the end result; they differentiated between the letter and the spirit, the image and the truth, even though they belong together in practice – since Moses without the inclusion of Christ is not the eternal Word of God. Yet each should remain in its proper order. And they adjusted their true message to correspond with Jewish understanding. Thus, they referred to all commandments, judgments, and ceremonies as the Law, whether or not they were included in the bare letter of the law as described by Moses. For in all

* * * * *

8 Valentin Crautwald. Cf. above headnote.
9 Cf. Rom. 9:31–2.

these things, which the letter reveals, the Jews considered themselves to be righteous.[10]

Now, when the Law is placed in opposition to the gospel, it is naturally nothing other than the letter of Moses without Christ and without the Spirit. The reason and free will of a God-fearing man may attempt to hold to this letter very earnestly, yet he does so through his own strength and without the grace of Christ and the Spirit. And he may flatter himself, taking it for something beautiful. In fact, it is a bit of hypocrisy and a futile and false presumption, since evil is attached to the old self through its very nature. Indeed, man, by virtue of his membership in that nature, lies imprisoned under the law of sin, from which he cannot escape until the Saviour himself releases him from his bonds and leads him into the realm of freedom. For the law requires a good and upright heart, but it causes significant damage, since all those who seek their salvation and security in works desire to justify themselves through the law and exclude God's righteousness, as in Tim.[11] But God himself has established for them that he who believes is already saved.[12]

Distinction between the law of the Truth and the revealed gospel.

If you wish to understand the distinction between the law and the gospel, you must keep in mind that the law can be understood in two different ways. First, it can be understood in and of itself with the entirety of its contents, just as it was given by God through Moses, interpreted in the prophets, and revealed to believing hearts. This is his eternal Word, which, though it was previously shrouded in clouds and prefigured dimly in the shadows and figures of the law, in the fullness of time, appeared in the flesh. Second, the law can be understood in terms of the Mosaic observance, followed out of fear, or as it has always been and will continue to be followed and understood through reasoning which does not come from God. Scripture treats the law in both these ways and in both cases distinguishes the law from the gospel. Indeed, the law in itself – that is, for God and in truth – is God's divine counsel and his delight.[13] Through it, he decided for himself from eternity to make man after all other creatures to be the crowning achievement of his magnificence and, after man's fall, to raise him up once again through the incarnation of

* * * * *

10 Meaning of phrase unclear: 'Wie der buchstab vff den gantzen inhalt die ... [two words illegible] davon hynnoch wyters.'
11 Cf. 1 Tim. 1: 9.
12 Cf. Rom. 10:4.
13 Cf. Ps. 1:2.

his Word in the flesh – that is, the work of Jesus Christ, his only begotten Son – and to introduce man to a share of the heavenly bounty.

Such counsel and Word of God are called the Law of Moses, since it introduces and anticipates our Lord Jesus Christ, whom all the figures and ceremonies depict. Therefore, the entirety of the Law of Moses is directed toward this: that it should bear witness to such work of God and that it should lead to Christ, for thus the Holy Spirit is finally seen through the law. The commandments are seen as necessary for this reason, in that they reveal sin and the natural inconstancy of the heart. In the same way, the judicial guidelines and penalties bear witness in the law to show that God does not desire those things that are sinful to go unpunished. In fact, he has commanded that worldly evil be punished strenuously, insofar as worldly evil and unrighteousness may be recognized in the world. Now then, through the law, the wrath of God is shown and the unrighteousness of man is made recognizable. And through the law, sin will be forgiven, the wrath and punishment of God taken away, and the heavenly kingdom established, which is the very image of the fatherly heart. It follows, therefore, that all such things – the Word of God, the counsel of God, his gifts, his grace, his mercy, and many other things which one receives spiritually in the heart from God – are and ought to be called the law.

Therefore, the kingly prophet David describes the law in this manner, Psalm 19: *The law of the Lord is unchanging and refreshes the soul*, etc.[14] This statement ought not to be understood as referring to the letter of Moses, since such an external law is insufficient until Christ himself writes it on the heart through the Holy Spirit, and thus makes the law reveal and share not only sin but also the forgiveness of sin. Thus, on the one hand, the law, if it accomplishes its purpose, rouses the conscience and is a type of knowledge, an internal comprehension, a heavenly wisdom, an understanding of God, a friend of the heart, an enlightenment of the eyes, and it remains in force throughout eternity. In contrast, the letter of the law remains external; it frightens, leading into despair, lacking all understanding of heavenly gifts, filled with sorrow of the heart and blindness of the eyes, and it does not have any understanding.

This first law is spiritual and has its peace and resolution in Christ. It renews the old birth. Everything that is established in the gospel is also present in this law, and it is thus one with the gospel. For this reason, Paul says: *The law is spiritual*.[15] It is spirit and brings spirit and life.

* * * * *

14 Ps. 19:7.
15 Rom. 7:14.

What, then, is the difference? Augustine and the other fathers generally answer that the law is the hidden gospel, and the gospel is the law explained.[16] That is to say that the grace and gift of God were not revealed to the world under the law, and that after Christ's resurrection there is nothing to be sought in the law, in the shadows, except for witnesses to the light. For the incarnation of light, our Lord Jesus Christ, illuminated the darkness of hearts after his resurrection and publicly revealed the truth – that is, himself – which the shadows had previously only shown prophetically. Some true believers saw that the law has as its end the Lord Jesus Christ, who was foreseen externally and who endowed their hearts with strength, illuminating and renewing them. Indeed, kings and prophets saw precisely the same things that the apostles saw. Yet many of the two groups desired to see, but were unable. The law is not opposed to grace. Before the law, Abraham believed and saw the Lord's Day with joy, because the Lord Christ, through the Holy Spirit, pacified his heart. Why should this not be possible under the law? David and Isaiah have shown that this is the case. How far the law of life goes, which Moses promoted through his observance and external practices, will now be shown further.

Distinction of the law, according to Mosaic observance and the revealed gospel.

The eternal law, which enlightens the heart, has always been administered by the Son of God, since the law is spiritual, and Christ has been, is, and will always be in the presence of God. In the following section, we will treat Mosaic observance, to what extent the law still concerns itself with Mosaic observance, what the difference is between the office of Moses and that of Christ, and what use the Law of Moses and its observance are today. If one understands and grasps these things, he is freed from many errors that still press upon those of weaker understanding.

The law according to Mosaic observance is the eternal will of God described earlier, but it is written on a stone tablet and fixed in letters, as it was received externally, without the Holy Spirit of the resurrection of Jesus Christ, through the spirit of fear, or without spirit through the old nature.

This description has three main points: first, that the law is an external exercise; second, that it instilled fear and that it could not accomplish anything else until it came out of the hand of Moses; and third, that the Law of Moses was not undertaken for the ceremonies alone but rather for its entire

* * * * *

16 Augustine, *Sermons on the New Testament*, 95.3.

contents, which has no relevance for us at all, as well as for its strength and influence.

Regarding the first point: the law is an external action. That can be seen in this manner. The office of the New Testament is an office of the Spirit, and that Spirit is made alive through the grace and gifts of God. Thus, our intercessor Christ Jesus resides within us in his Holy Spirit and changes our hearts internally, making of us new, heavenly men so that we might no longer dwell upon earthly things and instead be turned to heavenly things. In contrast, Mosaic observance is external. It is directed at and oversees the external man in the external worship of God, although it leads to the internal. For its power remains in the old birth and in natural man, since the servant of God is able to do nothing that is reserved for the Almighty Father alone, and that can only come to fruition through the divine and supernatural influence of grace, whose office belongs to our beloved Lord, the man Jesus Christ, the true son of God, and to no one else in heaven or on earth, as God's eternal will and counsel points to, Eph.: *anakephalaiosasthai*.[17] For this reason, Paul calls Mosaic observance in the old covenant or Old Testament observance of the letter, whose letter kills.[18] More about this later.

The apostle, in his letter to the Galatians, interprets Moses in this way: *Dear brothers, I wish to speak according to human understanding: no one despises a man's testament*, etc. until *430 years later*.[19] That is to say: although the Holy Spirit in the covenant of Abraham intended Isaac to be the seed and the recipient of Canaanite land, he was also referring ultimately to the true seed, through whom all generations of mankind are blessed, and to the heavenly inheritance, the full comprehension of God through a true recognition in faith. This is the kingdom of the living, and outside of the Word of God, our Lord Christ Jesus, there is no life: *In him is life, and the life is the light*, etc.[20]

All of us who believe are blessed through the blessed seed of Abraham, our Jesus Christ. In fact, we ourselves are that same seed, since we are all one in Christ to the extent that we are grafted onto him, and, as members, receive life from the head through his Spirit.[21] That is to say: we are one in

* * * * *

17 Eph. 1:10. The word *lendet* (points to) is apparently Capito's translation of *anakephalaiosasthai*, which means either 'to head toward' or 'to sum up.' Capito has chosen the former definition; most modern biblical translations choose the latter.

18 2 Cor. 3:6.

19 Gal. 3:15–18.

20 John 1:4.

21 Cf. Rom. 11:17–24.

Christ insofar as we have been freed from our old birth and restored in our nature to the status of God's children. Thus we are renewed in our share in the inheritance, which is given to us freely, as it was to Abraham, by grace in accordance with the covenant.

Now this heavenly covenant and this divine compact of Christ has been revealed in our consciences without mediation by any element or mortal creature. It was prefigured and depicted through Isaac, the natural son of Abraham, and through the land of Canaan 430 years before the arrival of Moses and his Law. This shows that this testament and covenant of God in Christ Jesus was established, sealed, and confirmed without the contribution and help of the Law of Moses, which, in Abraham's time, did not yet exist. Indeed, whereas the law has an external organization in the letter, the order and movement of grace is internal.

It was a fully sufficient compact that God concluded with Abraham, Genesis 15, for his faith was reckoned to him as righteousness and, after sundown when it had grown dark, a torch moved between the pieces of the sacrificial victims.[22] In this way God confirmed the agreement.

This compact of grace depended solely upon the covenant of God and his Truth; it required no merit other than simple belief. Thus, the external agreement [i.e., the law], which followed afterward, cannot be the true essence of God's covenant despite the Holy Spirit's presence in it. Rather, it is a shadow of God's existing covenant, since the Holy Spirit always directs all things toward his own work, and his work consists of the cleansing of our conscience through the shedding of Christ's blood, etc.[23] Now one may therefore conclude: if the compact of Abraham was not complete and sufficient prior to the arrival of the Law of Moses, the scriptures are then false in referring to Abraham's sacrifice. For scripture says: *On that day, the Lord made an agreement with Abraham, saying, 'I will give this land to your seed.'*[24] Here he indicates that a covenant was already in place, for a covenant is a secured and confirmed compact, an unalterable affirmation. And indeed, this agreement was confirmed through that covenant and, as the apostle writes, confirmed in Christ;[25] it may not be voided or changed through the Law. For God's gifts and summons may not be changed.[26] He is God and unchanging; his Word is eternal.

* * * * *

22 Cf. Gen. 15:6–18.
23 Cf. Heb. 9:14.
24 Gen. 15:18.
25 Rom. 15:8.
26 *Gerwen*, i.e., dye, press, knead, mix.

In the meantime, the Law of Moses neither gives nor takes anything from the compact, because the agreement had already been guaranteed and established by God as sufficient. *I*, he said, *will be your God.*[27] The Law cannot add anything to this complete and perfect will of God, lest it be found to be flawed. For if this were the case, the Law would have the strength of the compact, and would justify by its own power and initiate a covenant of grace through Mosaic observance. Indeed, such a thing pertains to the covenant and to God's Truth. And Moses is unable to reach the spirit and the internal person with his office, for he is created only for truly good works and thus is taken into the eternal covenant. For this reason, this office belongs to Jesus Christ, through his Holy Spirit, and he works and renews through it. It follows, therefore, that the Law of Moses is an external exercise and must remain so. Without this exercise, the entirety of God's compact in Christ is still efficacious.

This means that [the Law of] Moses did not create a people for God. Rather, God sent him to his people Israel, who were already his people, in order to lead them out of Egypt, Exodus 3,[28] and he called them his son and his firstborn, Exodus 5.[29] Although they were practically destroyed by the Egyptians' vice, Ezech.,[30] they were still God's people according to the old compact. Indeed, God's pledge cannot be made void by evil. The entirety of Israel is and remains a people of God and children of God, although God is not pleased with them. Those who remain after the election of grace, that is, those who are Jews internally and who are circumcised in their hearts, who desire praise from God and not from men, who will not be recognized by natural men, those are the true people of God and the honourable children of God to whom the eternal, lasting, etc. compact applies. However, in order that God might show this light and life to the people, to mortal believers through external representations, figures, and shadows, he adopted the entirety of Israel through Moses for such a purpose, even though many of them will never come to the eternal covenant. And they are called his property, his people, who have been set apart from the heathens and whom he led out of the slavery of Egypt into the temporal compact of the Canaanite land. Afterwards, they were received by God into the external covenant of ownership, written on stone tablets. Through this covenant, God confirmed them

* * * * *

27　Gen. 17:7.
28　Cf. Exod. 3:10–15.
29　Error for Exod. 4:22–3.
30　Ezek. 29:16.

as his people, and he became their God, just as he had promised Abraham, Isaac, and Jacob. Understand, however, that the compact of the patriarchs was completely accomplished in the confirmation of the old covenant before the Lord God, as the above-mentioned words were spoken by the mouth of Moses on the plains of Moab. For the Holy Spirit in him foresaw Christ's deed and the eternal Truth. There they had a temporal kingdom, an external priesthood, a temple, the sacrifice of dumb animals, an external rite of worship, and a worldly holiness, all of which are shadows and lead the way to the source of light, Christ Jesus, through their meaning and show how things are to be done until the day of grace arrives. For all of the commandments of the external law have departed, and the commandments of the spiritual law have arrived. The eternal kingdom of God has been installed in the place of David's transitory kingdom, and in that heavenly kingdom righteousness has the upper hand among believers. Likewise, in the place of Aaron's priesthood is placed the spiritual priesthood of Christ, who, in the Holy Spirit, sacrificed himself once to the Father on the cross for us, and thus established our eternal salvation. The temple is demolished, but Christ, through the Holy Spirit, consecrates and hallows us, making us into a temple and dwelling-place for God, one built upon the ground of the apostles and prophets.[31] For this reason we *present our bodies as a living sacrifice, holy and acceptable to God, which is our spiritual worship,*[32] just as the Lord was made a victim for our misdeeds, and has given obedience to God.

This, our worship, is an internal matter, for we do not butcher ourselves or cut ourselves with a meat knife. Rather, through the word of the cross we destroy the old Adam with his carnal desires and pray everywhere to the Father in spirit and truth, not only in Jerusalem or on Mount Gerizim.[33] All worldly holiness has passed away, but we strive for spiritual and heavenly holiness, which remain hidden externally. For this reason it ought to be determined how the figures in the law point to Christ, bearing witness to him and affirming the one upon whom they have all been built.

Take, for example, Abraham, who, before he had sacrificed and received circumcision, recognized the divine answer as righteous on account of his faith – recognized because he believed in the Lord: and this was reckoned to him as righteousness. The external sacrifice of the severed pieces followed after his justification, and the external circumcision was done as a sign

* * * * *

31 Cf. Eph. 2:20–2.
32 Rom. 12:1.
33 Cf. John 4:21–4.

and outward symbol of the internal faith through which he had been made righteous. Therefore, the law accomplishes nothing in terms of righteousness; righteousness depends solely upon the promised grace. The later Law of Moses and its entire office comes after faith, just as Abraham's sacrifice and circumcision came after his faith. Thus, the law is nothing other than an external exercise through which the great mystery, which does not depend on any transitory element, is revealed to the body of the faithful. So much for the first article.

Regarding the second article: The end of the law and of Mosaic observance is indeed the fear of God, as all of its contents indicate. But the end of the spiritual law, as it stands for God, is his fatherly heart, the love of God, which is poured out upon our hearts through the Holy Spirit, which is given to us. This is the grace in which we stand through Christ. Therefore, it is called the end of the law;[34] for it is the fatherly counsel and the love of God in which the elect are loved by God.

Now the law is, in and of itself, unified and undivided, and yet it has been practised and applied in two different manners. When it is controlled and applied by Christ, by the Holy Spirit, it is an eternal, true, and divine exercise. However, it remains only a transitory and figurative human exercise, although still useful in terms of God's worship, when the servant Moses is made the overseer and supervisor only in the observance of external things. For this reason, we still speak about the Law of Moses insofar as Moses might fulfil it through observance. Indeed, the apostles themselves did not write about his personal understanding or grace; rather, they wrote about his office and his commands. Thus, Moses' holiness does not add or subtract anything, but his office must be correctly understood. Otherwise, we run into serious difficulties.

The fact that Moses' service does not attain the end of the law (as it stands for God) is sufficiently clear to anyone who recognizes that no mortal man can give the spiritual and heavenly gifts and grace of God, since Jesus Christ alone, the heavenly man, does this. In fact, Moses himself shows this, for although the people [of Israel] in the wilderness had experienced themselves for forty years the trials of Pharaoh, the plagues of Egypt, and the great deeds and wonders and, what more, even though they had Moses, the true servant of God, as their leader for twenty-eight years, nevertheless there was no true fruit among the people as a result. Shortly before his death, he himself said as much with these words: *To this day the Lord has not given you*

* * * * *

34 Cf. Rom. 10:4.

a heart suited to understanding, eyes to see, or ears to hear, Deut. 29.[35] Notice that the Lord grants a heart capable of understanding divine things; otherwise, our nature is dumb, blind, and deaf, even though the Mosaic office had already been truly revealed by Moses and the power of the Law had already been given. Had it been possible to learn anything reliable about God from the practice of the law and its exercise, certainly it would have been revealed under Moses, the diligent, highly-enlightened man, and true servant of God. Yet despite hearing Moses for so many years and seeing for themselves the wonders of God, the people still remained ignorant and had neither the eyes nor ears to comprehend the secret nature of God. If Moses did not provide these people with anything reliable regarding God, then clearly no one else was able to do so with any other people either, since, otherwise, his office and authority would be considered higher than Moses'. In order to be able to understand, see, and hear, this ability must be placed in the heart by the Holy Spirit. The servant Moses is unable to do this. The Son of God received this promise from the Father, and he gives the Holy Spirit and renews the soul according to the internal man.

That Mosaic observance is fully directed toward the fear of God.

What, then, does Moses achieve among the people of the Old Testament?[36] Answer: when he is at his best, he brings to the people a fear of God, which leads to obedience to the law, to action, and to refraining from action in accordance with God's desire.

It was for this reason that God gave the law with such unprecedented fear. Indeed, the mountain was lit by fire halfway up into the heavens, and there was murkiness, clouds, and darkness. Lightning and thunder appeared, and the blare of horns increased. In the midst of this, God spoke the ten words upon which the covenant stands. Yet the people, seeing the thunder, the lightning, and the voice of the horn, and seeing that the mountain smoked, were afraid. They trembled and stood at a distance and went up to Moses, saying: *You speak with us, we will obey, and do not let God speak with us, lest we die.*[37] Read the nineteenth and twentieth chapters of Exodus and the fifth chapter of Deuteronomy, and be mindful of how often God calls himself a consuming fire. Here there is a great deal of anxiety regarding fire, smoke, thunder, lightning, the blaring of a horn, and earth tremors. The people fear and flee; they cannot hear the law and require an intermediary

* * * * *

35 Deut. 29:4.
36 *by dem alten volk.*
37 Exod. 19:19.

between themselves and the jealous, terrifying God. Here, Moses is indeed an intermediary but only as a servant who cannot bring the law into the heart and will. He therefore shows the will of God to these people of the Old Testament through words and deeds, and he indicates that God desires to be feared until the other intermediary, who was consecrated by God and who leads to God through his very existence, inscribes the law in the heart, making people truly devout and righteous and bringing them peace and joy and true love according to God's fatherly will.

Indeed, Moses himself bears witness to the fact that his office pertains to fear. He says: *Do not be afraid; God has come in order to test you so that his fear will be in your sight so that you will not sin*, Ex. 20.[38] And he speaks regarding the arrival of God upon Mount Sinai: *Indeed, the Lord said to me at Mount Horeb: 'Gather the people to me; I desire to let them hear my Word, which will teach them how to fear me for all the days that they live upon the earth,'* Deut. 4.[39] Moses is part of God's plan to make known his Word, meaning his Law which he commanded to Moses and which teaches us to fear the Lord. Therefore, Mosaic observance is directed toward the fear of God and can do nothing else. Indeed, the Lord himself demanded nothing else of Moses at the time.

In order to confirm this fear, Moses, in accordance with the agreement he made between God and the people, commanded that the six sons born from maids should curse [the people] as violators of the law upon Mount Ebal, particularly of those portions of the law which might be hidden from him, the external commander, and he confirmed the curse, Deut. 27,[40] but he kept silent on the blessing of those standing upon Mount Gerizim, since that blessing will be granted secretly to the children of God and will be made public on the day of the last judgment.

And just as, under the hand of Moses, the law was bound up with fear and was confirmed with curses and maledictions, so Moses even called the Law a curse in the twenty-ninth chapter of Deuteronomy: *You should enter into the covenant of the Lord your God and into the curse, which the Lord your God makes (or directs) with you this day*,[41] and shortly thereafter: *I make this covenant and this curse not just with you who are here today and stand with us before the Lord your God, but also with those of you who are not with us today.*[42] And again: *so that he should hear the word of this curse and bless himself in his heart, etc.*[43]

* * * * *

38 Exod. 20:20.
39 Deut. 4:10.
40 Deut. 27:13ff.
41 Deut. 29:12.
42 Deut. 29:14–15.
43 Deut. 29:19.

Therefore, the law of God would not have been given without fear, nor would it have blossomed without fear, for the fear of God is its express purpose: *If you will not observe all the commandments of this law which are written in this book, fearing the wondrous and terrifying name of the Lord your God, then you will, etc.,* Deut. 28.[44] In summation, the whole purpose of all of the words of Moses rests on fear, especially the twenty-sixth chapter of Leviticus and the twenty-seventh and twenty-eighth chapters of Deuteronomy. For this reason, Paul likens the covenant given on Mount Sinai to that of servitude, like Hagar, who was not of the promise but rather of the flesh.[45]

The difference between the Law of Moses and the law of nature.

Before the end of chapter twenty-eight of Deuteronomy, Moses shows that the contents of the Law are directed toward fear, and in the beginning of chapter twenty-nine, he says: *Therefore, keep the commandments of this covenant and act in accordance with them so that you may be wise in all that you do.*[46] Thus, in contrast to the two earlier passages, this makes it clear that the fear of the Lord God and the keeping of his Word is to be wise in all one's actions. And the words of Deuteronomy 4 follow from this: the law of the people will be called wisdom and understanding.[47]

The book called the Preacher Solomon[48] flowed from this same inspiration. In it, the wise man reveals the vain, toilsome, unsteady and difficult nature of all human activity and thought, and he therefore concludes: *The purpose of the things I have told you is to make you fear God and keep his commandments, for this is the whole duty of man. For God will bring all works, whether good or bad, to judgment, even those that are kept hidden.*[49] In short, he wishes to say: many efforts and wise thoughts have been proposed by men, but from these it is clear that man in death and life and in all his deeds is ultimately vain, useless, and miserable. Such thoughts lead to the conclusion, which everyone acknowledges, that man is not able to have anything permanent other than the fear of God and keeping his commandments. That is in accordance with the divine will, to order one's life and heart toward God. He comes to this conclusion because it is completely clear from his consideration of all conceivable activities that nothing else is lasting, and that the Lord God will weigh both actions and the secret counsels of the heart.

* * * * *

44 Deut. 28:15.
45 Cf. Gal. 4:24.
46 Deut. 29:9.
47 Cf. Deut. 4:6.
48 I.e., Ecclesiastes.
49 Eccles. 12:13–14.

In the Preacher Solomon, it is sufficiently brought to light how much of an advantage Israel has over other nations. The heathens, lacking God, depend upon their senses; they seek holiness, but gain nothing other than toil and work even if they avoid vice and fleshly lust and strive for wisdom and virtue. Therefore, all worldly wisdom will be put to shame, for they know that there is one God, but they do not worship him as a god. They are fixated upon themselves, upon their well-being and their own attractiveness. Thus, they have become vain in their thinking and have closed off their hearts, which are unable to understand. *Because they count themselves wise, they have become fools*, Rom. 1.[50] For this reason they *have no hope and are without God in the world*, Eph. 2.[51] They ascribe all things to their senses, to luck, or to other creatures. Among them it is accounted the greatest achievement to separate themselves from all religion and fear of God, for they consider it heresy and stupidity to walk in the sight of God. And as a cardinal recently said, they think that it is a stupid, irresponsible, and irrational thing to endure danger to one's body and goods on account of faith, and this is still the opinion of the world. Where there is peaceful trade and fleshly freedom, which they prize, and where wealth and lust are not lacking, there they desire to live, and there they practise the worship of God, as Isocrates says,[52] living in the world truly without the experience of divine power and without God.

Brave Israel feared the Lord their God in all their works and thoughts, and they daily came to know him better. They have the Law, through which they are included in the covenant; they have the promise and hope for abundant grace; they have a system of worship, which they did not invent but which God himself granted to them, *in which they persevere*:[53] Antiochius.[54] God is with them so long as they remain in the fear of God and keep in mind that their wisdom and glory is for the whole world, so that the heathen must also say: Oh, what wise and understanding people they are, an excellent people. For where is there such an excellent people whom the gods approach so closely and call to them so often, Deut. 4?[55]

This, then, is to be said regarding the difference between nature and the law: it is like the difference between the heathens, who live outside of the Law, and Israel, which lives under the Law; for among the people of the

* * * * *

50 Rom. 1:22.
51 Eph. 2:12.
52 Perhaps an allusion to Isocrates, *Ad Demonicum*, 13.
53 The text in italics is in Latin.
54 Cf. 1 Mac. 1:43–67.
55 Cf. Deut. 4:6–7.

Law, the fear of God is wisdom and understanding in works, but among those who are outside of the Law, there is only personal well-being, curiosity, vanity, and idle thoughts, no understanding, no wisdom, and no God at all. Indeed, the more these lawless ones concern themselves with God, the less they know about him or obey him. Thus it is that the people of the Old Testament belong to God and are distinct from other peoples, and that in Judaism God alone can redeem them, as David says.[56]

The difference between the Mosaic office and the office of Jesus Christ.

Nevertheless, nature and the Law of Moses are similar to one another in their piety, in that both the one outside the Law and the one under the Law proceed from their common sense and their own judgment. For the world has a natural piety which people receive from the exercise of their own strength and diligent application. This is the worldly-wise piety and virtue, a wondrous, glorious thing, but it has no permanence. It is and remains an external habit through which the philosophers probably avoided vices, but at the same time they took up different vices, which are worse. Seneca cursed the honorary offices in common usage in Rome; yet in doing so, he sought tranquillity and thus an honour that can be achieved without any special effort.[57] Conversely, Cicero performed great services for the government of Rome in his capacity as civil leader and in other ways; yet in doing so, he sought a glorious name, which he and all worldly people have no tendency to avoid.[58] And although philosophers write against ambition, they seek their own glory in the very same text, and they reject haughtiness with great haughtiness. And so each one of them manifests a particular aspect of this piety. Yet, he also brings forth a licence for more serious vices and does not truly have the piety on which he focuses. He has it only in terms of external appearances, in that he pays attention to his actions and his lack of action, through which he can achieve a good name. This is all made up and without grounding in the truth. Genuine piety will not be found through natural practice, since no one can make himself other than what he is, and man struggles and strives from his youth onwards and is evil by his very nature.

This is the type of superficial piety and false delusion that characterizes clever Pharisees, who are arrogant and well-satisfied with themselves, as if they knew God's will and could actually determine the best course of action

* * * * *

56 Ps. 73:2.
57 The Stoic philosopher Lucius Annaeus Seneca (4 BC–AD65), who advocated this ideal, for example, in his essay *On Tranquillity*.
58 Quintus Tullius Cicero (107BC–AD44), renowned Roman statesman.

from the instruction of the Law. They do great works on a daily basis, fasting, praying, giving alms, diligently and continuously occupying themselves with the correct interpretation of the words and commandments of God, but they do all of these works in order to be seen by other people. The heathens hold within their toilsome virtue the hope of honour and praise before the world. The Pharisee loves sitting in the place of honour at table and in the synagogue, and is quite pleased to be greeted in the marketplace and called rabbi.[59] They hold on more tightly to their own honour than to God's. The gospels bear witness to this, as do the nonsensical books of the Pharisees themselves, which say that a special punishment is prepared for those who do not treat the rabbis honourably (*Perek Nesikin*).[60]

The worldly people, then, who live outside the Law, have a few sayings and reasonable rules among their customs; the Pharisees fix God's law in writing. In both cases, however, it amounts to one's own interpretation and trust in one's own deeds. And this vice is at its worst among the Pharisees, in that they gain greater knowledge from the Law than the heathens are able to gain from their teachers, just as in our own time the stricter the monastic order, the more arrogant and intolerable they are. May God grant that our own chosen works not be given only the appearance of our gospel or be coloured by the strict letter of the New Testament. May they not be done with such fleshly certainty, which leads only to the destruction of all better order. The common people have never wanted to be tied down. They desire Christian freedom and conscience, although many have nothing but bold ignorance. O gracious Father, let your light, Jesus Christ, shine in our hearts so that we do not blindly stumble over one another, even though our ingratitude and lack of diligence deserve such misery. May God help us to improve. Amen.

This is the righteousness of the hypocrite, who, not believing God, seeks honour from others, weighing people down with high teachings and commandments, which they will not touch with their fingertips.[61] This figure is discussed by the Lord himself in the gospel. But the Holy Spirit speaks about Mosaic observance in a different way than it is interpreted by the superficial and externally holy ones. For they speak of two different things: there is observance in and of itself, and there is the description of those who interpreted it. Observance has an effect, but they [i.e., observance and its effect] are not to be taken for the same thing. The sun makes clay hard and wax soft. This

* * * * *

59 Cf. Matt. 23:6–7.
60 I.e., 'chapter on damages' (Seder Nezikin, Babylonian Talmud, Sanhedrin 99b).
61 Cf. Matt. 23:4.

is not the fault of the sun but of the material itself. There is a much greater difference between people [than between these materials].

When Paul himself describes the Mosaic office, he judges it when it is at its best. Similarly, when he speaks generally of the rulers of this world, he speaks of them in the best possible terms as well. He says: *If they had recognized the wisdom of God, they would not have crucified the Lord of splendour.*[62] Nevertheless, they were sure of themselves, although they did not recognize God the Father: *If I had not come, they would not have sinned,* etc.[63] Again: *The works bear witness to me.*[64] And again: *Since you say 'We see,' your sin will remain.*[65] If they had had God's honour in mind, Christ would not have remained hidden from them, for he often revealed himself through his words; yet they could not embrace him with their whole hearts. Yet the Holy Spirit looks for the best in everyone until he must rebuke a person in order to bring about improvement, as Christ spoke harshly to the Pharisees in Matthew, chapter 23.[66] It ought, therefore, to be noted that among these superficially holy men, as the gospels describe them, the Mosaic office was not understood. Rather, they understood it in the sense in which it might be interpreted through reason, and they could not understand it in any other way.

If you wish to understand the fundamental nature of Mosaic observance, consider a God-fearing Jew, whose devotion to God is based upon the righteousness of the law. For it is quite another thing to consider oneself pious, holding others in contempt, and to be pious before God according to the law of righteousness. The first one has the fear of God and desires salvation. The other is without the fear of God, for he renounces many of his duties and feels no need for a Saviour. In his mind, he is the cause of his own salvation. The Mosaic office is designed for the God-fearing man and can be seen clearly in him. Consider Zechariah, the father of John the Baptist: he was happy that his son should be the one to prepare the way for the Lord as a sign of the redemption that comes from the forgiveness of sins. And he was glad that the mercy of their God would direct their feet along the path of peace. He earnestly requested the righteousness that would be acceptable before God, and he did not depend upon his own righteousness, as the Pharisees did.[67] God-fearing Simeon presents a similar case: he was very happy to have

* * * * *

62 1 Cor. 2:8.
63 John 15:22.
64 John 5:36.
65 John 9:41.
66 See Matt. 23:13–33.
67 Cf. Luke 1:11–17.

seen the Saviour, the light and glory for all the people of Israel.[68] These and other God-fearing people were blameless according to the law of the Lord, but still they considered their hearts to be unrighteous and were eager for the eventual resolution through Christ. These individuals were guarded under the law and were locked into the faith, which then had to be opened up. The law was their disciplinarian during their wait for Christ, so that they would be made righteous through their faith. Take, for example, the tax collector in the temple, who would not lift up his eyes to heaven. Instead, he beat his breast and said: *'God, be merciful to me, a sinner.'*[69] These are the men who are visited by him who calls sinners to repentance and is present as a doctor to the sick.

In order to emphasize the power and results of the Law of Moses or the Mosaic office, consider how it stood in the thought of those Romans and Galatians, who, after their initiation by the Holy Spirit, thought to turn their attention once again to the Law and did not take into account whether they were Jews or heathens before they came to Christ. See how fear drove them to maintain the letter of the law in addition to Christ, so that they might be completely obedient to God. They wanted to fulfil his Word and did not want to be condemned as violators of the law, as if the entire counsel and will of God were not included in the one and only Christ, and as if these things were not fulfilled and reckoned through faith in him.

In the first place, then, it must be clear to you that the law demands fear. It was not simply passion that mistakenly placed them under such a worldly law. Rather, it was the fact that they feared God and did not wish to be found disobedient to him. They feared the curse, which affects those who do not adhere to everything that is written in the book of the Law, Deut. 27.[70] For this reason they took care ...[71]

Letter 458: 25 December 1531, Basel, Capito to Nicolaus Kniebs

The manuscript of this letter is in the Copenhagen, Det Kongelige Bibliotek, ms. Thott 497, f.81. For Kniebs see above, Ep.184 headnote.

Grace and peace, most respected patron. On the day before yesterday when I was about to leave, Bucer and I looked for Your Lordship in the chancel-

* * * * *

68 Luke 2:32.
69 Luke 18:13.
70 Deut. 27:26.
71 The text breaks off at this point.

lery, intending to ask for a leave of absence. For I had in mind to be absent a few days for the benefit, as it seemed to me, of the churches. But at that time you were perhaps with the prisoners, nor was I at leisure to attempt to call on you a second time in person, as I would have liked. Therefore I gave the task to Bucer, asking him to speak on my behalf. It turned out that I arrived here[1] safely, and so many good things happened in one short day that I did not regret my plan to travel at all. Therefore I decided, once I have completed my business here, to visit also the remaining churches.[2] For it seemed useful, and the nature of our office requires it. That region needs help, being in dire straits with its affairs in ruins,[3] which the Lord no doubt will repair. When matters are going well, piety is neglected; in adversity it is kindled. I myself have experienced that. Bucer will tell you the rest. May I be commended to Your Excellent Lordship. On the day of the birth of our Lord, Basel, at the end of the year 1531.

Yours, Wolfgang Capito.

Letter 459: 30 December [1531, Strasbourg], Capito, Martin Bucer, and their colleagues to Simon Grynaeus

Printed in BDS 10:111–19, #8. Although addressed to Grynaeus, this 'letter' states the Strasbourgers' opinion on King Henry VIII's 'Great Matter' and was meant for the King (cf. above, Epp. 447, 448, 449). Grynaeus sent it to England in January. Henry's reaction to the advice of the Strasbourgers is not known.

[*Summary*]: The Strasbourgers are providing an answer to the best of their ability, but 'no one can give more than he has received from heaven.' In their response they seek God's Truth, not the interest of the state. 'The king has people whom he may consult about doing everything according to his royal dignity; of us he only asks the Truth.' Grynaeus has asked them four questions concerning the legitimacy of marrying a brother's wife: (1) Did the prohibition in Lev. 18:16 apply even if the brother was dead? (2) Do the execrations in the passage apply to Henry's case? (3) Were Jews ever allowed to marry a brother's wife without dispensation? (4) Does Old Testament law apply in the context of evangelical freedom? The Strasbourgers answer only

* * * * *

1 Basel.
2 Capito subsequently visited Bern, Constance, and Lindau (in January 1532), Memmingen and Augsburg (February and March 1532).
3 After the deaths, on 11 October and 22/3 November 1531, respectively, of the leading Swiss reformers, Zwingli and Oecolampadius.

the first question: It was lawful for Henry to marry his late brother's wife, especially since 'the marriage was sanctioned by secular and ecclesiastical authorities.' Furthermore, 'the external laws of the Old Testament need not be observed by us.' Earlier, they approved of a divorce in Henry's case, if it was in the interest of the state, but they have changed their minds. Zwingli and Oecolampadius were wrong in permitting a separation. The Strasbourgers have consulted with Ambrosius Blaurer before giving their answer.

Letter 460: [1531, Strasbourg], Otto Brunfels to Capito

> The original autograph of this letter is in AST 154, #26; the text is also printed in Ficker-Winckelmann II, 77. On Brunfels, see CWC 1, Ep. 25 headnote.

To his dearest friend, Dr Wolfgang Capito, greeting.

I do not want you, my dear Capito, to ascribe to lack of diligence or inexperience my failure to send the requested purgatives immediately, as I first promised. I would have acted more promptly, if I wanted to be regarded as a charlatan or pseudo-physician,[1] the kind of people who are totally intent on their tricks and know nothing beyond them. But you are too dear to me to try out on you the effect of the hundreds of prescriptions of this sort. Therefore do not take it ill. I do not want to experiment with the thousand medications I could name, even if you asked me. I send, however, those that seem to me rather innocuous and which you may try without any danger. But it matters a great deal of what you want to purge yourself – choler, pituita, or melancholy[2] – that is not the smallest part of medicine, indeed the central tenet of the pharmacists, which you must at some time broach. If I knew that it was agreeable to you, I would write a whole volume to you about the use of purgative medicines. In the meantime, make use of these few medications, and fare well.

Otto Brunfels.

* * * * *

1 Literally 'mule-physician.'
2 Three of the traditional four humours, cf. Burton, *Anatomy of Melancholy* 1.2.1: '*Pituita,* or phlegm, is a cold and moist humour ... in the liver; ... *choler* is hot and dry and bitter ... gathered in the gall; ... melancholy, cold, dry, thick, black and sour ... is purged from the spleen.'

Appendix

1. Documents concerning Capito's provostship

a) 15 July 1521, Halle, Albert of Brandenburg to the Dean and Chapter of St Thomas

The manuscript of this letter is in Strasbourg, AST 16, #8. The archbishop's letter, addressed to Nicolaus Wurmser, dean of St Thomas (see CWC 1, Ep. 57 headnote), reinforces Capito's claim to the provostship. Capito himself wrote to the dean on the same date (CWC 1, Ep. 99) and on the same matter. Indeed, it is likely that Capito composed both letters. Compare with CWC 1, Epp. 81, 93, 106, 114, 115, which concern the provostship and bear Albert's name, although the drafts are in Capito's handwriting.

Albert, by divine grace cardinal priest of St Peter ad vincula, Archbishop of Mainz and Magdeburg, First of the Electors, Primate, etc. Administrator of Halberstadt, Margrave of Brandenburg.

Honoured and dearly beloved sirs, Wolfgang Fabricius Capito has, through briefs of our most Holy Lord,[1] the right to the prebend of the canonry and to the provostship of your church, whose possession a certain Jacob Abel previously extorted from you.[2] Therefore, we urge and gently request Your Paternities to obey the apostolic mandates and concede [Capito] the possession of the prebend and provostship, for he is properly entitled to them. In this matter, although you are under obligation to act, you will earn our goodwill and gratitude, since we greatly favour Capito on account of his faith and industry, and you will strengthen the ties between us, although he

* * * * *

1 Pope Leo X.
2 Capito's rival claimant had been installed as provost on 14 November 1520. Cf. CWC 1, appendix, p. 261.

is already most closely linked to us. Given at Halle, our city, at the castle of St Moritz, on 15 July 1521.

b) Autograph statement of Capito assuming the provostship of St Thomas, 14 March 1523

The manuscript is in Strasbourg, AST 19, #41. Since Abel (see above, Appendix 1a) persevered in his claim, Capito was forced to appeal to Pope Leo's successor, Adrian VI, who reconfirmed his possession in February 1523 (see CWC 1, Epp. 149,152). At that point Capito was finally able to assume his post.

I, Wolfgang Fabritius Capito, doctor of theology, clergyman of the diocese of Strasbourg, canon, prebend and provost of St Thomas there, have begun residency for a full year on Saturday after Dominica Oculi, which is the fourteenth day of the month of March in the thousandth five-hundredth and twenty-third year, which I will complete and fulfill, Christ willing, according to the statutes and legitimate and laudable custom of the same church. Acted as above, etc.

c) A statement concerning Capito's resignation of the provostship, 1527

The manuscript, an autograph, is in Strasbourg, AST 19, #58. For the circumstances, see above, Epp. 248a, 248c. The document is dated on the basis of the magistrates mentioned: Jacob Sturm was *Stettmeister* and Matthis Pfarrer was *Ammeister* (in charge of the *Schöffen*) in 1527. On Sturm see CWC 1, Ep. 48 headnote; on Pfarrer see above, Ep. 456, note 9.

Let it be known to each and every person that in the year of the Lord's birth 1524 pamphlets were circulating and speeches were made encouraging the peasants not to pay the tithes and the assessed tax, and the public heatedly asked for the same. Wolfgang Fabritius Capito, as a faithful minister of the Word, who knew that Christ looked only for a change of heart, not for a change in the political state except when it was found to be evil and harmful to the Word of the Lord, objected to these pernicious efforts strenuously and not without risk. Thereupon, he was obliged to hear that he was doing so for his own sake, because he was provost of St Thomas, and was worried about his tithes and income – for unfair people are very much inclined toward insults. The aforesaid Capito pondered this and, having previously devoted himself to God and the public welfare, decided to give up the provostship to give the detractors less material for slander, as their impudent slander detracted from the glory of God. However, since he was distracted by various concerns, he deferred his plan to 15 October 1525, on which day he freely relinquished his provostship before the chapter of the church of St Thomas in favour of Lorenz Schenckbecher. Schenckbecher was afterwards unanimously elected provost, and thus has the title and is considered provost with respect to all rights and privileges of the said provostship.

Furthermore, because we are all mortals, [Capito] had decided prior to his resignation to reserve for himself the right of regress, and did so in the presence of certain witnesses, as is permitted to him legally and in fairness.[1] For whatever he did, he did for the sake of promoting piety. Thus, kindness and the common sentiment of what is right would seem to favour him in turn, as he deserved. May God our Lord see to this, to whom [Capito] entrusts himself with a most simple heart.

Furthermore, considering the hospitable nature of the former provost, Wolfgang Fabritius Capito, whose house was like a hostel for exiles, as the house of a bishop ought to be according to Paul's teaching, and considering that Capito is very generous in giving to the poor and indigent, Lorenz Schenckbecher, the provost, promised to give him all the usufructs of the provostship and has given them to him from the time he took possession to this time, and has vowed before you to a notary that he would do so in future, as long as Capito lived, excepting only 20 gulden and the lawful fees and emoluments connected with investiture and the seal. These have been given to him so far for his labours, and ought to be given to him in the future. However, after Capito's death, if he should die first, Schenckbecher may convert the entire income of the provostship to his own use, without anyone preventing him either in Capito's or anyone else's name. If the present provost happens to die before Capito, he wishes the regress to be valid, so that Capito would again be his successor that he may help others during his lifetime.

But since Jacob Abel is said to have recently brought letters executorial against Capito in Rome because he publicly contracted a marriage, which is against the powers of the pontiff, the same Capito promises before you, the notary and witnesses, to indemnify Lorenz Schenckbecher and his heirs now and in future with respect to the income [from the provostship] being seized and costs being incurred in a lawsuit, if Jacob Abel or anyone else wins a judgment for costs by way of an agreement or through legal channels concerning the provostship and the income of which he was deprived. To ensure this, Capito has appointed trustees and co-debtors with the princi-

* * * * *

1 For discussions about Capito resuming the provostship in 1528, see above, Ep. 367b.

pal,[2] and he is now naming them: Ulrich and Johann Röttlin, his brothers-in-law, who guarantee in the presence of the notary the income received and to be received in future, together with Capito and Agnes Röttlin, his wife and their sister, and they assume the legal obligation of the debt together with the principal in case the aforesaid matter comes to pass, in all the better forms and ways that are and should be valid in the law. If death happens to put an end to the obligation of one or both of the guarantors, Capito now takes on the obligation to substitute another or other guarantors in place of the deceased, to provide sufficient surety for the lord provost. This obligation shall prevail until the day of Capito's death, but not beyond, for after that date, as said before, the provost will have the use of future income [from the provostship] in its entirety, and may respond on his own behalf to any adversaries that might appear, unless either Abel and other challengers die, or an agreement is reached with them on the basic points in the name of Capito.

Finally all the persons previously mentioned, that is, Lorenz Schenckbecher the provost, Wolfgang Capito and Agnes Rötlerin his wife, the principals, Ulrich and Johann Rötlin, the guarantors and co-debtors, beg and beseech, in the presence of the notary, the noble and well-known Jacob Sturm, *Stettmeister*, and the worthy Matthis Pfarrer, the magistrate in charge of the *Schöffen* in the city of Strasbourg, to approve this action, as it happened, with their seal. We acknowledge that Jacob Sturm and Matthis Pfarrer have done so nominally in response to the requests of the parties, but without prejudice to us or our heirs, or to their expense, in any way. About each and all of these points we request in your, the notary's, presence two official documents, one to remain with me, Wolfgang Fabritius Capito, the old provost, and the other to remain with Lorenz Schenckbecher, the new provost.

2. A statement concerning the Catholic party in the three collegiate churches, 1525

The manuscript of the statement is in Strasbourg, AST 22 (3). For the context see above, 234b.

On 13 November 1525, several persons of the three collegiate churches, now residing outside of Strasbourg in Freiburg im Breisgau, issued and publicly posted a declaration and appeal to the honourable council of the city of Strasbourg and the persons of the collegiate churches still resident in Strasbourg.

* * * * *

2 See Capito's reservations about this arrangement, above, Ep. 367b.

In this statement a claim is made with regard to our collegiate church of St Thomas, namely that in a chapter assembly here at Strasbourg Nicolaus Wurmser,[1] then dean of our collegiate church, was entrusted with our seal and confidential papers and asked to keep it safe. We reply with the truth: Dr Nicolaus, then dean, called a special assembly contrary to our sworn statutes, circumventing several persons of our chapter, and more specifically, the provost at the time,[2] although some of them were in residence and others could have been reached. The seal was taken without the knowledge and agreement of the bearers of the seal, together with our collegiate church's briefs, seal, treasure, ornaments, reliquaries, book of statutes, and whatever else concerns the administration of the collegiate church. They took these with them from Strasbourg to Molsheim. And after much negotiation, when they and those who were incited by them, who did not understand the full seriousness of the matter and did not realize that such an error would do serious damage to our collegiate church, the persons of the three collegiate churches residing outside Strasbourg finally decided to return to Strasbourg the goods they had taken, as they had agreed and promised in a message to the council. And the persons of the collegiate church of St Thomas had specifically in plain words commanded that Dr Nicolaus Wurmser should also hand over the seal, which he had taken to Offenburg.

But he did not follow the order, for the goods of the collegiate churches were afterwards brought back, but without the things that concern the deanery and the house of the Beguines, as well as the seal. We therefore made a public declaration in writing that Dr Nicolaus Wurmser, dean of St Thomas, took the seal without legal title and against the will of the others, including those who lived outside of Strasbourg. Thus we established another seal for ourselves and our successors in the administration of the collegiate church of St Thomas, as publicly posted on 27 January 1525 in Strasbourg and elsewhere for the purpose of giving everyone notice. Now, once again in response to their above-mentioned declaration, we wish to give notice to the public that the persons of the collegiate church have their residence here in Strasbourg, where we were founded and have lived so far, where we have our sworn administrators, briefs, seals, treasures, book of statutes, and other things, which we have in hand and keep with the agreement of those who are still living abroad. Their recently issued so-called proclamation and invalid revocation of our actions and transactions has no force, especially since they are not in residence proper, and refused to appear here in response to several

* * * * *

1 For Wurmser see CWC 1, Ep. 57 headnote.
2 I.e., Capito.

earnest requests. For we cannot recognize anyone as canon or associate of the chapter, unless they are present and obedient to us, the provost, vice-dean and chapter, according to their obligation. We, the members of the chapter, cannot be prevented from buying and selling, from good and legal actions, as the occasion arises, in the interest and for the honour of our praiseworthy foundation. If, however, anyone either before or after this, our proclamation, relies on the worthless, invalid seal which Dr Nicolaus Wurmser has taken and still holds without legal title, and wanted to do any transactions or wishes to do so in future, we revoke these transactions and declare them invalid, according to our previous proclamation and the earnest avowal of our collegiate church to apply legal and proper means within our ability and our obligations. For the collegiate church of St Thomas is not the property of Dr Nicolaus Wurmser; rather, it is the right of the chapter and persons of the choir in common, each according to his due, to possess and hold it, not to act individually concerning what pertains to us all together, but to administrate as a chapter what belongs to us jointly, as is the custom. This we proclaim publicly and attest before you notaries and the witnesses present here, with the request to prepare and give us one or more statements, as may be necessary, etc.

3. An admonition from the City Council of Strasbourg to the Preachers, 19 July 1526

The manuscript, a rough draft of a speech, is in AST 84, #9. A note following the text indicates that Jacob Zorn (see above, Ep. 275, note 1) was delegated by the city council to admonish the preachers to keep the peace. The note runs: 'This command was tendered by Jacob Zorn zum Riet to doctors Matthis Pfarrer, Capito, Hedio, Anton [Firn], Bucer, Sebastian [Meyer], to the magisters Matthew [Zell], Antonius [Engelbrecht] the pastor of St Jacob, Symphorian [Altbiesser], Diebold [Schwartz], and their assistants, and gave them a friendly warning in Christ to obey this command. They agreed, but also asked that the insults of their opponents should be stopped. Transacted on 19 July 1526.' From a follow-up note, we learn that the preachers had to be admonished a second time. The admonition should probably be seen in the context of the controversy with Johannes Fabri (see above, Ep. 288a).

Dear sirs and friends, you are aware that our lords on the council and the XXI[1]

* * * * *

1 The expression 'Council and XXI' refers to the entire legislative body of the city council.

have, in their earnest desire to increase the praise of the Lord and to maintain brotherly concord, issued a decree[2] that you, the parish priests and preachers, should preach and spread the holy gospel and the Word of God with all mildness and without words of reproach or anything that might incite the common man to rebellion or hatred of their fellow human beings. It was only fair that you should promise to do so, as it is not only a brotherly obligation but is also owed to divine law. Contrary to that, reports have reached our lords from several sides, and they furthermore know it from hearsay, that you have acted contrary to your promise and have used insulting words in your sermons against specific persons, that is, the pope, emperor, bishops, princes, and also the imperial diet and [other ill practices were pointed out],[3] which are not only to the detriment of the holy gospel and the concord of the citizens, but also affect simple people who go to hear your sermons and are scandalized by such strife. Thus it is the request of our lords, since such unseasonable and harmful utterances cause no mean disadvantage to our city and …[4] It is therefore our lords' earnest admonition and command to you all and individually that each one of you should keep to the previously issued Christian decree, and preach the Word of God with all mildness and for the edification of the people, to punish the sins in the community, and not touch on specific persons or incite and upset the common man. We wish you especially to show in your sermons and prove that each of you is a Christian and peaceful preacher and is entirely seen as such. Otherwise, if anyone does not conform to or show themselves in conformity with the earlier and present commands, and acts contrary to them in his sermons or otherwise, my lords will punish him and will deprive him of the right to preach. They will not have such a man in the city as an evangelist of the word of God, and you must not thereafter have such a man among you and take care not to protect him but to point him out by way of warning.

4. Capito's Hebrew Library

The following note and the transcription of Pappus' catalogue have been supplied by Stephen Burnett.

When Johannes Pappus briefly taught Hebrew at the Strasbourg academy between 1569 and 1575, he copied out a list of the Hebrew books held by the Strasbourg academy library. He wrote the titles on several blank leaves of his

* * * * *

2 1 December 1523. See above, Ep. 406.
3 The reading and meaning of the text is uncertain at this point.
4 Illegible.

copy of Elias Levita, *Meturgeman: Lexicon Chaldaicum* (Isny: Fagius, 1541), now HAB Sig. 205.1 Th. 2° (2). Some of them (including at least two copies of the rabbinical Bible and the Jerusalem Talmud) were very likely Bomberg imprints. A number of these books almost certainly belonged to Wolfgang Capito, and may have been donated to the library of the academy after his death in 1541. As early as 1526, Capito owned a Talmud and wished to study it (cf. above, Ep. 289 to Pellicanus), and in his remarkable letter to Guillaume Farel (above, Ep. 388) he quoted from the following books, all of which appear in Pappus' list: Pesachim u-Khetavim of R. Israel b. Petahia Isselin, Jacob ben Asher, Arba Turim, and both the Jerusalem and Babylonian Talmuds. Further study of both Capito's published works and his correspondence may reveal more about the size and scope of his personal collection of Hebrew books.

Index Librorum Haebraeorum, qui hodie extant, ubi reperiantur, in Bibliotheca Academiae Argent. Hi sunt:

In pulpito VII, ordine I
1. Perusch R. Bachai in Pentateuchum
2. Pentateuchus cum Targume item com. R. Sal. item R. Chiskum
3. Perusch in Pentateuchum, qui inscribitur Breschith Rabba
4. Perusch in Pentateuchum, qui inscribitur Midrach Tanchuma vel Yelammedenu
5. Perusch in Legem Mosii Abraham Hispani, qui inscribitur Zeror Hamor. Primus fasciculus Mynae
6. Perusch in Legem Mosi R. Mose, Bar Nachman

Ordo II

1. Concordantiae Haebreae
2. Biblia in 2 tomis cum Targume item 2 Peruschim R. Sal. Item Abenezrae
3. Biblia in 2 tomis cum Targume item com. R. D. K. Perisol, Rab Venaki

Ordo III
1. Perusch Legis Mosaicae, R. Menachen Racanati
2. Perasch in Perusch R. Sal. in Pentateuchum Eliae orientalis
3. Commentarius R. Isaac a Barbenell in prophetas posteriores
4. Commentarius in Legem inscriptus Sepher Siphra
5. Liber Menora Hamar R. Isaac Abenhaff Hispani; item Liber Schulkan Arba; item Liber Kad, Hakemach, R Bachai
6. Rabi Mose Dux dubiorum
7. Masmiah Jeschua autore Rabi [Isaac] a Barbenell

Ordo IIII

1. Siddur Haberacha
2. Sepher Rosch aemana R. Isaac a Barbannell; item Schaare Theschusa R. Jonae; item Sepher Halichoth olam R. Jeschuasi Levitae; item Pirke R. Elieser
3. Nahalath Avos Aboth R. Isac a Barbenel
4. Arba Turim in duobus tomis
5. Sepher Therumath Hadescham R. Israel; item Pesikim ve-Kafaphim eiusdem; item Sepher Hachimuth R. Aaronis
6. Sepher Ikkarim R. Joseph albo autore
7. Sepher Missoch Haggadul R. Mose [of Coucy]
8. Sepher Colbo (was man sucht der find man do)

In pulpito VIII ordo I

1. Seder olam; item Josiphon
2. Sepher Hajaschar Sepher dibbre Hajamim, chel Mose Raben
3. Sedar olam Rabba Vesuta Ukabala
4. Petrus Galetinus
5. Grammatica R. Abraham a Balmes
6. Michlol R.D.K.
7. R. Mosche Kimhi; item Petach defarai; item Sepher Mosnaim Abenesrae; item Sepher Zachut eiusdem
8. Sepher Bachur Eliae Levitae; item Sepher Thisbi eiusdem; item Perusch Thora R. Jacob Turim; item Sebach Pesach R. Isaac a Barbenell

Ordo II

1. Grammatica & Lexicon Reuchlini
2. Liber radicum R.D.K.
3. Meturgeman Eliae
4. Aruch autore R. Nathan Bar Jehiel

Ordo III & IV

Thalmud Ierusolymitanum tribus tomis
Thalmud babylonicum quinque tomis
Alcoranus cum refutatione pulp. 6 ord. 2

Table of Correspondents

Chronology of Capito's Life

1478?

Born Wolfgang Köpfel in the imperial city of Haguenau, north of Strasbourg, to Agnes and Hans Köpfel, a smith; educated at the Latin school at Pforzheim.

1501–1503

Matriculates at the University of Ingolstadt (October 1501), leaves on account of unrest caused by Bavarian War of Succession.

1504

Matriculates at the University of Heidelberg (May 1504), leaves once again on account of the Bavarian War of Succession.

1505

Resumes studies at the University of Freiburg (BA by 1505); attends Ulrich Zasius' lectures in jurisprudence.

1506–1507

Promoted to MA in the winter of 1506–7; begins study of theology.

1509

Takes over as lecturer in philosophy from Georg von Hechingen.

1510–1511

Promoted *baccalaureus biblicus* (December 1510); lectures on the OT and NT, and on Aristotle's *Ethics*; promoted *baccalaureus formatus* (1511); begins lecturing on the *Sentences*.

1512

Obtains license in theology (January 1512); appointed *professor extraordinarius* with a salary of 25 gulden.

1512–1515

Accepts a call from Philipp von Rosenberg, Bishop of Speyer, to become preacher in Bruchsal; begins study of Hebrew with the converso Matthaeus Adrianus.

1515–1520

Promoted Doctor of theology (July 1515); called to Basel by Bishop Christoph of Utenheim; serves as cathedral preacher and professor of theology; associates with scholars at the Froben press: Johannes Oecolampadius, Conradus Pellicanus, the Amerbach brothers, Beatus Rhenanus, Desiderius Erasmus; in 1518, Capito publishes a Hebrew grammar and persuades Froben to publish a volume of Luther's writings for which he provides a preface and glosses; in 1519 he publishes a translation of Chrysostom's *Paraenesis prior*.

1520

Moves to Mainz (April 1520) as cathedral preacher and advisor to the archbishop, Albert of Brandenburg; tries to secure the provostship of St Thomas in Strasbourg, but is challenged by Jacob Abel, who continues to press his claim over the next decade.

1521

Advises Albert to decline the post of inquisitor general for Germany in the wake of Luther's condemnation at the Diet of Worms; has a falling out with Luther over the latter's radical tactics.

1522

Visits Wittenberg; reconciles with Luther; asks for a two-month leave of absence during which he meets with Oecolampadius; rejoins Albert at the Diet of Nürnberg in June.

1523

Unauthorized publication of sensitive correspondence between Capito and Luther; Capito resigns his position at Albert's court; assumes provostship of St Thomas on 14 March 1523; takes out citizenship in Strasbourg.

1524

Invited by parishioners of Young St Peter in Strasbourg to become their preacher (February 1524); officially joins the evangelical cause, assisting Martin Bucer, Matthew Zell, and Caspar Hedio in their efforts to reform Strasbourg; defends clerical marriage and citizenship (*Appellation der Eelichen Priester von der vermeinten Excommunication; Das die pfaffheit schuldig sey*

Burgerlichen Eyd zuthun); engages in controversy with Conrad Treger (*Antwurt ... auff Bruder Conradts Augustiner ordens Provincials vermanung*); marries Agnes Roettel, the daughter of a city councillor (August 1524).

1525

Nicolaus Wurmser, dean of the chapter of St Thomas, and a group of Catholic canons flee Strasbourg, taking with them the seal and part of the treasure, and claiming to be the legal representatives of the chapter; Capito and the evangelical canons who have remained behind protest the claims (*Der Stifft von sanct Thoman zu Straßburg ußschryben und protestation; Von drey Straßburger Pfaffen und den geüsserten kirchen güttern*); a revised edition of Capito's Hebrew grammar is published; Capito and his colleagues are involved in consultations with the city council of Strasbourg over the Reformation, urging the abolition of the mass; Capito resigns his provostship (October 1525). Lorenz Schenckbecher is elected in his stead.

1526

Capito's commentary on Habakkuk is published; he co-authors the *Warhafftige verantwortung* with Matthew Zell, rejecting accusations of having encouraged the rebellious peasants in Alsace; Capito writes a preface to an unauthorized publication of the proceedings of the Disputation of Baden (*Warhafftige handlung*); a letter from Capito to Zwingli about his involvement in the edition is intercepted and published in a tendentious German translation by Johannes Fabri. Capito publishes an apologetic tract, *Der nüwen zeytung und heymlichen offenbarung ... bericht und erklerung* (Strasbourg, 12 August 1526).

1527

Publishes German translation of Hosea and a catechism (*De pueris instituendis*; translated into German as *Kinderbericht und fragstuck von gemeynen puncten christlichs glaubens*).

1528

Invited to attend the Disputation of Bern together with Bucer as observers; continued efforts by Bucer and Capito to have the mass abolished in Strasbourg; Capito negotiates with Schenckbecher about resuming the provostship, but the status quo is maintained; publishes commentary on Hosea (dedicated to Marguerite of Navarre).

1529

Mass is abolished in Strasbourg; Bucer attends Marburg Colloquy (illness may have prevented Capito's attendance); in the Sacramentarian controversy, Capito sympathizes with Zwingli's spiritual interpretation of the Lord's Supper (*Apologia und erclerung*).

1530

Travels with Bucer to the Diet of Augsburg; collaborates on the formulation of the Tetrapolitan Confession signed by Strasbourg, Lindau, Memmingen, and Constance; he disagrees with Bucer over the severe treatment of Anabaptists; his tolerance and his assocations with Anabaptists arouse suspicion.

1531

Death of Zwingli and Oecolampadius; Capito ill with the plague; his wife dies; Michael Servetus visits Strasbourg; Capito criticized for associating with Servetus.

1532

Capito visits the churches of Bern, Zurich, Constance, Lindau, Esslingen, Augsburg, Kempten and Ulm (January to March); acts as *de facto* chairman at the Synod of Bern (9–13 January 1532); marries Oecolampadius' widow, Wibrandis Rosenblatt.

1533

Strasbourg synod; Capito collaborates on the draft of the Sixteen Articles, the city's official statement of doctrine; he edits Oecolampadius' commentary on Jeremiah and translates Erasmus' *De concordia ecclesiae* into German.

1534/5

Capito distances himself from the Anabaptists and supports the measures taken by the city against radical sects; he experiences financial troubles because of investments in Matthaeus Apiarius' press; he edits Oecolampadius' commentary on Ezechiel, prefacing it with a life of Oecolampadius; Capito sent to advise Frankfurt on church order.

1536

Accompanies Bucer and co-signs the Wittenberg Concord, which unites the adherents of the Tetrapolitan Confession with the Lutherans; Capito fails in his efforts to persuade Basel, Bern, and Zurich to sign as well; he publishes *Precationes Christianae*.

1537

Advises Duke Ruprecht of the Palatinate-Zweibrücken on reforms in his territory; publishes *Responsio de missa, matrimonio, et iure magistratus in religionem* (addressed to Henry VIII).

1539
Publishes *Hexemeron Dei opus.*

1540
Attends the Colloquy of Worms, but expresses pessimism about the possibility of a concord between Catholics and Protestants; a statement advocating Nicodemism is circulating under Capito's name; resumes provostship of St Thomas (December 1540).

1541
2 November 1541, Capito dies of the plague; his widow marries Martin Bucer.

Index